Second Edition

Home
Work
& Play

Situating
Canadian
Social History

Edited by James Opp and John C. Walsh

OXFORD

UNIVERSITY PRESS

OXFORD

UNIVERSITY PRESS

8 Sampson Mews, Suite 204, Don Mills, Ontario M3C 0H5
www.oupcanada.com

Oxford University Press is a department of the University of Oxford.
It furthers the University's objective of excellence in research, scholarship,
and education by publishing worldwide in

Oxford   New York
Auckland   Cape Town   Dar es Salaam   Hong Kong   Karachi
Kuala Lumpur   Madrid   Melbourne   Mexico City   Nairobi
New Delhi   Shanghai   Taipei   Toronto

With offices in
Argentina   Austria   Brazil   Chile   Czech Republic   France   Greece
Guatemala   Hungary   Italy   Japan   Poland   Portugal   Singapore
South Korea   Switzerland   Thailand   Turkey   Ukraine   Vietnam

Oxford is a trade mark of Oxford University Press
in the UK and in certain other countries

Published in Canada
by Oxford University Press

Library and Archives Canada Cataloguing in Publication

Home, work, and play : situating Canadian social history, 1840–1980 / edited by
James Opp and John C. Walsh. — 2nd ed.

ISBN 978-0-19-543124-7

1. Canada—Social conditions—20th century.
2. Canada—Social conditions—19th century.
I. Opp, James William, 1970–   II. Walsh, John C., 1969–

HN103.H56 2010   971   C2009-907350-1

Cover image: filo/iStockphoto (top), Hugolacasse/iStockphoto (middle),
and A-Digit/iStockphoto (bottom)

This book is printed on permanent acid-free paper ∞.
Printed and bound in Canada.

1 2 3 4 — 13 12 11 10

Contents

Acknowledgements

When we were unexpectedly thrust together to teach a course in Canadian social history at Carleton University in the fall of 2003, we had no idea that many of the concepts we set out in class would evolve into this work. Although the readings and articles assigned in History 2304 have changed considerably, the students have always been exceptional participants in sharpening our sense of purpose and clarifying how space could be used to structure and communicate the importance of social history. Their responses, their enthusiasm, and their generosity are constant reminders to us that the classroom is truly a two-way learning experience.

In taking on a second edition of this book, our debts to the work of others have also grown. The sharp eyes of Maja Villarroel, a standout student from our first social history class, brought the Eveready battery ad to our attention. Susan L. Joudrey and Val Minnett were invaluable research assistants who also served as teaching assistants for the course. Laura Jackman introduced the 'lady cyclist' both to our class and this book. Doug Fischer from the *Ottawa Citizen* graciously shared digitized images, while Melissa Pitts from UBC Press, Glenn Bergen from the University of Manitoba Press, and Gerry Friesen were all instrumental in helping us to secure permissions for works that were not quite published at the time of compilation. Another former teaching assistant for our course, Jessica Dunkin, gave the entire manuscript a careful read, and provided excellent editorial feedback. And we remain grateful to the faith and support that Laura Macleod extended to us in making *Home, Work, and Play* such an important part of our professional lives.

We also continue to receive a great deal of encouragement and feedback from instructors, students, and scholars from across the country. In particular, Tamara Myers and Kathleen Lord both took time to comment on our table of contents for this current edition, and their insights are greatly appreciated. As editors, we are always surprised and heartened by the variety of ways that our book is used, and we continue to urge historians to seek out new and innovative strategies for designing courses and delivering materials. We hope that this second edition will open even more doors and offer more options in relation to the themes, methodologies, and theoretical approaches that characterize the rich diversity of social history today.

The first edition of this book was developed at a time when we both found ourselves taking on new roles as fathers. Since then, our families have continued to expand. Far too much of our work has followed us home, but Karen Reyburn and Pamela Williamson have seen us through the many highs and lows that have accompanied the production of this edition. And finally, thanks to Emily, Hope, Nevan, and Celia for reminding us every day about the spectacular importance of play.

James Opp and John C. Walsh
Mary Lake, Ontario
August 2009

THE BRIGHT WAY IS THE RIGHT WAY . . .

AT HOME

'Safety First is a rule in our home! From basement to attic, wherever light is needed — we use an "Eveready" flashlight for safety and convenience.'

AT WORK

'In my job, I can't afford to be without an "Eveready" flashlight. I keep mine in the glove compartment of my ambulance. And of course I use "Eveready" "Nine Lives" Batteries — they last longer!'

AT PLAY

'For camping trips and other outdoor fun, my "Eveready" flashlight is the best protection against the unseen dangers in darkness. Powerful "Eveready" "Nine Lives" Batteries light the way to safety.'

WITH NEW 24% LONGER LIFE . . .

*According to A.S.A. 2.25 and 4-Ohm General Purpose Tests.

Make *your* life easier and safer with "Eveready" Flashlights and Batteries. These amazing Batteries not only recover power between uses for longer life ..they're now packed with 24% more power. Insist on "Eveready" "Nine Lives" Flashlight Batteries and get a bonus of 24% more hours of light.

"Eveready", "Nine Lives" and the Cat Symbol are registered trade-marks of

NATIONAL CARBON LIMITED
MONTREAL   TORONTO   WINNIPEG

FM3-52

EVEREADY
TRADE-MARK

"NINE 9 LIVES"
TRADE-MARK

FLASHLIGHT BATTERIES

Figure 1.

Introduction:
Situating Canadian Social History

———— James Opp and John C. Walsh ————

In a 1952 advertisement for Eveready batteries (Figure 1), the flashlight is heralded as an essential tool for Canadian consumers, whether at home, at work, or at play. Although the flashlight remains the same in each setting, the context for its use suggests dramatically different social and physical environments. From illuminating the inside of an oven for a housewife to exposing an ambulance's engine for a driver to lighting the way in a dark forest for a group of young adults, the social relations surrounding the device are depicted in very specific ways that shift across space, gender, and age. In this example, the three fields of home, work, and play are deeply gendered; domestic labour is a feminine activity, while a masculine mechanical aptitude is required outside the home in order to accomplish paid labour. Leisure activities, such as camping, are characterized by young adults, who are at a stage in life when courtship and sexual relations are in flux and individuals' own home and work lives have not yet been defined. The ad suggests that the flashlight is useful from 'basement to attic', reinforcing the broad post-war middle-class conception of home ownership. Furthermore, the fact that all the actors in these images are white has the effect of normalizing a particular racial identity as typically Canadian. While the intention of this ad is clearly to sell batteries, it communicates a great deal more in evoking a set of cultural ideals that characterized Canada in the 1950s.

Such idealizations were not, of course, descriptions of reality as much as they were the projections of a comforting social order defined by an advertising agency. Nevertheless, the advertisement serves as a useful starting point for considering how historians situate history in terms of social and physical space, real or imagined. In bringing together a diverse selection of articles in recent Canadian social history, this volume calls attention to how historians, implicitly and explicitly, frame their work in relation to these spatial categories. The inclusion of visual primary sources offers readers an opportunity to go one step further, developing their own analysis of spatial meanings. Home, work, and play are not, as the battery advertisement suggests, self-evident or natural categories. Ultimately, our objective is to unsettle simplistic notions of how such spaces are constituted and made meaningful.

As spatial categories, home, work, and play operate in this collection in two different but complementary ways. First, the articles shed light on how these spaces were historically understood and experienced by various peoples in multiple contexts. For example, Franca Iacovetta and Valerie J. Korinek explore how the consumer choices and homemaking of immigrant mothers were viewed by authorities as agents of acculturation and assimilation in Cold War Canada. Making Jell-O was not only a way to put a smile on children's faces, but it was also considered to be an important element of cultivating good citizenship. Andrew Parnaby explains how Aboriginal men were at the heart of labour organization and labour relations around Vancouver's Burrard Inlet. His article demonstrates how working for wages affected these men and how their experiences and identities were essential to broader local and regional patterns of working-class formation. Suzanne Morton deftly shows how the gendered spaces of gambling were elements of an alternative social geography of Montreal during the 1940s, where play both reaffirmed gender identities and provided opportunities for men and women to transgress the normal codes of conduct. Despite the different historical settings, all three essays demonstrate that the spatial context in which people lived, worked, and played was an active component of their identities and experiences. This theme can be observed in each essay in this volume through different sources and can be understood from a variety of methodological and theoretical positions. While this collection makes no pretense to being comprehensive, the selections reorient how we can and should think about home, work, and play.

Second, we have used the terms 'home', 'work', and 'play' as an organizational framework. These categories operate as a map to help readers (most of whom we expect are newcomers to Canadian social history) navigate what might otherwise seem a dense and incomprehensible field of study. Through our own teaching experience, we wanted to develop something more than a strictly chronological structure or an endless list of themes with little in common. At the same time, we understood that chronology is critical to historical understanding and that social history is as diverse as the peoples whose stories it tells. The spatial organization of this text offers students a means to see shifts in social relations over time in focused areas.

Although we have organized our selections into three discrete categories, our intent is not to insist on their strict separation. Rather, this structure allows for readers to challenge the very artificiality of such predetermined classifications. Many of the selections point to the permeability of these boundaries. The male patrons who frequented the high-end 'supper clubs' of West End Vancouver or the working-class nightclubs of the East End might have viewed their activity as leisurely 'play', but, as Becki Ross and Kim Greenwell explain, the women dancing on stage were most certainly at work. While many readers may take it for granted that their home, work, and play lives are interconnected, thinking about these connections historically is unsettling because it compels us to embrace the messiness of the past.

The porous nature of the boundaries that surround home, work, and play also extends to the political borders that define Canada and its regions. Social historians have long been interested in mobility and movement through space and across territory, but new studies of borderlands and border crossings are revitalizing how we think about where (and when) 'Canadian' social histories were made and experienced. Colin D. Howell's analysis of sport in the Maritimes points to the region's strong cultural connections and exchanges with New England, while Anthony W. Lee's work on labour unrest in a Massachusetts factory town traces the significance of francophone migration from Quebec and the Maritimes to that region. Whereas Howell provides us with the view from the Maritimes, demonstrating how Boston and the northeastern United States were regarded as much closer to home than Montreal or central Canada, Lee offers insight on those who left their 'home' in search of work across the border. Both authors, however, position their narratives against a backdrop of industrial transformation that was global in nature, reshaping spaces of home, work, and play in the Western world.

In designing and updating this collection, we deliberately sought out recent work. While new is not necessarily better, we wanted readers to have a clear sense of the diversity of interests, methodologies, and approaches that currently characterize the field. We were also aware that framing our volume in terms of social space shifted the focus away from other major themes such as immigration, industrialization, and urbanization.[1] These large-scale transformations and the dislocations they triggered are not absent from this collection, as noted in the examples of Howell and Lee above. Instead, they are framed in relation to other concerns, reflecting new directions in social history that have emerged in the last decade.

Among these new directions is a perceptible shift in the relationship between historians and the archive. Historians have long relied on archives to provide the facts in order to reconstruct and analyze the past. The historian's task was first to describe what could be seen through these 'windows' into the past and then to explain the broader historical significance. Today, however, there is an increasing awareness that archives are not simply transparent windows but that the histories we produce are shaped and given meaning by the very organization, arrangement, and preservation of documentary materials. Social historians are now much more willing to incorporate the archive, and their archival experiences, within their narratives as an essential part of the story rather than leaving such encounters buried in the footnotes. Telling stories about where our histories come from, and how they are produced, offers a strategy for destabilizing the hidden forms of knowledge and power that present 'the archive' as a neutral and apolitical space.

If archives are today a contested site memory, a closely related development has been an explosion of interest in various forms of 'memory' as sites for historical analysis. Since the 1970s, social historians have been at the forefront of pioneering oral histories, but often the aim was to separate 'memory' from 'history', recovering only that which could be verified with other 'facts' and archives. For Stacey Zembrzycki, the stories told to her by Ukrainian-Canadians offer more than just insights about childhood; they are also memories that define the individual and collective selves. Rather than looking for 'bias', Zembrzycki is more interested in understanding why men and women remember their Depression-era childhoods as they do. Steven High shares an interest in oral history and memory, but in his essay he tells the remarkable story of how a paper mill in Sturgeon Falls, Ontario, became a powerful and highly contested site of memory. As High shows, two intrepid workers collected and preserved a wide range of materials in the 'mill history binder', an act that resisted the company's efforts to erase the mill from the landscape.

Along with the organizational structure, another innovative feature of *Home, Work, and Play* is the incorporation of visual primary sources. Historians tend to rely solely on textual sources, and images (when noticed at all) often serve as little more than inert illustrations. In recent years, however, visual culture has emerged as an important resource for scholars interested in how social spaces were represented. In paintings, photographs, advertisements, cartoons, maps, and architectural plans, social space is portrayed, reshaped, and given meaning by producers and consumers of such images. The inclusion of illustrations in this volume is therefore not a means simply to 'visualize' the past—we want to encourage readers to 'read' visual imagery critically in light of the questions raised by the essays. As with the Eveready advertisement, we need to be aware of how visual images create and reinforce the social constructions of gender, class, and race just as they represent the spaces of home, work, and play.

Making Social Histories

When social history emerged on university campuses in the 1960s, it was often defined against the dominant tradition of political history. Self-consciously revolutionary, social historians declared that they were doing history 'from the bottom up' or writing a more complete 'total history'. Over the past 30 to 40 years, however, the field has evolved. Perhaps a better way to define social history is as an attempt to relate the social experience of the lived past to the social structures that limit and define such experiences. Karl Marx famously said that individuals make their own histories (what social historians often call 'agency') but that they do so within parameters defined for them by others ('structure'). Most, if not all, Canadian social historians would agree with this basic proposition, although they would differ on the relative importance of agency and structure. Indeed, there is an enduring and underlying tension between the two in the broad landscape of Canadian social historical writing.

Agency and structure were central questions for social historians in the 1960s and 1970s who sought to restore a place for those marginalized by the traditional focus on national politics and the elite classes. For some, the path to recovering this history lay in a social science methodology that mined new and different types of sources, such as wills, baptismal and wedding registers, tax assessment records, city directories, and census returns. Like their colleagues in sociology and economics, historians became adept at statistical analysis and eventually produced a startling array of figures about the historical identities and behaviours of Canadians, from child-rearing to marriage patterns to kinship and community relations. This research was both interdisciplinary and international, as Quebec historians drew upon the work of the French Annales movement while English-speaking historians found inspiration in demographic studies of the Cambridge Group for the History of Population and Social Structure. The use of statistical analysis also owed much to the social scientific history emerging in the United States, which made an explosive entrance into Canada via the work of American-born and -trained Michael Katz and his well-funded project on Hamilton.[2] These works produced large amounts of data that spoke to large-scale economic structures related to industrialization, urbanization, and family strategies. For some historians, however, the social scientific approach offered little room for recovering the actual voices of the historically marginalized—the working class, immigrants, and women. A parallel, and occasionally overlapping, impulse within social history sought to go beyond these structures to explore how people were agents of history in their own right.

In particular, these scholars drew upon the work of British Marxist E.P. Thompson, whose classic *The Making of the English Working Class* (1963) is still regarded as the seminal text in the field. In his preface, Thompson famously remarked that his objective was to recover workers 'from the enormous condescension of posterity'.[3] For him, the key to recovering working-class agency lay in taking working-class culture seriously and in analyzing class-based organizations, customs, rituals, songs, and poems as expressions of political resistance that 'made' the working class as much as it 'was made' by the economic forces of capitalism and industrialization. Canadian working-class historians followed this lead, focusing on topics such as the organization and rituals of the Knights of Labor, the parades of the Orange Order, and the use of the charivari as markers of working-class culture.

Thompson's influence extended beyond his scholarly conclusions. In his political activism, most famously his campaigning for British disarmament in the 1980s, Thompson demonstrated a social role for the intellectual in contemporary society. Social historians in Canada similarly engaged with Marxist, New Left, and feminist concerns. The creation of the journal *Labour/Le Travailleur* (later *Labour/Le Travail*) in 1976 reflected the interest in creating dialogue between intellectuals and Canada's working class, and the journal actively sought outside contributors and cultivated a broad readership. Social historians' pursuit of agency and voice was viewed as a meaningful contribution to present-day politics. Concerned over the apparent rising tide of subversive activity among historians, the RCMP even sent spies to observe what went on at the annual meetings of the Canadian Historical Association.[4]

In the 1980s and 1990s, the interests and approaches of social historians evolved, but agency and structure remained central. Increased interest in immigration, ethnicity, and women's lives raised questions about whose experience was being reconstructed by historians. Labour and working-class historians had acknowledged the role of ethnicity in shaping working-class experience, but immigration historians focused their efforts on family and community bonds, framing their work as part of a narrative of migration and relocation. Women's historians called attention to the public and private aspects of women's lives, but in turn discovered that women's experiences varied with class and ethnicity. This broad-ranging dialogue called attention to the complexity of peoples' identities, shaped by multiple and overlapping factors, including sex, class, and ethnicity. Textbooks in Canadian history reflected these trends through titles such as *A History of the Canadian Peoples* and *The Peoples of Canada*, which implicitly rejected a single national narrative in favour of a more pluralistic perspective.

However, this embrace of multiple voices and identities produced new debates over the ethical position of historians and their unspoken assumptions. How accessible are past experiences, and who has the right to speak for those whose voices were denied or lost over time? How do we understand historic actions and events when the only records we have were written by those in power, such as housing inspectors, Indian agents, and court officials? The claim to understanding the experience of others was critiqued particularly by historians who worked with First Nations, Metis, and Inuit. The representation of Native voices produced heated debates at academic conferences as Aboriginal peoples demanded a role in representing their own histories. Social historians struggled to bridge a cultural divide between academic interests and collective memory.

The search for agency raised troubling questions for historians in many fields, and, drawing again on similar developments in the social sciences, new tools were developed to differentiate social realities from historically produced social constructions. In the 1980s, gender historians rejected the too-common assumption that women's history could simply be appended to a mainstream, national narrative. Rather than divide history by biological 'sex' into women's and men's stories, gender historians focused on the dynamic relations between masculine and feminine identities, social constructions that were fundamental in naturalizing the perceived 'truth' of sex. Whereas women's history sought to give women a voice and narrate their experience, gender history examined the fluid representations of femininity and masculinity that infuse and structure our understanding of social actions, behaviours, and spaces.[5]

The use of gender as a category of analysis offers historians a powerful tool to understand the structure of social history at a very different conceptual level. In their study of urban transit in the 1940s, Donald F. Davis and Barbara Lorenzkowski go beyond the experience of women riding and working on streetcars to explore how work and public space were gendered. From the very design of the streetcars to the battles between 'smokers' and 'shoppers', gendered assumptions lay at the heart of the debate over public transit in the war years. With bodies crowded together in such close proximity, the question of whether passengers' social actions are defined as 'proper' feminine or masculine behaviour takes on heightened significance. Gender historians argue that we cannot grasp the full meaning of individual experience without first understanding the structures of gender that have historically surrounded women and men.

In the 1990s, other socially constructed categories of analysis emerged. In particular, social historians turned their attention to the way perceptions of racial difference have changed over time. Writing about 'race' is not simply a matter of narrating the story of various ethnic groups. Rather, it exposes how essentialized notions of the Chinese 'character', or Native peoples, or 'whiteness' were produced and performed through social and cultural codes of belief, behaviour, and the presentation of the body. Gender and race are not competing levels of analysis but should be understood as overlapping spheres. As Pamela Sugiman explains in her chapter, black men were able to find work in southern Ontario auto plants in the 1940s. The work they were assigned in the factories was especially difficult and physically taxing, something that factory managers celebrated when they gave tours to journalists. Black masculinities were thus deemed 'appropriate' when this particular work was set within these spaces. Here the elements of class, gender, and race were all essential to making this historical moment possible.

Power lies at the centre of questions surrounding race and identity, and scholars have increasingly turned to post-colonial theories in unravelling how power is embedded in the cultural knowledge of 'Others'.[6] In their chapters, Sharon Wall and Gillian Poulter point to the appropriation of Native cultures and identities in such disparate settings as Ontario summer camps and Montreal winter carnivals. Native peoples themselves had little control over these representations, but as Andrew Parnaby points out, as dock workers Aboriginal men employed strategies that played upon these very stereotypes as a form of economic resistance.

Sexuality has also come to the forefront as another site of contested meanings. Mary Louise Adams's discussion of crime comics and pulp novels calls our attention to the postwar anxiety over defining heterosexuality as 'normal' and how these perceptions shaped understandings of homosexuality as a danger to the social order. Against the backdrop of the Cold War, such 'abnormal' behaviour was seen as part of a moral unmaking of the nation through the corruption of children and young adults. Little wonder, then, that the reading of comic books and pulp novels was subject to both social and political forms of governance. Rather than a history of comics or pulp fiction, Adams's chapter thus focuses on the constructed and historically specific categories of sexuality, gender, class, and race.

To explore how meanings within these categories are produced, scholars have turned to a wide variety of linguistic theories. Broadly speaking, such postmodern approaches to history question the ability of primary source texts to represent 'truths' or 'facts' of the past and instead suggest that social meanings are ultimately produced through language and 'discourses'. Since the past is ultimately unknowable, postmodernists suggest that scholars should turn their attention away from 'reality' and onto questions of 'representation', including visual, spatial, and literary sources. This critique cuts to the heart of the historical enterprise. Can historians truly claim to reveal how others experienced the past when we know 'reality' only through layers upon layers of 'discourse' and language? Indeed, are the historical meanings we draw from these fragments representative of past experience or the product of our own present understandings? Critics warn that an exclusive focus on discourse leaves little room for analyzing experience or for recovering a sense of agency on the part of oppressed groups. They also worry that such a focus pushes us farther away from our historical subjects rather than bringing us closer to them.[7]

While it may never be entirely possible to reconcile such oppositions, many historians are increasingly attuned to the significance of local resistance. For example, in Paige Raibmon's article, Aboriginal domestic space is put on display and carefully constructed as a spectacle of either 'primitiveness' or 'civilization'. And yet Native peoples themselves reconfigured their houses to suit their own needs, subverting the attempt to establish assimilation through domesticity. By viewing space itself as a form of language, Raibmon allows us to envision domesticity as a site where everyday life was both culturally constructed and materially contested. In understanding the surrounding context of representation and performance, agency is not lost but gains new meaning.

These are neither the first nor the last debates within Canadian social history. One of the defining elements of social history has been a willingness to question itself, to ask difficult and sometimes discomforting questions about what social history is and should be. In the 1990s, conservative critics lamented the loss of a national narrative in the face of multiple perspectives and the fragmentation of history into specialized subfields. We would argue that the proliferation of perspectives and new areas of interest testifies to the continuing vitality of Canadian social history. The essays in this collection are derived from fields as diverse as urban history, sport history, Native history, religious history, labour history, cultural history, and rural history. And yet all of them speak to larger issues surrounding themes of class, gender, and race. In addition, they are included in this particular volume because they speak to another overarching theme: space.

Thinking about Space

The continuing tension between agency and structure, experience and constructed identity, is also reflected in how social historians approach social space. Many focus on how the material conditions of home, work, and play shaped the experience of those who inhabited these spheres. Questions surrounding working conditions, standards of living, and family structures have been prominent in Canadian social history for decades. In this volume, Catharine Anne Wilson traces the value of the work bee for rural economies and analyzes how these work spaces reinforced 'neighbourliness' and particular social interactions that were, in turn, shaped by gender and class.

Recently, historians have also explored how such spaces are conceptualized, socially constructed, and represented. Chris Dummitt examines how barbecues were sold to consumers as a manly form of cooking rather than probing their actual use in the home. The particular words and phrases used to describe a cooking implement reflected masculine concerns, reinforcing a gendered notion of the 'outdoors' as an acceptable space for men to engage in an activity traditionally considered feminine.

It is worth noting the differences in sources employed by these two authors. Whereas Wilson turns to the diaries and writings of farmers who participated in nineteenth-century work bees, Dummitt focuses on advertisements and the language describing barbecues. This is not to suggest that the two approaches are mutually exclusive; most of our selections combine both perspectives in their analyses. For example, Kate Boyer explores how the new 'office girl' of the 1920s and 1930s was an essential element of advertising related to the new Remington typewriter. In comparing the depictions offered in these advertisements with other forms of evidence such as company journals and employee records, Boyer reveals a significant by-product of new office technologies: in 'saving' time and effort, as these advertisements claimed, new technologies actually tethered women to their desks, limiting their career choices and opportunities. Here the social space of the office is both 'real' and 'constructed', existing simultaneously as a sphere of lived experience and as a wider representation of waged labour and technology.

On a wider geographical scale, the spaces and landscapes of the city and country are themselves infused with moral assumptions. Thus Becki Ross and Kim Greenwell map the racial and class boundaries of nightclubs in Vancouver, distinguishing between West and East Ends. In a similar vein, Dale Barbour's chapter points to how categories of gender were deployed in remaking post-war alcohol regulations in Manitoba, where the working-class male beer parlour was frowned upon in favour of more respectable drinking establishments marked by the welcome presence of women. Both articles demonstrate how moral geographies are continually being remade, remapped, and reinscribed upon the spaces and places that surround us.

From these examples it is apparent that social space can be viewed from many perspectives. Spaces are never neutral or empty of meaning, especially those designated as proper sites of home, work, and play.[8] In the very classification of certain activities as 'naturally' belonging to these spheres, a multitude of historical assumptions are brought to bear in defining domesticity, labour, and leisure. Social spaces function materially and symbolically in shaping everyday life. In situating Canadian social history, we want to stress the active nature of these processes. Although not all the articles in this volume directly address the question of social space, they all point to the dynamic negotiation of power, whether imposed from above or resisted and restructured from below.

Visualizing Space

It is important to note the distance between experience and representation, especially when examining visual sources. The idyllic world portrayed in the Eveready advertisement offers a sense of how the social spaces of home, work, and play were represented to consumers, but without further research this would serve as a poor guide to understanding the everyday experience of Canadians in the post-World War II era. No doubt many working-class women who were employed outside the home relied on flashlights in their work lives, and men certainly used them in the home. The representations of space, whether seen in visual or textual sources, might encourage us to consume, to desire, or to fear.

As Sean Purdy argues in his chapter on Toronto's Regent Park, films produced by the National Film Board recast the area first as a 'slum' that required redevelopment and then later as a site of poor government planning dominated by crime and drugs. These representations were not only ideologically charged but also had very real effects on Regent Park's development and public perceptions of it. Purdy also notes how these spatial constructions were resisted by the voices of residents, who saw their community very differently. For Purdy, envisioning the problems of Regent Park as simply the logical outcome of poorly planned space ignores the deeper economic and social problems that lay beneath these representations.

From a very different perspective, Gillian Poulter explores how Montreal's anglophone elite lay claim to a geography of the city, allowing them to define a 'Canadian' identity through winter activities and carnivals in the late-Victorian period. And yet, this narrative was challenged by francophone participants, who narrated their own history through parades and processions. Poulter's sources range from cartoons to newspaper reports, calling attention to how the making, publication, and circulation of representations are also central to the envisioning of spaces and geographies.

What these authors, and many others in this collection point to, is that visual sources, like textual material, require a critical eye. Even photographs, which appear to offer an objective view of the past, are subject to multiple interests and cultural constructions. The photographer selects what to include within the frame and what to leave out. The subjects may willingly pose, or they may resent the intrusion. Technological limitations and cultural aesthetics influence what is captured on film and what is not. Publishers routinely recrop images to suit other needs, often adding captions that may have little to do with the original intention. As James Opp suggests, photographs of Winnipeg's North End do not reflect reality as much as they construct spaces of moral concern. And, as with any public image, what the producer *intends* to portray is not necessarily what the audience takes from it.

Visual sources actively contribute to the construction of meanings that surround and infuse social space. Sometimes they explicitly reinforce existing ideologies, and sometimes they articulate unspoken assumptions and attitudes.[9] What is clear, however, is that we cannot dismiss such sources as simply illustrations or 'pretty pictures'. For example, during the preparations of the first edition of *Home, Work, and Play* two major banks denied us permission to reprint advertisements that had appeared in *Maclean's* in the 1950s. At a time when the banks were facing lawsuits over past labour practices, the re-circulation of these visualizations was not deemed to be in their corporate or legal interest. Visual sources matter, then as now, and by including images for readers to analyze, critique, and evaluate, we hope to encourage discussion of perspective, evidence, and methodology. Ultimately, there is no simple way to determine how such images were received or what their creators intended. However, the insight provided by the articles in this collection may help readers to think about the visual representation of social space in new ways.

Conclusion

The obstacles facing historians in recovering social experience and social structures in many ways mirror the difficulties inherent in drawing out meanings and understandings from images. Social historians face a daunting task in trying to produce historical narratives that capture the multiple voices, meanings, textures, and complexities of past social worlds. The choices we make as historians are not dissimilar to the choices a photographer makes in framing his or her subject. In selecting what to focus on, a great deal is left out. The picture, like history, is never entirely complete.

Social history has changed a great deal in the last 40 years. A field once dominated by a focus on labour and the working class has now expanded to include issues of gender, race, and sexuality. Domesticity and home life are no longer marginal areas of concern but are viewed as fundamental elements of nation-building, colonization, and imperialism. A new interest in popular culture has led to wide-ranging studies in leisure, recreation, the environment, and spaces of play. New sources, including oral history, photographs, and advertisements, have led to new questions surrounding identity and representation. Yet, for all that is new, social historians remain committed to seeking understanding of and respect for the diversity of peoples who made Canada, a project that was as fundamental to scholars in the 1960s as it is today. *Home, Work, and Play* is a testament to the determination of social history to push the boundaries of our knowledge and understanding of the past while remaining unapologetically humane in its concerns.

Notes

1. For social history collections that explicitly approach these topics, see Franca Iacovetta and Robert Ventresca, eds, *A Nation of Immigrants: Women, Workers, and Communities in Canadian History, 1840s–1960s* (Toronto: University of Toronto Press, 1998) and Ian Radforth and Laurel Sefton MacDowell, eds, *Canadian Working Class History: Selected Readings*, 2nd edn (Toronto: CSPI, 2000).
2. Michael B. Katz, *The People of Hamilton, Canada West: Family and Class in a Mid-Nineteenth-Century City* (Cambridge, MA: Harvard University Press, 1975) and Michael B. Katz, Michael J. Doucet, and Mark J. Stern, *The Social Organization of Early Industrial Capitalism* (Cambridge, MA: Harvard University Press, 1982).
3. E.P. Thompson, *The Making of the English Working Class* (London: Penguin Books, 1980 [1963]), 12.
4. Steve Hewitt, 'Intelligence at the Learneds: The RCMP, the Learneds, and the Canadian Historical Association', *Journal of the Canadian Historical Association* 8 (1998): 267–86.
5. Joan Wallach Scott, 'Gender: A Useful Category of Historical Analysis', in Scott, ed., *Gender and the Politics of History* (New York: Columbia University Press, 1988). See also Scott's recent response to a forum discussion of her seminal work in 'Unanswered Questions', *American Historical Review* 113 (Dec. 2008): 1422–30.
6. Edward Said, *Orientalism* (New York: Vantage 1994 [1978]).
7. Bryan Palmer, *Descent into Discourse: The Reification of Language and the Writing of Social History* (Philadelphia: Temple University Press, 1990).
8. An important work in theorizing space that has influenced not only historians but also geographers, sociologists, and anthropologists is Henri Lefebvre, *The Production of Space*, trans. Donald Nicholson-Smith (Oxford: Blackwell, 1991).
9. This is particularly strong in the case of maps, as historians of cartography are continuing to explain. See the essays in J.B. Harley, *The New Nature of Maps: Essays in the History of Cartography*, ed. Paul Laxton (Baltimore: Johns Hopkins University Press, 2001).

Part One

—— At Home ——

Before the 1970s, the question of the home rarely found its way into the pages of Canadian history. Even the earliest works in women's history tended to focus on the pioneering roles of women outside the home, instead of viewing the home itself as an important historical space. However, in the 1970s and 1980s, social historians interested in women, children, the family, household structures, immigration, and kinship placed the home and household at the centre of their analyses rather than treating domestic spaces as marginal to the larger narrative of national (and political) history. For many historians, researching and theorizing the 'private' world of home and family offered a useful way for recovering the voices, work, and actions of women and children, which had been sidelined by historians' traditional understandings of the nation and citizenship.

As scholars delved into new issues such as domestic labour, child care, and women's property rights, the distinction between public and private was called into question. The conceptualization of diametrically opposing social worlds, also known as the ideology of 'separate spheres', was itself a historical construction of the Victorian period (c. 1830–1900). In the shift from an agrarian society to an industrial economy, the middle classes physically separated home from work, as fathers no longer worked with their families but instead found employment in factories and offices. This separation produced new ideals of domesticity, which reflected middle-class concerns over the nature of industrialization and established new boundaries of gender. Women were viewed as 'naturally' embodying domestic virtues, such as fidelity, compassion, and moral strength. In contrast, men were seen as the 'breadwinners', more capable of rational thought, and uniquely suited to the public affairs of politics and work. Within this binary context, the home served as a 'haven in a heartless world', a moral centre that counteracted the ruthless competitiveness that marked nineteenth-century economics and politics. This middle-class, Victorian ideology was critical to the work of early feminist historians who focused on the home as the space where women lived and made history, where they were agents rather than passive spectators of historical change.

By the 1990s, however, historians realized that the ordering of society as 'naturally' divided into public and private broke down in multiple ways. Studies of the Victorian era demonstrated that the waged labour of immigrant domestic servants betrayed the notion that 'work' did not take place in the home, while the realities of working-class family economies compelled many women and children to work for wages, both inside and outside their homes. Apart from the industrial heartland of southern Ontario and Quebec and the Lower Mainland of British Columbia, the majority of Canadians continued to live in rural settings well into the twentieth century, and it was clear that the ideal of 'separate spheres' had limited relevance for understanding the everyday experiences of rural families, where work and home often remained firmly intertwined. Historians even began to question how urban, middle-class women themselves fit the domestic ideal in light of their 'public' activities, such as participating in religious societies and social reform movements. The conclusions drawn from this research understandably led to a new questioning of the boundaries between the spheres. The simple division of public and private could not be sustained, since most people have historically inhabited some portion of both worlds simultaneously.

But rather than jettison the concept of separate spheres, historians discovered new ways of incorporating it into their analyses of the home. The emergence of gender history and a renewed focus on the social organization of masculine and feminine identities has been particularly influential. Instead of viewing 'public' and 'private' as static categories of a strictly defined society, gender historians emphasize the overlaps, ambiguities, and distance between the cultural conceptualization of private life and the material complexities of lived experience. The use of gender as an analytical tool allowed scholars to demonstrate the fluidity of the meanings that surround space, calling attention to the shifting representations of masculine and feminine attached to particular sites even within the home, such as the kitchen, the dining room, the study, and the parlour. Rooms occupied by both sexes could nevertheless be gendered very differently. Further complicating the picture, gendered perceptions of domesticity also intersected class and race. As the following essays demonstrate, the home is not simply a physical place inhabited by people; it is also a space that has historically been embedded with contradictory social meanings.

Beyond the overlapping spheres of public and private, new questions are being raised about the meaning of the home. How did the material spaces of the home function in relation to everyday life? And why was so much 'political' capital and energy invested in maintaining idealized conceptions of domesticity? These themes run through many of the articles included in this section. The home as a space for raising families was seen as the key to the future of the nation, and domestic ideals were central to middle-class perceptions of Native peoples, immigrant communities, and the working class. As these essays illustrate, inside and outside the physical space of the home a broad range of domestic relations were infused with moral tensions, especially marriage, sexuality, and the family. The public surveillance directed at the domesticity of 'others' points to the depth of anxiety that the white middle class felt about the future of Canada and the state of its 'race'. In the post-war period, suburban perceptions of home clashed with massive urban renewal projects, as the lines between 'safe' and 'dangerous' spaces continued to be redrawn and reinscribed. Cold War anxieties over the cultural challenge of immigration were assuaged by a consumerist ethos of abundance, both in the kitchen and beyond. From these articles, we therefore learn that such issues were not marginal, nor were they confined to the private sphere. Instead, the home emerges here both as a site of lived experience and as a space central to the culture and politics of state formation in the nineteenth and twentieth centuries.

For Further Reading

Adams, Annmarie. *Architecture in the Family Way: Doctors, Houses, and Women, 1870–1900.* Montreal and Kingston, 1996.

Baillargeon, Denyse. *Making Do: Women, Family, and Home in Montreal during the Great Depression*, trans. Yvonne Klein. Waterloo, ON, 1999.

Bradbury, Bettina. *Working Families: Age, Gender, and Daily Survival in Industrializing Montreal.* Toronto, 2007 [1993].

Christie, Nancy, ed. *Households of Faith: Family, Gender and Community in Canada, 1760–1969.* Montreal and Kingston, 2002.

Davies, Megan Jane. *Into the House of Old: A History of Residential Care in British Columbia.* Montreal and Kingston, 2003.

Dennis, Richard. *Cities in Modernity: Representations and Productions of Metropolitan Space, 1840–1930.* Cambridge, 2008.

Fahrni, Magda. *Household Politics: Montreal Families and Postwar Reconstruction.* Toronto, 2005.

Harris, Richard. *Creeping Conformity: How Canada Became Suburban, 1900–1960.* Toronto, 2004.

Morton, Suzanne. *Ideal Surroundings: Domestic Life in a Working-Class Suburb in the 1920s.* Toronto, 1995.

Parr, Joy. *Domestic Goods: The Material, the Moral, and the Economic in the Postwar Years.* Toronto, 1999.

Perry, Adele. *On the Edge of Empire: Gender, Race, and the Making of British Columbia, 1849–1871.* Toronto, 2001.

Swyripa, Frances. *Wedded to the Cause: Ukrainian-Canadian Women and Ethnic Identity, 1891–1991.* Toronto, 1993.

I

Women's Agency in Upper Canada: Prescott's Board of Police Record, 1834–50

——— Katherine M.J. McKenna ———

Just before midnight on a dark, chilly November night in 1837 in Prescott, Upper Canada, Mary Greneau was startled out of her sleep by the sound of a mob outside her house. Male voices shouted, 'Kill her' and 'By God I'll fix her!' Her attackers pounded on her door, heaving against it until the hinges burst and her home was broken open. Spilling inside were six horrifying figures, dressed in grotesque imitation of Native Indians. Their faces were blackened and streaked with red and they wore blanket coats. As they whooped and hollered, they went on a destructive rampage, smashing her windows, breaking her furniture, and throwing her possessions out into the street. Mary and the two women living with her, Jane Craig and Elizabeth Brady, felt entirely defenceless and in real terror for their lives. Only when a neighbour threatened to shoot them if they did not desist did the six marauders depart.[1]

Although this incident bears some resemblance to the classic charivari, there are important differences. Mary Greneau was, it is true, a well-known local figure. She was a constant nuisance to those living near her, and in particular had an ongoing feud with her neighbours across the street, John and Catharine Kelleaugher. They were fed up with her running what was then called a 'disorderly house', a place of entertainment operating at all hours and outside the law. She sold liquor, employed a fiddler, and entertained drunken men with 'dancing and indecent conduct'.[2] Women of doubtful

reputation were living there and going in and out at all hours, on at least one occasion fighting in the street. Catharine Kelleaugher later testified that, on one May evening, Bridget Savage and Margaret Doneghan disturbed the peace as they were coming out of Mary Greneau's house by engaging in a shouting match, calling each other 'bitch', 'whore', and 'bastard' for all to hear.[3] The Kelleaughers took to displaying their displeasure in a non-violent but pointed manner. Crossing to the drainage ditch in front of their disruptive neighbour's house, they emptied their slops and chamber pots there. When she complained to them, they replied with very 'insolent answers'.[4]

Earlier that November, Mary had clashed with some of her patrons as well. Late one Saturday night, she brought back three men to her home in a state of intoxication, giggling and laughing. One, William Glazier, called for four glasses of liquor, one for him, one for her, and one each for James Campbell and John Honeywell. The latter whispered to her, perhaps in jest, that because Glazier was a newcomer to Prescott from Glengarry 'that she might skin him'. When Mary tried to cheat William out of his change, he declared 'he would have the change or the worth of it before he left the house.' They scuffled, falling against the stovepipes with such violence that they were knocked over. She finally chased the men out of the house at gunpoint, firing a warning shot into the street in the wee hours of the morning.[5] This was too great an insult to the pride of John Honeywell, who promptly went to

Katherine McKenna, 'Women's Agency in Upper Canada: Prescott's Board of Police Record, 1834-1850'. Published in *Histoire sociale / Social History*, vol. 36, no. 72 (2003), 347-70. Used by permission of the publisher.

the authorities and charged her with firing the gun, and on the Sabbath, too, a double bylaw violation. Mary Greneau was duly fined, but was not prepared to take this passively. She counter-charged Campbell and Honeywell, perhaps angry with them for not defending her against Glazier, for having 'abused her in her own house'. The public testimony that resulted was not to her advantage. One witness asserted that 'for some weeks past' she had 'kept a very noisy house, after hours, Sunday evenings not excepted'. The whole story about the evening's doings became a matter of public record. Samuel Indicott, who had been employed by Mary as 'waiter and fid-dler', tried to put a good face on it, testifying that he only 'saw drunken people there occasionally, saw some dancing and indecent conduct some-times, heard singing frequently'. Pandering to racist sentiment, he asserted in her defence that he 'never saw the coloured people use her famil-iarly'. As for the accusation of carrying on such activities on Sunday, he assured his listeners that he had in fact seen 'some say grace before drink-ing'.[6] This did not persuade local authorities of the justice of her case. The charges against Campbell and Honeywell were dismissed, and Greneau assessed steep costs of £1.3.6.[7]

This victory did not appease John Honeywell. A few days later, he and some others launched the attack on her house, wreaking revenge on a woman who they thought needed to be put in her place. Their intentions were well known locally. One witness had 'heard it frequently said that she ought to be rid on a rail'. Others had been invited to join the raiding party but had declined. Honeywell's band hatched their plot at the store of Alexander Thomas, where they met to put on their costumes. A passerby heard them say, 'damn the old devil, she'll not know us.' They carried the charade to the point that they 'spoke in imitation of the Indians' when spoken to on the street, responding 'Chip, Chip, Chuck' in a crude mimicking of Native dialect. After the raid was over, they conveniently left their dis-guises at Thomas's store, where they were easily found and later presented as evidence. The men

then repaired to Beale the barber's for a drink to celebrate their triumph over Mary Greneau.[8]

Charivaris were a not uncommon form of 'rough justice' in Upper Canada.[9] This one devi-ated from the norm because it was not a political protest and was less an expression of commun-ity censure than the settling of a personal quar-rel.[10] Even though it is clear that there were many in the Prescott community who objected to the behaviour of Mary Greneau, the raid on her premises was not accepted by her neighbours as 'rough justice'. After some initial delay in recog-nizing that the attack was something more than just the usual carousing heard from her home, they turned out in her defence. Surprisingly, it was the short-changed Glazier who finally drove the rioters off with the threat of shooting. Other members of the community, Mr Deneau and Mr Cavalier, had not only refused to join the party, but also testified against Honeywell's band.[11] Mary Greneau herself, as we have seen, was not one to accept attack passively, and she quickly sought her own revenge through legal means, successfully prosecuting Alexander Thomas, Thomas Meredith, and John Honeywell for disturbing the peace. As an expression of com-munity censure, they were handed exceptionally punitive fines of £2.10 with costs of 17 shillings, 3 pence each.

Such a remarkable story about a woman of the popular class is rare in Upper Canadian history. That it has survived is due to the existence of an equally remarkable document—the Minute Book of the Board of Police for Prescott, Ontario. For almost 150 years this record has sat virtually untouched in the vault of the municipal offices of Prescott.[12] What it reveals is an unparalleled source of social history on many aspects of Upper Canadian life. Standards for acceptable community behaviour on everything from con-trol of livestock, health regulations, road main-tenance, keeping the Sabbath, licensing alcohol and entertainment, and even what language was permissible to use in public space are recorded in the 400 densely written pages of this Minute Book. Of particular interest are the cases brought to the Board of Police that involved women as prosecutors or plaintiffs or were brought on their behalf by men during the 16 years it presided over Prescott life, from 1834 to 1850.

In the 1830s and 1840s Prescott was at the peak of its success, a rapidly growing small town of more than 2,000 persons.[13] Situated just above a section of the St Lawrence River made unnavigable by rapids and with a natural, deep harbour, it was an important transfer point for goods and people arriving overland from Montreal en route to Ogdensburg to the south and points west such as Kingston and Toronto. This forwarding trade meant that merchants prospered, and associated activities such as shipbuilding and marine insurance developed.[14] During the 1837–8 Rebellion, the decrepit Fort Wellington was rebuilt, and from 1843 to 1854 it was garrisoned with a company of men from the Royal Canadian Rifle Regiment.[15] After the Montreal–Toronto railway was built in the 1850s, Prescott subsided in importance. The time covered by the Board of Police Record, then, coincided with the town's height of prosperity and activity.[16]

. . .

. . . [In] the 1830s a new governing model was implemented in eight rapidly developing communities across Upper Canada, incorporating them as towns and establishing local Boards of Police to take over the comprehensive duties of the Quarter Sessions. If the Quarter Sessions was flexible and well suited to frontier needs, so too were the Boards of Police. They were also more democratic and more closely tied to their communities. In Prescott, presiding Board members were chosen from among local male property holders of at least £60 assessed value and elected by men who were British subjects owning a dwelling house and a plot of land or paying rent of at least £5 per annum within the boundaries of the corporation. . . . This system held sway until a new Municipal Act in 1849 called for the establishment of a mayor and council, with a separate Police Court.[17] . . .

. . . As Allan Greer has observed, early Upper Canadian justice was a 'ramshackle affair' which

'could not function as the instrument of an external and superior state power to anything like the degree that modern police forces later would'.[18] Only after the change in government in 1850 do we see a few charges brought to trial on behalf of the Board as a corporate body, despite the fact that the Board often asked town officials to perform bylaw enforcement duties.

In keeping with this personalized model of justice, cases were summarily dealt with, often the same or the next day. There were no judges, lawyers, prosecutors, or police witnesses, only the members of the Board, sometimes the bailiff or constable, the plaintiff, defendant, and the witnesses whom they had brought. The Board members themselves were not remote from those who appeared before them. Although some professionals such as lawyers and physicians served, for the most part the members were practical men of business, local merchants and manufacturers.[19] In their daily affairs they rubbed shoulders with those brought before them, even if they did have the authority to impose taxes and fines and to imprison defaulters for up to 30 days. Despite the fact that many of the individuals who appeared in front of this informal tribunal were not able to elect its members, it was nonetheless a community-responsive and immediate form of justice.

As a record of the public activities of ordinary women, the Board record provides us with rare insight into their transgressive behaviour, as well as the gender-based and class-linked sanctions increasingly brought to bear on them by the Prescott town fathers throughout this period. There was a rough total of 139 cases involving women between 1834 and 1850. Only 12 of these were brought on behalf of women by men. Of the 139, more than half (about 76) were independently initiated by the women themselves as prosecutors. Overwhelmingly, these were ordinary labouring women of the popular class, most of whom did not skirt the boundaries of the law in their daily lives like Mary Greneau. More often, they appeared at the court to settle everyday disputes that arose in their community. To a greater extent than the more formal Court of Quarter Sessions or the Police Courts established after 1850, the Board of Police was a practical means of dealing with community problems. . . . It was not costly; it was informal and conveniently located in the town. . . . More often, it was a tool used by the local populace for their convenience, as a strategy for negotiating dissent within their neighbourhoods. . . .

On the other hand, it is worth underlining that the Board of Police was a coercive institution, ultimately representing the interests of the wealthier male members of the Prescott community. It was no idealized, democratic, grassroots body. Yet, since it did not always control the charges brought before it, but only sat in judgment, it was easily used by common citizens as a tool in negotiating social difficulties. Katz, Doucet, and Stern still see this occurring in the Hamilton Police Court of the 1870s. They observe, 'To Hamilton's working class the Police Court was not remote. Rather, as the assault cases in particular show, it was used to settle disputes within families or between friends and neighbours and to resolve the tensions that resulted when the strains of everyday life erupted into minor incidents of violence.'[20] Those who appeared before the court were not criminals, but were using the courts for their own private purposes.

Public records such as the Prescott Board of Police Minute Book, it has been argued, reveal at least as much about the institutions that created them as they show about the subjects whose histories are recorded in their pages. All too often the entries followed a prescribed script that undermines their value as authentic sources of information about people's lives.[21] Although this problem can never be totally removed, the Board of Police for Prescott is perhaps less prone to it, due to the Board's informality and the fact that in 1834 it was a new Upper Canadian institution with little in the way of established practice to follow. Although not totally unmediated, the Board record appears to provide a summary of actual testimony recorded by the Clerk, taken verbatim from the lips of those who testified,

complete with grammatical mistakes and colloquialisms. It is likely to be as close as one is going to get to hearing the real voices of women of plebeian origin for this early nineteenth-century period. This is a record, then, that can provide us with rare insight into the public roles of ordinary Upper Canadian women.

Many of the women of Prescott who brought charges before the Board were married with their spouses still living, despite the fact that, according to British law, they were not supposed to act as legal entities apart from their husbands. Constance Backhouse's path-breaking work on women and the law in early Canada indicates that, in particular, married woman were legally subjected to patriarchal control.[22] Law and custom do not always coincide, however. Women in Prescott could and did take the law into their own hands, acting as full citizens in the eyes of the Board of Police, if not in any other capacity in Upper Canadian society. . . . There is even at least one recorded instance of a woman successfully charging her own husband with disturbing the public peace by striking her.[23] Married as well as single women in Prescott could and did have their day in court, acting independently of their husbands despite the fact that law might dictate otherwise.

In this public role, women of the popular class of Prescott differed from their bourgeois sisters. Throughout the nineteenth century in Upper Canada, a new consensus was emerging about middle-class gendered social and moral values.[24] 'The Cult of True Womanhood' prescribed that women's role was in the private domestic sphere. Purity, chastity, delicacy, and retirement from the male world of politics, law, and business were requisite to this ideal of femininity.[25]

The chasm that separated the classes in Upper Canada is dramatically revealed in the pages of the Board of Police record. Middle-class ladies were not to appear in public unescorted and were never to raise their voices. Compare this to the behaviour of Mrs Hannah Ahern and Mrs Catharine Murphy, screaming insults at each other in the street in a dispute over a pig.

This fracas was concluded by Hannah's employment of a favourite contemporary insult, placing, as the record shows, 'her hand upon her hind parts' and inviting her neighbour to kiss her there.[26] Contrast the ideal of the 'domestic angel' with the behaviour of Mrs Thursbay and Mrs Chamber toward Mr Reynolds, Mrs Chamber's former landlord. Mrs Chamber had departed without paying her rent, so Reynolds was holding as security a box of her possessions. The two women arrived at his door one day, in the company of 'one or two' soldiers, to reclaim her property. According to the court record, 'Chamber pretended to offer him 3/— being the balance due . . . but would not let him see the money. He refused to give up the box without the same.' The two women then left the house and 'commenced breaking his Windows' with their umbrellas. 'Both then made great confusion in the street cheering as they broke the glass crying out whores thiefs and villains.' Not many women behaved as outrageously as these two, and the stiff fines of 25 shillings each with costs of 2 shillings, 6 pence ensured that they would most likely have been sent to jail for 30 days in default of payment.[27] Still, their case and those of other women in the Board of Police record of Prescott show the striking differences between the genteel ideal to which the colony's social leaders aspired and the rough and ready nature of small-town street life. It is rare to locate such information about women of the popular class for this early period of Canada's history.[28]

The records of the Board of Police may have been dominated by the lower-class citizens of Prescott, but it was not a criminal court. It merely tried bylaw infractions, however broadly defined. . . . Although the behaviour that brought individuals to the Board of Police was deviant, it was not deviant enough to lead to exclusion from society. There are even accounts of prominent male citizens who appeared before the Board without seriously damaging their social position.

. . .

. . . The illustrious Jessup family, staunch Loyalists and founders of Prescott, were represented locally by two male descendants in the 1830s and 1840s. One, Hamilton D. Jessup, was a local physician who was a respectable pillar of his community and elected to the Board in 1837, 1843–5, and 1848. The other headed a decaying branch of the family tree. Henry James Jessup came up before the Board on many occasions, caused by either his hot temper or by his predilection for frequenting houses of 'disorder'. In 1844 Jessup was rumoured to be 'keeping a bad woman' at the house of Mrs Black, by the name of Mary Delany.[29] Two years later he had tired of her, but Mary was not taking his abandonment without protest. She took to following him around, accosting him in public barrooms, and calling him a 'damned whoremaster'. This got to be too much for him, and he charged her with 'annoying, insulting and abusing' him. The members of the Board were all too aware of the pair's former relationship and they sought to mediate the dispute. The matter was finally concluded when 'defendant agreed with Prosecutor that if he would give two pounds ten shillings and give up her cloths and she to give up his they were to part. He gave up her cloths, gave her the money. She gave up his cloths, they appeared to be satisfied at parting.' This settlement did not prevent the Board from fining Mary Delany 15 shillings plus court costs, however, which made a substantial dent in her £2 from Jessup.[30]

Henry Jessup may have already taken up with a new woman by this time, by the name of Marian or Mary Lang or Lane. She was living in Mrs McLean's house, which earlier that summer of 1846 had been such a nuisance to the neighbourhood. Jane McLean, Mary Lane, Mary Keating, and Bridget Wood were 'brought before the Board for a violation of the By-Laws' by their neighbour and later Board member, merchant Robert Headlam, for a 'Breach of Public Decency and good order and for intoxication'. Witnesses testified that they had been 'annoyed by these prisoners for a long time', but, on one particular night, 'a large party of drunken men [were] in and about the house creating a riot and disturbance in the door of the house where the prisoners live.' One 'saw men passing

and repassing with Bottles in their hands, drunk
. . ., saw one man pulling Mrs Lane by the arm
outside the house'.[31] This may have been the same
woman who, like Mary Delany, began shouting
abusive names at Jessup in the street a year later.
The first time Jessup charged her, the case was
dismissed, but a month later, when she added
threats to throw stones through his window to
her insults, she was fined 5 shillings plus costs.[32]
The comparatively light fine that she received may
have been an acknowledgement by the Board of
Jessup's role in provoking such behaviour from
two different women.

Perhaps Jessup should have followed the lead of
railway engineer Walter Shanley, who was always
on the lookout for sexual prey, but concluded
that Prescott was a dead loss in this respect.[33]
'There is a sad deficiency of anything *safe* in these
diggings,' he complained to his brother in 1851.[34]
Shanley had a highly tuned sense of what was
appropriate to what he considered his station
as an educated professional man. For example,
he was shocked when he heard that his brother
had entered a public bar frequented by some
railway labourers. 'Nothing I had heard for some
time "put me out" so much as your confession of
swilling porter in a public bar with my serfs,' he
complained. 'I keep all my staff at an immeasurable distance. How they must have laughed
in their sleeves at the porter drinking and in
what utter contempt . . . must hold you . . ., but
the subject is an unpleasant one to dwell on.'[35]
Shanley preferred not to 'slum it' with women
like Mary Delany and Marian Lang, but sought
out the more respectable elements of the popular
class. He particularly was attracted to innkeep-
ers' daughters. When he stayed for a while at
Gilman's Hotel in Prescott, he complained that
he was not allowed access to 'those sisters-in-law
of Gilman's' who were 'really very fine girls—but
so "severely proper" you can scarcely approach
them. . . . Mrs Gilman, who is as fine a looking
woman as I ever saw, keeps strict watch & ward
over them, & it is not easy even to see them.'[36]
. . . Yet, for all his frequent preoccupation with
sexual adventure in his letters to his brother,

Shanley scorned the society of women who kept
and frequented disorderly houses. After renting
a room in Prescott at Torr the baker's, he found it
to be 'a most Bawdy-house place' and determined
to move at the first opportunity.[37] Although some
men were able to get away with crossing the class
barrier, for the most part the women who turned
up in the Board records for disturbing the public peace were consorting with men of their own
class or nearly so. They most certainly did not
aspire to be middle-class angels of domesticity.

Still, in the earlier years of the Board of Police
records, even if disorderly houses were not appreciated, neither were they especially condemned.
Mary Anne Poutanen has observed a similar tolerance in Montreal neighbourhoods, provided
the peace was not disturbed.[38] The line between
them and houses of prostitution was not sharply
delineated. Katz, Doucet, and Stern note this later
in the century as well. 'In fact,' they observe, 'little
distinction was made between houses in which
prostitution took place and ones where loud,
uninhibited behaviour annoyed the neighbours
or attracted the attention of the police.'[39] Selling
a little bit of sex on the side was rarely a special-
ity for most popular-class woman, who adopted
a number of strategies of survival, which in
Prescott included, as Bettina Bradbury has noted
for Montreal, keeping pigs and other livestock
and taking in boarders.[40] Selling liquor and providing entertainment, as did Mrs Greneau, was an
easy way of augmenting one's income. Certainly a
ready clientele would be found among the soldiers
at Fort Wellington and the sailors and traders who
passed through Prescott. Such women did not
consider themselves to be prostitutes and might
even have had other occupations such as needle-
work or laundering that did not pay them enough
to survive.[41] Catherine Curry, for example, who
appeared before the Board on three occasions on
charges related to keeping a disorderly house,
was listed on the 1851 census as a dressmaker,
with two female 'servants' living with her.[42] Mary
Keating, Mary Lane, Bridget Wood, and Jane
McLean, when charged with public drunkenness,
were all women on their own who had combined

their households to stretch their limited means. Although they may very well have been providing sexual services to their patrons, they were not charged with prostitution.

In fact, there was no bylaw that specifically referred to prostitution, only a vaguely worded general ordinance that called for penalties for any breach of public decency or order, which included, among other things, breaking the Sabbath, cutting down shade trees, and defacing buildings.[43] Most of the charges against disorderly houses came under this bylaw. Although in testimony it was often mentioned that the defendants were keeping disorderly houses, on only three occasions before 1848 were women actually charged with this offence, and one of these charges was dismissed. In 1841, perhaps alarmed by the military presence of British soldiers at Fort Wellington after the Upper Canadian Rebellion, the Board for the first time brought in two bylaws dealing specifically with keeping bawdy houses and 'vagrant public Prostitutes loitering about the streets'.[44] No charges were ever brought under these new bylaws, however, and they were not renewed the following year.

Indeed, although almost all of the charges involving women included some element of public disorder, most were not for offences related to providing entertainment. A significant number—about 32 cases of the 139 involving women—were related to violence against women committed by men, in particular between husbands and wives. A much smaller number—about nine—involved violence against women committed by women. Often alcohol abuse was implicated, as when Henry Hughes disturbed the public peace by striking Mrs Anne Crowthers in the street outside the Dog and Duck tavern.[45] When labourer Jonathan Houlihan was charged by Constable Cavalier 'for being drunk on Sunday night and for abusing his wife' Teresa he admitted his guilt, but blamed it on the drink.[46] One case of wife assault complicated by racial discrimination involved a black man, Lewis Beale, the local barber. He first appears in the record when involved in a barroom brawl. Witnesses

said that he had 'ushered himself into some company he had no business with' and was accordingly refused service. Beale asserted in response 'that he was a Gentleman & would flog all the englishmen in the place' along with a number of other threats. When Joseph Wood called him 'a fool and a drunkard', Beale responded that 'if he could have the chance to shave him he would cut his throat,' hardly a statement that would be good for business. He was evidently a large man, too strong to be removed by those present. Later Beale's wife and child took the brunt of his anger and fled to the home of Obadiah Dixon and his wife in fear for their lives. When Dixon refused to deliver up Beale's wife, Beale drew a dagger. In the process of disarming him, Dixon suffered a bite on his thumb and a fight ensued. Although only charged 5 shillings for the first offence, this second time Beale was given a fine of £2.10 with costs, a serious deterrent. He did not appear on charges again, although he was living in Prescott until at least 1842, when a reference in another case was made to the 'nigger barber'.[47]

Sometimes violent cases involved some element of sexual coercion, as when Charles Gray and Joseph Webb were charged in 1848 'for disturbing the public peace, and abusing Mrs Webb this day and previously and for keeping a house of ill fame'.[48] One particularly disturbing case involved William Lee, who had been charged before for public intoxication and using profane language, and the young daughter of Mrs Keating. Lee was charged by Alexander MacMillan, a well-off farmer who had been a Board member for 10 years, 'for committing a breach of public decency'. Witnesses testified that, although 'Mrs Keating's daughter desired Lee to leave her Mother's residence,' he refused. Passersby heard the 'child cry murder' and call Lee 'a blackguard'. The record implies that perhaps she had resisted Lee's sexual advances. Apparently he beat her severely; others heard 'screeches from Mrs K's child, went there and saw the child almost breathless and in a state of suffocation from the ill treatment of Lee, and her face was covered with blood'. Lee was given a heavier fine than normal, 15 shillings, but it was still nothing close to what Beale had been fined for biting a white man's thumb.[49]

Popular-class women were not simply passive victims as these cases of assault have implied. More typical was the behaviour of Dorothy Erringy toward her husband Thomas, a local hotelkeeper. Their marriage was in crisis in the summer of 1850. Thomas had moved into the home of Minerva Coons (alias Finley, according to the record), who was considered to be keeping a house of ill fame. Rather than accept this abandonment, Dorothy went to the house, broke the windows, and 'called Mrs Finley a whore'. She then publicly berated her husband, calling him a 'whoremaster', and ended up in a violent argument which ended with him hitting her. Even though Dorothy had started the altercation, the neighbours charged Thomas and Minerva with disturbing the peace, and they were fined 25 and 20 shillings respectively. Thomas launched his own complaint against his wife for her role in disturbing the peace, but such was the community censure of his behaviour that, when the Board convened, he did not show up and was charged costs. In the 1851 census, Dorothy and Thomas were listed as occupying the same premises and Minerva Coons Finley had evidently moved out of town, so it appears that Dorothy's aggressive action had reclaimed her husband.[50]

Such violent cases were not typical of the charges brought to the Board, however. By far the greatest number, about 78 of the 139 cases involving women, had to do with name-calling. In any public dispute involving women, such as with Minerva and Dorothy, far and away the favourite insult was some variant of whore. Men, in contrast, were called a variety of names such as scoundrel, thief, villain, or blackguard, which more generally reflected on their character or integrity rather than their sexual behaviour.[51] Ethnic insults were relatively rare, according to the Board record. Cases of name-calling often involved women from the 'respectable' part of the popular classes, as well as the obvious easy targets of such insults. Anna Clark has studied

defamation cases involving women from 1770 to 1825 in the Church of England London Consistory Court. She argues that the frequency of cases involving insults to the sexual reputation of lower- and middle-class women reveals tensions and anxieties surrounding changing social values about women's honour. Prior to the development of a middle-class ideology of female domestic purity, being seen in public did not automatically mean that a woman was suspected of being a prostitute. Defamation charges were both examples of conformity and resistance to a new moral standard. The insult of whore served to restrict a woman's public life, for to be truly respectable a woman had to remain in the home. Clark argues that, when women called each other whore, 'they were succumbing to the reality of the importance of sexual reputation in women's lives, drawing upon the moral vocabulary of the dominant class to carry out their own vendettas. But they were also defying the linguistic constraints of ladyhood by being loud and aggressive and by refusing to accept the newly defined private domestic sphere.'[52] This was, then, a discourse of both repression and resistance. . . .

Insults which called into question a woman's moral honour could be used to put her in her place, as when Mr Desordie responded to Hannah Ahem's attempt to collect payment for bread by calling her a 'drunken woman'.[53] They could also be a way in which a woman whose reputation had been maligned might counter-attack, by discrediting her critics. When William Dove accused Christina Brogan of keeping a disorderly house, she replied by calling his wife a whore and a bitch.[54] . . .

It is important to note that these cases were not defamation charges, but usually complaints brought under the bylaws for disturbing the peace. It was a matter of utmost indifference to the Board whether the charges were justified or not, simply whether or not the breach to the public peace had occurred. Just calling a woman a whore in public was considered inappropriate, whether or not she actually was one. It was very likely that the size of the fines given reflected the Board's opinion of the woman's respectability, but only in exceptional circumstances was more than 5 shillings assessed for public insults. Although the many women who brought charges for name-calling obviously must have felt they were defending their honour, they did not have to prove it. Thus Catherine Curry was able, for example, immediately following a conviction for keeping a house of ill fame, to charge Henry James Jessup successfully with using insulting and improper language to her.[55]

Since it was so easy to obtain convictions, and the consequences for being found guilty were usually so minor, the women of Prescott came to use the Board more and more for settling personal disputes. This peaked in 1840–1, when about twice as many cases involving insults against a woman's reputation were heard by the Board than in the previous five years; this number was about the same as that of similar cases heard over the next eight years. Anxiety about the increased complaints may have been another reason that motivated the Board to enact the bylaws concerning streetwalking and keeping bawdy houses in 1841. It may have also been behind a stern warning issued in June 1840 reminding citizens 'that anyone after the date hereof entering complaint' should be aware that 'the Board will not hold themselves responsible for whatever costs the said complaint may incur to the Clerk or constable for said complaint.'[56] . . .

Particularly after 1848, however, the use of the Board changed. The steady drop in charges brought to it by women may have had to do with a growing sense that such public displays were damaging to female reputation. From a peak of 25 cases involving women in 1840, the number steadily dropped to only three by 1844. Then the numbers slowly began to rise, hitting a smaller peak of 13 by 1850. The cause of the second rise, however, was not more women themselves bringing charges, but rather more aggressive action by the town fathers, particularly aimed at reducing the incidence of disorderly houses.

In the mid-nineteenth century, a wave of Evangelical reform was sweeping over North America as well as Britain. Historians such as Jan Noel, in her study of temperance movements, documented a striking change in social values in Upper Canada in the 1840s and 1850s.[57] In Prescott, this may have also been fueled by concern over the number of destitute Irish immigrants who were arriving after 1847. In the summer of that year, the Board had been ordered by the Governor-General to take steps to prepare to deal with an expected onslaught of the ill and the desperate.[58] Nonetheless, although such steps were taken, in 1849 the Board responded to complaints about 'the occupation of a dilapidated house in the main street by emigrants, that said house being in a filthy state'. Orders were given to 'abate the aforesaid nuisance by ejecting the parties living in said premises and cleaning and securing the same from further annoyance to the Neighbourhood'.[59]

The same urge to clean up was directed toward alcohol consumption and public morality. After 1848 there are cases of applications for liquor permits being turned down, something that was unheard of before this time. Certainly a very large amount of alcohol was manufactured in Prescott. According to the 1851 Census, 30,937 gallons of spirits, wine, and fortified wine were sold annually, as well as 1,500 gallons of beer. Although some of this was surely sold away, it still is a remarkable amount produced in a town of 2,156 persons. J. O'Sullivan, who took the census, was a stonemason and a temperance man. He could not resist editorializing about this amount of alcohol. 'The Enumerator begs leave,' he wrote in an extraordinary notation concerning this use of grain products, 'to draw the Hon. Inspector General's attention to this large amount of the people's food [being] consumed into poison and prays that his noble efforts may be employ[ed] either in Council or in the legislature to suppress the crying evil of intemperance.'[60]

The Board was equally concerned about the 'crying evil' of female immorality and the public disorder it caused. In 1848 a new bylaw specifically prohibited prostitution and houses of ill fame occupied by 'loose' women.[61] The first three charges brought under this bylaw, however, were dismissed for lack of evidence. It is not clear who brought the charges, but obviously people were not willing to testify against their neighbours under the new law.[62] The local authorities then became increasingly involved in pressing charges, as when Constable Benjamin Cavalier charged Bridget Agar with 'riotous conduct', 'scolding', and keeping a 'bad house'. He actually entered her home and, when he 'saw part of a man's pantaloon stuck out of a hole', he pulled out the half-undressed Patrick Griffin. Fines also became stiffer, and thus imprisonment more likely. Bridget Agar was fined 20 shillings and sent to [the] Brockville jail in default of payment for 21 days, although Griffin was not charged.[63] A local lock-up was also built, so that miscreants such as Mary Hutton could be imprisoned locally while they awaited trial. Both she and her husband were found drunk and arguing in the street, but only Mary was locked up until the Board assembled on Monday.[64] Obviously this would send a strong message to women who were fond of drinking. Increasingly, women of the popular class stopped laying charges, and several charges before the court were delayed and then quietly died. Accordingly, the Board stepped up its role in prosecution. In late 1849 the Corporation took it upon itself to charge William Sanders with keeping a bawdy house. Even though he confessed, he was fined 10 shillings and had his liquor licence revoked.[65] Half a dozen other successful charges were brought after 1848 against women for keeping disorderly houses, the most notable of which was that against Catherine Curry, brought by none other than Henry James Jessup. Her neighbours turned out in force to defend her, asserting that they never saw men there, that the house was always quiet by 9:00 p.m., and that she did not allow gambling. Jessup, they said, was having a quarrel with her and had said publicly that 'he would perjure himself to have Mrs Curry turned out of town.' Jessup alone testified against her, and on that basis she was convicted. This was quite a departure from the judgments of earlier boards.[66]

Still, as we have already noted, Catherine Curry successfully countercharged Jessup the following day and was not run out of town. She was still in Prescott the next year and shows up on the census as a dressmaker.

In conclusion, it is illustrative to look at the career of one particularly notable user of the Board's services, Mrs Ann Black. She appeared before the Board for many different reasons a total of 15 times between 1839 and 1850. . . .

In 1843 Ann charged Mary McMannus with accusing her of 'bringing up bastards for Bill Johnston'. This had occurred in the context of an argument over whether Mary was entitled to stay in the room she was renting from Ann. Ann told her 'that two women had been looking at the house', and Mary replied that 'she would keep the key until her month was up . . . that no one should come in as long as she paid the rent.' During the course of this dispute, Ann had also insulted Mary by alleging that she lay in bed all day drunk. The board fined them each 5 shillings and split the costs between them.[67] Obviously, Ann could give as good as she got, and in 1844 she was charged by Louisa Fortier, as one witness attested, for saying 'that Mrs Fortier was taken out of a whore house in Quebec and was a whore to all the Canadians in Quebec' and for 'throwing stones into her house'. Although Ann was charged with using abusive language, her neighbours volunteered much more evidence. One witness said that she had heard 'noise throughout the night' from Ann's house, 'which from all circumstances the Witness considers . . . an indecent house. . . . [T]he defendant keeps a woman who is not a decent woman in her opinion, her house is open at all hours of the night.' The woman who was not decent was none other than Mary Delany, at that time the kept mistress of Henry James Jessup. Jane Wilson even alleged that she had 'lived in Mrs Black's house five months and caught a man in bed with Mrs Black'. Ann was given double the usual fine, 10 shillings plus costs.[68]

Between 1843 and 1850, Ann was involved in seven other cases in the record, one as witness, two as complainant, and four as defendant. She won both her cases, one in which the defendant had called her a 'poxed bitch' and the other in which the defendant had spit on her in the street.[69] Two of the charges against her were dismissed, and she was convicted and fined the standard 5 shillings on two others involving abusive language.[70]

Finally, in 1850 the respectable men of Prescott decided that Ann Black had troubled them enough. Thomas Gainford, MD, took it upon himself to charge her with keeping a house of ill fame. His testimony was recorded in detail:

> Dr Gainford sworn, Says that ever since she came to the neighbourhood, that her conduct was a specimen of depravity a little short of Murder. Debauched females are harboured in said house and incendiary conduct carried on therein. Says that Mrs Black did curse & swear on the night & morning as aforesaid & continued so doing for about the space of two hours—calling out infernal liars, Damn liars, and it would be impossible to repeat all that she said in the way of Cursing and Swearing, even said God Damn liars to some persons outside the door. . . .[71]

This language actually sounds fairly tame for Ann, but perhaps Gainford could not bring himself to repeat the full extent of her profanities. She was fined the incredible sum of 50 shillings, which of course she could not pay, and so was sent to Brockville prison for 30 days. . . . The most remarkable case, however, was the last recorded about her. In 1850 John Bodry assaulted Ann. She testified that 'she was in her house and [he] asked her if he would be allowed to lye down awhile, she would not allow him to lye down in her house then he commenced breaking several articles in said house and insisted that Complainant should go to bed with him, witness says that he used violence to effect his purpose.'[72] Bodry did not succeed in subduing the indomitable Ann Black. She fought him off, and, even

though he offered to settle with her by paying $1 in damages, she insisted on her day in court. He was fined 20 shillings and costs of 7 shillings, 6 pence. The mayor was paid 2 shillings, 6 pence; the court 8 shillings, 9 pence; and 8 shillings, 9 pence went to Mrs Black. This was a truly incredible result since, as a convicted keeper of a house of ill repute, she could not possibly have obtained a judgment against Bodry for attempted rape in a higher court.[73]

Although women like Catherine Curry and Ann Black could still have their day in court, by 1850 the Board of Police was playing a very different role in the Prescott community than it had in 1834. From a peak of cases brought by women in 1841, women's use of the Board declined as it became increasingly the instrument for a gendered and class-based agenda of social control and moral reform, led by professional men of the bourgeois class. The character of the record changes as well, and we no longer hear as much from the voices of the women themselves as we do from their accusers.[74] From 1850, municipal enforcement bodies such as the police and police courts were established, which were much more effective in asserting the power of local authorities. Throughout the latter part of the nineteenth century, the process of establishing the hegemony of gendered middle-class values of appropriate female behaviour was well advanced. By the late nineteenth and early twentieth century, if a women was raped or assaulted, she was the one on trial, and her male attacker's crime was mitigated by any failure on her part to live up to the domestic and moral ideal of 'True Womanhood'.[75] We still struggle with this legacy today.

What Ann Black's story, and those of the other women who used the Board of Police, can tell us today is that, despite the dictates of law, class status, and convention, they were publicly active in the pursuit of their interests. The Board of Police record gives us a glimpse of women's transgressive behaviour and shows that they could choose not to be compliant with the restrictive ideology of 'True Womanhood'. Women of the popular class of Prescott in this early period could and did take the law into their own hands and use institutions run by male community leaders for their own purposes, as agents in their own lives.

Notes

1. Board of Police Records, Prescott, Ontario, 28 Nov. 1937 (hereafter referred to by date).
2. 6 Nov. 1837.
3. 15 May 1836.
4. 2 Nov. 1835.
5. 6 Nov. 1837.
6. Nov. 1837.
7. 20 Nov. 1837.
8. 28 Nov. 1837.
9. On charivaris, see Allan Greer, 'From Folklore to Revolution: Charivaris and the Lower Canadian Rebellion of 1837', *Social History* 15 (Jan. 1990): 25–43; J.I. Little, *State and Society in Transition: The Politics of Institutional Reform in the Eastern Townships, 1838–1852* (Montreal and Kingston: McGill-Queen's University Press, 1997), 92–101; Bryan Palmer, 'Discordant Music: Charivaris and Whitecapping in Nineteenth-Century North America', *Labour/Le Travailleur* 3 (1978): 5–62 . . .
10. The attack also differed from usual Upper Canadian charivaris in the adoption of Indian dress. This suggests that one or more members of the raiding party may have come from the United States, where the assumption of Indian dress had a long tradition, dating as far back as the Boston Tea Party. See Philip J. Deloria, *Playing Indian* (New Haven: Yale University Press, 1998).
11. Deneau, Cavalier, and Greneau are names which suggest a common French-Canadian background, which may have been a reason why these men would not attack Mary Greneau.
12. I am indebted to the generosity of town officials for granting me access to this resource. In particular, I would like to thank Andrew Brown, Prescott Town Clerk. There is also now a microfilm copy of the Board of Police Record in the Queen's University Archives in Kingston, Ontario.
13. Toronto, Archives of Ontario (hereafter AO), 1851 Prescott Census.
14. Douglas McCalla, *Planting the Province: The Economic History of Upper Canada, 1784–1870* (Toronto: University of Toronto Press, 1993), 118–21, 158.
15. Katherine M.J. McKenna, *Family Life in a Military Garrison: History of the Routines and Activities of the Royal Canadian Rifle Regiment at Fort Wellington, Prescott, 1843–1854* (Ottawa: Canadian Heritage Parks Canada. Microfiche Report Series No. 533, 1995).
16. Ruth McKenzie, *Leeds and Grenville: Their First Two Hundred Years* (Toronto: McClelland & Stewart, 1967), 188.
17. On the history of municipal government and policing in Upper Canada, see James H. Aitchison, 'The Development of Local Government in Upper Canada, 1783–1850' (PHD thesis, University of Toronto, 1953); Paul Craven, 'Law and Ideology: The Toronto Police Court', in David H. Flaherty, ed., *Essays in the History of Canadian Law*, vol. II (Toronto: University of Toronto Press, 1983), 248–307 . . .
18. Allan Greer, 'The Birth of the Police in Canada', in Allan Greer and Ian Radforth, eds, *Colonial Leviathan: State Formation in Mid-Nineteenth-Century Canada* (Toronto: University of Toronto Press, 1992), 19.
19. Information on the occupations of Board members and of citizens who appeared before the Board has been obtained by checking names against the 1848 and 1851 Prescott censuses.
20. Michael Katz, Michael J. Doucet, and Mark J. Stern, *The Social Organization of Early Industrial Capitalism* (Cambridge, MA: Harvard University Press, 1982), 228–9.
21. Karen Dubinsky, 'Afterward: Telling Stories About Dead People', in Franca Iacovetta and Wendy Mitchinson, eds, *On the Case: Explorations in Social History* (Toronto: University of Toronto Press, 1998), 359–66; Franca Iacovetta and Wendy Mitchinson, 'Introduction: Social History and Case Files Research', in *On the Case*, 3–21; Annalee Golz, 'Uncovering and Reconstructing Family Violence: Ontario Criminal Case Files', in Iacovetta and Mitchinson, eds, *On the Case*, 289–311.
22. Constance Backhouse, *Petticoats and Prejudice: Women and the Law in Nineteenth-Century Canada* (Toronto: Osgoode Society, 1991) . . .
23. 7 Sept. 1841.
24. On the development of these new ideas about the gendered public and private spheres propagated by the middle class, see Andrew C. Holman, *A Sense of Their Duty: Middle-Class Formation in Victorian Ontario Towns* (Montreal and Kingston: McGill-Queen's University Press, 2000); Lynne Marks, *Revivals and Roller Rinks: Religion, Leisure, and Identity in Late-Nineteenth-Century Small-town Ontario* (Toronto: University of Toronto Press, 1996); Katherine M.J. McKenna, *A Life of Propriety: Anne Murray Powell and Her Family, 1755–1849* (Montreal and Kingston: McGill-Queen's University Press, 1994) . . .
25. On the genesis of the new ideal of middle-class womanhood in eighteenth- and early nineteenth-century

England, see Leonore Davidoff and Catherine Hall, *Family Fortunes: Men and Women of the English Middle Class, 1780–1850* (London: Croom Helm, 1987) . . .

26. 12 June 1840.

27. 8 Feb. 1841.

28. One exception is the information on women's work that Jane Errington has gleaned from newspaper sources in her book, *Wives and Mothers, School Mistresses and Scullery Maids: Working Women in Upper Canada, 1790–1840* (Montreal and Kingston: McGill-Queen's University Press, 1995) . . .

29. 29 Apr. 1844.

30. 4 Aug. 1846.

31. 26 May 1846.

32. 30 June and 6 July 1847.

33. A recent book on the Shanley brothers discusses their professional careers and their class status as 'gentlemen' in some detail, but not their views on women. Richard White, *Gentlemen Engineers: The Working Lives of Frank and Walter Shanley* (Toronto: University of Toronto Press, 1999).

34. AO, Shanley Papers, Box 68, Walter Shanley to Frank Shanley, Prescott, 23 June 1851.

35. Ibid., 6 Oct. 1851.

36. Ibid., 16 June 1851.

37. Ibid., 23 Nov. 1851.

38. Mary Anne Poutanen, 'The Geography of Prostitution in an Early Nineteenth-Century Urban Centre: Montreal, 1810–1842', in Tamara Myers, Kate Boyer, Mary Anne Poutanen, and Steven Watt, eds, *Power, Place and Identity: Historical Studies of Social and Legal Regulation in Quebec* (Montreal: Montreal Public History Group, 1998), 102.

39. Katz et al., *The Social Organization of Early Industrial Capitalism*, 231.

40. Bettina Bradbury, 'Pigs, Cows and Boarders: Non-Wage Forms of Survival among Montreal Families, 1861–91', *Labour/Le Travail* 14 (1984): 9–46.

41. Judith Fingard has also seen this type of practice of prostitution in Halifax; see *The Dark Side of Life in Victorian Halifax* (Porter's Lake, NS: Pottersfield Press, 1991), 95–113.

42. 24 Feb. 1848; 29 Jan. 1849; 8 May 1850.

43. See bylaws for Apr. 1834.

44. 7 June 1841.

45. 26 July 1839.

46. 1 July 1850.

47. 6 July and 7 Oct. 1837; 26 Sept. 1842. Beale, as noted earlier, does not appear in the 1848 and 1851 censuses.

48. 15 Sept. 1848.

49. 5 Sept. 1844.

50. 1 July 1850.

51. S.M. Waddams observes the same gendered pattern in name-calling in English ecclesiastical courts in his book, *Sexual Slander in Nineteenth-Century England: Defamation in the Ecclesiastical Courts, 1815–1855* (Toronto: University of Toronto Press, 2000) . . .

52. Anna Clark, 'Whores and Gossips: Sexual Reputation in London, 1770–1825', in Arina Angerman, Geerta Binnema, Annemieke Keunen, Vefie Poels, and Jacqueline Zirkzee, eds, *Current Issues in Women's History* (London and New York: Routledge, 1989), 238–9 . . .

53. 12 July 1837.

54. 26 Aug. 1850.

55. 9 May 1850.

56. 15 June 1840.

57. Jan Noel, *Canada Dry: Temperance Crusades Before Confederation* (Toronto: University of Toronto Press, 1995), 123–39 . . .

58. 7 June 1847.

59. 4 June 1849.

60. AO, 1851 Prescott Census, 75.

61. Mary Anne Poutanen also sees a sharp rise in the number of women arrested for prostitution in the 1840s in Montreal ('"To Indulge Their Carnal Appetites": Prostitution in Early Nineteenth-Century Montreal, 1810–1842', PHD dissertation, Université de Montreal, 1996, 233).

62. 28 Feb. 1848.

63. 13 July 1850.

64. 28 Apr. 1849.

65. 3 Dec. 1849.

66. 8 May 1850.

67. 12 May 1843.

68. 29 Apr. 1844.

69. 23 Mar. 1846; 30 Nov. 1848.

70. 20 July 1849; 9 Nov. 1849; 8 Sept. 1846; 12 Aug. 1848.

71. 25 June 1850.

72. 3 Oct. 1850.

73. On the difficulty of getting convictions related to rape, see Constance Backhouse, 'Nineteenth-Century Canadian Rape Law, 1800–92', in Flaherty, ed., *Essays in the History of Canadian Law*, vol. II, 200–47 . . .

74. Lykke de La Cour, Cecilia Morgan, and Mariana Valverde see this trend more generally in what they call a 'masculinization of public power' after the rebellions in Upper Canada. See 'Gender Regulation and State Formation in Nineteenth-Century Canada', in Greer and Radforth, eds, *Colonial Leviathan*, 163 . . .

75. On women's supposed responsibility for crimes committed against them, see especially Dubinsky, *Improper Advances: Rape and Heterosexual Conflict in Ontario, 1880–1929* (Chicago: University of Chicago Press, 1993); Golz, 'Uncovering and Reconstructing Family Violence'.

2

Nurture and Education: The Christian Home

Marguerite Van Die

In March 1871, when despite her husband's [Charles] frantic mining efforts the fear of bankruptcy began to loom, Hattie [Child Colby] reminded him, 'The quiet way we live now brings us all very near to each other, and I have great comfort in mother & Charley and our good little girls. It never can be just home without you but it is a duty to make it and feel it as pleasant as we can.'[1] Much has been written about the ways in which the Victorian home, presided over by the mother as the ministering angel of light, increasingly became a haven for businessmen caught up in the loneliness and frenetic activity of the commercial 'outside world'.[2] In this way, historians have seen it taking on a religious function, replacing the institutional church in a secularizing society by being a private site of Christian socialization and moral formation. As one historian has succinctly summarized the development, 'The outer world had become destitute, but the home was still endowed with the old, positive values; it had not relinquished tested standards and Christian morals; it was the place of the old order; it was the sanctuary of traditional principles. It was separated from the outside world and better for it.'[3]

On the surface, Hattie's comments to her husband fit well into this typology, as does his frequently reiterated desire to spend more time with his family. But the candour that surfaces at times in her letters, when referring to her shortness of temper and the long hours spent in housework,

suggests that the lives of real mothers often failed to live up to the prescriptive literature. Similarly, the prototype of the hard-pressed businessman exiled to the amoral marketplace has come under significant revision as gender historians such as John Tosh have drawn attention to the value that middle-class Victorians placed on paternal domesticity.[4] As the old patriarchy of [Charles's father] Moses Colby's day began to crumble and as the burden of providing a family livelihood shifted from land to the marketplace, fathers found that spending time with their children could be emotionally gratifying as well as giving them 'the satisfaction of fulfilling a critical role of adult masculinity—the ability to feed, clothe and shelter children'.[5] For Charles Colby, this found expression in a wide range of activities, from carrying out requests of his wife and daughters for purchases in the various urban centres to which his work took him, to assuring his children frequently by letter of his constant love, and, as they grew older, by taking them along when his travels allowed visits to distant relatives.[6]

For men as well as women, this domesticity was rooted in a livelihood derived from the marketplace. The form of patriarchy that Moses Colby had tried to ensure in his will by basing his family's security on land no longer worked for his sons. Having lost the land, they had to find other means to achieve economic security for their families. 'Do not think I had no feeling at parting with our old home the walls of which

Marguerite Van Die, 'Nurture and Education: The Christian Home', *Religion, Family, and Community in Victorian Canada: The Colbys of Carrollcroft* (Montreal: McGill-Queen's University Press, 2007). Reprinted by permission of the publisher.

I had reared under great difficulties and around and through which cluster so many associations of happiness and sorrow,' Charles wrote to Hattie two days after the sale of the stone house. Valuable as a house might be to a middle-class family's self-worth, other less tangible but more enduring forms of security had to be found in a world in which fortunes could be lost as quickly as they were acquired. As Charles elaborated, 'All the means which we are likely to have over and above the bare cost of living are needed to educate and fit out the children—and as they grow older they need more of our personal care.'[7]

At the time, the children consisted of Abby, age 12; Jessie, age 10; and Charles William, who had just turned five. As Charles intimated in his letter, education and self-formation had taken on new importance in the family's straitened circumstances, calling for careful distribution of their financial resources. This held true not only for his sons (John would be born the following year) but also for his daughters, whose only dowry would be their family name and reputation, their physical attributes, and their ability to excel in the graces of a developing middle-class society. As it turned out, Abby did not marry until the age of 28 and Jessie remained single. The two sons spent considerable time in post-graduate studies as preparation for careers in, respectively, university teaching and medicine. Paternal provision was therefore a lengthy process and fell entirely on the male head of the household—unlike the case with their parents and William's [Charles's brother] two daughters, all of whom worked briefly as schoolteachers to help with family finances.

Although practical in their purpose, education and formation were also, according to Victorian domesticity, to be shaped by love and order, two qualities that were notably absent in the unpredictable marketplace. Here religion, especially the domesticated heart religion of evangelical Protestantism, had much to offer, and historians have drawn attention to the close fit between evangelical family religion and the

home as its most perfect location.[8] How this fit took place, however, is less well understood. Did religion turn the home into a 'haven in a heartless world', into a surrogate church, as was argued above? Or—following the lead of research that has questioned the explanatory value of such dualisms as sacred and secular, material and spiritual, male and female, private and public— did religion in the home help the middle-class family adapt to the socio-economic order . . .?[9]

As this chapter will explore more fully, the Colbys, like many other Victorian families, did place very high expectations on the home. And as a businessman who in 1858 had experienced a 'new birth', which led him to exchange his understanding of a righteous, awe-inspiring God for a loving Father, Charles Colby tried to work out its implications for domestic life, just as he did for the marketplace. Meanwhile Hattie, drawing on her childhood formation, her training as a teacher, and her literary tastes, found her own ways of making religion a meaningful element in the nurture of their children. And though at times—as when the family's material fortunes plummeted—she wrote appreciatively of their quiet home life, the home emerges in many of the family letters not as a retreat but as the place of integration, from which gender, school, church, community, and nation ultimately assumed their significance. This was also the intention of evangelical ministers and educators. But as laypeople, the Colbys found their own ways of integration, which were sometimes at variance with the official tenets of religion. Through such means, their story enters into a much larger narrative of social and religious change in which the symbolic universe of religion begins to merge with the family as a source of ultimate meaning.

Since the seventeenth century, when the first Colbys and Childs emigrated to the New World, Puritan teaching had underscored the importance of the home as a 'nursery of virtue' in preparing children to take up their adult responsibilities in church and state. By law, the heads of the Colby and Child households in the

Massachusetts Bay colony had been required to catechize their children and servants at least weekly and to instruct them in the Scriptures.[10] The subsequent separation of church and state and the shift to revivalism had the potential to undermine this tradition, and ministers unrelentingly continued to emphasize the importance of family religious instruction by the head of the household.[11] Rather than seeing the eternal safety of their offspring depending on the experience of a 'new birth', or conversion, many clergy as well as laypeople such as [Charles's parents] Moses and Lemira Colby had chosen to uphold the old tradition of religious instruction in the home. This had been supported by the increasing prevalence of the Sunday school.[12] Even such revivalist denominations as Canada's Wesleyan Methodists, though equivocating on the need for the conversion of children raised in the faith, were beginning by the 1860s to emphasize the importance of childhood religious instruction.[13]

Roman Catholic priests in Quebec were equally zealous in pointing out to parents their duty to begin instructing their children in the truths of the Christian faith the moment the children's intelligence 'awakened'. Where Protestants relied on the Scriptures and a flood of tracts and moral publications, Roman Catholic parents had the *petit catechisme*. About 15 per cent of this was devoted to the sacrament of penance, which was the chosen vehicle for training the child's conscience by seeking God's forgiveness through repentance and monthly confession of sin.[14] In their theological stance on infant depravity, Roman Catholics, despite their many differences from Protestantism, held to a view of the human condition that was significantly closer to the Puritan understanding than the view beginning to hold sway among many middle-class Protestants. The liberalizing shift in Protestant theology from an emphasis on the atonement to the incarnation affected not only a businessman's self-understanding but also had profound implications for the religious nurture which parents provided for their children.

Officially, in their baptismal liturgies, mainline Protestant denominations continued to uphold the view that every infant entered the world tainted with the sin of Adam and was thus in need of regeneration. In the Wesleyan Methodist liturgy, for example, which was followed when baptizing Charles and Hattie's children and which faithfully reflected its Anglican predecessor (derived in turn from the Roman Catholic form), the minister, while sprinkling water on the newborn infant, solemnly intoned, 'All men are conceived and born in sin' and 'None can enter into the kingdom of God, except he be regenerate and born anew of water and of the Holy Ghost.'[15] How this rebirth was to take place, however, became a matter of theological controversy. Was it through the breaking of a child's will in order to experience a conversion by accepting God's forgiveness through the atonement, as the revivalists preached? Or could such a rebirth occur naturally and slowly, within the confines of a Christian home? In his highly influential book *Christian Nurture*, published in 1847, Horace Bushnell, Congregationalist minister in Hartford, Connecticut, argued that evangelical conversion, with its emphasis on sin, provided a negative model for the religious formation of the child and had every chance of turning the child away from religion as an adult. Instead, the child should be surrounded by loving parental influences from the time of its birth, enabling it to experience religion as part of the normal process of growth. Bushnell did not reject the belief in original sin, but his remedy placed a new emphasis on the role of parents to become positive agents of grace in the lives of their children.[16] Although its impact among mainline evangelicals was slow initially, in retrospect *Christian Nurture* has been seen as a critical turning point—away from revivalism and towards religious socialization. 'In its entirety,' historian Margaret Bendroth has succinctly summarized, 'Bushnell's theology brought God closer to human reach, an emphasis that places him at the forefront of an emerging liberal strain within Protestant

Christianity, emphasizing divine immanence in human reality.'[17]

. . .

Hattie held similar views, as a result of the religious nurture given her by her father, her interest in romantic poetry, and no doubt some of her reading as a teacher. Improvements in communication through train travel, mail service, and increased choice in periodicals and newspapers ensured that even in such villages as Stanstead, people were kept abreast of developments in social and religious thought. Although there exists no record of Hattie reading Bushnell's *Christian Nurture*, there were many other likeminded treatises. One that she did read enthusiastically described marriage and family as the earthly foretaste of the bliss of heaven. Since 'God we are told is love,' the author asserted, 'it is but reasonable to suppose that he would establish between his children a relation designed to inspire universal and eternal love.'[18]

In the course of the couple's economic woes, Hattie reassured her husband that their love for one another constituted the one certainty in life.[19] Implicitly endowing the family with an absolute value formerly reserved only for religion, she reflected the belief of Bushnell, Beecher, and other liberal Protestant writers that the love of family members for one another was truly the nursery of religion. The love that Charles and Hattie expressed for their children was indeed unconditional, total, and exuberant. 'Papa sends Charley three kisses—one on his two lips, each of his red cheeks and a Scotch kiss beside,' wrote Charles to his daughter Jessie after she and Charley had been sent to Weybridge during the fatal illness of their baby sister, Alice.[20] Cleaning up after a birthday party for one of the children, Hattie commented to her husband, 'Certainly nothing is wasted that tends to make home happy for children.'[21]

Although Bushnell had argued the importance of environment as a redemptive force and thus had cleared the ground for romantic views of childhood innocence, he had not rejected the Calvinist view of total depravity. Where his peers were critical of such theological inconsistency, laypeople were less troubled. Among Hattie's papers, for instance, can be found a poem, written by a friend but preserved in her own handwriting, entitled 'Little Hattie'.[22] Intended as comfort for a mother who is about to lose an infant daughter (and thus possibly written in 1871 during Alice's terminal illness), the lines place the new emphasis on childhood innocence side by side with an older belief in the inscrutable ways of God described in the hymn that Lemira had sung at the funeral of her daughter Emily. The updated poem was a humanized (and feminized) confession, in which a loving Saviour welcomes the 'gem . . . borrowed from Paradise':

Yea! thy cherished babe will slumber there
On the holy Saviour's breast
Perchance long years of woe mother
May be spared thy little one
For our Father sees not as we see,
His will not ours be done.

Although in Methodist circles the theological debate about infant depravity continued to rage for another 20 years, long before that, middle-class women such as Hattie had already rewritten official doctrine in ways that reflected their own experience.[23]

. . .

Middle-class evangelical families had at their disposal a number of ways in which 'gloomy piety' could be replaced by a religious nurture that was more in tune with the optimistic spirit of the age. Although the religious press continued to stress the role of the father when reminding readers of the importance of family devotions, the shift in responsibility for leadership from the father to the mother was part of a wide and well-documented pattern.[24] In the Colby household, since the father was often away and since Hattie had been a teacher as a young woman, it was the mother who took on the task of religious instruction. Early in her marriage, to mark Charles's infrequent periods at home, and reflecting the new interest in quality 'family time', Hattie had instituted a special Sunday domestic ritual after the usual church and Sunday school attendance.[25] Known as 'dressing and combing father's whiskers', the practice (and its much-regretted absence when he was away) surfaced regularly in family correspondence in the 1860s.[26] Juxtaposed with this family ritual, rich in its potential for physical intimacy, was an hour each Sunday afternoon when the children systematically read aloud to their mother a chapter of Scripture and committed to memory selected verses for Sunday school. Changed into 'prayers and psalms' once the children had ceased attending Sunday school, the practice continued well into the 1890s, with their father becoming a more frequent participant after his retirement from political life.[27]

Sunday Bible-reading in the home was a long-established Puritan tradition in children's lives, but in the nineteenth century the growing trade in inexpensively published books and Bibles offered a new context.[28] Gifts for the Colby children drew on the growing religious consumerism that by the nineteenth century was fuelling both Protestant and Roman Catholic piety.[29] To prudent parents, the educational purpose of religiously inspired children's gifts justified the monetary outlay.[30] When money was at its scarcest during the year of the bankruptcy, Hattie was able to justify the one-dollar purchase of a Noah's Ark, which delighted Charley during a visit to her friends, the Cowles. Birthday gifts for Jessie, who from an early age showed an interest in religion, included a gilt little Wesleyan hymnal from her uncle William, followed some years later by the gift of the Bible that had once belonged to her grandfather Moses.[31] Whether handed down or newly purchased, Bibles became coveted children's gifts in the religiously charged culture of the period; their contents were considered essential to furnishing a child's mind with a wealth of imagery, which later would inform an understanding of literature and poetry. Charles William, the eldest son, precociously already

reading at age three, was given an illustrated copy of *Pilgrim's Progress* by his grandmother and a Bible by his mother on his sixth birthday. 'He is pleased as can be with each gift, but regards the Bible, all his own, as most too good to be true,' Hattie proudly informed her husband. 'He returns to it again and again: reading now in the Old Testament and now in the New: finding alone the places he is familiar with.'[32] Thanks to such encouragement, a child's mind became richly furnished with biblical imagery, some of which could be put to remarkable use. When, for example, his careless playing with matches set the barn on fire and he was faced with a rare paternal use of the switch, young Charley was able to deflect his well-deserved corporal punishment by pointedly comparing his situation to the New Testament martyr Stephen, thereby seeing his solicitous and largely female audience dissolve into laughter.[33]

The fact that none of the children required encouragement in reading can in large part be attributed to their mother's example. A favourite family pastime, reading aloud to one another was begun by the couple in the first months of their marriage, and it was transmitted to the children, the two eldest daughters taking it upon themselves to read to their brothers, and all four later taking turns to read to their grandmother [Lemira] in her final years. Since their father had ready access to the parliamentary library in Ottawa after his election in 1867, requests for books surfaced regularly in the family letters. These included a request from Hattie for *Moods* by Louisa May Alcott, *Robinson Crusoe* for Charley, and a biography of the evangelical hymn writer Frances Havergal, which in 1883 was read aloud to Lemira and other household members, including Rosalie, the Roman Catholic servant. By his own account Charles Williams was 'a boyish bookworm'. At seven he was deeply enamoured of Richard the Lionheart and soon developed an admiration for the novels of Sir Walter Scott. By the age of 12 he had completed the extensive *Commonplace Book of Shakespeare*, and extending beyond the Anglo-Saxon corpus he read the Koran to his grandmother.[34] Thanks to this steady fare of books, literary and biblical images fuelled the children's imagination, as well as providing subject matter for games such as charades and their own theatrical productions.

Poetry and song, like reading aloud, especially when presented from a mother's lips, were seen by educators as ideal ways of inculcating early childhood religious influences. Hearth, home, and song figured prominently in the nostalgia of the later Victorians, and among Hattie Colby's happiest experiences was an evening of singing around the piano when her brother Jack made an unexpected visit with his young son.[35] Jessie and Abby were both given piano lessons, and their mother took every opportunity to have them display their musical talent before admiring house guests. Such accomplishments, in tandem with the family's exposure to literature, refined the taste of both adults and children.

In a society that placed a high value on self-formation, these also became an essential component to religious nurture. Here, too, historians have pointed to the influence of Horace Bushnell who, in addition to his interest in child nurture, expressed strong views about the difference between what he called 'fashion' and 'taste'. While fashion marked the values of an effete aristocracy, taste was a God-given quality through which people participated in God's creative work of beautifying the universe. Thus, the moral for middle-class evangelical Americans was, as historian Richard Bushman has pointed out, 'to cultivate taste and avoid fashion'.[36] Others have gone further, seeing in this 'refinement' of religion a new secular understanding of the process of sanctification, a practical updated expression of Christian perfection—the 'second blessing' (as Charles Colby called his 1858 experience of divine love). Given the social value placed on self-improvement, moral formation came to be seen as a religious duty, no longer the preserve of a small number of male intellectuals, as it had been in the eighteenth century, but a popular

ideal available to all. Since the literary culture of the period was polite, evangelicalism began to take on accents of this broader culture, aided by the availability of inexpensive printed material and its own emphasis on individual transformation. The true Christian was not only someone whose sins were forgiven but was also a person who was refined, balanced, and had benefited from the increasingly available opportunities for self-development.[37]

The marriage between good taste and religion inevitably challenged some forms of evangelical expression, and in the Colby household not all of the didactic material available to a juvenile audience received approval. A travelling panorama of *Pilgrim's Progress*, for example, performed at the Stanstead town hall, to which Hattie took the children, left her profoundly disappointed. Its pictures seemed 'fearful daubs', the angels' wings reminded her of 'half-worn store wings from the goose', and 'the pearly gates anything but what a fine faith sees'.[38] In like manner, the moralistic children's literature that flooded the evangelical book market and was highly favoured by adults as gifts did not escape the criticism of the Colby children (and, no doubt, other juvenile readers). 'Charley's book is beautifully illustrated,' Hattie wrote in a letter to Abby, 'but he doesn't care much about the story. It is written in the "goody-goody" style. Jess began reading it aloud to me, but would say every other sentence "now it's going to moralize."'[39] This literary form of self-development, redolent of an earlier generation and still solemnly extolled in children's literature, resonated little with the lives of well-read middle-class youth.[40]

An aversion to moralization did not mean that children should not be exposed to moral influences. In fact, such influences were seen to lie at the heart of the new understanding of religion, whereby children were socialized into the faith rather than being brought to conversion as had been the practice a generation earlier. Since refinement was no longer a capitulation to fashion but was seen as a desirable characteristic, it was to be cultivated like other virtues, such as courage and kindness. And it was the task of the mother, as the central figure in family religious nurture, to impart to the next generation the importance of good manners and good taste. Manners and morals went together. 'Charley waits upon me elegantly everywhere I go, and he did last night,' Hattie informed her daughters when describing a recent Methodist social, whose 'first rate' entertainment had included several duets, a violin solo, and sundry readings and declamations by Stanstead youth.[41]

This refinement assumed that religion was not simply a spiritual concern but also had an important material dimension. Nineteenth-century evangelical religion was a religion of the heart and could endure only if it remained sensitive to the changing material culture of its adherents.[42] 'All this material scene is but the homestead, the play-ground, the workshop and schoolhouse, of human nature,' one contemporary writer reminded his readers as he impressed upon them the value of childhood religious nurture.[43] In a Christianity that stressed the incarnation of God's love, high-toned poetry, literature, and tastefully manufactured religious commodities all became part of 'the material scene' of family religion. Since religious beliefs are in large part transmitted through image and language, refinement may well have been more instrumental than the well-publicized theological disputes of the period in bringing about the shift in evangelical Protestantism from an emphasis on the atonement to the incarnation.[44]

Studies of the Victorian middle-class home, with a few notable exceptions, have focused on the nuclear family—a claustrophobic unit comprising father, mother, and children—and they have devoted little attention to the wider context of kinship and community.[45] However, as social workers and psychologists emphasize, these networks play an indispensable role in child formation.[46] Victorian educators were no less assiduous in reminding parents of the importance of surrounding children and youths

with sound moral influences. 'The family is not a unit, cast alone into space,' Mrs Julia McNair Wright, author of *The Complete Home*, told her readers. 'It is one of many which make up the grand sum-total of the race; in every department of life we touch on our fellows: we were born social animals, and we will exercise our social instincts.'[47] Not every family had a resident grandmother and an assortment of cousins and family friends living with them for extended periods, as was the case with the Colbys. But nineteenth-century children, like their parents, were part of larger communal networks. Hattie and Charles Colby were therefore no less assiduous than Mrs Wright in ensuring that their children's social instincts were well shaped.

In their youth, the burden of moral formation had rested on the immediate family, on the church, and on whatever rudiments of a public/private system of education happened to be in place in the area. By the 1860s and 1870s, their children were able to benefit from a greatly widened circle, thanks to the large output of the religious presses, a host of material refinements, and an increase in voluntary societies such as Sunday schools and Bands of Hope directed at the young. As a result, decisions concerning formal education, the selection of marriage partners, and a career now took place in an environment permeated by religious and moral influences. Like the older custom of seeking patrons, the new emphasis on refining influences meant that young people needed to be part of a wide network of social interaction. Although not always borne out in practice, ministerial families were considered specially endowed to extend such refinement. 'It is good to get a little out of the commonplace talk of weather, health and servants which makes up the staple of our talk usually, and hear governments and aristocracy and literature,' Hattie appreciatively commented, with her daughters in mind, after a visit by the recently appointed Methodist minister and his wife.[48]

Leisure activities of a communal nature provided the children with opportunities for self-development unavailable a generation earlier. In a village such as Stanstead with a population of 575, rural and urbanized life frequently intersected, but for its children aged 14 and under . . ., activities associated with rural life predominated.[49] The letters of the Colby children abound with such traditional events as sugaring and taffy pulling, buggy rides in the area, and bathing in the region's large cool lakes. As well, there were family and community picnics, fishing and hunting for the boys, visits to the homes of local residents, and a steady stream of children's parties. Depending on the age and gender of the guests, such gatherings included long-established games such as blind-man's bluff, hide-and-go-seek, and charades, but the children also had the opportunity to learn dancing and card playing, whist being a favourite.[50]

Lemira, Charles, and Hattie had grown up in the shadow of a middle-class society whose evangelical ministers had frowned on moral 'dissipations' such as dancing and cards (though this had not prevented Hattie from enjoying a game of whist). By the 1870s, Stanstead claimed a number of prominent Universalists, and while Hattie tended to decline invitations from members of this more 'worldly' religious denomination, the children mixed freely and attended one another's parties. For children, dancing consisted largely of hopping in step with the music, but by the time the two Colby daughters had reached their early teens and were ready to learn more formal dancing, they encountered no parental opposition to what had become a general peer practice in Stanstead.[51] Nor, as long as one was not a church member, was there much ministerial opposition.[52] In 1886, implicitly acknowledging the prevalence of dancing, the Methodist denomination prohibited members from taking part not only in the 'buying, using, or selling' of liquor, but also in 'the dance, gambling games, the theatre, the circus, and the race course'.[53] Long before this effort to regulate the behaviour of the laity in an increasingly worldly society, Stanstead's ministers, like

some of their colleagues elsewhere, had already quietly accepted for adherents such 'refined' activities as dancing in homes and attending the theatre.[54] This was facilitated by the fact that Stanstead's Methodists, by then the most influential Protestant denomination in the region, usually managed to ensure that only ministers who shared their values were sent to them by the denominational stationing committee. There were evangelical families who resisted dancing, but in the eyes of the Colby children this made the socials they put on rather dull affairs.[55]

While there was some disagreement on the matter of dancing, this was not the case with 'dry socials', which were the prevalent form of entertainment among all the region's Protestants, young as well as old. Within the evangelical framework of individual moral responsibility, intemperance represented the greatest threat to family harmony and unity; but also, happily, it offered the greatest opportunity for social reform. The cold winters of the Eastern Townships and the availability of beer and rye whiskey (as the cheapest way of marketing hops and wheat in the early days) continued to be a formidable challenge to the temperance movement.[56] By the 1870s and 1880s, when the Colby children were reaching adolescence, support for Prohibition had become strong and widespread, especially among women, children, and civic leaders. Few families seemed to be immune from the ravages of alcohol—including, at one point, Stanstead's Anglican rector, whose wife's black eye and children's neglected state did not go unnoticed.[57] Closer to home, where the Colby children's own beloved Uncle William sometimes went on an extended spree, it was his wife Melvina who took forceful charge of the village's juvenile temperance organization, which was known as the Band of Hope. Whether they liked it or not, children were often harnessed into the good causes promoted by their parents. When, on her niece Mary's birthday, she had been requested to bring bread and butter to a parlour meeting which Melvina was holding to talk up the Band of Hope to the young guests, Hattie noted, tongue in cheek, 'I hope Mary will like that form of celebration.'[58] In Hattie's approach to nurture, this was putting Prohibition ahead of the children's need to enjoy themselves.

A major reason for juvenile involvement in Protestant voluntary societies was their role in character building and nation building.[59] In a world where evangelicals presented public duties as part of convivial pleasures and where a father's role in civic life was a way of impressing his children of his importance in the wider world, even the political picnics of the 1870s, with their endless speech making, were of interest.[60] 'It was a treat,' 15-year-old Jessie enthusiastically told her sister when describing 12 successive speeches (including two by her father, who 'spoke *splendidly*') delivered one fine July day in 1877 when Sir John A. Macdonald and his entourage visited Stanstead.[61] No less political, but more tuned to juvenile participation, was the temperance movement. During a temperance picnic held at Derby, a visiting niece (also called Hattie) decided to join the Temperance Lodge, and as the older Hattie confided to Jessie, joining the lodge in this small American border community would enable young Hattie to enter into contact with 'all the best portions' of its population.[62]

. . .

By the mid-1880s, the major Protestant denominations had become more concerned with attending to the social needs of young women and men by forming young people's societies.[63] Stanstead's Methodist Young People's Association, established in 1884, like many others, reflected the tastes and skills of its membership by offering such entertainment as piano duets, recitations, and related fundraising for church-related causes. These societies with their expected etiquette, like the ritualized entry of denominational youth into full church membership, were indicative of a pattern of carefully planned stages in religious socialization informed by commitment to family and community. In turn, young people who had been socialized

into religion took it upon themselves, through church groups, to transmit to the next generation some of the influences that had shaped their own outlook.[64] Nineteen-year-old Jessie's efforts through study and activities at 'children's meetings' evoked from her mother the approving comment: 'Grown people are what they are and cannot (generally) be materially changed—but youth is plastic and can be moulded to good purpose.'[65] In a variety of ways, therefore, the new ideals of Christian nurture were extended beyond the home to a younger generation and a wider community.

. . .

Abby's fragile health made her the first to embark on what became a female family tradition of travel in search of improved well-being. Accompanying her father on one of his western business trips in the spring of 1875, she spent some time with a great aunt's family in Chicago (where her mother, with an eye on the future, sent her a strong encouragement to 'get a taste of dancing').[66] . . . Hattie, who joined Abby in January 1880, found herself two months later faced with the delicate task of having to deal with the first of three western suitors for her daughter's hand. Regretting profoundly her husband's absence when his advice was so needed, she confided in a letter home, 'The fact is as you and I know, that Abby is qualified to adorn *any* position, the higher the better, and it would seem a sad waste, for her to accept anything or anybody who was second rate. With her good head and good heart and her very rare social qualities she is fairly entitled to the best.'[67] Although Hattie noted the family background of the suitors, including denominational affiliation, for her husband's information, she did not have to make a decision. Abby, who agreed with her mother's assessment of her attributes, decided that 'the best' was to be pursued not in the West but in the nation's capital, through the connections of her politician father. By the spring of 1881, therefore, she began to spend time in Ottawa, boarding with her father at the Russell Hotel, and after

1883 Jessie often accompanied her.[68] Marriage did not appear to be a priority for Jessie, but spending increasing amounts of time in Ottawa allowed her to perfect her musical training, and her letters home gave detailed accounts of the fun available in the national capital for two attractive young women of marriageable age.[69]

Their mother, at home in Stanstead, accompanied them vicariously, unable to restrain either her enthusiasm or her inclination to offer advice: 'Isn't papa lovely and elegant at the parties tho? I knew you w'd find it out. I think he w'd have been willing to see you dance a few times (I would just—) after supper and not disappoint the partners on your list.'[70] Abby, who as the more attractive and coquettish seems to have been especially receptive to her mother's coaching, received several proposals. Two of these were refused, one resulted in a brief but brilliant engagement to a Winnipeg business partner of her father, and a fourth, at first refused, ultimately led to marriage.[71] Concerned that her daughter's tempestuous road to engagement might have led to gossip in Ottawa and elsewhere, Hattie sought to reassure herself while giving her daughter a subtle reminder of the standard of true womanly behaviour: 'I am thankful to know that in every instance, where you have declined "the highest compliment", it has been through no fault of yours that it was offered—on the contrary that it has been [offered] notwithstanding very guarded conduct on your part.'[72]

The final choice, Somerset Aikins, was everything a mother could desire in a son-in-law. He was the second son of James Cox Aikins, a Conservative MP from Winnipeg, who had recently been appointed lieutenant governor of Manitoba and was an active Methodist.[73] Initially refused by Abby, the suitor had briefly transferred his affections to Jessie, but by the spring of 1887, upon the termination of Abby's earlier engagement, he was encouraged to make a second proposal. It was a time of major change in the lives of the Colby family. That May, thanks to improved material circumstances and the death of the previous owner of the stone house,

Charles was able to buy back the family home, henceforth to be called Carrollcroft. In addition, his son Charles William graduated from McGill with first-class honours and the Shakespeare gold medal in English. The final thread was tied down when Somerset Aikins arrived in Stanstead, stayed nine days, proposed to Abby, and in the words of Jessie's journal, 'went away happy'.[74] The next few months, in anticipation of Abby's wedding on 13 October, saw furious activity around the stone house before the family re-entered it in August. Since the bride was 'not strong' and her mother was 'very poorly', the decision was made to have a private wedding. As evidence of the extent to which a private family was also part of a larger public network, 800 invitations were sent out, but fortunately only 200 guests were able to attend. Conducted in Stanstead's small Anglican church, it was followed by a reception at Carrollcroft, which reflected in every way that taste and refinement had become well-entrenched evangelical values.[75]

As evidenced by this highly acclaimed wedding, the expanding marketplace of the 1880s and Charles Colby's growing success therein had indeed brought a remarkable change in the opportunities for self-definition available to at least some young people, when compared with those of their parents and grandparents. To the earlier emphasis on self-control, self-development had been added as an important way for members of the middle class to advance in a commercial society shaped by expanding economic opportunity. In this process, polite culture which, as a number of historians have observed, had earlier begun to shape the values of 'the middling sort' in Britain, had also begun to permeate the domestic life of middle-class evangelicals in North America.[76] Having proudly informed his mother that his costs in his first year at McGill had been significantly lower than those of his housemates, Charles William promptly received a stinging rebuke: 'Never sponge in any way—but take your share in paying for treats. To be prudent is one thing and to be "mean and small" is quite another. The family tradition & practice will warrant you in spending all you need to *spend*, and in doing it frankly like a man.'[77] Although Charles and John Colby's financial circumstances as students remained cramped, the concept of character had undergone a sea change since the days when their father as a student at Dartmouth had carefully noted his expenses in order to assure his parents that he was making every possible economy.

By the 1880s, frugality, which had once been seen as a commendable character trait in the middle class, had come to be equated with unmanly behaviour. Liberality in spending was no longer a trait that evangelicals associated with a wasteful upper class; it had become the noblesse oblige of upper-middle-class Methodists. Thus, the wedding of the older Colby daughter, her elaborate trousseau, and her lifestyle as a newlywed member of a prominent Winnipeg Methodist family were far removed from the experience of her mother. The latter's wedding had been noteworthy only in its soberness, and as a young bride she had had to defer material purchases and remind her husband that 'costliness is not happiness.' Abby, through her marriage, and Jessie, in her single life as a companion to her parents, had entered a way of life reminiscent of that of late eighteenth-century English gentlewomen, so well described by Amanda Vickery and others.[78]

By the latter part of the nineteenth century, Canadian Methodists as a group had become solidly middle class, respectable, and in many cases, 'refined'. . . . In a world in which God was seen to be immanent, the Christian family became the site where self-improvement and religious nurture worked together to prepare a child for this life as well as for eternity. From the time of the Puritans to that of Moses Colby's generation, the family had been seen as 'a little church' in which the child was taught the eternal truths of salvation. Evangelicals took a distinctive turn when they went further and added to their concern for salvation 'the conviction that the particular arrangements of family life could have

eternal consequences', to cite historian Margaret Bendroth.[79] It is not surprising, therefore, that some have seen the Victorian fascination with domestic religion as an important step in the gradual disenchantment of Western society.[80]

For late nineteenth-century evangelicals, however, the equation was precisely the reverse: instead of the family replacing religion, religion sacralized the family. As Hattie Colby had reminded her husband during the nadir of their economic fortunes, in the unpredictable world of industrializing North America, family was the one constant that promised stability and security. Taken together, family and religious moral formation provided security, order, and practical assistance, and it is not surprising that both were seen to be of divine origin and universal. . . . In the words of an 1865 publication, 'As the family is a divine institution and a type of the church and of heaven it cannot be understood in its isolation from Christianity; it must involve Christian principles, duties and interests; and embrace in its educational functions, a preparation not only for the State, but also for the church.'[81]

. . .

Notes

1. Hattie Child Colby (HCC) to Charles Carroll Colby (CCC), 1 Mar. 1871, HCC Papers, Series 1, Box 1:2, Fonds Colby (FC), Stanstead Historical Society.

2. For an early example, see Anne L. Kuhn, *The Mother's Role in Childhood Education: New England Concepts, 1830–1860* (New Haven: Yale University Press, 1947), and Barbara Welter, 'The Cult of True Womanhood, 1820–1860', *American Quarterly* 18 (1966): 151–74.

3. Maxine Van De Wetering, 'The Popular Concept of "Home" in Nineteenth-Century America', *Journal of American Studies* 28 (1984): 1, 5–28.

4. John Tosh, *A Man's Place: Masculinity and the Middle-Class Home in Victorian England* (New Haven: Yale University Press, 1999), 79–86, and Leonore Davidoff, *The Family Story: Blood, Contract, and Intimacy, 1830–1960* (New York: Addison Wesley Longman, 1999), 151–7.

5. Tosh, *A Man s Place*, 101.

6. See, for example, his description of purchases in anticipation of a trip to Vermont with his wife and youngest daughter; CCC to HCC, 4 Apr. 1870, CCC Papers, Series 4:A, Box 2:4, FC.

7. CCC to HCC, 30 Apr. 1872, CCC Papers, Series 4:A, Box 2:5, FC.

8. Davidoff, *The Family Story*, 109; Colleen McDannell, *The Christian Home in Victorian America, 1840–1900* (Bloomington: Indiana University Press, 1986); and Margaret Bendroth, *Growing Up Protestant: Parents, Children, and Mainline Churches* (New Brunswick, NJ: Rutgers University Press, 2002), 1–80. . . .

9. This has been well argued for Victorian England in Leonore Davidoff and Catherine Hall, *Family Fortunes: Men and Women of the English Middle Class, 1780–1850* (Chicago: University of Chicago Press, 1987), 76–148. For the United States, see Mary P. Ryan, *Cradle of the Middle Class: The Family in Oneida County, New York, 1790–1865* (Cambridge: Cambridge University Press, 1981). In both, however, the relation to the institutional church has received little attention.

10. Edmund S. Morgan, *The Puritan Family: Religion and Domestic Relations in Seventeenth-Century New England* (New York: Harper and Row, 1944), 87–108.

11. J.I. Little, 'The Fireside Kingdom: A Mid-Nineteenth-Century Anglican Perspective on Marriage and Parenthood', in Nancy Christie, ed., *Households of Faith: Family, Gender, and Community in Canada, 1760–1969* (Montreal and Kingston: McGill-Queen's University Press, 2001), 77–100. . . .

12. The most informative study on the Sunday school movement (for the United States) is Ann Boylan, *The Formation of an American Institution, 1790–1880* (New Haven: Yale University Press, 1988). . . . [F]or Methodism in Canada, see Neil Semple, *The Lord's Dominion: The History of Canadian Methodism* (Montreal and Kingston: McGill-Queen's University Press, 1996), ch. 14 . . .

13. In Canada the official resolution of the theological dispute about whether a child's eternal safety rested on conversion, rather than on baptism and childhood nurture, took significantly longer than in the United States; see Marguerite Van Die, *An Evangelical Mind: Nathanael Burwash and the Methodist Tradition in Canada, 1839–1918* (Montreal and Kingston: McGill-Queen's University Press, 1989), 25–37. See also Neil Semple, '"The Nurture and Admonition of the Lord": Nineteenth-Century Canadian Methodism's Response to Childhood', *Histoire Sociale/Social History* 14 (1981): 157–75.

14. Serge Gagnon, *Plaisir d'amour et crainte de Dieu: sexualité et confession au Bas-Canada* (Sainte-Foy: Presses de l'Université Laval, 1990), 79.

15. *Liturgy or Formulary of Services in Use in the Wesleyan-Methodist Church in Canada* (Toronto: S. Rose, 1867), 7.

16. For a succinct summary of Bushnell's thought, see Gary Dorrien, *The Making of American Liberal Theology: Imagining Progressive Religion, 1805–1900* (Louisville: Westminster John Knox Press, 2001), 111–78. . . .

17. Bendroth, *Growing Up Protestant*, 25.

18. George S. Weaver, *The Christian Household: Embracing the Christian Home . . .* (Boston: Tompkins and Musey, 1856), 36. The reference to its reading is in Journal, 10 Mar. 1861, HCC Papers, Series 2, Box 1, FC.

19. HCC to CCC, 1 Apr. 1873, HCC Papers, Series 1, Box 1:3, FC.

20. CCC to Jessie Maud Colby (JMC), 7 July 1872, CCC Papers, Series 4:A, Box 1:5, FC.

21. HCC to CCC, 26 Mar. 1875, HCC Papers, Series 1, Box 1:5, FC.

22. 'Little Hattie', HCC Papers, Series 2, Box 2, FC.

23. For the debate on infant depravity in Canadian Methodist circles, including recent historiographical controversy, see Van Die, *An Evangelical Mind*, ch. 1.

24. McDannell, *The Christian Home*, 108–16, and Bendroth, *Growing Up Protestant*, 14–16.

25. Tosh, *A Man's Place*, 84.

26. See, for example, HCC to CCC, 22 Sept. 1867, HCC Papers, Series 1, Box 1:1, FC.

27. HCC to CCC, 20 and 23 Mar. 1873, HCC Papers, Series 1, Box 1:3, FC; and Diary, 5 Apr. 1903, JMC Papers, Series 2, Box 1, FC.

28. See the fine study on Victorian Bibles as commodities in Colleen McDannell, *Material Christianity: Religion and Popular Culture in America* (New Haven: Yale University Press, 1995), 67–102.

29. McDannell, *The Christian Home*, 77–107.

30. Insightful commentary on the moral dimension of consumer choice, though for a later period, is found in Joy Parr, *Domestic Goods: The Material, the Moral and the Economic in the Postwar Years* (Toronto: University of Toronto Press, 1999).

31. HCC to CCC, 12 Nov. 1868, HCC Papers, Series 1, Box 1:1, FC.

32. HCC to CCC, 25 Mar. 1873, HCC Papers, Series I, Box 1:3, FCM.

33. Charles William Colby (CWC), 'Garrulities of an Octogenarian' (typescript), 21, CWC Papers, Series I:C, Box 11:3, FC.

34. Ibid. See also HCC to CCC, 2 Mar. 1883, HCC Papers, Series 1, Box 1:6, FC.

35. HCC to CCC, 31 Aug. 1874, HCC Papers, Series 1, Box 1:4, FC.

36. Richard L. Bushman, *The Refinement of America: Persons, Houses, Cities* (New York: Vintage, 1993), 326–31.

37. Daniel Walker Howe, *Making the American Self: Jonathan Edwards to Abraham Lincoln* (Cambridge, MA: Harvard University Press, 1997), 118–19.

38. HCC to CCC, 27 Mar. 1873, HCC Papers, Series 1, Box 1:3, FC.

39. HCC to Abby Lemira Colby Aikins (ALCA), 11 Apr. 1875, HCC Papers, Series 1, Box 2:4, FC.

40. This did not seem to deter the evangelical press. See David Paul Nord, 'Religious Reading and Readers in

Antebellum America', *Journal of the Early Republic* 15 (Summer 1995): 241–72.

41. HCC to girls, 23 Feb. 1883, HCC Papers, Series 1, Box 2:1, FC.

42. As argued in William McLoughlin, *Revivals, Awakenings, and Reform: An Essay on Religion and Social Change in America, 1607–1977* (Chicago: University of Chicago Press, 1978), which analyzes the close fit between nine-teenth-century experiential religion and its cultural expression.

43. Weaver, *The Christian Household*, 104.

44. This is also briefly noted in Bushman, *Refinement of America*, 351–2 . . .

45. For an example of the former, see Van De Wetering, 'The Popular Concept of "Home" in Nineteenth-Century America'. Notable exceptions include Davidoff and Hall, *Family Fortunes*, and Françoise Noël, *Family Life and Sociability in Upper and Lower Canada, 1780–1870: A View from Diaries and Family Correspondence* (Montreal and Kingston: McGill-Queen's University Press, 2003).

46. Peter N. Stearns and Timothy Haggerty, 'The Role of Fear: Transitions in American Emotional Standards for Children', *American Historical Review* 96, 1 (1991): 63–94.

47. Julia McNair Wright, *The Complete Home: An Encyclopedia of Domestic Life and Affairs* (Brantford, ON: Bradley, Garretson, 1879), 289.

48. HCC to JMC, 28 Aug. 1872, HCC Papers, Series 1, Box 2:7, FC.

49. Census of Canada, 1871, Stanstead (microfilm) C-10089-90, Library and Archives Canada (LAC).

50. A good entry into these varied activities can be found in CWC, 'Garrulities of an Octogenarian' (typescript), 22–4, CWC Papers, Series 1:C, Box 11:3, FC.

51. See, for example, HCC to JMC, 5 July 1874, HCC Papers, Series 1, Box 2:7, FC, in which she notes that Abby had been 'invited to a little dance on account of Johnny Foster's friends'.

52. Hattie told her husband of a female church member's announcement of a Ladies' Aid meeting at the parson-age for the purpose of arranging suitable entertain-ment 'for the young people who are church members want some kind of party that they may go to: and as they are so to speak forbidden to accept the invitations they do receive, they call for something suited to their case'. She did not attend. See HCC to CCC, 20 Jan. 1875, HCC Papers, Series 1, Box 1:5, FC.

53. This was done by adding a footnote to paragraph 35 of its official Doctrine and Discipline. For the wider context, see William H. Magney, 'The Methodist Church and the National Gospel, 1884–1914', *Bulletin* (Committee on Archives, United Church of Canada), 20 (1968): 3–95.

54. Charles William Colby (who married Emma Cobb, granddaughter of Wilder Pierce, member of another prominent Stanstead Methodist family) recounts that the dancing at his outdoor wedding in 1897 was wit-nessed by six ministers, who, though they did not par-ticipate, did not . . . object; see Diary, 23 June 1897, CWC Papers, Series 1:C, Box 12, FC.

55. HCC to ALCA, 31 Jan. 1875, HCC Papers, Series 1, Box 2:4, FC.

56. Jean-Pierre Kesteman, Peter Southam, and Diane Saint-Pierre, *Histoire des cantons de l'Est* (Sainte-Foy: Presses de l'Université Laval, 1998), 396–8.

57. HCC to CCC, 3 Aug. 1873, HCC Papers, Series 1, Box 1:3, FC.

58. HCC to CCC, 21 Oct. 1884, HCC Papers, Series 1, Box 1:7, FC.

59. Bendroth, *Growing Up Protestant*, 39–50.

60. On the relationship between public duty and paternal domesticity, see Tosh, *A Man's Place*, 124–41.

61. JMC to ALCA, 9 July 1877, JMC Papers, Series 1, Box 7:2, FC.

62. HCC to JMC, 10 and 14 Aug. 1874, HCC Papers, Series 1, Box 2:7, FC.

63. For the wider context, see Semple, *The Lord's Dominion*, ch. 14, and Christopher Coble, 'The Role of Young People's Societies in the Training of Christian Womanhood (and Manhood), 1880–1910', in Margaret Lamberts Bendroth and Virginia Lieson Brereton, eds, *Women and Twentieth-Century Protestantism* (Urbana: University of Illinois Press, 2002), 74–92.

64. Young Canadian Methodists in urban centres applauded the move away from the old barnlike build-ings, characteristic of their denomination's earlier architecture, and displayed their aspirations to taste and gentility in their fundraising and social activities.

65. HCC to JMC [early 1880s], HCC Papers, Series 1, Box 2:7, FC.

66. HCC to ALCA, 30 Apr. 1875, HCC Papers, Series 1, Box 2:4, FC.

67. HCC to CCC, 10 and 25 Feb. 1880, HCC Papers, Series 1, Box 1:6, FC.

68. Although they were very different in temperament, the two daughters were extremely close and, when not together in Ottawa or Stanstead, they shared a lively correspondence. . . . It may have been [Jessie's] attrac-tion to the more interesting male world that led her, at the age of 12, to announce that she would 'never marry anyone, because there wouldn't be *another* man *just like papa*'; HCC to CCC, 2 Apr. 1873, HCC Papers, Series 1, Box 1:3, FC.

69. JMC to HCC, and JMC to family, JMC Papers, Series 1, Boxes 1:1, 2 and 2:1, FC.

70. HCC to ALCA, 26 Feb. 1881, HCC Papers, Series 1, Box 2:5, FC.

71. By the spring of 1883, with both daughters well estab-lished in the Russell Hotel, letters between Ottawa and

Stanstead began to make frequent mention of Abby's engagement with a certain K.N. McFee. K.N., as he was generally known, was a Winnipeg entrepreneur who had won the confidence and admiration of her father, as well as the approval of her mother. A frequent visitor in Stanstead, McFee took up a number of business partnerships with Charles Colby in the Northwest.

72. HCC to ALCA, 24 Mar. 1883, HCC Papers, Series 1, Box 2:5, FC.

73. Upon hearing of Abby's engagement to McFee, Aikins had immediately transferred his affections to Jessie, the younger daughter. . . . See HCC to ALCA and JMC, 26 Mar. 1883, HCC Papers, Series 1, Box 2:1, FC.

74. Diary entries, 11 and 29 May 1887, JMC Papers, Series 2, Box 1, FC.

75. See also description in Diary, 31 Jan. 1881, JMC Papers, Series 2, Box 1, FC. The wedding notice in the *Stanstead Journal* stated that the couple were married on Thursday evening at 7 o'clock, Christ Church, Stanstead, followed by an At Home at 8 o'clock, Mr and Mrs C.C. Colby, Carrollcroft.

76. Amanda Vickery, *The Gentleman's Daughter: Women's Lives in Victorian England* (New Haven: Yale University Press, 1998), 161–94, and Marjorie R. Hunt, *The Middling Sort: Commerce, Gender, and the Family in England, 1680–1780* (Berkeley: University of California Press, 1996), 193–218. . . .

77. HCC to CWC, 23 July 1883, HCC Papers, Series 1, Box 3:1, FC. . . .

78. See note 76 above.

79. Bendroth, *Growing up Protestant*, 14.

80. 'It is the tie between parents and children which has been imbued with ever more poignancy as people's relationship to the transcendental realms of religion, folk belief and magic has gradually disappeared'; Davidoff, *The Family Story*, 81. John R. Gillis, *A World of Their Own Making: Myth, Ritual, and the Quest for Family Values* (New York: Basic Books, 1996), esp. ch. 4.

81. S. Phillips, *The Christian Home as It Is in the Sphere of Nature and the Church* (New York: Gurdon Mill, 1865), 23, donated to the Archives of the Stanstead Historical Society.

3

Living on Display: Colonial Visions of Aboriginal Domestic Spaces

Paige Raibmon

Notions of domesticity were central to colonial projects around the globe. They were part of the fray when metropole and colony collided and transformed one another. As Jean and John Comaroff put it, 'Colonialism was as much about making the center as it was about making the periphery. The colony was not a mere extension of the modern world. It was part of what made the world modern in the first place. And the dialectic of domesticity was a vital element in the process.'[1] The colonial desire to order domestic space had its correlate in broader attempts to impose discipline in the public sphere.[2] On the late nineteenth-century Northwest Coast, this process took shape for Aboriginal people who increasingly lived not only overseas from, but within, the society of the colonizing metropoles. Aboriginal people experienced extreme pressure to bring their lives into conformity with Victorian expectations about private, middle-class, bourgeois domesticity. This pressure came not only from isolated missionaries posted in lonely colonial outposts but also from a broad swath of colonial society. So intense was the interest in Aboriginal domestic arrangements, however, that colonial society brought Aboriginal domestic space into the public domain as never before, even as it urged Aboriginal communities to adopt the Victorian values of the domestic

private sphere. While missionaries and government officials pressured Aboriginal families to replace multi-family longhouses with Victorian-style nuclear family dwellings, anthropologists and tourists invaded Aboriginal homes, alternately in search of a rapidly receding ('savage') past or a slowly dawning ('civilized') future. Missionaries encouraged such voyeuristic investigations in the hope that the object lessons of everyday Aboriginal life would generate a flow of funds from Christian pocketbooks into missionary society coffers. Anthropologists such as Franz Boas fed their own form of economic necessity with these displays, which they hoped would encourage benefactors to provide funding for additional anthropological fieldwork and collecting. In a sense, as they transformed Aboriginal domestic spaces into spectacle, all of the members of these non-Aboriginal groups became sightseers.

Domestic space was transformed into spectacle, and attempts to effect greater separation between private and public spaces simultaneously blurred the two, creating a hybrid public/private domain. Colonialism is riven with such invariably ironic contradictions. But the importance of such contradictions runs deeper than postmodern irony. While with one hand colonial society held out the promise of assimilation, with the other it

Paige Raibmon, 'Living on Display: Colonial Visions of Aboriginal Domestic Spaces', *BC Studies* 140 (2003): 69–89. Reprinted by permission of *BC Studies*.

impressed upon Aboriginal people its lack of good faith. The history of Aboriginal people in North America is replete with 'sweet' promises gone sour; with 'final' promises turned final solutions.[3] How did colonizers reconcile these contradictions, these 'tensions of empire'?[4] A review of their views of Aboriginal domestic space provides an opportunity to address this question.

When curious, often nosy, sometimes aggressive members of colonial society entered Aboriginal homes, they brought the things they needed to make sense of the room around them. The significance of cultural practice may lie in the story we tell ourselves about ourselves, but the insight that the metropole has been defined by the colonies, and the 'self' by the 'other', forces us to acknowledge that culture is also the story we tell ourselves about others.[5] The colonial preoccupation with the domestic spaces of Aboriginal people provides a window onto stories that worked in both of these ways simultaneously. The stories that members of colonial society told themselves about Aboriginal people were also stories they told themselves about themselves. The stories that Canadians and Americans told themselves differed, as did specific policies and conditions on both sides of the border. However, during the late nineteenth century, public interest in 'authentic' Indians and pride in successful Indian policy were important components of both countries' sense of nationalism. Differences in policy did not preclude continuities in attitudes and assumptions. Colonizers' fascination with the domestic spaces of Aboriginal people offers us an important moment of cultural convergence.

The colonial narration of Aboriginal domestic space as spectacle generated a multiplicity of stories about, among other things, Aboriginal savagery, white civilization, colonial legitimacy, and modernity. Two assumptions of colonial thought recur in these stories. First, from their various, and admittedly diverse, vantage points, members of late nineteenth-century colonial society cast domestic spaces and domestic goods as material markers of civilization. But this alone

cannot explain the sway that these markers of domesticity held over the colonial imagination. The second assumption takes us this additional step. The evidence suggests that members of colonial society assumed that the significance of these markers was more than skin deep. They assumed that the markers were straightforward reflections of the inner state of the individual's soul and the family's moral state. They extrapolated from fixed material form to fixed immaterial self. If the space was civilized, then likewise its inhabitants; if the space was uncivilized, then so were its inhabitants.

Aboriginal domestic spaces were put on display in a variety of contexts and along a continuum of consent. Some Aboriginal people willingly participated in the public performance of their private lives, while others submitted somewhat more grudgingly to the public gaze. Sometimes Aboriginal people did not have the opportunity to grant or withhold consent at all, when non-Aboriginal viewers invaded their private homes without bothering to ask permission. All of these interactions were infused with relations of power. Whether they suffered public scrutiny willingly or not, most Aboriginal families could ill afford to forgo the material benefits that accompanied submission to the colonial view. Some form of direct or indirect remuneration usually accompanied the performance of everyday life. This sometimes came as wages, at other times it came from the sale of souvenirs to sightseers hoping to commemorate their excursions into Aboriginal domestic space.

In this article, I explore a selection of domestic spectacles that fall along various points of the aforementioned continuum of consent, and I also address the nature of some of the stories that these spectacles enabled colonizers to tell themselves. I conclude with some brief considerations of the quite different stories that Aboriginal people told themselves about domestic spaces. The transformation and narration of everyday life were central to colonial policy and culture alike. This article takes preliminary steps towards considering why this may have been so.

Exposition Space

The world's fairs and expositions of the late nineteenth century provide some of the clearest examples of Aboriginal people voluntarily submitting to living on display. Beginning with the Paris Exposition in 1889, colonized peoples became important attractions at world's fairs and expositions. In many respects, exhibit organizers intended these so-called 'live exhibits' to display and legitimate colonial narratives of modernity and progress. Early examples of mass advertising that helped generate public support for foreign and domestic policies, the expositions were themselves grand stories that members of colonial society told themselves about themselves.[6] While live exhibits at European fairs tended to come from distant overseas colonies, North American fairs, beginning with the 1893 Chicago World's Fair, featured displays of internally colonized Aboriginal people. While most of these performers spent at least some time in scripted song and dance performances, the bulk of their time as live exhibits was given over to the performance of everyday life.

The live exhibits at the 1893 Chicago World's Fair invariably revolved around domestic dwellings. Millions of tourists flocked to see Aboriginal people supposedly living 'under ordinary conditions and occupying a distinctive habitation'.[7] These dwellings fed into the fair's organizational theme: progress. They offered a relief against which visitors could measure the architectural achievements not only of the rest of the fair but also of dominant society in general. As one reporter wrote, the Aboriginal dwellings stood 'in amazing contrast to the white palaces stretching away to the north, that evidence[d] the skill and prosperity of their successors in this western domain'.[8] Against this backdrop of modernity, the Aboriginal dwellings lent themselves to a social evolutionist narrative that legitimated colonial endeavours.

Anthropologists and other exhibitors erected a 'great Aboriginal encampment',[9] consisting of the living spaces of Aboriginal people from across North America. While newspaper reporters might concede that Aboriginal people lived in 'stone, brick and frame houses'[10] when they were at home, they imagined 'authentic' Aboriginal dwellings as something quite different. For the duration of their time at the fair, Inuit families lived in skin tents; Penobscot families in birchbark wigwams; Navajo families in hogans; Menominee families in skin tepees; Winnebago families in 'sugar-loaf' woven reed mat wigwams; Chippewa families in birchbark longhouses; Iroquois families in elm and birchbark huts and longhouses; and Kwakwaka'wakw families in cedar plank longhouses.[11] Anthropologists simultaneously created and fulfilled expectations of authenticity among visitors to the fair by carefully stage-managing the forms of dwelling put on display.[12]

The Kwakwaka'wakw performers from northern Vancouver Island were, in several respects, typical of the live exhibits. Frederic Ward Putnam, Harvard professor and organizer of the anthropology display, explained that the 16 Kwakwaka'wakw participants would 'live under normal conditions in their natural habitations during the six months of the Exposition'.[13] In order to reinforce the aura of ordinary life, Putnam and his assistants worked to ensure that the Kwakwaka'wakw troupe consisted of family units. This principle was applied to most of the live exhibits, although the definition of 'family' in this context was a non-Aboriginal one. Organizers attempted to limit the performers to couples and their children, even when would-be performers expressed a desire to travel in larger groups.[14] The coordinator of the Kwakwaka'wakw troupe, George Hunt, arranged for his brother and his brother's wife to join the group, although his own wife did not come to Chicago.[15] Hunt's son and father also came. The group included two other couples and two small children. Another performer came with his brother. Hunt seems to have made an effort to meet the desires of his employer, anthropologist Franz Boas, by recruiting people in such a way as to approximate nuclear families. While the final group was not quite a Victorian nuclear family unit, neither was it an extended family of the kind that would have lived in a cedar longhouse.

Putnam's fixation with producing authentic, 'normal' conditions extended to his insistence that the domiciles be originals rather than faux reproductions. Thus, when the Kwakwaka'wakw from Vancouver Island arrived at the Chicago World's Fair, they reassembled the planks of a cedar longhouse that had been disassembled at a Nuwitti village on the northern coast of Vancouver Island before being shipped by rail to Chicago. The house's authenticity was heightened by the report that, when it was chosen for the exhibit, it had actually been occupied by a Kwakwaka'wakw family.[16] The house may even have been the property of one of the performers, which would have added an extra layer to the exhibit's patina of everyday life. The Kwakwaka'wakw house was situated alongside the fairground's South Pond, which stood in for the waters of the Johnstone, Queen Charlotte, and Hecate Straits. The houses faced a sloping 'beach' upon which canoes were pulled ashore.

The display of everyday life was about domestic goods as well as domestic space. 'Traditional' domestic goods completed the tableaux of Aboriginal domesticity presented by the familial scenes. Visitors could see the Kwakwaka'wakw living among items representative of everyday and ceremonial life, including canoes, house poles, totem poles, masks, and regalia. And if they strolled past the dairy exhibit to the nearby anthropology building, visitors could inspect hundreds of other implements integral to Northwest Coast Aboriginal life. Like other human performers, the Kwakwaka'wakw were living appendages of the vast displays of ethnographic objects, many of them drawn from domestic life.

The Kwakwaka'wakw exhibit in Chicago was an explicit realization of the colonial assumption that the 'normal'—that is, 'traditional' and 'authentic'—state of these so-called savages was most visible in their 'everyday life'. The enormous trouble and expense that exhibit

organizers took to ensure that the mock villages consisted of 'real' houses, filled with 'real' goods, was emblematic of their belief that inner meaning was inherent within outward form. They knew that the live exhibits did not 'normally' live beneath the intrusive eyes of millions of visitors. But they nonetheless assumed that the more subjective characteristics of everyday life could be held stable as long as outward conditions and characteristics were replicated as precisely as possible. This assumption was apparent in a number of other settings.

Migrant Space

The Kwakwaka'wakw who travelled to Chicago did so voluntarily and earned lucrative wages for their efforts. Less consensual examples of the performance of everyday life abound. When the domestic spaces of migrant labourers became spectacles, the degree of Aboriginal consent was much more ambiguous. In the late nineteenth century, thousands of Aboriginal people from British Columbia and Washington converged on Puget Sound for the fall hop harvest. Workers harvested a cash crop that was sold on a volatile world market. Yet while employers may have seen Aboriginal pickers as an emerging proletariat, many non-Aboriginal consumers of spectacle cast the labourers as remnants of a vanishing, authentic Aboriginal past, inexorably dying off to make way for the region's non-Aboriginal future. The migrant labour camps to which the influx of workers gave rise became tourist destinations for non-Aboriginal inhabitants of urban and rural Puget Sound. Entrepreneurs and sightseers converged to transform the migrants' temporary living quarters into spectacles. Although the migrant hop pickers had not set out with the intention to perform commodified versions of Aboriginal culture, their experiences in the migrant camps around Puget Sound bore striking resemblances to those of the Kwakwaka'wakw in Chicago's 'great aboriginal encampment'.

The workers were sights of interest even before they reached the hop fields. Local newspapers commented on them when they travelled through urban areas on their way to and from the fields.[17] The appearance of the hop pickers in Seattle was said to be as 'regular as the annual migration of water fowl or the rotation of the seasons, and . . . ever a source of attraction and interest'.[18] The most commonly referred to centre of Aboriginal activity in Seattle during the hop season was the waterfront area known as 'Ballast Island'. Aboriginal migrants began fashioning makeshift camps atop this pile of rocks and rubble in the 1870s, and by 1892 *Harper's Weekly* informed readers that Ballast Island was the place to go to see the pickers.[19] Other sites in and around Seattle and Tacoma also became known for the appearance of seasonal Aboriginal camps.[20]

Rural Aboriginal camps in the hop fields themselves provided an even greater spectacle for curious tourists. During the harvest season in late August and early September, each day hundreds of tourists descended on rural towns like Puyallup and the surrounding hop fields, travelling from Seattle or Tacoma in carriages and on the frequent interurban passenger trains.[21] In the late 1880s and early 1890s, day trippers turned into vacationers as businessmen opened hotels at or near the hop farms.[22]

These urban spectators converged around the domestic lives of the Aboriginal hop pickers. Local papers touted the temporary villages as being 'always worth a visit and study'.[23] John Muir found 'their queer camps' more striking than even the natural setting of 'rustling vine-pillars'.[24] When 400 Cowichan camped in the Puyallup Valley in 1903, visitors and residents alike flocked to watch the 'mode of life and habits of these fish-eating aborigines from Vancouver island'.[25] For tourists, these 'queer camps' were colourful spectacle with a measure of ethnographic education thrown in.

Physical conditions at these urban and rural encampments varied. Tents made of a variety of materials, ranging from cedar bark or rush mats to canvas sheeting, were common in city- and field-side camps alike. Along the urban waterfronts, some migrants erected structures on the ground, while others used their canoes as the foundation over which to hang canvas or mats.[26] At the fields, workers located wood with which to frame the canvas or mats that they had brought with them. Some farmers built houses or temporary huts for seasonal labourers.[27] Cabins, and even 'wooden houses, built after the style of the white man',[28] could also be found along urban waterfronts. Some Aboriginal people found the living arrangements substandard— even uncivilized. Twana subchief Big John visited the Puyallup hop fields and commented that the people living there had 'small huts, not like our houses, or even barns, but more like chicken coops, while we have houses and are civilized'.[29] For Big John, as for colonial viewers, domestic form and domestic character were interlocking.

For the non-Aboriginal viewer, the fact that these were migrant labourers living in temporarily erected tents did not detract from the attraction of the spectacle. The notion that they were viewing 'real' everyday life rather than reproductions (as they would at a world's fair) likely appealed to many. In the hop fields, they could believe that they were one step closer to the real thing than even Putnam, with all his attention to authentic details, could offer.

The transitory quality of the structures themselves also corresponded with common assumptions about Aboriginal people, who were presumed to be shiftless and wandering by nature. The assumption that Aboriginal people were incapable of permanently possessing property shrouded the self-congratulatory stories immigrants told themselves about the improvements they wrought with their transformation of the Pacific Northwest landscape from primitive (Aboriginal) to modern (non-Aboriginal). As railway investor, amateur ethnographer, lawyer, and (later) judge James Wickersham put it, 'the Indian doesn't care [about retaining reservation land]—clams, a split cedar shanty on the beach, a few mats and kettles, leisure and a bottle of rum once in a while are all he wants—anybody can have the land that wants it. Really why should our govt [sic] go to such enormous expense in trying to make a white man out of an Indian?'[30] Wickersham's bluntness may have been somewhat unusual, but his sentiment was not. North of the border, in British Columbia, newcomers applied a different land policy than that used in Washington, but it, too, systematically deprived Aboriginal people of the land base required to remain self-sustaining.[31] The scene that Wickersham described was much like the ones that non-Aboriginal viewers in Washington and British Columbia, or at the Chicago World's Fair, found when they sought out spectacles of Aboriginal domestic space: picturesque object lessons featuring the notion of the vanishing Indian. The hop pickers reinforced several dearly held assumptions for tourists who ventured forth to view the workers en route or in camp: Aboriginal people used land and resources sporadically and unsystematically; they were inevitably disappearing in the face of civilization and modernity; and investment in an Aboriginal future was an oxymoron.

These assumptions were apparent in popular assessments of how the pickers spent their hard-earned wages. Here again, domestic goods as well as domestic space came under scrutiny. Although Indian agents commented that Aboriginal pickers often returned with 'useful' goods such as furniture, harnesses, sewing machines, and stoves, tourists and reporters focused on items they deemed ridiculous and frivolous.[32] The belief that outer form mirrored an inner subjective state informed these assumptions as well. It elevated the brief glimpses non-Aboriginal viewers had of Aboriginal lives from anecdotal evidence to generalized and authoritative judgment.

Casual viewers who made afternoon or weekend excursions to the hop fields or waterfront did not see the rough migrant labour camps as a component of a hard-working and highly flexible Aboriginal economy, which is what they were. They read the seasonal itinerancy of the migrant workers as evidence of an underlying lack of connection to any fixed locale. The notion that Aboriginal people had no use for land or resources was a fiction; however, in the hands

and minds of a growing non-Aboriginal population, it was a powerful one. As in Chicago, spectacles of Aboriginal domestic space provided a jumping-off point for the stories viewers told themselves about themselves.

Home Space

As migrant labourers, the hop pickers faced constraints on the level of privacy they could maintain over their domestic spaces. The circumstances of travel would have subjected their spaces and processes of domestic life to a degree of public view, even without tourists' obsession with 'vanishing Indians'. Their presence as travellers was noticeable to local residents. As in Chicago, it had been temporary structures that were on display at the hop fields. Yet, along the late nineteenth-century Northwest Coast, even inhabitants of Aboriginal villages who remained at home had to deal with the intrusions of non-Aboriginal viewers. With the advent of tourist steamship routes along the Inside Passage in the early 1880s, adventurous non-Aboriginal travellers could now journey along the coasts of British Columbia and southeast Alaska. As Sitka, Alaska, became one of the prime ports along the Inside Passage tourist route, the Tlingit residents faced one of the most intrusive forms of assault on Aboriginal domestic space. For tourists the 'performances' of everyday life in Sitka seemed among the most 'authentic' to be found; the Tlingit, meanwhile, found themselves cast in the role of involuntary 'performers'. This latter point is of course not unrelated to the former. In Sitka the Aboriginal people stayed put; thus, the display of Tlingit lives falls among the least consensual examples of 'living on display'.

Sitka's tourist industry provided visitors with a dual view of Tlingit domestic life: (1) the 'civilized cottages' inhabited by Presbyterian mission school graduates and (2) the Tlingit village. The 'Ranche', as the latter was dubbed, was both the figurative and literal antithesis of the mission cottages located at the far end of town. Tourists arrived by steamer, and, as they disembarked, they had the choice of turning left towards the Ranche or right towards the mission school and cottages. This dichotomous division of domestic space was not unique to Sitka. Farther south, along the coast in British Columbia, missionary Thomas Crosby made the same distinction between what he called 'Christian street' and 'Heathen street'.[33]

Publications for visitors to Sitka invariably featured the Ranche as a 'must-see' sight. The local newspaper encouraged visitors to 'get off the beaten track' and, if possible, to find a local guide: 'Get some one who knows the village to conduct you through, as many places of interest will be otherwise overlooked. Don't confine your attention to the front row only, go in among the houses and see those on the back street.' This reporter urged visitors to penetrate the inner reaches of Tlingit domestic life, claiming that 'generally the natives do not object to visitors entering their houses.'[34] At least some visitors took this advice to heart. As Sir John Franklin's niece wrote of her visit in 1870, 'We went into several [houses], not merely to inspect, but in search of baskets & other queer things.'[35] Glimpsing the interior was important because this was sometimes the most distinctive aspect of the building: 'In exterior appearance [the houses] do not differ from those of the white man, but usually there is only a single room within on the ground floor.'[36] Although some Tlingit residents undoubtedly chafed at such intrusions, many took advantage of the situation that literally came knocking on their door. Pine doorplates appeared above the lintels of certain houses, directing visitors towards homes that gained renown in the tourist literature.[37]

Tourists carried their assumptions about domestic space as women's space with them to the Ranche. Although male residents such as 'Sitka Jack' and the hereditary chief, Annahootz, put up such doorplates, the 'palace of Siwash Town' had a matriarch on the throne.[38] Mrs, or 'Princess', Tom was the most sought-after resident of the village and was renowned throughout southeast Alaska. Visitors never failed to scrutinize her domestic situation. In some respects, her home sounded like the epitome of domesticity: 'a painted cabin with green blinds, and a green railing across the front porch'.[39] But it was other elements of her domestic situation that attracted the most attention from visitors in search of a savage authenticity: her excessive wealth in gold, silver, blankets, and furs; and her multiple husbands, one of whom was reported to have been her former slave.

While male and female visitors alike focused their travel writings on Mrs Tom, they told different stories about her. While female visitors used stories of Mrs Tom to argue obliquely for women's economic independence and sexual freedom, male writers decried Mrs Tom's behaviour. Eliza Ruhamah Scidmore's 1885 description of Mrs Tom was the basis for subsequent writers' accounts, and its transfiguration over time is telling. Scidmore wrote that Mrs Tom had 'acquired her fortune by her own ability in legitimate trade'.[40] Later male writers cast aspersions on her moral and sexual conduct, characterizing her as 'a disreputable Indian woman' who used 'doubtful methods' to amass her large fortune.[41] Female writers, on the other hand, viewed Mrs Tom's accomplishments of domestic economy in a more positive light. In 1890 a female traveller emphasized that this wealth allowed Mrs Tom to support two husbands and to still live in greater luxury than Chief Annahootz.[42] The 'regal splendor' in which she reputedly lived included silk, satin, and lace dresses; carpeted floors; a mirror; pictures; and a 'Yankee' cooking stove.[43] While female writers, beginning with Scidmore, stressed the neatness of Mrs Tom's home and self, Frederick Schwatka characterized her as a 'burley Amazon of the Northwest'.[44] When these visitors stepped inside Mrs Tom's house, they brought with them the narrative framework of the story they would tell.

Nearly a mile through and then beyond town, at the mission cottages, visitors could investigate the lives of the 'civilized', 'modern' Indians. They lived in two rows of neat, frame cottages built by Aboriginal labour but paid for by donations from

American churches. The local, Presbyterian-aligned newspaper articulated the purpose of the cottages: 'With their neat and inviting appearance, they are an object lesson which strongly contrasts with the filth and squalor of the Indian huts in other parts of the town.'[45] Not only were the Ranche houses presumably dirty, they were also said to 'cause trouble'; that is, to encourage uncivilized, tribal behaviour and relationships.[46] Missionaries worried that tourists' romanticization of 'uncivilized' Aboriginal life would hinder their missionary endeavours, but they also saw the money that the tourists spent on curios in the Ranche.[47] The mission came to rely on displays of domestic space in order to convince potential donors that mission work could be successful and that mission graduates had a future other than 'back-sliding' into Ranche life. By putting the object lesson of the cottages on display, missionaries hoped to elicit donations for their work.

The object lesson among object lessons was the Miller cottage (named for the pastor of the Pennsylvania church that donated the funds), in which the mission's star graduate, Rudolph Walton, lived. According to Presbyterian missionary Sheldon Jackson, the Miller cottage was 'a better and more comfortable house' than those of 90 per cent of the Americans in Sitka, 'one of the best dwelling houses in the place'.[48] But the donors were disappointed. When Walton sent them a sketch of the finished cottage, they complained that the structure did not look to have the character of a $500 house.[49]

The donors' concern with appearances makes sense in the context of the assumption that outer form reveals inner state. This non-Aboriginal assumption was as apparent in Sitka as it was at the Chicago World's Fair and in the Puget Sound hop fields. Visitors invariably subjected the domestic arrangements of cottage residents to close scrutiny and paid close attention to the bourgeois furnishings. When the mission doctor wrote an article about the Miller cottage he detailed everything from the furniture to the behaviour of the children. He commented on

'the neat board walk and gravel walks around the side'; the 'parlor and sitting room, about twelve feet square—carpeted, sofa at one side, rocking chairs, table and book case, as we should find in any comfortable home'. Continuing, he noted, 'in a small room adjoining this sitting room we find a cabinet with some pretty china and a few odd trinkets treasured by the family. The dining room and kitchen in the rear though less pretentious are neat, while upstairs the two bedrooms are furnished with bedsteads and the usual furniture.'[50] Such details were evidence that the family within had escaped the 'contaminating influences of the Ranch'.[51] Other cottages received similar evaluations by visitors. 'In many of their homes are phonographs, pianos, and sewing machines,' wrote local schoolteacher Dazie M. Brown Stromstadt in her promotional book on Sitka.[52] For Stromstadt, these items were evidence that their Tlingit owners were 'living a "civilized life"'.[53] The cottage settlement was meant to stand as objective material proof of the subjective spiritual transformation that had taken place in the lives of the resident Tlingit. The material circumstances of the cottages were critical measurements of civility and modernity. Missionaries and tourists alike assumed that the geographical and structural opposition between Ranche and cottages extended to the inner lives of the residents.

Needless to say, reality was not as simple as this idealized picture would have it. Close attention to the written descriptions of Ranche and cottage life reveals that some of the similarities are as striking as the differences. Much like the cottage settlement, the Ranche, too, had neat boardwalks and a general tidiness about it.[54] Ranche homes also contained modern domestic goods such as furniture and stoves (often of the 'modern type').[55] The cottages, too, were less severed from Ranche life than many missionaries liked to admit. While living in the cottages, Rudolph Walton and other Tlingit residents sustained familial ties with Ranche residents and participated in important Tlingit ceremonies and community events.[56] They also followed similar cultural practices. The family unit within Miller cottage was not a nuclear one but, rather, included Rudolph Walton's widowed mother and grandmother, who spoke Tlingit to Walton's children.[57] Moreover, it was not just Ranche residents who were likely to offer baskets, carvings, or 'curios' for sale to visitors but also cottage residents.[58] However, in the minds of white observers, the larger context—either Ranche or cottage—of each domestic interior seemed to carry overriding importance.

The notion that outside mimicked inside was less a statement of the status quo than it was a wishful prescription—an interpretation that observers attempted to impose, against the natural grain of the evidence before them. It was the story they *wanted* to tell themselves. Not surprisingly, the contradictions inherent within such an exercise frequently broke through to the surface, rending the oppositional social fabric of Ranche versus Cottage. At such times, observers worked hard to repair the damage and to restore the impression of easy opposition. Visitors might attribute the 'civilized' signs of cleanliness and order in the Ranche to the influence of white discipline (through the police and military) or white blood (through interracial sex).[59] Either way, they countersunk their narratives in the common plank of domestic space as social text.

The stakes of sustaining domestic space as transparent social text become clearer when we realize that challenges to the Ranche-Cottage dualism came not only from Aboriginal people but also from white frontier residents. While interracial sex and marriage might explain signs of civilization found within Tlingit homes, they might just as easily engender new contradictions when white 'squaw-men' adopted the domestic habits of their Aboriginal wives. In places remote from white settlement such behaviour could be attributed to the poverty that prevented the men from travelling to find white wives.[60] Such rationalizations were less tenable in busy settlements like Sitka. There, the Russian fur trade had given way to American settlement, and the domestic

choices of 'squaw-men' became increasingly difficult to reconcile with the standard colonial dualisms of Indian and white, primitive and modern, savage and civilized. Too many white men failed to enact the bourgeois values that middle-class society worked to impress upon Aboriginal people. The narrative power of domestic space could justify the marginalization of men whose race ostensibly should have ensured them a measure of colonial privilege. It could likewise broadcast the price that would-be 'squaw-men' faced if they failed to conform to the bourgeois values of the modern settlement frontier.

Non-Aboriginal viewers used Aboriginal domestic spaces as a trope through which to tell themselves stories about themselves. Even when Aboriginal people did not intentionally or willingly place their homes and goods on display, non-Aboriginal viewers sought them out, often penetrating the inner reaches of Aboriginal home life. The contradictions of such a situation run deep. While the forces of colonial society urged Aboriginal people to adopt bourgeois values of privacy and domesticity, they simultaneously transformed Aboriginal homes and private spaces into public spectacles. Even missionaries, who were among the most aggressive proponents of bourgeois domestic values, encouraged the public to view the Aboriginal domestic space of 'civilized' Christian converts. The homes of families who became mission success stories were as subject to inquiring eyes as were those who resisted missionary overtures. While missionaries promised that Aboriginal converts could earn equality through outward conformity to colonial, Victorian values, they broke this promise from the very start. Aboriginal homes—whether civilized or uncivilized—were *always* subject to different rules than were non-Aboriginal ones. Voyeurs implicitly judged *all* Aboriginal domestic space as savage when they subjected it to a degree of scrutiny that they would never have tolerated in their own homes. The display of domestic space became not just a story white people told themselves but also a story they told *to* the Aboriginal spectacles.

Aboriginal Stories

Non-Aboriginal viewers were not the only ones who narrated domestic space. They were not the only ones telling stories. While the display of domestic space did not always begin with Aboriginal consent, Aboriginal people invariably took advantage of the situation when they could, catering to tourists' desire for souvenirs and 'curios', thus creating added income opportunities for themselves. 'Traditional' Aboriginal domestic goods circulated as commodities, the returns from which sometimes allowed the vendors to purchase 'modern' domestic goods that tourists would later judge, depending on the context, as either material markers of civilization or laughable markers of pretense.

Aboriginal people did not tell themselves the same stories as non-Aboriginal people told themselves. Aboriginal transformations of domestic spaces, and the adjustments they made to nineteenth-century colonialism, suggest a storyline out of keeping with any straightforward correlation between outward form and inner nature. Sometimes cottage life was literally a facade concealing traditional practices. For residents of Sitka's cottage community, the outer trappings of civilization fit easily over sustained hereditary obligations and practices. Similarly, the Christian homes in Metlakatla, British Columbia, looked, from the street, like workers' cottages. Past the door, however, they opened up into large communal spaces with sleeping areas to the sides, just like the interiors of old longhouses.[61] Sometimes, when the main floors of houses were conjoined (with only the second storey separate), the communal space extended to more than one 'house'.[62] The model Christian Indians of Metlakatla also refused to relinquish the longhouses they kept at Port Simpson.[63] The outward forms of Christian life at Sitka and Metlakatla distracted missionaries from the continuities of practice and value within cottage walls. Cottage residents could live in accord with Aboriginal values and simultaneously placate missionaries, thus reaping the material and spiritual benefits that accrued to converts.

It seems likely that chiefs mimicked Victorian architecture in order to speak to both colonial and Aboriginal society. When Christian Tsimshian chief Alfred Dudoward built himself a Victorian mansion, he moved in with a large lineage-based group and continued to fulfill his hereditary obligations.[64] His wife, Kate, confused missionary women with her syncretic domestic habits. On one occasion, she concluded a respectable afternoon gathering with a slightly suspect biscuit giveaway. When the white women returned the following day, they watched, shocked, while Kate and other Tsimshian women performed in front of them, 'painted and dressed in their skins blankets and other old fixtures', before sending them off with more tea biscuits.[65] Like Dudoward, Musqueam chief Tschymnana built a colonial house; his was in imitation of Colonel Moody's residence. When Bishop George Hills visited the house in 1860, he found the chief's *three* wives at home.[66] These prominent chiefs' houses engaged colonial notions of form and content as well as indicating Aboriginal awareness of colonial scrutiny. They also demonstrate a degree of confidence and flexibility that culture inheres not in the post-and-beam structure itself but in something else: the idea that form can change without foreclosing continuity. Indeed, the forms of these houses may have offered an added measure of prestige within Aboriginal communities.

With the advent of colonialism, high-ranking individuals sought new ways of displaying power and status.[67] Engaging with 'modern' colonial culture is one example of this. Shingles, hinged doors, milled lumber, and windows functioned as status symbols.[68] They marked new forms of expression within an age-old system. This hybrid facility extended to domestic goods as well as to structure. Nineteenth-century photographs reveal Aboriginal interiors to be 'contents displays' of status items of both Aboriginal and non-Aboriginal origin.[69] These new styles and objects joined older symbols of wealth and power that marked the status of Aboriginal homes and their residents. Crest art painted on house fronts or carved on house posts has long asserted the status and hereditary rights of the inhabitants.[70] A house's size, materials, and position relative to other houses rendered the intravillage hierarchy visible—a pattern dating back over 4,000 years on the Fraser River.[71] The spatial distribution within pre-contact longhouses designated the relative status of the family units within,[72] and, similarly, the styles of pit houses can be correlated to wealth and status.[73] Such examples hint at the contours of Aboriginal narratives of domestic space.

Present Space

Through the twentieth century, agents of colonial policy continued to target Aboriginal homes for transformation. Reserve houses constructed by the Department of Indian Affairs continued in the 'cottage' tradition of attempting to reshape Aboriginal domestic life socially as well as architecturally.[74] At the same time, twentieth-century Stó:lō families who had the means continued to build European-style frame homes that could accommodate the large extended family and community gatherings of Stó:lō social tradition.[75]

The preoccupation with 'traditional' Aboriginal domestic space has likewise survived. The 'Indian house' has remained the ethnographic artifact par excellence, somehow imbued with an unstated yet assumed ability to speak for Aboriginal culture and history writ large. When the Civilian Conservation Corps of the New Deal looked to define a project in Alaska in the 1930s, it chose, at the urging of the local non-Aboriginal population, to undertake a meticulous and authentic restoration of Chief Shakes's house at Wrangell.[76] Some members of Wrangell's Tlingit population initiated a further restoration of four house posts in 1984.[77] When the Canadian Museum of Civilization designed its Grand Hall, which opened in 1989, it decided to construct a composite Northwest Coast 'village' with houses and totem poles from various nations placed side by side, although still in geographical order.[78] The similarity in form with Chicago's 'great

Aboriginal encampment' is too striking to ignore. However, unlike the world's fair, the Grand Hall intends to celebrate rather than to condemn Northwest Coast culture. The difficult question comes in deciphering the relationship between this colonial form and its post-colonial message. To pose a familiar question: can new meanings transcend old forms?

Conclusion

More than just an ironic contradiction of private turned public, an analysis of the spectacle of Aboriginal domestic space reveals some underlying colonialist assumptions. The audiences of Aboriginal people living on display defined themselves as modern through a dialectic of stories: stories they told themselves about themselves; stories they told themselves about others; and stories they told others about themselves. Colonial society presumed that civilization and modernity were as easy to read as an open book. This assumption, although false, shaped myriad interactions. Various groups, Aboriginal and non-Aboriginal alike, have had an interest in the spectacle of Aboriginal domestic life, with money and prestige always at stake. Missionaries' and anthropologists' interests dovetailed in the contrasting displays of uncivilized and civilized domestic spaces. For missionaries, the former demonstrated that reform was needed while the latter demonstrated that it was possible. Anthropologists focused on the former to display the ethnographic strangeness and value of their work and on the latter to establish that such work was urgent because Aboriginal disappearance was imminent. For many other non-Aboriginal members of colonial society, the display of domestic spaces reinforced comfortable stories about themselves and their position in a colonial world. The souvenirs they brought home to their 'curio-corners' played a role of their own in bringing middle-class status to Victorian homes.[79]

Aboriginal people also linked domestic and social space to individual and group identity. Traditional elites might manipulate domestic forms to shore up their personal power and status over other Aboriginal people as well as in relation to colonial society. Ambitious nouveaux riches might play with old and new markers of domestic space in their move to climb the social status ladder. It seems certain, however, that Aboriginal people conceived of the connections between domestic space and identity in a radically different manner than did colonizers. The form and content of domestic spaces did not obviously offer the key to the interior of residents' sense of self and community responsibility. The links that existed were not clearly visible to outsiders. Looks could indeed be deceiving, at least for those with colonial eyes.

Colonial society from the nineteenth century through to the present has focused on houses as representative material forms of culture—as culture in practice. And Aboriginal people have consistently inhabited their houses in ways that prove the simplistic nature of this assumption. Still, scholars today continue to find it remarkable that Aboriginal people can proceed with traditional values and practices in 'untraditional' contexts. Twentieth-century Tlingit potlatches held in 'Western-style buildings' indicate to one writer, for example, that 'the presence of proper joinery and other architectural devices that refer to past form, the "classic building blocks", are not required for traditional practice.'[80] The history of Aboriginal domestic spaces suggests that we should not be taken aback by the realization that the presence of 'knowledgeable people' and witnesses from other clans is more important than are the specifics of a particular architectural form.[81]

The endurance of domestic space as a trope for the narration of Aboriginal culture gives rise to many questions. Why has domestic space proven such a powerful symbol? What is it that imbues domestic spaces with the power to shape judgments about inner selves? How did the fixed material forms of houses and household goods come to signify fixity of character and culture? Perhaps we are more prone to naturalize the values and arrangements of domestic spaces

because they are the most familiar environments we have. The intimacy with which bourgeois domestic space has been experienced since the Victorian age may set off the alleged strangeness of other ways of living. And perhaps it is the very changelessness of material form that lends itself to rendering accessible the otherwise amorphous concepts of self and culture.

Members of colonial society have been searching for the location of culture since they first arrived on the Northwest Coast. Just when we think we have it cornered, it escapes out the back door. Maybe what these stories of domestic space tell us is that we should begin looking somewhere other than architectural plans.

Notes

I wish to acknowledge SSHRC, whose support made this research possible. I would also like to thank Kathy Mezei, who encouraged me to present this as a conference paper and then to write it up as an article; Tina Loo, who offered editorial suggestions; and Jean Barman and Susan Roy, who pointed the way to useful primary sources.

1. John and Jean Comaroff, *Ethnography and the Historical Imagination* (Boulder, CO: Westview Press, 1992), 293.
2. Dipesh Chakrabarty, 'Postcoloniality and the Artifice of History: Who Speaks for "Indian" Pasts?', *Representations* 37 (1992): 13.
3. J.R. Miller, *Sweet Promises: A Reader on Indian-White Relations in Canada* (Toronto: University of Toronto Press, 1991); Frederick E. Hoxie, *A Final Promise: The Campaign to Assimilate the Indians, 1880–1920* (Lincoln: University of Nebraska Press, 1984).
4. Frederick Cooper and Ann Laura Stoler, eds, *Tensions of Empire* (Berkeley: University of California Press, 1997).
5. Clifford Geertz, *The Interpretation of Cultures* (New York: Basic Books, 1973), 448.
6. Robert W. Rydell, *All the World's a Fair: Visions of Empire at American International Expositions, 1876–1916* (Chicago: University of Chicago Press, 1984), 6, 8; E.A. Heaman, *The Inglorious Arts of Peace: Exhibitions in Canadian Society during the Nineteenth Century* (Toronto: University of Toronto Press, 1999), 7.
7. 'The Man Columbus Found', *New York Press*, 28 May 1893, Scrapbook, vol. 2, Frederic Ward Putnam Papers (hereafter FWPP), Harvard University Archives (hereafter HUA).

8. *The Dream City* (St Louis: N.D. Thompson Publishing Co., 1893), n.p.
9. 'All Kinds of Indians', *Daily Inter Ocean* (Chicago), 20 June 1893.
10. See, for example, *Daily Inter Ocean* (Chicago), 9 July 1893, Scrapbook, vol. 2, FWPP, HUA.
11. Clipping, 8 Feb. 1893; *Daily Inter Ocean* (Chicago) 9 July 1893; *Pioneer Press* (St Paul, MN), 15 Mar. 1893, Scrapbook, vol. 2, FWPP, HUA.
12. In a strange wrinkle in the authentic fabric of the fair, the Midway included Sitting Bull's 'log cabin'. The presence of the log cabin was unusual, as all other Aboriginal performers lived in dwellings that fair organizer's deemed 'traditional'. Perhaps Sitting Bull's fame imbued the cabin with the necessary aura of authenticity that, in other cases, only a teepee could have offered. Or perhaps the log cabin conveyed a grudging respect for the Sioux chief. *Official Catalogue of Exhibits on the Midway Plaisance* (Chicago: W.B. Conkey Co., 1893), box 38, FWPP, HUA; Gertrude M. Scott, 'Village Performance: Villages at the Chicago World's Columbian Exposition, 1893', PHD dissertation (New York University, 1991), 329–30.
13. Rossiter Johnson, ed., *A History of the World's Columbian Exposition Held in Chicago in 1893* (New York: D. Appleton and Co, 1897), I: 315.
14. See, for example, Antonio, an Apache, to F.W. Putnam, 25 July 1892, box 31, FWPP, HUA; F.W. Putnam to Antonio, 4 Aug. 1892, box 31, FWPP, HUA.
15. For the most complete account of the identities of the Kwakwa̱ka'wakw performers that I have been able to compile, see Paige Raibmon, 'Theaters of Contact: The Kwakwa̱ka'wakw Meet Colonialism in British Columbia and at the Chicago World's Fair', *Canadian Historical Review* 81, 2 (June 2000): 175.
16. Clipping, July 1893, Scrapbook, vol. 2, FWPP, HUA. Organizers went out of their way to apply this principle to other Aboriginal groups at the fair as well. On the Navajo performers, for example, see F.W. Putnam to Antonio, 4 Aug. 1892, box 31, FWPP, HUA.
17. 'Siwashes Again Seek the Street', *Seattle Post-Intelligencer*, 31 May 1904, 9; 'Great Influx of Indians', *Seattle Post-Intelligencer*, 10 Sept. 1899, 6; 'Indians Returning from Hop Fields', *Seattle Post-Intelligencer* 1 Oct. 1906, 16.
18. J.A. Costello, *The Siwash: Their Life, Legends and Tales, Puget Sound and Pacific Northwest* (Seattle: The Calvert Company, 1895), 165.
19. W.H. Bull, 'Indian Hop Pickers on Puget Sound', *Harper's Weekly* 36, 1850 (1892): 546.
20. 'Indians Returning from Hop Fields', *Seattle Post-Intelligencer*, 1 Oct. 1906, 16; Photo NA–698, Special Collections, University of Washington (UW); Paul Dorpat, *Seattle: Now and Then* (1984), 45; photo NA–897, Special Collections, UW; photo 15,715, Museum of History and Industry, Seattle, Washington (MOHI); 'Indian Life on Seattle Streets', *Seattle Post-Intelligencer*, 10 Dec. 1905, 7; 'Siwash Village on Tacoma Tide Flats', *Seattle Post-Intelligencer*, 15 Apr. 1907, 20.
21. 'Hop Picking', *Washington Standard*, 24 Sept. 1886, 2; *Puyallup Valley Tribune*, 3 Oct. 1903, 6.
22. 'A Western Hop Center', *West Shore* 16, 9 (1890): 137–8; 'Meadowbrook Hotel Register', Snoqualmie Valley Historical Society, North Bend, Washington.
23. 'Picturesque Hop Pickers', *Puyallup Valley Tribune*, 10 Sept. 1904, 1.
24. John Muir, *Steep Trails* (Boston: Houghton Mifflin, 1918), 257.
25. 'At the Indian Village', *Puyallup Valley Tribune*, 19 Sept. 1903, 1.
26. Photos 2561 and 6123–N, MOHI; photos NA–1508, NA–1501, NA–1500, NA–698, NA–680, Special Collections, UW.
27. 'Hops in Washington', *Pacific Rural Press*, 3 Jan. 1891.
28. 'Indian Life on Seattle Streets', *Seattle Post-Intelligencer*, 10 Dec. 1905, 7; 'Siwash Village on Tacoma Tide Flats', *Seattle Post-Intelligencer*, 15 Apr. 1907, 20.
29. Myron Eells, *The Indians of Puget Sound: The Notebooks of Myron Eells*, ed. George Pierre Castile (Seattle: University of Washington Press, 1985), 270.
30. Quoted in George Pierre Castile, 'The Indian Connection: Judge James Wickersham and the Indian Shakers', *Pacific Northwest Quarterly* 81, 4 (1990): 126.
31. Cole Harris, *Making Native Space: Colonialism, Resistance, and Reserves in British Columbia* (Vancouver: University of British Columbia Press, 2002), 88, 109, 111.
32. Canada, Department of Indian Affairs, Annual Report, 1886 (Sessional Papers 1887, no. 6), 1x; W.H. Lomas to J. Johnson, Commissioner of Customs, 3 Nov. 1886, Cowichan Agency Letterbook, 1882–7, vol. 1353, RG 10; Bull, 'Indian Hop Pickers', 545–6; E. Meliss, 'Siwash', *Overland Monthly* 20, 2nd ser. (Nov. 1892): 501–6.
33. Susan Neylan, 'Longhouses, Schoolrooms, and Workers' Cottages: Nineteenth-Century Protestant Missions to the Tsimshian and the Transformation of Class Through Religion', *Journal of the Canadian Historical Association* 11, n.s. (2000): 76.
34. *The Alaskan*, 5 June 1897, 1. See also 'Sitka and Its Sights', *The Alaskan*, 7 Dec. 1889, 1.
35. Sophia Cracroft, *Lady Franklin Visits Sitka, Alaska 1870: The Journal of Sophia Cracroft, Sir John Franklin's Niece*, ed. R.N. DeArmond (Anchorage: Alaska Historical Society, 1981), 24.
36. George Bird Grinnell, *Alaska 1899: Essays from the Harriman Expedition* (Seattle: University of Washington Press, 1995), 157.
37. E. Ruhamah Scidmore, *Alaska: Its Southern Coast and the Sitkan Archipelago* (Boston: D. Lothrop and Company, 1885), 176.

38. Ibid.
39. Ibid.
40. Ibid., 177.
41. H.W. Seton Karr, *Shores and Alps of Alaska* (London: Sampson, Low, Marston, Searle and Rivington, 1887), 59.
42. 'Journal of a Woman Visitor to Southeast Alaska, ca 1890', fol. 4, box 7, MS4, Alaska State Historical Library (ASHL), 20. See also Anna M. Bugbee, 'The Thlinkets of Alaska', *Overland Monthly* 22, 2nd ser. (Aug. 1892), 191.
43. Bugbee, 'The Thlinkets of Alaska', 191; 'Journal of a Woman Visitor', 20.
44. Scidmore, *Alaska: Its Southern Coast*, 176; 'Journal of a Woman Visitor', 20; Bugbee, 'The Thlinkets of Alaska', 191; *New York Times*, 3 Oct. 1886. Quoted in Frederica de Laguna, *Under Mount Saint Elias: The History and Culture of the Yakutat Tlingit* (Washington: Smithsonian Institution Press, 1972), 191.
45. *The Alaskan*, 23 Jan. 1891, 4. See also 'A Visit to the Cottages', *The Alaskan*, 30 Oct. 1897, 2.
46. Brady to Rev. J. Gould, 30 Dec. 1905, J.G. Brady, *Letters Sent*, vol. 9, Nov. 1905–May 1906, files of the Alaska Territorial Governors, roll 7, microcopy T–1200, National Archives Microfilm, AR25, ASHL.
47. 'The Orthodox Indian Temperance', *The Alaskan*, 10 July 1897, 1.
48. J. Converse to W.H. Miller, 30 Aug. 1888, Sheldon Jackson Correspondence, reel 97–638, Sheldon Jackson Stratton Library.
49. J. Converse to W.H. Miller, 25 July 1888, Sheldon Jackson Correspondence, reel 97–638, Sheldon Jackson Stratton Library.
50. B.K. Wilbur, 'The Model Cottages', *The North Star* 6, 8 (1895): 1.
51. Ibid.
52. Dazie M. Brown Stromstadt, *Sitka, The Beautiful* (Seattle: Homer M. Hill Publishing Co., 1906), 9. See also *The North Star* 5, 8 (Aug. 1892) in *The North Star: The Complete Issues*, 228.
53. Stromstadt, *Sitka, the Beautiful*, 9.
54. 'President's Message', *The Alaskan*, 9 Dec. 1905, 3; Bertand K. Wilbur, 'Just about Me', box IB, no. 8, MS4, ASHL 220–1.
55. Wilbur, 'Just about Me', 220–1; J.G. Brady to Geo. C. Heard, Attorney at Law, Juneau, 19 June 1905, fol. 86, box 5, John G. Brady Papers, Beinecke Library, Yale University.
56. For examples, see Rudolph Walton, 'Diaries', 1900–4, 1910, 1919. Private possession of Joyce Walton Shales.
57. *The North Star*, 6, 1 (1895): 1.
58. Wilbur, 'The Model Cottages', 1.
59. Scidmore, *Alaska: Its Southern Coast*, 175; 'Journal of a Woman Visitor', 24; E. Ruhamah Scidmore, *Appleton's Guide-Book to Alaska and the Northwest Coast* (New York: D. Appleton and Co., 1896 [1893]), 120; Francis C. Sessions, *From Yellowstone Park to Alaska* (New York: Welch, Fracker Co., 1890), 92; Wilbur, 'Just about Me', 221.
60. *The Alaskan*, 5 Aug. 1893, 2.
61. Neylan, 'Longhouses, Schoolrooms, and Workers' Cottages', 81.
62. Ibid.
63. Ibid., 82.
64. Ibid.
65. 28 and 29 Jan. 1884, Kate Hendry, Letterbook, 1882–9, EC/H38, British Columbia Archives.
66. Roberta L. Bagshaw, ed., *No Better Land: The 1860 Diaries of Anglican Colonial Bishop George Hills* (Victoria: Sono Nis Press, 1996), 75. Even allowing for the distinct possibility that Hills misinterpreted the exact nature of the relationship between the women and the chief, this domestic space clearly housed an extended rather than a nuclear family.
67. Judith Ostrowitz, *Privileging the Past: Reconstructing History in Northwest Coast Art* (Vancouver: University of British Columbia Press, 1999), 31.
68. Neylan, 'Longhouses, Schoolrooms, and Workers' Cottages', 79–80; Ostrowitz, *Privileging the Past*, 32.
69. Ostrowitz, *Privileging the Past*, 30. See also Tony Bennett, 'The Exhibitionary Complex', in David Boswell and Jessica Evans, eds, *Representing the Nation: A Reader* (London: Routledge, 1999), 333.
70. Neylan, 'Longhouses, Schoolrooms, and Workers' Cottages', 79; Ostrowitz, *Privileging the Past*, 9.
71. Keith Thor Carlson, ed., *A Coast Salish Historical Atlas* (Vancouver: Douglas & McIntyre, 2001), 36, 41.
72. Ibid., 43.
73. Ibid., 46.
74. Ibid., 44.
75. Ibid., 43, 45.
76. Ostrowitz, *Privileging the Past*, 33–9.
77. Ibid., 39–43.
78. Ibid., 51.
79. As one writer put it, 'every well-appointed house might appropriately arrange an Indian corner.' George Wharton James, 'Indian Basketry in House Decoration', *Chautauquan* (1901): 620. See also Lloyd W. MacDowell, *Alaska Indian Basketry* (Seattle: Alaska Steamship Company, 1906).
80. Ostrowitz, *Privileging the Past*, 39.
81. Ibid.

4

Re-imaging the Moral Order of Urban Space: Religion and Photography in Winnipeg, 1900–14

—— **James Opp** ——

When the Methodist minister J.S. Woodsworth published his first book, *Strangers within our Gates*, in 1909, the 'problem' of the city took up one small chapter. By 1911, however, the city formed the main topic of his second book, *My Neighbor*, reflecting the growing sense of urgency over the new urban space created by the rapid expansion of Canadian cities: 'As we penetrate more deeply into [the city's] life, we discover evils of which we had hardly dreamed. . . . We get behind the scenes; we see the seamy side. We look beneath the glittering surface and shrink back from the hidden depths which the yawning darkness suggests.'[1] Addressing the social conditions of the city required a new way of 'seeing' the 'seamy side' of life 'behind the scenes'. By the twentieth century, proponents of the social gospel such as Woodsworth had decided that the old methods of Christian charity work and a focus on individual salvation needed to be replaced with a collective approach that emphasized building the kingdom of God through new forms of social reform based on more scientific principles. To 'penetrate' the darkness required not only moral courage and converted hearts, but data, statistics, and comprehensive city 'surveys'.

The emergence of the social gospel marked an important transition in the visual metaphors employed by the Methodist Church in Canada. Mission work among the urban poor had traditionally been seen as the light of the gospel displacing the darkness within. But Woodsworth's language in *My Neighbor* operated differently. Now the goal was to expose the darkness, to see through it in order to reveal its very existence. To observe the darkness was the first step towards producing a collective strategy of changing the environment. The act of seeing was in itself a 'light', and so it is not surprising that the language of the social gospel is overlaid with visual metaphors. The Reverend Hugh Dobson wrote that the church's pursuit of 'Social Service' involved two stages: the first, and 'most vitally constructive', was 'to observe and set down and look squarely in the face of the facts of our social life'; the second was to 'establish and fix in reality the vision made visible by the preacher and evangelist, to build cities and plan towns and rural communities patterned after what they saw in the mount, and guided by the knowledge gained by the survey of facts'.[2] In a public recommendation for *My Neighbor*, the Reverend S.D. Chown made the same point, noting that the 'fulness of knowledge displayed indicates intimateness of opportunity for study and observation and gives a satisfying sense of authority to the statements made. It is

James Opp, 'Re-Imaging the Moral Order of Urban Space: Religion and Photography in Winnipeg, 1900–1914', *Journal of the Canadian Historical Association* 13 (2002): 73–93. Reprinted by permission of the Canadian Historical Association and the author.

well that those who are at ease in our Canadian Zion should be made to see so clearly and forcibly how the "other half" lives.'[3] Constructing the New Jerusalem upon a righteous moral order first required an accurate assessment and a visualization of current conditions.

While the principles and theology of social reform have been studied, and the activities of social gospellers like J.S. Woodsworth have been detailed extensively, one area that remains to be explored is how the 'modern' techniques of social reform entailed a new way of visualizing urban space. In carrying out their appointed tasks, social reformers compiled statistics and constructed detailed charts and graphs, but one of the most powerful tools for re-visualizing the city was photography. The social documentary style of photography had evolved from the startling exposés of Jacob Riis's *How the Other Half Lives* (1890), which sensationalized New York slums, to a more 'scientific' form in the hands of social reformers such as Lawrence Veiller, secretary of New York's Charity Organization Society. Veiller incorporated more than 1,000 photographs in his famous Tenement-House Exhibit of 1899, and the power of photography to document social conditions was felt across North America as health departments started to develop their own photographic records.[4] Photography was incorporated into a 1911 study of Toronto's slums by the city's Medical Officer of Health, Dr Charles Hastings, and it was prominent in Montreal's Child Welfare Exhibit of 1912.

For Protestant reformers such as Woodsworth, photographs served an indispensable function in bringing the 'real' conditions of the city to the public mind, creating visual reference points from which the new emphasis on a social gospel could be launched. In their extensive publishing efforts that incorporated photographs, Protestant churches in Canada played a key role in publicly framing the moral boundaries of the modern city. The Methodist Church in particular, through the efforts of the Young People's Forward Movement for Missions (YPFM), distributed photographs

through multiple channels that included its own journals, photographic exhibitions, and lantern slide shows. The YPFM also served as the publisher for both of Woodsworth's books, each of them amply illustrated with photographs drawn from the YPFM's own files. Toronto and Montreal were both featured in the new social documentary style, but the city that attracted a disproportionate amount of attention from the Methodists was Woodsworth's own Winnipeg. As a rapidly growing metropolis, a centre for immigration, and a symbol of the future direction of Canada, Winnipeg embodied the potential dangers of urban growth across the country.

In focusing on the photographic representations of the city of Winnipeg in the published materials of the Methodist Church before the First World War, the purpose is not to assess the real conditions of urban poverty, but rather to analyze the transformation that occurred in visual representations of the city. Although historians have been far from reluctant to incorporate such images into their own books as illustrative material, there has been remarkably little analysis of the photographic medium and the relation between visual representation and social reform. While the choice and placement of photographs were the responsibility of a small group of editors, authors, and publishers, it is important not to underestimate their impact on the public perception of urban space. As Susan Sontag suggests, photographs 'do not simply render reality realistically. It is reality which is scrutinized, and evaluated, for its fidelity to photographs.'[5] The increasing use of photography in the early twentieth century shaped a modern sense of vision, and these images offered particular narratives and realities that were difficult to ignore.[6]

The first decade of the twentieth century marked a definite shift in the visual strategy of representing the city. Photography was not a new technology, but photographic images were invested with a new authority, a power of scientific observation that exuded an 'evidential force'.[7] The appearance of documentary photographs of poverty and unsanitary living conditions in Canadian cities within the context of religious publications marked a conscious attempt to make 'surveying' and 'seeing' society a part of the work of social redemption. And yet, while the value of photography lay in its dispassionate representation, such images were produced and read within a particular moral and spiritual context. To examine Methodist photographic representations of Winnipeg at the turn of the twentieth century is to witness a 're-imaging' of the moral boundaries and order of urban space.

Picturing Religion

When the aspiring photographer Lewis B. Foote arrived in Winnipeg in 1901, his first foray into marketing his photographic skills was to take pictures of every single church in the city, superimpose the prints with portraits of the ministers, and then sell the pictures to the churches.[8] This photographic narrative, linking the visible landscape of religious institutions with portraits of those called to religious service, was the same framework for photographic illustrations used by the *Christian Guardian*, the official denominational journal of the Methodist Church of Canada, and other religious magazines in this period. Popularized in the 1890s, the half-tone printing process made the reproduction of photographs feasible, and pictures of churches and portraits of the ministers who served them dominated the visual imagery of religious journals, especially denominational organs such as the *Christian Guardian*. There were important exceptions to this pattern, however. Missionary pictures offered both similarities and differences to the standard photographic practices. For the most part, the focus remained upon heroic missionaries and the mission buildings constructed in foreign lands, but they also strayed into more scenic explorations of exotic landscapes. Occasionally, a direct moral commentary was offered to explain the intended meaning of photographs of subjects that lay, geographically

and morally, outside of the church. For example, underneath a 1905 photograph of a 'Vancouver Island Indian Home' in the *Christian Guardian*, the caption noted that its inhabitants had 'grown old in paganism'.[9]

The *Guardian*'s use of photography increased noticeably in 1903 when it introduced a new format, transforming itself from a newspaper-style serial into a longer magazine with a smaller layout. With the shift, photographs became noticeably larger and more prominent. However, the role of photography remained the edification of the church and its ministers. In 1906, a photograph of Calgary's Central Methodist Church was featured on the cover of the *Guardian*, with a caption underneath that read: 'Completed February, 1905; seating capacity, nearly 2,000; cost, including furnishings and organ, $75,000. Beginning at the very first, Methodism has been in Calgary only 23 years.'[10] The spiritual health of the church found a direct corollary in the increasing number and size of stone monuments in the nation. Churches, especially large, new buildings in rapidly expanding parts of the country, represented growth, progress, and the post-millennial optimism that shaped Protestant thought at the turn of the century.

In 1907, the *Christian Guardian* devoted a special issue to the city of Winnipeg. The explosive growth of the Canadian Prairies from the waves of immigration in the early years of the new century had quadrupled the size of Winnipeg; between 1901 and 1916 the city's population jumped from 45,000 to 187,000, making it Canada's third-largest city.[11] The *Guardian*'s photographic representations offered visual confirmation of the expansion of the city and the fulfillment of its motto: 'Commerce, Prudence, Industry'. Banks, warehouses, department stores, and the city hall all spoke to the material progress of Winnipeg, while the detailed history of Methodism was interwoven with photographs of the impressive churches that now stood as the monuments and confirmation of spiritual progress. For the moment, the public vision of building the kingdom of God was concentrated upon demonstrating that Methodist work was expanding in Winnipeg just as fast as the city itself.

The growth of the West, and Winnipeg in particular, was an important issue for Methodists. Membership in Anglican and Presbyterian churches was increasing at faster rates in the city and the region because of their direct links to the religious background of a greater proportion of recent British immigrants. Far fewer Methodists were emigrating, and many feared that Methodism would be left behind if the West fulfilled its growth potential.[12] The front-cover status of Calgary's Central Methodist Church and the interweaving of Methodist growth in Winnipeg with the expansion of the city itself assuaged anxieties that the Methodist Church was in danger of losing its pre-eminent position as the dominant Protestant denomination in Canada.

The growth of the city itself, however, posed new social and spiritual problems. In its commemorative issue, the *Guardian* editorialized that Winnipeg could, by most accounts, be called a 'great city'. But at the same time, it cautioned that the 'problem of the great city is one of the most serious that faces an enlightened civilization in this twentieth century'.[13] Indeed, in the same issue, the Reverend S.P. Rose warned that the religion of the city was different than the religion of the country because the city 'demands of the Christian religion that it shall pre-eminently express and apply itself socially'. It was not enough to lift people from despair, 'their feet must be placed upon the rock. A purified environment must be found for the regenerated life.'[14] Visually, however, photographs illustrating the particular social or spiritual problems of Winnipeg remained off the page. For the moment, the moral uplift of the city was directly connected to the ability of Methodists to raise impressive stone churches that matched the progress of the city itself.

The 1907 pictorial display coincided with an important shift within Winnipeg Methodism that would ultimately mark the beginning of a new photographic strategy. J.S. Woodsworth's arrival as the new superintendent of All Peoples' Mission in Winnipeg's North End heralded the introduction of a social documentary style that offered a very different visual representation of the city. On the verge of resigning from the ministry altogether, Woodsworth saw the superintendent's position as a perfect opportunity to engage in a more 'practical' Christianity, and he dedicated himself to increasing the profile of the North End mission.[15] It was in the course of promoting this work that a new visual representation of the city emerged in Methodist publications. The photographic images produced during Woodsworth's tenure offered bleak assessments of conditions in the North End in the social documentary style; it was no longer a celebration of material progress.

In Winnipeg, L.B. Foote was the most prominent photographer that Woodsworth and other social reformers turned to for photographic evidence to document social conditions of the city. By this time, Foote had established himself as a freelance commercial photographer who supplied images to a variety of newspapers. Although he was familiar with the diversity of Winnipeg's population, Foote himself was no crusader in the mould of Riis or the child labour activist Lewis Hine, preferring to take pictures of visiting royalty than raise awareness of the North End. Nevertheless, it was Foote's work that made its way into the pages of the *Christian Guardian* in August 1908 as social reformers started to reshape the image of the city through documentary photography. In stark contrast to the prosperous, progressive images of Winnipeg laid before its readers only a year earlier, Foote's picture of the back of a double-decker tenement house (Figure 1) marked the first time that a photographic representation of poor urban living conditions had been published in the magazine. The same image had accompanied a *Winnipeg Free Press* story a month earlier on 'Social Settlement Work in Winnipeg', an article which Woodsworth saved for his scrapbook.[16]

The paucity of archival material leaves only speculation as to the actual relationship between Woodsworth and Foote. Even though a number of mission activities were documented photographically by Foote, there is no direct evidence that he was actually commissioned for this work. Woodsworth himself wrote nothing about photography, and was certainly not an innovator in adopting the social documentary style, which had already made significant inroads within the American social reform movement. Many of Foote's images of Winnipeg's North End appear to have been taken primarily for use in newspapers, and only later incorporated within Methodist magazines and books. Nevertheless, Woodsworth clearly embraced this new photographic strategy, and put the images to use in many different places. The 1908 tenement-house picture was later republished on the second page of All Peoples' Mission annual report and included as an illustration within Woodsworth's *Strangers within our Gates*.[17]

The introduction of a social documentary approach to photographic representations in Methodist publications was neither abrupt nor absolute. Traditional forms continued to dominate, and hybridized versions also emerged. Woodsworth may have wanted to make mission work more scientific in nature, but he still had to raise money and support for All Peoples' through publicity, and photography was an important avenue for demonstrating both the need and the work accomplished by the mission. Even prior to Woodsworth's arrival, photographs of All Peoples' had been printed, largely focusing upon the mission buildings and the types of classes and activities that occurred within. In 1905, an image published in the *Christian Guardian* (Figure 2) displayed a kindergarten class arranged outside of the mission.[18] The traditional progressive vision was confirmed in this representation by placing the class in front of the sign with the English phrase 'A House of Prayer for All People' clearly visible, while the German text underneath was blocked from view. Assimilation through Canadianization was the goal of such educational efforts, and the bodies of the children are situated as vehicles for assimilation. Pictures of Sunday

Figure 1. The back of a tenement house in Winnipeg. Photographer: L.B. Foote, c. 1908. Reprinted from J.S. Woodsworth, *Strangers within Our Gates* (Toronto: The Missionary Society of the Methodist Church, 1909).

schools, kindergartens, and 'fresh air' camps were visual images that spoke to the work of the mission itself, and reinforced the message that the hope for the future of Canada, and Methodism, lay in the children of immigrants.[19]

After 1907, however, the work of the mission was increasingly conceptualized as taking place not only within the mission building itself, but also in the homes of the North End, and film was used to capture this form of broader community outreach. For example, a series of images produced around 1910 documented the activities of All Peoples' in conducting Christmas charity drives and delivering baskets to the needy. One photograph (Figure 3) presents the exchange between the Mission and the North End as a personal interaction between a deaconess, helped by a boy, and a needy family who are receiving a Christmas basket. These pictures were a form of public appeal for the mission, an effort to demonstrate the concrete action being taken by its workers. The class lines are clearly distinguishable between the warmly clothed workers and the poor family, whose faces are marked by dirt. The picture is obviously posed, requiring the mother and children to step outside into the cold in order for the photograph to be taken. Published

as part of the mission's 1911–12 annual report with the simple caption 'Christmas Cheer',[20] the family and location are not identified.

This type of documentation offered proof that mission workers were engaged in active, 'practical' Christianity, and that the work of the mission was indeed reaching the poor. In their namelessness, the family on the step became the embodiment of poverty in Winnipeg's North End, a passive entity exposed by the camera to prove both the necessity of relief, and the ability of the mission to deliver it. . . .

Such photographs were useful for publicity purposes, but this portrayal of mission workers in action was actually quite rare. . . . The new photographic strategy of 'surveying' existing conditions, such as the tenement house in Figure 1, relied upon an 'objective' visual regime that required a detachment from the subject. To place mission workers in direct contact with slum dwellers within the frame implied subjectivity and personal connections. The place of the scientific social worker was behind the camera, directing the view, gathering photographic exposures as a form of data, rather than being caught in front of it as a participant or an object of inquiry.

Figure 2. All Peoples' kindergarten class, Winnipeg. Writing on the image identifies the teachers as Annie Kelly and J.K. Lothrop. Photographer unknown, c. 1904. Winnipeg: Provincial Archives of Manitoba, No. N13261.

A parallel theological shift accompanied this changed photographic strategy. As the social gospel shifted attention away from individual salvation towards more collectivist approaches to building the kingdom of God, the camera similarly directed attention away from the individual subject and onto the environment that surrounded the body. Unlike the carefully documented pictures of churches and portraits of ministers, which offered a comprehensive, progressive narrative that drew image and text together, the new visual representations of Winnipeg's North End were largely disconnected from direct textual references, and their subjects were rarely identified by name. However, reproducing images of social conditions did not necessarily mark a secularization of the Methodist urban vision as much as it created a new moral ordering of urban space. The presence of photographic images of the North End within religious publications drew an explicit connection between environment and salvation. As Rose wrote in his series of articles on religion and the city, the church should 'intentionally set herself to the correction of specific abuses and evils, which threaten the well-being of modern civilisation, particularly in great centres of population'. Through the teaching and living of the

'truth', a 'purifying atmosphere' could pervade the political, commercial, and social realms. In this way, 'the truth of the Gospel pervades society, corrects its errors, and thus effects marvellous changes in the environment in which men live.'[21]

Before such a task could be accomplished, however, the existing environment needed to be surveyed and documented. Out of the documentary photography of Winnipeg and other cities in the first decades of the twentieth century, a new visual representation of the city entered the public consciousness. However, such images did not simply fill a vacuum; rather, they were read within a particular moral and spiritual context. Despite the perception that the camera was positioned to simply capture an objective reality, the employment of this new visual regime ascribed a moral order to urban space that reflected a wide range of underlying anxieties and concerns about the city itself.

The Danger of Urban Space

In their very ability to reproduce detail and context, photographic images made the environment that surrounded the subject an aspect that was impossible to ignore. In many of the

Figure 3. A posed photograph of mission workers delivering Christmas hampers to a home in Winnipeg's North End. Photographer unknown, c. 1910. Winnipeg: United Church of Canada Archives—Manitoba and Northwestern Ontario Conference, J.M. Shaver fonds, PP53, No. 2484.

examples already given (such as Figure 1), individuals and their bodies practically merge with their surroundings, or become dominated by the conditions around them. Woodsworth argued that if unchecked, the social problems of the urban environment threatened to turn the city into 'a hateful thing, from which we would flee in despair—a monstrous blot on the face of God's fair earth'.[22] Following the lead of the newspapers, church publications participated in a certain degree of sensationalism in publishing images of the 'monstrous blot' of urban slums.

Photography served the purpose of documenting the threatening condition that the city had become, but the underlying danger of this environment was conceptualized not in the mere existence of poverty or slums, but rather as a relationship between urban space and the body. While the city itself was generally seen as an unhealthy place compared to the country, the deeper tension lay in how specific urban spaces could lead to both physical and moral failings. This moral ordering of urban space was explicitly and implicitly related to the bodies that occupied it. Under the new photographic strategy of social documentary, when bodies enter the frame, the bodies are usually those of children. Woodsworth's *My Neighbor* included 44 different photographs, 15 of which were devoid of any human subjects. Of the remaining 29 pictures, 21 included children as part of the subject matter.

Children were prominent in the documentary activities of social reformers for a number of reasons. It was obviously easier to capture images of children than to take photographs of adults, who might have resisted the imposition. More importantly, however, the bodies of children drew attention to moral codes ascribed to the social space that surrounded them. By the second half of the nineteenth century, Methodists had started to remove the spectre of original sin from children, arguing that their innocence kept them in a state of grace. More controversial views suggested an environment of

Christian nurture even removed the necessity of a traditional conversion experience.[23] While the exact theological relationship of children and the church remained in dispute, most agreed that without a healthy Christian home, based on Anglo-Saxon Protestant values, the moral lives of children were at risk. The pliable nature of children in the face of their environment indicated that the space surrounding the child's body held a particular moral significance.

In making children the subject of photographic representations of urban slums, the 'problem' of the city became a problem for the future of the nation. For middle-class social reformers at the turn of the century, children were central to the welfare of Canada,[24] and Methodists, the most self-consciously 'national' Protestant denomination, repeatedly expressed these concerns. The *Guardian* editorialized that slum conditions and neglect would turn children into a 'class of thugs and hooligans and criminals', and the church's greatest task lay in 'safeguarding the moral and physical health and well-being of the children, and especially the children of our rapidly growing cities. The destiny of the church of the city, and of the nation rests upon the way we accomplish that task to a far greater extent than we can at all realize.'[25]

The physical environment of the city, however, posed a number of difficulties to the creation of productive citizens out of children. Rather than offering a pure and wholesome environment, the *Guardian* characterized the atmosphere of crowded downtowns as 'vitiated with smoke and tainted with a thousand inevitable odors that do not make for health'. Children needed to play, but their choices were limited geographically to playing indoors or on the street: 'To shut healthy children indoors to play is little short of murder . . . But, in the cities, to step outdoors is to step into the street . . . And unfortunately the streets are not a school of virtue, but of vice.'[26] To place children photographically in the street was to document the moral boundaries that threatened the nation. Unsupervised children on the street were subjected to the vices of the street. Only the urban reform of cities, creating more playgrounds to provide a safe space for children, could solve the problem. As the *Guardian* put it, 'Let the boys and girls have plenty of vigorous physical exercise, and the probability is they will be far less apt to become lawbreakers, and much more likely to become good citizens.'[27]

But the moral boundaries of urban space were not gendered equally. Parks and playgrounds were necessary reforms to prevent crime and disease, but they were particularly important for boys. As articles in the *Christian Guardian* outlined, the nature of boys made urban space particularly problematic. R.B. Chadwick, Alberta's Superintendent of Dependent and Delinquent Children, explained that 'the boy is a little savage, who prefers the free, natural, simple life of his aboriginal forebears to the ridiculous customs and conventionalities of civilization . . . His savage instinct demands that he live close to nature.' As Canadian cities became crowded, an 'insufficiency of grounds' prevents the boy from 'finding an outlet for his desire to run and play'. The result was predictable: without a safe space in which to express his natural inclination, the boy would 'become outlawed or a criminal'.[28] The streets of

the city were defined as a moral space that produced criminal bodies, an area that threatened the health of boys in particular, and by extension, the manhood and leadership of the nation.

While it was common to find photographic images of both girls and boys in the street, often with captions that commented on the lack of playground space, pictures of girls alone on the street were practically non-existent. The same was not true of boys, however. *My Neighbor* included a photograph (Figure 4) of a line of boys with the caption 'Boys of school age on the street'. The same image was published in a special 'city' issue of the *Missionary Outlook*, the magazine of the Young People's Forward Movement. F.C. Stephenson, secretary of the YPFM and Woodsworth's publisher, excerpted part of *My Neighbor* for the issue and had some of the photographs reprinted. Underneath the image of the boys, the caption starkly asked 'NEGLECTED NOW—WHAT OF THEIR FUTURE?' and included a subtitle that implied the voices of the boys themselves, stating, 'We run the streets all day.'[29]

Girls needed parks as well, but the moral space of greatest concern for them lay not in exterior spaces, but within interior spaces. Streets were dangerous, but the greater danger of moral

Figure 4. This image of boys on the street was used in a variety of Methodist publications. Photographer unknown. Reprinted in J.S. Woodsworth, *My Neighbor* (Toronto: The Missionary Society of the Methodist Church, 1911).

corruption for girls lay in the largely unspoken fear of sex and girls becoming 'fallen' in their morals. At a time when the domestic space of middle-class households emphasized separate bedrooms and offered girls' bodies a private space, the emergence of tenement houses and slums with overcrowded conditions raised fears that the environment was corrupting girls. Families sharing a single room, and sometimes a single bed, was a sight fearful enough. The greater worry was when families took in boarders, often single men; girls mixed with this uncontrolled element would find their moral state under threat.

Unlike the relatively straightforward campaign for playgrounds, however, raising the issue of sexuality was complicated by social sensibilities. The Reverend James Allen, Secretary of the Home Mission Department of the Methodist Missionary Society, caused an uproar in Winnipeg when he gave a sensational address to an Ottawa audience, claiming that living conditions were so poor in Winnipeg's North End that 'whole sections of the female population were being driven into virtual prostitution.' An outraged Winnipeg newspaper broadcast the headline 'Winnipeg Given Bad Reputation', and the city council was up in arms at the remarks.[30]

Respectable Winnipeg did not want its reputation sullied by such generalizations about prostitution, but the underlying visualization of moral boundaries within the interior of the homes remained. The *Winnipeg Tribune* sensationalized a case in which a fine had been levied against a boarding-house owner with the headline, 'Girls and Men in Same Room'. The item went on to report that 'the house consists of three rooms and a cellar and is large enough to hold seven people, but the accused was found to have 25 people living in his domicile, three of whom occupied the cellar and in one room girls and men slept.'[31] In Toronto, a missionary worker related similar stories on the 'secret sufferings and horrors of Toronto's "Ward"', where girls grew up 'without privacy, without self-respect'.[32]

Photographs taken by L.B. Foote of domestic interiors from the North End were framed within this context of moral concern. One image (Figure 5) juxtaposes the bodies of men, all of working age, with the bodies of children (boys and girls) within the cramped quarters of the home. Although one of the men is holding two children in his arms, perhaps signifying a paternal relationship, the other men remain detached from any clear familial ties.

Figure 5. Interior of a North End home, Winnipeg. Photographer: L.B. Foote, c. 1911. Winnipeg: Provincial Archives of Manitoba, No. N2438. The image was published in the *Winnipeg Tribune*, 28 Sept. 1911.

My Neighbor reproduced similar images that problematized the issue of gender and beds. . . .

Mariana Valverde argues that for most reformers the 'sexual secret of the slum' was incest, an 'unmentionable vice lurking deep beneath the crust of civilization'.[33] Despite Woodsworth's oblique reference to it through the use of a quotation from Tennyson (included as an epigraph in *My Neighbor*), the general characterization of crowded living conditions in Methodist publications does not substantiate Valverde's claim. Rather, in reports from the North End of Winnipeg of how the 'other half' lived, the greatest expression of anxiety concerned the problem of unattached male boarders. When the Reverend S.P. Rose took readers on an imaginary 'pilgrimage' to some North End homes, he described one domestic household as being occupied by a 'Ruthenian woman' and two children in a room that is 'neat and fairly clean', but in which danger lay, not in the close quarters of the family, but in the presence of five male boarders, which made 'decency and morality . . . inconceivable'. In contrast, another one-room household of two parents and four children, including an 18-year-old daughter, was described as a 'more hopeful' situation largely because there were no boarders.[34]

The moral implications of bodies crowded together extended into images that ostensibly documented environment alone. Foote's photograph of an unkempt bed (Figure 6) was originally published in the *Winnipeg Telegram*, complete with the prominent headline 'Six were Sleeping in This Room.'[35] Without physically placing the bodies onto the frame, the moral implications were read through the context which problematized such conditions on multiple levels. Although the accompanying article on visitations to the poor in preparation for distributing Christmas funds did not refer explicitly to the photograph, it did complain about Winnipeg's familiar problem of overcrowding. Single-room homes that contained both large families and male boarders produced circumstances where the 'sanitary conditions were something to appal

one and the moral atmosphere under each surroundings can be imagined.'[36] The same image was reprinted as an illustration for an article on All Peoples' Mission in the *Canadian Epworth Era*.[37] The absence of bodies did not lessen the moral boundaries ascribed to urban space, given the ability of readers to 'imagine' it.

Conclusion

The meaning of the social gospel is traditionally framed in connection with issues such as secularization, the rise of the welfare state, or class-based theories of social control. However, a deeper epistemological engagement with modernity within the social gospel has been overlooked, especially in the Canadian context. The new focus upon social conditions at the turn of the century required a new way of 'seeing' and 'surveying' the city. The progressive vision of churches and church workers within the photographic representations of Methodist publications had to make room for an objective exposure of how the 'other half' lived. The arrival of the social documentary style produced a dramatic shift in the visualization of Winnipeg within Methodist publications at the turn of the century.

One of the major differences between the two different photographic strategies, however, lay in how the images related to the text. When photographs were used to exemplify the progressive expansion of the church, they were carefully linked to the accompanying narrative; through captions or references within articles, people and places were carefully identified. In contrast, there was a remarkable discontinuity in the narrative when images that offered a social documentary were published. People are rarely identified by name, and often even the name of the city is absent, let alone more specific indications of place. This absence of narrative reinforced the underlying notion that the subjects were not important as individual people, but rather served as bodies framed by the environment. Such a 'depersonalized' approach was, as John Tagg has

Figure 6. Photograph of a one-room home for six people in Winnipeg. Photographer: L.B. Foote, 1908. Courtesy of United Church of Canada/ Victoria University Archives, No. 93.049P/3117N.

noted, indicative of the practices of 'professional social technicians' who believed that social problems could be solved through environmental change.[38] Set within the context of Methodist publications, the namelessness of subjects overshadowed by the details of their surroundings had a particular theological resonance that implicitly downplayed the importance of individual conversion and reinforced a collective moral understanding of the urban environment.

Referring to the photographs within a 1911 study of Toronto slums, Mariana Valverde observed that there were 'many more dirty outhouses than criminal human beings', and suggests that 'this shift in focus from the poor people to their habitat reflects not a shedding of moralism in favour of science but simply the ascription of moral deviance to physical objects.'[39] However, objects in themselves did not reflect a moral order as much as they created a moral space which produced moral bodies. The bodies of children in particular offered social reformers malleable material, but the meanings of these bodies could be understood only as products of their environment. Woodsworth summed up this relationship when he claimed that 'crime, immorality, disease and misery vary almost directly as the size of the

plot, the breadth of the street and the number of parks.'[40] As sin was increasingly seen as the product of an environment, the environment itself required surveillance.

Documenting the shift in visual imagery in Methodist publications is a much simpler task than analyzing its meaning. Peter Burke suggests that visual images are both 'an essential and treacherous source' for historians, in part because 'Images can bear witness to what is not put into words.'[41] While we can only speculate as to the exact intentions of Woodsworth and others who promoted this strategic shift to the social documentary style, the wordlessness of photographs should not obscure or diminish how such images operated within the historical context of their production (and reproduction). This visual ordering was not simply symbolic of social reform ideals, but actively constructed a view of the city through its own technological authority, an objective claim to dispassionate representation of the urban space surrounding the body. In return, the very context in which this re-imaging took place invested the urban landscape with multiple layers of moral boundaries, where the dangers to physical and spiritual health were clearly exposed. Although they were disconnected from the overt narratives of missionary work, social documentary photographs spoke to a broader narrative that positioned the religious response to the city as both a moral and environmental issue.

Notes

Financial support for this project was provided by a University of Lethbridge Research Fund Grant. The author wishes to thank Janet Friskney for her comments on early drafts of this work.

1. J.S. Woodsworth, *My Neighbor* (Toronto: Missionary Society of the Methodist Church, 1911), 22.
2. Toronto, United Church of Canada Archives (UCA), 73.102C, Methodist Church Department of Evangelism and Social Service papers, box 1, file 2, Board of Temperance and Moral Reform, Annual Meeting, 21–2 Oct. 1913.
3. S.D. Chown, 'Introduction', in Woodsworth, *My Neighbor*, 6; see also *The Missionary Outlook* 31, 8 (Aug. 1911): 177.
4. As Alan Trachtenberg notes, the 'documentary' label was applied retrospectively to the work of Lewis Hine and Walker Evans as a way to classify an aesthetic that appeared to be neither 'art' nor purely journalistic in its intent. Alan Trachtenberg, *Reading American Photographs: Images as History, Mathew Brady to Walker Evans* (New York: Hill and Wang, 1989), 190–2. On the transition from Riis to Veiller, see Maren Stange, *Symbols of Ideal Life: Social Documentary in America, 1890–1950* (Cambridge: Cambridge University Press, 1985), 28–46.
5. Susan Sontag, *On Photography* (New York: Dell, 1977), 87.
6. On the relationship between photography and a 'modern vision', see Suren Lalvani, *Photography, Vision, and the Production of Modern Bodies* (Albany: State University of New York Press, 1996).
7. The phrase 'evidential force' is Roland Barthes's, but John Tagg takes the same notion in a different direction by pointing out that the 'very idea of what constitutes evidence has a history'. See John Tagg, *The Burden of Representation: Essays of Photographs and Histories* (Basingstoke: Macmillan, 1988), 2.
8. Doug Smith and Michael Olito, *The Best Possible Face: L.B. Foote's Winnipeg* (Winnipeg: Turnstone Press, 1985), 2–3.
9. *Christian Guardian* 76, 40 (4 Oct. 1905): 9.
10. Ibid., 77, 21 (23 May 1906): 1.
11. Paul Voisey, 'The Urbanization of the Canadian Prairies, 1871–1916', *Histoire Sociale/Social History* 8 (1975): 84–5.
12. George Emery, *The Methodist Church on the Prairies, 1896–1914* (Montreal and Kingston: McGill-Queen's University Press, 2001), 104–25.
13. 'Problems and Policies', *Christian Guardian* 78, 14 (3 Apr. 1907): 5.
14. S.P. Rose, 'The Religion of a Great City', *Christian Guardian* 78, 14 (3 Apr. 1907): 6.
15. Nancy Christie and Michael Gauvreau suggest that the threat to resign was not based on theological issues but was rather a 'ploy' to secure the position at All Peoples' Mission. . . . See Nancy Christie and Michael Gauvreau, *A Full-Orbed Christianity* (Montreal and Kingston: McGill-Queen's University Press, 1996), 8–12. In contrast, George Emery reasserts the radical position of Woodsworth, but claims that this was balanced by a mainstream evangelicalism that characterized most of the mission workers. See Emery, *The Methodist Church on the Prairies*, 147–50. Whether mainstream or radical, Woodsworth's ascendance certainly marked a shift at All Peoples' that was reflected in the realm of visual representation.
16. *Christian Guardian* 79, 34 (19 Aug. 1908): 9. The image was published the previous month in the *Free Press*. Ottawa: National Archives of Canada (NAC), J.S. Woodsworth fonds, Woodsworth Scrapbooks, newspaper clipping, 'Social Settlement Work in Winnipeg', *Winnipeg Free Press*, 11 July 1908.
17. NAC, J.S. Woodsworth fonds, box 15.8, microfilm H-2278, *All Peoples' Mission, Winnipeg, Report, 1907–1908*; J.S. Woodsworth, *Strangers within our Gates* (Toronto: Missionary Society of the Methodist Church, 1909), facing p. 262.
18. *Christian Guardian* 76, 40 (4 Oct. 1905): 5.
19. For an even earlier image of All Peoples' Mission, and one that included signage in multiple languages, see *Christian Guardian* 70, 30 (26 July 1899): 467.
20. NAC, J.S. Woodsworth fonds, box 15.8, microfilm H-2278, *Organized Helpfulness: All Peoples' Mission, 1911–1912*, 22.
21. S.P. Rose, 'The Religion of a Great City: Part III', *Christian Guardian* 78, 16 (17 Apr. 1907): 8.
22. Woodsworth, *My Neighbor*, 23.
23. Neil Semple stresses the development of the Christian nurture ideal, while Marguerite Van Die notes that Nathanael Burwash maintained the more traditional evangelical viewpoint well into the twentieth century. Although Burwash reasserted the doctrine as official church policy in 1906, the model of Christian nurture promoted by Horace Bushnell had clearly won out by 1918. See Neil Semple, '"The Nurture and Admonition of the Lord": Nineteenth-Century Canadian Methodism's Response to "Childhood"', *Histoire Sociale/Social History* 14, 27 (May 1981): 157–75; Neil Semple, *The Lord's Dominion* (Montreal and Kingston: McGill-Queen's University Press, 1996), 363–7; Marguerite Van Die, *An*

Evangelical Mind: Nathanael Burwash and the Methodist Tradition in Canada, 1839–1918 (Montreal and Kingston: McGill-Queen's University Press, 1989), 26–37, 191. As Phyllis Airhart notes, these issues were further complicated by psychological views of religious experience itself. Phyllis Airhart, *Serving the Present Age: Revivalism, Progressivism, and the Methodist Tradition in Canada* (Montreal and Kingston: McGill-Queen's University Press, 1992), 97–103.

24. See Neil Sutherland, *Children in English-Canadian Society: Framing the Twentieth Century Consensus* (Toronto: University of Toronto Press, 1976).

25. 'Giving the Children a Chance', *Christian Guardian* 82, 13 (29 Mar. 1911): 5.

26. 'The City and the Children', *Christian Guardian* 78, 5 (30 Jan. 1907): 5.

27. Ibid.

28. R.B. Chadwick, 'The Boys: A Social Problem', *Christian Guardian* 81, 52 (28 Dec. 1910): 9–10.

29. *Missionary Outlook* 31, 11 (Nov. 1911): 251.

30. UCA, 78.099C, Methodist Church of Canada Board of Home Missions, box 7, file 3, unidentified newspaper clippings, 11 Oct. 1909.

31. Ibid., *Winnipeg Tribune* newspaper clipping *c.* 1909.

32. 'Sad Picture of Toronto's Slums', *Toronto Star*, 19 Oct. 1909, 1.

33. Mariana Valverde, *The Age of Light, Soap, and Water: Moral Reform in English Canada, 1885–1925* (Toronto: McClelland & Stewart, 1991), 139. Valverde also notes the problem of male boarders, but prioritizes the issue of incest.

34. S.P. Rose, 'The Raw Material of Canadian Citizenship: A Closer View', *Christian Guardian* 79, 34 (19 Aug. 1908): 9–10.

35. Woodsworth Scrapbooks, *Winnipeg Telegram*, 16 Dec. 1908.

36. Ibid., 'Some of Children to be Gladdened by Fund', *Winnipeg Telegram*, 16 Dec. 1908.

37. Ibid., *Canadian Epworth Era* (Mar. 1909): 68.

38. Tagg, *Burden of Representation*, 131–2.

39. Valverde, *Age of Light, Soap, and Water*, 133.

40. Woodsworth, *My Neighbor*, 47; also quoted in Valverde, *Age of Light, Soap, and Water*, 130.

41. Peter Burke, *Eyewitnessing: The Uses of Images as Historical Evidence* (Ithaca, NY: Cornell University Press, 2001), 31.

5

'There Were Always Men in Our House': Gender and the Childhood Memories of Working-class Ukrainians in Depression-era Canada

—— **Stacey Zembrzycki** ——

When Bill Semenuk recently shared his memories about growing up in Depression-era Sudbury, Ontario, as one of seven children born to a Ukrainian immigrant worker employed at the International Nickel Company (INCO) and his wife, he highlighted a number of personal narratives. One was a happy narrative of how, when the family moved from a neighbouring farm to 'the Donovan' area of Sudbury, Bill always had 'places to play', stating 'there were ball fields, [we played] cowboys in the rock mountains . . . [and in] the winter there was a lot of sliding [and] we used to crawl up the telephone poles and then drop ourselves into snow piles underneath.' Another was a moving narrative about his mother's illness and eventual death. When his mother, Mary, became sick, he told me, 'I used to ask to leave school early to take care of her.' Sadly, Mary died in 1932 when Bill was nine years old. 'It was very hard for a while after mother died,' Bill explained, noting that often the family was 'just glad to eat' and that 'sometimes us kids would fight over potatoes.'

Bill also pointed out that his 'father always worked day shift' and thus he marvelled at the thought of how this man had looked after the whole lot of them: 'He would leave at six in the morning and return at six at night. Father would do everything. I remember him sewing clothes, [and putting] patches upon patches.' In addition, since many men could not find jobs in the Depression, there were always Ukrainian men who would come to Sudbury, a place where job opportunities actually existed, and stay with Bill's family. 'These men,' Bill said, 'were good friends of my father [and they] looked after us when mother died.' He added: 'I remember the kitchen being the main room of the house where everyone congregated and told stories. We [children] would sit around and listen.'[1]

Bill Semenuk's childhood narrative, which takes place against the backdrop of a family home that became a boarding house for Ukrainian male workers during the 1930s, is not an abstract discussion about the general conditions of the Great Depression. As we sat at his kitchen table and he recounted his childhood years, Bill, a member of Sudbury's Ukrainian Catholic community, structured his narrative around what he considered to be his most important Depression-era memory: the death of his mother. Her death, he makes clear, dramatically affected his life and that of his father and siblings. By turning the history of this period into a biographical memory, Bill acted as a subjective and central historical actor in his narrative. In elucidating his general experiences in deeply personal terms, Bill's narrative provided a means by which he could both order and validate his childhood experiences and understand the meanings of his life.[2]

Excerpt from Stacey Zembrzycki, '"There Were Always Men in Our House": Gender and the Childhood Memories of Working-Class Ukrainians in Depression-Era Canada', *Labour/Le travail*, 60 (Fall 2007), 77–105. Reprinted by permission of the publisher.

It is also entirely possible that the gender dynamics of our kitchen table interview, in which a now elderly man shared his boyhood memories with a much younger Ukrainian-Canadian female researcher, affected how Bill told his tale. As oral historians note, the interviewer and the interviewee both participate, although perhaps to varying degrees, in the making of an oral history and/or memory text.[3] Taking this insight one step further, and explicitly gendering it, feminist labour and immigration historian Franca Iacovetta has demonstrated how when female historians interview older immigrant male workers about their pasts, asking gendered questions, they may well encourage their male informants to reflect more fully on the women in their lives and on their gendered understandings of their pasts.[4] The gendered character of female narratives of the past has also been well demonstrated by feminist scholars, including labour and immigration historians, but perhaps most forcefully by those who have probed the silences and gaps in women's recollections of such deeply traumatic events as war-time rape and internment; such silences can represent coping strategies to protect fragile memories.[5]

Of course, Bill was not alone when it came to constructing biographical memories about growing up ethnic and working class in Sudbury during the thirties. Specifically, there were plenty of other Ukrainian working-class men and women who also lived out their boyhood and girlhood years in Depression-era family homes that doubled as boarding houses. In significant respects, both Ukrainian men and women who grew up in the Sudbury region during this period understood and viewed the Depression in similar ways. Many of them, for example, did not focus on the economic crash of 1929, an event that few children appreciated before they reached adulthood, but rather remembered the personal difficulties that their families faced during the Depression era as well as the years that preceded and followed it. As recent immigrants of humble and/or poor rural backgrounds, many working-class Ukrainians in Canada were accustomed to subsistence living and penny capitalism and thus the collapse of the wider economy in the thirties did not have as great an impact on their daily lives as was the case for many middle- and upper-class Anglo-Canadians.[6]

Still, the Depression years were trying ones and my informants generally filtered their narratives into personal stories about struggle and despair. Their accounts of the difficulties, however, went hand in hand with memories that spoke to the issue of immigrant and working-class pride as well as stories about coping strategies and ultimately survival. At the same time, it must be noted that there were significant gender differences in how boys and girls lived and remembered their daily lives during this period, especially in regard to social relationships with male boarders, household work, and leisure pursuits that took place inside and around their immigrant boarding houses. To paraphrase the European oral historian Alessandro Portelli, all of these subjective—and gendered—narratives 'tell us not just what people did, but what they wanted to do, what they believed they were doing, and what they now think they did'.[7]

As an exploration of the childhood memories of working-class Ukrainians who grew up in Depression-era boarding houses (or houses with a few boarders) in a heavily immigrant northern Ontario town, this paper treats the oral histories as the subject, not merely the method, of analysis and highlights, in particular, the gendered differences that emerge in the narratives of the men and women that I interviewed. Moreover, this article argues that even within a politically polarized immigrant group such as the Ukrainians, where left/right, progressive/nationalist, and secular/religious splits were so pronounced, and thus central to shaping the histories and historiographies of both camps, it was the influence of dominant gender roles rather than politics, religion, or ideology that most directly informed the differing memories of experience that men and women had of growing up Ukrainian and working class in Sudbury.[8] The political egalitarianism professed by progressive Ukrainians, for instance, did not transgress the boundaries of their households and thus traditional gender roles were assumed by inhabitants. This article therefore focuses on my informants' recollections regarding three areas of activity that were part of everyday boarding house life: children's relationships with male boarders, their domestic chores, and leisure activities.

. . .

When it came to conducting the interviews for this project, I was both an outsider and an insider to Sudbury's Ukrainian community. Although I grew up in the city, I neither participated in any community-sponsored activities, nor joined any Ukrainian organizations. My paternal *Baba* (grandmother), however, was very active in the organized life of the community, devoting much of her spare time to St Mary's Ukrainian Catholic Church. While *Baba*'s stories about the community undoubtedly provided me with an insider perspective about the narratives which had shaped its history, I also struggled to understand and clarify aspects of the narratives which I found unclear as an outsider.[9] With *Baba*'s help—she often telephoned Ukrainian men and women that she knew and convinced them to grant me an interview—I interviewed 82 of her friends and acquaintances in English using a life story approach.[10] It must be noted that *Baba*'s connection to the church did not hinder my ability to interview Ukrainians who belonged to other institutions; my informants had Catholic, Orthodox, nationalist, and progressive affiliations. Moreover, my relationship with *Baba* was something that could be discussed with the men and women that I interviewed, opening up the conversations because it provided a level of trust in the interview spaces.

While I certainly consider social and material conditions when turning to childhood memories of the Depression, my main intention is to 'communicate with the past more directly'.[11] Childhood is a separate and socially constructed

stage of existence which complicates the creation of a memory text; in terms of age, all of my interviewees were under the age of 13 prior to 1939. Since as Neil Sutherland notes, adults tend to use childhood memories that are 'really a reconstruction of what is being recalled rather than a reproduction of it', this article will pay particular attention to the form, content, and silences of these Ukrainian narratives.[12] In making the act of remembering just as important as the memories themselves, we will be able to explore and evaluate how Sudbury's Ukrainians used memory, experience, and history to construct their subjective Depression-era narratives.[13] . . .

My interviewees tended to couple their childhood memories about financial instability with those that recalled the many men in their lives, namely the boarders with whom they shared their private domestic spaces. . . . As one of the most common survival strategies during the Depression years, boarding was a normal occurrence in this heavily masculine resource town and thus directly and indirectly touched the lives of most working-class residents. This is reflected in my sample: a majority of my interviewees, roughly 66 per cent, recalled having boarders or roomers living in their houses at this time. Together, these domestic working-class childhood narratives shed light on the collective and shared experiences as well as the noteworthy gender differences experienced by Ukrainian men and women. Different political or religious affiliations, for example, did not produce dramatically different memories. Whether they frequented the Ukrainian Labour Farmer Temple Association (ULFTA) hall, St Mary's Ukrainian Catholic Church, St Volodymyr's Ukrainian Greek Orthodox Church, or the Ukrainian National Federation (UNF) hall, the Ukrainians who shared their stories with me recalled the boarding-house or rooming-house culture in which they grew up in a similar fashion. . . .

In considering the economic importance of boarding among Sudbury's Ukrainians, we must also understand it as part of a wider family economy and as a strategy, among others, for surviving in a particular set of economic conditions. As an ethnic entrepreneurship most often managed by my interviewees' mothers, it was a way for the family to earn extra money during these difficult years, improving its ability to pay the mortgage as well as the bills at the local grocery store. In addition to supplementing a father's wages, boarding was also an informal insurance policy when a father lost his job. Since Ukrainians with foreign surnames, or alleged links to communism, were the first to be fired during this period, a wife's boarding business ensured some steady income that allowed the family to survive such a disaster.[14] Moreover, since most fathers' days were spent at work or looking for extra work if they lost their jobs or had their shifts cut back, the mothers were the dominant figure in their children's lives.[15] Heavily male resource towns offered women few opportunities for earning incomes and this, of course, affected the gendered family strategies employed by those who lived in these kinds of environments. . . . Ukrainian women may have had few formal job opportunities, but they were able to create their own economic opportunities at home. By taking in boarders, they either supplemented their husbands' incomes or managed to be financially independent, supporting themselves and their children if their husbands had either lost their jobs, or abandoned them, or died prematurely. In many cases, women were the primary breadwinners and housewives in these spaces. By placing memories at the heart of this analysis it is thus possible to illuminate the ethnic and gendered roles performed by Ukrainian women in these boarding houses. Since these memories belong to children who grew up in these spaces, getting 'inside' these boarding houses also enables a discussion of the gendered contributions girls and boys made to these family economies.

It is also important to note that Sudburians had a unique Depression experience. In contrast to other parts of the country, this region remained relatively unscathed because of its nickel and the global demand for it. As Carl Wallace shows, the local market nearly collapsed in 1931 and 1932 but it quickly recovered between 1933 and 1937, stumbling in 1938 and then exploding with the outbreak of war.[16] Sudbury thus became a 'destination city' during this period.[17] . . .

Those men who made the decision to come to Sudbury during the 1930s, both single and married men with children, settled in a variety of working-class neighbourhoods, both multicultural and ethnically homogeneous; the majority of my interviewees recounted what it was like to grow up on the streets of the Donovan, the West End, the East End, and Polack Town, in the INCO company town of Coniston. It must be noted that these neighbourhoods were not ideologically, religiously, or politically ordered; it was not unusual for a Ukrainian Catholic to live down the street or next door to a Ukrainian who was a member at the local ULFTA hall.

. . .

Boarding was always a risky business but during the Depression it was particularly precarious.[18] A successful business depended upon reliable and employed clientele who paid their bills regularly, and this was made difficult with the uncertainty of the times.[19] Boarding either eliminated the effects of the Depression or it brought them right into the home, adding yet another challenge for the immigrant family to overcome. Nick Evanshen, a Ukrainian with no organizational affiliations, recalled the ways that his life changed when his parents, Steve and Mary, moved from their house on Whittaker Street to their new one at 268 Drinkwater Street; this was a large boarding house that had enough space for 30 boarders and roomers. Before undertaking this business, Nick remembered how his 'mother went for days with very little food so she could scrape up enough to feed all five children', remarking 'it wasn't very pleasant during the [. . . early days of the] Depression.' After moving into the boarding house, he recalled how his mother would wake at three or four o'clock in the morning to make lunch pails and then she would spend her day cooking, cleaning, and doing laundry. He also understood that her labours mattered: the boarding fees 'helped the family income, [and] improved the situation', and it meant that they 'always had enough food [to eat] when they lived on Drinkwater [Street]'.[20]

For others, boarding proved to be more of a hassle than a solution to their family's economic difficulties. Olga Zembrzycki (née Zyma), a lifelong member of St Mary's Ukrainian Catholic Church, stated: 'If times were tough some roomers left father holding the bag. They would leave to look for work elsewhere and never pay their rent. They always said that they would come back to pay [but] they never did.' . . .[21] Pauline Kruk's (née Mykoluk) parents, both of whom were members of Holy Trinity Roman Catholic Church, faced a similar fate, nearly losing their only house in the Depression because of the pressures of providing for a large family which included 10 children and sometimes up to three Ukrainian boarders who were often unable to pay their fees. Had it not been for one boarder who was particularly close to Pauline's parents, and paid regularly, Malanka and Jacob would have lost their home. . . .[22] Engaged in a difficult and sometimes uncertain venture, especially during the Depression, boarding-house keepers could not always find reliable boarders.

One way of trying to ensure more trustworthy boarders was to have relatives, such as uncles, cousins, or grandfathers, stay in the home. This proved to be a better arrangement for some interviewees. Financially, these family members helped to pay the bills; splitting the cost of living made it possible for more families to buy homes rather than rent them. Their presence could also ease the emotional difficulties that came with immigrating to a new country. For example, those who knew their *Gidos* (grandfathers) and *Babas* (grandmothers), even if only for a brief period before they sojourned back to the old country, considered themselves lucky.[23] Still, some relatives took advantage of the situation. Bernice Crowe (née Haluschak) had a vivid

childhood memory of the four uncles (her father's brothers) who came to live with her family after getting jobs at Falconbridge Mine. When her mother, who spent some of her 'leisure' time cooking in the ULFTA kitchen, got angry about this arrangement and confronted the men, they replied: 'well he's our brother and we don't have to pay.'[24] Taking on family members, then, could also involve considerable economic risk.

. . . Unless they had family in the region, most of my interviewees' parents came to Sudbury only after they settled in another part of the country and failed to obtain the standard of living that they had envisioned. Men saw advertisements for jobs in Sudbury or they learned about them from co-workers. John Stefura's father, Alec, one of the founding members of Sudbury's UNF hall, received a letter from friends in the region who told him that 'if you wanted a job INCO was hiring for 25 cents an hour and you could work for 6 1/2 or 7 days a week.'[25] If the men had family or friends in the region, they usually stayed with them until they could get settled and send for any immediate family members who were living in other parts of Canada or in Ukraine. In contrast, those men without a connection to anyone living in Sudbury would ride the rails to the town and when they arrived they would either hear about a boarding house from the men that they encountered or they would visit the local Ukrainian church, the ULFTA hall, or the UNF hall where they would be welcomed and recommended to a boarding-house operator. Thus, in contrast to the mixed neighbourhoods of the town, these boarding houses tended to be ethnically, ideologically, politically, and religiously homogenous; a progressive Ukrainian would not have boarded with a Catholic family for instance. Unless one of the operators was familiar with the men recommended to them, they always took a chance when taking in boarders. The desperation of the times meant that one could not be particularly fastidious.

Children who grew up in these kinds of households thus recalled that there were always men in the house, usually eating or sleeping. This was especially true for Paul Behun's family, all of whom were devout members of St Michael's Ukrainian Catholic Church. When his father, John, died in 1932, his mother collected $30 a month in mother's allowance to raise Paul and his older brother Bill. To supplement that income, Anna took in three boarders, one for every shift at the nearby INCO smelter. While one man slept, the second man worked, and the third man remained awake. Anna had to do this in order to qualify for mother's allowance, rotating the men to prove to officials that she did not have a constant breadwinner in the house.[26] It is significant to note that although Anna's strategy was meant to help her evade officials, other Ukrainian women also employed bed rotation schedules to accommodate more men. By having the men sleep in shifts, a three-bedroom home with two beds in each room, for instance, could then meet the needs of 18 men who worked the day, afternoon, and night shifts at the local mines. According to Anne Matschke, 'the beds were always warm.'[27]

In these childhood memories, the boarders occupy different ranks with respect to the family. Some male interviewees elevated the men to the status of 'uncles' while others could rarely remember the names of those with whom they had shared their domestic space. As the opening story tells us, after Bill Semenuk's mother, Mary, died in 1932, his father, John, a devoted member of St Mary's Ukrainian Catholic Church, had to raise seven children alone. Luckily he worked steady day shift at INCO's Frood Mine and so he could come home in time to meet the children when they arrived from school. In those instances when he needed a babysitter, the male boarders looked after the children, congregating in the kitchen where they would play cards and tell stories that the children would sit around and listen to. For Bill these men were like family.[28] Taciana*, who frequented St Mary's and the UNF hall, also remembered the men who lived in her parent's home fondly; she reminisced about the many Ukrainian holidays spent with them

at her mother's kitchen table, eating traditional Ukrainian dishes and listening to stories about the old country.[29] It is, in this case, important to stress that adult memories about childhood are fallible and thus these now nostalgic stories may have been transformed with the passage of time.[30]

Other interviewees had very different memories of the boarders who had lived in their homes. These stories do not move toward a 'happy ending', but rather interviewees remembered these men as simply strangers who had shared their space. For instance, Mary Brydges (née Ladyk), who took mandolin lessons at the ULFTA hall, stated that the men 'used to come through the back door, through the kitchen and go straight upstairs', eating with her family but otherwise living separately. Mary left school at the age of 13 to help her mother run the family's boarding house, and although she vividly recalled waking every morning to make 13 or 14 lunch pails to send to work with the men, she could not remember any particular man.[31] . . . Angela Behun (née Bilowus), a member of St Michael's Ukrainian Catholic Church, echoed this sentiment, emphasizing that there were always different men staying with her family. Her house was like a 'temporary stop-over', a place where the men would stay before switching to another boarding house or getting married.[32]

If a child developed a relationship with a boarder, he was usually the son, not the daughter, of the family. The girls spent a significant amount of time helping their mothers, while boys usually had few domestic chores. Nellie Kozak (née Tataryn), one of five daughters in her Ukrainian Catholic family, remembered that when the one boy, her brother, Steve, arrived '. . . God was born. For Ukrainian people, the son was everything and the girls were nothing. The girls would just have to work.'[33] Lynne Marks has well documented the different gendered dimensions of working-class leisure and certainly there were important gender distinctions in Sudbury as well.[34] Boys like Steve tended to have more spare time than their sisters. Consequently, some boys spent much of their leisure time with the men who lived in their homes, often getting to know these men better than their own fathers who worked long 12-hour shifts at the local mines. It must be noted that boarders, with whom boys formed bonds, often did not work at the mines. Rather they worked odd jobs and thus had more time to spend at home. Peter Chitruk remembered developing close relationships with many of the men living in his home, but one particular man, 'Bill', stood out; Bill worked odd jobs in and around the region. They had a close bond and a special Sunday morning routine: Bill would buy the *Toronto Star* and read it to Peter while he sat next to him and looked at the pictures.[35] Nick Evanshen developed a similar bond with two brothers who boarded at his house, John and Peter Buyarski. When they were not working at the nearby East End Bakery, a job which took them away from home in the morning, John and Peter would babysit Nick, taking him swimming in the summer and skating in the winter. Nick admitted to seeing these men more often than his father, fondly recalling that they bought him his first pair of skates.[36] . . .

While girls may have had less time to spend with male boarders because their workload in the home was heavier than that of their brothers, we must also address the other ways in which parents regulated these relationships. Parents subtly limited the time their daughters spent with these men and monitored any interaction they may have had with them to ensure that relations did not turn sexual. For instance, girls often ate at different times from the men and slept in bedrooms that were located on separate floors. I say that these measures were subtle because when asked about their relationships with boarders, my interviewees noted that their memories contained no recollections of undue sexual anxiety about having had men living in their homes. Although these silences seem to indicate that sexual anxiety was not a part of my interviewees' experiences, it is important to recognize that the Ukrainians with whom I spoke may have

suppressed, transformed, and/or chosen not to reveal these kinds of incidents to me when asked about boarding-house culture.

We must, as Gabaccia and Iacovetta argue, nevertheless view boarding houses as sexualized spaces of pleasure and danger. Although the childhood memories of the Ukrainian men and women that I interviewed downplayed the fear and/or alarmism expressed by social reformers who argued that crowded domestic spaces threatened girls' sexuality, there is no doubt that sexual tensions and sexual misconduct of various types did occur in some of these households.[37] Instances of boarders guilty of sexually assaulting the girls with whom they lived can be found within the written record even if they were not reported by my informants.[38] Despite their silences on the issue of sexual assault, some intriguing stories did emerge in these interviews which give us insight into some of the sexual tensions which occurred in these homes. One woman recalled that certain boarding-house keepers treated the younger men as a pool of potential husbands for their daughters, in some cases making their choices very clear to the community so as to avoid unnecessary competition for their daughters.[39]

. . . Although we may not be able to determine whether my interviewees' houses were sexually charged places, some of the men and women were forthcoming when it came to telling negative stories about other boarding houses and their operators; gossip is therefore essential to shedding light on those issues which my interviewees refrained from discussing. . . . While stressing that their parents' boarding houses had been filled with respectable men, they referred to certain Ukrainian boarding-house operators as 'floozies' who had left their husbands for boarders. These women became outcasts in the Ukrainian community because in leaving their husbands they also often left their children. At least this was the case with religious Ukrainians; no one from the progressive community raised this matter. Those Catholics who did share their memories of 'bad' women stressed that these women never returned to church. Living in a common law situation, or as Ukrainians negatively referred to it, living *na bushwel*, was unrespectable. If a Ukrainian woman married, then the belief was that she had chosen a life partner. Regardless of whether a woman's husband abused her or their children, drank excessively, or lost his job, divorce was not considered to be an option. . . . The immigrant generation believed that there was no right or wrong reason for a woman to divorce, let alone abandon, her husband. Stories such as these therefore remind us that we need to study the silences that occur when doing oral history. Memories about boarders who became 'uncles' need to be read alongside those of men who were cunning or abusive; memories of boarding houses as sites of pleasure alongside those that spoke to danger.

Although the sexual dynamics within boarding houses varied, all successful boarding businesses required thriftiness and this was especially true during the Depression. This burden fell upon the woman of the household. In performing this type of paid labour in the home, the boundaries between a woman's public and private spheres were inevitably blurred. Despite this compromise and the fact that boarding created more work for women and led to extra expenditures and infringements on their private spaces, this domestic business, as Bettina Bradbury reminds us, offered women a source of income comparable to a wage.[40] During the Depression, this wage came with a catch. . . . The boarding-house keeper had to prepare enough food for her boarders and, at the worst of times, try to financially break even.

Not surprisingly, this was often difficult to do when boarders did not have enough money to pay their boarding fees. Ukrainian women responded to this challenge by preparing ethnic food. . . . Ukrainian women, like most immigrant women feeding families on tight budgets, took their role as food providers seriously and drew on customary ways of stretching meals to feed

their households.[41] A pot of borscht or a roast pan of perogies or cabbage rolls fed many hungry mouths and these foods could be made in large quantities for a relatively low price; it must be noted that these dishes were often made with seasonal ingredients. Such ethnic foods were a staple, made at least once a week to satisfy the boarders' hunger as well as the family's budgetary constraints. Boarding-house operators also made a variety of soups. Like perogies made with flour and potatoes, and cabbage rolls made with cabbage and rice, large quantities of soup made with water, a small portion of meat and some kind of vegetable could be made quite inexpensively. Anne Matschke (née Kuchmey), a member at St Mary's Ukrainian Catholic Church, remembered her mother preparing a different pot of soup for her boarders almost every day, especially during the Depression. If she did not have enough food to feed her boarders as well as her seven children, her mother, Malanka, would just 'add more water to the soup'.[42] Like perogies and cabbage rolls, soup was a cost-efficient answer for those struggling to feed many hungry mouths on a small budget.

. . . Interestingly, the children said that taste was never compromised; nearly every one of my interviewees made sure to report that their mothers had been exceptional cooks. Preparing ethnic food was an economically efficient way for women to provide their boarders with the calories that they needed to work underground for 12-hour shifts. Ethnic food may have helped to preserve Ukrainian traditions but it was above all a way for women to ensure that their boarding businesses were successful in tough times.

Boarding was also a labour-intensive business and thus many mothers asked for assistance. While some hired single or married women looking to make some extra money, most relied on their children, whose labour was free and often readily available. In addition to managing their boarding businesses and overseeing their family's finances, mothers supervised their children, assigning them tasks to be done in and around the home.[43] Although mothers and their children conversed in Ukrainian, the tasks assigned to them were not ethnic but gendered: girls undertook domestic tasks within the household while boys performed masculine chores and errands outside of the home.

After Bernice Crowe's (née Haluschak) father passed away in the late 1930s, her mother, Stella, a member of the ULFTA, decided to take in boarders to support her family. Although six men lived with them at a time, Stella cooked for about 25 to 30 men a day, serving as a type of restaurant cook for those who were rooming in the area. In speaking about the ways that she helped her mother, Bernice explained: 'Every Saturday I would help mother with the cleaning, and I would sweep and then scrub those darn wood floors. It was hard. [During the week] I was going to school and I would have to come home and do the afternoon dishes and set the table.'[44] Helen Cotnam (née Cybulka), who attended a French Catholic school and had no Ukrainian organizational affiliations, also helped her mother with her rooming business. They did not cook meals for the men but every week Helen had to help her mother clean the rooms that they had rented. Although they were lucky enough to have indoor plumbing, she emphasized that this was a mixed blessing because she had to clean the bathrooms the men had used. As she vividly recalled, it only took her a few dirty toilets to issue an ultimatum, insisting that her mother buy her a toilet brush before she would clean another toilet.[45] . . .

Running a boarding business was always hard work. Those girls who helped their mothers often undertook daily domestic chores, mainly cleaning. Surprisingly, few of them learned to cook from their mothers. Cleaning was a task that could be assigned to a child. If not done properly, it would not send the business into disarray. But as the women interviewed explained, cooking was a greater responsibility—while men may not have minded coming home to a house with dirty floors and unmade beds, they would have been upset to find that a meal was not waiting

for them at the end of a 12-hour shift—and so it was left up to the older women in the household. . . . In addition to these domestic duties, girls were also responsible for caring for their younger siblings. When the oldest daughter in the household married—they often did so at a young age to alleviate the financial strain placed on the family—the next oldest female sibling would take over her domestic and child-rearing responsibilities. This familial female cycle was another essential ingredient for a successful boarding business.

Boys' chores often took them outside of the home. Whenever Paul Behun's mother needed wood for the stove, he and his brother Bill would go into the bush, cut logs, and then haul them home, splitting them before stacking them close to the house.[46] If boys were not splitting firewood, they were collecting coal and shovelling it through the chute which carried it into the basement. Many mothers also kept a number of farm animals in the backyard, including cows, pigs, and chickens. Most often it was the boys in the home who were responsible for milking the cows and cleaning the chicken coops and then delivering milk or eggs to customers in the neighbourhood. Blueberry picking was another way for a Ukrainian family living in northern Ontario to supplement its income and it was usually the boys in the household who were responsible for picking them. It was laborious and hot work, usually done during late July and early August.[47] Although he now enjoys picking blueberries, Stanley Hayduk, a Roman Catholic who attended St John the Evangelist Church, remembered when he hated doing this task, recalling that he would only be allowed to play ball after he had filled a basket.[48] Like Stanley, Bill Semenuk spent many mornings during the 1930s picking blueberries to earn extra money. He looked forward to it though, as a morning of picking often went hand in hand with an afternoon of swimming at Ramsey Lake.[49] Boys rarely helped their mothers when it came to domestic chores although many, including Frank Makarinsky, have fond memories of watching their mothers cook, waiting for such things like fresh bread to come out of the oven.[50] In highlighting memories like those recalled by Frank, I am not trying to deny that boys worked less than their sisters. Certainly chopping wood, shovelling coal into the house, and picking blueberries were difficult tasks. However, it is important to note that these chores were done less frequently than the daily domestic tasks assigned to girls.

As this description of the gendered division of child labour suggests, Ukrainians, like other immigrant and Canadian parents, had gendered expectations of their children, and those expectations reflected a response to economic realities as well as cultural and ideological factors. Daughters were trained to be future wives while boys emulated their fathers and learned what it took to be a successful breadwinner. By sending their boys to deliver milk or pick blueberries, parents gave them not only independence but also financial responsibility, teaching them the value of a dollar at an early age. Ukrainian immigrants who arrived in early twentieth-century Canada brought a distinct peasant culture with them. This baggage, as Frances Swyripa shows, included a set of clearly defined gender roles and stereotypes: 'They [women] were essential to the functioning of the family as the basic unit of production and consumption, yet they were regarded as inferior beings subject to the authority of their menfolk.'[51] But this view was not limited to Ukrainians or even immigrants more generally. In Denyse Baillargeon's study about the Depression experiences of French-Canadian women who lived in Montreal, one of her informant's comments was similar to the one made by Nellie Kozak (née Tataryn): 'Little boys were like little kings. Very few homes made the boys work. They couldn't be touched. If there was something to be done, the girls did it.'[52] Within the wider Anglo-Celtic society, an enduring Victorian ideology of separate spheres (which in practice were never separate) did not necessarily justify male privilege (the point was that boys and girls were to be trained for separate

but complementary worlds) but it could and did lead to a double standard. Boys were encouraged to undertake roles that would train them to be breadwinners while girls were trained for the domestic roles that they would eventually assume. Economic factors led many working-class families to make strategic decisions about children's work. If a boy could make more money than a girl in the public sphere then he was sent to work, not his sister.[53] These gendered roles, then, reflected the interplay of a number of economic and cultural factors, including the dynamics of the mining town and the differing job opportunities available to men and women. But transplanted old world ideas about what it meant to be a 'Ukrainian man' and a 'Ukrainian woman' reinforced such gender roles.

Accounting for the situation and living it are two different things. It must be stressed that in reflecting upon their childhoods, my interviewees, especially females, were well aware of the gender dynamics that ordered their households.[54] In the women's opinions, boys were valued more than girls and were treated accordingly. Indeed, decades later there is still a great degree of bitterness in the voices of women who recall the broken dreams and the many limitations placed on them. Some remain upset that their parents did not encourage them to stay in school; they are haunted by the memory of the rhetorical question that their father had put to them: 'Why go to school [when] you are going to scrub floors and do housework anyway?'[55] Most of them, however, shrugged off their feelings and subtly warned me not to stress these gender inequalities because 'this was normal' for that time. As Michael Frisch warns, we must be sensitive to such differences when doing oral history or we risk creating a 'discursive disconnect', essentially causing us to lose touch with the people we interview and the narratives we hope to reconstruct.[56] While we should listen attentively and read our interview transcripts carefully for trends and silences, we must not pass judgment on the opinions of past generations. Rather it is vital to note that these gendered notions structured the ways in which boarding houses operated and therefore they are central to the collective experience of Sudbury's Ukrainians. Moreover, these gendered notions of work are vital to understanding the child-rearing practices of most parents, not just Ukrainian parents, who struggled to raise a family during the first half of the twentieth century.

When it came to reminiscing about their pasts, Ukrainian men and women used deeply personal biographical memories to understand their boyhood and girlhood experiences. In particular, boarders and boarding-house culture left indelible marks on the memories of Sudbury's Ukrainians. Regardless of their Catholic, Orthodox, nationalist, or progressive affiliations, my informants recounted similar working-class experiences, uniting an otherwise ideologically, politically, and religiously divided community in a collective struggle to survive.[57] There is no doubt that Sudbury's Ukrainians had very different experiences when they stepped onto the streets of their neighbourhoods or into their halls or churches; however, an examination of their domestic spaces reveals that boarding-house culture was a gendered, working-class experience shared by all those who lived it. Catholic girls who were chased down their streets by May Day protesters and progressive girls who were called communists in their schoolyards at recess both washed floors when they went home at night. Progressive boys who learned to speak Ukrainian and play the mandolin at the ULFTA hall and Catholic boys who spent their Sunday mornings as altar boys both ran errands for their mothers and spent their leisure time telling jokes to the boarders who lived in their houses. Mothers who sang in the church choir or slaved over the ULFTA stoves all prepared perogies and cabbage rolls to satisfy their boarders. In noting such similarities, I am not denying that difference is important; indeed, it is quite central to the story of Sudbury's Ukrainians. It is however meant to bring attention to an underdeveloped but ever-present theme in the stories of men and women who grew up working class and Ukrainian in one northern Ontario town.

Notes

This article is based in part on a chapter of my doctoral dissertation. I would like to thank Franca Iacovetta, John Walsh, Steven High, Marilyn Barber, Rhonda Hinther, Myron Momryk, Kristina Guiget, Andrew Burtch, and Bryan Palmer for their comments on this article. An earlier draft of this article was presented at the Oral History in Canada Conference and therefore I would also like to thank all of the people who offered astute comments throughout the proceedings of that conference. These insights, along with those of *Labour/Le Travail*'s anonymous reviewers, have enhanced this article. Above all however, I am indebted to those who shared their stories with me.

1. This article is based upon 82 oral history interviews conducted with Ukrainians who were . . . born or raised [in Sudbury] or came to the Sudbury region prior to 1945; 50 of these interviewees were women and 32 were men. These interviews took place between October 2004 and June 2005. Those interviewees who wished to remain anonymous were given the opportunity to choose an alias. When quoted, an interviewee's alias will be followed by an asterisk. Moreover, interviewees' maiden names have been included in the body of this article as well as in the footnotes. Many female interviewees married men who descended from other ethnicities and thus they now have non-Ukrainian surnames. This inclusion is meant to denote their Ukrainian heritage. Bill Semenuk, interview by author, Sudbury, 11 Nov. 2004.

2. . . . Michael Frisch, *A Shared Authority: Essays on the Craft and Meaning of Oral and Public History* (Albany, 1990), 12–13.

3. See, for instance, Paul Thompson, *The Voice of the Past: Oral History* (Oxford, 1988), 271–5; Alessandro Portelli, 'The Peculiarities of Oral History', *History Workshop* 12 (Autumn 1981): 103–04; Virginia Yans-McLaughlin, 'Metaphors of Self in History: Subjectivity, Oral Narrative, and Immigration Studies', in Virginia Yans-Mclaughlin, ed., *Immigration Reconsidered: History, Sociology, and Politics* (Oxford, 1990), 261–2; Joan Sangster, 'Telling Our Stories: Feminist Debates and the Use of Oral History', *Women's History Review* 3 (Mar. 1994): 10–13 . . .

4. Franca Iacovetta, 'Post-Modern Ethnography, Historical Materialism, and Decentring the (Male) Authorial Voice: A Feminist Conversation', *Histoire sociale/Social History* 32 (Nov. 1999): 286.

5. For a Canadian discussion about the silences which result when informants are asked to recall events that have been deeply traumatic, see, for instance, Marlene Epp, *Women Without Men: Mennonite Refugees*

of the Second World War (Toronto, 1999), 48–63; . . . Paula Draper, 'Surviving Their Survival: Women, Memory, and the Holocaust', in Marlene Epp, Franca Iacovetta, and Frances Swyripa, eds, *Sisters or Strangers? Immigrant, Ethnic, and Racialized Women in Canadian History* (Toronto, 2004), 399–414; . . . [and] Pamela Sugiman, '"These Feelings That Fill My Heart": Japanese Canadian Women's Memories of Internment', *Oral History* 34 (Autumn 2006): 78–80.

6. For a discussion about the ways in which Ukrainian immigrants structured their daily lives see Frances Swyripa, *Wedded to the Cause: Ukrainian-Canadian Women and Ethnic Identity, 1891–1991* (Toronto, 1993), 20–62. It must be noted that Denyse Baillargeon makes a similar point about working-class housewives in Montreal, noting that they were already used to unemployment, low wages, and frugal living before the Depression crippled the economy. Baillargeon, *Making Do: Women, Family, and Home in Montreal During the Great Depression*, Yvonne Klein, trans., (Waterloo, 1999), 107. . . .

7. Alessandro Portelli, *The Death of Luigi Trastulli and Other Stories: Form and Meaning in Oral History* (Albany, 1991), 50.

8. . . . For a more sophisticated discussion about these contrasting identities, see, for instance, Frances Swyripa, *Wedded to the Cause*; Rhonda Hinther, '"Sincerest Revolutionary Greetings": Progressive Ukrainians in the Twentieth Century', PhD Dissertation, McMaster University, 2005; and Orest Martynowych, *Ukrainians in Canada: The Formative Period 1891–1924* (Edmonton, 1991).

9. Paul Thompson and Sherna Berger Gluck discuss the ways in which insider/outsider relationships can impact the interview space. Unlike Thompson, Gluck also highlights the important roles that gender, class, and ethnicity play during an interview. See Thompson, *The Voice of the Past*, 140–1; and Gluck, 'What's So Special About Women? Women's Oral History', in Susan Armitage, Patricia Hart, and Karen Weathermon, *Women's Oral History: The Frontiers Reader* (Lincoln, 2002), 3–26.

10. See Robert Atkinson, *The Life Story Interview* (Thousand Oaks, 1988). It is significant to note that all of my interviewees were of working-class status. . . .

11. Frisch, *A Shared Authority*, 8.

12. Neil Sutherland, 'When You Listen to the Winds of Childhood, How Much Can You Believe?', in Nancy Janovicek and Joy Parr, eds, *Histories of Canadian Children and Youth* (Oxford, 2003), 23. . . .

13. For a discussion about the subjective nature of oral history and the importance of interpreting the silences which result in oral history narratives, see, for instance, Luisa Passerini, *Fascism in Popular Memory: The Cultural Experience of the Turin Working Class*, Robert Lumley and Jude Bloomfield, trans, (Cambridge, 1987), 67–70; and Joan Sangster, 'Telling Our Stories: Feminist Debates and the Use of Oral History', 7–10.

14. See, for instance, 'Coniston – Letter From Maksym', *Ukrainski robitnychi visti*, 20 Feb. 1930; 'Sudbury', *Ukrainski robitnychi visti*, 8 July 1930, articles translated by Larissa Stavroff.

15. This was a generalized statement made by the majority of my interviewees. Ukrainian men and women regarded their mothers as dominant figures because in addition to running their households, they handled most of the disciplining that occurred in these spaces. Nick Evanshen, for instance, recalled that his mother, Mary, was very strict: 'If I did something that wasn't right she would make me go outside, get a handful of rocks, and then I would have to kneel in the corner on the rocks with a broom over my head . . . She was too busy to chase me around or spank me [and] that punishment stuck.' See Nick Evanshen, interview by author, Sudbury, 14 May 2005.

16. C.M. Wallace, 'The 1930s', in C.M. Wallace and Ashley Thomson, eds, *Sudbury: Rail Town to Regional Capital* (Toronto, 1993), 143. . . .

17. Wallace, 'The 1930s', 139.

18. Although working-class Ukrainians who lived in Sudbury used boarding as a coping strategy, it must be noted that working-class families living in other parts of the country did not have the means to follow suit. In particular, Denyse Baillargeon notes that because of small and often crowded urban living spaces, boarding was not an option for working-class housewives living in Montreal during the thirties. See Baillargeon, *Making Do*, 97.

19. It is unclear how much men paid for boarding arrangements. Children were not involved in the financial end of these businesses and thus interviewees could not comment on these fees.

20. Nick Evanshen, interview.

21. Olga Zembrzycki (née Zyma), interview.

22. Pauline Kruk (née Mykoluk), interview by author, 20 Jan. 2005.

23. Anonymous interview, interview by author, Sudbury, 18 May 2005.

24. Bernice Crowe (née Haluschak), interview by author, Sudbury, 17 May 2005.

25. John Stefura, interview by author, Sudbury, 24 Jan. 2005.

26. Paul Behun, interview by author, Coniston, 12 May 2005. For a discussion about mother's allowances and the moral regulation of women, see Margaret Jane Hillyard Little, *'No Car, No Radio, No Liquor Permit': The Moral Regulation of Single Mothers in Ontario, 1920–1997* (Oxford, 1998) . . .

27. Anne Matschke (née Kuchmey), interview by author, Sudbury, 7 May 2005. . . .

28. Bill Semenuk, interview. Employing the work of pre-industrial British historian Naomi Tadmor, it is important to broach the term 'like family' critically, noting that the boundaries of Ukrainian families were quite fluid at times and thus emanated from relationships of co-residence and authority. See Tadmor, 'The Concept of the Household-Family in Eighteenth-Century England', *Past and Present* 151 (May 1996), 113 and 120–5.

29. Anonymous interviewee, interview by author, Sudbury, 16 Nov. 2004.

30. Sutherland, 'When You Listen to the Winds of Childhood, How Much Can You Believe?', 20.

31. Mary Brydges (née Ladyk), interview by author, Sudbury, 28 Oct. 2004.

32. Angela Behun (née Bilowus), interview by author, Coniston, 12 May 2005.

33. Nellie Kozak (née Tataryn), interview by author, Sudbury, 6 June 2005.

34. See Lynne Marks, *Revivals and Roller Rinks: Religion, Leisure, and Identity in Late-Nineteenth-Century Small-town Ontario* (Toronto, 1996).

35. Peter Chitruk, interview.

36. Nick Evanshen, interview.

37. For an examination about the ways that social reformers depicted the moral boundaries of urban space and, in particular, the boarding house, see Jim Opp, 'Re-imaging the Moral Order of Urban Space: Religion and Photography in Winnipeg, 1900–1914', *Journal of the Canadian Historical Association* 13 (2002), 86. . . .

38. See, for instance, Archives of Ontario (AO), Record Group (RG) 22–392, Box 151, File: Swerda, John, Sudbury, 1920, Carnal Knowledge of Girl Under 14.

39. Olga Zembrzycki (née Zyma), interview.

40. Bradbury, *Working Families*, 175–8.

41. Food is central to understanding the narratives of immigrants, especially immigrant women. See, for example, Franca Iacovetta, *Gatekeepers: Reshaping Immigrant Lives in Cold War Canada* (Toronto: Between the Lines, 2006), 137–69; Franca Iacovetta and Valerie Korinek, 'Jell-O Salads, One-Stop Shopping, and Maria the Homemaker: The Gender Politics of Food', and Marlene Epp, 'The Semiotics of Zwieback: Feast and Famine in the Narratives of Mennonite Refugee Women', in Epp, Iacovetta, Swyripa, eds, *Sisters or Strangers?*, 190–230, 314–40 . . .

42. Anne Matschke (née Kuchmey), interview.

43. For a discussion about the ways in which women were financially responsible for budgeting the family income, see, for instance, Bettina Bradbury, *Working Families*.

44. Bernice Crowe (née Haluschak), interview.

45. Helen Cotnam (née Cybulka), interview by author, Sudbury, 2 May 2005.

46. Paul Behun, interview.

47. Generally, interviewees stated that blueberry picking lasted about three weeks a year and supplemented the family income nicely. Although many interviewees recalled that this extra income helped to pay for groceries others, like Ernie Lekun's mother, Mary, saved the money they earned. Mary, who made about 50 cents a basket, spent a number of years saving and, in the end, purchased her first refrigerator with the money around 1947. Ernie Lekun, interview. Also see '88, 000 Quarts of Blueberries are Harvested', *Sudbury Star*, 20 July 1932; and '4,500 Baskets Sent to Toronto Each Day From District Points', *Sudbury Star*, 12 July 1933.

48. Stanley Hayduk, interview by author, Garson, 19 May 2005.

49. Bill Semenuk, interview.

50. Frank Makarinsky, interview by author, Sudbury, 4 May 2005.

51. Swyripa, *Wedded to the Cause*, 26. Rhonda Hinther also draws on Swyripa's argument and provides a convincing discussion pertaining to the ways in which this gendered cultural baggage was a part of the Ukrainian left. See Hinther, '"Sincerest Revolutionary Greetings": Progressive Ukrainians in the Twentieth Century', 128–9. . . .

52. Baillargeon, *Making Do*, 42.

53. See Bradbury, *Working Families*; and Bradbury, 'Gender at Work at Home', 177–98.

54. Although the Ukrainian men that I interviewed openly admitted to being treated in a more superior manner than their sisters, they did so in more hesitant and guarded ways than women, making sure to indicate that they had contributed to the family economy nevertheless. See, for instance, Joseph Maizuk, interview by author, Sudbury, 25 Jan. 2005.

55. Olga Zembrzycki (née Zyma), interview. Nellie Kozak's (née Tataryn) mother echoed this sentiment, stating '. . . you don't need to go [to school] to wash dishes and diapers.' See Nellie Kozak (née Tataryn), interview.

56. Michael Frisch, 'Working-Class Public History in the Context of Deindustrialization: Dilemmas of Authority and the Possibilities of Dialogue', *Labour/Le Travail* 51 (Spring 2003), 153–64.

57. Despite the egalitarian views that progressive Ukrainians maintained in the public sphere, especially in their ULFTA hall, they did not transfer these beliefs to their homes. 'Equality,' as Swyripa notes, 'often remained an elusive and contentious ideal.' See Swyripa, *Wedded to the Cause*, 151.

6

Jell-O Salads, One-stop Shopping, and Maria the Homemaker: The Gender Politics of Food

—— **Franca Iacovetta and Valerie J. Korinek** ——

Food is about more than recipes, cooking, nutrition, and eating. The practices surrounding its purchase, preparation, and consumption have long been a matter of conflict and contest. Food campaigns have been the site of clashes and accommodations between health professionals and beleaguered mothers told to forsake folk routines to 'scientific' regimes; between food fashion-makers and discerning or ostentatious culinary consumers; and between gatekeepers of receiving societies and immigrants bearing allegedly exotic or offensive cuisine and smells. Forced to consider our own food habits, many might see them as a matter of personal choice, yet such claims overlook the ways in which food tastes and customs are informed, prescribed, or mediated by government, education, social services, multinational food corporations, and mass media. In short, food and its attendant practices are also about power. Food traditions evolve in social and cultural contexts that are shaped by economic conditions and class politics, racial–ethnic relations, and other factors.

Food can also act as a signifier of difference. Historically, 'ethnic' foods have been relegated to the margins of receiving societies, dismissed as unhealthy or inappropriate, or pilloried by food experts in search of new ideas to pick up the palates of bored eaters. Bastardized versions of 'foreign' recipes, with most of the chili peppers or other pungent spices removed, are one aspect of the homogenizing process that comes from adapting ethnic cuisine to mainstream culture. Yet, immigrants have also transformed (albeit unevenly) the cuisine of mainstream cultures even as their own food habits were modified. Though hardly a new phenomenon, the current allure of 'multicultural' dining has brought some immigrant and minority food cultures into the forefront, where, ironically, they have become middle- and upper-middle-class demarcators of status and taste.[1]

Here, we grapple with the complex politics of food through the prism of early post-1945 Canada, a period marked by a mix of social optimism and Cold War hysteria; economic expansion and persistent poverty; heightened domesticity and social and sexual non-conformity.[2] These tensions coincided with another major trend, mass immigration; by 1965, 2.5 million newcomers, many of them women and children, and members of young families, had entered Canada.[3] The Canadian context thus permits us to explore how the dominant gender ideologies of capitalist democracies in the Cold War—including a middle-class model of homemaking and North American-defined standards of food customs and family life—influenced reception work and social service activities among immigrant and refugee women. Did efforts to reshape the culinary and homemaking skills of female newcomers overlap or diverge from the wider campaigns aimed at transforming all Canadian women into efficient shoppers, expert consumers, nutrition-wise

Franca Iacovetta and Valerie J. Korinek, 'Jell-O Salads, One-stop Shopping, and Maria the Homemaker: The Gender Politics of Food', from *Sisters or Strangers?: Immigrant, Ethnic and Racialized Women in Canadian History*, Marlene Epp, Franca Iacovetta, Frances Swyripa, eds (Toronto: University of Toronto Press, 2003), pp. 190–230. © University of Toronto Press Incorporated 2004. Reprinted with permission of the publisher.

cooks, and nurturing wives and mothers? Did Canadian and New Canadian women respond in similar ways to popular post-war campaigns designed to teach women the benefits of modern homemaking, meal planning, and nutritional guides? . . . In tackling such themes and questions, we adopt a comparative approach that probes the varied situations and responses of Canadian- and foreign-born women and of middle- and working-class women from both dominant and immigrant cultures in English Canada. So doing, we hope also to help bridge the continuing gap between what is generally seen as Canadian women's history and the history of immigrant and refugee and racialized women in Canada.[4]

Canadian 'Affluence' in a World of Hunger

. . .

Canadian propagandists promised immigrant and refugee women a better life. Their promotional materials, including films made by the National Film Board [NFB] in conjunction with the federal Citizenship Branch, featured enticing images of the modern conveniences and range of choices that helped define Canadian ways. The film *Canadian Notebook* presented the modern store and mail-order catalogue as products of Canadian post-war affluence now within the reach of the New Canadian homemaker. A Maritime rural scene sings the praises of the mail-order catalogue, which brings 'the largest city shopping centres' to the homemaker's 'fingertips'. Greater praise was reserved for the urban department store (a 'meeting place' with a 'wide range of items and variety of styles') and the one-stop, self-serve 'groceteria'. As the following sequence featuring a white, slim, and attractive 'Mrs Sparks' indicates, depictions of the modern Canadian supermarket emphasized convenience and order, abundance of items, and quality and cleanliness of food. It also delivered messages about the sort of priorities that should preoccupy the Canadian homemaker:

Mrs Sparks finds cellophane-wrapped meats in different quantities and grades on the refrigerated shelves. And now for some things for the picnic tonight! Prices, grades, and weights are all clearly marked, and Mrs Sparks can finish her shopping very quickly. As all her food needs are here, Mrs Sparks usually buys her whole week's groceries at one time. If she wishes, she can get a few other articles here too: magazines, cigarettes, and candies. When finished, Mrs Sparks leaves through the cash register aisle, where the cashier totals her bill and gives her an itemized receipt.

Canadians, the narrator concludes, 'find the self-service store well-suited to the faster pace of city life, where a busy housewife has to buy the week's groceries, go to the bank and the hairdresser's and still get home in time to prepare supper'.[5] Another NFB film enthused over that 'newest' trend in post-war merchandising, 'the suburban Shopping Centre, with its "one-stop" buying, and ample parking space for several hundred cars'.[6]

While the Cold War alone cannot explain its renewed popularity as post-war ideology, the homemaker ideal, in that it symbolized the stability and superiority of Western democratic families, took on great political import. That it reflected a misplaced or cultivated nostalgia for a bourgeois ideal that never entirely reflected most people's lives, and a conservative reaction to women's wartime gains, has been well documented.[7] It was also part and parcel of contemporary debates over women's roles engendered by the growing presence of working mothers, daycare lobbies, increasing divorce rates, and other signs of women's changing status in post-1945 society.[8] That many war-weary immigrants and refugees quickly married or remarried and started families does not negate the argument that dominant definitions of family and gender, well encapsulated by the phrase *breadwinner husband and homemaker wife*, privileged middle-class, heterosexual, Christian, and North American ideals.[9] The large presence of immigrant wives and mothers in paid labour did not stop reception workers from encouraging eventual domesticity. Indeed, the greater emphasis now placed on parents' obligations to produce mentally fit as well as socially productive children[10] made not only working mothers (whether Old or New Canadian), but also stay-at-home immigrant mothers allegedly cut off from mainstream (English) Canadian society, highly vulnerable to professional scrutiny. However, being 'othered'—or marginalized as social problems to be resolved—hardly meant being ignored. Immigrant women, who were part of a wider campaign to reform Canadian women and elevate post-war family life, were isolated for special attention. As women, female immigrants were considered essential to modifying the social habits of family members. As front-line English teachers in Toronto put it, the most effective way to encourage the newcomers' adaptation was to target 'the key person' in the immigrant family, 'the housewife and mother', and ensure that she was sufficiently exposed to Canadian ways.[11]

. . .

Canada's racist restrictions on the admission of 'not-white' peoples were post-war nation-building devices intended to keep Canada (mostly) white. It is thus not surprising that most early post-war newcomers before the 1970s were white Britons, Europeans (led by Italians and Germans), and white Americans, all of whom came in the hundreds of thousands.[12] Canadian officials restricted the number of Jewish refugees largely by bureaucratic means, but Jewish-Canadian lobbies helped secure safe passage for tens of thousands of them. Newcomers settled across Canada but Ontario attracted a majority of them. And while countless villages, towns, and cities felt the impact of their presence, Toronto became home to most of them.[13]

Canada's early post-war female newcomers were thus largely 'white ethnics' who shared a British or European heritage but they were not a homogenous group. . . . These women would be joined by a continuing mix of peoples, including West Indians and South Asians,[14] but in the early post-war decades, white newcomers, considered far better suited for Canadian citizenship, garnered the lion's share of attention. Indeed, all this handwringing on the part of reception workers reflected the centrality of these immigrants to the remaking of the post-war Canadian nation.[15]

. . .

Nutritional Experts, Food Fashion-makers, and Women

. . .

Food and health campaigns aimed at immigrant women and their families were varied and numerous. Early efforts began in European refugee camps, where Canadian relief workers taught 'Canadian ways' with Canadian magazines, newspapers, school texts, films, and, most popular of all, Eaton's and Simpsons catalogues.[16] The British war brides, whose integration was closely defined in homemaking terms, were the target of better organized culinary campaigns designed to ensure that 'when [they] set up their new homes in the Dominion, they will have a good idea of what's expected of them in the cooking line.'[17] As part of a state-funded and chaperoned scheme to resettle the wives of Canadian servicemen, cooking classes and health lectures for British war brides dominated orientation programs delivered in London; professional dieticians like Canadian Red Cross officer Ruth Adams stressed the importance that Canadians attached 'to well-balanced diets'. 'Time spent in planning meals,' she also advised 'would payoff in saving doctor and dentist bills.' Adams counselled the women 'not to forget their own specialties such as scones and Yorkshire pudding' but 'urged' them 'to get busy and practise on pancakes and Canadian-style salads'. To demonstrate what Canadians 'like to eat', she brought along 'a real apple pie, tea biscuits, a white cake with fudge icing, several types of salads, [and] the biscuit part of a strawberry shortcake'.[18]

This training continued in Canada. In Ontario, Red Cross staff in North Bay, St Catharines, and elsewhere gave courses in cooking (where women made muffins, tea biscuits, cream sauces, salads, and cakes, and learned to cook vegetables), canning techniques, nutrition, and participated in Department of Health home visits for meal planning and budgeting. One war bride evidently prompted local staff to begin a pastry-making class with her declaration that 'the ambition of every British bride was to make a good lemon pie.'[19] In these records, favourable assessments abound (though other sources, especially oral testimonies, tell more complicated stories).[20] 'The girls,' declared their teachers, gained 'practical experience in actual cooking', grew familiar with Canadian equipment (including wooden spoons),[21] and enjoyed the chance to socialize, over tea and cookies or cigarettes. Graduates received an appropriately Canadian gift—a set of plastic measuring spoons. Beyond specialized cooking courses, many reception programs for immigrant women included nutrition and food lessons as part of a larger orientation program. English classes in settlement houses, for instance, could become forums for discussing children's food needs and shopping trips.[22]

Chatelaine and Canadian Culinary Ways

For nutrition experts, the first priority was to teach all Canadians, especially mothers, sound nutritional advice and healthy food habits. (They never tired of praising the Canada Food Guide as a simple and flexible teaching tool for raising nutritional awareness.)[23] A good diet, they stressed, improved children's growth rate and physique, resistance to disease, and meant longer lives; a faulty diet established early in life might not show immediate results but could produce far greater damage than a vice such as adult drinking. In dispensing advice, food editors and health experts often prioritized middle-class food customs and efficiency regimes derived from capitalist time-management principles, and emphasized cleanliness. Descriptions of the family meal, especially dinner, invariably assumed (or pictured) a nuclear family, its well-groomed members assembled around an attractively set table in a dining room, happily engaged in conversation while eating mother's nicely presented and healthy meal. Their awareness of the myriad of 'families' inhabiting inner-city flats, boarding houses, and suburban bungalows, did not alter their pitch.

. . . An excellent source of Canada's post-war health and homemaking campaigns is the country's premier women's magazine, *Chatelaine*. Although usually dismissed as a bourgeois women's magazine, *Chatelaine* was an affordable, mass-market periodical that by the late 1960s enjoyed the largest circulation of any Canadian magazine in the country. Circulation figures, surveys, and letters to the editor show that its audience came from across Canada and included urban and rural as well as working- and middle-class women and some men and children. The primarily female readership was English-speaking and Anglo-Celtic but included some ethnic Canadian and immigrant women. . . .

The magazine's food features were largely the creations of the Chatelaine Institute kitchen staff or recipe entries in the annual Family Favourites Contests that had been adjudicated and tested by the Institute staff. Founded in 1930 and modelled after the US-based *Good Housekeeping* Test Kitchen, the Chatelaine Institute was staffed by professional home economists whose white robes and laboratory-style kitchen lent a scientific air to the departmental features. Efficient and economical meal preparation, with a focus on nutrition, was their central message. As female professionals operating in the overlapping worlds of health and fashion, they took their job seriously: taste testings on in-house recipes, inspection visits to factories, and product test runs to determine which items would receive the *Chatelaine* Seal of Approval (again mimicking the *Good Housekeeping* Seal of Approval). . . . The particular gender dynamics that gave Chatelaine Institute nutritionists a degree of autonomy not enjoyed by their counterparts in the United States are also noteworthy. In contrast to the United States, where male editors vetted materials submitted by female writers, *Chatelaine*'s editorial and advertising departments were separate, sundering the usual cozy relationship between editorials and advertising. *Chatelaine*'s male publishers complained about women editors who refused to be dictated to. In the budget features, women food editors who, theoretically, should have been promoting the advertiser's products (many of them processed goods) refused, on the grounds that they were too expensive.[24]

While undergoing some transformations in the two decades under review, *Chatelaine*'s food features remained remarkably consistent. Even amid the changing food fads that appeared, the Canadian way was most commonly represented by images and texts extolling the virtues of affordable abundance. As in the NFB films, recurring images of attractive . . . WASP women pushing over-flowing grocery carts or posed near well-stocked freezers and store shelves attested to the Canadian homemakers' good fortune. So did recipe and cooking contests. Proud contest winners photographed alongside their prize-winning Jell-O-mould salad, carrot medley, casserole, or dessert parfait promised women readers ease of preparation and family fun. The come-on ads of brand-name food corporations of prepared products, such as canned soups and vegetables, stressed how convenience foods offered maximum return for minimal preparation. By contrast, the advertisers of baking supplies preferred labour-intensive treats to enchant husbands and children. Invariably, their ads drew on women's supposed virtues for self-sacrifice, sending out the message that a mother's proof of her devotion to husband and family was literally in the pudding, or in homemade bread and pies. Indeed, despite the prominence of convenience food corporate advertisers, the majority of recipes in *Chatelaine*'s departmental pages (as

opposed to those in name-brand advertisements) involved cooking 'from scratch'. As to economical eating, the magazine increasingly featured frozen foods as a cheaper and healthy alternative to fresh items, though the higher price of frozen goods compared to the tinned variety, and the limited freezer space of the older refrigerators that most fridge-owning Canadian homes had, could put even frozen food beyond the grasp of many struggling families. Not so with canned foods, which were consistently promoted as the cheapest way of attaining the well-balanced meal. Particularly in winter, women were encouraged or cajoled to buy tinned foods instead of more expensive fruit and vegetable imports.

. . . Only infrequently did *Chatelaine*'s food articles acknowledge that many Canadian wives worked outside the home, and some of them offered less than solid advice. 'Seven Dinners on the Double' tantalized working wives with this appealing fantasy: 'You're home at six and dinner's on the table in thirty minutes. Here's how you do it in a small apartment kitchen: work to plan and let your husband help.' The accompanying photo essay depicts a cheerful heterosexual couple, both wearing aprons, preparing food in a tiny kitchen. Some examples from the 1960s highlighted working women who made ends meet by preparing meals the night before or shopping at a well-stocked deli counter. The affordable meals in *Chatelaine*'s sixties repertoire were also slightly more glamorous than their fifties counterparts, though casseroles remained popular. One of the quickest ways of interjecting novelty was to feature 'ethnic' ingredients and food—a process, that as Harvey Levenstein and others have described for the United States, usually meant modifying 'foreign' fare for more timid North American palates. *Chatelaine*'s examples of this homogenizing process include the following 1960 recipe for Easy-to-Make Pizza Pin Wheels: biscuit mix, tomato soup and ketchup, pressed meat, cheese wafers, cheddar cheese, and modest amounts of oregano, green pepper, and onion. Clearly, authenticity was not a hallmark of such recipes.[25]

. . .

Greater attention to ethnic foods—both inside the pages of women's magazines and beyond—. . . reflected an increasing interest on the part of North Americans in the sort of 'gourmet' cuisine associated with such successful food writers as Julia Child (who sparked interest in French cuisine with the publication of her cookbooks in the early 1960s) as well as a greater degree of culinary experimentation and the internationalization of foods more broadly speaking. Whether dubbed as hippies, radicals, bohemians, or brown-ricers, many middle-class youth were enticed by the alternative tastes of global foods. Their rebellion against the standard 'meat-mashed-potatoes-and-peas' family fare was part of a larger interest in cultural and for some political and sexual experimentation. It suggests the need to pay more attention to what Levenstein aptly referred to as people's growing appreciation of the 'sensuality' of food.[26]

Changes were also taking place in mother's kitchen. A summary of the recipes submitted for *Chatelaine*'s 1965 Family Favourites Contest suggests that many Canadian housewives were incorporating ethnic cuisine into the meal plans. 'Chinese food' was 'the most popular dish, followed by Italian'[27]—though such nods towards multicultural eating should not be exaggerated. Even by the end of the 1960s, the 'Canadian way' was best exemplified by the homemaker who had the major burden of food preparation, and the food standard usually meant updated classics like 'hamburgers with class' or 'ten ways with a pound of hamburg', rather than experimental cuisine.[28]

From the Point of Nutrition?

Other sources, including a popular postwar nutritional guide, *Food Customs of New Canadians*,[29] speak more directly to the concerns and practices of health and food experts serving immigrant communities. Produced by an organization of nutritionists and dieticians (Toronto

Nutrition Committee [TNC]), the guide appeared in 1959 and was revised and expanded in 1967. A part of a cookbook project launched by the International Institute of Metropolitan Toronto, the city's largest immigrant aid society, the guide's claims to be objective and social scientific, like its rejection of an overtly assimilationist approach, reflects the general approaches of postwar reception activists like those who staffed the Institute. The TNC's liberal perspective is clearly evident in their counselling of flexibility when assessing immigrant food customs—'From the viewpoint of nutrition, some food habits may be better than our own, and changes may not be necessary'—but the committee's presumption of expert authority is equally evident. Notwithstanding its constant reference to immigrant groups and New Canadians, the guide's main target is the homemaker whose schooling in Canadian ways was seen as crucial to affecting desired changes in the whole family.

The guide profiled the food customs of 14 of Toronto's significant ethnic groups,[30] with the British conspicuous by their absence. The data collected (from published texts, military surveys, international agencies, and interviews with immigrants) was organized into categories. For each group, there is a detailed table of food customs both in the Old World setting and in Toronto, with the relevant information broken down into subcategories: food groupings (milk, fruits and vegetables, bread and cereals, meat and fish), meal patterns, and cooking facilities, Vitamin D, fats, sweets, beverages, and condiments. Another category, Food for Special Ages, dealt mainly with prenatal education for mothers, childfeeding patterns, and public health facilities. Conclusions and recommendations were then grouped together under Teaching Suggestions. With two exceptions,[31] the guide used national groupings (Chinese, Portuguese), but was careful to document regional and rural/urban variations in Old World contexts, to highlight patterns in areas of out-migration, and to note changes (for better or worse) in food habits that pertained in

Toronto. In most cases, however, stark contrasts are drawn between the more 'primitive' and time-consuming cooking facilities of rural homes, where running water is scarce and women operate charcoal, wood stoves, or clay stoves, and the 'modern' urban homes equipped with gas, electricity, and running water. Although such differences undoubtedly reflected class as much as city residence, only the West Indian entry draws explicit class distinctions.[32] The desire to be precise and comprehensive makes for some very terse summaries, as indicated by the following German-Austrian entry:

> German and Austrian food habits are combined since differences are more regional than national. North Germans like sweet soups and sugar on salads, serve potatoes and vegetables regularly, and drink beer with meals. South-West Germans and Bavarian-Austrians do not eat sweet soups and salads; South-West Germans replace potatoes with noodles and use less vegetable while Bavarian-Austrians use dumplings and fewer vegetables except for sauerkraut. Although South-West Germans replace beer with wine at meals, the Bavarian-Austrians do not.

The guide's claim to neutral assessments of immigrant food customs and liberalism was inexorably mingled with the presumption of scientific, even cultural, authority to define standards for newcomers. Indeed, the guide was designed precisely to inform health and social service personnel 'helping' newcomers 'adapt the familiar food patterns of their homelands to the foods and equipment available in Canada'. The aim was to gradually change the food and eating habits of immigrants so as to bring them in line with Canadian ways and standards. . . .

The wisdom encoded in *Food Customs* was meant to be objective, yet the advice involved an act of cultural imperialism: advising conformity to North American health regimes meant deliberately bringing about changes in the daily habits,

and social and cultural values, of those being counselled. It might be unfair to equate this guide with the blatantly assimilationist intentions of nineteenth- and early twentieth-century domestic science professionals or residential school staff who taught African-American, Native, and immigrant children to reject their mother's cooking and customary foods in favour of mainstream choices.[33] Still, definitions of health and nutrition can be culturally constructed. Despite its scientific language, the guide reflected a shared normative discourse regarding dominant bourgeois definitions of Canadian 'ways' and 'standards' that were as much about class and capitalist notions of efficiency and budgeting as about nutrition and food. For instance, it held the North American pattern of three meals per day as sacrosanct. 'Canadians,' it said, 'follow a pattern of three meals a day which fits into school and working hours.' That newcomers had to adapt to this industrial pattern was not in dispute.

. . .

The nutrition committee's preoccupation with the shopping habits of immigrant and refugee women also reflected the experts' class and cultural bias. In short, they pathologized this behaviour, seeing it as the consequence of poverty (lack of storage, refrigeration) or rural underdevelopment, and all but ignored its cultural and social significance. In the bakeries, butchers, fish shops, and other specialty stores of Old World towns and villages, women developed important lines of trust and credit with shopkeepers, and maintained critical gossip networks of information and support. For Canadian nutrition experts, however, efficiency concerns predominated: access to clean, well-stocked stores meant shopping less frequently and more efficiently. Such practices were equated with modernity, as suggested by a German-Austrian entry: 'Shopping is done less frequently than before, mostly at neighbourhood stores, but supermarkets are increasing.' Such views also ignored the fact that many thousands of working-class immigrants would live for years in inner-city flats and basement apartments without modern stoves or fridges, and thus rely on daily shopping of perishables. Equally important, the modern supermarket being promoted—large chain stores such as Dominion, Loblaws, and Power—were hardly places where immigrant women well versed in marketplace 'haggling' could practise their craft. Ethnic shops and open markets made greater economic sense than urban or suburban supermarkets. Frequency of contact helped women to forge bonds of trust with local shopkeepers, who often extended credit to families in financial straits.

Harsher professional judgments accompanied discussion of nursing mothers and childfeeding regimes. These evaluations, usually grouped under Food for Special Ages, noted childfeeding practices (breastfeeding or artificial) in each country, availability of specialty foods for children, level of public instruction for mothers, and the state of prenatal health services.[34] Again, immigrant mothers were evaluated in terms of their conformity to 'modern' health regimes. As in the past, post-war nutrition experts showed little respect for the folk traditions and mothering remedies of Europe, Asia, and elsewhere. Rural Chinese women's supposed inadequacies on the childfeeding front, for instance, was attributed to their devotion to folk practices. The entry in *Food Customs* reads:

No special foods prepared. Mothers increase only their starch intake during pregnancy and, although prenatal health services are improving, the authorities recognize that there is still a need for education of mothers in the kinds of foods required for an adequate pregnancy diet. Following birth of the baby, mother does not eat fruits or vegetables or drink cold water for a month. She eats as much meat, poultry, and eggs as the family can afford. Eggs coloured red are sent to the mother to celebrate the birth.

Women of other countries were depicted as more closely resembling Canadian or North American standards. Of women in Czechoslovakia, the guide observed: 'In rural areas, breast feeding is prevalent although increasing attention is paid to modern methods' (presumably, use of baby formula). . . . Highest praise of all went to Dutch women whose childfeeding patterns—which followed a progression from formula feeding to gradual introduction of solid foods—were decidedly modern. In Holland, 'formula feeding is generally accepted' and 'a variety of evaporated milk formulae and canned infant foods', as well as vitamin supplements, were widely used. . . .

Amid the details emerge some broad patterns. First, the nutrition experts were careful not to give any group an entirely negative evaluation. They commended most groups for varied diets that combined in-season fruits and vegetables, meat, and fish. Here, Chinese food customs scored well because of the 'economical use of meat, varieties of fish, crisp-tender method of cooking vegetables and consistent use of fruit'. They also acknowledged the fine-honed skills of women from modest rural backgrounds accustomed to stretching economical cuts of meat with starches and vegetables or producing one-dish meals using meat alternatives such as fish. The assessment of the Polish homemaker in Toronto echoed that of most European women under review. She could make 'a small amount of inexpensive meat' go 'a long way in soups and stews', and she often substituted 'legumes, eggs and fish in all forms' for meat. She had adapted easily to new foods, such as citrus fruits, that had been prohibitively expensive back home, though she did need to learn to cook vegetables for a shorter time and to cook a 'more substantial breakfast'.

Nor did any group receive an entirely positive evaluation; there was always room for improvement, and the experts identified precisely where. Since immigrant children 'become very fond of candy and sweet carbonated beverages', social service personnel were told to discourage 'the increasing use of sweet fruits' among all newcomers. The TNC also insisted that most immigrant women had to be taught the value of canned or frozen fruits, vegetables, and fruit juices as substitutes for expensive, out-of-season fresh imports.

The guide established a food customs hierarchy of immigrant groups, and it closely resembled Canada's historic racial–ethnic preference ladder. The basis of ranking was the comparative ease with which newcomers made the transition to Canadian foods and customs. Without exception, the most positive evaluations were of Canada's more 'preferred' groups of Europeans: North and West European whites. The 'similarity of foods in the home countries and Canada', the guide observed of Germans and Austrians, for instance, 'makes adjustment relatively easy'.[35]
. . .

By contrast, women and families belonging to Canada's 'less preferred' immigrants—Chinese, southern Europeans, and West Indians—appear in the guide as less equipped to adopt modern culinary standards. As we have seen, Chinese hygienic standards needed serious upgrading. Serious adjustments were required of Italians, particularly southern Italians (who regularly use 'strong spices and hot peppers' and 'highly seasoned meats like salami'), before they would better conform to Canadian food ways. This, even though Italians, like other Europeans, earned good marks for a varied diet, use of fresh foods, and a three-meals-a-day pattern. Still, serious adjustment problems plagued Italian newcomers, a low income group, in part, the nutritionists claimed, because they preferred expensive, imported goods, such as olive oil, meats, and cheeses, when cheaper Canadian alternatives (such as corn oil) were available. Hence, the TNC counselled social service personnel to encourage Italian women to forgo familiar items, now dubbed expensive luxury foods, in favour of affordable Canadian products. . . .

Culinary Pluralism from the Bottom Up?

Historically, food customs have offered some racial minorities, such as First Nations, African-Americans, and urban immigrants, a resource, albeit limited, in resisting the forces of cultural hegemony. Although wary of intruding middle-class professionals, working-class immigrant mothers might more willingly heed the advice of nutrition experts because good health, especially in a child, reflects certain universal qualities.[36] The capacity for choice or resistance greatly differed among Canadian and New Canadian women and, as recently documented for Toronto's post-war inner-city neighbourhoods, low-income women from humble or impoverished rural regions bore the greatest brunt of Canadian professional discourses and front-line practices that singled out immigrant women for special attention or blame. In the late 1950s and 1960s, for example, Portuguese and Italian mothers were branded as too ignorant, isolated, backwards, stubborn, and/or suspicious to access 'modern' health care facilities or to trust the school nurses and visiting homemakers who dispensed advice.[37] Still, neither group should be treated as monolithic categories, and within each group, women displayed a differing willingness and/or capacity to embrace or resist professional interventions. New and Old Canadian women responded in selective and varied ways to external and internal pressures to recast themselves in ways promoted by bourgeois image-makers.
. . .

Refugee and immigrant women . . . responded selectively to post-war health and homemaking campaigns. Like surviving written sources, oral testimonies, including our sample of 28 taped interviews,[38] reveal patterns that defy easy categorization: immigrant mothers who steadfastly stuck to 'traditional' meals at home and those keen to experiment with Canadian recipes or convenience foods; refugee husbands who pressured wives to stick to familiar meals and those who encouraged wives to incorporate some Canadian foods; and endless permutations of hybrid diets in the households of working- and middle-class immigrants who increasingly combined familiar and Canadian foods and 'ethnic' foods from elsewhere.

Post-war immigrant and refugee narratives contain their own versions of the theme, homeland scarcity and Canadian abundance. Hunger and fears of starvation dominate the war-time stories of early post-war arrivals, including Holocaust survivors. Female survivors recall the smaller rations of food given to women in the camps, and of the courage of Jews and Gentiles who sneaked food into Nazi-created ghettos and camps. When English soldiers arrived to liberate Bergen-Belsen, recalled Amelia S-R., they found 'everyone running to the planted areas to dig beet roots and potatoes out with their hands'. English soldiers helped them to find food, and she and others suffering from typhus and other illnesses were slowly nursed back to health by Red Cross personnel in quarantined hospitals in Sweden. But even there, Amelia added, the fear that they might yet starve never subsided. A Dutch war bride describing the days before Holland's liberation spoke of 'starving under German occupation'. The anti-Soviet DPs had also endured prolonged hunger and inadequate sanitation facilities in the refugee camps, forcing many to take up jobs or begin families in Canada while still suffering from malnourishment and related diseases.[39]

No wonder, then, that many newcomers reacted with astonishment to the comparative abundance of food in Canada. Some, including Dutch newcomer Maria B., marvelled at the stock in Canadian 'self-serve' grocery stores. Many recalled their first taste of new foods, such as 'Canadian-style' bread or cereals, and the joy of eating fresh fruits in scarce supply back home. A German woman, Helga, who arrived with her husband in 1952, swore the apples and oranges 'tasted just like heaven'; they lived on McIntosh apples for months, she added, while her husband, a former electrician, looked for work. A Czech refugee who settled in Hamilton in 1949 recalled her excitement at tasting cornflakes and at once again eating eggs. Financially strapped, she also learned how to bargain shop at the market.[40]

Not everyone enthused over Canadian food, however. Some much preferred their dense dark bread to the light and airy Canadian fare and complained about unappetizing meat. As an East European refugee woman declared 'only the immigrants . . . brought good taste in food to Canada.' Whether Baltics from the post-war DP camps, Hungarian 56ers, or Iron Curtain escapees, many refugees expressed their disgust with what they considered Canadian wastefulness, especially in restaurants, where, they noted, people were served an appalling amount of food and an evening's leftovers could have sustained several refugees for weeks at a time.[41] As most volunteer immigrants arrived with little cash or capital, they too could endure a spartan diet—something that worried Canadian nutritionists. Yet, as the example provided by the Portuguese couple who lived for several years on bread and coffee, bean soup, and pigs feet while saving money to start a small family business indicates, the diets were not outrageously unhealthy.[42] Still, illness or injury could cut into a modest food budget, creating yet more pressures for women.

. . . The evidence does suggest that some East European refugees who eventually found work in former or alternative professional or white-collar jobs more quickly moved into suburbs and integrated Canadian foods and customs into family meals and holiday celebrations. . . . But other women put up greater and longer resistance, and shopped in their 'old' city neighbourhoods to get the necessary ingredients. Working-class immigrants such as Italians, Portuguese, and West Indians could largely reproduce their homeland diets precisely because they relied on low-budget food items such as rice and pasta and comparatively little meat though this kind of cultural continuity, at least early on, was more easily attained in large cities like Toronto, which already had a wide range of ethnic foods, or in smaller cities like Sudbury, which had established Ukrainian, Finnish, and other ethnic businesses.

Women's efforts to negotiate a complex culinary terrain emerges clearly from oral testimonies. Our sample also underscores the importance of individual choice and of differing family and household dynamics. For example, while many mothers experimented with tinned soups, tuna fish sandwiches laden with mayonnaise, hot dogs and hamburgers, and Jell-O in response to their children's persistent requests, others resisted, even for years. An East German refugee woman who liked to supplement her 'mostly German' diet with various foods also recalled the 'tensions' between her and her children over her husband's domineering approach to maintaining 'strict' German standards in food and child-rearing.[43] By contrast, Austrian-born Susan M., who married an Italian immigrant she met in Toronto, said she never cooked 'in any particular style' for her family. . . . For Nazneed Sadiq, a young and recently married upper-caste Pakistani woman who emigrated with her accountant husband in the early 1960s, learning to cook in her North Toronto apartment building (where everyone else was white) meant experimenting with both 'Indian' and North American foods. The resulting weekly meal pattern: Pakistani food two to three times a week, a lot of salads, and the occasional Canadian-style barbeque.[44] Such experimentation led to many multicultural family diets, of which holiday food customs are perhaps most emblematic: Italian households that combined antipasto and lasagna with turkey for Thanksgiving, Ukrainian mothers who added Canadian cakes and hams to the family favourite, perogies, and so on.[45]

The *Chatelaine* stories dealing with immigrants devoted considerable space to culinary customs or reactions to Canadian patterns of consumption and domestic images. Published in 1957, when the plight and arrival of the Hungarian 56ers had captured the imagination of many Canadians, Jeannine Locke's 'Can the Hungarians Fit In?' about Frank and Katey Meyer illuminates key themes under scrutiny.[46] Like other Iron Curtain 'escape' narratives, Locke's article drew a sympathetic and compelling portrait of the young refugee couple as freedom fighters who fled the Hungarian revolution, spent some harrowing time 'crouched in a ditch' near the Hungarian-Austrian border, and now looked forward to a

'good' life in Canada. The caption that accompanies the cover photograph of an attractive, smiling Katey declares: '[She] resembles that mythical creature, the average young Canadian housewife. In a straight-cut skirt, soft sweater and low-heeled shoes, her brown hair and eyes healthily bright, her skin rosy as a schoolgirl's, she is inconspicuously attractive.' Although she and her engineer husband occupied a small flat in Toronto, Locke added that Katey, 'could fit into any setting from St John's to Saanich'. The domestication of Katey is all the more telling given that she was a professionally educated woman who first worked in Canada as a hospital cleaner and then a bank teller.

. . . Under the provocative subtitle 'Katey Discovers Supermarkets and Limps to Mass in Red Leather Shoes'—Locke describes Katey's first exposure to a modern Canadian household and then grocery store. In Budapest, the couple had shared a three-room apartment with three other family members; they had had no electrical household appliances and endured a 'perpetual chill' due to the scarcity and high cost of fuel. By contrast, their Toronto patrons, a doctor and his large family, had given the couple commodious accommodations: a suite of two rooms, a new refrigerator and stove, and their own bathroom. While living there, Katey discovered the wonders of the Canadian supermarket: one day 'she came home staggering under a load of newly discovered delicacies—sardines, instant coffee, canned soups, ham and chicken legs,' and 'so much ice cream that they used it in great scoops even in their coffee'. In a statement that would have pleased Canadian boosters, Katey, wrote Locke, told her husband: 'There is everything you could want to buy in the supermarket . . . not like the little shops at home where there was little to buy and what we wanted we could never afford.' Next came department stores. When husband Frank told Katey to buy herself a present, Katey had decided on a pleated nylon slip but on impulse bought high-heeled red leather pumps that cost about $35 (nearly a week's salary for Frank), and then 'limped, painfully but persistently around their rooms in her tall, thin pumps until she was accomplished enough to manoeuvre them, for the first time in public, to Sunday morning mass'. 'Katey's new red shoes,' added Locke, 'were part of their celebration of three most happy events': mail from home; Frank's (and brother Louis's) acceptance, with scholarship, into the University of Toronto engineering school; and Katey's bank job.

Canadian nutritionists might have disapproved of Katey's culinary indiscretion (all that ice cream!) but enjoyed the depictions of a Canadian paradise of goods and the Meyers's eagerness to become Canadian consumers. Locke spelled out the stages of their acculturation: learning English, landing a job, one-stop shopping, plans to purchase a suburban home, and their first car. The couple's enthusiasm for all things Canadian was tempered by wistful memories of Hungarian food and gypsy music—which, much to their delight, they rediscovered in a Hungarian restaurant, the Csarda, in downtown Toronto. 'Transported home by the smells and sounds' of Csarda, the Meyers, writes Locke, 'eat goulash and cheese strudel' and 'believe they are back in their favourite restaurant' at the lakeside resort near Budapest where they spent vacations. Although the couple never enjoyed the traditional gypsy music back home (a sign of their class status), Katey is 'amused' to find that the same songs heard here please her very much. So do the Hungarian cafe's slightly tart desserts that remind her of mother's cooking. Katey has even absorbed North American women's obsession with weight: at home, she yearned for expensive cream-fllled eclairs but, here, where she can and, at first, did buy them, '[she] is suddenly calorie conscious.'

The role played by food in the Meyers's tale of escape and redemption is a complex one, at once signifying Canadian abundance, novelty, and satiety, while in the couple's obvious enjoyment of 'traditional' Hungarian cuisine a romanticization of their 'older' ways. As with most public articulations of post-war cultural pluralism, the tension between assimilation and acculturation is never completely resolved, yet its success at weaving a compelling Cold War narrative of a Canadian democratic paradise is suggested by the positive letters the article engendered.[47]

. . .

Conclusion

In adapting ethnic cuisine to mainstream culture, food fashion-makers drew, explicitly or implicitly, on liberal notions of celebrating diversity—a theme that post-war Canadian officialdom encouraged, within limits—but early post-war culinary pluralism also produced uneven and contradictory results: Canadians were encouraged to appreciate immigrant customs while newcomers themselves were often transformed into (or, rather, reduced to) colourful folk figures bearing exotic foods and quaint customs but never accorded an equal status with 'real' Canadians. The emergence in these years of 'multicultural' cookbooks with a 'unity in diversity' theme were financed with some federal government funds because officials considered them 'an excellent medium to further the idea of Canadian unity'.[48] Such texts reflect the contradictory features of post-war cultural pluralism: celebrating ethnic customs and encouraging 'multicultural' cuisines while at the same time perpetuating cute and patronizing stereotypes of immigrants as static folk figures. By stripping immigration of its more threatening aspects, they reduced ethnic diversity to entertainment and novelty.[49]

When post-war Canadian health and welfare experts, food fashion-makers, and mass-market magazines promoted a Canadian way of cooking and eating, they prioritized pro-capitalist, middle-class food practices, household regimes, and family values. Approved patterns included careful meal planning, strategic shopping in 'modern' stores, three nutritionally balanced meals per day—all washed down with countless glasses of milk. The bourgeois experts encouraged all Canadian women, and particularly low-income and immigrant mothers, 'to get the most for their food dollar' through planned grocery shopping trips using a seven-day menu plan, taking advantage of grocers' specials, and following the casseroles and roasted-meat diet favoured by Canadians. The Canadian way held centre stage while ethnic dishes were relegated to the margins as novelty items to entice North American palates (and often bastardized in the process) or as a source of economical meals.

We should be wary of imputing too much influence on the prescriptive literature, however. The different kinds of evidence mined for this paper indicate a range of responses to post-war food and homemaking campaigns. For those eager to embrace all facets of Canadianism, . . . eating Canadian was very important. In contrast, . . . many other adult newcomers expressed their desire to be Canadian but drew the line at Canadian food, while for others, incorporating Canadian food customs meant neither abandoning their previous food culture nor a passive acceptance of 'modern' childfeeding regimes that front-line health and welfare workers tried to impose on them. The differing capacities of both Canadian and New Canadian women to incorporate, ignore, or modify the suggestions of experts should not be overlooked. Indeed, it suggests that the relationship between food experts and newcomers is perhaps best understood as a series of negotiations and encounters that transformed both food cultures, though not equally. Anglo-Canadian experts had the power and position to define 'ethnic' food as un-Canadian, while the *Food Customs* guidebook and other projects for newcomers suggest that nutrition experts and food fashion-makers, like other experts involved in immigrant and refugee reception work, sought to modify, not obliterate the food (and other) cultures of emigrating groups, but liberal intentions did not eliminate cultural chauvinism. In turn, the vast number of post-war immigrants and refugees actually transformed Canadian cuisine even as they incorporated Canadian foods into their own diets. Through *Chatelaine*, some, perhaps many, post-war Anglo-Canadian housewives experimented with their first Italian, Chinese, Indian, and Caribbean dishes. If the recent allure of multicultural dining experiences and conspicuous dining has brought immigrant food cultures into the forefront of North American bourgeois standards of 'taste', the 1950s and 1960s were more tentative, contested contexts. Still, current food wars—including the recent 'wok wars' in Toronto sparked by an Anglo-Canadian couple who complained about their Chinese neighbours' food smells—remind us that class and cultural conflict continue. . . .

Notes

1. Our discussion draws on the emerging literatures on food and accompanying practices and issues, such as Stephen Mennell, Anne Murcott, and Anneke H. van Otterloo, *The Sociology of Food: Eating, Diet and Culture* (London: Sage, 1992). On social histories of food, see, for the United States, Harvey Levenstein's pioneering works, *Revolution at the Table: The Transformation of the American Diet* (New York: Oxford University Press, 1988) and *Paradox of Plenty: A Social History of Eating in Modern America* (New York: Oxford University Press, 1993) and more recently Donna Gabaccia, *We Are What We Eat: Ethnic Food and the Making of Americans* (Cambridge, MA: Harvard University Press, 1998). A comprehensive survey of the Canadian scene remains to be written, but worthwhile forays into the field are Margaret Visser, *Much Depends on Dinner* (Toronto: McClelland & Stewart, 1986) and *The Rituals of Dinner* (Toronto: HarperCollins, 1991) and Anne Kingston, *The Edible Man: Dave Nichol, President's Choice and the Making of Popular Taste* (Toronto: Macfarlane Walter & Ross, 1994). . . .

2. For a sample of the emerging social and gender history of post-1945 Canada, see Gary Kinsman, *The Regulation of Desire*, 2nd edn. (Montreal: Black Rose Books, 1996); Franca Iacovetta, *Such Hardworking People: Italian Immigrants in Postwar Toronto* (Montreal and Kingston: McGill-Queen's University Press, 1992); essays in Joy Parr, ed., *A Diversity of Women: Ontario 1945–80* (Toronto: University of Toronto Press, 1998) and in Gary Kinsman, Dieter K. Buse, and Mercedes Steedman, eds, *Whose National Security? Canadian*

State Surveillance and the Creation of Enemies (Toronto: Between the Lines, 2000). . . .

3. The literature on post-Second World War immigration to Canada is extensive, but useful studies include the relevant chapters in Donald H. Avery, *Reluctant Host: Canada's Response to Immigrant Workers, 1896–1994* (Toronto: McClelland & Stewart, 1995) and in Irving Abella and Harold Troper, *None Is Too Many: Canada and the Jews of Europe 1933–1948* (Toronto: Lester and Orpen Dennys, 1982); and, on the impact of Cold War policy on immigration, Reginald Whitaker, *Double Standard: The Secret History of Canadian Immigration* (Toronto: Lester and Orpen Dennys, 1987).

4. Marlene Epp, Franca Iacovetta, Frances Swyripa, eds., *Sisters or Strangers? Immigrant, Ethnic, and Racialized Women in Canadian History* (Toronto: University of Toronto Press, 2004), 3–19. On this topic and on recent efforts at such integration see the discussion in the introduction.

5. National Film Board Archives (hereafter NFBA), Montreal, file 51-214, *Canadian Notebook*, produced by NFB for Department of Citizenship and Immigration, Information Sheet (Apr. 1953). On the NFB and Cold War, see Reg Whitaker and Gary Marcuse, *Cold War Canada: The Making of a National Insecurity State, 1945–1957* (Toronto: University of Toronto Press, 1994).

6. NFBA, file 57-327, *Women at Work*, produced for Department of Citizenship and Immigration (Gordon Sparling, producer and director) (1958). . . .

7. The vast international literature on the professionalization and medicalization of 'mothercraft' and on 'homemaking' in the pre-1945 period includes valuable Canadian studies such as Cynthia Comacchio, *Nations Are Built of Babies* (Montreal: McGill-Queen's University Press, 1993) and Kathryn Arnup, Andrée Lévesque, and Ruth Pierson eds, *Delivering Motherhood* (London: Routledge, 1990). For studies that deal more explicitly with immigrants and minorities, including First Nations, see J.R. Miller, *Shingwauk's Vision: A History of Native Residential Schools* (Toronto: University of Toronto Press, 1996); Gabaccia, *We Are What We Eat*, and Levenstein, *Paradox of Plenty*. On post-1945 trends, see, for example, Parr, *A Diversity of Women*; Mary Louise Adams, *The Trouble with Normal* (Toronto: University of Toronto Press, 1997); and Mona Gleason, *Normalizing the Ideal* (Toronto: University of Toronto Press, 1999).

8. For Canada, see, for example, Susan Prentice, 'Workers, Mothers, Reds: Toronto's Postwar Daycare Fight', *Studies in Political Economy* 30 (1989); and Veronica Strong-Boag, 'Home Dreams: Canadian Women and the Suburban Experiment', *Canadian Historical Review* 72, 4 (1991). . .

9. Doug Owram, *Born at the Right Time: A History of the Baby Boom Generation* (Toronto: University of Toronto

Press, 1996), chs 1 to 3; Franca Iacovetta, 'Remaking Their Lives: Women Immigrants, Survivors, and Refugees', in Parr, *Diversity of Women*; Marlene Epp, *Women without Men: Mennonite Refugees of the Second World War* (Toronto: University of Toronto Press, 2000).

10. Gleason, *Normalizing the Ideal*.

11. City of Toronto Archives (hereafter CTA), Social Planning Collection (SPC), SC 40, box 56, file 9 – c 'Immigrants, Migrants, Ethnic Groups – English Classes – West Toronto, 1954, 1959–1962, 1966', *Report of the Committee on English Language Instruction*, June 1961.

12. Not until the 1970s did migration streams from 'non-white' nations reach significant numbers. Government recruitment policies of Caribbean women for domestic service brought only handfuls of these women into Canada before 1965. A modest number of Chinese women arrived by 1965, but their presence was significant: in 1947, Canada rescinded the racist Chinese Immigration Act (1923) (and that had been preceded by the infamous Chinese head taxes dating back to 1895).

13. For details, see Avery, *Reluctant Host*; Abella and Troper, *None Is Too Many*.

14. Iacovetta, 'Remaking Their Lives'; Epp, *Women without Men*; Joyce Hibbert, *The War Brides* (Toronto: PMA Books, 1978); Agnes Calliste, 'Canada's Immigration Policy and Domestics from the Caribbean: The Second Domestic Scheme', in Jesse Vorst et al., eds, *Race, Class and Gender: Bonds and Barriers* (Toronto: Between the Lines, 1989) . . .

15. On race, racialized women and nation-building—an important theme in recent multi-disciplinary work on immigrant and refugee women and women of colour—see, for example the essays in the special theme issue, 'Whose Canada Is It?' of *Atlantis*, co-edited by Tania Das Gupta and Franca Iacovetta.

16. Jean Huggard, 'From Emigrants to Immigrants: Hungarians in a European Camp', *Canadian Welfare* 33 (Feb. 1958). On women in South Korean refugee camps, for example, see Pierre Berton, 'The Ordeal of Mrs. Tak', *Maclean's* 15 June 1951.

17. On this and other examples, Canadian Red Cross, Ontario Division, News Bulletin. Special Issue on the British War Brides (September 1946). Thanks to Frances Swyripa for this source.

18. CRC, Ontario Division *News Bulletin* (Ruth Adams) (Sept.–Oct. 1945). No doubt strawberries were not easily obtained in post-war London; see also ibid. (May 1946).

19. CRC, Ontario Division, *News Bulletin* (Sept. 1946).

20. For contrasting examples of war-bride experiences, including women's stories of intense loneliness, conflicts with Canadian in-laws, and difficult marriages, see, for example, Iacovetta, 'Remaking Their Lives'; Hibbert, *The War Brides*; and Estella Spergel's collection

of oral testimonies (including her own) in her 'British War Brides, World War Two: A Unique Experiment for Unique Immigrants – The Process that Brought Them to Canada' (MA thesis, University of Toronto, 1997). With thanks to Estella for sharing her material.

21. The British measured liquids by weight, North Americans by volume.

22. For examples, consult: YWCA, MU3527, *Annual Reports, 1941–9; Annual Report*, 1949 Weston Branch; University Settlement, Social Planning Council, vol 24, Nl, box 1, Staff Meeting Minutes 1948–65, 4 June 1957 report.

23. Rather than specifying foods, the Canada Food Guide listed food groupings based on their nutritional value—vegetables, and meat and fish, and so on—and then offered general guidelines for their consumption while allowing for choice and variety. In 1950, a revised guide was issued.

24. For more details, see Korinek, *Roughing It in the Suburbs: Reading Chatelaine in the Fifties and Sixties* (Toronto: University of Toronto Press, 2000).

25. Marie Holmes, 'Meals off the Shelf' (Feb. 1955); Elaine Collett, '98 Cent January Specials' (Jan. 1960); 'Seven Dinners on the Double'; and 'Easy-to-Make Pizza Pin Wheels' (1961), all in *Chatelaine*. Levenstein, *Paradox of Plenty*; see also Gabaccia, *We Are What We Eat*.

26. Levenstein, *Paradox of Plenty*, 218. We also thank the members of the Toronto Labour Studies Group, the faculty at several universities where we delivered this talk (individually or collectively), and other colleagues 'of a certain age' who shared their stories of culinary (and other forms of experimentation) in the 1960s and 1970s!

27. Editors, 'What's New with Us' (Mar. 1965).

28. For example, see Elaine Collett, 'Ten New Ways with a Pound of Hamburg' (Sept. 1961).

29. This and the following references are from the AO, International Institute of Metropolitan Toronto, MU 6410, file: Cookbook Project, booklet: Toronto Nutrition Committee, *Food Customs of New Canadians*. Published with funds from the Ontario Dietic Association.

30. The revised guide profiled Chinese, Czechoslovakian, German and Austrian, Greek, Hungarian, Italian, Jewish, Dutch, Polish, Portuguese, Spanish, Ukrainian, and West Indian 'food customs'.

31. The entries for Jewish and German-Austrian.

32. Although the guide does not explicitly state it, these class distinctions, in turn, overlapped with racial distinctions between wealthier whites and poorer blacks more likely to emigrate.

33. Miller, *Shingwauk's Vision*; Gabaccia, *We Are What We Eat*; Comacchio, *Nations Are Built of Babies*.

34. Another entry noted the availability and use of vitamin D for mothers and children.

35. As for improvement, it stated: 'If income low the use of more poultry might be encouraged' and 'The cost and relative value' of sugar-coated cereals and milk was explained.

36. For a valuable discussion see Comacchio, *Nations Are Built of Babies*.

37. Franca Iacovetta, 'Recipes for Democracy? Gender, Family and Making Female Citizens in Cold War Canada', *Canadian Woman Studies* 20, 2 (Summer 2000).

38. The sample is of 28 interviews conducted in the 1970s with immigrant women and couples asked to comment on food customs and with the following national, regional, and ethnoreligious breakdown: European (18), including European Jewry (4), Asian (2), Caribbean (1), and South Asian (mainly from India) (3). This sample was selected from Iacovetta's database of more than 60 interviews with post-1945 immigrants culled from the Oral History Collection, Multicultural History Society of Ontario (hereafter MHSO), Toronto.

39. MHSO sample, interviews with Amelia S-R. and Maria B. Similar reports come from POWs, including Lotta B., a Polish Gentile woman who fought in the Polish Resistance until her arrest during the Warsaw insurrection in 1944. For her, the Germany POW camp meant lack of food, poor sanitary conditions, and total isolation from world events.

40. MHSO sample, interviews with Maria B., Helga A., and Dagmar Z.

41. MHSO sample; the theme also comes up repeatedly in the recordings of reception workers.

42. MHSO sample, interview with Iusa D.

43. MHSO sample, interview with Annemarie H.

44. MHSO sample, interviews with Susan M., Helga A., and Nazneed S.

45. For one example, see Franca Iacovetta, 'From Jellied Salads to Melon and Prosciutto, and Polenta: Italian Foodways and "Cosmopolitan Eating"', in Jo Marie Powers, ed., *Buon appetito!* (Toronto: Ontario Historical Society, 2000).

46. Jeannine Locke, 'Can the Hungarians Fit In?' (May 1957).

47. All were favourable though for varied reasons. . . . Mrs M. Filwood, Toronto to Editors, 'Letters to *Chatelaine*' July 1957); Letter from a new reader, Halifax, to Editors (Aug. 1957); Rev. G. Simor, SJ, St Elizabeth of Hungary church, Toronto, to Editors (Sept. 1959).

48. For example, see NA, MG31, Citizenship Branch, D69, co112, file: 1950, Liaison Officer, Dr V. Kaye, Report of Trip to Toronto and Hamilton, 27 Sept.–2 Oct. 1950.

49. For example, AO, IIMT, file: Cookbook Project, *Special Greetings in Food Christmas 1963* (homemade pamphlet). A more detailed discussion of this theme is in Iacovetta, *Making New Citizens in Cold War Canada* (in progress).

7

Finding a Place for Father: Selling the Barbecue in Post-war Canada

Chris Dummitt

Daily household chores do not figure prominently in images of 1950s manliness. Domesticity enters our remembrance of men's lives at that time as an absence; a point of wry humour for women, sly humour for men. But post-war men and women did label some household tasks as masculine; this paper looks at one such task, outdoor cooking. Men were central to the image of barbecuing, which advertisers introduced into the Canadian market and backyard during the late 1940s and 1950s. In this new form of household cookery the chief steak griller was male.

What should we make of men and barbecuing? In an era known for its strict gender division of labour, men's barbecuing transgressed normative gender roles.[1] Typically, preparing the evening meal was considered part of a homemaker's responsibilities. Why, then, did women not become the spatula-toting barbecue chefs of popular imagination? Certainly male cooks were not unknown. The army cook and the gourmet chef are two possible precedents. But both World War II and the Korean War had ended by the mid-1950s and the backyard barbecue was not often celebrated as haute cuisine. And although hunting and fishing were popular pastimes, men's outdoor cooking in these areas need not have translated into their position as the family

backyard cook. So why did men become the family barbecue chef? What made barbecuing different from other forms of post-war cookery?

In this paper, I argue that barbecuing's masculine status arose out of broader changes in both post-war gender relations and notions of fatherhood; namely, an increased expectation that fathers be more involved in family domestic life. Men occupied an ambiguous place in post-war Canada's renewed cult of domesticity. Being a distant breadwinner was no longer sufficient, but a gender division of labour which assumed fatherly absence for much of the day remained unchecked.[2] It is within this narrow cultural space, a search for an appropriately modern place for men in 1950s domestic life, that we should read the emergence of the male barbecue chef.

Masculine Domesticity

Besides barbecuing, men were central participants in a wide assortment of family leisure activities in the 1940s and 1950s. Along with family outings, coaching youth sports, and hobbies like model-train building, barbecuing was one of a variety of masculine endeavours amidst the relative cornucopia of post-war family leisure. The period's increased time for, and emphasis upon,

Chris Dummitt, 'Finding a Place for Father: Selling Barbecue in Postwar Canada', *Journal of the Canadian Historical Association* 9 (1998): 209–23. Reprinted by permission of the publisher and Christopher Dummitt, Assistant Professor, Trent University.

leisure fit in with longer-term changes in ideologies of fatherhood. In these narratives, the 'new father' took more interest in matters of daily family life, including leisure-oriented child care and the psycho-sexual development of sons and daughters. Such developments did not represent a change in men's position as breadwinners, but expanded fatherhood's realm into new, more domestic, areas.[3]

In fact, the post-war father was not altogether 'new'. Increasingly, gender historians have been lured towards men's household activities, towards tantalizing and perplexing evidence of what Margaret Marsh has labelled 'masculine domesticity'. This historiographical movement follows the work of Catherine Hall and Leonore Davidoff. Their study of the early nineteenth-century English middle class, *Family Fortunes*, challenges the usefulness of a strict and literal reading of separate spheres ideology to convey the complexity of women's and men's lives. For our purposes, they point towards the interpenetration of public and private as relational categories. They urge us to inquire into the process whereby the public/private dichotomy is created. Americans Robert Griswold and Michael Kimmel follow up these insights in examining the place of domesticity in ideologies of fatherhood and masculinity, respectively. Both recognize that by treating breadwinning as the meta-narrative of fatherhood, we obscure the way fathers have been both public and private figures as well as the power relations that have worked to make this complex social position appear one-dimensional.[4]

Twentieth-century Canadian historians have similarly commented on the inadequacy of breadwinning discourses to wholly capture the history of fatherhood. Historians such as Suzanne Morton and Joy Parr note that men's domestic travails have often been labelled as 'help' to distinguish them from similar activities performed by women. To explain this linguistic posturing in the context of 1920s Halifax, Morton argues that 'there was no language

available to recognize the male contribution to domestic production' so men's gardening, hunting, and alcohol manufacturing were said to be 'hobbies' or 'leisure activities'. Morton's and others attempts to understand the relationship between men's wage labour and domestic life are still tentative, certain that there is more to be told, uncertain how to proceed. As one gender historian notes, 'There is clearly something more to the family man than the imagery of economic man can comprehend, something more complicated governing his relations with the others in his household, both female and male, than his relation to the market alone can explain.'[5]

This paper attends to the 'something more' of the family man implicated in barbecuing's commercial speech. Cookbook writers, journalists, retailers, and advertisers packaged a particular image of domestic masculinity to sell along with the barbecue. But bringing men into domestic matters was not straightforward. Men's barbecuing raised eyebrows. Many agreed with the author of a 1955 *Maclean's* exposé on outdoor cooking who described the phenomenon as 'weird' and 'odd'.[6] Even so, sellers of barbecue culture prepared themselves for such doubters. They went to great lengths to convince Canadians that barbecuing was an acceptable masculine leisure pursuit. Barbecuing's commercial speech did not merely replicate a routine designation of some pre-existing masculine essence. The intensity of efforts to masculinize the barbecue belies the naturalness claimed for outdoor cooking's masculinity. Instead, barbecuing's commercial speech presented, to use Foucault's terms, a 'proliferation of discourse'—a veritable orgy of linguistic posturing that linked outdoor cooking to symbols of virile masculinity and manly leisure.[7]

But why did domesticity form such a crucial part of this image of the post-war masculine good life? And how did creators of barbecuing's commercial speech sell masculine domesticity to post-war Canadians? To ask such questions is not to equate commercial speech with daily life. Daily interaction and understanding do not flow unproblematically from ad copy. Yet, to examine how commercial speech envisioned the link between masculinity and domesticity is crucial. Although the promotions of commercial speech could be modified, this discourse formed the basis of post-war Canada's barbecue culture.[8]

Making the Barbecue Masculine

The barbecue's entry into Canadian backyards followed a two-stage process. The federal government's 1947 *Emergency Exchange Conservation Act* restricted imports of domestic appliances and other allegedly 'luxury' consumer products, barbecues included. Accordingly, Canadians who wished to enjoy outdoor cooking in the late 1940s were largely limited to building their own permanent brick and cement barbecues. 'How to' articles in *Canadian Home and Gardens*, *Home Building*, and *Handy Man's Home Manual* provided substantial promotion of this fad. But although such articles boasted how easily the average family man could build such contraptions, it was not until import restrictions were lifted in the early 1950s that the cultural phenomenon of backyard cooking became firmly established in Canada.[9]

The extent of the move to outdoor cooking is difficult to discern. Unlike electric stoves, census takers and other statisticians of family commodities did not regularly track rates of barbecue ownership. Even if such records were gathered, they may not have included home-built barbecues or the use made of picnic sites and campground firepits. Despite these limitations, we can uncover the barbecue's cultural significance in other areas. Retailers and manufacturers, for example, regularly reported boom sales. An Ontario home barbecue building company reported in 1955 that 'for every barbecue [we] built ten years ago, [we] build a hundred today.'[10] Cookbooks added new sections on 'Outdoor Cookery' and 'Outdoor Meals' to their regular list of chapters. In 1959, Sears made grilling central to its advertising strategy, devoting the cover of its summer catalogue to the barbecue.[11] It is safe to say that by the late 1950s barbecuing's commercial speech had grilled its way onto the Canadian consciousness.

Journalists, advertisers, and cookbook writers set priorities for certain aspects of barbecuing. In particular, sellers of barbecue culture found its location outside the home to be significant. *Maclean's* writer Thomas Walsh suggested a genetic link between masculinity and the outdoors as the reason for men's proclivity to pick up the barbecue tongs. He noted that, 'one theory for the increasing number of male cooks is simply that barbecuing is done outdoors, which is man's natural domain. It's the same inherited impulse that makes him take over at a corn roast.' Many advertisers backed up Walsh, consistently describing outdoor cooking, which primarily included meals served in the relatively domestic suburban backyard, as qualitatively distinct from cooking done inside the home.[12]

The barbecue was also potentially rustic and old-fashioned. The *Art of Barbecue and Outdoor Cooking* went out of its way to note that grilling was 'an age-old method of preparing meat'. Others contrasted this 'age-old' process with the exigencies of modern life. Unlike cooking done by homemakers in a modern kitchen, barbecuing hearkened back to an earlier time. According to Tom Riley, author of *How to Build and Use Your Own Outdoor Kitchen*, 'It seems, along with a rocket soon to the moon, we want the goodness of a simple thing—the heartiness and friendliness of outdoor cooking.' For Riley, the bustle of modern life explained men's barbecuing:

The time was when a fellow cooked a meal over an open fire just plain and simply because he had to. When he received a chance to eat elsewhere, any kind of chance, he dropped everything and ran—his one fear he might be late. But the world does change. In these hurried days of supersonic aircraft and pushbutton kitchens, amidst the myriad of marvelous things we possess, the same fellow has no desire to hurry out to dinner alongside the superhighway. Instead, he is tantalized by the idea of donning a chef's cap and leisurely barbecuing a sizzling supper in the backyard.

In this vein, the barbecue represented a brief respite from modern life and, presumably, modern gender roles as well.[13]

Those who sought out historical precedent for men cooking over fire took the imagined nature of barbecuing's rustic lineage to its furthest extremes. Cookbook writers with an eye on the past found no paucity of historical barbecue chefs. The *Canadian Cook Book* credited the cave man for this 'very popular form of cookery'. Then, the culinary expert turned historian went on to trace a more recent, though still distant, ancestry: 'Some of the most efficient barbecues can still be seen in the remains of medieval castles where great spits held suckling pigs, fowl, and all forms of succulent meats over coals of enormous hearths.' Moving south and east, the origins of the shish kebab received similar treatment. *The Art of Barbecue and Outdoor Cooking* told its readers that 'long, long ago Armenian soldiers and migrating mountain folk speared pieces of wild game or lamb on their swords and roasted it over a roaring camp fire. This they called "shish kebob" meaning skewered pieces of meat.' With a slight geographical twist, another writer claimed the shish kebob was 'a Turkish term for roasting food over a fire on the point of a sword'. What had changed since the ancient Turks and Armenians? 'Today, metal skewers replace swords. And, many more foods such as fish, vegetables and even fruits are skewered to add interest to the menu.' Lest North Americans feel left out of barbecue history, Tom Riley asserted that 'the American Indian of the east coast was doing a fair job with a spit long before Columbus.' Later, Riley brought many of these themes together. 'Luckily for our times,' he mused,

there were some blessed persons throughout the ages of outdoor cooking who took

an interest in their campfires. They experimented. The native who first roasted on a spit, his friend who tried a pit. The Chinese epicurean who first basted a fowl in a low chimney, the fellow who first broiled over charcoal, the soldier who stuck a combination of meat and vegetables on his sword for the first shish kebab—slowly throughout the ages they found the rudiments of good barbecuing.[14]

To recall barbecuing's ancient lineage in this way became part of the genre of writing on outdoor cooking. These were not serious attempts to historicize the barbecue. Instead, journalists and cookbook writers made sense of men's outdoor cooking by invoking its history in terms redolent of muscular and military manhood.

Meat was key to such invocations. Throughout the 1950s almost no visual image of a barbecue was complete without the requisite steak, hamburger, or pork chop. Journalists' and cookbook writers' language complemented the visual imagery, suggesting hot dogs, hamburgers, deluxe steaks, individual steaks, and chops as the ideal grilling foods. One cookbook established a hierarchy of food to be served at a barbecue, with meat at the top: 'Usually when a complete meal is being served outdoors, it is the meat course that is barbecued, perhaps with one or more vegetables. When serving a crowd, unless the barbecue is equipped with a spit, it is often impossible to accommodate more than the meat over the fire box.' In this listing, vegetables could be accommodated but only if there was room.[15]

For obvious reasons, Canada Packers sought to strengthen the association between meat and barbecuing. In the summer of 1955, the company offered a free portable brazier to consumers who purchased a specified amount of their canned meat products, including beef stew, bologna, beans with wieners, and Klik pork luncheon meat. In the image accompanying the offer, a smiling apron-clad man serves a Fred-Flintstone-size steak to an appreciative female onlooker, suggesting that Canada Packers could continue its service to the virile, meat-hungry new barbecue owner. Similarly, the cover of Canadian Tire's 1961 summer catalogue unabashedly connected red meat with manly virility. Throughout the 1950s and into the 1960s, Canadian Tire catalogue covers hosted a series of cartoons with the same stock characters and stock plots. Each centred on the efforts of a white, middle-aged man chasing after, and making sexual advances upon, a much younger, 'full-bodied' woman (usually blonde). In the barbecue rendition of this post-war misogynistic male fantasy, the older man serves a large T-bone steak to an admiring younger woman. Two 20-something-year-old men stare on incredulously, looking back and forth between the woman's succulent steak and the hot dogs they had received.[16] Through this overt symbolism, advertisers asserted a direct relationship between meat, barbecuing, and virile heterosexual masculinity.

Advertisers assured potential owners that the physical structure of the barbecue was just as masculine as the meat it was designed to grill. The 'tough' descriptions of barbecue advertisements are noteworthy for their mere repetitiveness. 'Heavy steel', 'sturdy steel', and 'heavy-gauge steel' were the descriptors of choice. An advertisement for Eaton's Spring/Summer Catalogue provides a representative flavour: 'Top . . . is made of heavy-gauge aluminum to be completely rust proof. Firebox is a durable stainless steel. Grill, spit and supporting uprights are steel finished in gleaming nickel plate. Legs and wheels are of braced steel in baked-on enamel finish with cross braces.'[17] Eaton's promised prospective buyers that this was a sturdy contraption that would hold up under extreme conditions. The type of steel with which a barbecue was constructed was undoubtedly important in determining both its effectiveness and its longevity. But advertisers' rhetoric of strength and durability sought to reassure consumers about more than the equipment's functionality. Eaton's 1954 spring/summer catalogue boasted that a 'light weight' barbecue,

ideal for trips away from home, was still capable of a 'man's sized job of outdoor cooking'.[18]

Advertisers went on to gender the movement of the barbecue's 'heavy' and 'sturdy' parts. Unlike advertisements for the modern electric stove, barbecuing's commercial speech did not describe their product's machine-like functions in easy-to-understand language. Instead, with barbecues, a 'crank mechanism' worked to adjust heat control by raising and lowering the 'extra heavy grid'.[19] Unlike the celebrated easy, modern dials on the electric stove, the barbecue worked with 'cranks'. Sociologist Susan Ormrod found a similar tactic at work in the gendering of technical commodities in 1980s Britain. Jargon-filled language prevailed with allegedly masculine items, while advertisers employed comprehensible and non-expert language to describe products deemed feminine.[20] In our case, barbecuing's pseudo-industrial language differentiated it from stoves and other 'feminine' cooking appliances in the home.

These linguistic devices were also used for barbecue utensils. Such items were often labelled 'tools'. An advertisement accompanying a Canadian Home and Gardens article on barbecue culture listed, 'five members of a gadget set, namely large fork, soup ladle, flapjack flipper, vegetable spoon, spoon for odd jobs. . . . The last item is a real old-fashioned butcher knife for carving steaks. . . .'[21] This description boasts a number of gender assumptions. First, the advertisement labelled the group a 'gadget set' despite the fact that all of its objects were relatively common household items. As well, the butcher knife's 'old-fashioned' status conveyed the image of barbecuing's rusticity. In this way, advertisements inserted a cultural mélange of masculine symbols into the language of barbecuing; they distinguished between a butcher knife used to carve a grilled T-bone from a butcher knife used to carve an oven-broiled T-bone.

Cookbook writers extended these distinctions to include the barbecue cook's clothing. Advertisements often depicted men clad in apron, chef's hat, and, sometimes, heat-protecting mitts. The inclusion of the chef's hat cast allusions to another acceptable male cook, the fine-dining chef. In fact, writers often used this title in tandem with images of men in the customary duck hat or toque. The *Canadian Cook Book* highlighted protective needs to further distinguish barbecue dress from apparently similar items worn by housewives. It warned that, due to the dangers of cooking over fire, barbecue apparel should consist of 'a large, heavy, non-frilly apron and thick oven mitts'. Such warnings did not normally accompany other sections of the cookbook.[22] Finally, advertisements presented barbecue attire as humorous. Lest readers miss the comical association, manufacturers emblazoned sayings such as 'call me cookie', 'hotdog', or 'wot'll it be' on aprons as a reminder. Sears summed up the appropriate barbecue costume in its 1959 summer catalogue; beside a tiny picture of barbecue garb, the description read, 'Asbestos palm mitts, white duck hat, apron. Humorous.'[23]

Commercial speech presented humour, especially self-deprecating humour, as central to barbecue culture. Irony was the tool of choice. Articles on outdoor cooking overflowed with images of men beaming proud smiles one moment and dousing a raging fire the next. Journalist James Bannerman openly admitted his own incompetence:

> All I know about barbecuing could be tattooed in large letters on the south end of a thick gnat. [Barbecuing] sounds easy and I don't doubt it would be to a person of normal intelligence. It so happens, however, that I am not a person of normal intelligence and for a while it looked as if I was never going to get anything more out of my barbecue than the odd puff of pallid smoke.[24]

In taking on this humorous tone, Bannerman fit his work into a wider genre of writing on masculine domesticity in post-war Canada. The image of the hapless father recurred in a variety of 1940s and 1950s media. This genre portrayed

men as more than adequate breadwinners but ridiculed their status in the home. For example, in a 1952 *Maclean's* article, 'Timetable of a Father Looking After the Children', a fictitious mother leaves home at 7:25 for a meeting on child guidance, instructing her husband to put the two children to bed 20 minutes later at 7:45. A carnivalesque evening ensues in which hapless dad is stripped of all dignity in a blatantly incompetent, though energetic, attempt to put his children to bed. The kids, the woman next door, and, presumably, the reader, mock father's feeble efforts to assert control in domestic matters. Yet, ultimately, this ritualized mocking did not challenge men's position in the family. Instead, it reasserted that men's 'true' position, the position in which they were not mocked, lay outside the home.[25] By treating men's barbecuing as a joking matter, barbecuing's commercial speech appealed to this wider discourse that linked domestic incompetence with normal masculinity.

Barbecuing and Post-war Leisure

In order to sell barbecues and barbecue products, advertisers enticed men to try barbecuing because of the enjoyment they would receive. Despite the fact that men would be cooking a meal, something considered work for women, barbecuing's commercial speech maintained that grilling steaks was 'fun'. The language was repetitive: 'Enjoy Outdoor Living', 'It's fun to cook and eat on the patio', 'Outdoor meals can provide enjoyment and good eating. . . .'[26] Yet, in claiming the barbecue as 'fun' entertainment, advertisers employed a gendered strategy to neatly situate the barbecue within post-war family leisure. They incessantly sought to enlarge what could be a very fine distinction between leisure and work in barbecuing.

A number of journalists suggested that barbecuing required an altered, more relaxed, dining etiquette. For one commentator, to eat a meal '"picnic style" included a consideration of all the elements of informality plus a change of atmosphere and even a different type of menu'. Writing in the Halifax *Chronicle-Herald*, Steven Ellingston agreed that the 'relaxed, camp-out, carefree attitude' was key. According to yet another journalist, 'The barbecue has added its weight to the general breakdown of formality in the home, which [has] daily become more functional and less formal. . . . People who a generation ago wouldn't have eaten in their shirt sleeves are now sitting around barbecues in shorts, bathing suits, pedal pushers and blue jeans.' Not all appreciated the new barbecue dining style. *Canadian Home and Gardens* food columnist, Frederick Manning, criticized barbecuing's effect on social mores. 'If it's all the same to you,' he appealed to readers in August 1948, 'I'll cook mine in the kitchen and carry it out, wind and weather permitting, but only if the dining room is knee deep in a paper and painting job. After all, what is wrong with a dining table in summer anyway?'[27] By making dinnertime into leisure time, barbecuing upset traditionalists like Manning and established its gendered distinctiveness.

To further differentiate barbecuing from the more mundane forms of cookery, journalists and advertisers maintained that the family barbecue was an 'event'; a special, and irregular, occurrence. Advertisers envisioned and promoted a family eating schedule supplemented by occasional bouts of male interest and involvement. For example, in 1958, Simpson's told wives of prospective barbecue cooks that the barbecue appliances they advertised were 'for his outdoor cooking *sprees*'.[28] Others presented the barbecue as an ideal way to entertain guests or celebrate a family outing. The 1957 promotional film, *Barbecue Impromptu*, celebrated the wonders of stainless steel through the fictional occasion of a couple preparing a barbecue dinner party for the husband's business associates. In this simulation, the dinner provided a direct link between the man's public business life and his private home life. Both husband and wife shared the responsibilities for preparing the meal for the

guests. While the husband greeted his guests and operated the barbecue itself, his wife prepared most of the meal.[29] Whether celebrated as a dinner party or a family meal, commercial speech highlighted the specialness of men taking part in meal preparation at a barbecue.

This part-time co-operative spirit exemplified idealized notions of post-war gender relations. A *Canadian Home and Gardens* article suggested Sunday morning as a time to 'gather the home circle around [the barbecue] and have brunch. . . . Somebody can make coffee while dad flips the flapjacks, scrambles the eggs, or grills the bacon and the youngsters take over fixing the table or distracting the pup from too close attention.' Another writer claimed that the 'ideal picnic will be turned into a "family game" if everyone has particular duties and responsibilities. Dad is responsible for the fire and icing of the beverages and perishables: the girls help mom with the food and the young man takes care of the game equipment, bats and balls, portable radio, playing cards and perhaps the paper plates, cups and silverware.' In these scenarios, the barbecue meant more than just the father fixing the fire; it represented collective effort and collective enjoyment. The change in the sex of the cook was, therefore, only one part of a wider narrative of changing values and mores.[30]

As part of this collectivist and informal narrative, advertisers and cookbook writers cast the barbecue chef's responsibilities in a language of sly humour. One cartoon depicted an apron-clad barbecue chef taking care of the after-dinner cleanup by spraying water from a garden hose onto dishes piled up in a children's plastic pool. Thomas Walsh's description of what men did to prepare a meal on the barbecue reflected a similar lackadaisical attitude: 'A man who ten years ago did nothing about supper but sniff under the saucepan lids and who wouldn't dream of setting a table, today doesn't mind building a fire and putting some meat on it.' Walsh played on the assumption that not many men would mind the not-so-arduous task of 'building a fire and putting some meat on it'. Here the discourse on leisure made a double movement; barbecuing was leisure for men but work for women. Walsh went on to quote a suburban housewife on her husband's new-found love of barbecuing:

> My husband takes care of all our barbecue meals. He comes home and starts right in. 'Get me the garlic salt. Hand me the tongs. Get me the fork. Hand me a bay leaf. Put some more charcoal on the fire. Bring the plates over here.' Holy cow! There's more to cooking than holding a couple of pork chops over the fire.[31]

The truncated cooking responsibilities suggested here made barbecuing truly appear, as the advertisements boasted, 'easy'.

Conclusions

Barbecuing's commercial speech was a prescriptive discourse. We should not expect it to offer realistic descriptions of daily life. And when cookbooks and popular magazines described barbecue culture, it appeared as a uniformly white, middle-class, and heterosexual phenomenon. The visual imagery, especially in high-end publications like *Canadian Home and Gardens*, presented idealized nuclear families in middle-class suburban backyards as the norm. In this way, barbecuing's commercial speech was part of a larger middle-class advertising discourse that offered up a homogenized world of post-war abundance.

We can see that not all participants in barbecue culture accepted unproblematically the rhetorical flourishes of its commercial speech. Certainly, *Maclean's* satirist Robert Allen disputed the benefits of barbecuing as relaxing leisure. In a brief moment of seriousness, Allen decried leisure that focused on 'doing': 'If we're going to keep shortening the work week,' he argued in *Maclean's* in 1957, 'we should start realizing that we can't fill up the other end with hobbies. . . . Relaxation is a lot like happiness: the harder we chase it, the farther it moves away.'[32] For Allen, barbecuing and other masculine hobbies required too much hustle.

At the same time, Allen still dismissed the significance of the new post-war domestic leisure; he argued that barbecuing was not leisure, but neither did it equal men's real work. Allen's dismissal of barbecuing's significance may lead historians to do the same, to treat the barbecue as an insignificant aside to 1950s masculinity. Certainly, other household items such as cars, lawnmowers, and fix-it tools appear to have been more pivotal in men's lives. But a close reading of barbecuing's commercial speech militates against such an interpretation. The barbecue's insignificance, its status as a humorous sidebar to the 'real' story of men's breadwinning obligations, did not stem automatically from its material conditions. To read the barbecue as an inconsequential aberration is to accept the myth of barbecuing sold by cookbook writers, journalists, and advertisers.

Alternatively, we can read in barbecuing's commercial speech a proliferation of discourse on the subject of masculinity and domesticity in 1950s Canada, not, as popular lore might hold, an absence of such discourse. Taking our cue from Foucault's insights into the fascination behind Victorian sexual repression, we can see that the incitement to speak of barbecuing as humorous and insignificant formed a discourse of disavowal and repudiation. The sellers of barbecue culture were incessantly concerned about domesticity. Advertisements and cartoons may have been lighthearted, but they were also earnest. The creators of barbecuing's commercial speech sought to assuage any anxiety caused by the transgression inherent to barbecue culture by enfolding it in a masculine discourse of dismissal.

What does the existence of this discourse suggest about gender relations in the 1950s? How do we read such refusals? First, our uncovering of the intensity of barbecuing's commercial speech fits into an emerging revisionist history of the 1950s.[33] Here, we find the gendered insecurities of the decade. Where would men fit into the post-war era's domestic life? How could men's changing place in the family be reconciled with normative ideals? Far from being a period of static gender relations, barbecuing's commercial speech demonstrates that cultural negotiation and conflict underlay the decade's social life. We like to remember this period as a time of placid tranquility but contemporaries more often described a world of rapid change.

Barbecuing's commercial speech points out the direction of some of these changes. The Victorian division between public and private, however tenuous and artificial, had supported cultural divisions between masculine and feminine. But as suffragists, women war workers, and others assailed this cultural construct, and the ideology of gender relations it supported, individuals looked elsewhere to shore up their belief in the naturalness of gender difference. If the division between public and private had eroded, what replaced it? Can we view men's involvement in domestic matters as one small step in a progressive evolution? Should we replace the previous history of post-war gender relations that characterized the period as a step backward with a new history emphasizing slow but steady advancement? Our exploration of gender and barbecuing again points in a different direction. Gender hierarchies based on the division between public and private had faltered but new dichotomies took their place. New gendered divisions between leisure and work redefined and rearticulated older divisions between public and private and masculine and feminine. Ultimately, the story of barbecuing and post-war gender relations is not a tale of simple progression or descent, but a complex narrative of cultural change.

Notes

For both constructive criticism and support during the time I spent revising this article, I thank Joy Parr, Jack Lillie, and Karen Ferguson as well as the audiences at the annual meeting of the Canadian Historical Association and at Simon Fraser University's Border Crossings series. I especially thank my former advisor, Shirley Tillotson, for her commitment and even-handed guidance during my time at Dalhousie and since.

1. On gender relations in the immediate post-war decades, see Mary Louise Adams, *The Trouble with Normal: Postwar Youth and the Making of Heterosexuality* (Toronto, 1997); Doug Owram, *Born at the Right Time: A History of the Baby Boom Generation* (Toronto, 1996); Veronica Strong-Boag, 'Home Dreams: Women and the Suburban Experiment in Canada, 1945–1960', *Canadian Historical Review* 72, 4 (1991): 471–504; Strong-Boag, 'Canada's Wage-Earning Wives and the Construction of the Middle Class, 1945–1960', *Journal of Canadian Studies* 29, 3 (1994): 5–25; Mona Gleason, 'Disciplining Children, Disciplining Parents: The Nature and Meaning of Advice to Canadian Parents, 1945–1955', *Histoire Sociale/Social History* 29 (May 1996): 187–209. Useful counterpoints in the American literature include Elaine Tyler May, *Homeward Bound: American Families in the Cold War Era* (New York, 1988); Joanne Meyerowitz, ed., *Not June Cleaver: Women and Gender in Postwar America, 1945–1960* (Philadelphia, 1994).

2. On the place of fathers in post-war domestic life, see Robert Rutherdale, 'Fatherhood and Masculine Domesticity During the Baby Boom: Consumption and Leisure in Advertising and Life Stories', in Lori Chambers and Edgar André Montigny, eds, *Family Matters: Papers in Post-Confederation Canadian Family History* (Toronto, 1998), 309–33; Rutherdale, 'Fatherhood and the Social Construction of Memory: Breadwinning and Male Parenting on a Job Frontier, 1945–1966', in Joy Parr and Mark Rosenfeld, eds, *Gender and History and Canada* (Toronto, 1996), 357–75; Owram, *Born at the Right Time*.

3. There is some question as to whether notions of fatherhood that Robert Griswold has described for the United States as the 'new fatherhood' also developed in Canada before World War II. On the origins of the 'new fatherhood' in Canada, see Cynthia Comacchio, '"A Postscript for Father": Defining a New Fatherhood in Postwar Canada', *Canadian Historical Review* 78, 3 (Sept. 1997): 385–408. For studies which treat post-war parenting and fatherhood more generally, see Neil Sutherland, *Growing Up: Childhood in English Canada from the Great War to the Age of Television* (Toronto, 1997); Owram, *Born at the Right Time*; Mona Gleason, 'Psychology and the Construction of the "Normal" Family in Postwar Canada, 1945–1960', *Canadian Historical Review* 78, 3 (1997): 442–77 . . .

4. Margaret Marsh, 'Suburban Men and Masculine Domesticity, 1870–1915', *American Quarterly* 40 (June 1988): 165–86; Marsh, 'From Separation to

Togetherness: The Social Construction of Domestic Space in American Suburbs, 1840–1915', *Journal of American History* 76 (Sept. 1989): 506–27; Leonore Davidoff and Catherine Hall, *Family Fortunes: Men and Women of the English Middle Class, 1780–1850* (Chicago, 1987); Robert Griswold, *Fatherhood in America: A History* (New York, 1993); Michael Kimmel, *Manhood in America: A Cultural History* (New York, 1996). . . .

5. Joy Parr, *The Gender of Breadwinners: Women, Men, and Change in Two Industrial Towns, 1880–1950* (Toronto, 1990), 90–2, 191, 200; Suzanne Morton, *Ideal Surroundings: Domestic Life in a Working-Class Neighbourhood in the 1920s* (Toronto, 1995), 129.

6. Thomas Walsh, 'How to Cook Without a Stove', *Maclean's* (9 July 1955).

7. I borrow here from Foucault's insights into the 'repressive hypothesis' of Victorian sexuality. He argues that an excitable and interested 'incitement to discourse' lay behind Victorian prohibitions, warnings, and regulations on sexual matters. See Michel Foucault, *The History of Sexuality: An Introduction*, trans. Robert Hurley (New York, 1978). In the case of the barbecue, we can see that the elaborate rituals, language, and humour of barbecuing's commercial speech worked in a similar fashion. At the same time as this discourse refuted men's incorporation into feminine domesticity, the intensity of its refusal and the meanings of its privilege point both to the existence of men's domesticity and to a language that sought to make it masculine.

8. In this paper, I examine barbecuing through what I refer to as 'commercial speech'. I include in this definition sources that might not otherwise be considered 'commercial'. My concern is with the manner by which the barbecue was sold as a cultural concept. Advertisements in catalogues and newspapers were one way the barbecue was sold. But cookbooks that added new sections on 'Outdoor Cooking' and journalists who expounded on the eccentricities of the new fad were also essential in the selling process. Together they presented potential buyers and casual onlookers with a language which, although it could be taken up, rejected, or distorted, nonetheless formed the initial framework through which barbecuing was understood.

9. Joy Parr, 'Gender, Keynes, and Reconstruction', paper presented to the Department of History, Simon Fraser University, 1998; 'How to Build Your Own Barbecue', *Canadian Home and Gardens* (June 1948); 'The Barbecue Anyone Can Build', *Canadian Home and Gardens* (May 1949); 'Barbecues for Outdoor Living', *Home Building* (June–July 1952); *Handyman's Home Manual* (New York, 1960).

10. 'Barbecue Grills Pace Housewares Sales Rise', *Weekly Retail Memo*, 27 June 1955; 'Food Chains Plan Big Outdoor Eating Promotions', *Weekly Retail Memo*, 4 June 1956; '"Outdoor Dining Room" to Spur Summer Food Sales', *Weekly Retail Memo*, 17 June 1957; Walsh, 'How to Cook Without a Stove'. Published by the *Vancouver Sun*, the *Weekly Retail Memo* was a digest of news from publications in the United States and Canada relevant to retailers who might wish to advertise in the paper.

11. Cookbooks which followed this trend include, *The Ogilvie Cook Book* (Toronto, 1957); Nellie Lyle Pattinson, *Canadian Cook Book*, revised by Helen Wattie and Elinor Donaldson (Toronto, 1961); Agnes Murphy, *The American Everyday Cookbook* (New York, 1955); *Dishes Men Like: New and Old Favorites. Easy to Prepare . . . Sure to Please* (New York, 1952). Although some of these works were published in the United States, all were in use in Canada during the period covered by this paper. All cookbooks referred to in this paper are held in the collections of the Halifax Public Library, the Vancouver Public Library, and in the personal collections of Lynda Laton, Tena Neufeld, and the author.

12. Walsh, 'How to Cook Without a Stove'; See also *Eaton's Summer Catalogue* (1960): 10–11; *Sears Spring and Summer Catalogue* (1959): 448; Halifax *Chronicle-Herald*, 15 June 1956, 14.

13. Tested Recipe Institute, *The Art of Barbecue and Outdoor Cooking* (New York, 1958), 22; Tom Riley, *How to Build and Use Your Own Outdoor Kitchen* (Chicago, 1953), 3–4. Seeming to contradict Riley's argument that families wanted to flee the superhighway at mealtime, Andrew Hurley has traced the transformation and growth of roadside diners into family restaurants in post-war America. See Andrew Hurley, 'From Hash House to Family Restaurant: The Transformation of the Diner and Post-World War II Consumer Culture', *Journal of American History* (Mar. 1997): 1282–1308.

14. *Canadian Cook Book*, 193; *The Art of Barbecue and Outdoor Cooking*, 86; Walsh, 'How to Cook Without a Stove', 41; Riley, *How to Build and Use Your Own Outdoor Kitchen*, 4–5.

15. 'Let's Have a Picnic . . . and Make it a Success', Halifax *Chronicle-Herald*, 18 June 1954, 16; *Canadian Cook Book*; Halifax *Chronicle-Herald*, 7 June 1955, 7.

16. Halifax *Chronicle-Herald*, 7 June 1955, 7; *Canadian Tire Summer Catalogue* (1961).

17. *Eaton's Spring/Summer Catalogue* (1954): 548. For other examples, see *Sears Summer Catalogue* (1953): 35–6; *Eaton's Summer Catalogue* (1959): 187; Halifax *Chronicle-Herald*, 15 June 1956, 14; Halifax *Chronicle-Herald*, 19 June 1959, 14.

18. *Eaton's Spring/Summer Catalogue* (1954): 548.

19. *Eaton's Summer Catalogue* (1959): 187; *Eaton's Summer Catalogue* (1960): 10–11. Joy Parr explores the gendered tactics of electric range manufacturers and salesmen in Ontario between 1950 and 1955 in her 'Shopping for a Good Stove: A Parable About Gender,

Design and the Market', in Parr, ed., *A Diversity of Women: Ontario. 1945–1980* (Toronto, 1995), 75–97.

20. Susan Ormrod, '"Let's Nuke the Dinner"': Discursive Practices of Gender in the Creation of a Cooking Process', in Cynthia Cockburn and Ruza Furst Dilic, eds, *Bringing Technology Home: Gender and Technology in a Changing Europe* (Buckingham and Philadelphia, 1994), 42–58.

21. Advertisement accompanies Frederick Manning, 'Summer Eating and Some . . .', *Canadian Home and Gardens* (Aug. 1948).

22. Actually, the section on pressure cooking did give various warnings to housewives about how to avoid an explosion. However, unlike in the section on outdoor cookery, the authors do not suggest wearing protective clothing in case of such an explosion!

23. *Canadian Cook Book; Eaton's Summer Catalogue* (1959): 187; Halifax *Chronicle-Herald*, 15 June 1956, 14; Halifax *Chronicle-Herald*, 19 June 1959, 5; *Canadian Tire Summer Catalogue* (1961); Walsh, 'How to Cook Without a Stove'; *Sears Summer Catalogue* (1959): 448.

24. James Bannerman, 'Me and My Barbecue: Adventures in barbecuing, past and present—a harrowing tale with a happy ending', *Canadian Home and Gardens* (May 1949). On a similar theme, see Robert Allen, 'But I Don't Want the New Leisure', *Maclean's* (23 Nov. 1957); Walsh, 'How to Cook Without a Stove'.

25. Barry Mather, 'Timetable of Father Looking After the Children', *Maclean's* (15 Jan. 1952). See also Robert Allen, 'How to Endure a Father', *Maclean's* (31 Jan. 1959); 'You Too Can be a Perfect Parent', *Maclean's* (15 Mar. 1951); 'How Children Remodel Their Parents', *Maclean's* (6 Aug. 1955); Victor Maxwell, 'So Daddy's a Dope!', *Maclean's* (15 June 1947).

26. *Eaton's Summer Catalogue* (1960): 10–11; *Canadian Tire Spring and Summer Catalogue* (1960): 104; *Canadian Cook Book*, v; *The Art of Barbecue and Outdoor Cooking*, 6; *Ogilvie Cook Book*, 219.

27. 'Let's Have a Picnic', Halifax *Chronicle-Herald*; Walsh, 'How to Cook Without a Stove', 43; Steve Ellingston, 'Barbecue Table, Benches Make Eating Out Easy', Halifax *Chronicle-Herald*, 14 June 1958, 11; Manning, 'Summer Eating and Some . . .'.

28. Halifax *Chronicle-Herald*, 14 June 1958, 18 [emphasis mine].

29. National Archives of Canada, ISN-25327, *Barbecue Impromptu*, International Nickel Co. of Canada, 1957. Others have commented upon the distinction between family men and single men both in business and in community affairs. See Parr, *Gender of Breadwinners*; Kimmel, *Manhood in America*; Griswold, *Fatherhood in America*.

30. 'Let's Have a Picnic', Halifax *Chronicle-Herald*; 'Every Meal's a Picnic . . . With a Barbecue!', *Canadian Home and Gardens* (May 1949). On the co-operative nature of barbecuing, see also Manning, 'Summer Eating and Some . . .'; *Canadian Cook Book; The Art of Barbecue and Outdoor Cooking*, 149; *How to Build and Use Your Own Outdoor Kitchen*, 12–13.

31. Walsh, 'How to Cook Without a Stove', 43.

32. Allen, 'But I *Don't Want* the New Leisure'.

33. The conservatism of the immediate post-war decades is a point of debate in many recent Canadian works. See Owram, *Born at the Right Time*; Jeff Keshen, 'Getting it Right the Second Time Around: The Reintegration of Canadian Veterans of World War II', in Peter Neary and J.L. Granatstein, eds, *The Veterans Charter and Post-World War II Canada* (Montreal and Kingston, 1998), 62–84; Keshen, 'Revisiting Canada's Civilian Women During World War II', *Histoire Sociale/Social History* 30, 60 (Nov. 1997): 239–66; Adams, *The Trouble With Normal. . . .*

8

Framing Regent Park: The National Film Board of Canada and the Construction of 'Outcast Spaces' in the Inner City, 1953 and 1994

—— **Sean Purdy** ——

. . . down came the verminous walls, the unclean, the unhealthy buildings and down came the fire hazards, the juvenile delinquency, the drunkenness, the broken marriages and up rose, something new, the nation's first large public housing project.[1]

In 1953 and 1994 the National Film Board of Canada (NFB) produced two documentary films about Canada's first and largest public housing project, Toronto's Regent Park. *Farewell to Oak Street* charted the dramatic 'before' and 'after' effects of public housing on the family, social, and cultural life of the inner-city dwellers whose 'slum housing' was demolished in the late 1940s and early 1950s to make way for the pioneering housing scheme. The film was didactically scripted and shot to highlight the striking shift in the built and social environment from the untidy, rundown, row housing of the working-class 'slum' to the spotless modernism of the houses and walk-up apartments of Regent Park. *Farewell* would be widely trumpeted by the City of Toronto until the late 1960s to publicize the triumph of its urban renewal campaign. Forty years later, the NFB made a *Return to Regent Park*. This time round, the film centred on the abject failure of public housing and urban renewal in Toronto and the efforts of activists to combat

drugs, crime, and the physical/social stigma of the project. Using interviews with activists, local politicians, and planners, and deftly punctuating its narrative with clips from its 1953 predecessor, it offers a much more subtle portrait of a state-created 'ghetto' and its residents.

I argue in this article that both NFB films contributed to the powerful *territorial stigmatization* of inner-city workers and public housing tenants as social and cultural deviants. Such stigmatizing renderings were not free-floating ideological and spatial representations, but reflected and reinforced real spatial and social divisions in the city and had concrete political, economic, and social consequences for tenants. . . . The NFB reflected and reproduced a symbolic external representation of the old slum area and the new housing project as modern day Babels, perilous problem areas full of dysfunctional families and cultural misfits. In a concluding section, I underscore how this powerful place-based stigma, brought to national prominence by Canada's influential state film agency, would complement the damning and pervasive characterizations of Regent Park residents by social workers, academics, and the media. In general, therefore, I aim to open up critical windows on the politics and ideology of urban redevelopment in Canada's premier metropolis.

Sean Purdy, 'Framing Regent Park: The National Film Board of Canada and the Construction of Outcast Spaces in the Inner City, 1953 and 1994', *Media, Culture and Society* 27, 4 (July 2005): 523-49. Copyright © 2005, SAGE Publications. Reprinted by permission of SAGE.

Reading and Mapping the Documentary Film in Historical Context

Scholars of film studies have long paid attention to non-fiction films as important cultural artifacts of society. At the risk of simplifying a diverse and complex literature, film studies specialists have focused their research on three key areas involved in the documentary form: technological factors, sociological dimensions, and aesthetic concerns. . . . Historians, on the other hand, have tended to view non-fiction films uncritically, as rich repositories of primary sources. As Robert Rosenstone aptly notes, historians frequently accept documentaries as 'a more accurate way of representing the past, as if somehow the images appear on the screen unmediated'. Documentaries, of course, may reveal previously unknown facts about places, people, and events. Taken as a whole, however, it is crucial to remember that we do not see in the documentary film 'the events themselves, and not the events as experienced or even as witnessed by participants, but selected images of those events carefully arranged into sequences to tell a story or to make an argument'.[2] . . . Cultural geographers, too, have studied both the industrial geographies of the film industry and the depictions of places and people within documentaries and fiction films. They have focused on mapping the 'representational' spaces of these particularly prominent media texts.[3]

. . . In this article, I adopt an interdisciplinary approach, drawing on elements of film criticism as well as historical and geographical studies. . . .

The Documentary, the City, and the NFB

Numerous studies have revealed the poignant effects of photographs in the popular construction of the 'slum' in the late nineteenth and early twentieth century.[4] Yet surprisingly few researchers have highlighted the potent role played by film in shaping popular attitudes towards the inner city and the urban poor. Yet from its origins in the late nineteenth century, film has frequently utilized the city as its subject. . . . [I]t was in the 1930s with the rise of John Grierson and the British documentary movement that film most pointedly engaged with the 'urban' for a mass audience.

Grierson, a one-time director with experience in Hollywood, founded and administered the semi-state agencies, the British Empire Marketing Board's Film Unit (1930–4), and the General Post Office Film Unit (1934–9). From 1939 to 1945, he headed the NFB in Canada and later tackled similar assignments in Australia and New Zealand.[5] From 1929 to 1952, he 'gave impetus to a movement' that resulted in the production of over 1,000 films and helped shape the technical, social, and aesthetic elements of documentary filmmaking for more than a generation.[6]

. . .

Grierson would put his ideologically charged ideas on 'slums' and the necessity of public housing to good use in the 1930s. Numerous films he oversaw in Britain charted the decrepit state of working-class housing and its effects on 'slum' dwellers. The slum clearance and public housing movement was seen as a panacea and symbol 'of progress that provides hope for the future'.[7] As Gold and Ward emphasize, however, what is left out is equally important. There is little attention to the causes of overcrowded and dilapidated housing: they are just regarded neutrally as the 'result of history and unenlightened practices'.[8] Filmmakers also purveyed a simplistic environmental determinism that portrayed blighted areas and their residents as rife with social pathologies. Moreover, working-class residents are always seen as unequivocally welcoming the new public housing developments even though we know that many communities were uprooted and destroyed with little input or consent from the actual residents. In some cases, they openly resisted the destruction of their neighbourhoods.[9] In general, 'slum dwellers' are seen purely as objects of state social policy, which downplayed structural explanations for poverty and ignored the agency of the poor.

Historians of the Grierson-founded NFB tell a similar story in the Canadian context. They have demonstrated that both management and the creative staff were imbued with a social mission to highlight the trials and tribulations, diversity and achievements, of post-war Canada. . . . While it may have been largely free from direct political intervention by its government paymasters and willing to engage with more controversial issues, it nevertheless depicted a middle-class view of the world with hackneyed images of women, workers, and the poor. It celebrated a rational and efficient ordering of the tumultuous post-war capitalist world, advocating modernizing social change within gradualist boundaries.[10] Part and parcel of this vision was the rigorous advocacy of the 'advantages of democracy' to counter the ever-present threat of Communism. . . .

The NFB of the early 1990s was, of course, a different organization than the one founded by Grierson in 1939. Highly acclaimed over the years for its innovative approaches to animation, short films, and documentary, it has received over 70 Oscar nominations. It continued to engage with a wide variety of politically controversial topics in the 1960s and in 1974 created Studio D, a production unit dedicated solely to films on women's issues by women filmmakers. It has gained a reputation for producing socially critical material and has continued to engage with themes unpalatable to the mainstream commercial studios. . . .

Regent Park and Post-war Reconstruction

Public housing in Canada emerged as part of the broader reform impulse of governments at all levels during the post-Second World War reconstruction period. The federal government constructed some dwellings for war workers and established a veterans' housing program but shortages remained severe in most urban centres throughout the 1940s and early 1950s.[11] During the war, unions, veterans' organizations, the Communist Party of Canada, and other socialists were instrumental in organizing mass demonstrations, occupations of public buildings, and militant defences of homeowners and tenants threatened with foreclosure and eviction—all of which were effective in pressuring the state for more action on the housing front.[12] . . .

Unlike the tumultuous 'Red Years' of the post-First World War era, during this time the government could count on an 'evangelistic' middle-class housing reform movement as a key ally in the 1940s and 1950s.[13] Composed of Keynesian-influenced social scientists, intellectuals, and community activists, reformers believed that comprehensive urban revitalization programs could allay the impact of post-war economic and social volatility. . . . These 'public housers' envisioned the project as a spatially and socially ordered community, free from the debilitating vagaries of 'slum life'. From the 1930s onwards, they made a successful financial and moral case for the benefits of slum clearance and rebuilding and won the local government over to an interventionist policy. The City of Toronto put a question on the 1947 municipal election ballot asking voters (at this time, only property owners and long-term leaseholders) for financial and political support for a large-scale public housing project; 62 per cent of the voters answered in the affirmative.[14] Two years later, Regent Park North, the ground-breaking effort in Canadian public housing, would open its doors amid much fanfare and celebration by City Hall and the reform lobby.

Regent Park was constructed in the working-class neighbourhood of Cabbagetown in downtown Toronto. The majority of inhabitants were descendants of English, Scottish, and Irish immigrants who worked in local factories and businesses. The area had long been characterized as a blighted area by what Seán Damer aptly calls 'slumologists'.[15] The northern section was composed largely of three-storey walk-up apartments and row houses; it began accepting low-income families and some senior citizens in 1949 and was completed by 1957. Regent Park

South, completed in 1959, exclusively housed families and comprised a mix of townhouses and five large apartment buildings. By 1960, the two sections of the development contained approximately 10,000 people, a figure reduced to approximately 7,500 residents by the 1990s. . . .

Constructing 'Outcast Spaces'

. . . Considerable historical research has been conducted on external, often racialized, depictions of 'slum' neighbourhoods, for instance, showing that the substance and rhetoric of slum representations revealed more about distinctly white, middle-class notions of what constituted a proper neighbourhood and requisite behaviour than they did about the actual physical, social, and cultural environments of the poor and minorities.[16] From the disorderly, Victorian slums of the nineteenth century to the dangerous 'no go' neighbourhoods of today, these slum representations have had a tenacious hold on the imaginations and practices of twentieth-century urban reformers, the media, state officials, and the wider public in both developed and developing nations.[17]

The Cabbagetown area razed to build Regent Park, and its residents, were subject to such a nefarious representation from the 1930s onward, which assisted the state and the reform movement in making their case for slum clearance and public housing. Most historians have overlooked the spatial dimensions of these brutalizing images of the poor. Identity and place were firmly entangled, nonetheless, in the minds of the growing cadre of slumologists. 'Deviant' spaces—frequently the urban conglomeration itself, but more particularly, disreputable slum areas of the city—produced 'deviant' people.[18] For urban reformers, as David Ward contends, slums expressed 'the presumed causal links between social isolation, and adverse environment and deviant behaviour'.[19] Thus, the urban reform campaign constructed a powerful slum narrative of Cabbagetown punctuated by exotic images of social pathology and 'dangerous spaces', such as back alleys and streets where people congregated

in a disorderly and often sexually licentious fashion. Images of poor housing conditions, poverty, filth, and moral wickedness were condensed into one striking picture of abject misery that was propagated en masse by the reform lobby, state officials, and the main media outlets in Toronto and nationally. Exoticizing the physical shabbiness of dwellings and neighbourhoods and the troublesome behaviours ostensibly produced by them was not only an instrument of moral indictment, it was also a rhetorical technique intended to sufficiently unsettle the social imagination of the public to acquire support for slum clearance and public housing.[20]

For a short period in the 1950s, the discourse of housing betterment focused on how the residents of the newly built Regent Park had been economically, socially, and morally transformed due to the new public housing environment. These arguments essentially centred on how residents had adopted 'decent' ways of living in line with the norms of post-war middle-class notions of family and community. From the 1960s to the 1990s, however, a series of economic, political, and social shifts within public housing and the larger socio-economic context shaped a new slum discourse. By the late 1960s, the project itself would increasingly be characterized as a 'slum', similar in many respects to the Cabbagetown neighbourhood that was destroyed to build it. Condemned as too large and badly designed by academics, as a haven of single mothers, welfare families, and deviants by governments and the media, a magnet for crime and drug problems by police and law and order advocates, and the site of potentially explosive 'racial' problems by many popular commentators, it had come full circle in the public mind from the 'ordered community' of the 1940s.

The media played a crucial role in constructing Regent Park as a dangerous problem area. As a number of scholars have established, the mainstream media tends to cover poor working-class, immigrant, and/or black neighbourhoods in such a way as to stress anything that runs counter to the accepted social, economic, and moral order.[21] In such a way, Regent Park was almost always characterized in all forms of the local and national media as solely a site of poverty, behavioural problems, and crime.[22] The wider public, with little or no direct experience of the project or its tenants, only received the 'bad' and the sensational from the media, significantly distorting their opinions on the project and its tenants. . . . Such harmful portrayals reinforced stigmatization by obscuring structural explanations for poverty and concealing the agency of tenants in contesting these brutalizing characterizations.[23] It is in this context that we need to situate the spatial representations of Regent Park in documentary films.

A Farewell to Oak Street

. . .

Farewell to Oak Street[24] enjoyed a mass audience markedly larger than the specialist expositions of social workers and academics. Conceived as part of an ongoing project boasting of the resilience of the country in the post-war era, the *Canada Carries On* series, it was mainly shown across the country as an introduction to popular films in the theatre. With the advent of television, it was probably rebroadcast on television numerous times, as was the custom with NFB shorts. The Housing Authority of Toronto (HAT), which managed Regent Park North, used it as one of its key propaganda tools. In 1949, Henry Matson, secretary of HAT, heeded the advice of his counterpart in the Detroit Housing Authority, J.H. Inglis, to overcome opposition to slum clearance by using visual images such as films and photographs 'to illustrate the dilapidated character of the buildings you propose to demolish' and therefore win over a sometimes reluctant public.[25] HAT personnel would play a close collaborative role in the making of the film, making suggestions for scenes and delighting in the positive publicity the film offered.[26] Throughout the first 20 years of Regent Park's history, *Farewell to Oak Street* would be shown regularly to university and high-school audiences as well as diverse community groups. In 1965, it was running

twice weekly to 'interested' groups in the community and was compulsory viewing for nurses in Toronto-area hospitals on their annual field trips to the development.[27] . . .

The film was written and produced by Gordon Burwash and directed by Grant Maclean, seasoned staffers at the NFB. Extraordinarily, it was made over a five-year period and, for a 17-minute short, its $29,000 price tag was remarkably costly at the time, demonstrating the NFB's commitment to constructing well-wrought images of the progress of the nation. Shooting of the exteriors of existing houses slated for demolition and the beginnings of construction began in the summer of 1948. Filming of the interior of 'slum' habitations commenced in the spring of 1949 and editing and voiceover narration was completed over the next four years. . . .

Burwash continued the tradition of the wartime NFB founder, John Grierson, in didactically scripting the film to make a crystal-clear propaganda statement about the physical and social depravity of the Cabbagetown slums and the modern promise of public housing. In 1949, he wrote to Matson that for the interior shots 'we would like to shoot a family in its old residence (*the more slum-like the better*), the family's moving activity (van, wheelbarrows, or what have you), and the family *joyfully taking possession of the new home*' (author's emphasis).[28] As in the classic documentary film, it aimed to project 'a generalized reality or social truth'[29] which, in the eyes of the filmmakers and contemporary reformers, consisted of the shameful contrast between the decrepit disorder of Cabbagetown and the efficiency of the new housing development.[30] To accomplish this, it mixed a real contemporary development—the ground-breaking urban renewal scheme of Canada's largest city—with fictional vignettes of the frustrations of the 'old' and the joys of the 'new' juxtaposed throughout the film to emphasize the striking contrast.

Despite its extensive use of fictionalized dramatic scenes, therefore, it was crucial that the film convey an air of authenticity and realism.[31] Each of the scenes was carefully crafted, acted, sequenced, and narrated to construct this 'realist' vision. Locations were used rather than studios; the majority of actors were either residents themselves or non-professionals, which was intended to drive home to the viewers that what they were seeing was the genuine thing; the voiceover narration by well-known veteran of CBC radio and later American television star, Lorne Greene, aimed to express the 'authority' of pro-urban renewal commentary. The NFB's press release gave viewers a hint of what to expect in the screening:

This is the story of how many Toronto families, jam-packed in the squalor of the city's slums, were transplanted to a new spacious life in the homes of Canada's first large public housing project, the Regent Park development. The film depicts the corrosive misery of six families, 19 persons in all, sharing one bathroom, one source of running water and the common shame of a life where home is a place to get out of, and tavern, moviehouse and street are refuge from sub-standard living. But the Brown's, the Bennett's and the Biggs's of the film, like 5,000 other Cabbagetown dwellers of Toronto's East End, were fortunate. The camera follows them from their Oak Street shambles to the comfort and dignity of four and five room apartment units in the 42 acres of Regent Park. There, paying rent according to their income, they find life has a new face and home is a place in which to live.[32]

Above all, the images in the film would be depicted as if they were real scenes in real lives. In this way, the filmmakers meant to emphasize the overriding social and political necessity to do away with slums and construct efficient dwelling units for the urban poor and working class.

The film opens with a conspicuous still photograph of a dilapidated Cabbagetown house. The accompanying classical music is sombre and the dreary scene is enveloped in dim and eerie light. Immediately, the vista brightens as the first buildings of Regent Park are shown in the backdrop of the project's wide-open spaces as a grocer's delivery boy makes his rounds on his bike. While Lorne Greene authoritatively announces 'not a trace' of the slum 'remains, except its people. They're still here, still occupying the same stretch of space but in a different way. Everything is sparkling, and new, and tidy and kept that way,' the camera pans to a set of clean windows and a woman sweeping the floor. The documentary switches back and forth in this way, contrasting the daily irritations and larger pathologies produced by slums with the virtues of modern project living.

The boost to social life within the home is strongly emphasized in *Farewell*, reflecting the widespread concern about inharmonious relations between husbands and wives, parents and children. One scene shot in the cramped slum home shows a family sitting down for supper, everybody strangely quiet and morose. 'Supper time for the Browns,' Lorne Greene narrates, 'is the high point of any families' day. School behind, rest and relaxation ahead, the day's adventures to talk about. Hardly a time for silence. Trouble was, the Oak St day was often best forgotten. There weren't many good days.' The frustration of the slum existence also exacerbated domestic disputes. Another section of the film depicts a husband and wife verbally sparring against the backdrop of a dark and dreary room. The narration continues, 'Not all tempers flared, some were diverted and dulled by escape' as the camera switches to an equally lifeless and dark tavern. By contrast, project life is bright and cordial. Families moving into their new units are smiling and curious. One young boy gleefully jumps into the shiny, new bathtub and the accompanying music reaches a crescendo as the whole family watches the bathwater run. The film cuts to the 'brighter and more interesting and friendlier' kitchen with its well-placed, modern, and efficient appliances. The husband puts his arm around his wife as they contemplate their new surroundings. The new supper table shows the family excitedly conversing. Other scenes tell a similar story: the father relaxing in the living room, reading the paper, and the mother joyfully carrying out domestic chores.

The film especially accentuates women's enhanced roles as mother and housewife. Yvonne Klein-Matthews has shown that NFB films of the 1940s–50s only validated women's roles as mothers and housewives, celebrating their natural homemaking virtues and warning against the perils of joining the male-dominated workplace.[33] *Farewell to Oak Street* was no exception. The flaking paint, grimy walls, filthy floors, and crowded rooms are distinguished conspicuously from the spacious rooms, new-fangled appliances, and hardwood floors of Regent Park. Domestic work by women is duly celebrated: 'A great deal of washing and scrubbing goes on nowadays. The Maclean kitchen has a new modern look as do the Maclean ladies.' In Cabbagetown, on the other hand, 'keeping clean was a daily battle and a lost cause.' One dramatized scene shows a woman futilely attempting to kill a cockroach, expressing symbolically the frustration of women's life within the slums. Disorder and confusion are represented in the slum housing by showing six separate families trying to use the same bathroom: 'Things mislaid, everyone getting in everyone's way.'

Farewell to Oak Street prominently engages with the question of children's lives as well. Kids playing happily in the new project are juxtaposed in the same scene with a group of boys playing road hockey in an area not yet demolished. The message is that the orderly play spaces of 'trees, grass, playground' are better than the 'cars [and] pavement' that plague disorderly road hockey games. Greene adds that there are 'backyards too and private entrances to homes', emphasizing the privatized orderliness of Regent's row houses. Even children's physical and sexual health is dealt with in the film. One shot portrays a teacher or nurse bringing kids home with lice in their hair. Boys and girls are shown sleeping in the same bed in the slum house, a taboo frequently condemned in the contemporary literature on housing reform. And, in probably the first depiction of sexual abuse in Canadian film, a young girl is assaulted in old

Cabbagetown by a neighbour.[34] Greene gravely states: 'Sometimes the vermin was human and the shame was secret,' playing on the widespread, if false, notion that children were more vulnerable to sexual abuse in poor neighbourhoods. Such a sensationalist tactic was also a useful means to attract wider support for public housing.[35]

The documentary also deliberates on the practical difficulties of finding affordable housing and how the rental system works at Regent Park. It ends on a shot of residents industrially going about their business while Greene sounds off on the NFB's liberal modernization appeal that there are 'too many Oak Streets for such a resourceful nation'. The soundtrack ends on a triumphal note as the camera displays an impressive aerial view of the vast development.

The NFB joined contemporary sociologists, social workers, and the media in contributing to the powerful stigmatization of inner-city workers. Even if the slum environment itself was largely to blame in these accounts, working families in Cabbagetown were portrayed as dirty, disreputable, and prone to various pathologies, a condition only redeemed in the eyes of the national film agency and reformers by the top-down, modernization of urban renewal and public housing. Only public housing, moreover, could reinstall women in their valid roles as housekeepers and mothers, and families to their central role as the bedrock of society and nation. Children, too, would benefit from a safe and orderly setting within the home and the neighbourhood, free from the lures of delinquency and sex. The medium of film with a mass, popular audience was a convenient and effective means to get across this message of the urgent necessity of social engineering.

The very tenants whose homes and lives were maligned were the first to respond to the documentary. A tenants' and homeowners' political association had been active since the outset of the Regent Park development, demanding a say in the process, criticizing high rents and other HAT policies, and the low compensation offered for their houses. They particularly resented the 'slum' label and, on the release of the film, communicated their disgust to their Conservative Member of Parliament, Charles Henry. They were upset because they had no chance to view the film beforehand or make suggestions, a right reserved only for housing officials. In the House of Commons, Henry criticized the negative portrayal of Cabbagetowners and requested that the film be withdrawn from circulation.[36] It is difficult to gauge the reception of the film among the wider population but certainly the weight of the modernizing reform impulse and its support by the media suggests that the film's central message was accepted as authoritative. The *Toronto Telegram* and the *Ottawa Citizen* defended the portrayal of the 'slums' and, even though some members of the NFB Board of Governors were sympathetic to Henry's appeal, the NFB soldiered on with the marketing and distribution of the film.[37] . . . In the process, it contributed to negative characterizations of inner-city workers and the poor in Cabbagetown, a set of harmful assumptions and ideas that would soon be applied to Regent Park dwellers themselves.

Return to Regent Park

Since this film was made only a decade ago, we have no archival records about *Return to Regent Park*;[38] I will rely on a reading of the film in the context of public housing in the 1990s. Directed by Bay Weyman, the film was financed and produced by the NFB, Weyman's Close-Up Productions, and the Canadian Broadcasting Corporation (CBC), Canada's public broadcasting network. It first aired on 6 May 1994 on CBC Newsworld's *Rough Cuts*, a weekly program that brings new national and international documentaries to the small screen. We have no viewing figures for the documentary, but it has been replayed periodically on public television in Canada and is widely available in university, public, and community libraries. In 1995, NFB head Sandra Macdonald told a federal parliamentary committee on Canadian Heritage that she was particularly proud of Weyman's film. In her nationalist vision of the NFB's role, she opined that, 'We dream of the day when . . .

Central Park West [a popular American show] will be replaced by a broadcast of *Return to Regent Park*'.[39]

The film's promotional blurb gives a good introduction to the themes of the film and deserves full citation:

> Ten thousand people live in Toronto's Regent Park, Canada's first large-scale housing project. Built in a spirit of post-WWII optimism that social problems could be corrected through urban renewal, Regent Park replaced a working-class neighbourhood with a modern, park-like community of apartment buildings.
>
> But, forty years later, it has become a paradigm of city planning failure. The physical isolation of Regent Park from the surrounding community has created a unique ghetto-like environment. Within its confines, many residents feel as if they are under siege by an army of outsiders who are using the Park as a haven for drugs, prostitution and violent crime.
>
> Frustrated by the apparent 'benign neglect' of the Metro Toronto Housing Authority, groups of Regent Park residents have banded into committees organized by residents-turned-social activists. They are now persuasive advocates of the concept that Regent Park requires radical physical redevelopment in order to be successfully reintegrated within the larger social community.
>
> Bay Weyman lets the people of Regent Park tell their own story of desperation and hope. Featuring interviews with residents, activists, community organizers, local politicians, academic planners, and the police, the film compresses three stories into one: the failure of traditional urban renewal schemes, the impact of drugs and crime on an enclosed environment, and the positive effects of social redevelopment in which people are empowered with a newborn self-respect, changing the way they think about themselves and their community.[40]

Unlike its 1953 predecessor, then, the film provides substantial room for (some of the) residents themselves to discuss life in what tenants nickname 'Regent' or simply the 'Park'. In a narrative quite similar to *Farewell to Oak Street*, however, *Return to Regent Park* sets out to engage in social criticism, directing its fire at the superblock public housing design that enclosed the project's buildings within its own discrete borders. While its techniques are more subtle and elegant, the latter film also relies on the theme of the contrast between the 'old' and 'new' to tell its story. Reflecting a common technique in socially critical documentary filmmaking,[41] it constantly juxtaposes interviews with talking heads and residents and shots of the project with old archival footage from newsreels, television, and *Farewell to Oak Street* itself, contrasting the overly optimistic and top-down planning of 1940s–50s urban reformers with the drug and crime problems in the project today and the efforts of activists to sell a physical redevelopment plan to the City of Toronto.

The 'outcast space' narratives of the 1940s and 1950s are evident in *Return to Regent Park* even if the pathologies have changed. The problem of drugs and crime in Regent Park take up a good portion of the documentary, although residents also intersperse positive comments about living in the project. In one of the first scenes, a teenage crack dealer is interviewed on the street, expressing his frustration about the lack of economic opportunities: 'Police don't care. Government don't care. They're just trying to get elected.' Yet he concludes by saying, 'Despite all the bad publicity we get, I love this park.' Betty Hubbard says, 'My old man is from the States and lived in a ghetto and he says this is heaven compared to a ghetto.' She goes on to say she's from a middle-class family and, as the camera pans out over the park from her balcony, she relates, 'When I first come here the place was great and then when the crack came out it got really bad and we started having beatings, shootings, robberies . . . .' Visibly weak and sullen, Tina Thibeault, a prostitute and crack addict who grew up in the project, talks about the nice times she had when she was

a kid and contrasts it to the problems now, seeing her own history as illustrative of the change, 'I'm to blame because I'm involved, right?'

Interspersed with the interviews are clandestine shots of drug dealing happening on the public streets and dark lanes of the development, and brutal police arrests of alleged traffickers. In one scene, one young black man threatens to break the camera and orders the crew to stop filming. Perhaps the most revealing scenes of the drug problem in the film involve George Burkle, an ex-crack addict, who was one of the key activists in the North Regent Park Residents Steering Committee (NRPRSC). As he speaks in his apartment, the camera (again clandestinely) surveys the street below showing a fistfight and the brutal beating of a black suspect by the police. Burkle explains that it is 'welfare night' when social assistance cheques are delivered and, according to him, it regularly sparks drinking, drug-taking, and fighting until the money from the cheques is all gone. In another scene, he discusses how his life has changed and how activism has given him a focus. While we listen, the viewer is shown shady scenes of drug dealing, limousines pulling up to buy drugs, and prostitutes plying their trade on the project's many narrow lane ways and courtyards. The themes of hope and despair are continually emphasized as the camera juxtaposes the 'bad' with the 'good'.

As in the slum images of *Farewell to Oak Street*, much of the film focuses on the physical deterioration of the built environment. 'The buildings are falling apart,' one resident says early on in the film. One scene shows a family moving out, quoting the father as saying, 'The people and the place you can adapt to but the housing seems to deteriorate so much. Nothing gets done too much about it.' Close-up shots of graffiti ('Fuck the Police'), 'tagging', holes in the walls, and overflowing garbage bins are revealed as the police and members of the redevelopment committee take the filmmakers on a tour of the project. While searching the corridors of one of the buildings for drug dealers, one policeman exclaims, 'If only the camera could pick up the smell.' The documentary actually aims in this scene to reveal the tangible sensual experience of physical deterioration.

As the promotional blurb emphasizes, great effort is expended in the film to highlight the role of resident activists involved in the NRPRSC. In conjunction with a new breed of urban reformers, the tenant committee rallied around a plan to physically redevelop a section of the project, which proposed to combine private-market rental units and various new commercial outlets with the traditional subsidized units. . . . Some of the most poignant scenes show the palpable frustrations of activists as they are stonewalled in their earnest efforts by the Metropolitan Toronto Housing Authority and Toronto mayor June Rowlands. The mayor misses an important meeting with the redevelopment committee and the homemade lasagna that residents had prepared for the gathering sits uneaten on a table. The sense of let-down on the part of activists is palpable as they express their anger and frustration.

. . .

One of the most remarkable scenes of the documentary actually comes near the beginning. In a suitably postmodern twist on representing the represented, the filmmakers shoot a scene of a local Toronto television station reporting in the project. Speaking from one of the internal streets of the project, the reporter comments on the crime rates, the drug problem, and the lack of jobs. Then he interviews a woman, who argues sharply,

> They should get the truth before they start reporting. I was watching it at home and it made me angry. The dark-haired reporter saying that we're 'ridden'. We're not 'ridden'! Where's the shooting going on in Regent Park if we're so ridden? Where's the drug dealing going on right now. It's not that bad. Yes, we do have it bad in the Park. But it's outsiders coming into the Park. We're not bad. I love living in Regent Park. I'm raising my kids in Regent Park, I'm raising my grandchildren in Regent Park. You've been in the Park, have you been shot yet?

A raucous debate follows between the tenants gathered on the street about the problems of the project with one woman focusing on poverty and another arguing that these problems are everywhere, showing the contested nature of the causes of stigmatization among tenants. Unfortunately, this sense of debate among tenants and alternative arguments about the problems of project living (e.g. media stigmatization, poverty) is never revisited in the documentary. From then on, the focus is on how physical redevelopment will transform the project.

Return to Regent Park offers a more stylish and less preachy look at Regent Park than *Farewell to Oak Street*. Its inclusion of the voices of the tenants themselves is a welcome addition to the documentary form. However, it also (unintentionally) produces a damning characterization of the homes, neighbourhood, and residents of Regent Park by what it focuses on and what it omits. Drugs and crime, for example, are not discussed in any kind of social or historical context. As in its predecessor, the viewer gets little sense of the whys. Why are public housing residents so poor? Why does Regent Park have a drug problem? Many of the socio-economic and ideological developments that have shaped material misery and driven a minority of residents to drug dealing and anti-social behaviour in public housing are never discussed in the film. Yet it is in this context of bitter despair that we need to place the widely publicized rise in violence and drugs in the project and elsewhere in the 1990s.[42] As the state increasingly cut funding and programs, material deprivation intensified, and a related increase in hard drug dealing has plagued the project. Drug dealers, many of whom live outside the project, have sunk roots in the project,[43] providing much-needed monetary and social benefits to young people with no futures. Despite the long-standing propensity of the Toronto media to sensationalize and blow crime figures out of proportion, particularly in regard to public housing, it is apparent that the problems of violence and drugs had increased to worrying proportions for many tenants in the early 1990s. The film leaves us with no explanation for this, lending credence to the common-sense idea that tenants themselves are individually responsible.

The image of criminality in the project, increasingly racialized in the 1980s and 1990s, was nevertheless always more powerful than the reality. Social geographers have demonstrated the powerful spatial associations of racialized representations, which link race, crime, and neighbourhood. They have argued persuasively that racialized depictions of minority groups and criminality are enhanced when linked with certain identifiable places.[44] This is only hinted at in *Return to Regent Park* when one of the (largely white) activists in the redevelopment committee claims that the 'multicultural' atmosphere of the project has impeded the establishment of law and order due to the fears of the police of being labelled racist. The film otherwise neglects the lengthy history of tensions between black tenants and the police, which has centred on allegations of police brutality and other forms of unfair 'racialized' policing.[45] As numerous studies of police culture have commented, many police officers perceive certain parts of the 'public' to be their enemy, especially those populations labelled as problematic and dangerous—the poor, communities of colour, and ethnic minorities.[46] The activists cited in the film complained of a lack of security in the project and police ineffectiveness in patrolling the project. We are not told that this same group of tenants has persistently lobbied for a firmer police presence based on a mix of 'hard-nosed zero tolerance' and 'community policing' with extensive foot patrols, an approach that has put it at odds with many black tenants.[47] Indeed, frustration with the police had reached an explosive boiling point by the mid-1990s. It came as little surprise that soon after social assistance rates were savagely chopped by 21.6 per cent by the Ontario Conservative government in 1995, pent-up frustration with police brutality and desperation with living conditions led to a riot

against police in Regent Park involving several hundred residents and 100 police officers.[48] Yvonne Beasley, mother of Sydney Hemmings, a young black man murdered in the project on 5 July 2001, angrily expressed these frustrations when confronting the police in a public forum: 'My question to you is, how exactly do the youth of Regent Park trust the police in the neighbourhood, when all it is to them is niggers killing niggers?'[49] *Return to Regent Park* gives us little sense of the tensions and frustrations lying beneath the surface of daily life in the project in the early 1990s.

The frequent resort to juxtaposing historical archival footage of urban planners from the 1950s and 1960s with contemporary 'experts' to show up the 'naiveté of the past'[50] also implicitly comes down on the side of the new 'experts' without acknowledging that they too have their own political axe to grind. Structural deterioration of the buildings has been a mainstay of recent criticism but the housing form and site design of Regent Park have long been the target of academic and popular criticism. Almost all commentary on the built environment of the project highlights the 'ugliness' of the buildings, the unsuitability of high-rises for children, the segregation of the development from the surrounding neighbourhood, and the lack of individually definable and private space within the project. Much of this criticism takes as its starting point Jane Jacobs' 1961 book, *Life and Death of Great American Cities*, which argues that urban design elements themselves can enable healthy and safe social interaction by providing spaces that encourage natural meetings and other friendly interactions. She believed that modernist planning, especially public housing projects, had destroyed this 'natural' urban fabric.[51] . . . *Toronto Star* reporter Christian Cotroneo describes Regent Park as sprawling 'in all its Soviet sameness, flanked by anonymous apartment blocks'.[52] . . . The only solution to Regent Park's problems, these authors conclude, is wholesale redevelopment of the built environment to create safe and orderly communities.

Such arguments, echoed in the Regent Park redevelopment proposal discussed in the film, tread dangerously close to the same 'environmental determinism' of post-war planners and the state. Physical form does influence human life and behaviour but it cannot be treated as an independent phenomenon or factor. . . . Environmental determinist arguments not only deflect attention away from the wider socio-economic problems of poor project dwellers, they discourage, as Keith Jacobs and Tony Manzi argue, 'new possibilities and alternative visions' to deal with the crisis of affordable housing.[53]

It also stretches belief to argue . . . that the problems of crime in public housing can be solved by mere changes to the built environment. Design changes making it less easy for drug dealers to hide or escape from the police, or to integrate living with public spaces, may enhance some tenants' sense of well-being, but it does nothing to deal with the root problems of economic misery, which fuel the drug trade and other security concerns. . . . David Harvey makes a similar point in arguing that such general design approaches falsely contend 'that the shaping of spatial order can be the foundation for a new moral and aesthetic order'[54] bringing us back to the authoritarian utopianism of 1950s urban renewal.

. . . Certainly Regent Park needs substantial renovations due to the aging buildings and infrastructure. Improving design may be worthwhile but it does not provide jobs or adequate funding for local schools. Nor does it tackle police brutality against black youth. These are the key reasons for socio-economic marginalization and it is this lack of power in society that leads to the often exaggerated but nevertheless real anti-social and harmful behaviour that is wrapped up with drugs and violence. In *Return to Regent Park*, we are told that redevelopment may promise a sense of stability and social order in a time of rapid socio-economic change. Yet it also 'serves to legitimize the ideological shift presenting the problems of housing as attributable to individuals

rather than a failure of government' as Jacobs and Manzi argue for the similar British case.[55]

Conclusion

. . .

Farewell to Oak Street meshed neatly with the housing reform, social work philosophy, and media attitudes of the 1940s and 1950s, which prescribed that the poor needed to live in 'efficient' and 'harmonious' communities purportedly like the rest of society. The film envisioned that this desired homogeneity and social cohesion could only obtain within a profoundly middle-class paradigm of private family life and responsible conduct in line with the social order. Neither the NFB nor public housing observers ventured structural explanations for the social problems of poor families, such as unstable employment, pitiful social services, a biased educational system, and sheer lack of socio-economic opportunities for those falling outside the accepted norms of suitable family and social life such as single parents. In the tumultuous post-war social and economic context, however, the scientific legitimacy of liberal modernization plans and the popular saliency of 'realist' documentary film ensured that it sold well to the public. In this respect, Paula Rabinowitz's argument that, 'documentary films provide a stability to an ever-changing reality, freezing the images for later instructional use' is particularly pertinent.[56] The 'visual ideological' arguments in *Farewell to Oak Street* helped paint a nefarious portrait of the inner-city poor that would be used for two decades to bolster the arguments of the urban renewal movement.

In contrast with its 1953 counterpart, *Return to Regent Park* allows some residents of Regent Park to speak themselves directly about their problems and hopes for the future. Nevertheless, its steadfast concentration on the physical design deficiencies of the project provides only a very partial understanding of the problems that tenants face. Lacking any sense of social, economic, and political context concerning why Regent Park and its residents were territorially stigmatized, the documentary leaves the viewer with the impression that marginalization stems largely from the individual problems of tenants themselves. Moreover, we get little indication in the film that tenants contested this stigmatization in various ways. The film, therefore, unwittingly assists in the social construction of the project as an 'outcast space', contributing to the damning social and economic exclusion faced by project dwellers.

Notes

This article was first presented at the International Geographical Union Conference, Commission on the Cultural Approach in Geography, Rio de Janeiro, June 2003. The author would like to thank conference participants and organizer, Mauricio Abreu, the editors of *Media, Culture & Society*, Bryan D. Palmer and Richard Harris for helpful suggestions. Special thanks to Philip Alperson, Richard Immerman, and members of the Department of History at Temple University for a welcoming and stimulating intellectual atmosphere.

1. National Film Board of Canada (NFB), *Farewell to Oak Street*. Directed by Grant Maclean. Narrated by Lorne Greene. 1953.
2. Robert Rosenstone, 'History in Images/History in Words: Reflections on the Possibility of Really Putting History onto Film', *The American Historical Review* 93, 5 (1988): 1179–80.
3. Chris Lukinbeal, 'Reel-to-reel Urban Geographies: The Top Five Cinematic Cities in North America', *The California Geographer* 38, 1 (1998): 64–78.
4. Peter B. Hales, *Silver Cities: The Photography of American Urbanization, 1839–1915* (Philadelphia, PA: Temple University Press, 1984). . .
5. Erik Barnouw, *Documentary: A History of Non-fiction Film*, 2nd edn (New York: Oxford University Press, 1993), 87–99.
6. John R. Gold and Stephen V. Ward, 'Of Plans and Planners: Documentary Film and the Challenge of the Urban Future, 1935–52', in David B. Clarke, ed., *The Cinematic City* (London: Routledge, 1997), 63.
7. Ibid., 65.
8. Ibid.
9. Kevin Brushett, 'Blots on the Face of the City: The Politics of Slum Housing and Urban Renewal in Toronto, 1940–1970', PhD thesis (Queen's University,

2001), and Sean Purdy, 'From Place of Hope to Outcast Space: Territorial Regulation and Tenant Resistance in Regent Park Housing Project, 1949–1999', PhD thesis (Queen's University, 2003).
10. A list of all NFB films dealing with urban issues over a period of 50 years can be found at the NFB English Language Collections Website, Urbanism—Housing and Public Housing, www.nfb.ca (consulted 10 Nov. 2003).
11. Richard Harris and Tricia Shulist, 'Canada's Reluctant Housing Program: The Veterans' Land Act, 1942–75', *Canadian Historical Review* 82, 2 (2001): 252–83.
12. John Bacher, *Keeping to the Marketplace: The Evolution of Canadian Housing Policy* (Montreal and Kingston: McGill-Queen's University Press, 1989); and Brushett, 'Blots on the Face of the City'.
13. 'Evangelistic' was the word used to describe the efforts of the reformers of the period by one of their leading members, Humphrey Carver, in his memoirs (*Compassionate Landscape* [Toronto: University of Toronto Press, 1978], 82). For a fuller treatment, see Sean Purdy, 'Scaffolding Citizenship: Housing Policy and Nation Formation in Canada, 1900–1950', in Robert Menzies, Dorothy Chunn, and Robert Adomski, eds, *Canadian Citizenship: Historical Readings* (Peterborough: Broadview Press, 2002), ch. 6.
14. Albert Rose, *Regent Park: A Study in Slum Clearance* (Toronto: University of Toronto Press, 1958).
15. Seán Damer, *From Moorepark to 'Wine Alley': The Rise and Fall of a Glasgow Housing Scheme* (Edinburgh: University of Edinburgh Press, 1989).
16. Kay J. Anderson, *Vancouver's Chinatown: Racial Discourse in Canada, 1875–1980* (Montreal and Kingston: McGill–Queen's University Press, 1991).
17. Gerry Mooney, 'Urban Disorders', in Steve Piles, Christopher Brook, and Gerry Mooney, eds, *Unruly Cities?* (London: Routledge, 2000), 54–99.
18. Marianna Valverde, *The Age of Light, Soap, and Water: Moral Regulation in English Canada, 1900–1920* (Toronto: McClelland & Stewart, 1991), 132.
19. David Ward, 'The Progressives and the Urban Question: British and American Responses to Inner-city Slums, 1880–1920', *Transactions, Institute of British Geographers* 9, 4 (1984): 304.
20. Purdy, 'From Place of Hope to Outcast Space', and Judith Walkowitz, *City of Dreadful Delight: Narratives of Sexual Danger in Late-Victorian London* (Chicago: University of Chicago Press, 1992).
21. Robert M. Entman, 'Blacks in the News: Television, Modern Racism and Cultural Change', *Journalism Quarterly* 69, 2 (1992): 341–61, and Patricia M. Evans and Karen J. Swift, 'Single Mothers and the Press: Rising Tides, Moral Panic, and Restructuring Discourses', in Sheila M. Neysmith, ed., *Restructuring Caring Labour:*

Discourse, State Practice, and Everyday Life (Don Mills, ON: Oxford University Press 2000), 73–92 . . .

22. Purdy, 'From Place of Hope to Outcast Space'.

23. Sudhir Venkatesh, *American Project: The Rise and Fall of a Modern Ghetto* (Cambridge, MA: MIT Press, 2000), and Rhonda Y. Williams, 'Living Just Enough in the City: Change and Activism in Baltimore's Public Housing, 1940–1980', PhD thesis (University of Pennsylvania, 1998). It is important to emphasize that Regent Park residents were not ill-fated spectators of their own futures or empty recipients of the ideological messages conveyed by outside critics. Stigmatization was contested at all levels over the years (see Purdy, 'From Place of Hope to Outcast Space', . . . and Purdy, 'By the People, For the People: Tenant Organizing in Toronto's Regent Park Housing Project in the 1960s and 1970s', *Journal of Urban History* 30, 4 (2004): 519–48.

24. NFB, *Farewell to Oak Street*, 17 minutes.

25. James H. Inglis, 'To Henry Matson', City of Toronto Archives, Housing Authority of Toronto Papers, RG 28, B, Box 33, File: 'Regent Park Rate Payers and Tenants' Association, 1947–1954', 1 June 1949.

26. Henry Matson to Donald Mulholland, City of Toronto Archives, Housing Authority of Toronto, RG 28, B, Box 41, File: Central Mortgage and Housing Corporation, 1947–1949, 7 Feb. 1949.

27. Robert Bradley and Gordon Noble, City of Toronto Archives, Housing Authority of Toronto Papers, RG 28, B, Box 41, File: '1965–1968 N', 1 June 1965.

28. Gordon Burwash, 'To Henry Matson', City of Toronto Archives, Housing Authority of Toronto Papers, RG 28, B, Box 41, File: 'CMHC Progress Reports, 1947–1945', 29 Apr. 1949.

29. Peter Morris, 'After Grierson: The National Film Board, 1945–1953', *Journal of Canadian Studies* 16, 1 (1981): 7.

30. Donald Mulholland, 'To H.L. Luffman', City of Toronto Archives, Housing Authority of Toronto Papers, RG 28, B, Box 41, File: 'CMHC Progress Reports, 1947–1945', 27 Apr. 1949.

31. Morris, 'After Grierson', 7–9.

32. NFB, Press Release for *Farewell to Oak Street*, City of Toronto Archives, Housing Authority of Toronto Papers, RG 28, B, Box 36, File: 'Regent Park North: Statements by Mayor, 1949–1955', 1953.

33. Yvonne Klein-Matthews, 'How They Saw Us: Images of Women in the National Film Board Films of the 1940s and 1950s', *Atlantis* 4, 1 (1979): 20–33.

34. Gary Evans, *In the National Interest: A Chronicle of the National Film Board of Canada from 1949 to 1989* (Toronto: University of Toronto Press, 1991), 37.

35. Brian Low, *NFB Kids: Portrayals of Children by the National Film Board of Canada, 1939–1989* (Waterloo: Wilfred Laurier University Press, 2002), 85–6.

36. Brushett, 'Blots on the Face of the City', 97.

37. Evans, *In the National Interest*, 37, n29, 346–7.

38. NFB, *Return to Regent Park*. Directed by Bay Weyman. 1994, 55 minutes.

39. Parliamentary Committee on Canadian Heritage, URL (consulted Apr. 2003): http://www.parl.gc.ca/committees/heri/evidence/114_95–12–14/heri114_blk101.html. 1995.

40. NFB, *Return to Regent Park*.

41. Dan Georgakas, 'Malpractice in the Radical American Documentary', *Cinéaste* 16 (1987–8): 46–9.

42. Iain Ferguson and Michael Lavalette, 'Postmodernism, Marxism and Social Work', *European Journal of Social Work* 2, 1 (1999): 27–40 . . .

43. Don Gillmor, 'The Punishment Station', *Toronto Life* January (1996): 46–55.

44. Peter Jackson, 'Policing Difference: "Race" and Crime in Metropolitan Toronto', in Peter Jackson and J. Penrose, eds, *Constructions of Race, Place and Nation* (London: University College Press, 1993), and Peter Jackson, 'Constructions of Criminality: Police–Community Relations in Toronto', *Antipode* 26, 2 (1994): 216–35 . . .

45. *Toronto Star*, 'Treatment Differs by Division', 19 Oct. 2002, URL (consulted Jan. 2003): www.thestar.com.

46. Neil Websdale, *Policing the Poor: From Slave Plantation to Public Housing* (Boston: Northeastern University Press, 2001), ch. 6.

47. Jim Ward Associates, *The Report on a Study to Identify and Address Police–Community Issues in Regent Park* (Toronto: Jim Ward Associates, 1996).

48. Gillmor, 'The Punishment Station'.

49. CBC (Canadian Broadcasting Corporation), 'Making Peace, Ending the Violence', Town Hall Discussion, CBC Toronto; URL (consulted 3 June 2002): http://www.cbc.ca.

50. Paula Rabinowitz, 'Wreckage Upon Wreckage: History, Documentary and the Ruins of Memory', *History and Theory*, 32, 2 (1993): 133.

51. Jane Jacobs, *Life and Death of Great American Cities* (New York: Bantam Books, 1964), Introduction.

52. Christian Cotroneo, 'Dynamic Duo Delivers Christmas', *Toronto Star*, 16 Dec. 2002, URL (consulted 2 Mar. 2003): www.thestar.com.

53. Keith Jacobs and Tony Manzi, 'Urban Renewal and the Culture of Conservatism: Changing Perceptions of the Tower Block and Implications for Contemporary Renewal Initiatives', *Critical Social Policy* 18, 2 (1998): 170.

54. David Harvey cited in Peter Marcuse, 'The New Urbanism: Dangers So Far', *DISP Online* (2000), URL (consulted 2 Mar. 2003): www.orl.arch.ethz.ch/disp/pdf/140_1.pdf.

55. Jacobs and Manzi, 'Urban Renewal and the Culture of Conservatism', 167–8.

56. Rabinowitz, 'Wreckage Upon Wreckage', 120–1.

9

—— Visualizing Home ——

The cult of domesticity that arose in the Victorian era produced a wide range of imagery about domestic space, a trend that certainly continues today. Presented here are three forms of visual culture in which the ideals of home were cultivated: floor plans, photography, and advertisements. Of these three, it is perhaps easiest to acknowledge the subjectivity of advertisements, for they were intended to convince audiences that they 'needed' to fill their homes with consumer goods. Yet it is important that we do not privilege floor plans and photographs simply as objective images of domestic space-as-it-was; each played active roles in the societies that produced and used them. Indeed, it is hardly coincidental that the advertisements included here used both photographs and floor plans to sell their wares.

While we can 'read' these images to better appreciate how Canadians have historically ordered their domestic spaces, we learn even more from these images about the ideals of domestic space dominant in the period. Keep in mind, then, the content, the form, and the intended audience of these images.

Series 1: Domestic Visions

Architects designed buildings for both urban and rural Canada, but it was in the exploding cities of the late nineteenth and twentieth centuries where their work changed how public and private spaces were being built. In doing so, architects were fundamental in constructing urban landscapes and, thus, the face of modern, industrial Canada.

Figures 1 and 2 are floor plans for a middle-class Victorian row house on Jarvis Street in Toronto. This architectural style was imported from Britain, and although rarely found in rural areas or small towns, row houses were common in many Canadian cities.

1. In what ways does the floor plan depict an ideal Victorian society with respect to gender and class? How is work in the home separated from play and family? What other separations can you see?

2. Examine the floor plan and note which rooms are located closest to the street and which rooms are located at the back of the house. What is the significance of this distinction? Which rooms are privileged by this organization and why?

Figure 3 is a floor plan of a Kwakwaka'wakw (Kwakiutl) longhouse, and Figure 4 is a photograph of a Kwakwaka'wakw village, both produced in the late nineteenth century. The photograph was taken in 1881 by Edward Dossetter, travelling through by ship. The floor plan was sketched by anthropologist Franz Boas (1858–1942), who spent much of his professional life studying the First Nations of Canada's west coast and, like many of his fellow anthropologists, was very interested in Native domestic spaces. In the name of science, Boas used rigorous schematic plans, photographs, and material specimens to produce an 'objective' representation of everyday Kwakwaka'wakw life.

However, the cultural context of nineteenth-century anthropology indelibly shaped these scientific views, as noted in Paige Raibmon's study (Chapter 3). Therefore, such sources require a careful reading, set against the cultural perspective of the fieldworker.

The legend and symbols on the floor plan are from the original, and the language in the legend is also that of Boas. Terms in quotation marks, such as 'middle forehead', represent Boas's translation of the Aboriginal term. Also, only the exterior lines on the plan represent walls. The other lines represent beams that were used to frame the longhouse as well as the embankments that were built around the interior to create a separate level in case of flooding.

1. What would social reformers and missionaries approve and disapprove of in the ordering of domestic space in the longhouse (Figure 3) and in the organization of the village (Figure 4)?
2. How has Boas sought to 'prove' the cultural worth of the Kwakwa̱ka'wakw? Why, for example, does his diagram suggest the presence of walls around the 'bedrooms'?
3. Compare the arrangement of space in Figures 3 and 4 with that of the first two floor plans from urban Canada. What are the similarities and differences in the organization? What accounts for these differences? How might Boas's reading of the Kwakwa̱ka'wakw interior space be shaped by an understanding of 'civilized' domesticity as embodied in Figures 1 and 2?

Series 2: Exhibition and Surveillance

In early twentieth-century Canada, the surveillance of homes went beyond Native communities. Facing rapid urbanization and immigration, expanding cities across Canada struggled to manage and regulate chronic poor housing conditions. As James Opp demonstrates in Chapter 4, social reformers used a documentary style of photography to 'expose' slum conditions and draw moral lessons. In different forms, the practice of 'experts' deploying visual evidence to construct dangerous urban spaces has continued up to the present, as Sean Purdy argues in his analysis of two NFB films about Toronto's Regent Park (Chapter 8).

The photographs included in this series were taken by Arthur Goss, a photographer employed by Toronto's Department of Public Works. Goss's images were used by the city's Department of Health in its efforts to produce a wide-ranging social survey. Filed alongside photographs of the working poor were promotional advertisements from Mott's Ironworks, a New York-based manufacturer of plumbing fixtures which offered illustrations of ideal domestic spaces. The gap between these two sets of images is not one of 'ideal' versus 'reality'; both should be regarded as social constructions of space, projecting middle-class assumptions of how health, environment, and cleanliness relate to each other. Such images were staples of multiple exhibits of public health that toured the country, including the annual Canadian National Exhibition (CNE) in Toronto.

1. Unlike the photographs analyzed by Opp, these images focus on kitchens and bathrooms. Why would social reformers consider these spaces areas of concern?
2. Analyze the compositional elements of the images, especially noting the use of light and darkness. How do these aspects reflect middle-class assumptions?
3. How could such images be put on display as part of a public education campaign? What kind of narrative would this visual evidence suggest?

Series 3: Home and Consumption

The 1921 census was the first to show that as many Canadians were living in cities as in rural areas, and the gap between urban and rural populations only grew in subsequent decennial censuses. Becoming increasingly 'urban' carried with it a number of significant changes for the social history of Canada. For example, a market culture solidified itself even as Canada's economy underwent tremendous upheaval and a debilitating depression during the 1930s. Advertising became more systematic and scientific in its methods, seeking to promote and naturalize consumption as an act of everyday life as both need and pleasure. In both regards, women as consumers were of particular importance. Women's periodicals, such as the fashion magazine *Chatelaine* and the housekeeping magazine *Canadian Home Journal*, provided outlets for these advertisers while also providing advice and instruction for their readers. The following two images (Figures 10 and 11) are examples of how advertisers sought to navigate the urban market culture of the interwar years and to speak to the variety of women consumers in this era of changing gender identities and experiences.

1. What does the Lux advertisement suggest about gender and power relations in the 1930s?
2. How does each advertisement lay claim to a 'modern' lifestyle for newlywed women? How do the advertisements appeal to gender roles to encourage consumption in the midst of the Great Depression?
3. Although both advertisements appeared in 1934, what elements in each suggest they were intended for different audiences?

Series 4: Suburban Landscapes

The post-1945 era gave rise to a new era of suburban living. Empowered by the creation of new financing options, government programs, and a general boom in the economy, a generation who had lived through a massive depression and another world war enthusiastically

made their way into the hundreds of thousands of new homes being built on the peripheries of Canada's major cities. As Chris Dummitt emphasizes in Chapter 7, this era was defined in part by a return to 'normal' gender relations. Looking back at the turbulence of the Depression era and the upheavals of World War II, many felt that women's roles had strayed too far from the traditional Victorian ideals of home and family. Set against the backdrop of the Cold War, by the mid-1950s a suburban, nuclear family was celebrated as the epitome of the democratic West's superior way of living, a bulwark against the threat of communism. The food, kitchens, and consumerism associated with Western abundance were, according to Franca Iacovetta and Valerie Korinek (Chapter 6), key ingredients in facilitating the assimilation and acculturation of immigrants in the post-war era. When examining the images in this series, carefully read the text in the advertisements and consider the following questions:

1. Examine the floor plans of Figures 12 and 13. What has been the most significant shift in domestic space compared to the Victorian period (Figures 1 and 2)? What room(s) are located most centrally and would receive the most traffic?
2. How are these houses designed to fit a 'suburban' lifestyle? What are the expectations of the builders in relation to the people who might occupy these homes?
3. How do the advertisements in Figures 14, 15, and 16 produce gendered assumptions regarding domestic space? How do they define or reinforce the proper social roles occupied by men and women? How have representations of masculinity shifted from the 1950s to the 1970s?
4. Carefully examine the representations of children in the advertisements. How are the expectations for children gendered? What roles do children play in defining suburban spaces?

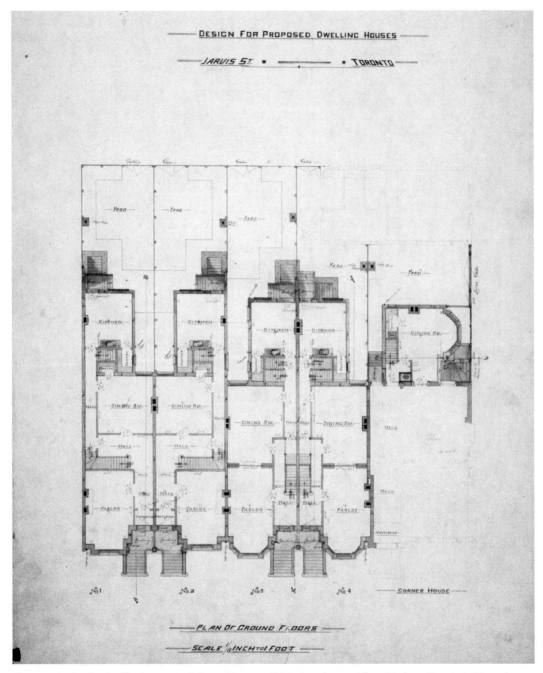

Figure 1. Design for dwelling house, Jarvis Street, Toronto, 1887, plan of ground floor, Mathew Sheard. Archives of Ontario, J.C.B. and E.C. Horwood Collection, C11–658–0–1 (628a)7. Also printed in Peter Ward, *A History of Domestic Space: Privacy and the Canadian Home* (Vancouver: University of British Columbia Press, 1999), 32.

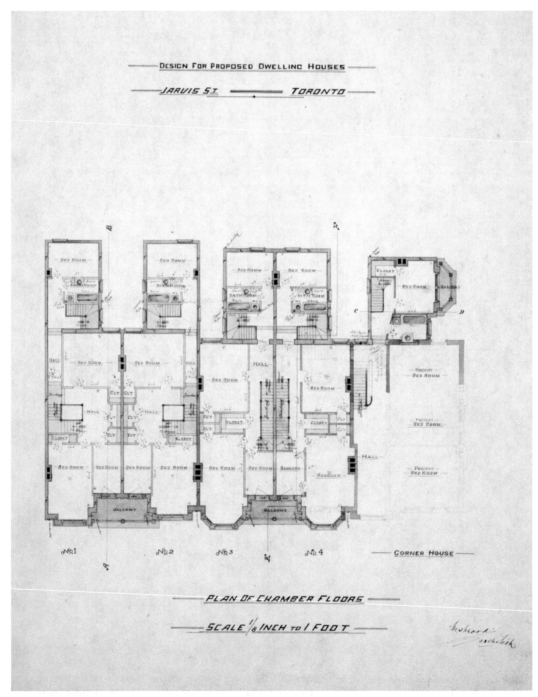

Figure 2. Design for dwelling house, Jarvis Street, Toronto, 1887, plan of chamber floor, Mathew Sheard. Archives of Ontario, J.C.B. and E.C. Horwood Collection, C11–658–0–1 (628a)8. Also printed in Peter Ward, *A History of Domestic Space: Privacy and the Canadian Home* (Vancouver: University of British Columbia Press, 1999), 33.

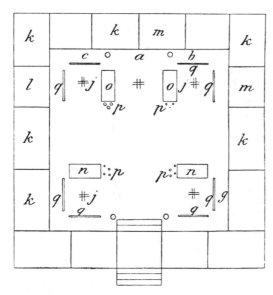

Legend
a - 'middle forehead'
b - 'right forehead'
c – 'left forehead'
f – 'upriver'
g – 'downriver'
j – 'house fire' (which Boas also uses '#'
    to signify)
k – bedrooms (on embankments)
l – firewood
m – boxes containing provisions
n, o – seat of the housewife
p – cooking utensils
q – other seats

Note: Some information has been removed
from this image for the sake of clarity.

Figure 3. Plan of a Kwakw<u>a</u>ka'wakw longhouse, from Franz Boas, *The Jesup North Pacific Expedition*, vol. V, part II (Leiden: E.J. Brill Ltd, 1909; reprint, AMS Press, 1975), 415.

Figure 4. Edward Dossetter, photograph of Humdaspe, Vancouver Island, 1881. Image 42298, courtesy the Library, American Museum of Natural History.

Figure 5. Arthur Goss, photograph, 1913. City of Toronto Archives, Series 372, ss0032, it0247.

Figure 6. Arthur Goss, photograph, 1913. City of Toronto Archives, Series 372, ss0032, it0251.

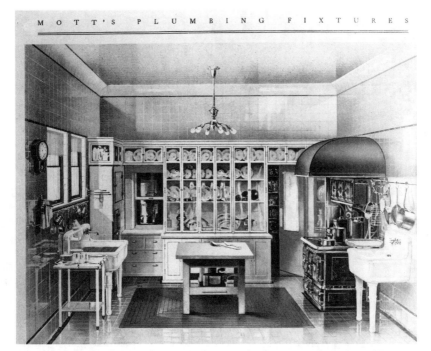

Figure 7. Illustration from catalogue, Mott's Ironworks, 1912. City of Toronto Archives, Series 372, ss0032, it0124.

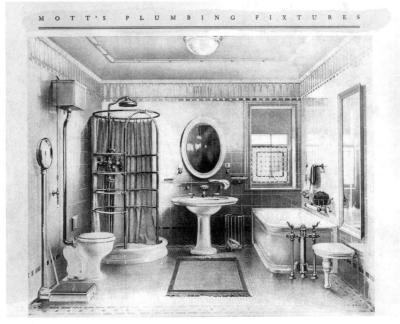

Figure 8. Illustration from catalogue, Mott's Ironworks, 1912. City of Toronto Archives, Series 372, ss0032, it0127.

Figure 9. Advertisement for Lux (laundry soap), 'More Stocking Runs?—You'll Ruin me Babs', *Chatelaine*, Feb. 1934. Lux is a trademark of Unilever.

Figure 10. Advertisement for *Canadian Home Journal* (Consolidated Press, Ltd), 'Meet Mrs. Modern', *Saturday Night*, 8 Sept. 1934. Reprinted with permission of *Chatelaine*.

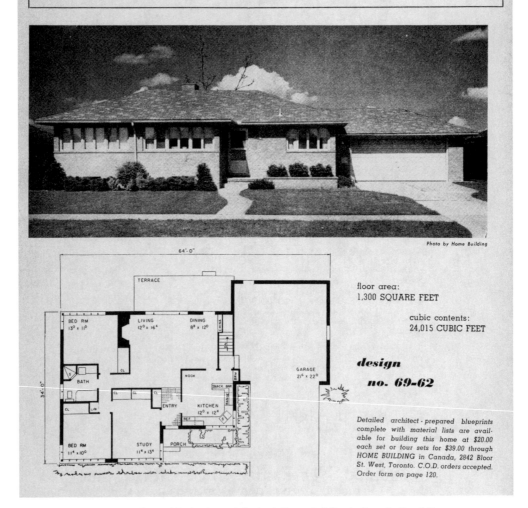

CONVENIENCE-PLANNED
for lasting satisfaction

THIS home is sure to be a favourite with SH readers for it meets just about every planning requirement of the average Canadian family. Attractively landscaped with well placed foundation shrubbery, the exterior combines bark face buff brick (veneer), brown-and-grey shaded roof, and very light mist green for trim and garage door.

The centre hall arrangement provides excellent traffic circulation. While the room to the left of the entry hall is indicated in the sketch plan as a study, most families will of course use it as a third bedroom. The vanity-equipped bathroom is much above-average in size—boasts a separate shower in addition to the bath.

The 145 square foot kitchen is brought up to the front and comes complete with built-in snack bar, corner sink, broom closet and dining nook. Notice its excellent placement in relation to basement stairs and the garage. A full basement is provided. Plans give full details for all built-ins.

Photo by Home Building

floor area:
1,300 SQUARE FEET

cubic contents:
24,015 CUBIC FEET

design

no. 69-62

Detailed architect - prepared blueprints complete with material lists are available for building this home at $20.00 each set or four sets for $39.00 through HOME BUILDING in Canada, 2842 Bloor St. West, Toronto. C.O.D. orders accepted. Order form on page 120.

Figure 11. 'Convenience—Planned for lasting satisfaction', *Home Building in Canada: Small Homes*, 1960 edition (Toronto: Walkers Publishing, 1960), 100.

J. E. HOARE, Architect

Owner S. J. Reid of North Toronto, Ontario, is full of praise for this new ranch-style home. His only regret was that our picture was taken before a flagstone terrace had been added, and the landscaping completed!

We agree that the plan is particularly good, and the exterior most attractive. Outer walls are red brick, combined with white vertical boards. Roof is black. House was erected by H. A. Hoare, builder, and contains 25,600 cubic feet, without garage.

The home owner says:

"It's Comfortable and Convenient"

Figure 12. 'The home owner says: "It's Comfortable and Convenient"', *Home Building in Canada: Small Homes,* 1951 edition (Toronto: Walkers Publishing, 1951), 140.

"To the King's Taste!"

...AND THAT PRACTICAL *CRANE* SINK
IS TO THE LADY'S!

IT'S JUST the kind she wanted for *her* step-saving kitchen — a flat rim, lightweight, stain-proof Porcelain-on-Steel model that's installed flush with a continuous counter top. Low in cost, it has enduring easy-to-clean finish — handy swinging spout faucet and finger-tip "Dial-Ese" controls.

Your plans may call for something a little different and more elaborate—for a sink-and-drainboard combination, perhaps. If so, you'll find it, too, in the complete Crane line—which includes dozens of modern types, with single or double basins, single or double drainboards—

from which you can select the right sink for your particular needs, with the size, depth and work area you desire — to fit your taste, your space and your budget.

For complete information ask your Plumbing and Heating Contractor. He'll be glad to tell you all about Crane-quality sinks, built for endurance, convenience and easy cleaning.

For every home... For every budget

The Preferred Plumbing   1-5224

CRANE LIMITED • GENERAL OFFICE: 1170 BEAVER HALL SQUARE, MONTREAL • 6 CANADIAN FACTORIES • 18 CANADIAN BRANCHES

Figure 13. Advertisement for Crane Ltd (Montreal), 'To the King's Taste!', *Canadian Homes and Gardens*, Sept. 1952.

This floor is composed of Dominion Jaspé Linoleum tiles. Patterns J-720 and J-72

This floor reflects a thoughtful husband!

"The floor in your kitchen," said my husband when we were planning it, "must be the kind that will save you work. I want you to have lots of leisure to enjoy yourself."

That's how linoleum came in. Our dealer told us it was the only answer — easy to keep colourful and clean even on the muddiest days, easy on the feet and — this really pleased my husband — easy on the budget!

I'm delighted with the result. Linoleum has everything!

If *you* are planning to build or renovate, consult your dealer or flooring contractor. Ask for comparative prices of linoleum and other floors. And keep in mind that linoleum is colourful, resilient, easy to keep clean . . . and that its durability has been time-tested by forty year's wear on Canadian floors.

The kitchen above and breakfast nook here say a cheery "Good morning" 365 days a year. Let us have your name and address so that we can send you colourful FREE literature which will open your eyes as to what is being done to create individual, delightful, durable floors for every room in the house. Sixty-five colours and patterns to choose from.

DOMINION *Jaspé* LINOLEUM TILES

BEAUTIFUL · RESILIENT · TIME-TESTED

Also Marboleum · Battleship (plain) in tiles or by the yard . . . products of

DOMINION OILCLOTH & LINOLEUM COMPANY LIMITED
MONTREAL

1952 is our 80th Anniversary

Figure 14. Advertisement for Dominion Oilcloth and Linoleum Co. (Montreal), 'This floor reflects a thoughtful husband!', *Canadian Homes and Gardens*, Sept. 1952.

Figure 15. Advertisement for Campeau Corporation, 'Kanata: for the two of you', *Ottawa Citizen*, 4 July 1978. Also reprinted in Doug Fischer and Ralph Willsey, eds, *Each Morning Bright: 160 Years of Selected Readings* (Ottawa Citizen Group Inc., 2005), 382.

Part Two

—— At Work ——

Work is the most thoroughly studied subject in Canadian social history, and it has also been central to the debates that have swirled around and within the field. In part, this is a reflection of the subject matter. The challenges of everyday life, as well as many of its opportunities, have historically involved questions of labour in one form or another. It is hardly surprising, then, that historians concerned with the study of social life—both its experiences and the structures that shape them—should spend so much time researching, thinking, and writing about the historical conditions of work. Labour, work, and the working class have been and remain among the most vibrant and innovative fields of social historical scholarship.

Historians of work have reshaped our historical understanding of Canada's transition in the late nineteenth and early twentieth centuries from a mostly rural, agrarian country to a mostly urban, industrial country. Until the 1970s, the study of this 'great transformation' usually focused on broad economic patterns, various government trade policies, and the accomplishments of merchants and businessmen. After 1970, however, historians increasingly called attention to the experience and identities of workers and argued that their blood and sweat had made possible a more industrial Canada. Epitomized by the now classic studies by Bryan Palmer and Greg Kealey, historians were especially interested in understanding how workers organized themselves into craft guilds, fraternal orders, and unions. They explored how workers accommodated and resisted such things as the deskilling of labour through new technologies and the reorganization of factory work under the scientific management theories of Frederick W. Taylor. At the heart of these analyses was an argument that a distinct working-class culture was produced in Canada that owed much to worker organizations and to the often tense relationships that existed between workers, their bosses, and a government that was often little more than a handmaiden to the interests of capitalists.

The 1980s and 1990s brought some change to the historical study of work. The convergence of this early social history of labour with other areas of social historical research, especially the history of women, the history of families, and the history of education, deepened our understanding of the impact of industrialization in all sectors of everyday life. Feminist scholarship was particularly important in calling historians' attention to the non-waged work of women and children within the home. Immigration historians demonstrated how work could function as a form of social currency, reinforcing and delimiting community boundaries as new arrivals turned to earlier generations of immigrants for assistance in the settlement process. Education historians showed us how the decision to send or not to send children to school was contingent on their contribution to the family economy. The sum total of this and other research was that we gained a much more complete understanding that gender, ethnicity, race, age, and sexuality also affected the experience and identities of workers. Awareness of social class remained of paramount importance to these scholars, but it became more complicated, and thus more fragmented, by other categories of analysis. At the same time, this complexity has produced some important depth and breadth to our historical understanding of what it has meant to work, including how work spaces were as diverse and complex as the workers themselves.

Among the most enduring scholarly contributions to this area of study are the importance of regulation to the historical experiences of work. While the sources of regulation have been multi-faceted, including shop foremen, union stewards, co-workers, family members, consumers, and factory inspectors, the overall effect has been similar. Consistently, historians have demonstrated that workers have been subjected to various practices and technologies of discipline. Equally important, though, historians have shown how confronting, resisting, and accommodating discipline have been central to the experiences of work and the formation of workers' identities.

Disciplining work time and work space, however, took many different forms. It could be overt and sometimes brutal, including beatings, whippings, and other forms of corporeal punishment, as well as verbal abuse or the threat of withholding wages. Discipline could also be covert. It might include codes of worker conduct, uniforms, punch clocks, scheduled washroom breaks, or an unspoken threat of social isolation. As many of the chapters in this section demonstrate, workers themselves also disciplined and regulated their own work, work spaces, and other workers. In situations such as the docks of early twentieth-century Vancouver, where jobs were parcelled out among a large body of workers on a near-daily basis, the relationships among workers could be as important as that between workers and employers in even getting paid work. Whether it was the barn raisers in rural Ontario, the pit boys in Nova Scotia coal mines, or French-Canadian and Chinese shoemakers in New England, discipline and work were strongly affected by the formation of at-work class cultures.

Readers might be well served to keep some questions in mind as they explore the readings and documents in this section. What historical situations have existed where a person worked for reasons other than a wage? Whether people worked for a wage or not, what was this work environment like? What rules did one follow? How was the labour divided among the workers? How were individuals identified at work? How did those at work identify themselves as workers? How did work experiences affect other areas of everyday life? Such questions not only connect these diverse stories and documents of work, but they also allow us to see what has historically connected rural women from the mid-nineteenth century to boy miners in late nineteenth-century Cape Breton to black auto workers in post-World War II Ontario. In doing so, perhaps we also learn a little bit more about ourselves and our ideas and assumptions about what it means to work.

Further Readings

Craven, Paul, ed. *Labouring Lives: Work and Workers in Nineteenth-Century Ontario.* Toronto, 1995.

Danysk, Cecilia. *Hired Hands: Labour and the Development of Prairie Agriculture, 1880–1930.* Toronto, 1995.

Gidney, R.D., and W.P.J. Millar. *Professional Gentleman: The Professions in Nineteenth-Century Ontario.* Toronto, 1994.

High, Steven. *Industrial Sunsets: The Making of North America's Rust Belt, 1969–1984.* Toronto, 2003.

Kealey, Gregory S., and Bryan D. Palmer. *Dreaming of What Might Be: The Knights of Labor in Ontario, 1880–1900.* Cambridge, 1982.

McPherson, Kathryn. *Bedside Matters: The Transformation of Canadian Nursing, 1900–1990.* Toronto, 1996.

Palmer, Bryan D. *Working-Class Experience: Rethinking the History of Canadian Labour, 1800–1991,* 2nd edn. Toronto, 1992.

Parnaby, Andrew. *Citizen Docker: Making a New Deal on the Vancouver Waterfront, 1919–1939.* Toronto, 2008.

Podruchny, Carolyn. *Making the Voyageur World: Travelers and Traders in the North American Fur Trade.* Toronto, 2006.

Ramirez, Bruno. *On the Move: French-Canadian and Italian Migrants in the North Atlantic Economy, 1860–1914.* Toronto, 1991.

Sangster, Joan. *Earning Respect: The Lives of Working Women in Small-town Ontario, 1920–1960.* Toronto, 1995.

Stephen, Jennifer A. *Pick One Intelligent Girl: Employability, Domesticity and the Gendering of Canada's Welfare State, 1939–1947.* Toronto, 2007.

I O

Reciprocal Work Bees and the Meaning of Neighbourhood

Catharine Anne Wilson

The reciprocal work 'bee' deserves to be understood as a vital and characteristic element of nineteenth-century rural Ontario. It was as much a part of Ontario folk culture as the potlatch was for west coast Natives, and much more common than the charivari.[1] The bee was an integral part of the farm economy and an important social resource. Through reciprocal work, individual farm families who lacked self-sufficiency in labour and skills were given a measure of insurance against hard times while they established and maintained a workable farm unit. The bee was also a key component in the structuring, operation, and definition of neighbourhood.

The study of reciprocal work bees takes us directly into the construct and concept of neighbourhood. Neighbourhood is not generally understood as part of the larger social system, but tends to be treated peripherally in relation to such categories as class, ethnicity, and gender, if it is not ignored entirely.[2] As such, a disjunction exists between the family unit and the wider world. By examining the structure and process of reciprocal work bees, we reach a deeper understanding of the relationship between the individual, the family, and the larger social order. Neighbourhood, however, is a nebulous idea. Most commonly it is recognized as comprising

people at a certain time who live near each other. In this article it goes beyond this spatial and temporal definition to include interaction, process, and a sense of belonging.[3] In the nineteenth century, neighbourhood was not just the people who lived near you but the basis for economic activity, social support, and the organization of day-to-day living. Though some settlements may have been made up of independent and isolated families that kept to themselves, or tightly knit groups united by ethnicity and religion, others used the bee to develop highly effective networks of interaction. At the bee, people from diverse cultural backgrounds came together and were incorporated according to their genealogy, wealth, age, gender, and skills. Thus the bee helped to create a structural and cognitive order in the neighbourhood. Like the potlatch, it was not only an economic and social exchange but also a process through which shared values and a collective identity were created and communicated. Like the charivari, the bee was a mechanism of social integration identifying those who belonged and those who did not. As such, neighbourhood might, but did not necessarily, include the generosity and kindness that came with 'neighbourliness'.

. . .

Catharine Anne Wilson, 'Reciprocal Work Bees and the Meaning of Neighbourhood', *Canadian Historical Review* 82, 3 (2001): 431–64. © 2001 University of Toronto Press. Reprinted by permission of University of Toronto Press (www.utpjournals.com).

'Busy as Bees'

What settlers called a 'bee' was a neighbourly gathering where people worked together industriously with the bustle of bees in a hive.[4] Bees occurred with regularity and frequency throughout the calendar year in early Ontario. In the spring, bees were called for raising houses and barns, shearing sheep, picking the burrs from fleece, plowing and dragging the land for planting, and piling logs to clear the land. In the hot, dry days of summer, farm folk gathered together at bees to clean water courses, mow and cradle hay, shell peas, and cut grain. Once the busy harvest season slowed down, a new round of bees began. There were bees for spreading manure, husking corn, plowing fields, picking and peeling apples, and hunting squirrels and pigeons. Fanning and threshing bees were often held in the barn in the winter months. This was also the time when neighbourhoods turned their energies to processing clothing and food. Bees for butchering livestock, plucking fowl, spinning wool, and sewing quilts and carpets enlivened the long winter months, and sawing and chopping bees kept the family warm and ready for the next round of clearing and building in the spring.[5]

. . .

'The Still Bee Gathers No Honey': The Economics of the Bee

Reciprocal work was typical of all agricultural communities, but especially frontier areas where land was readily available and capital and labour were in short supply. In early Ontario, few settlers had cash with which to hire labourers. With land readily available, labourers were costly and hard to come by, especially in the backwoods.[6] Most families, particularly those with young children, were simply unable to perform all the tasks themselves without assistance from neighbours. This was especially true of chopping, logging, and building, which required special skills and immense physical strength. As cultivated acreages

increased, it was also true for certain periods of the year such as harvest time, when work demands reached their peak and time was of the essence. By holding a bee, individual farming families who were not self-sufficient in terms of meeting the demands of peak labour periods in the year or possessing all the skills and equipment required to establish a home and farm could attain those ends. The bee was, in effect, an informal labour exchange, part of the hidden economy overlooked by census takers and economic historians. It was a forum for labour in a variety of ways. It served to concentrate labour for those events requiring large numbers. It provided families with extra labour in emergencies that might never be fully repaid. But, most often, it simply redistributed labour over time so that families had more at certain times in the year, in their personal settlement history, or in their life course, a debt that was then fully repaid at a later date.

The beeing phenomenon, therefore, was an essential part of the farm economy. Through reciprocal labour, the farm family was able to create capital. It was also better able to cope with risks. With a low standard of living, no insurance, and the possibility of sudden and unexpected calamities, it was essential to be on good terms with your neighbours. This was especially true in newly settled areas where population was highly dispersed and kin networks were not yet established. If your barn burnt, your fields were flooded, or your husband was killed, you needed to be able to rely on reciprocal aid rather than face these disasters on your own. If you were not part of this neighbourhood exchange system, the backwoods could be a frightening, risky, even hostile place.[7]

. . .

Bees were also an important part of the exchange economy of early Ontario. A tendency exists for scholars of nineteenth-century Ontario to place too much emphasis on wheat exports and, thus, the importance of cash in the economy. The economy was much more complex, involving a system of exchange that included not only cash but also the barter of goods that the family produced and the credit that settlers extended to neighbours and received in return. Indeed, anything that 'earned credit in the local economy . . . would help to sustain farm making'.[8] Certainly the giving and receiving of labour as found in the custom of bees was a part of this exchange system.

Like most significant interaction, an accounting process was at work. It may have been subtle and hidden beneath the rhetoric of neighbourliness, but it was present nevertheless. Participation was part of an exchange of labour, skills, equipment, information, hospitality, and goodwill. Reciprocal work operated much like a bank, in which all made their deposits and were then entitled to make their withdrawals or acquire small loans. One could even attain personal credit for the contributions made by ancestors or close relatives. It was possible to borrow and then abscond, but most settled families probably contributed and received in equal quantities. Was beeing, however, viewed by the participants as a business transaction or, in an attempt to make sense of this phenomenon, are we projecting our twentieth-century capitalist values on the past? The farm diaries do not clarify the mentality at work. On the one hand, the researcher senses that farmers who did not trust a mental system of checks and balances began their diaries as a way of keeping track of bees and other forms of reciprocal labour. Bees were frequently recorded and clearly identified as such. Walter Beatty, near Brockville, carefully noted the participant, the location, and the type of bee his family attended. For example, on 18 September 1849 his entry reads, 'Jock goes to George Toes Dung Bee.' Return labour was just as carefully accounted. For example, on 24 May 1849 he wrote, 'Thomas Davis sent his horses and son to Plow.'[9] When W.F. Munro gave advice to farmers on calculating their costs in the backwoods, he reminded them to 'take into account the "bees."'[10] It was clearly not as strict an accounting, however, as we might expect. When costs were itemized,

they were rarely given in monetary terms, but were generally a day's work for a day's work. But the rule had to be flexible. Inequalities were bound to exist—someone would have a bigger field to harvest, a smaller pile of wood to chop. A family raising a frame barn and having 70 people at the bee would not be expected to attend 70 bees in return. The major players might be repaid with labour, the skilled framer paid cash, and the others paid with the feast and frolic that followed. Clearly they did not have a strict accounting, but it was understood that the same effort would be returned and, in the end, a redistribution of skills, equipment, labour, and hospitality would occur.[11]

Reciprocal work, therefore, played an integral role in the exchange economy, assisting individual farm families to establish a workable farm unit and ensure against hard times. In this manner, it contributed to the extensive growth of the larger provincial economy.

'He That Handles Honey Shall Feel It Cling To His Fingers': The Influence of Association

Beyond contributing to the economic structure of neighbourhood, the bee was a social resource. In the early settlement period, with a scarcity of religious and educational institutions and with kin networks stretching back generations, this factor was especially important. The need to co-operate brought people of diverse backgrounds and potentially divisive lines of affiliation together. The bee provided the mechanism for social integration and bonding. Each and every individual raising or quilting can be viewed as an interaction episode where patterns of association and meaning were confirmed and sometimes initiated or reshaped.[12] By participating and abiding by the rules as they were understood, people of various ages, classes, genders, skills, and experiences were incorporated into the group.

A code of behaviour developed regarding communal labour that extended beyond a mere accounting system to encompass social relations. Those giving advice to new settlers urged them to take heed that every favour conferred required a return favour. As Catharine Parr Traill, a leading authority on life in the backwoods, told her readers, 'It is, in fact regarded in the light of a debt of honour; you cannot be forced to attend a bee in return, but no one that can does refuse, unless from urgent reasons; and if you do not find it possible to attend in person you may send a substitute in a servant or in cattle, if you have a yoke.' Though this might be an inconvenience, this 'debt of gratitude ought to be cheerfully repaid.'[13] This generalized reciprocity, 'I'll help you with something later,' implied a certain degree of trust and closeness. The request to return the effort at another bee could be met in three ways: accept it, discharge the debt later, and reinforce the bonds; accept to return the favour in another form, maybe discharge the debt, and reinforce the bonds; or refuse to attend, renege on your repayment, and risk breaking the social bond. Few risked exclusion from the system altogether because alienating your neighbours could be costly financially and socially.[14]

Because of this obligatory reciprocity, work groups could become highly stable among a core of persistent farmers, or even last for a generation or more.[15] It was unlikely that all labour obligations would be repaid in the same season, but they might linger for years, cementing and lengthening the lines of obligation, especially among people who shared the same values of hard work, neighbourliness, and trust. The stability of the group was essential to mutual aid. As such, the self-interest of individual families conjoined with the shared interests of the neighbourhood.

Constant social contact and mutual dependency did not necessarily imply deep affection, as work groups could be torn asunder by a serious accident or quarrels between families. Tensions simmering beneath the surface of neighbourhood life frequently erupted at bees, especially those where whisky was liberally served. Patrick Dunigan, for example, who had accused a neighbour of stealing his valuable oak tree, was stripped and tortured with hot irons by his neighbours at a bee. Hatred between Patrick Farrell and James Donnelly Sr over possession of 50 acres culminated at a bee in June 1857 when Donnelly killed Farrell with a handspike.[16] Such violence, even verbal disagreements, acquired significance in the rumour mill. Someone drunk, disorderly, uncooperative, or insulting was clearly breaking the code of neighbourliness and was a nuisance, if not a serious liability, to completing the job efficiently and without incident. Such behaviour not only threatened life and property but also jeopardized the working relationship of the group. That person was apt to be ostracized.

In this manner, the bee was a way of asserting community identity and belonging: one either adhered to the shared values of hard work and neighbourliness and belonged or was left out. For example, two young Englishmen who considered themselves above assisting at a logging bee in Douro Township in the 1830s were ridiculed with laughter.[17] In another case, Thomas Niblock, who had gained the reputation of not paying his debts on time and disparaging his neighbours' company, was not included in the beeing circle in Delaware and had to hire men to help him clear and harvest.[18] So important was a 'neighbourly' attitude that responsible, cheerful, and generous effort even took precedence over the actual quality of the work done. The neighbourly quilter was still asked to a quilting even if her stitches were uneven. Sloppy work could always be ripped out and replaced at a later date; a fissure of friendly relations was more difficult, time-consuming, and costly to repair.[19]

Besides the cheerful repayment of labour, hospitality was an integral part of the exchange and one of the most valued virtues of the social code. Just what constituted appropriate, neighbourly hospitality changed over time. In the early days of sparse settlement and rough ways, hospitality took the form of simple food, entertainment, and plenty of whisky. Whisky, in particular, was the measure of hospitality. Commentators were quick to point out in the 1820s that you simply could not raise a barn without it.[20] Generally it took 16 men to raise a building, and five gallons of whisky was the recommended store to have on hand.[21] An inexperienced grog-boss, as at Moodie's bee, inadvertently wreaked havoc by being too generous too early in the day. Susanna Moodie's 'vicious and drunken' guests stayed on after the logging bee with their 'unhallowed revelry, profane songs and blasphemous swearing', and left her to pick up the broken glasses, cups, and strewn remnants of the feast. Not surprisingly, Susanna condemned bees as being 'noisy, riotous drunken meetings, often terminating in violent quarrels, sometimes even bloodshed'.[22] Concern over the accidents, quarrels, expense of provisions, and damage to property occasioned by such drinking brought about a contest between the whisky supporters on the one side and the evangelicals and temperance advocates on the other in many communities. Evangelicals and temperance advocates met with considerable resistance in their attempt to redefine traditional patterns of hospitality as sinful. For example, a Waterdown man wishing to raise a sawmill without whisky had to send to the Indian mission on the Credit before he could obtain willing men.[23] In another case, men turned out to a raising in Nissouri Township, but once the foundation was laid, refused to raise the barn unless whisky was served. When no whisky appeared, the men left.[24] At times resistance could take a nasty turn. For example, when Thomas Brown, who had previously been part of a gang of young men who caroused at any bee within riding distance, took the pledge, he became a target of ridicule. When he next attended a bee and refused to drink, whisky was forcibly poured down his throat and he was beaten.[25] By the 1870s, however, as the farming population became more established, older, and respectable, and as evangelicalism gained converts, strong drink was either not offered or limited to moderate amounts after the job was done.[26] Though hospitality continued to

be a vital component of the exchange, elaborate meals and entertainment replaced generous quantities of whisky.

By reciprocating in the appropriate fashion through hospitality and labour, people demonstrated their support for reciprocal labour and the shared values that supported it. In so doing, they became or continued to be part of the neighbourhood. This process of incorporation worked to integrate newcomers and established settlers, young and old, rich and poor, women and men not as equals, but with clearly defined identities within the larger group. Though Catharine Parr Traill viewed the coming together of the educated gentleman, the poor artisan, the soldier, the independent settler, and the labourer in one common cause as the 'equalizing system of America', it was neither so romantic nor so revolutionary. Although the bee publicly identified people as belonging, it also established, confirmed, and renegotiated their status in the rural hierarchy, whether that standing was based on experience, skills, age, class, or gender.

Bees constituted a rite of passage for new settlers, a time when they were incorporated into the group values and understandings that could make them into useful and valued members of the neighbourhood. Reciprocal labour tied new and established families together. On the one hand, established farmers who expanded their operations needed additional labour. On the other hand, new settlers relied on more experienced settlers for their skill, equipment, advice, and any older children they could spare.[27] When Mr Sinclair arrived in Howard Township (Kent Co.) in the 1830s, for example, he had a neighbour accompany him to summon the locals to his raising. As newcomer, he had no outstanding favours to call upon, no reputation established as a trustworthy and hard worker, and therefore needed William Anderson to provide an introduction. With no house of his own, and his wife sick with lake fever, Sinclair had to rely on another neighbour to assist in preparing for the feast and festivities that followed. In repaying all these favours in the customary way, the Sinclair family could establish its claim to membership in the neighbourhood and the rights and responsibilities that status conferred.[28]

The bee, like the farm operation itself, incorporated people of all ages into its service while publicly acknowledging their status within the group. The very young and the very old, for example, were relegated to the sidelines to watch, cheer, and pass judgment. Those able to participate in the work were given responsibilities according to their perceived capabilities and talents. It was standard practice, for example, for dangerous, strenuous work, such as raising or logging, to get experienced young men. Though an older man might shout the orders to 'heave ho', only someone with a 'steady head and active body' could go out on a beam.[29] On several occasions while raising barns, seasoned men had let a bent slip and someone had been killed.[30] Novices, therefore, had to be kept away from dangerous work. In John Geikie's account of a logging bee at his father's farm in the 1830s or 1840s, John and his brother (who were under 15 years of age) were allowed only to watch on the sidelines and do the 'lighter parts of the business'. They lopped off branches, made piles of brush, brought the men pails of water, and kept the animals out of danger of falling trees. The men did the chopping and the 'wild work' of rolling the logs together.[31] As power saws and threshing machines were introduced later in the century, the specialized knowledge required to run the machines and ownership of this technology reinforced the age-based social hierarchy. Boys, or men past their prime, were limited to carrying the logs and pitching blocks at the sawing bee, or pitching grain at the threshing bee. Only experienced, active men in their prime could take their place next to the saw blade or the threshing machine. When a worker was considered to be too old to be trusted with the serious or dangerous work, the meaning of his aging was publicly recognized, his status altered, and he was relegated to the sidelines.[32]

The bee also incorporated people of different classes. Gentlemen farmers such as the Langtons, the Stricklands, and the Moodies invited the educated gentleman, the independent settler, the tenant farmer, and the poor labourer alike to join together in common cause. That such a meeting of classes and temporary laying aside of differences was invariably cause for comment suggests that people were well aware of the social hierarchy. After raising their house in 1833, Traill concluded that, 'in spite of the difference of rank among those that assisted at the bee, the greatest possible harmony prevailed.'[33] Such patterns of dependence cutting across classes did not lessen inequality. As scholars studying festive labour in primitive societies have observed, the exchange was not always between equals and was, in fact, a way of reinforcing or establishing one's place in the social hierarchy.[34]

Gentlemen farmers admitted that bees, especially raisings, were essential and unavoidable. They participated in reciprocal labour, but took pains when possible to distance themselves from the lower classes and express their superiority. Both could be achieved in a number of ways. Usually the host was the work boss when a bee was convened, but where inequality between the host and workers was great, the host hired a foreman. John Thomson, a retired half-pay officer who held several properties in the Orillia area, did so when he ordered his hired hand to invite neighbours and Natives, procure supplies, and conduct the raising. It was only when workers threatened to leave because of rain and poor preparation that Thomson got involved and set about cajoling and flattering them to stay for another day.[35]

A typical way to use the bee to express one's place in the social hierarchy was through conspicuous giving—to serve a lavish feast and throw a better party than most participants could afford. Settlers expected the well-to-do to throw a good bee. To live in a commodious frame house and serve your guests only pork and peas outside was not meeting the code of hospitality. It was a challenge for most settlers to acquire and prepare enough simple fare for their guests, given the primitive storage and cooking facilities of early settlement life, but they were all expected to do their best, even if it turned out to be a very modest affair. At the Sinclairs' raising in 1831, for example, the men sat on the beams, ate bread, butter, and meat, and drank water and whisky. They had no plates, only their pocket knives.[36] In contrast, the Stewarts, gentlemen farmers in Douro Township, threw a splendid affair at their raising. The guests sat down in the kitchen and parlour to a feast of roast pig, boiled and roast mutton, fish pie, mutton pie, ham, potatoes, and a variety of vegetables, followed by puddings and tarts. In the afternoon, when rain broke up the work, tea and cakes were served. Guests were entertained by a pianist throughout the afternoon, danced to fiddle music throughout the evening, and, at 11, sat down to another feast of a wide variety of meat, desserts, and decanters of currant cordial. Dancing continued thereafter, and everyone was bedded down for the night under buffalo robes and bear skins. At the end of it all, Frances Stewart was able to look back in satisfaction and conclude, 'Altogether it looked very respectable.'[37] The Stewarts had succeeded in meeting their guests and their own expectations of fitting hospitality, given their station in life, and had confirmed their position of superiority in the neighbourhood.

On such occasions it was expected that the host would at least temporarily cast aside class differences and condescend to rub shoulders with his workers. Such had been expected of the landed class in the Old World at festive occasions.[38] It was the host's way of demonstrating his goodwill, mutual respect, generosity of spirit, and appreciation towards workers. These were integral parts of the concept of hospitality and necessary components of a continuing social relationship. When a well-to-do host was not forthcoming, guests might demand festivities fitting his station. For example, when an owner of 500 acres called a raising, but hadn't planned any entertainment, a large group of young women cornered him

during the proceedings and forced him to consider how the evening should be spent.[39] When the host succumbed, dancing and games were organized. Likewise, after rain postponed John Thomson's raising, he and two gentlemen friends retired to his dining room while the remaining workers were relegated to the kitchen for the rest of the day. This division caused 'some envious feelings among certain yankiefied personages' of what Thomson called the 'no-Gent' class. To keep the workers satisfied and willing to stay overnight, Thomson and his friends had to be 'mixed up among them' as they did all they could 'to do away with any bad impression'.[40] Thereafter, Thomson resumed his distance.

In the months that followed, Thomson, like other gentlemen, paid his return labour not by attending what was deemed an 'odious gathering', but by sending his hired hands or a yoke of oxen.[41] The gentleman class participated in reciprocal labour only as long as it was necessary. As an ex-settler flatly stated, 'A gentleman . . . has no business with it—the idle riff-raff are they who will surely come, getting drunk, eating up all your pork and flour, and fighting like Irishmen.'[42] John Langton considered establishing a gentleman's logging association to avoid bees altogether, and Moodie simply stopped going or even sending anyone or anything in his place.[43] Clearly the bee was not the democratizing agent it was sometimes characterized to be.

The bee incorporated people of different age, background, and gender. The view of farm men as commercialists working alone for exchange and profit, while women worked together building neighbourhood and kin ties, needs further examination.[44] The study of bees suggests that both men and women were part of the world of mutuality. Reciprocal work has generally been viewed from the separate spheres ideology. A tendency exists to see logging, raising, and threshing bees as purely male events, and as examples of a 'male community' from which women were excluded.[45] In contrast, feminist scholars have viewed quiltings and other forms of female reciprocity as part of a 'female community' of empathy, spirituality, support, and non-hierarchical arrangements.[46] Scholars now recognize, however, that gender is best understood as a relational system. Through the interaction of men and women, the meaning of gender is created, reinforced, and transformed. More attention is now given to the construction of gender in everyday experience and in settings where men and women operate together. Scholars of rural communities recognize that, unlike urban men and women, who were increasingly defined by their differences from one another, rural men and women continued to share many of 'the tasks which produced their income and sustained their families'.[47] Bees viewed as interaction episodes are exceptionally good opportunities to examine men and women working together, because this form of reciprocal work rarely occurred without the participation of both sexes.

Men were the principal actors in reciprocal labour that involved physical strength and danger. They also exchanged labour among themselves. Women were the principal actors in reciprocal labour that involved the preparation of clothing and food. They also exchanged labour among themselves. Rarely did men and women exchange labour with each other. Beyond these significant differences there was much commonality. Both men and women were involved in bees for the capital development of their farming operation (cleared fields, buildings, household goods), for market (grain, fowl, cloth), and for basic family sustenance (food and clothing). A successful bee—where work was done well, no incidents occurred, and guests were pleased with the hospitality—required the participation of both men and women. Their work, responsibilities, and space intersected at various points throughout the event. Even though they were main actors in different kinds of bees, men and women shared the values and experience of diligence, skill, competition, hierarchical working structures, and neighbourliness. Gender, nevertheless, was an essential variable in understanding their lives.

Logging bees were substantively about men and the rituals of manliness. The loggers formed gangs in different parts of the field and competed to see who would finish logging their section first. It was very strenuous work shifting and heaping logs. In the hottest days of summer, the hours were dreadfully long, the logs terribly heavy, the work tiring and dirty, the grog foul-tasting and plentiful. It took physical stamina to last the day. It took bravery to run the risk of breaking a leg or losing one's life. And it took a great deal of self-control to keep a clear head. As Munro explained in *Backwoods Life*, logging was what 'tries a man's mettle'.[48] Just to participate as a main actor (one who rolled and piled the logs) was a mark of one's prowess. Being allowed to drive the oxen marked the beginning of manhood, and, by participating and observing, boys soon learned what was expected of them once they graduated to the status of main actors. Strength, speed, and energy were all valued, and skill was deeply appreciated and critically evaluated. Lives were at stake. Save for the skill of a good axeman, a tree might fall on man or beast. Men gained and lost reputations at these events as the strongest, the fastest, or the most skilful. Such identities were created in the heat of work and confirmed in the competitive sports that often followed. As Geikie recounted after attending a logging bee in Bidport Township in the 1830s, there was much bragging about chopping prowess, much comparison between men regarding their skills, and much laughing at those who had accidents or used inferior equipment.[49] Heavy drinking, smoking, and fights were part of the equation too, though the 'rough back countryman' style of manhood exhibited by Monaghan, who attended Moodie's bee on a hot July day in 1834 'in his glory, prepared to work or fight', gradually lost favour to the more morally upright male who was esteemed for his strength, skill, stamina—and his self-restraint.[50]

Women played a supporting role at bees where men held centre stage and were a valued audience. As anthropologists who study spectacles argue, the role of spectator is not passive or neutral, as spectacles require exchange between actors and audience.[51] At barn raisings, for example, women cheered the men on as they competed to see which team raised their side first. As Russel Clifton recalled from his barn-raising youth, he was often one of the first lads to ride up with the bent, and 'usually there was some girl among the women that I hoped would worry about my falling.'[52] Even at logging bees, the dirtiest and roughest events of all, women might participate as spectators. For example, Anne Langton and her kitchen helpers walked down and took 'a view of the black and busy scene' at their logging.[53] At hunting bees, women swarmed the fields, supporting their teams by bringing the hunters provisions and relieving them of their game.[54] In the exchange, men and women confirmed their own and each other's gendered identities. To defy these identities was to court disapproval.[55]

Even more important than their valued role as spectators was women's role in preparing and executing the feast and festivities; these were essential components of any successful bee, the first installment in the pay-back system, and an integral part in developing the farm.[56] Women were indispensable in this capacity. If a family could not supply enough female labour itself, additional women were hired or, more commonly, neighbouring women gave their labour, crockery, cooking utensils, and, on occasion, their kitchens, with the understanding that they would receive help in return.[57] It was hard work. For most women, even with help, it took two to three days to prepare the house and food, in order to set out what was considered 'a respectable table' and to make room for the dancing or games that followed. Great activity then ensued on the day of the event, with cooking, keeping the fires going, serving food, minding children, and being the cheerful hostess.[58] Once the festivities were over, the cleanup began.

In a sense, the roles of actor and spectator were reversed at the feast, as the hostess took centre stage. As fictional accounts portrayed it, 'supper was the great event to which all things moved at bees.'[59] Considerable pressure existed for women to perform. Isabella Bishop concluded in *The Englishwoman in America* (1856) that the 'good humour of her guests depends on the quantity and quality of her viands.'[60] Being hostess to a bee gave women a rare occasion to exhibit themselves, their skills, and their homes. Though men might eat with a 'take what you have and you won't want fashion,' they nevertheless took stock of the meal. In their accounts of bees, men carefully and, if the host, proudly itemized the menu and often evaluated the hostess. Wilkie, for example, after attending a chopping bee, noted [of] Mrs Webb [that she was a] 'provident dame [who] had busied herself to some purpose'.[61] Women, however, were the most exacting critics when it came to the meal. As men competed with and assessed each other while logging, women evaluated each other at the feast. As Stan Cross recalled of his parents' barn raising, senior women eagerly offered their assistance so that they could 'see first-hand how my mother, who was one of their peers, would approach such an undertaking especially with three babies in tow.'[62] So great was the competition and the pressure to prepare a fine feast that M.E. Graham, in an article entitled 'Food for Bees', urged Ontario farm women not to give themselves 'dyspepsia preparing bountiful, fancy and varied threshing feasts'. She went on to say, 'I know for truth that we simply cook that we may equal or excel the other woman in the neighbourhood.'[63] A lot was at stake, for the quality of the hospitality could determine the family's reputation and its continuing membership in the ring of reciprocity. It was only after the feast and the festivities were over and the guests had gone away happy that the host and hostess could relax and congratulate themselves on having held a successful event.

The quilting was the female counterpart of the male logging bee. As men were the central actors at a logging bee and women played a supporting role, the reverse was true of quiltings. It was an event organized and held by and for women which combined work with socializing. For days the hostess prepared the house and the food for the event, made arrangements for the children, and pieced scraps together to form the top of the quilt. Whereas a general call might be sent out for a barn raising, women were individually invited to a quilting. The guests would secure the top, wool, and backing to a frame, quilt it, and remove it from the frame, ready for use, in the same day. To be invited to a quilting generally meant you were not only a member of a particular social circle but also accomplished in sewing skills. Whereas men were esteemed for their strength, stamina, and bravery, women were praised for their detail and dexterity. The good seamstress sewed fast, short, even stitches and wasted no thread. The hostess was evaluated on her hospitality, and the artistry and skill exhibited by her quilt top. As experienced men took the lead at loggings, experienced women took the lead at quiltings and were known as the 'queen bees'. Young girls learned how to sew from their mothers and grandmothers on doll quilts. Once they were experienced enough, they would be invited to participate in their first bee. In this manner, quilting skills were passed down through the generations, reaffirming the female role and female connectedness.[64]

Usually we think of the quilting bee as a female-only affair, but in the nineteenth century, though women held centre stage, men played significant supporting roles. When young women were present, the hostess, who controlled the social space of the marriage market, invited young men too.[65] A.C. Currie, a young bachelor in Niagara, got invited to several quilting bees over the winter of 1841. Sometimes he had two a week.[66] While the women sat around the quilting frame, the men, under the supervision of the queen bees, would sit on the sidelines and aid by threading needles, chatting, and flirting. As spectators, they were to appreciate the women's domestic skills and social charms; as supporting actors, they were to mingle with the young women

at the 'frolic' of charades, dancing, singing, and flirtations that usually followed. Such flirtations at apple-paring and corn-husking bees, where men and women participated as equals, took priority over the actual work accomplished, at least in the retelling. At paring bees, men might peel apples and throw them to the women, who cored, quartered, and strung them. Once the old folks retired for the evening, the young people kissed, danced, and played all sorts of games. Wilkie excitedly recounted his experiences at such a bee when, alone in a moonlit room, amid much whispering and gentle tittering, a game of forfeit ensued and he found himself holding a 'bonnie lass' on each knee.[67] In this manner, bees provided an opportunity for courtship under the supervision of the community.

At the bee, one's identity was confirmed within the neighbourhood. Though people might work together in harmony like bees in a hive, they took their place within a non-egalitarian and differentiated group. While initiating, reshaping, and confirming patterns of association between individuals, the bee also served a variety of functions for the neighbourhood as a whole. One contemporary deemed it to be 'the fete, the club, the ball, the town-hall, the labour convention of the whole community'.[68]

. . .

'To Bee or Not To Bee'

What the bee actually meant to participants can only be judged from their actions and the evaluations they have left. Contemporary accounts repeatedly revealed that if a bee functioned well—the job got done, money was saved, people had fun and knew their place—the communal effort was applauded. Participants, however, were well aware of the exchange system that underlay this event and were reluctant to depict reciprocal work as selfless behaviour.[69] They knew that both the communal and the individual ethic were in operation. While selfish ambition and the man who did not do his share were clearly frowned upon, individual gain had an acknowledged place in the system. The barn raising, for example, was a momentous achievement in an individual family's measure of material success. It symbolized not only their reasons for emigrating and their years of saving and planning but also their material wealth, social improvement, and independence. Indeed, private property and individual ownership were never in question. Though people agreed to share their labour, tools, and time, it was always clear whose field had been logged, whose cattle would use the newly raised barn, and who could sleep under the quilt. Most participants would have been baffled to find twentieth-century writers casting the bee as the embodiment of the selfless communal ideal and the polar opposite of the capitalistic spirit of individualism and material gain. Instead, most farm families understood that work was a commodity and also a means to foster neighbourly relations. Their lively networks of reciprocal labour fostered both individual prosperity and mutual reliance. This social reality flies in the face of a number of dichotomies that have been developed by scholars, such as use versus exchange, sufficiency versus commercialization, and the moral economy versus the market economy.[70] That reciprocal work often resulted in a warm sense of generosity, belonging, and security within a larger community was an important by-product deeply appreciated by people at the time and lamented later when lost. When given the opportunity to be released from the constraints of scarce labour and capital, however, many people chose to leave the obligations and inconvenience of co-operative work behind for other ways over which they had greater control.

The main complaints levelled against bees had to do with managing people. Co-operation is not easy. As with any kind of communal work, industrious workers had to share with the idle, and individual decisions were constrained by the decisions of the group. One common complaint was that it was difficult to control the workers. Some came with the attitude that the host was lucky to have them and they drank and ate heartily while leaving little in the way of quality workmanship. Farmers felt they had more control over their workers and the quality of work if they hired labourers. Furthermore, bees could be costly if the work was shoddy, yet the host was bound to feast and entertain the workers. After her logging bee had gone wrong, Susanna Moodie went out of her way to declare, 'I am certain, in our case, had we hired with the money expended in providing for the bee, two or three industrious, hard-working men, we should have got through twice as much work, and have had it done well, and have been the gainers in the end.'[71] The main disadvantage with the bee was being called upon at an inconvenient time for return work. Just when a farmer needed to seed or harvest his own fields, he was called upon by others to work theirs.[72]

Given the difficulties in managing people, it is not surprising that once other viable alternatives arose, bees declined. Bees persisted in remote areas where hired labour was hard to find and the price of labour was high. They also continued to operate in situations such as the Middaughs' where persistent farm families of similar status had a tradition of reciprocal work firmly established. In other populous and longer-settled areas, however, where farmers were expanding their operations and entering into a cash economy, it was more convenient to hire workers, and the cash payment—an immediate reciprocity—took into consideration the quality and quantity of the work done.[73] Farmers were then free of the obligations of reciprocal labour and could attend to their own farms—and according to their own schedule. The growing availability of cash and hired labour removed the necessity of relying on bees.

Technology was not as central as some have argued in the decline of bees.[74] The introduction at mid-century of patented iron apple peelers, the self-raking reaper, and, later, cross-cut saws reduced the need for bees by cutting the time and labour needed in processing apples, harvesting, and sawing.[75] Some of the new technology, such as threshing machines in the 1880s and later silo-filling equipment, did not alter the tradition of collective work, but was often co-operatively owned and operated. Threshing bees and silo-filling bees continued well into the twentieth century. Only after the First World War, with the introduction of combines and tractors, was one man able to do the work that had previously taken a neighbourhood.[76]

The need for bees also declined with the rise of more formal strategies for security and new forms of entertainment. Insurance companies offering compensation for damage done by fire, fraternal orders offering sickness and death benefits, and eventually the welfare state all played their part in reducing the effect of hard times and families' reliance on traditional networks of neighbourhood support.[77] Furthermore, bees now competed with lodge meetings, Sunday school picnics, school concerts, and agricultural fairs for the visiting and courtship opportunities they provided.

As the economics, technology, and social aspects of farm life changed, bees slowly became a thing of the past.

Conclusion

Though often idealized as the epitome of the selfless communal ideal, participants in bees behaved as though there was no inherent or insurmountable conflict between individual and communal goals. Both men and women participated in reciprocal labour using the ties born of geography and genealogy to build their resources, increase their own productivity, and shape their future opportunities. Through this sharing, many individual farm families were able to acquire the extra labour, skills, and equipment necessary for capital improvements, so that profitable farming could proceed. Such structural dependence on neighbours reduced the risk of life in the backwoods. Many people found that, through reciprocal work, they could succeed individually and that it was in their own material and social interests to be neighbourly. The network of labour exchange, in effect, produced individual prosperity and mutual reliance. In the process, neighbourhoods were created that could be defined by their spatial dimension, membership, shared values, and collective identity. Such neighbourhoods were dynamic entities, with fluid patterns of interaction particular to each family and responsive to the social networks and social space that individual participants brought to bear on the network as it developed. Finally, though the bee facilitated neighbourhood and often neighbourliness, it did so in a way that incorporated differences in class, age, gender, and skill and acknowledged the importance of private property and social hierarchy.

Notes

I would like to thank my research assistants, Karen Kennedy and James Calnan. The helpful comments of my colleagues Terry Crowley, Kris Inwood, Jamie Snell, and Richard Reid on earlier versions of this article are greatly appreciated. A version of this article was presented at the 2001 annual meeting of the Canadian Historical Association in Quebec City.

1. Bryan D. Palmer, 'Discordant Music: Charivaris and Whitecapping in Nineteenth-Century North America', *Labour/Le Travail* 3 (1978): 5–62; Allan Greer, 'From Folklore to Revolution: Charivaris and the Lower Canadian Rebellion of 1837', and Tina Loo, 'Dan Cranmer's Potlatch', both in Tina Loo and Lorna R. McLean, eds, *Historical Perspectives on Law and Society in Canada* (Mississauga, ON: Copp Clark Longman, 1994), 35–55, 219–53; Pauline Greenhill, 'Welcome and Unwelcome Visitors: Shivarees and the Political Economy of Rural–Urban Interaction in Southern Ontario', *Journal of Ritual Studies* 3, 1 (1989).

2. Studies such as those done by Bradbury, Parr, and Marks come close to examining neighbourhood, but still link families only with the larger urban area and economy and bypass the neighbourhood as a unit of analysis. See Bettina Bradbury, *Working Families: Age, Gender and Daily Survival in Industrializing Montreal* (Toronto: McClelland & Stewart, 1993); Joy Parr, *The Gender of Breadwinners* (Toronto: University of Toronto Press, 1990); Lynne Marks, *Revivals and Roller Rinks: Religion, Leisure, and Identity in Late-Nineteenth-Century Small-Town Ontario* (Toronto: University of Toronto Press, 1996). . . .

3. A vast literature exists on community. For the most recent overview of this literature in a Canadian context, see John C. Walsh and Steven High, 'Re-thinking the Concept of Community', *Histoire Sociale* 32 (Nov. 1999): 255–73. . . .

4. Samuel Strickland, *Twenty-Seven Years in Canada West*, vol. 1 (Edmonton: Hurtig Publishers, 1972 [1853]), 35; Martin Doyle, *Hints on Emigration to Upper Canada* (Dublin: Curry, 1832), 61; George Easton, *Travels in America* (Glasgow: John S. Marr & Sons, 1871), 89. . . .

5. Queen's University Archives, Walter Beatty Papers, Walter Beatty Diary, 1838–92, box 3057; ibid., Ewan Ross Papers, John MacGregor Diary, 1877–83, series 3, binder 94, no. 2504; ibid., Ewan Ross Papers, James Cameron Diaries, 1854–1902, series 3, binders 25–33, no. 2504; Lucy Middaugh Diary, 1884–7, private possession of Jean Wilson; John Tigert Diaries, 1888–1902, private possession of Tigert family; Joseph Abbott Diary, 1819, reprinted in his *The Emigrant to North America* (Montreal: Lovell & Gibson, 1843); James O'Mara, 'The Seasonal Round of Gentry Farmers in Early Ontario', *Canadian Papers in Rural History* 2 (1980): 103–12.

6. For the most comprehensive study of rural labour in nineteenth-century Ontario, see Terry Crowley, 'Rural Labour', in Paul Craven, ed., *Labouring Lives: Work and Workers in Nineteenth-Century Ontario* (Toronto: University of Toronto Press, 1995), 13–102. For frontier labour, see Daniel Vickers, 'Working the Fields in a Developing Economy: Essex County, Mass., 1630–1675', in Stephen Innes, ed., *Work and Labor in Early America* (Chapel Hill: University of North Carolina Press, 1988), 60.

7. Immigrant guidebook writers were well aware of the necessity of reducing risk in the backwoods and urged their readers to take part in bees. See William Hutton, *Canada: Its Present Condition, Prospects, and Resources Fully Described for the Information of Intending Emigrants* (London, 1854), 42–3; Catharine Parr Traill, *The Backwoods of Canada* (Toronto: McClelland & Stewart, 1929 [1836]), 121; Easton, *Travels in America*, 90–3, 168.

8. Doug McCalla, *Planting the Province: The Economic History of Upper Canada, 1784–1870* (Toronto: University of Toronto Press, 1993), 82, 146.

9. Beatty Diary; see also Tigert Diary and Middaugh Diary. . . .

10. W.F. Munro. *The Backwoods Life* (Shelburne: The Free Press, 1910 [1869]), 38.

11. A day's work for a day's work was generally the custom throughout North and South America. See Basil Hall, *Travels in North America, in the Years 1827–1828* (Edinburgh: Cadell & Co., 1829), 311–12; Charles Erasmus, 'Culture Structure and Process: The Occurrence and Disappearance of Reciprocal Farm Labour', *Southwestern Journal of Anthropology* 12 (1956): 445. . . .

12. I first came across the use of 'interaction episode' as an analytical tool in Rhys Isaac's *The Transformation of Virginia* (Chapel Hill: University of North Carolina Press, 1982), ch. 'A Discourse on the Method'. My thanks to Richard Reid for drawing my attention to this work. . . .

13. Traill, *Backwoods of Canada*, 122.

14. Contemporary writers urged new settlers to repay the favour: Hall, *Travels*, 312; Edward Allan Talbot, *Five Years' Residence in the Canadas* (London: Longman, Hurst, Rees, Orme, Brown & Green, 1824), 69; Doyle, *Hints on Emigration*, 45. See also Paul Voisey, *Vulcan: The Making of a Prairie Community* (Toronto: University of Toronto Press, 1988), 147; Jane Marie Pederson, *Between Memory and Reality: Family and Community in Rural Wisconsin, 1870–1970* (Madison: University of Wisconsin Press, 1992), 154.

15. Kimball, 'Rural Social Organization', 47; Erasmus, 'Culture Structure and Process', 447; Anthony Buckley, 'Neighbourliness—Myth and History', *Oral History* 2, 1 (1983): 49.

16. *Globe*, 10 Sept. 1880, 6; 6 Feb. 1880, 1. For other examples, see Ray Fazakas, *The Donnelly Album* (Toronto: Macmillan of Canada, 1977), 10–14. . . .

17. James Logan, *Notes of a Journey Through Canada* (Edinburgh: Fraser & Co., 1838), 46.

18. National Archives of Canada (NAC), Niblock Letters, MG 24, 180, microfilm A-304, Thomas Niblock to Edward Niblock, 27 Jan. 1850. For those who broke the code and were considered divergent or outsiders, see Kimball, 'Rural Social Organization', 41; Conrad M. Arensberg and Solon T. Kimball, *Family and Community in Ireland* (Cambridge, MA: Harvard University Press, 1948), ch. 12.

19. Interview with quilters at a quilting bee, Martin House, Doon Village, 1 July 1996.

20. Thomas Brush Brown, *Autobiography of Thomas Brush Brown (1804–1894)* (private printing by Isabel Grace Wilson, 1967, available at the Oxford County Library), 17–18. For the importance of whisky and hospitality, see also David Wilkie, *Sketches of a Summer Trip to New York and the Canadas* (Edinburgh: J. Anderson Jr & A. Hill, 1837), 173, 176–7 . . .

21. Patrick Shirreff, *A Tour through North America* (Edinburgh: Oliver & Boyd, 1835), 125. For the usual amount of whisky per man, see Rev. T. Sockett, ed., *Emigration: Letters from Sussex Emigrants* (London: Phillips, Petworth and Longman & Co., 1833), 28; Centennial Museum, Judicial Records, Peterborough County, Peterborough. MG-8-2V, Inquest of Charles Danford, Smith Township, Accession No. 71–007, box 5, 1876, no. 30.

22. Susanna Moodie, *Roughing It in the Bush* (Toronto: McClelland & Stewart, 1962 [1852]), 156–62; and also Wilkie, *Sketches*, 176; Shirreff, *A Tour*, 125.

23. Emily Weaver, *Story of the Counties of Ontario* (Toronto: Bell & Cockburn, 1913), 165; Pederson, *Between Memory and Reality*, 142, 217, 219.

24. Brown, *Autobiography*, 25.

25. Ibid., 23–4.

26. Charles Marshall, *The Canadian Dominion* (London: Longmans, Green, 1871), 63; see also Easton, *Travels in America*, 169.

27. Doyle, *Hints on Emigration*, 60–1.

28. Alexander Sinclair, *Pioneer Reminiscences* (Toronto: Warwick Bros & Rutter, 1898), 11–12.

29. Frances Browne Stewart, *Our Forest Home* (Montreal: Gazette Printing, 1902 [1889]), 174, 177; *Canada Farmer* 2, 9 (15 Nov. 1870).

30. Trent University Archives, Court Records of the United Counties of Northumberland & Durham, Coroners' Inquests, Inquest of James Hill, 84–020, series E, box 49; Judicial Records Peterborough County, Inquest of Charles Danford. A bent was made of two posts connected with a beam. It was laid on the foundation and then raised to form the frame of the barn.

31. John C. Geikie, ed., *Adventures in Canada: Or Life in the Woods* (Philadelphia: Porter & Coates, 1882), 40–4, 47–8; see also Logan, *Notes of a Journey*, 45.

32. Jim Brown, 'Memories of Work Bees', *Up the Gatineau!* 21 (1995): 9; Royce MacGillivray, *The Slopes of the Andes: Four Essays on the Rural Myth in Ontario* (Belleville, ON: Mika Publishing, 1990), 90.

33. Traill, *The Backwoods*, 135; see also Moodie, *Roughing It*, 156; Logan, *Notes of a Journey*, 46.

34. Erasmus, 'Culture Structure and Process', 458.

35. Archives of Ontario, John Thomson Diary, MU-846, part 2, 22–4 Apr. 1834. This was done elsewhere as well; see Erasmus, 'Culture Structure and Process', 448.

36. Sinclair, *Pioneer Reminiscences*, 12; see also Wilkie, *Sketches*, 177; Strickland, *Twenty-Seven Years*, 35–6.

37. Stewart, *Our Forest Home*, 174–6.

38. Catharine Anne Wilson, *A New Lease on Life* (Montreal and Kingston: McGill-Queen's University Press, 1994), 110.

39. *Canada Farmer* 2, 9 (15 Nov. 1870).

40. Thomson Diary, 22–4 Apr. 1834.

41. For example, see Thomson Diary, July, Oct., and Nov. 1833, June 1834. John Langton and Moodie sent their hired men to bees also. Anne Langton, *A Gentlewoman in Upper Canada* (Toronto: Clarke Irwin, 1964), 167; Moodie, *Roughing It*, 162.

42. Ex-Settler, *Canada in the Years 1832, 1833 and 1834* (Dublin: Hardy, 1835), 115.

43. Langton, *A Gentlewoman*, 166; Moodie, *Roughing It*, 162.

44. Nancy Osterud goes further than most historians in understanding the rural family and community as gendered relationships. While she acknowledges that men participated in co-operative work, she still tends to see men as part of the commercial world and argues that women were the ones who sustained co-operative relations. In fact, she goes as far as to argue that women advocated a model of interdependence as an alternative to male dominance and capitalist social relations. She states that women used mutuality as a strategy of empowerment. Nancy Grey Osterud, *Bonds of Community: The Lives of Farm Women in 19th Century New York* (Ithaca, NY: Cornell University Press, 1991).

45. John Mack Faragher, *Women and Men on the Overland Trail* (New Haven: Yale University Press, 1979), 112, 116.

46. Carroll Smith-Rosenberg, 'The Female World of Love and Ritual: Relations between Women in Nineteenth-Century America', *Journal of Women in Culture and Society* 1, 1 (1975): 1–29; Marjorie Kaethler and Susan D. Shantz, *Quilts of Waterloo County* (Waterloo, ON: Johanns Graphics, 1990), 12; Ruth Schwartz Cowan, *More Work for Mother* (New York: Basic Books, 1983), 112.

47. For gender as a relational system, see Joan W. Scott, 'Women's History', in Peter Burke, ed., *New Perspectives on Historical Writing* (University Park: Pennsylvania State University Press, 1995); for rural communities, see Pederson, *Between Memory and Reality*; Osterud, *Bonds of Community*; Royden Loewen, *Family, Church, and Market: The Mennonite Community in the Old and the New Worlds, 1850–1930* (Toronto: University of Toronto Press, 1993).

48. Munro, *Backwoods Life*, 55.

49. Geikie, ed., *Adventures in Canada*, 41–3.

50. Moodie, *Roughing It*, 158; and for similar accounts of logging bees, see Logan, *Notes on a Journey*, 45; William Johnston, *Pioneers of Blanchard* (Toronto: William Briggs, 1899), 188–9, 227; Wilkie, *Sketches*, 174–5. . . .

51. Bonnie Huskins, 'The Ceremonial Space of Women: Public Processions in Victorian Saint John and Halifax', in Janet Guildford and Susanne Morton, eds, *Separate Sphere: Women's Worlds in the 19th Century Maritimes* (Fredericton: Acadiensis Press, 1994), 147.

52. Cited in West Oxford Women's Institute, *The Axe and the Wheel: A History of West Oxford Township* (Tillsonburg, ON: Otter Publishing, 1974), 17.

53. Langton, *A Gentlewoman*, 94.

54. Abbott, *The Emigrant to North America*, 42.

55. An extreme, but nonetheless suggestive, case occurred in 1918 when a young Quebec girl dressed in male attire participated in a log-driving bee, and, when exposed, was sentenced to two years at the Portsmouth Penitentiary in Kingston. Original 11 June 1918, reprinted in *Toronto Star*, 19 May 1992.

56. Elizabeth Jane Errington, *Wives and Mothers, School Mistresses and Scullery Maids: Working Women in Upper Canada, 1790–1840* (Montreal and Kingston: McGill-Queen's University Press, 1995), 96.

57. Catharine Parr Traill, *The Female Emigrant's Guide and Hints on Canadian Housekeeping* (Toronto: MacLear, 1854), 40; Sinclair, *Pioneer Reminiscences*, 12; Geikie, ed., *Adventures in Canada*, 44.

58. Munro, *Backwoods Life*, 55; Stewart, *Our Forest Home*, 172–6; Wilkie, *Sketches*, 176–8; Isabella L. Bishop, *The Englishwoman in America* (London: W. Clowes & Sons, 1856), 205–6; Louis Tivy, *Your Loving Anna: Letters from the Ontario Frontier* (Toronto: University of Toronto Press, 1972), 89.

59. Ralph Connor, *The Man from Glengarry* (Toronto: Westminster Co., 1901), 211.

60. Bishop, *The Englishwoman in America*, 205–6.

61. Wilkie, *Sketches*, 176.

62. Stan Cross, 'The Raising', *Up the Gatineau!* 21 (1995): 7.

63. M.E. Graham, 'Food for Bees', *The Farming World* 18 (11 Sept. 1900): 104.

64. Strickland, *Twenty-Seven Years*, 2: 295–6 . . .

65. Peter Ward, 'Courtship and Social Space in Nineteenth-Century English Canada', *Canadian Historical Review* 68, 1 (1987): 35–62.

66. University of Western Ontario, Regional Collection, William Leslie Papers, box 4178, A.C. Currie to Richard Leslie, 25 Dec. 1841; see also Strickland, *Twenty-Seven Years*, 2: 296; Munro, *Backwoods Life*, 57; Thompson, *Tradesman's Travels*, 37.

67. Wilkie, *Sketches*, 182–6; see also Canniff Haight, *Country Life in Canada Fifty Years Ago* (Toronto: Hunter, Rose & Co., 1885), 67–8; Geikie, ed., *Adventures in Canada*, 326–7; Traill, *Female Emigrant's Guide*, 75;

Gavin Hamilton Green, *The Old Log House* (Goderich, ON: Signal-Star Press, 1948), 109.

68. Marshall, *Canadian Dominion*, 62.

69. Doyle, *Hints on Emigration*, 61–2; Traill, *The Backwoods*, 122.

70. See Stephen Innes for his insightful discussion of the need for greater caution when using such dichotomies to describe the past. 'John Smith's Vision', in Innes, ed., *Work and Labour in Early America*, 36–40.

71. Moodie, *Roughing It*, 13; see also the Diary of William Proudfoot, 12 June 1833, cited in Edwin Guillet, *Pioneer Days in Upper Canada* (Toronto: University of Toronto Press, 1975 [1933]), 127; Ex-Settler, *Canada*, 115.

72. John J.E. Linton, *The Life of a Backwoodsman; or, Particulars of the Emigrant's Situation in Settling on the Wild Land of Canada* (London: Marchant Singer & Co., 1843), 14; Langton, *Gentlewoman*, 155, 166; *Canada Farmer* 2, 12 (12 Dec. 1870); Traill, *Backwoods*, 122. . . .

73. Traill, *Backwoods*, 121; Strickland, *Twenty-Seven Years*, 1: 37.

74. Kimball, 'Rural Social Organization', 42, places significant weight on technology as a factor in the decline of co-operative labour. Erasmus disagrees, placing more emphasis on the growth of a money economy and on more intensive agriculture that makes co-operative work inconvenient and inefficient in terms of the costs and quality of work done. 'Culture Structure and Process', 456. . . .

75. *Farmer's Advocate* 59 (10 Apr. 1924): 548; McCalla, *Planting the Province*, 225; Lois Russell, *Everyday Life in Colonial Canada* (London: B.T. Batsford, 1973), 90.

76. Pederson, *Between Memory and Reality*, 151–4.

77. McCalla, *Planting the Province*, 161 . . .

11

What the Crispins Saw

——— Anthony W. Lee ———

. . .

Although Quebec in the late 1850s and early 1860s was overwhelmingly rural—more than 80 per cent of its population was still living on farms—the province was hardly the sort of place where a French Canadian farmer thrived. . . .

For the least successful farmers, life was a struggle for survival. They barely kept their heads above the poverty line and sometimes sank below it and became part of the floating population of indigents. In harsh times, families with no grains in storage had to buy their food, sometimes from the marginally better-off farmers who lived side by side in the old plots of the seigneurial system. Those with modest means got a little richer; the poor got much poorer. The near destitute survived by their rural wits, hiring themselves out as farmhands, picking up the back-breaking jobs that even their poor neighbours didn't want (including removing the seemingly ubiquitous stumps), begging, stealing, smuggling, doing whatever they could to hang onto the small patch of land inherited from their parents, often without success. . . .

It is no surprise that when recruiting agents from American factories traipsed across the border looking for new hands, Quebec's farmers leaped at the chance. Between 1850 and 1870, more than 250,000 farmers, about a third of the

population, moved south.[1] The exodus was dramatic, felt in every town and village. Despite the fact that Quebec was having a hard time feeding its population or that the Catholic parishes and church councils were earning a nice cut in American dollars from the recruiters, the mass movement caused a palpable level of alarm and feeling of doom and gloom among the remaining Quebecois, already feeling oppressed by British rule and squeezed out by an English commercial class. The emigration was the 'great haemorrhage' and portended, as Antoine Labelle, cure of Saint-Jerome, feared, the absolute 'graveyard of the race'.[2] In the villages, new songs were sung and poems recited warning not only of the death of a people but also of the travails across the border. 'Où allez-vous?' a popular song asked. 'Dans les Ètats,' the audience replied. 'Vous courez après le misère. Virez de bord, n'y allez donc pas!'[3] But the fears of an ethnic apocalypse and even greater poverty abroad could not stem the tide. The conditions at home seemed to inure the French Canadians to the risks and hardships on the road. The poor men and women had a reputation for taking the lowest-paying jobs, acclimating themselves to the most minimal standards of living, and travelling by the most modest means. With cheap manpower seemingly everywhere north of the border, New England's factory owners and managers happily welcomed them and soon dubbed them . . . the 'Chinese of the Eastern States'. Most of the farmers-turned-industrial labourers headed for the southern New England and upstate New York mill towns; some went to work on the Erie and Champlain canal networks.

Many of the French Canadians who left . . . took their whole families.[4] They transformed these towns into suddenly thickly populated, French-speaking communities. Sometimes husbands, wives, and children entered the factories as one; in those cases farming families became industrial labourers almost overnight, trading the axe and spade for the spindle and loom in a radical transformation of their daily lives. But that wholesale relocation and transformation was never entirely the case, either in the coastal mill towns or especially in North Adams. Perhaps it was the relative proximity of the northern Berkshires to the border. Perhaps it was the connection of waterways from the Saint Lawrence River to the Richelieu in southern Quebec to Lake Champlain in Vermont and down through a series of tributaries to the Hoosic River that made North Adams seem within easy reach (it was a difficult but passable route, although winter crossings were usually out of the question and the trains had to be used). . . . Whatever the many reasons, the French Canadians at first did not view North Adams as a place to resettle entire families. Young men arrived alone, most of them probably the second and third sons of impoverished farming families, many leaving young wives and children behind.[5]

This was not an unusual scenario. At least as early as the 1830s, parts of Maine, New Hampshire, and Vermont had served as places for seasonal work for French Canadians, a migrant workforce that baled hay and cut wood in the autumns and returned home with a few coins in their pockets or a few supplies in their knapsacks to help their families face the cold winters. The thick, forested region of the entire northeast quadrant of the continent made their skills felling trees transferable from place to place. There was

talk of regular work in Montana, Idaho, and even the Klondike whenever the men wanted it.[6] . . .

The young men arriving in North Adams at first understood the town as a seasonal locale, albeit in the factory, and viewed their incomes as part of an effort to augment the household economies back home. Some may have continued chopping wood and baling hay during the months when they were not pegging shoes for the American manufactories. Others may have made North Adams the very southern terminus of a well-travelled route between Quebec and western Massachusetts, picking up jobs along the way in Vermont, maybe stopping in Burlington for a spell when the barges came in and needed loading or when the labourers were flush with a little spending money. The vacuum left by New England men off at the battlefront during the Civil War made all kinds of patched-together jobs available for the Quebecois. The rhythm of Berkshire shoe manufacturing, in which the hired help tended to be temporarily let go in the slow months of December and January, fit neatly into the already established patterns of migrants and poor farmers living by their wits and allowed them to dovetail shoemaking with other kinds of work. Whatever the mixed-and-matched employment, the working life of the young French-Canadian shoemaker was as wide and varied as the path he traced back and forth across the border. . . .

***

The French Canadians crossed the border to find and make a decent living—that much is abundantly clear. . . . [T]hey did not wander in the picturesque frontier but travelled with a sense of purpose through the industrial landscape. Compared to the miseries of a near-indigent farming life, living for extended periods in the overcrowded New England tenements and toiling in the mills were often worthwhile trade-offs. The days tending the looms or spindles were numbingly long, true, and the wages provided little more than subsistence, and sometimes less. But the majority of French Canadians were marginally better off than they were in the fields. Some received pay for the first time in their lives.[7] Along with the sheer massing of so many workers in the mills and tenements, this sense of obtaining means, however minimal, brought about a shift in the social relations among the former Quebecois farmers. . . . In the English-speaking New England mill towns, the sense of an inherited francophone social identity survived, even magnified; but the economic disputes, when they took place, changed dramatically. They did not usually pit workers against each other but rather against capital and management. Far from fissuring or dispersing the French Canadians, as some in Quebec feared, the mill experience tended to collectivize them, providing not only a ready-made community in the sheer numbers who were gathered together but also giving the various workers a shared cultural *and* economic interest.

This claim for a collective sensibility among the French Canadians contradicts the usual claim for them offered by their Yankee contemporaries.[8] The idea of a bedraggled, hopelessly fractious people was elaborated in all sorts of invidious characterizations. The workers from across the border were selfish, penurious, and untrustworthy; they had no loyalty to anything larger than individual gain; they squabbled relentlessly with each other; they were so preoccupied with hoarding what little they earned that they could not act communally and cared nothing for the welfare for their own children; they had no desire to put down proper roots. Of course these descriptions were the usual fare for foreigners taking up residence in the Northeast (the Chinese got versions of them out West, the Mexicans in the Southwest) but what is significant—and not wholly surprising—is the vehemence with which they were offered of the French Canadians, not only from the xenophobic or nativist townspeople but also from labour's most sympathetic supporters. Read, for example, the single description of French Canadians that

appeared in the report by the Massachusetts Bureau of Statistics and Labor . . .

With some exceptions the Canadian French are the Chinese of the Eastern States. They care nothing for our institutions, civil, political, or educational. They do not come to make a home among us, to dwell with us as citizens, and so become a part of us; but their purpose is merely to sojourn a few years as aliens, touching us only at a single point, that of work, and when they have gathered out of us what will satisfy their ends, to get them away to whence they came, and bestow it there. They are a horde of industrial invaders, not a stream of stable settlers. Voting, with all that it implies, they care nothing about. Rarely does one of them become naturalized. They will not send their children to school if they can help it, but endeavor to crowd them into the mills at the earliest possible age. To do this they deceive about the age of their children with brazen effrontery. . . . To earn all they can by no matter how many hours of toil, to live in the most beggarly way out of their earnings they may spend as little for living as possible, and to carry out of the country what they can thus save: this is the aim of the Canadian French in our factory districts.[9]

They work endlessly, they live beggarly, they send their children to the factory. How easy it was to ascribe to the French-Canadian personality the conditions imposed on them by American industry. How convenient it was to forget the role and promises of recruiting agents and the mad rhythms inside the factories. Of all the bile and displaced responsibility, the most telling was the simple declaration: 'their purpose is merely to sojourn.'

Beginning roughly in 1867 and in contrast to the official state findings, the evidence for a large, generous, tenuously stable community and communal sensibility among the workers was everywhere. To combat the mindless effects of the factory, the French Canadians, like nearly all foreign workers who arrived in the Northeast, initiated and maintained a wide spectrum of social and cultural institutions to bring life to the few hours they had off: fire brigades, church groups, musical bands, fraternal clubs, pubs, music and dance halls, cockfights and revivalist meetings, a Young Men's Catholic Literary Association in nearby Cohoes, a French newspaper defiantly called *Le Patriote* in Burlington, another equally defiant in Cohoes called *La Patrie Nouvelle*, and on and on.[10] Vulgar songs got composed extolling the naughty pleasures of sinning, breaking the rules of the Catholic priests in the new French-Canadian parishes, or simply remarking on the more lenient aspects of New England-style French Catholicism ('Les curés du États, ils nous conduis'nt mieux qu'ca,' one of them went, 'ils nous font des veillées, c'est pour nous fair' danser').[11] Of course all these social and cultural extravagances, even the silly French ditties, could be chalked up as further evidence of an insular and resistant foreignness, traces of a stubborn *la survivance* mentality, rather than also being attempts to cope as an alienated community in the New England mill towns. But for our purposes the larger point is that these were all signs of new social relations among the former Quebecois farmers as they found each other as a working class in American industry. This is not to say they were blessedly free of feuds and rivalries; there were plenty of complaints about favouritism, the rankling air of superiority worn by some, the impossible jealousies of others. Nor is it to deny the greater fluidity between the old farmlands and the new factories for the Quebecois, a mobility that was in practice impossible for other foreigners, the Irish especially. But in general, the old village relations that had once characterized the farming countryside were being replaced by something entirely new, not homegrown in Quebec but grafted on foreign, urban soil—a collective resolve, often based on social and cultural pursuits, to accommodate and withstand the rigours of industrial life. Despite the fact that the

Bureau of Statistics and Labor could not conceive the French Canadians as anything more than miserly, rootless, and hopelessly unassimilable—in essence, unsuited for the needs of organized labour—the people from across the border were in their own way being proletarianized.

***

There is a temptation to consider the French-Canadian formation of local lodges of the Knights of St Crispin separately from the more obviously language-based social and cultural institutions described above, but that would be a mistake. Although easily the clearest sign of a new economic consciousness and cohesiveness among the former farmers, the Crispin lodge, especially as the old medieval shoemakers guild had been revived and developed during and immediately after the July Monarchy in France, possessed an important social as well as economic dimension. Whatever else it might connote, shoemaking also possessed a 'delightful princely and entertaining history', according to the Crispins.[12] They concocted plays and colourful stock characters, not only of Crispin and Crispianus, the saints who gave the order its name, but of entirely new figures like John the Frenchman, whose many adventures revolved around a 'Shooe-maker's Glory' (fellowship and fortune) and trysts with his many fair customers (usually a mayor's or banker's wife). The earnest pursuit (or fabrication) of medieval stories, poems, sayings, and songs—all of them available in the mother tongue—surely appealed to the French speakers. Even the crazy blanket-tossing initiation rite must have been a social experience, if nothing else. At some fundamental convivial level, then, the local Crispin lodges must have been on a par with the music and dance halls, the drinking clubs and corner pubs—places to gather, swap gossip and stories about the farms and factories, contrive tall tales about crossing the border or hazing the British, and sing the new drinking songs that put to melody both homesickness and American opportunity.

Of course the lodges were based on a trade, too, and developed in relation to a specific kind of industry and manufactory so dismissive of its workers, so jaundiced in its view of the interchangeable nature of cheap labour, that it forced the shoemakers to organize. In the manufacturer's logic, one worker was as good as another; and the cheaper the wage, the better, for after all, even a hardscrabble farmer could learn how to operate the stitching machines. In that industrial climate, the goals of the lodges were clear: above all to monopolize the skills needed to run the new machines, and to maintain a closed shop and keep 'green hands' from entering their workspace and devaluing their work. There was the sense among some contemporaries . . . that the Crispin lodges were resistant to new technology—romantic primitives unable to fathom the coming of modernity—and that they organized simply to prevent or retard the transformation of shoemaking from the artisan's craft to the industrialist's assembly. But this was the manufacturer's typical lament (if only he could get more machines!) and not at all characteristic of North Adams shoemakers' attitudes. Besides, hardly any of them made more than an occasional shoe prior to leaving the Canadian farms, and they had no long-standing devotion to the hands-on, leather-to-finished craft of the cobbler. For most of them, their introduction to the trade in North Adams took place when machines had already begun to structure most of the processes in the manufacture of shoes. This is not to suggest they were either lackadaisical or unskilled when it came to the art of making shoes. But it is to suggest that . . . the Crispins were sober about the ubiquity of machinery and their economic prudence to master and monopolize it.

. . .

The first signs of conflict could be seen only a few years after the French Canadians started work. [Factory owner Calvin] Sampson brought lasting machines into the factory, and the men, believing the machines would begin to shrink their numbers, simply rebelled. Short of striking,

the usual methods of rebellion were slowing the pace, making bad shoes, or tinkering with the machines to make them malfunction—small acts of sabotage. Perhaps the shoemakers did all three; whatever the means, 'the men managed to make it cost me more than to do lasting by hand,' Sampson complained.[13] Their resistance to machinery must have irked him sorely. While the Lynn manufactories and the Blackinton mill had been almost completely mechanized, Sampson admitted the he had 'not as yet been able to do the greater part of my work by machinery'.

In 1869, in a move of either colossal arrogance or blithe indifference, Sampson purchased a new factory and attempted to introduce, once again, more machinery and regimentation.[14] The new building was huge—115 feet wide, 120 feet long, three stories high, a main carriage entrance for the traffic of raw materials coming in and finished shoes going out, a central courtyard, and perhaps most importantly, direct access to the Hoosic River, whose flowing waters the manufacturer 'may use . . . for the purposes of power or otherwise in any manner [he] shall deem fit', as the deed of sale is careful to elaborate.[15] He was preparing for large steam power. He broke the building into three parts, each floor corresponding to a different aspect of shoemaking: the top for the uppers, the midlevel for the bottoming, the ground floor to hold the steam engines, for storage, and for crating and shipping the finished merchandise. The building was no longer an empty husk in which the shoemaking process was arbitrarily fit; the architecture began to have a logical design function. The men and women were split apart; the berths were organized around the central courtyard, where windows illuminated the stations; the belt-driven stitching and sewing machines were organized in neat rows and the overhead pipes carrying the steam were positioned to deliver optimum pressure; and the various pieces for assembly were conveyed to and from the several departments using rolling carts, chutes, and a system of pulleys. . . . The shoe assembly worked top down, literally, as the process began on the upper floor and the ladies' shoe, as it began to take shape, travelled downward toward the shipping crates and wagons. It was the first time such a comprehensive assembly logic—it is not quite right to call it an assembly line yet—was introduced into Berkshire shoemaking.

Sampson must have been extraordinarily proud of the new factory. It was a visible sign of his reach, and while it did not quite rival the Lynn manufactories in sheer size, it began to approach that level of industrial splendour and order. . . . The local papers poured unrestrained praise, took their readers on a detailed walking tour, as if the factory were a wondrous monument to industry, and delighted in all the mechanical advances. 'It is a model establishment,' the *Transcript* declared.[16] Turn this way and that, look at 'boiler rooms, coal house, and other store rooms—all arranged and adapted for convenience, dispatch and safety'. Take the elevator upstairs, where '30 sewing machines, 1 punching machine and 3 eyelet machines' are humming along. Stand in the central courtyard and be amazed that the 'entire building is heated by steam, lighted by gas, supplied with wash rooms, cloak rooms and conveniences of every kind.' Take notice that all the work 'is executed upon a careful system and proceeds with the regularity of machinery'. And remember this prediction: 'Large as the business now is, we have good reason to believe that plans are in contemplation for its enlargement, which in the end will make this the most extensive manufactory of this style of work in the state.'

The French Canadians responded to the factory by organizing into a union.

. . .

***

. . . [B]y 1870 the French Canadians had organized the pegging rooms in all the shoe factories in North Adams. When Sampson refused to accept their demand for a closed shop and when he refused to pay them a decent wage (or at least one in proportion to his profits), they all went out on strike. For nearly a month in late spring

1870, the protesting Crispins shut down every shoe manufactory in town.

. . .

. . . Seemingly surrounded everywhere by those unruly, demanding Crispins, Sampson sent his superintendent, George Chase, to San Francisco to hire a gang of Chinese. Chase left for the coast in late April or early May 1870, in either case less than a year after Sampson's model establishment had opened. By late May, the superintendent had rounded up a crew of 75—a Foreman, two cooks, and 72 would-be shoemakers—and on 1 June set off with them for North Adams.

. . .

Bruised by the Chinese appearance, the French-Canadian Crispins almost immediately responded. Of course there were the expected schoolyard pranks; one shoemaker scaled Sampson's fence and scrawled 'No Scabs or Rats Admitted Here' on the factory wall. . . .[17] There was simple thuggery; some of the Chinese were beaten when they attempted to walk through town during their time off. Others had buckets of dirty water poured on them.[18] There were attempts at intimidation of the shoe manufacturer himself; Sampson was sent threats, the factory put in danger of 'being blown up or set on fire'.[19] And there was a good bit of loud moaning; the Crispins held a mass rally in the centre of town, invited Samuel Cummings, the national leader, to speak, and bellyached about Sampson, whose name they shuddered to say because they 'did not wish to pollute [their] lips with it oftener than possible'.[20] Needless to say, none of these bad manners helped their cause among the shoe manufacturers or nativist townspeople, and in general the Crispins responded with more sophisticated strategies, though most of them may strike us as astonishingly contradictory.

The first was to go back to work at the other factories just a week after the Chinese had arrived. Given the presence of the Chinese in Sampson's bottoming room, they went back under a black cloud, but the circumstances were even worse than that. A journalist for the *Transcript* happily listed them: 'The suspension of work in the other shoe factories caused by this event, has ended and work has been resumed. Parker Bros., Cady Bros., Millard and Whitman and E.R. and N.L. Millard offered their old hands work at a reduction of ten per cent, but this was not accepted. They then resolved to employ new help and so many of the old as chose to accept the new terms, and on Tuesday commenced work.'[21] All the names of North Adams' shoe factories were carefully spelled out, making clear that manufacturing had combined its might to confront the Crispins in unison, determine an across-the-board wage (and cut), and follow through on the threat to turn to 'new help' if the union (not the manufacturers) did not yield. As if to punctuate the fresh resolve of the shoe manufacturers and the precarious position of shoemakers who remained out, the *Transcript* concluded that Parker, Cady, Whitman, and all the others 'expect to be able to procure fresh hands and in the end to be as well supplied as before.'

Why did the Crispins return? Had the presence of the Chinese—and the potential for more 'new help'—so rattled them? . . .

A good guess is that a majority of North Adams shoemakers had no more money to sustain their strike, and no help from the national Order. (It did not help that so many of the other lodges out on strike were Irish and English; what little available money surely was not distributed evenly.) Some were forced back to the factory to put food on the table; their decision must have caused spleen among the more principled. No wonder Samuel Cummings was so quick to the scene in North Adams; in addition to berating Sampson, he was trying to keep the lodge from splintering or collapsing. Only a few shoemakers, who had stored up enough food or money or had income from the mixed-and-matched jobs along the Quebec–Massachusetts corridor, could weather the storm a bit longer.

In addition to going back to work, the Crispins kindled a larger discussion on the East Coast about labour's relationship to the Chinese, a discussion that had been raging for years on the West Coast. They gathered all of North Adams' unions together in late June, just two weeks after the Chinese had arrived, assembling at the Wilson House (of all places, the heart of the nouveau riche), and putting the 'Chinese question'—what to do about them—in the context of the larger labour movement. Although the papers were barred from covering the union meeting—all they could report was that a 'Labor Reform Meeting will be held . . . to consider and discuss, among other things, the Chinese question'—there is sufficient evidence to suggest what took place.[22] The union men had discussed the wholesale exclusion of the Chinese and agreed to put the subject up for national debate. Some may have wanted exclusion outright; others, it is clear, began to parse the distinction between immigrant and coolie labour (the venerable and useful distinction among manufacturers, as we have seen) and finesse the question; and still others, themselves recent arrivals in the country, wanted no part of exclusion. The positions played out in a whole sequence of meetings and rallies afterward among unionists in Albany, Boston, Chicago, New York, Rochester, and Troy.[23] The summer was rife with heated debate as labour tried to feel its way toward a proper stance regarding the Chinese. By August, the positions had hardened. At the National Labor Union meeting in Cincinnati, the Crispins introduced a resolution to establish a separate labour party to bring their platform to national elections—in effect, to put their views to the ballot box. What did they want voted on? They pushed through a new official Union stance, that the old Burlingame Treaty between the United States and China—the treaty that had made provisions for the free flow of Chinese labour across the Pacific—be completely abrogated and the Chinese, having suddenly penetrated east of the Mississippi, be excluded from the country entirely.[24]

. . .

***

At one obvious level, the Crispins saw in the Chinese a class of competitors—competitors for their jobs, yes, but also competitors and instigators for their claims to belonging. . . . I earlier suggested that such an identity or way of naming this complex sense of belonging might be understood by way of current theories about diaspora. Diaspora, the dispersion or scattering of a people, has several key features of particular relevance to the French Canadians in North Adams. It connotes not only a history of dispersal (whether forced or voluntary), but also a strongly held memory (or set of myths) about the homeland from which its people have been scattered; a difficult relationship with the new country (the 'belief [that the people] are not—and perhaps cannot be—fully accepted by their host country', as William Safran writes); a desire for an eventual return, however distant, but in the meantime a commitment to the maintenance or maybe even the restoration of a homeland and its downtrodden people; and a sense of community with others, often living in quite separate places, who are kept in contact with each other by some important homeland circulation (of goods, money, photographs, perhaps even just a bit of gossipy news).[25] It differs from exile insofar as exiled persons are prevented from returning home, destined because of legal or political obstacles to remain forever outside the land of their dreams. Indeed, for the exile, the continuous experience of loss is much more intensely constitutive of identity. There was nothing that absolutely kept the French Canadians from returning; in fact quite the opposite, most of the townspeople would have preferred that they went home. The border was completely porous, as the migrants up and down the Quebec–Massachusetts corridor knew well. But the idea of return—to home, but perhaps more importantly to a condition of ethnic solidarity and cultural richness and to a place and time (usually mythologized out of all proportion) where the benefits and privileges of citizenship were simply assumed—helped give form to the community living on an alien soil.

The Crispins did not pack their bags and return to Canada. It must have been tempting; the old farms were still there, the old community,

no matter how embattled under the 1867 British North America Act, must have seemed familiar and comforting. A popular song made them dream of a future there. 'C'est là l'endroit d'ma naissance,' it reminded the French Canadians, 'Là où que j' suis toujours resté. Nous achèt'rons une terre qui nous sera parfaite en beauté.'[26] Instead, they chose to stay, and in doing so augmented the condition of living in the diaspora. The presence of the Chinese had somehow activated in the Crispins, who were everywhere reminded of 'l'endroit d'ma naissance' and their responsibility to *la survivance*, an awareness that they were committed to North Adams as well and made them recognize that they had multiple attachments, as all diasporics do. In this sense, the diasporic identity was shaped not only by a transnational sensibility and network but also in response to another foreign workforce claiming a place on the host land. It was formed relationally and characterized a way of framing one's relationship to local constituencies and circumstances and a means of communal survival—and community making—amidst Others.

. . .

***

In late June 1870, only a few weeks after the Chinese arrived in North Adams, 31 Crispins purchased and began operation of a worker-owned shoe factory, a commune to compete directly with Sampson.[27] The name for such a commune was 'co-operative' (the socialist inflection lessened) and was much in the news. Short of dismantling industrial capitalism, which only the most fervent or delusional radical envisioned, the co-operative was seen by many as a good compromise and an antidote—maybe the only kind—for the embattled labourers to use. Capital is 'too subtle and fugacious a thing' the editor for *The Nation* proclaimed, and the shoemakers 'have but one means of protecting themselves against its tyranny, and that is, becoming capitalists themselves and co-operating'. Neither the strikes nor the violence throughout 1869 and

1870 had brought manufacturers to their knees, everyone understood. 'It is becoming clearer and clearer every day that this [the co-operative] is the only road out of [the shoemakers'] difficulties,' *The Nation* concluded.[28] The national Order of the Crispins agreed and encouraged as many lodges as possible to begin their own shops, decreeing after a spate of unsuccessful strikes in 1869 that 'cooperation [is] a proper and efficient remedy for . . . the evils of the present iniquitous system of wages.'[29] The North Adams Crispins were not the first group of shoemakers to form a co-operative; French Canadians had already done so in February 1869 in Saint John, New Brunswick. They were followed in March by shoemakers in Stoughton, Massachusetts; in June by shoemakers in North Bridgewater, Massachusetts; and soon by men in New York, Brooklyn, Baltimore—in all, between 30 and 40 new shops nationwide by midyear.[30] . . . The North Adams Cooperative Shoe Company, as it was called, was followed in town by another just a few months later in September 1870, led by William Vial, a former lead shoemaker at Sampson's, and a third—it turned out to be stillborn ('we mention no names,' the *Transcript* reported with relief)—shortly after that.[31]

The first North Adams co-operative was a small enterprise, its ability to compete tested from the start. The Crispins could afford only six sewing machines and a single pegging machine, compared to 35 sewing and three pegging at Sampson's, and 26 sewing, three pegging, and even three new heeling machines at Millard's. At top speed, working day and night, they produced a hundred cases of shoes a month; Sampson produced over 400, Millard over 400, the Cady Brothers over 300, among several other top-flight factories.[32] The disadvantages apparently did not diminish the Crispins' feistiness. Whether feeling more competitive than other lodges, more rancorous, or perhaps having fewer building options open to them, they settled on a spot only a hundred yards uphill from Sampson's manufactory, putting themselves in open view of their former boss. It must have seemed an amazingly brazen act.

Equally brazen, the co-operative Crispins had a picture made of themselves soon after opening their doors, as if they too were going to pronounce in visual terms their stake in the new economy (Figure 1). Although they numbered only 31 (they appear mostly in the back row and off to the left), they saw fit to include the other men and women they had to hire to fill out the berths, bringing their mass to a size roughly comparable to the Chinese workers at Sampson's, competing with them not only in the manufacture of shoes but also in the sheer mass of bodies. We should be struck by other details that were in dialogue with those in the first picture of the Chinese. Although the co-operative was housed in a 'smaller wooden shop', as the *Transcript* reported, the Crispins had decided to set themselves against a large brick wall.[33] A closer look reveals the facade was not just some convenient factory face in North Adams but in fact the north wall of Sampson's. . . . It was a deliberate, pugnacious, provocative gesture, not to say an indication of stealth and wiliness. One can only imagine how they managed getting inside and pulling off the picture. In the photograph's logic, the Crispins pour out of Sampson's back door; men crowd the steps, pushing the rest of the men and women off to the right, three and four deep. Some chairs or benches must have been hastily set up in order to allow the shoemakers in the back to stand high enough to be seen. The arrangement is orderly, even meticulous. The lineup against the plain exterior, the reduction of the factory to windows and walls, the care of the mass of people not to overflow the limits of the lens, to crowd in such a way so as to touch but not trespass the picture's borders—in all these, the Crispins had looked closely at the competition and responded point by point. . . . The outpouring of men from the open door and the streaming of men and women along the north wall are signs of an exodus, as if the factory once belonged to these people—once their

Figure 1. Unknown photographer, The Crispins of the Co-operative, 1870.

vocational home—and, with the Chinese on the other side, as if they were being booted out the back. One of the men at the left descends from the lowest step to the bare ground, hat in hand, jacket and vest buttoned tight, as if he were leaving the factory.

. . .

***

Just as the Chinese shoemakers went to the photography studios, the Crispins started going too. Unlike the Chinese, who may have initially found those sessions to be an extension of Sampson's long reach and viewed their portraits as mediated by his patronage, the Crispins took it as an opportunity to lay claim to a different kind of identity, closer to an artisan's sense of self derived from a craft. It is a curious identification, since few of the Crispins had actually been cobblers in the old sense of the trade. But because it became the stock type by which industrial shoemakers still got identified . . . and because it fed

so neatly into the enthusiastic recall of the medieval artisan, as the French so loved, the cobbler was happily enlisted to help characterize the Crispins' devotion to skill. In a tintype portrait, a shoemaker has brought the instruments of the old trade to the photographer's studio (Figure 2). A toolkit is placed carefully off to the side. A shoe, its sole turned upward for repair, sits on his lap. The sitter wears the simple apron of a shoemaker, like the kind used by shoe repairers everywhere throughout the Berkshires, as later pictures attest. The upper flap on his apron sags, the result of years of being pressed upon by his chin and neck. The shoemaker's fingers hold the thread and needle to stitch the leather strips together; his head and shoulders droop slightly to give him better advantage over his work, one leg forward to balance the sole, the other back to brace his weight, the elbows splayed at a light angle so to manage the sharp needle and thick thread properly. It is a position this man claims to have assumed many times before and

Figure 2. Unknown photographer, Cobbler, *c.* 1870.

can take up again instantly, even in the artificial environs of the studio. Sometimes called occupational portraits, these pictures make the photographer's fancy screens in the background appear more ludicrous than is normally the case. The Victorian wallpaper belongs to someone else, the middle-class parlour fantasy of a tropical paradise far removed from the conditions of labour.

. . . [T]his shoemaker insists upon the cobbler's work clothes, daily habits, and long facility with tools as the proper markers of an identity. And in this sense, he is less a shoemaker, as it was being practised in the new manufactories, and more like a medieval Crispin cobbler, an artisan of long-standing and singular skill, whose kind of labour and identity predates those permitted by the newfangled, steam-powered machines. The portrait is an argument for the endurance of a craftsmen's integrity and the values inscribed in it, values worth recovering and proclaiming during a moment of its imminent erasure, when craft became mechanized and the Chinese and

other green hands could learn shoemaking right off the train. He clings to (or fabricates) this identity when he and his brethren in the Crispin lodge are hardly earning a living in the way that is pictured here. The portrait is a conjuring of a pre-industrial aura, even as the sitter, once back in the co-operative factory, must necessarily put himself on different competitive ground. In a sense, the lack of fit between conjuring the cobbler's old skills and the reality of the new factory, where steam power had taken firm hold of the industry and transformed the nature of labour, is mirrored in the portrait itself, where the hand-sewing shoemaker seems a cutout from another place and set like a specimen in a world that does not belong to him.

. . .

***

The co-operatives struggled along for a number of years. The effort required to succeed was prodigious. In November 1870, normally the beginning of the winter slow period when most manufacturers began to lay off their workers and shut down the machines for two months, the Crispin co-operatives remained open, trying to squeeze out all the pennies from the tight market.[34] (Of the big manufacturers, only Sampson stayed open; he had huge new contracts to fill.) The same thing happened the next year and the one following. While most of the manufactories gave their machines a rest and put them up for yearly maintenance, the co-operatives kept their six or seven stitching and single pegging machines chugging for three years straight. Although they boasted to the local papers in early 1871 that their businesses were 'in prosperous condition, having all the orders [we] can fill and being free of debt', they were having difficulty penetrating the lucrative Boston markets.[35] It surely did not help when Sampson combined with other shoe manufacturers to pressure the state's wholesalers into refusing Crispin-made goods.[36] After the autumn of 1873—the beginning of the Panic of 1873—there was no hope of success; the nation's economy went into a tailspin, and massive unemployment ruled throughout the Northeast, eliminating the market for any sort of luxury item like the dainty shoes being pumped out of North Adams. But even before then, the co-operatives were in danger, since they were always on tenuous footing and deeply susceptible to even the tiniest shifts in the market. A single lost order or an unpaid bill, a refusal of credit or the demand that a debt be paid immediately could set them back. They began to close one by one. The closings were slow deaths, the men departing the co-operatives in twos and threes and leaving their remaining brethren to try to keep the hope alive with increasingly smaller numbers of hands. The shops struggled along in a nearly comatose state for weeks on end, the membership slowly leaving and yet shoes still trickling out from the machines in smaller and smaller bundles. Even the North Adams Co-operative, the first and largest and most militant of the bunch, could not keep its membership intact. 'Look out for a smash

up,' the credit reports warned their creditors, because 'the best men have left the concern.'[37] The prognosis was accurate. In March 1873, the North Adams Co-operative shut its doors and advertised the small wooden factory building on Brooklyn Street for rent.[38] As if to drive the wound of failure deeper, Sampson quickly declared to the papers that while other manufactories were closing he was refurnishing his office 'in a very elegant and tasty manner' and, oh yes, 'putting a new boiler, suitable for driving a 40-horsepower engine'.[39] Later that year, the North Adams Crispin lodge, like nearly all the lodges throughout New England, quietly folded.

***

. . .

The decades after the Civil War comprised the great age of working-class formation, to which the French Canadians throughout the industrializing Northeast contributed. A key aspect of that larger story is how various workingmen from across the immigrant spectrum solidified as both a white working class and proper citizens and how that solidifying was brokered through their repeated efforts to position themselves against unorganized, non-white labourers, especially the Chinese—against an 'indispensable enemy', as the historian Alexander Saxton once described them.[40] In that negotiation, white working-class consciousness obtained economically, politically, and socially through an oppositional, sometimes violent, form of race relations.[41] Its most concrete political embodiment appeared in 1877 with the founding in San Francisco of the secret, working-class Order of the Caucasians, whose 'bounden and solemn duty' was to 'pursue and injure' the Chinese and agitate for their exclusion.[42] Through the efforts of the Caucasians and groups like them, whiteness and class mixed, fortifying each other, a kind of alchemy that resulted in a means for immigrants to claim rights in the public sphere and, eventually, citizenship. The French Canadians would eventually pursue that route.

The situation in 1870s North Adams between the French Canadians and Chinese would seem an early example of that larger story, but we ought to be mindful of an enormous gray area, a historical moment when the path to citizenship was for many nominally 'white' immigrants not easy to discern or follow. The French Canadians were, after all, the 'Chinese of the Eastern States', caricatured by the same invidious features of penury, babble, mindless efficiency, and rootless sojourn normally offered about the Chinese. And they were hardly 'white'—they did not even make it into the spectrum of variegated whiteness proposed in an 1877 series of *Harper's* articles concerned with ethnographic differences among the 'white races'—and were usually considered by the representatives of labour to be no better or sometimes even worse than the horde of Chinese threatening to come across country.[43] Sampson certainly came to think so. Of course the French Canadians went some way toward becoming more aligned with the Irish and English by becoming an activist Crispin lodge and helping to generate a pro-labour and anti-Chinese platform in national politics. But as the ungenerous, niggardly reports from the Bureau of Statistics and Labor and the special agent for the Bureau of Labor suggest, they could be accommodated in an image of labour only to a point. In a bizarre way, the features that we have identified and valued as enabling their entry into class politics . . . were the same ones that kept them consistently construed as other, as unassimilated, unassimilable, and even racialized. They were non-white labourers hoping to gain a foothold in a white working-class polity.

. . .

Notes

This chapter compiled from the chapters 'What the Shoe Manufacturer Saw' and 'What the Crispins Saw' in Anthony Lee's *A Shoemaker's Story: Being Chiefly about French Canadian Immigrants, Enterprising Photographers, Rascal Yankees, and Chinese Cobblers in a Nineteenth-century Factory Town* (Princeton: Princeton University Press, 2008).

1. These numbers are middle-of-the-road. Estimates vary wildly. For examples, see Yolande Lavoie, 'Les mouvements migratoires des Canadiens entre leur pays et les Etats-Unis au XIXe et au XXe siècles', in Hubert Charbonneau, comp., *La population de Québec: Études rétrospectives* (Montreal: Boréal Express, 1973), 78; and Dyke Hendrickson, *Quiet Presence* (Portland, ME: Guy Gannett Publishing, 1980), 51.
2. The 'great haemorrhage' is by Raoul Blanchard. Both this quote and 'the graveyard of the race' by Antoine Labelle are offered in Paul-André Linteau et al., eds, *Québec: A History, 1867–1929* (Toronto: James Lorimer, 1983), 28. This reference for the following quote as well.
3. 'Where are you going?—To the States.—You are headed for poverty. Turn around, don't go there!' As transcribed in Donald Deschênes, 'The Dream of a Better Life in the Songs of Departure for the United States', in Claire Quintal, ed., *Steeples and Smokestacks: A Collection of Essays on the Franco-American Experience in New England* (Worcester, MA: Assumption College, 1996), 438.
4. Though not as plentiful as studies devoted to other immigrant groups, studies of how French Canadians settled in New England factory towns are growing. For typical examples, see Frances Early, 'French-American Beginnings in an American Community: Lowell, Massachusetts, 1868–1886', PhD dissertation, Concordia University, 1979; and Tamara Hareven and Randolph Langenbach, *Amoskeag: Life and Work in an American Factory* (New York: Cambridge University Press, 1982). A good example of a comparative study (in this case, between Irish and French-Canadian immigrants) is the early and venerable Daniel J. Walkowitz, *Worker City, Company Town: Iron and Cotton-Worker Protest in Troy and Cohoes, New York, 1855–1884* (Urbana: University of Illinois Press, 1978).
5. The 1860 census for North Adams is helpful in making these assessments. It lists categories for age, employment, and place of origin for each person. The common profile of the French-Canadian immigrant was a man in his twenties who worked as a 'day laborer'.
6. Pierre Anctil, 'The Franco-Americans of New England', in Dean Louder and Eric Waddell, eds, *French America: Mobility, Identity, and Minority Experience across the Continent* (Baton Rouge: Louisiana State University Press, 1983), 43.
7. Anctil, 'Franco-Americans', 44.
8. It is a claim often repeated by historians in otherwise sympathetic accounts and is the basis for the related claim that French Canadians did not organize into unions as enthusiastically as other groups. See, for example, Hugh Mason Wade, *The French Canadians, 1760–1945*, vol. 1 (Toronto: Macmillan of Canada, 1968), 337–43.

9. H.A. Dubuque, as quoted in *Thirteenth Annual Report of the Bureau of Statistics and Labor, Embracing the Account of Its Operations and Inquiries From March 1, 1881, to March 1, 1882* (Boston: Wright and Potter, 1882), 12.

10. The literary association and Cohoes paper are noted in Walkowitz, *Worker City, Company Town*, 161 and 172. The Burlington paper is noted in Hendrickson, *Quiet Presence*, 47. . . .

11. 'The priests in the States, they lead us better than that. They hold parties for us where we can dance.' As transcribed in Deschènes, 'Dreams of Better Life', 442.

12. Blanche Hazard, *The Organization of the Boot and Shoe Industry in Massachusetts before 1875* (Cambridge: Harvard University Press, 1921), 170.

13. 'Testimony of C.T. Sampson', *Report of the Bureau of Statistics and Labor, Embracing the Account of Its Operations and Inquiries From March 1, 1870, to March 1, 1871* (Boston: Wright and Potter, 1871), 99. This reference for the following quote as well.

14. Deed, 2 October 1869, book 119, p. 3, Northern Berkshire District Registry of Deeds. The purchase price was $17,000.

15. Deed, 2 October 1869, book 119, p. 3, Northern Berkshire District Registry of Deeds.

16. 'A Model Shoe Factory', *Adams Transcript* (24 Mar. 1870). This reference for the following quotes as well.

17. Andrew Gyory, *Closing the Gate: Race, Politics, and the Chinese Exclusion Act* (Chapel Hill: University of North Carolina Press, 1998), 41.

18. *New York Times* (9 July 1870), 2.

19. *The Nation* (23 June 1870), 397.

20. The rally was widely covered. See *New York Herald* (26 June 1870); *Springfield Republican* (25 June 1870); and *Albany Journal* (23 June 1870).

21. 'Chinese Notes', *Adams Transcript* (23 June 1870). This reference for the following quote as well.

22. 'A Labor Reform Meeting', *Adams Transcript* (23 June 1870).

23. This is a huge point of contention among scholars of labour and the Exclusion Act. Most proclaim the anti-Chinese sentiment among eastern labour. Gyory proclaims otherwise; see his *Closing the Gate*, especially 42–7 for his assessment of labour's attitudes in the many rallies during the summer of 1870. . . .

24. John R. Commons et al., *History of Labor in the United States*, vol. 2 (New York: Macmillan, 1918), 148–51.

25. Understanding 'diaspora' is a scholarly industry in its own right, but for a useful introduction, see Safran's full essay, from which my quote is taken, 'Diasporas in Modern Society: Myths of Homeland and Return', *Diaspora* 1 (1991), 83–99. . . .

26. 'That's where I was born. It is there that I always lived. We'll buy a farm that will be perfectly beautiful.' As transcribed in Deschènes, 'Dream of Better Life', 443.

27. The details of the company and its shareholders are described in 'The North Adams Cooperative Shoe Company', *Adams Transcript* (6 Oct. 1870). An interesting aspect of this 6 October essay is that it was written by a journalist from the *New York Tribune* and picked up by the *Transcript*. The local paper had not bothered to cover the co-operative on its own.

28. *The Nation* (14 July 1870), 18.

29. As recorded in Don Lescohier, *The Knights of St. Crispin, 1867–1874: A Study in the Industrial Causes of Trade Unionism*, University of Wisconsin Economics and Political Science Series (Madison, 1910), 49.

30. Lescohier, *Knights of St. Crispin*, 49–55.

31. 'New Shoe Manufacturing Company', *Adams Transcript* (15 Sept. 1870).

32. Comparisons between the town's factories are offered in 'The Shoe Manufacturing Business of North Adams', *Adams Transcript* (6 Oct. 1870). Although the town had many more shoe manufactories, the *Transcript* compared data for only five.

33. 'Cooperative Shoe Company'.

34. *Adams Transcript* (24 Nov. 1870).

35. *Hoosac Valley News* (5 Apr. 1871), 2.

36. *New York Times* (31 Dec. 1870), 2.

37. Massachusetts, vol. 5, p. 37, R.G. Dun and Co. Collection, Baker Library, Harvard Business School.

38. *Adams Transcript* (13 Mar 1873).

39. *Adams Transcript* (15 May 1873), 2.

40. Alexander Saxton, *The Indispensable Enemy: Labor and the Anti-Chinese Movement in California* (Berkeley and Los Angeles: University of California Press, 1971). See also David Roediger, *The Wages of Whiteness: Race and the Making of the American Working Class* (NewYork: Verso, 1991); and my *Picturing Chinatown: Art and Orientalism in San Francisco* (Berkeley and Los Angeles: University of California Press, 2001), 59–99.

41. Readers will hear echoes of Noel Ignatiev's argument, which I wish gratefully to acknowledge. See his *How the Irish Became White* (New York: Routledge, 1996).

42. From the Order's bylaws, as quoted in Matthew Frye Jacobson, *Whiteness of a Different Color: European Immigrants and the Alchemy of Race* (Cambridge: Harvard University Press, 1998), 160. My reference to the 'alchemy' of race and class is indebted to Jacobson.

43. See the several articles in *Harper's Weekly* for January 1877 and March 1877 and *Harper's New Monthly Magazine* for June 1877 and October 1877.

12

'The best men that ever worked the lumber': Aboriginal Longshoremen on Burrard Inlet, British Columbia, 1863–1939

Andrew Parnaby

Aboriginal people in Canada, like Aboriginal people across the continent, have been engaged in wage labour for centuries. Yet despite a long and diverse history of paid employment, this dimension of Aboriginal life is under-studied by Canadian scholars.[1] Generally, anthropologists and ethno-historians have focused on 'traditional' Aboriginal cultures and Native-newcomer relations, while political scientists and legal experts continue to probe questions of treaty rights and government policy. This intellectual orientation is not surprising. To some extent, it reflects scholars' engagement with contemporary Aboriginal politics: documenting the existence and persistence of a customary way of life—the occupation and use of a certain territory or the practice of a specific ritual—has been, and continues to be, a critical dimension of the ongoing struggle for title to land and rights to resources. As a consequence, however, the significance of wage labour to Aboriginal communities—a phenomenon that suggests change, not continuity; modernity, not custom—has been neglected. It does not fit easily into scholarship aimed, to varying degrees, at bolstering Aboriginals' historical and moral claim to self-determination.[2]

... Of interest, now, is not whether Aboriginal people worked for wages, but why they chose to do so, what that experience meant, and how long it lasted.[3]

This cluster of questions is at the core of this essay, an examination of Aboriginal longshoremen, most of whom belonged to the Squamish First Nation, a linguistic subdivision of the Coast Salish, on Burrard Inlet, British Columbia, from 1863 to 1939. ... Organized into four sections, this essay begins with an analysis of the Squamish's adaptation to wage labour in the mid-to-late nineteenth century. It then considers the ways in which Aboriginal workers negotiated the daily demands of longshoring—an occupation characterized by hard physical labour, intense competition for work, and raw employer power. Throughout their long tenure on the waterfront, Aboriginal dockers adopted numerous strategies to bolster their collective power as workers and their particular objectives as Aboriginal people. The third and fourth sections of this essay explore these tactics, and in doing so, highlight some of the ways that Aboriginals' workplace struggles influenced, and in turn were shaped by, the Squamish's wider search for autonomy in the face of sweeping economic, political, and demographic change in British Columbia's Lower Mainland. Often mentioned in the scholarly literature, but never studied in a systematic

Andrew Parnaby, '"The best men that ever worked the lumber": Aboriginal Longshoremen on Burrard Inlet, BC, 1863–1939', *Canadian Historical Review* 87, 1 (Mar. 2006): 53–78.

way, the 'Indian' waterfront provides a window into the importance of waged work to Aboriginal people on Burrard Inlet and the sophisticated ways that the Squamish responded to Canadian colonialism *and* capitalism.

***

Cheakamus Tom understood the history of Native-newcomer relations in British Columbia very well. 'For many years, our people could and did gain a living suitable for our wants from the forest and the sea,' he stated in a letter written to the Royal Commission on Indian Affairs, which was holding hearings in the province from 1912 to 1916. 'The different tribes or bands had their own territory in which they fished and hunted, and over which they had control,' he continued. 'But when the White man came he was allowed to go where he pleased to hunt, trap, or fish. Then our troubles began.'[4] Pithy and succinct, Tom's assessment evokes an era prior to European settlement, when his people, the Squamish, utilized a swath of land between Howe Sound and Burrard Inlet in southwestern British Columbia; seasonally harvested aquatic and terrestrial resources in groups of family or extended family members; and, with these resources in hand, periodically held potlatches—a collection of ceremonies that reaffirmed the prestige, status, and influence of particular leaders or families through feasting, dancing, and gift-giving.[5] Flexible and mobile, this kin-ordered social formation, and the rituals lodged deeply within it, underwent an important adjustment after the first sawmill appeared on Burrard Inlet in 1863. Shortly after its construction, Squamish families gravitated to the area, incorporating wage labour into their seasonal migrations.[6] . . . 'A great number of these Indians live and exist by the work of their hands,' Indian Agent Peter Byrne observed in 1913, referring specifically to those Squamish resident on the North Shore. 'They work in the sawmills, at longshoring, and . . . at other occupations of a like character.'[7]

As this short list of jobs suggests, sawmills—Sewell Moody's on the North Shore, then Edward Stamp's on the south shore—were harbingers of things to come. From the mid-nineteenth century to the early years of the twentieth century, British Columbia underwent a far-reaching economic transformation, a shift illustrated well by the rise of Vancouver as an important Pacific Coast port. Spurred on by the completion of the Canadian Pacific Railway in 1886 and the opening of the Panama Canal in 1914, large piers, grain elevators, and warehouses were constructed up and down Burrard Inlet, while numerous rail lines were laid along both its north and south shores (see Figure 1).[8] Like the physical environment of the port, capital was reorganized too. Individually, shipping companies in Vancouver invested in iron hulls, steam technology, and larger vessels; collectively, shipping, railway, and stevedoring companies banded together to form the Shipping Federation in 1912 to better manage the increase in maritime traffic and the waterfront's burgeoning labour force.[9] . . . By the interwar period, the paternalism and single-staple exports of the mid-to-late nineteenth century had given way to more sophisticated economic structures. As David Montgomery has remarked, 'The waterfront of a great port dramatized both the organizational achievements and the social chaos of industrial capitalism.'[10]

Squamish men and women were important, if unequal, actors in this new industrial context. They stacked lumber in the mills, acted as guides for recreational hunters and fishers, built fences on farms, felled trees in the coastal forests, gutted fish in the canneries, piloted small boats in the salmon fishery, and loaded and unloaded cargo on the waterfront, usually combining a range of occupations to earn a modest livelihood. That all of the occupational pursuits undertaken by Aboriginal workers were seasonal is important, hinting at the ways in which the temporal and spatial rhythms of a customary, kin-ordered way of life articulated with the logic of a burgeoning capitalist labour market.[11] The result was a mixed economy in which Squamish men and women deployed some of their labour power some of the time in a new way—working for wages—while simultaneously maintaining older methods of

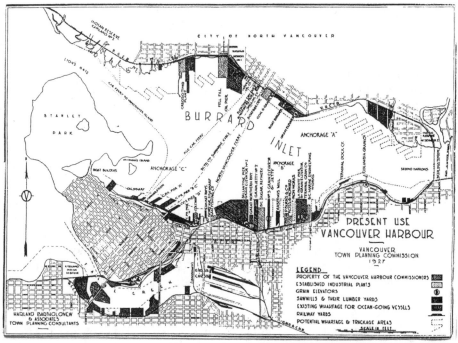

Figure 1. Port of Vancouver, 1927. Note the Squamish Reserves on the North Shore in North Vancouver and at the mouth of False Creek in Vancouver. Source: Vancouver Town Planning Commission, *A Plan for the City of Vancouver* (Vancouver, 1929).

regulating access to resource sites and affirming links between their families and larger Aboriginal groups. There was a culturally specific logic in operation here that was internal to Coast Salish society: it is likely that Squamish men and women engaged in wage labour because their earnings could be used to purchase the goods necessary to hold a potlatch—a rationale shared by the Lekwammen and Kwakwaka'wakw of Vancouver Island. Fragmentary evidence reveals that the Squamish continued to hold potlatches throughout this period of economic adjustment, although it is difficult to assess their size and frequency.[12] In short, cash and culture were connected, the persistence of the latter tied, to some degree, to the successful acquisition of the former.

Decisions about the utility of wage labour were not always made under conditions of the Squamish's own choosing, however. As an 'old man' who could 'remember when there was no Indian agent,' Cheakamus Tom knew this: 'The

White man thought we ate too much fish, too much game, and passed laws to prevent our people from killing game or fishing except for a short time each year.'[13] From the earliest days of the colonial project in British Columbia, the state played a critical role in setting limits on, and erecting boundaries around, the scope of Aboriginal life—a dynamic particularly obvious in the context of land. By the late 1870s, the Squamish, who, along with other Coast Salish groups bore the brunt of white encroachment, occupied a clutch of reserve sites in and around Howe Sound and on the North Shore of Burrard Inlet, an archipelago of Aboriginal territory in a sea of white pre-emptions.[14] Urban development, population growth, and economic expansion in the Lower Mainland, backed by a state that refused to recognize Aboriginal title to land, eroded this modest land base even further.[15] 'A long time ago, the Indians depended upon hunting and fishing as their only means of living,'

Mathias Joseph, a Squamish leader, observed in 1913. 'Now things have changed.'[16] While the Squamish were drawn into the capitalist labour market by a desire to continue potlatching, they continued to work for wages because, as time went on, they possessed few other options, save for selling their labour power in the canneries or on the waterfront.

***

For waterfront workers on Burrard Inlet, as for longshoremen the world over, the experience of work was shaped by the demands of both a casual labour market and the 'shape-up' method of hiring—a combination that persisted, in various guises, from the mid-nineteenth century until the 1920s. Typically, when vessels arrived in port, men swarmed the docks, and there, in a ring around a foreman, cargo hooks in hand, they jostled for position in hopes of securing a day's work.[17] In this context, work came in fits and starts, earnings fluctuated, and competition among men was often intense. Not surprisingly, then, waterfront workers tended to stress different skills and abilities in order to carve out a degree of security in an otherwise chaotic labour market. Organized into gangs, some men worked on ship, others laboured on shore, and within both categories men specialized in handling a particular cargo or operating a piece of technology. As long-time longshoreman Joe Gagnier recollected, referring specifically to the early twentieth century, 'There were gangs who regularly worked the Australasian boats and those same gangs worked general cargo and practically nothing else.' 'You cannot get lumbermen to trim grain,' echoed a waterfront employer in 1928.[18]

Socially constructed, and sometimes bitterly defended, demarcations of skill and ability intersected with cleavages of race and ethnicity on the job to produce a complex and hierarchical occupational milieu. Between 1908 and the late 1930s, the years for which solid evidence is available, white longshoremen dominated general cargo, Italian men tended to work as coal

heavers, and Aboriginal workers monopolized logs and lumber.[19] . . .

Lumber handling gangs loaded cut wood into a ship's hold. On a sailing ship, lumber was transported by hand over the stern or through a porthole, each piece sliding down a series of ramps to the hold. Alternatively, the cut wood, what longshoremen sometimes called 'boards', 'sticks', or 'timbers', was placed inside a sling, which was then fastened by a series of cables to a portable steam-powered engine called a 'donkey'; the donkey engine, which was situated on a barge or on the wharf, lifted the 'sling load' to the sailing ship to be stowed. Steam-powered vessels, which had all but replaced sailing ships in the lumber trade by the mid-to-late 1920s, utilized deck-mounted winches, as well as derricks or cranes, to accomplish the same task, albeit at a much faster pace. Once inside a ship's hold, the load was disassembled and each 'stick', which ranged widely in length, width, and weight, was carefully packed away.[20]

Each member of a lumber handling gang was assigned a specific task. The gang leader, or 'hatch tender', coordinated the efforts of the men on ship, shore, and/or barge: he called for loads, sent signals to the donkey or winch driver, and dealt with personnel from the ship or stevedoring company who meddled in the work process ('Look, do this') and pushed the men to move faster ('Come on, you guys down there, move').[21] 'Wire pullers' assisted the donkey driver; 'slingmen' assembled loads; and 'side runners' organized the men in the ship's hold— the men who, in pairs, handled each 'timber'. Experienced men, like 'the Indian Charlie Antone', were able to work at a variety of jobs within a single gang; '[He] could run side pretty darn good,' long-time waterfront worker Axel Nyman recollected. 'Good man on the boom, [too].'[22] Above or below the ship's deck, lumber handling was both physically demanding and repetitive. It was not, however, without skill. On the 'top side', winch drivers and slingmen prided themselves on being able to manoeuvre long pieces of lumber through a small hatch into the ship's hold; ''tween decks', gang members valued men who understood how to stow lumber no matter what the configuration of a ship's hold. As one Squamish longshoreman observed, reflecting on his skills as a lumber handler, 'When I was running side I used to watch the load coming down the hatch. There might be six or eight timbers in the load and I would size it up as soon as it landed I would know where each timber was going.'[23]

The number of 'Indian' gangs working on Burrard Inlet between 1863 and 1939 varied over time. Estimates by veteran longshoremen, who were thinking specifically about the early 1900s, put the number between four and six—which means that, depending on the size of the vessel, and whether or not it was being loaded or unloaded, anywhere between 40 and 90 'Indian' lumber handlers could be found on the docks on a given day. The figures available for the early 1920s, drawn from the records of a longshoremen's union and the Department of Labour, are higher, placing the number at approximately 125. Almost entirely absent from the docks in the mid-to-late 1920s, for reasons that will be explored later, 'Indian' longshoremen turn up in greater numbers after 1935; personnel records kept by waterfront employers indicate that between 40 and 55 men were actively handling lumber in the early 1940s.[24] In the context of the waterfront, 'Indian' was an elastic category that included individuals born to Squamish parents, as well as those, Aboriginal and non-Aboriginal, who married Squamish women. An assortment of other workers, drawn from a range of national, cultural, and racial backgrounds, including other First Nations, rounded out the ranks of the 'Indian'-dominated gangs. This diversity is captured well by the personnel histories of William Nahanee and Joe Jerome. Nahanee, who started on the waterfront in 1889 and remained a longshoreman for over 50 years, was of Hawaiian and Squamish ancestry, while Jerome, who, it appears, began his career on the docks sometime

in the 1930s, was born to Tsimshian parents and married to a Squamish woman.[25]

The 'Indians'' status on the waterfront as lumber handlers flowed, in part, from their long history of paid employment in and around Burrard Inlet. They had been handling logs and lumber, either in the sawmills or in the woods, for a long time.[26] With this employment history, it is no surprise that they emerged as adept waterfront workers: both logging and longshoring were physically demanding jobs, and the skills acquired in one occupational context—the ability to run a donkey engine, for example—were easily transferred to another.[27] Specialization in a particular commodity helped Aboriginal longshoremen shore up their prestige as well, for it enabled them to gain greater knowledge of a specific cargo and, over time, a strong reputation for loading and unloading it. 'The Indians were "it" on the sailing ships,' one old-timer recollected. 'They were the greatest men that ever worked the lumber,' observed another.[28]

Great, but not quite equal: while Aboriginal dockers chose to work 'the lumber' because they possessed the right skills, and specialization helped to bring some predictability to casual work, they did so in an occupational context in which their options, although not closed off entirely, were constrained. Significantly, white waterfront workers tended to dominate general cargo, which was less dangerous and more lucrative than working the lumber.[29] Their position of relative privilege was girded by a sense of entitlement that all whites possessed by virtue of being white in a society in which race mattered. In British Columbia, this structure of feeling was deeply imbricated in culture, discourse, and space, formalized in law, and bound up in the province's political economy. In the specific context of the waterfront, it was reinforced by employers who benefited from competition from racially distinct gangs and who tended to hire non-Aboriginal men to handle general cargo—day-to-day decisions that, over time, helped to create the conditions in which such divisions were naturalized and legitimated. It is not hard to see how white longshoremen's own sense of powerlessness on the job would make them more receptive to the authority derived from, to borrow from David Roediger, 'the fiction that they are "white"'.[30]

Aboriginal men negotiated the politics of waterfront work in a variety of ways—individual and collective struggles marked by the tensions associated with being both a longshoreman and being an 'Indian'. '[My Indian friend] George Newman, he was always full of fun. He would holler down the hatch in Indian language and then he would start to laugh,' Edward Nahanee observed, the punch line being that white workers ''tween decks' did not understand George's orders: 'Those Indian boys could talk behind their backs.'[31] On the Vancouver waterfront, longshoremen's use of a shared language—nicknames, slang, profanity, and occupational jargon—accentuated the differences between employers and employees, and distinguished dockers from other ostensibly more respectable and skilled workers.[32] As this anecdote suggests, however, the use of the 'Indian language' on the job reinforced *internal* divisions of allegiance and identification as well—a dynamic that likely subverted white workers' sense of racialized camaraderie and entitlement, if only for a moment. At times, the 'Indian language' could be more physical than verbal. During his tenure on the waterfront in the late 1910s and early 1920s, Dan George, who became chief of the Squamish band in the 1950s, perfected what he called his 'big dumb Indian look'. Intimidating, defiant, and mocking in equal measure, it was used by George and other Squamish men to protest harsh working conditions, enforce standards of appropriate behaviour on the job, or to communicate, silently, between themselves.[33]

In other situations, Squamish men sought to neutralize white privilege in a more forceful way. 'There was a one eyed [Indian] fellow running . . . side and he hated the sight of a white man. Sure enough, inside of two hours he threw a plank on [Moose] Johnson's foot and he had to go home,' one docker recalled.[34] On the docks, physical strength was both an occupational requirement and a badge of working-class masculinity; as such, it played a key role in shaping longshoremen's sense of themselves as working men and, by extension, the wider dockside world that they inhabited. Yet, as the plight of Moose Johnson suggests, physical strength could be used to set boundaries around a particular type of cargo, job classification, or the composition of a work gang—dimensions of waterfront labour that were simultaneously defined in racial terms. In Vancouver, as in other port cities, a longshoreman's success or failure in the competition for work was dependent on a wide range of factors, not the least of which was the ability of racial groupings to mobilize in defence of their particular occupational niches, no matter how undesirable or difficult the work within that niche was.[35] Use of the 'Indian' language and physical confrontation were part of this process; so, too, was labour recruitment. It was not uncommon for the sons and nephews of Aboriginal longshoremen to follow their fathers and uncles to the waterfront, and, in the process, learn the arts and mysteries of 'working the lumber'. On other occasions, experienced Aboriginal longshoremen could be found enticing 'young fellows' from the Mission and other reserves to work on a specific lumber ship—a manoeuvre facilitated by the extensive familial relationships that characterized Aboriginal life on the North Shore and elsewhere.[36]

The experience of Simon Baker illustrates this final point. Born in 1911, Baker was raised on the North Shore of Burrard Inlet by his grandfather (and longshoreman), Squamish chief Joe Capilano, and his grandmother, Mary Agnes Capilano. As a young man, Baker attended a residential school, where he 'organized' a 'strike' to protest poor food and harsh discipline, and worked in a variety of occupations, including waterfront work. 'After I got back home [from hop-picking], Dan Johnson, who is a relative of ours, asked me to go with him. I knew why he asked me, because we're good longshore-men,' Baker recalled in his autobiography. 'Joe Horton, the boss of the longshoremen, came to Westholme Reserve, near Duncan [on Vancouver Island], and came to Dan's house. "Dan," he said, "do you want to go to work?" "No," said Dan, "I'm tired but I have a young man; he's a good long-shoreman." So that was my first [job] longshor-ing [in 1926] at fifteen years of age.' . . . 'Our legend began in the 1800s during the days of the sailing ships. They had one mill at the time on the North Shore. They hired all the Indians on the North Shore who were able to work,' Baker observed. 'Five generations of our family have worked on the waterfront.'[37]

Baker's recollections are significant for another reason: they illustrate the ways in which long-shoremen, in the context of the waterfront labour market, utilized the idea of race to sort out who should have access to the docks, what gang to join, and which cargo to handle. Key to white longshoremen's monopoly on general cargo, race was deployed simultaneously by Aboriginal long-shoremen to defend their status as skilled men on the lumber and to facilitate the entry of other 'Indians' into waterfront work, thereby perpetu-ating their presence on the docks over time. In a more intimate way, working the lumber, and all the associations of race that went with it, helped Baker to further establish a dichotomy between himself as an Aboriginal person and other non-Aboriginal individuals. That understanding of difference, as his autobiography suggests, was critical to the formation of his identity as an Aboriginal man, and to his understanding of the need for political action, on the job and off. That specific idea—the ways in which working on the waterfront helped to mark off the boundaries of identity, and the political questions that flowed from that differentiation—is particularly evident in the context of political action and class conflict.

***

Labour relations on the waterfront were rarely peaceful. Between 1889 and 1935, Vancouver's

waterfront workers joined a wide range of unions—from the conservative to the Communist—and went on strike at least 18 times, a pattern of mil-itancy that was matched by few other occupa-tional groups, either provincially or nationally.[38] Aboriginal longshoremen were deeply involved in these struggles. In 1906, lumber handlers on Burrard Inlet, most of whom were Squamish, founded Local 526 of the Industrial Workers of the World (IWW), a radical organization that offered up a heady mix of revolution and reform to those workers who did not fit well into the established craft union structures: the unskilled, the migra-tory, and the marginal.[39] Its highly decentralized form of union organization, which was rooted in part in the itinerant lifestyle of its members, likely suited Squamish lumber handlers well, for they continued to hunt, fish, and work season-ally. Limited evidence suggests that Local 526 included approximately 50 or 60 men and held its meetings on the North Shore's Mission reserve.[40] A nasty waterfront strike in 1907, which, accord-ing to one source, was characterized by impres-sive levels of racial solidarity, apparently marked the local's demise.[41]

That Aboriginal workers were pioneers of industrial unionism in British Columbia is important to note, for it was this commitment to organizing the unorganized that would inform the challenge mounted by the Socialist Party of Canada and the One Big Union—radical alterna-tives to the Trades and Labor Congress—on the waterfront and in other workplaces in the years running up to and immediately follow-ing the Great War.[42] Equally striking is the fact that the IWW emerged at the same time that coast and interior Salish peoples were experi-menting with new forms of resistance. In 1906, representatives from both communities met on Vancouver Island. There they nominated a dele-gation of three chiefs, including Joe Capilano, to take their demands directly to King Edward in London. Although the mission was unsuccess-ful—the British government maintained that the question of title to land was strictly a Canadian issue—the unity of coastal and interior groups was, as Paul Tennant has argued, 'a step in the evolution of pan-Indianism' that set the stage for future political innovations in the 1910s and 1920s.[43] Without question, the assertion of Aboriginal rights, particularly title to land, was part of a specific history of resistance among the Squamish that stretched back to the earliest days of white settlement and drew upon the cultural resources of their community. At the same time, however, it is important not to underestimate the political contribution of their participation in the industrial economy. Travelling great distances and working in a variety of occupational settings likely enhanced the Squamish's understanding of the breadth and depth of the changes wrought by white society and allowed for the wider dissemination of political ideas among different Aboriginal groups. 'In my young days . . . we lived in shacks with outside toilets. . . . We didn't seem to know that we could have things, the same as the white man,' Simon Baker recalled. 'It wasn't until I was young and traveled to other places in BC [to work] that I realized that we could do better.'[44]

The importance of migration, and the realizations it prompted, is particularly evident in the realm of waterfront work. . . . In this context, the links between the emergence of the IWW and the first pan-Salish organization comes into sharper focus. Not only were the same people involved in both movements—Joe Capilano paid for his trip to England with money earned on the waterfront—but, on a wider canvas, both were attempting to assert control over an economic and political context in which the balance of power had shifted decisively in favour of white society with the emergence of industrial capitalism and the incursion of the colonial state.[45] This dialectic of politicization is captured by the nickname adopted by Aboriginal dockers for Local 526: it was called the 'Bows and Arrows', an assertion of difference and identity at a time when white society was bent on political marginalization and cultural assimilation.

After the demise of Local 526, Squamish waterfront workers formed Local 38-57 of the International Longshoremen's Association (ILA) in 1913, about a year after white workers had established ILA Local 38-52 in Vancouver. 'The Indians used to handle nothing but lumber and the whites, the general cargo. Sometimes they'd be working in the next hatch to each other and they'd get talking. That's how some Indians learned English and that kind of talk led to the formation of the ILA,' one lumber handler recalled. 'Things were dying out and ILA was getting bigger and bigger,' remarked another.[46] Communication across divisions of race and specialization was no doubt important in this process of union building, but so too were the broader structural shifts taking place in the shipping industry, which brought larger numbers of workers together to load and unload a wider range of commodities on a single vessel. By the eve of the First World War, only a handful of ships took on large volumes of lumber, while sailing vessels, once the domain of Aboriginal dockers, continued to disappear.[47]

The decision to disband the Bows and Arrows and join the ILA sparked a debate among Squamish workers. While no transcripts or minutes of this discussion survive, the memories of Ed Long, a lumber handler during these years, suggest that Aboriginal workers were politicized both as workers and as 'Indians'. During this debate they laid bare an agenda that linked workplace struggle to other Aboriginal concerns: 'A lot of the old Indian boys didn't like it because they could go to work and quit and the boss would go and get him because he was a good lumber handler. They couldn't do without him.'[48] Long's recollection highlights one dimension of casual work that many longshoremen—Aboriginal or not—valued: the ability to choose when and where to work, even if that choice meant taking one's chances on the daily shape-up.[49] More specifically, it suggests that at the core of the 'Indian boys'' critique was an abiding sense of pride in their status as skilled men 'on the lumber' and a desire to protect their usual practice of merging waterfront work with other pursuits, such as waged work in the hop fields or hunting and fishing.[50] In the end, according to one source, about 90 per cent of the Bows and Arrows backed a move into their *own* ILA local—the men, evidently, opting for political separation in order to maintain control over their union affairs.[51]

. . .

From the emergence of the IWW to the creation of the ILA, Aboriginal men were involved in the political fermentation that characterized working-class life in Vancouver in the early twentieth century. Presumably they took part in the debate surrounding the amalgamation of ILA locals 38-57 and 38-52 in 1916, the new union's subsequent support for the One Big Union, and the strike wave that gripped Vancouver during and after the Great War. Edward Nahanee was among the waterfront workers barricaded inside the ILA hall on 3 August 1918 when it was attacked by returned soldiers who were protesting the dockers' unanimous support for the 'Ginger Goodwin' general strike. 'There were swarms of soldiers storming the doors, and on the roof of one of the warehouses, three machine guns were trained on us by the RCMP, so close I could practically see down their barrels,' he recalled.[52] Woven into this wider pattern of collective action were moments when Aboriginal longshoremen's language and tactics addressed issues that were specific to them as 'Indian' workers in a workplace segmented by differences ascribed to race: the desire to work the lumber, influence the composition of work gangs through labour recruitment, and take on other jobs when the need or desire arose. Significantly, the politics of work influenced, and in turn were shaped by, the emerging struggle for Aboriginal rights. . . .

That specific goal—independence—would become increasingly difficult to secure on the job after 1923 as class conflict, coupled with a plan by waterfront employers to reform the dockside labour market, threatened to marginalize 'the best men that worked the lumber' from an occupation they had possessed since the mid-to-late nineteenth century.

***

The 1923 longshoremen's strike was a lengthy all-or-nothing affair that marked a turning point in the organization of the waterfront workplace.[53] In that conflict, the Shipping Federation moved decisively to break the ILA, establish an open shop, and reconfigure the local labour market. For its part, the longshoremen's union, which had played an important role in fomenting 'the spirit of discontent' that accompanied the Great War, was pushing for a five-cent wage increase and greater control of hiring through a union-run despatch hall.[54] Fragmentary evidence from the 1923 saw-off suggests that Aboriginal dockers were opposed to going on strike at first, but later took an active role in 'holding the fort'. William Nahanee, Edward's father, was a member of the union's negotiating committee, rubbing shoulders for a time with veteran radical and longshoreman William A. Pritchard.[55] An anecdote from the pages of the ILA's strike bulletin hints at involvement at the rank-and-file level as well. 'It is beyond the ability of my mental apparatus to understand why those who boast of having a higher degree of intelligence and civilization than that of the Indian will be so base as to scab on their fellow workers when the Indian will not do so,' an anonymous writer opined. 'Were scabs able to understand the Indian language they would receive an education on an Indian's opinion of a scab.'[56] After two months on the picket line, the ILA, which had mounted 'one hell of a fight', was broken, its efforts undercut by the Shipping Federation's effective use of strikebreakers, limited unity among Pacific Coast waterfront workers, and the conservatism of the labour movement—locally, provincially, and nationally—after the heady days of 1919.

Aboriginal workers paid a heavy price for their activism. After decades of class conflict, the Shipping Federation embraced a new philosophy of workplace relations: welfare capitalism.

Inspired by similar innovations in other industries, it sought to secure long-term industrial peace by building institutional and social bridges across the chasm of class difference and decasualizing the local labour market. Dubbed a 'good citizens policy', the latter initiative took aim at the use of the shape-up method of hiring and the overabundance of casual workers who, it was thought, were 'inclined to agitation'. Under the terms of the post-strike settlement, members of the ILA, if they were not blacklisted outright, were entitled to only a small portion of available work; the lion's share of employment opportunities was reserved for strikebreakers who, after the end of the strike, were enrolled in a new company-sponsored association, the Vancouver and District Waterfront Workers Association.[57] In this context of defeat, whatever unity existed between Squamish longshoremen and their white counterparts dissolved. By January 1924, former members of the Bows and Arrows, in particular Andrew Paull, were pressing the Shipping Federation to create a new lumber handlers' organization, the Independent Lumber Handlers' Association (ILHA). Not only did they want to control their own political affairs, but they objected 'to being placed in [full-time] gangs because of the necessity of working whenever the gangs in which they were placed were equipped'—a practice key to the Shipping Federation's vision of decasualization.[58]

. . .

Aboriginal longshoremen were marginalized from waterfront work after the 1923 confrontation. Placed at a considerable disadvantage by the blacklisting of former ILA men and the creation of a company union, their desire for some control over when and where their gangs were 'equipped' was at odds with the Shipping Federation's long-term vision of creating a permanent pool of full-time longshoremen under its direction.[59] The logic behind the ILHA's position reflected a preference among its Aboriginal members for a more migratory working life, one that combined a variety of occupations with other customary forms of support, such as hunting and fishing.[60] Not only did this attachment to mobility resonate with their specific histories as Aboriginal people, but, in the context of waged work, it provided a means to assert their independence on the job. At the same time, however, a migratory working life was born of necessity. The terms of the post-strike settlement, which reduced the earning power of the ILHA's membership, coupled with the limits placed on other Aboriginal economic practices by the colonial state, made it difficult for them to make ends meet without working on the docks, aboard a fishing vessel, or in the hop fields in a single year. 'In ten days it was all over,' Edward Nahanee observed, referring to the 1923 strike. 'We lost our jobs and everything.'[61]

Aboriginal workers' absence from the waterfront lasted until 1935, when they returned to work in the midst of a gruesome six-month confrontation between the Shipping Federation and the Vancouver and District Waterfront Workers Association, which had forged links with the Communist Party of Canada in the early 1930s and become more and more militant as the Depression wore on.[62] Leaflets identifying 'scab' workers circulated by the longshoremen's strike committee contained the names of several Aboriginal men; one Communist-backed newspaper, *Ship and Dock*, asserted that the Department of Indian Affairs was helping waterfront employers in recruiting replacement workers.[63] 'Some would call us strikebreakers,' Tim Moody recollected. 'But that is a matter of opinion. The men whose jobs we took were those who broke the strike in 1923 . . . My father said my grandfather had been a longshoreman and we had to hang on to what he had started. It was all we had.'[64] Hanging on in the aftermath of the 1935 strike meant being members of the North Vancouver Longshoremen's Association (NVLA), a union created by the Shipping Federation, with the assistance of the North Vancouver Board of Trade, to both reward 'Indian' workers for opposing the 'forces of disruption' and act as a bulwark against bona fide unions that were active in other Pacific Coast ports.[65] The new organization was guaranteed 10 per cent of waterfront work and possessed 86 members, 40 to 55 of whom were Aboriginal.[66] In many cases, the men who belonged to this cohort worked alongside other members of their family or extended family, suggesting that the link between kin relations, labour recruitment, and working the lumber remained strong. Dan George and seven of his relatives belonged to the new North Shore union; so, too, did Simon Baker and five members of his family.[67]

Strikebreakers, not strikers, this time around, 'Indian' dockers fared better in the wake of the 1935 confrontation than they did after the 1923 strike. Indeed, in the mid-to-late 1930s, they dominated the union's executive and worked nearly as often as other gangs that handled similar cargo, despite the ongoing effects of the Depression on maritime traffic. After a long hiatus, the Bows and Arrows were back 'on the lumber'—an occupation that they would retain during the Second World War and after.

***

Aboriginal men on Burrard Inlet figured prominently in the industrialization of British Columbia, taking up longshoring, among other occupations, almost from the moment that sawmills first came to the area in the early 1860s. On the docks, they worked in an occupational setting characterized by turbulent labour relations, strong competition for work, and sharp distinctions of specialization. The intersection of class and race was significant in this complex context, shaping the day-to-day decisions that Aboriginal longshoremen, most of whom were Squamish, made about what job they might do, whom they might work with, and what their political options were, on the waterfront and off. That waterfront unionism and organizations dedicated to Aboriginal rights emerged at the same time illustrates this point well. Men who were politically active on the 'Indian' waterfront were also involved with the Salish delegation to London, the Allied Tribes of British Columbia,

and the Squamish Tribal Council—a cross-pollination that persisted into the early 1940s, when Tim Moody of the NVLA joined the Native Brotherhood of British Columbia, a group created by coastal First Nations in 1931 to advance the concerns of Aboriginal commercial fishers.[68]

Skilled and knowledgeable longshoremen, Aboriginal workers' longevity on the waterfront was due to many factors, not the least of which was their ability to specialize in a particular cargo and, over the span of several decades, ensure that 'Indian' men were available to work it. Family relations were vital to this process of labour recruitment; so, too, was the passage of workplace knowledge from one generation of Aboriginal waterfront workers to the next. Absent from waterfront work after the 1923 strike, the Bows and Arrows returned to the docks in 1935, and in short order, they made up about half of the NVLA's membership and dominated its executive.

By that time, the waterfront workplace had changed considerably. Decasualization was firmly in place. Within the ranks of the newly formed North Shore lumber handlers' union, however, casual sensibilities—the desire to work where and when one wanted—persisted into the late 1930s, 1940s, and 1950s, a structure of feeling evident throughout Aboriginal workers' lengthy tenure on the docks. . . . 'It was murder at first [to give up fishing],' recalled one Aboriginal longshoremen after deciding to work on the waterfront full time. 'But now we've got no squawks. I wanted to live here in town and it was getting too hard to make any money fishing.'[69]

Inspired by Rolf Knight's pioneering *Indians at Work*, this analysis illustrates the significance of wage labour to Aboriginal life on Burrard Inlet between 1863 and 1939. Rooted in a specific location, time period, and configuration of power relations, the Bows and Arrows' history of waged work was, simultaneously, part of a more general phenomenon: the expansion of capitalism on a global scale. Indeed, indigenous people from southeast Alaska to Puget Sound faced broadly similar challenges with the advent of paid labour from the mid-nineteenth to the early twentieth century; so, too, did waterfront workers from Seattle to London, Montreal to Mombassa, who struggled with decasualization as it took hold in other labour markets in other ports during the same time.[70] Perhaps the experiences of Tlingit cannery workers or London dockers were known to the Bows and Arrows—information, as well as commodities, circulated in port cities—and, from their vantage point on Burrard Inlet, they recognized a common pattern of conflict, resistance, and adaptation to capitalist development.

For the 'best men that worked the lumber' that pattern was intimately connected to their encounter with colonialism. As a consequence, their struggle for autonomy not only embraced questions of land, resources, and self-government—as the existing literature suggests—but issues related to the day-to-day realities of life 'on the hook' as well. By bringing Aboriginal history and labour history into closer contact, two disciplines that are typically conceptualized and researched separately, the very notion of Aboriginal politics expands and changes shape. Class, as a structured reality and a lived daily experience, mattered to the Squamish. To ignore or downplay this dimension of their lives is to obscure many of the key issues that they thought about often, struggled with daily, and hoped, in the end, to be free from.

Notes

Gregory S. Kealey, Mark Leier, and Todd McCallum read drafts of this essay and provided important feedback; special thanks to anonymous 'Reader B' whose close reading of this text and lengthy evaluations proved invaluable. The research upon which this essay is based was supported by the Social Sciences and Humanities Research Council.

1. A 'bibliography of major writings in aboriginal history' that appeared in [*The Canadian Historical Review*] illustrates the point well. Of the 130 books published between 1990 and 1999, only six focused on 'economics', and of those six, three were editions of books that originally appeared in the 1930s and 1970s. See Keith Thor Carlson, Melinda Marie Jetté, and Kenichi Matsui, 'An Annotated Bibliography of Major Writings in Aboriginal History, 1990–99', *Canadian Historical Review* 82, 1 (Mar. 2001): 122–71. Writing in 'Top Seven Reasons To Celebrate and Ask More from *Labour/Le Travail*', *Labour/Le Travail* 50 (Fall 2002): 88–99, David Roediger argues that Aboriginal workers have fared even worse in the context of Canadian labour history where the experiences of newcomers, not natives, dominates the literature concerned with race and ethnicity.

2. For the Canadian context see Steven High, 'Native Wage Labour and Independent Production during the "Era of Irrelevance"', *Labour/Le Travail* 37 (Spring 1996): 243–64. For the American context see Alice Littlefield and Martha C. Knack, eds, *Native Americans and Wage Labor: Ethnohistorical Perspectives* (Norman and London: University of Oklahoma Press, 1998). . . .

3. John Lutz, 'After the Fur Trade: The Aboriginal Labouring Class of British Columbia, 1849–1890', *Journal of the Canadian Historical Association* (1992): 69–94; Lutz, 'Gender and Work in Lekwammen Families, 1843 to 1970', in Kathryn McPherson, Cecilia Morgan, and Nancy M. Forestell, eds, *Gendered Pasts: Historical Essays on Femininity and Masculinity in Canada* (Toronto: Oxford University Press, 1999); Lutz, 'Making "Indians" in British Columbia: Power, Race, and the Importance of Place', in Richard White and John M. Findlay, eds, *Power and Place in the North American West* (Seattle and London: University of Washington Press, 1999), 61–84.

4. Chief Cheakamus (Tom) to 'Honourable Gentlemen', [n.d., likely 1912 to 1916], file 520c, vol. 11021, RG 10, British Columbia Archives (hereafter cited as BCA). I consulted RG 10, the records of the Department of Indian Affairs, in both the British Columbia Archives and Library and Archives Canada (LAC); for this reason, citations for RG 10 may refer to either the BCA or the LAC.

5. Homer Barnett, *The Coast Salish of British Columbia* (Eugene: University of Oregon Press, 1955); Cole Harris, *The Resettlement of British Columbia: Essays on Colonisation and Geographical Change* (Vancouver: UBC Press, 1997), 68–102; and Wayne Suttles, *Coast Salish Essays* (Vancouver: Talonbooks, 1987).

6. 'Sproat's Report on the Squamish River Reserve, 1877', file 3756-7, vol. 3611, RG 10, BCA.

7. Testimony of Peter Byrne, 20 June 1913, Union of BC Indian Chiefs, Add.Mss 1056, BCA.

8. On the transformation of the port of Vancouver, see Alexander Gibb, *The Dominion of Canada: National Ports Survey, 1931–32* (Ottawa: King's Printer, 1932); Leah Stevens, 'Rise of the Port of Vancouver, British Columbia', *Economic Geography* (Jan. 1936): 61–71.

9. Andrew Yarmie, 'The Right To Manage: Vancouver Employers' Associations, 1900–1923', *BC Studies* 90 (Summer 1991): 40–74.

10. Robert A.J. McDonald, *Making Vancouver: Class, Status, and Social Boundaries, 1863–1913* (Vancouver: UBC Press, 1996). The quotation is in David Montgomery, *The Fall of the House of Labor* (New York: Cambridge University Press, 1987), 97.

11. This generalization is based on the annual reports of the Department of Indians Affairs published by year as part of Canada, *Sessional Papers* (1877–1930). See Andrew Parnaby, 'On the Hook: Welfare Capitalism on the Vancouver Waterfront, 1919–1939' (PhD thesis, Memorial University of Newfoundland, 2001), 204–7, 453, 454.

12. References to potlatches held by the Squamish can be found in Byrne to assistant deputy, 3 Feb. 1914, vol. 1479, Letterbook, RG 10, BCA; Devlin to Vowell, 16 July 1896, file 121,698-53, vol. 3944; Charles Hill-Tout, 'Notes on the Skqomic of British Columbia', in Charles Maud, ed., *The Salish People* (Vancouver: Talonbooks, 1978), 49; testimony of Chief Mathias Joseph and Chief Harry, 1913, Add.Mss 1056, BCA; 'Gilbert Malcolm Sproat's Summarized Report . . . 1877,' file 3756-11, vol. 3611.

13. Chief Cheackmus (Tom) to 'Honourable Gentlemen'. . . .

14. Cole Harris, *Making Native Space: Colonialism, Resistance, and Reserves in British Columbia* (Vancouver: UBC Press, 2002), maps 3.6, 5.1, and 5.2 on 67, 110, and 111 respectively.

15. The sale of the Kitsilano reserve captures this development well. See William John Zahoroff, 'Success in Struggle: The Squamish People and Kitsilano Indian Reserve No. 6' (MA thesis, Carleton University, 1978).

16. Testimony of Mathias Joseph, 1913, Add.Mss 1056, BCA.

17. The global perspective is detailed in Colin J. Davis, David de Vries, Lex Heerma van Voss, Lidewij Hesselink, and Klaus Weinhauer, *Dock Workers: International Explorations in Comparative Labour History, 1790–1970* (Aldershot: Ashgate, 2000). For Vancouver see John Bellamy Foster, 'On the Waterfront: Longshoring in Canada,' in Craig Heron and Robert Storey, eds, *On the Job: Confronting the Labour Process in Canada* (Montreal and Kingston: McGill-Queen's University Press, 1986), 281–308; ILWU Pensioners, *Man Along the Shore! The Story of the Vancouver Waterfront as Told by the Longshoremen Themselves, 1860s–1975* (Vancouver: ILWU Pensioners, 1975), 8–61; Robert McDonald and Logan Hovis, 'On the Waterfront', in Working Live Collective, ed., *Working Lives* (Vancouver: New Star Books, 1985), 71–2; Parnaby, 'On the Hook'.

18. ILWU Pensioners, *Man Along the Shore!* 40; 'Meeting . . . the Shipping Federation . . . and a Committee from North Vancouver City Council', 17 Oct. 1928, file 10, box 5, Add.Mss 279, Shipping Federation of British Columbia records, City of Vancouver Archives (hereafter cited as CVA).

19. ILWU Pensioners, *Man Along the Shore!* 27, 29, 41, 45, 99.

20. Ibid., 16, 24–9, 36–7, 44–5, 55–6.

21. Interview with Ed Long, tape 17:35, International Longshoremen's and Warehousemen's (ILWU) records, University of British Columbia, Special Collections (hereafter cited as UBC-SC).

22. Interview with Axel Nyman, tape 17:19, ILWU records, UBC-SC.

23. ILWU Pensioners, *Man Along the Shore!* 56.

24. Ibid., 15, 33, 41, 80 (early 1900s); *Longshoremen's Strike Bulletin*, 9 Nov. 1923 (early 1920s), vol. 37; 'North Vancouver Longshoremen's Assn., membership' (post-1935), file 3, box 46, Add.Mss 279, CVA.

25. According to 'Squamish Longshoreman Has Watched Vancouver Grow into Great Port', *Vancouver Daily Province*, 10 May 1941, Nahanee's father was Hawaiian and his mother was a 'Capilano Indian'. . . .

26. 'Agricultural and Industrial Statistics, 1899–1919', vol. 1493, RG 10, BCA.

27. Hilda Mortimer with Chief Dan George, *You Call Me Chief: Impressions of the Life of Chief Dan George* (Toronto: Doubleday, 1981), 113–14; ILWU Pensioners, *Man along the Shore!* 74.

28. ILWU Pensioners, *Man Along the Shore!* 27, 29. Similar sentiments are expressed in an interview with Paddy McDonagh, tape 17:4, ILWU records, UBC-SC.

29. 'Accidents for the 1st Half of 1925', file 1, box 36, Add. Mss 279, CVA.

30. David Roediger, *Towards the Abolition of Whiteness: Essays on Race, Politics, and Working-Class History* (New York: Verso, 1994), 8.

31. Interview with Edward Nahanee, tape 17:9, ILWU records, UBC-SC.

32. David De Vries, 'The Construction of the Image of the Dock Labourer', in Davies et al., *Dock Workers*, 695–700.

33. Mortimer and George, *You Call Me Chief*, 115.

34. ILWU Pensioners, *Man Along the Shore!* 29.

35. Bruce Nelson, 'Ethnicity, Race, and the Logic of Solidarity', in Davies et al., *Dock Workers*, 655–80.

36. ILWU Pensioners, *Man Along the Shore!* 56; Dorothy Irene Kennedy, 'Looking for Tribes in All the Wrong Places: An Examination of the Central Coast Salish Social Network' (MA thesis, University of Victoria, 1995), 122–6.

37. Simon Baker, *Khot-la-cha: The Autobiography of Chief Simon Baker*, ed. Verna J. Kirkness (Vancouver: Douglas and MacIntyre, 1994), 2–4, 8–11, 36–7, 53–60, 76–8.

38. Parnaby, 'On the Hook', 1–15. For the national strike trends see Gregory S. Kealey and Douglas Cruikshank, 'Strikes in Canada, 1891–1950', in Gregory S. Kealey, ed., *Workers and Canadian History* (Kingston and Montreal: McGill-Queen's University Press, 1995), 345–418. . . .

39. Mark Leier, *Where the Fraser River Flows: The Industrial Workers of the World in British Columbia* (Vancouver: New Star Books, 1990).

40. Herbert Francis Dunlop, *Andrew Paull as I Knew Him and Understood His Times* (Vancouver: Order of the OMI of St Paul's Province, 1989), 80, 166; ILWU Pensioners, *Man Along the Shore!* 33, 46; interview with Axel Nyman, tape 17:19, ILWU records, UBC-SC.
41. *Industrial Union Bulletin*, 2 Nov. 1907.
42. Allen Seager and David Roth, 'British Columbia and the Mining West: A Ghost of a Chance', in Craig Heron, ed., *The Workers' Revolt in Canada, 1917–1925* (Toronto: University of Toronto Press, 1998), 231–67.
43. Paul Tennant, *Aboriginal People and Politics: The Indian Land Question in British Columbia, 1849–1989* (Vancouver: UBC Press, 1990), 85.
44. Baker, *Khot-la-cha*, 98.
45. Knight, *Indians at Work*, 124; William John Zaharoff, 'Success in Struggle: The Squamish People and Kitsilano Indian Reserve Number 6' (MA thesis, Carleton University, 1978), 143–4.
46. ILWU Pensioners, *Man Along the Shore!* 46; Stuart Bowman Philpott, 'Trade Unionism and Acculturation: A Comparative Study of Urban Indians and Immigrant Italians' (MA thesis, University of British Columbia, 1963), 44.
47. ILWU Pensioners, *Man Along the Shore!* 46–7.
48. Ibid.
49. On this point see Klaus Weinhauer, 'Power and Control on the Waterfront', in Davies et al., *Dock Labour*, 580–603.
50. Dunlop, *Andrew Paull*, 80, 163–6; interview with Axel Nyman, tape 17:19, ILWU records, UBC-SC.
51. ILWU Pensioners, *Man Along the Shore!* 46–7.
52. Mortimer and George, *You Call Me Chief*, 115–16.
53. Logan Hovis, 'The 1923 Longshoremen's Strike', in Working Lives Collective, *Working Lives*, 175.
54. *Longshoremen's Strike Bulletin*, 24 Oct. 1923, vol. 37, Add.Mss 279, CVA.
55. Ibid.
56. Ibid., 9 Nov. 1923.
57. For an introduction to welfare capitalism see the entire issue of *International Labor and Working-Class History* 53 (Spring 1998). For the Vancouver waterfront see Parnaby, 'On the Hook', 26–74.
58. McVety to Harrison, 23 Feb. 1924, Strike 95 (vol. 2), vol. 332, RG 27, LAC.
59. Crombie to Labour Committee, 11 Feb. 1924, file 4, box 23, Add.Mss 279, CVA.
60. On the importance of migration to other Aboriginal workers in BC see Paige Raibmon, 'Theaters of Contact: The Kwakwaka'wakw Meet Colonialism in British Columbia and at the Chicago World's Fair', *Canadian Historical Review* 81, 2 (June 2000): 157–90.
61. Philpott, 'Trade Unionism', 45.
62. Richard McCandless, 'Vancouver's "Red Menace" of 1935: The Waterfront Situation', *BC Studies* 22 (Spring 1974): 56–70.
63. 'Where are these men working?' file 10, 75-E-5, series 200, Vancouver Police Department fonds, CVA; 'Indian Agency Is Used To Break Strikers' Ranks', *Ship and Dock*, 14 Nov. 1935, Strike 87A, vol. 369, RG 27, LAC.
64. Philpott, 'Trade Unionism', 47.
65. Canadian Transport to Johnson, 18 Feb. 1938, file 2, box 46, Add.Mss 279, CVA.
66. 'Agreement . . . 25 Day of March . . . 1937', file 9, vol. 25, Add.Mss 332, ILWU Local 501 records, CVA; assistant labour manager to president, 14 Aug. 1941, file 3, box 46, Add.Mss 279, CVA. The low number is taken from 'North Vancouver Longshoremen's Assn., Membership', file 3, box 46, Add.Mss 279, CVA; the high number appears in Philpott, 'Trade Unionism', 46.
67. 'North Vancouver Longshoremen's Assn. membership'.
68. Philpott, 'Trade Unionism', 48–9; Tennant, *Aboriginal People and Politics*, 114–24.
69. . . . Philpott, 'Trade Unionism', 22; the quotation appears on 52.
70. Russell Lawrence Barsh, 'Puget Sound Indian Demography, 1900–1920: Migration and Economic Integration', *Ethnohistory* 43, 1 (Winter 1996): 65–97; Frederick Cooper, 'Dockworkers and Labour History', and Klaus Weinhauer, 'Power and Control on the Waterfront: Casual Labour and Decasualisation', in Davies et al., *Dock Workers*, 523–41, 580–603; Cairn Elizabeth Crockford, 'Nuu-chah-Nulth Labour Relations in the Pelagic Sealing Industry, 1868–1911' (MA thesis, University of Victoria, 1991); Victoria Wyatt, 'Alaskan Indian Wage Earners in the 19th Century: Economic Choices and Ethnic Identity on Southeast Alaska's Frontier', *Pacific Northwest Quarterly* 78, 1–2 (Jan.–Apr. 1987): 43–9.

13

Boys in the Mining Community

—— Robert McIntosh ——

Boys in coal towns are 'particularly rough and uncultivated'.

> Nova Scotia teacher, 1886

At the centre of the boy's life in coal towns and villages was the mine. He was raised within sight of it; the smell of coal dust was as familiar to him as the sounds of steam pumps and hoists. The boy may have seen for years his father and older brothers leave for the pit. For most boys raised within these communities, the day arrived when they too surrendered their childhood to it. In the nineteenth century, boys raised in coal-mining towns and villages were expected to enter the mine. The class, gender, and cultural identities the community defined for boys encouraged them in this aim. But as childhood was reconstructed in the urban centres of late nineteenth-century Canada, reservations over child labour filtered into coal communities. Teachers and school and mines inspectors arrived to enforce the new laws reflecting emerging views of childhood. Although they were seldom numerous, they helped to constitute a respectable, reforming middle class in coal towns. Organizations dedicated to the reconstructed childhood also entered coal towns and villages: the Woman's Christian Temperance Union (WCTU), Bands of Hope, Boy's Brigades, and the YMCA in the nineteenth century; in the twentieth, the Scouting movement, Children's Aid Societies, and public health nurses. More importantly, early trade unionists were also drawn to the emerging new standards of appropriate childhood. Advocates of compulsory education and restrictive mining legislation, they were instrumental in enforcing the legal redefinition of childhood in the coalfields. By the early twentieth century, the mining community was clearly ambivalent about boys' presence in the pit.

The coal community was marked by the mine, literally overshadowed by the prominent bankhead at the top of the pit housing its hoisting, dumping, and screening equipment. In close vicinity were pump and winding-engine houses, their large smokestacks and engines 'blowing and snorting away most furiously', the lamp cabin, the fan house, stables, carpenter's and blacksmith's shops, and mine offices.[1] Various storehouses were also distributed about the mine surface, the one for explosives at a distance from the rest. Huge mounds of coal, awaiting shipment out, were adjacent to the bankhead, as were the substantial mounds of waste removed from the coal at the picking table. Piles of lumber to buttress the roof of working places and underground roads were collected prior to transport into the mine. A pond or reservoir to supply water for the steam engines was in the vicinity, as was a waste pond to collect the water pumped out of the mine. Also on the mine surface was the transportation infrastructure to ship coal out: rail lines inland, loading wharfs

Robert McIntosh, 'Boys in the Mining Community', from *The Boys in the Pits*. McGill-Queen's University Press, 2000. Reprinted by permission of the publisher.

at the seaside. By the turn of the twentieth century, compressor sheds, coal-fired electrical generating stations, with their large chimneys, and wash houses for miners had been added to the colliery landscape.

Never far from the mine were the community buildings: churches with their adjacent cemetery, a schoolhouse, the company store, possibly independent retailers beyond company property, the temperance hall, and drinking establishments. Other community halls were erected by fraternal societies or trade union locals. The manager's residence, commonly on a hill overlooking the community, was a prominent landmark. The miners' far more modest dwellings clustered closer to the pit. Larger communities would have a town hall, hotels and restaurants, a bank, a post office, a variety of merchants, perhaps even a newspaper office or a small hospital.[2]

. . .

. . . [A]t least to the end of the nineteenth century, boys were raised in these coal towns with the strong expectation that they would enter the pit at some point in their life. Far more than elsewhere in Canada, boys were bred to the mine in Nova Scotia. Coal mining was a way of life, a lifelong occupation. Dan J. McDonald recalled: 'I was just a boy when I first went down in the pits. I never thought much about it one way or another because it was natural for all the miners' sons in those days. You just followed on.'[3] As late as 1927 a Springhill miner complained to the UMWA [United Mine Workers of America] local that 'he got three boys laying around and eating every thing and the Company won't give them work.'[4] Coal companies made a practice of hiring on a preferential basis men and boys inhabiting company dwellings—and indebted at the company store—for mine employment.[5] F.C. Kimber, manager at the Reserve Mine on Cape Breton Island, indicated in 1888 that he took boys when they reached the age of 13—'They are always our own boys who live in the place.'[6] Of the 937 boys 12 years of age and older resident in Dominion Coal-owned housing in 1907, an estimated 811

were working in the mines.[7] These coal towns and villages were generally able to reproduce the mining labour force, although in periods of rapid growth, such as from 1900 to 1914, demand far outstripped the local supply of boys.

Class in the Coal Community

Class profoundly marked coal towns and villages. In single-industry coal communities, there were few merchants, professionals, or clergymen to form an intermediate class between mine management and mine workers. Coal companies exercised wide authority within the community, as employers, as landlords, and as merchants. 'Everybody in Glace Bay,' reported the *Canadian Mining Journal* in 1908, 'is either the servant of the Coal Company, or the servant of the servant of the Coal Company.'[8]

Considerable investment in community infrastructure was required to draw and retain a workforce, particularly if the mine was located in an isolated or remote district. Companies built and maintained schools and encouraged the construction of churches by providing free land.[9] Most importantly, coal companies built houses. The General Mining Association [GMA] erected company housing on a large scale, setting a pattern for Nova Scotia, where the construction of company houses continued throughout the nineteenth century, particularly in Cape Breton. By the turn of the twentieth century, the Dominion Coal Company owned 1,200 houses.[10] In the isolated mining communities of the western interior, companies typically erected bunkhouses.[11] On Vancouver Island, single-family dwellings were built by coal companies from the time of the Hudson's Bay Company.[12] James Dunsmuir was so wedded to the company town that when he opened the Extension mine a few miles south of Wellington in 1897, he insisted that miners employed there, many of whom had built houses in the vicinity, move (at their own expense) to the company village of Ladysmith, better isolated from unionized Nanaimo.[13]

The class gulf was clearly expressed in housing. Mount Rundell, a two-storey building constructed by the GMA for its manager at the Albion Mines in 1827, contained 22 large rooms. Situated on a 75-acre property overlooking the mine and entered by a long curved carriage drive, the estate had a cricket pitch, a fruit orchard and gardens protected by a wooden palisade, stables, servants' quarters, and outbuildings for guests.[14] The slightly smaller Beech Hill was built at Sydney Mines in 1829 for manager Richard Brown.[15] Miners, in contrast, inhabited tenements.[16] Typically, these were brick houses built in one-storey terraces on an English model. The smallest houses had one room and a kitchen, the largest two or three rooms, a kitchen, and sleeping space in the attic. The backyard would usually have an outhouse and large garden, with perhaps a cow, pigs, and chickens.[17] Although by the twentieth century 'miners' rows' were no longer built, having been supplanted by 'cottages' comprising two homes, company houses were reputed for their dilapidation and overcrowding. . . .[18]

Whatever its quality, company-owned housing was an effective tool of corporate control. In a sequence of events frequently repeated in coal communities throughout Canada over the years, a strike at Sydney Mines in the spring and summer of 1876 was followed by evictions from company-owned houses. The arrival of strikebreakers at the end of July led to violence along the picket lines and the arrival of militia units.[19] The coal operators most likely to employ these tactics were the Dunsmuirs, on Vancouver Island. Participation in a strike led to prompt eviction. And efforts to resist eviction led to prompt calls for the militia.[20]

In addition to owning housing, coal companies frequently operated retail outlets. Company stores were originally established to offer merchandise to miners that might otherwise have been unavailable; to offer credit to miners to carry them over periods (during winter especially) when there was little work at the colliery; and, crucially, to ease financial pressure on coal companies by paying workers in goods rather than cash. A store was established at Sydney Mines as early as 1809.[21] GMA manager Richard Brown alleged that the early mine owners on Cape Breton Island 'made more profit by the sale of their stores than of their coal'.[22] The Hudson's Bay Company operated what was effectively a company store, but its successor, the Vancouver Coal Mining and Land Company, instead encouraged independent merchants to establish themselves at Nanaimo.[23] Alberta mining camps, in contrast, typically contained a company store.[24]

Where they persisted, company stores emerged as a lightning rod for controversy. A slow mining season could rapidly inflate the extent of a miner's indebtedness to the company store and deepen his subjection to the coal company.[25] As a resident of Cape Breton observed in 1881, company stores 'are a fertile source of disease. It is true they keep on hand all articles the men require, but the prices are most exorbitant. Such being the case, when work is slack, the workmen, especially if they have large families, are soon head and ears in debt, hopelessly I might add, and completely under the will of the agent [manager], who uses the men as one uses a football. Under these circumstances if the workman sees a chance of bettering his position and pay, he requires to ask permission of his lord and master, which request is often met with a point blank refusal, or a declaration to the effect that he *may* leave *when* the store debt is paid.'[26] The requirement to pay wages in currency—rather than, for instance, in credit at the company store—was not legislated in Nova Scotia until 1899. Company stores persisted into the twentieth century.[27]

The nineteenth-century manager wielded wide power in the community. He ruled on access to company housing and to consumer goods in the company store; he determined the nature of local services, including streets (frequently named after corporate officials), policing, and schooling.[28] Small wonder that Pictou County boys doffed their caps when the manager of the Acadia Company drove by in his carriage or sleigh.[29] As late as 1946, the Royal Commission on Coal condemned closed camps in the western interior, where 'the local coal operator controls all land within convenient distance of the mines, owns all housing and controls all stores, hotels and service facilities.'[30]

The power of the colliery manager was tempered by the authority that miners retained underground, for at least as long as board-and-pillar mining continued, and the need for ongoing negotiation of working conditions in the mine. It was also mediated by paternalism: a relationship marked by mutual obligations whereby the powerful offer protection and direction; the weak, obedience and loyalty. Even at the largest nineteenth-century mines managers knew all employees by name. R.H. Brown noted in his diary in 1874 that the '[b]oy Alex McAskill [was] hurt in pit today, driving tubs on No.1 Level. One tub got off road and jambed [sic] his leg. [N]o bones broken.'[31] Similarly, when a boy broke his leg at Springhill in 1890, manager Henry Swift reported this event in his regular correspondence with company officials.[32] Reinforcing paternalist relations were the ties of family, which frequently bound miners and mine officials. Into the twentieth century, the majority of mine officials were former working miners.[33]

Paternalist overtures gave mine managers a more compliant workforce. As one correspondent wrote in 1881, 'I know of no instance where an employer has displayed a concern for the social well being and improvement of his workmen, in which he has not been amply repaid, by their increased respect and zeal on his behalf.'[34] Paternalism offered employees a range of benefits. Companies might provide coal free or at cost to employees.[35] The Hudson's Bay Company offered miners at Nanaimo in 1862 a house, fuel, and medical attendance.[36] In Pictou County, the General Mining Association purchased uniforms for a volunteer rifle company in the 1860s.[37] Boys at the Caledonia Mine received a traditional Christmas treat, which they forfeited in 1888 when one of their number inadvertently broke a piece of mine machinery.[38] In the twentieth century, coal companies commonly provided sports fields and open-air rinks.[39]

Paternalist gestures in the mining community extended to a contest run by the Provincial Workmen's Association [PWA] in 1884 for the most popular mine manager in Nova Scotia.[40] Respected officials could expect periodic tokens of the miners' regard. G.M. Appleton, engineer at the Vale Colliery, was presented in 1885 with 'a very valuable box of Drawing Instruments and a Writing Desk'. Shortly before mine manager Leckie left Springhill it was suggested that '[o]n the eve of his departure there should be a big meeting of the workmen and the presentation of something tangible that he might take away with him—as a memorial of the good wishes of the men—and be able to show his friends.'[41] As Ian McKay has pointed out, gift-giving carried significance both as a 'gesture of subordination' but also as reflecting notions of 'reciprocal rights and obligations'.[42] Paternalism placed limits on the powerful by embodying expectations about how power could legitimately be exercised.

Only gradually was corporate strength within the company town eroded. Fraternal orders, whereby miners combined to provide mutual death, disability, or medical benefits in exchange for the payment of dues, carved out a niche for mine workers outside of the ambit of the company (although members of the lodge of Freemasons formed at the Albion Mines in 1860 asked permission of the local manager before they marched through the town).[43] Miners also established co-operatives. As early as the 1860s, co-operative retail stores were organized in the Nova Scotian coalfields. A store established at Albion Mines (later Stellarton) in 1861 may have been the first in Canada. Some, including stores at Stellarton and Sydney Mines, enjoyed considerable longevity.[44] The British Canadian Cooperative Society in Cape Breton, with nearly 3,500 members and $1.5 million in annual sales by the 1920s, was a significant counterweight to the extensive chain of company stores operated by the Dominion Coal Company in Cape Breton.[45] Retail co-operatives were also formed in western Canada: at Nanaimo before the end of the nineteenth century and in the Crowsnest Pass in the first decade of the twentieth.[46]

Miners also organized for electoral politics. They formed political clubs, including one in Stellarton in 1882.[47] In 1886 the PWA entered provincial politics, unsuccessfully running two candidates for the House of Assembly.[48] The incorporation of mining towns from late in the nineteenth century and the extension of the franchise to miners in company housing in Nova Scotia in 1889 encouraged political organization.[49] But the political education the PWA attempted to provide only slowly overcame a tradition of deference to the company in mining towns. 'For a long time,' David Frank quoted a former miner, 'the miners themselves wouldn't vote for a miner. They'd figure he wouldn't know enough.' It was not until the 1910s that numerous trade union municipal councillors were elected, determined to restrict company police and evictions from company housing and to review the modest levels of municipal taxes paid by mining companies. A miner was elected mayor of Glace Bay in 1918.[50] During the 1920s, four Farmer-Labour candidates were elected to the provincial legislature from Cape Breton County.[51] Paralleling the changing political orientation of Nova Scotian miners, a Socialist Young Guard emerged in provincial coalfields in the early twentieth century.[52] Coal miners enjoyed more success in electoral politics in western Canada. In Alberta, they were represented in the provincial legislature between 1909 and 1913, and from 1921 to 1930.[53] And in British Columbia, labour candidates were repeatedly elected: in fact, with the exception of the years 1894 to 1898, miners were represented in the provincial legislature continuously from 1890 to 1930, a unique accomplishment, as Allen Seager observed, for working-class constituencies of the period.[54] Nanaimo even sent miner Ralph Smith to Parliament in 1900.[55]

Most importantly, corporate domination was challenged by the growth of unions in the coalfields. . . . Trade unions allowed mine workers to carve out a margin of manoeuvre. As part of this process, they allowed them to re-examine child labour in light of class, to question its value to the boy, and to explore options, such as the acquisition of formal education that would open broader opportunities, both within and outside of coal communities, for their sons. Organized miners . . . were strong advocates both of compulsory education provisions and of laws restricting child labour in the mines. Mine owners, in contrast, resisted these legislative initiatives. . . .

Boys raised in coal towns and villages learned their class identity in various ways. During the UMWA recognition struggle of 1909–11 in Nova Scotia, few non-union children ventured to attend school, where they were subjected to scorn, even blows.[56] At the same time, children boycotted one of Glace Bay's Sunday schools because it was led by a Dominion Coal manager.[57] Similarly, the UMWA recognition strike on Vancouver Island produced a boycott of school classes in 1912.[58] Two boys were among those jailed after the riots of 1913 at Nanaimo.[59] At the times of greatest industrial conflict, class identity was most keenly felt.

Gender in the Mining Community

If class was the basic social division boys encountered in coal towns and villages, gender also divided the residents of coal communities. Manhood was defined most fundamentally against women. A miner unhappy about his pay, yet not voting for a labour candidate, was told to give his wife 'the pants' and 'go home with the children and wear the skirt'.[60] The sexes were distinguished in other ways. Men were rugged. Women were not. A manager at Springhill, Henry Swift, remarked favourably on a badly cut young boy: 'He never flinced [flinched] . . . being a smart, handy little fellow.'[61] Sydney Mines manager R.H. Brown recorded in his diary that his wife was 'bled in the right arm by the Doctor for her giddy head'.[62] Men fought. Women swooned. 'The excursion of the athletic association [at Springhill] ended in a row. I believe the boys had the best of it although some of the women fainted.'[63] Most importantly, men worked for wages in the mines; women did not. A man was a breadwinner.

Masculine identity, based in men's work, shifted over the turn of the twentieth century. In the nineteenth-century coalfields, the model for manliness was the craftsman, an independent contractor, paid on the basis of the quality and quantity of coal he produced. He took pride in his ability to produce large coals efficiently and safely. Victor Belik, a Crowsnest Pass miner, observed: 'You know, a coal miner is just like a fisherman with his fish tales. In the bar, we dig more coal than in the mine, because everyone brags about what they do.'[64] But masculinity, when defined around craftsmanship, was exclusive.[65] Thomas Keating, a British immigrant miner, considered the mine labourer 'in the light of the weak brother, unskilled, requiring all our aid'.[66] Similarly, the elderly mine worker, no longer capable of work as a miner, was no longer a complete man. An expression current in the anthracite coalfields of Pennsylvania at the turn of the twentieth century held that 'twice a boy and once a man is a poor miner's life.'[67]

Boys learned that their masculine identity—their integrity as men—hinged on their ability both to acquire a craft and to earn a living. To linger at school was effeminate—even disreputable. Boys looked forward to their start in the mine as a mark of approaching manhood, assuring them added respect in the family and within the community. Their initiation to the mine consisted largely of 'pit-hardening', the acquisition of the required toughness. The *Springhill News and Advertiser* wrote admiringly about a 'young lad who walked uncomplainingly for a good mile from the mine with a severe scalp injury, which was ultimately treated with 11 stitches'.[68] After the explosion at Springhill in 1891, only a handful of survivors were able to stagger out of the stricken pit unaided. Two boys particularly distinguished themselves in

the eyes of journalist R.A.H. Morrow. Fifteen-year-old Dan Beaton, 'on hearing the explosion, immediately ran to the place where he knew his younger brother was working, and found him burnt, wounded, and his clothes on fire. After extinguishing the fire he put him on his shoulder, and would not give up his charge to any one who offered assistance until he had taken him out of the mine and laid him on a lounge in his own home.'[69] Fourteen-year-old driver Dannie Robertson only survived the explosion because his horse, Jenny, absorbed the brunt of the blast, which threw Robertson back into a box. Momentarily dazed, he was aroused by the noise of timber cracking as the roof collapsed. Almost delirious, with bad burns on his head, face, arms, and side, he started to make his way out of the pitch-black mine. Hearing the cries of 12-year-old trapper Willie Farris, he groped his way to his side. Because of his burns, Robertson could not take hold of the boy to assist him out. Instead, he instructed Farris to climb on his back, and supporting him as best he could, he ran out of the mine. Once on the surface, Robertson asked the men carrying him home on a sled 'that he be allowed to walk into the house, so that his mother might not be alarmed'.[70]

The craft-based definition of manliness—hard-working, respectable, breadwinning, reasonable—was challenged in its day by 'rough' behaviour in the coal towns—hard drinking, gambling, improvident. But it was also under increasing stress as the transformation of mine work and skills lessened miners' autonomy and scope for independent judgment, and as the crisis in the coal industry threatened miners' livelihood. If one pillar of manhood in nineteenth-century coalfields was the miner's skill, a second was his ability to bring home a living family wage. A resident of Glace Bay underscored to the Nova Scotia premier in 1924 the humiliations of economic distress 'that rob a man of his last ounce of self-respect he possesses'.[71]

The transformation of the skilled miner's work from the 1890s and the decline of the coal industry after the First World War produced a crisis in the definitions of masculinity carried over from the nineteenth century. The new basic 'test of manhood' was reconstructed less around skill than around class loyalty.[72] Trade unions built support by appeals to manliness. Strikebreakers were excoriated as effeminate (or female-dominated).[73] But long strikes created a dilemma for the miner, torn between his loyalty to fellow workers and his responsibilities as the family breadwinner. As one New Waterford miner pointed out in a letter to the Sydney *Post* during the lengthy Cape Breton strike in 1925, 'The miners can stand the gaff [strain] far better than their wives and little children can.'[74] Employers were quick to apply pressure to this tender point. 'As between the wives and families on the one hand and the Western Federation of Miners on the other,' Vancouver Island miners were lectured in 1903, 'I should think the families have the highest claim upon the husband.'[75] Likewise, a striking Glace Bay miner was told by the mine manager in 1909 that if he 'thought more of the United Mine Workers than he did of his wife and family, then he had better pack his traps and leave the country'.[76]

Unlike the male role, women's place in the community did not change. Girls were raised to be wives. The miner's wife's status was based on her ability to 'make do', her demonstrated capacity to maintain a home. Within this sphere, women could exercise considerable influence.[77] In addition, women were the mainstay of the community's social and religious networks, as Bill Wylie has observed, 'keeping up the ties within families and with neighbours, ensuring the observance of religious traditions, and pulling together with other women in times of crisis'.[78] Women shared the stress of uncertainty, the possibility faced daily that their husband[s] and sons might not live to return home from the mine.[79] They also bonded together to support male trade unionists in women's auxiliaries, where they organized dances, dinners, picnics, excursions.[80] They also embarked on limited self-organization through

participation in Women's Labour Leagues, which sponsored educational programs.[81]

Women also learned of wage earners' superior entitlements. Unequal consumption patterns within mining communities are most clearly illustrated with respect to alcohol. Like mine work, alcohol consumption was gendered. If accounts of drunken men and boys were common in mining communities, there were none of women.[82] These reports are emblematic of more than merely the rough aspects of the colliery town; they also illustrate males' superior access to leisure and drink.[83]

Corporate challenges to family livelihood forced women into unusual roles. At times of industrial conflict, they paraded, demonstrated, and appeared on picket lines. During a strike at the Albion Mines in 1842, miners' wives and children attacked the mansion of the company agent, smashing kitchen windows, hurling insults at him.[84] At Wellington in 1877, women 'discouraged' strikebreakers, meeting them at the pit with their infants, jeers, and missiles.[85] A generation later, miners, their wives, and their children collectively harassed strikebreakers at Nanaimo.[86] Women took a prominent part in the riots of 12 August 1913 on Vancouver Island, shouting 'Drive the scabs away,' throwing stones, urging others on.[87] On Cape Breton Island, women participated in the riots and looting that followed decisions on the part of company stores during the major strikes of the early 1920s first to suspend the sale of anything but basic foodstuffs and then to cut off credit sales altogether.[88]

Women's public role was recognized very reluctantly. Their voices were seldom if ever heard before the numerous government commissions of inquiry that toured the coalfields.[89] Newspapers hesitated to report their role in riots, preferring to depict women (and children) as victims. The police did not arrest or charge women, and consequently the courts did not try them.[90] Miners too may not always have accepted a public role for their wives. Striking miners at Minto, New Brunswick, for instance, distanced their wives from the conflict in 1937 by failing to inform them of picket locations.[91]

Women did not share the intimate relation with the mine that their menfolk had. Marking the distinction within the family between those who earned wages in the mine and those who did not was 'pit talk', conversation about the experience of the mine which—to their frustration—excluded women.[92] There is some evidence to suggest that women were the first to resist boys' entry into the mine.[93] Alberta miner Frank Wheatley, for instance, acknowledged in 1919 that although he advocated boys' traditional apprenticeship to the craft, his wife was 'keen that [their sons] don't go into the mine'.[94]

Culture in the Coal Community

Nineteenth- and early twentieth-century coal towns and villages were also marked by a cultural divide that reflected contested views of class and gender identity. In these communities, a traditional culture characterized by irregular work habits, tolerance of disorder, superstition, and questionable leisure activities—such as the 'rum-hole' and fist fights, the brothel, gambling, and blood sports—had become the target of an emergent liberal ethic, one that found the coarse, turbulent behaviour within the coal community abhorrent.[95] Early trade unionists, who congregated at the 'respectable' end of the cultural spectrum, devoted considerable energy to hectoring miners to counter a public perception that they were '[r]ough in speech, in mind and in manners; reckless of reason and right; regardless of law, of order, and morality'.[96] Traditional, rough culture in coal towns and villages tolerated child labour. Respectable culture grew increasingly intolerant of boys' early start to work in the mines.

Most characteristic of traditional culture—and a target of early trade unions—was miners' irregular mode of working.[97] 'What our miners should aim at,' the PWA urged in Nova Scotia, 'is to be steadily industrious.'[98] Sydney Mines manager R.H. Brown, searching for means of 'making them work steadily', noted in 1874 the number of occasions when the majority of mine workers were absent, severely curtailing or even stopping coal production: on the twelfth night of Christmas 'many men and boys were off work,' on St Patrick's day 'not half the men [were] out,' on Good Friday, and on 1 May, when the 'Queen Pit night shift [was] idle, [because] only 9 pair men and no boys came out.'[99] Because 'the pits were very frequently idle owing to the number of holy days or saints days that were celebrated,' mine managers requested the assistance of the PWA. Robert Drummond suggested that they enlist the aid of the clergy, 'telling them that commemoration days were abused and offering to collect church dues through the office in return for their intervention'. The clergy was amenable and was rewarded with the check-off.[100]

Absenteeism was also related to superstition. Arbitrary death in the pit, while spurring organized miners to lobby for safety measures, including miner certification, also encouraged folk beliefs. At Springhill, it was held that a life was lost whenever company owners visited.[101] Madame Coo, an Aboriginal Nova Scotian credited with predicting the explosions at the Foord Pit in 1880 and at Springhill in 1891, wielded influence with many Nova Scotian miners.[102] On one occasion, even the pits at distant Sydney Mines were closed, as their manager complained, 'on acc[oun]t of [a] prophesy [of a mine disaster] of [an] old woman at New Glasgow'.[103] This manager protested a few years later to the local Roman Catholic and Presbyterian clergy about their superstitious congregations after a very low turnout at work one day because 'one foretold for an explosion.'[104]

There were other causes of absenteeism. When a death occurred in the mine, work ceased immediately and did not resume until after the deceased was buried. Companies resisted these pit closures, and by 1887 the tradition of suspending work from death to burial was not always respected.[105] In 1909 C.O. MacDonald observed that whereas miners might remain idle on the day of an accident, they would be at work on subsequent days 'unless the number of men desiring to actually attend the funeral prevents its being worked on that day'.[106] But the tradition of closing a pit for a funeral continued at least into the 1920s.[107]

The lure of pleasant weather also took mine employees from work. Spring led to a 'picnic scourge', when high levels of absenteeism were 'not unusual'.[108] 'The miners are strong on picnics,' reported the trade publication the *Canadian Mining Journal*, 'preferring a day's picnicking to a day's pay at any time, and this year the month of August was prolific in picnics.'[109] Much absenteeism was closely linked to the traditional 'idle spell' after payday to attend to chores around the house, in the garden, or to do some shooting or hunting.[110] The lure of a circus or a game of baseball also periodically drew enough boys away from smaller mines to force a temporary closure.[111]

Absenteeism was also the child of a binge. According to a report from Westville, Nova Scotia, in 1883, 'Things were lively round the streets on pay Saturday. All the Rumholes were in full blast.'[112] A Stellarton correspondent observed that '[a]ny stranger coming into our village last Saturday night would have said "Well I've heard that miners were rough and thriftless, but I never thought they were quite so bad."'[113] A description of Joggins in 1885 included 'one general store . . . and twenty grog shops'.[114] Nearby Springhill boasted 40 rum-holes.[115] Neil A. McDonald, a PWA official from Glace Bay, wrote candidly in 1882: 'Work is very brisk and there is plenty of Shipping, but the output is often very short of what it should be. Too much rum the cause.'[116] The issue of absenteeism began to be raised with greater insistence by mine managers in the twentieth century. An industrial publication claimed in 1914 that on post-payday Mondays up to 1,500 Nova Scotian miners were absent from work.[117] Senior British Empire Steel Corporation officials condemned miner absenteeism, which they alleged to reach 10 per cent on Mondays, before the Duncan Royal Commission in 1925, linking it with drinking.[118]

Drink produced irregular work habits. It also led to violence. Although the claim of local Salvation Army converts that Westville was 'the worst place this side of Hades' was likely exaggerated, coal towns and villages were notorious for their rough behaviour.[119] In one account, 'The first public pugilistic exhibition, for a long time, was held on the street [in Westville] last Friday night, and some say it was splendid, and I'm sure it must have been refreshing after such a long interval of quiet; and especially after so much Scott Act [prohibition by local option] talk. What would the village, or in fact any place, be without the "wee drop" that gives us more than school or college, that wakens wit, and kindles lore, and bangs us full of knowledge.'[120] A correspondent sent this report from Springhill in 1883: 'Last Saturday, pay day, there was considerable drink and noise. Quiet drunks before dark, raging ones after dark. . . . Big bloody fight in Rogues corner [a popular local gathering point].'[121] Druggist John D. Higinbotham, newly arrived in Lethbridge from Ontario in 1885, remarked of payday brawls that '[i]t was a surprise . . . that any of the eighteen saloons were still standing.'[122] Drink also led to domestic violence. An immigrant to Nanaimo from Scotland early in the twentieth century remarked that 'a lot of the men would get drunk to drown out their troubles and come home and sometimes would beat up the wife and kids.'[123] On occasion it drew a public response. The *Trades Journal* referred in January 1885 to a 'wife beater [who] got quarters in the jail'.[124] More commonly, domestic violence was privately endured.[125]

Drink and disproportionate numbers of young single men encouraged other coal-town vices. Efforts in one Nova Scotian coal town to close a brothel were recounted in the *Trades Journal*: 'There is one house that has a very questionable name, and which a large number of the young men visit. It is kept by a fair charmer and goes by the name of "Over the Garden Wall." It is a pest to the neighborhood.'[126] When a citizens' vigilante group assembled to destroy the Garden Wall, its female proprietor threw a brick, striking the leader of the group bent on tearing it down. Her assailants withdrew.[127] Informal mechanisms for the maintenance of propriety were more successful in Springhill. A disreputable house at 'Rogues' Corner' was raided between four and five one Sunday morning. The crowd 'horse-whipped a temporary lodger up the street to his boarding house'. The residents of the house were told to leave town.[128] Prostitution flourished less in the settled communities of Nova Scotia than in the frontier camps of western Canada.[129]

Gambling was a popular leisure activity.[130] One PWA lodge meeting in Springhill was particularly poorly attended because of the number of miners 'having to at[t]end the preformance [*sic*] of a Card Sharper and patent med[icine]s hack'.[131] Races of all varieties also drew wagers.[132] So did traditional blood sports. 'The barbarous custom of dog fighting prevails largely at present,' reported one indignant coal-town journalist. 'When people are coming from Church on Sunday, it is common to see large crowds running madly hither and thither to witness a dogfight.'[133] Cock-fighting was also reported.[134]

For boys, the cultural divide in coal communities revolved on school attendance, increasingly the badge of youthful respectability. By the late nineteenth century, if the family had money for appropriate clothing and books, children were spending some time in school. Nineteenth-century schools were generally of poor quality and teachers of uncertain qualification.[135] Information was drawn from textbooks, memorized by sing-song chant, and reproduced on demand in overcrowded primary classrooms that grouped several dozen children in perhaps six or eight grades.[136] The harassed teacher, increasingly female, soon discovered that if she could keep children in their seats and teach them to read, 'she would be safe from interference on the part of parents and trustees.'[137] The relevance of the curriculum to working children was unclear and the lasting legacy of the school years uncertain.[138] While Robert Drummond claimed that of the hundreds of pit boys in Nova

Scotia 'we would be surprised, if told that more than a dozen could not read or write,' the federal labour commissioners repeatedly encountered illiterate boys in 1888.[139] A Cape Breton miner, testifying that the youngest pit boys were nine or 10 years of age, was asked if they could read and write. 'I think they have a small chance,' he responded.[140] The experience of the mine distinguished the pit boys of the mining community from those boys who did not work. Hostility between pit and school boys was embodied in an event as innocuous as a snowball fight. When 'missiles' broke school windows in the course of an exchange of snowballs between pit and school boys at Stellarton, the responsible pit boys were brought before a justice of the peace and fined 50 cents apiece. Such was the price of the pit boys' probable triumph.[141]

Pit boys' participation in rough culture demarcated them from schoolchildren. Wage-earning relieved them from the domestic chores that had previously had the first call on their time outside of school. It also liberated them of the more circumscribed behaviour required of the schoolchild. Once boys started to work, parental control of their leisure activities was substantially diminished. 'Now that I was a wage-earner,' recalled one English pit boy in writing his autobiography, 'I could go out at night for as long as I liked and where I liked.'[142] The community offered a range of attractions. A Halifax journalist observed of Springhill's pit boys that 'they meet in little groups on street corners or wherever there happens to be an attraction, and make things as lively as possible.'[143] They would lounge, exchange news, chew tobacco, stare at girls and women, and observe other street activity. Street-corner idling was free and, as Lynne Marks has underlined, one of the few alternative leisure pursuits to uncomfortable, overcrowded homes.[144]

Other sites of boys' activity included the bowling alley (when Springhill's burned down, the *Trades Journal* reported that 'mothers of boys . . . are heartily glad') and the shooting gallery.[145] Although the youngest pit boys' leisure activity did not generally involve girls, older boys might be drawn towards them. One censorious journalist noted in 1885: 'Dance-Halls are the rage. Morality is at a discount.'[146] The ubiquitous rum shops led to frequent accounts of intoxicated boys[147]—'Last Saturday there were quite a number of drunks to be seen on the streets, a few of whom were boys.'[148] In 1888 two particularly 'drunk and disorderly' boys aged 12 and 14 were jailed in the course of their merry-making.[149] Similarly, a year later, '[s]everal small boys not more than ten to twelve years, were seen paralyzed through drink.'[150] '[T]he rum fiends,' complained the *Canadian Mining Review* in 1894, 'serve the devil by dispensing liquid poison to the miners, boys as well as men.'[151] When driver Malcolm Ferguson was asked if boys were 'generally sober', he responded, 'Some of them.'[152] The drunken and blasphemous boys reported at Springhill in 1887 were the despair of Robert Drummond.[153]

By the 1880s, the charivari, a mock serenade to a couple on their wedding night, belonged to the young.[154] 'Of all the forms, kinds, species and degrees of blackmail,' complained one writer in 1884, 'certainly the worst kind of all is that which goes by the name of charivari.' He told of a couple on their wedding night 'being bombarded by tin tea kettles, bake pans, old dinner horns, bone crackers and old horse pistols'. He advised: 'Boys give it up once and for ever. Don't be a charivarist.'[155] His advice was unheeded. One charivarist rashly used a two-dollar bill as wadding for a gun salute later in the decade. 'After the salute had been successfully fired, he recovered consciousness and bethought him of the bill. Parts of it were found but the glory of the whole had faded.'[156] Hallowe'en demanded its rituals of youth also. The *Trades Journal* commended boys on their behaviour on that evening in 1887: 'They contented themselves with waving torches and doing a little shouting.'[157]

Boys' views of organized religion were evident when they disrupted church services. 'Young Rowdies' disturbed a Primitive [Methodist] service in 1870, and another service at Stellarton in 1885.[158] Two lads were fined two dollars apiece and costs after disturbing a Salvation Army meeting in 1888.[159] Three boys were fined the following year in Springhill for the same reason.[160] 'Unruly' boys attempted to burn the Presbyterian Mission at Nanaimo in 1900.[161] Temperance groups were similarly targeted. The *Trades Journal* complained in 1889 that boys in Sydney Mines 'make what they think great sport by tearing away [the] door-steps' of the new temperance hall.[162]

Lynne Marks has observed that, in late nineteenth-century Ontario, regular church attendance and participation in church organizations were the 'central focus of local respectable culture'. She also noted that this culture—in contrast to local rough culture—was dominated by women, who had far higher rates of church attendance than men.[163] Church groups and temperance associations were further hallmarks of respectability in the coalfields. Associated with the Protestant churches were a great range of temperance societies. The Sons of Temperance, the Church of England Temperance Society, the Cadets of Temperance, the International Order of Good Templars, and the Juvenile Templars were all active in coal communities.[164] In the 1880s, an active Vigilance Society prosecuted liquor-sellers in Springhill.[165] The PWA, a strong advocate of temperance, denied membership to anyone engaged in illicit liquor-selling.[166] It readily acquiesced in the allotment of punishment by mine managers to mine workers for liquor offences.[167] Robert Drummond repeatedly urged that miners be paid on some day other than Saturday, in light of the ensuing drunkenness.[168]

Fraternal societies, with some reservations on account of the alcohol consumed on certain occasions, were deemed respectable. Commonly organized on ethnic lines, they were the most popular form of voluntary association. Major ones included the Masons, the Loyal Orange Lodge, the Odd Fellows, the Knights of Pythias, and the Ancient Order of Foresters. Using the Masons as the model, these groups developed elaborate rituals and degrees of hierarchy, and their rhetoric centred on a brotherhood of male virtues such as independence. Initiation into a fraternal order was seen as a rite of passage into manhood.[169] Fraternal orders had a significant place as means of working-class self-help, sponsoring a variety of insurance programs.[170] They also encouraged occasions of community sociability: parades, balls, dinners, and picnics. Although women were not members of fraternal orders, much of the activity these groups sponsored—unlike 'rough' pastimes within the mining community—included women. The Orange Society of Westville, after parading through the town behind the lodge banner, retired to a supper and ball in November 1882.[171] Fuller Lodge, of the Independent Order of Odd Fellows, marked the arrival of the New Year of 1885 with a 'Supper and Ball'—described in the local press as 'a most recherché affair'.[172] On other occasions, the activities of fraternal orders could be marked by heavy drinking. The revelry associated with the Orangemen's Glorious Twelfth picnic in 1904 led to considerable absenteeism in Pictou County the following day.[173]

. . .

Into the twentieth century, a traditional view of boys dominated coal communities: they were competent to labour, their early initiation to work was valuable to them and their families, schooling was of uncertain worth. Gainful employment was fundamental to male respectability: to remain a schoolchild was effeminate, even disreputable. C.W. Lunn, a railwayman, journalist, and labour advocate, contributed a serialized story to the Halifax *Herald* over several months in 1905 about a young boy, Tommy Barnes, who entered the mine at the age of 10 as a trapper to support his widowed mother. Diligent in his studies at home in the evening, a fine sportsman, organizer of a boys' junior PWA lodge while still an adolescent, committed to 'wise councilling and clever negotiating', Barnes was distinguished as a youth who was going 'to make a mark'.[174] The pit boy was not offensive to the respectable mining population.

But shifting notions of respectability and the new views of appropriate childhood led to changing commentary on the pit boy. A growing commitment to children's schooling among the mining population put into question a boy's early start to mine work in coal towns and villages. Their behaviour, as child wage labour was defined ever more commonly as a social problem, led to frequent claims that the mine brutalized boys. While O.R. Lovejoy offered an extreme opinion in claiming that the pit boys of his experience were 'so tainted by vicious habits that an almost insuperable obstacle to a maturity of virtue and intelligence is presented', his views were widely shared within the urban reforming classes.[175] Boys in coal towns and villages were 'particularly rough and uncultivated' claimed a teacher in 1886; another educator affirmed in 1912 that pit boys were 'chiefly interested in learning how to chew tobacco and in acquiring an extensive vocabulary of picturesque profanity'.[176] With increasing frequency, pit boys were defined as violating liberal society's new and universal prescriptions for childhood.[177] Respectable society was increasingly hostile to the employment of boys in the mines.

Within the mining community, new views of class interest led organized miners to scrutinize boys' early start to work at the mine. At the same time, women began to raise doubts about sending their boys into the pits. Concern also arose among men about the integrity of their craft, about whether it was a suitable basis of earning a livelihood. The redefinition of respectable culture in coal communities also undermined the popular view that local boys' appropriate place was the mine. By the early twentieth century, the expectation had weakened that boys raised in coal towns and villages would work in the mines.

Notes

1. Victoria *Daily British Colonist*, 27 Jan. 1861.
2. Bertha Isabel Scott, *Springhill, a Hilltop in Cumberland* (Springhill, NS: n.p., 1926); E. Blanche Norcross, *Nanaimo Retrospective: The First Century* (Nanaimo, BC: Nanaimo Historical Society, 1979); A.A. Den Otter,

Civilizing the West: The Galts and the Development of Western Canada (Edmonton: University of Alberta Press, 1982), 161–96; 238–65.

3. Bill McNeil, *Voice of the Pioneer* (Toronto: Macmillan, 1978), 61.

4. See Angus L. Macdonald Library, St Francis Xavier University, United Mine Workers of America, Local 4514, *Minutes*, 8 Jan. 1927.

5. C. Ochiltree Macdonald, *The Coal and Iron Industries of Nova Scotia* (Halifax: Chronicle Publishing Co., 1909), 57.

6. LC, *Evidence*, 459.

7. Macdonald, *Coal and Iron Industries*, 72.

8. *Canadian Mining Journal (CMJ)*, 11 June 1908, as quoted in David Frank, 'Company Town, Labour Town: Local Government in the Cape Breton Coal Towns, 1917–1926', *Histoire Sociale/Social History* 14, 27 (May 1981): 178.

9. James M. Cameron, *The Pictonian Colliers* (Halifax: Nova Scotia Museum, 1974), 103–4. The Hudson's Bay Company provided a teacher at Nanaimo as early as 1853. Norcross, *Nanaimo Retrospective*, 40–6.

10. *Canadian Mining Review (CMR)*, June 1902, 166.

11. See David Bercuson, ed., *Alberta's Coal Industry* (Calgary: Historical Society of Alberta, 1978).

12. Charles Forbes, *Vancouver Island, Its Resources and Capabilities as a Colony* (Victoria: Colonial Government, 1862), 57.

13. John Douglas Belshaw, 'The Standard of Living of British Miners on Vancouver Island', *BC Studies* 84 (Winter 1989–90): 53.

14. William N.T. Wylie, *Coal Culture: The History and Commemoration of Mining in Nova Scotia* (Ottawa: Historic Sites and Monuments Board of Canada, 1997), 172; Cameron, *Pictonian Colliers*, 24–5; Joseph Howe, *Western and Eastern Rambles*, ed. M.G. Parks (Toronto: University of Toronto Press, 1973), 159.

15. Wylie, *Coal Culture*, 182.

16. Ian McKay, '"By Wisdom, Wile or War": The Provincial Workmen's Association and the Struggle for Working-Class Independence in Nova Scotia, 1879–97', *Labour/ Le Travail* 18 (Fall 1986): 18–19.

17. Stephen J. Hornsby, *Nineteenth-Century Cape Breton: A Historical Geography* (Montreal and Kingston: McGill-Queen's University Press, 1992), 103–5, 178; LC, *Evidence*, 412.

18. LC, *Evidence*, 412; *CMJ*, 1 July 1914, 442.

19. These events were also commonly followed by legal action against striking miners. Ian McKay, 'The Crisis of Dependent Development: Class Conflict in the Nova Scotian Coalfields, 1872–1876', in Gregory Kealey, ed., *Class, Gender, and Region: Essays in Canadian Historical Sociology* (St John's: Committee on Canadian Labour History, 1988), 37–9.

20. Jeremy Mouat, 'The Politics of Coal: A Study of the Wellington Miners' Strike of 1890–91', *BC Studies* 77 (Spring 1988): 8.

21. Macdonald, *Coal and Iron Industries*, 219.

22. Richard Brown, *The Coal Fields and Coal Trade of the Island of Cape Breton* (Stellarton, NS: Maritime Mining Record Office, 1899), 53.

23. Belshaw, 'Standard of Living', 50–1.

24. See Bercuson, ed., *Alberta's Coal Industry*, 127, 133.

25. Hornsby, *Nineteenth-Century Cape Breton*, 171.

26. *Trades Journal (TJ)*, 16 Mar. 1881, cited in McKay, '"Wisdom, Wile or War"', 20.

27. Macdonald, *Coal and Iron Industries*, 219–22.

28. Frank, 'Company Town, Labour Town', 181.

29. Cameron, *Pictonian Colliers*, 103.

30. Canada, *Report of the Royal Commission on Coal, 1946* (Ottawa: Edmond Cloutier, 1947), 599. Similar concern over company towns in Cape Breton had been expressed earlier. See Nova Scotia, Royal Commission Respecting the Coal Mines of the Province of Nova Scotia, *Report* (Halifax: Minister of Public Works and Mines, 1926), 10.

31. Public Archives of Nova Scotia (PANS), RG 21, series A, vol. 38, no. 10, Richard Brown diary, entry for 7 Feb. 1874.

32. PANS, RG 21, series A, vol. 32, Letter Books, Henry Swift to J.R. Cowans, 24 Nov. 1890.

33. In 1903 nearly all Nova Scotia's colliery managers were former workmen. Even at the massive Dominion Coal Company, in 1910 virtually all officials 'were ex-miners trained in the mining schools'. See Donald MacLeod, 'Colliers, Colliery Safety and Workplace Control: Nova Scotian Experience, 1873–1910', Canadian Historical Association, *Historical Papers* (1983): 251. Mine-owner Robert Dunsmuir first entered the mines as a boy of 16. See Daniel T. Gallacher, 'Robert Dunsmuir', *Dictionary of Canadian Biography (DCB)*, vol. 11 (Toronto: University of Toronto Press, 1982), 290–4.

34. *TJ*, 20 Apr. 1881.

35. Companies would levy a charge, for instance, just for the cost of delivering the coal. Macdonald, *Coal and Iron Industries*, 59.

36. Forbes, *Vancouver Island*, 57.

37. Cameron, *Pictonian Colliers*, 104.

38. *TJ*, 9 Jan. 1889.

39. A.W. Macdonald, 'Notes on the Work of the Industrial Relations Department of the Dominion Coal Company Ltd. and the Dominion Iron and Steel Company Ltd.', *Transactions of the Canadian Mining Institute* (1916): 326; Scott, *Springhill*, 51.

40. McKay, 'Wisdom, Wile or War', 31.

41. *TJ*, 28 Jan. 1885, 27 Mar. 1889.

42. McKay, 'Wisdom, Wile or War', 31.

43. Cameron, *Pictonian Colliers*, 122.

44. Macdonald, *Coal and Iron Industries*, 223–5. Others, such as the Pioneer Co-operative at Springhill, lasted only a few years. See *TJ*, 21 June 1882, 4 May 1887. On reasons for the failure of co-operative stores in mining communities, see Ian MacPherson, *Each for All: A History of the Co-operative Movement in English Canada, 1900–1945* (Toronto: Macmillan of Canada, 1979), 23.

45. Ian MacPherson, 'Patterns in the Maritime Cooperative Movement, 1900–1945', *Acadiensis* 5, 1 (Autumn 1975): 68–70.

46. Lynn Bowen, *Boss Whistle: The Coal Miners of Vancouver Island Remember* (Lantzville, BC: Oolichan Books, 1982), 197–8; Sharon Babaian, *The Coal Mining Industry in the Crow's Nest Pass* (Edmonton: Alberta Culture, 1985), 77–8.

47. *TJ*, 8 Jan. 1882.

48. McKay, 'Wisdom, Wile or War', 43.

49. Ibid., 45.

50. Frank, 'Company Town, Labour Town', 181–6.

51. Wylie, *Coal Culture*, 121.

52. David Frank and Nolan Reilly, 'The Emergence of the Socialist Movement in the Maritimes, 1899–1916', *Labour/Le Travailleur* 4 (1979): 99.

53. Allen Seager, 'Miners' Struggles in Western Canada, 1890–1930', in Deian R. Hopkin and Gregory S. Kealey, eds, *Class, Community and the Labour Movement in Wales and Canada, 1850–1930* (n.p.: Society for Welsh Labour History and the Canadian Committee on Labour History, 1989), 176.

54. Ibid., 176–7.

55. Allen Seager, 'Socialists and Workers: The Western Canadian Coal Miners, 1900–1921', *Labour/Le Travail* 16 (Fall 1985): 37–42; Carlos A. Schwantes, *Radical Heritage: Labor, Socialism, and Reform in Washington and British Columbia, 1885–1917* (Seattle: University of Washington Press, 1979), 73–4, 100–1.

56. Halifax *Herald*, 26 Sept. 1910.

57. Ibid., 31 July 1909.

58. Nanaimo *Free Press*, 28 Nov. 1912, cited in Alan John Wargo, 'The Great Coal Strike: The Vancouver Island Coal Miners' Strike, 1912–1914', BA essay (University of British Columbia, 1962), 94.

59. *CMJ*, 1 Nov. 1913, 690.

60. *Maritime Labour Herald*, 15 Apr. 1922, cited in Steven Penfold, '"Have You No Manhood in You?": Gender and Class in Cape Breton Coal Towns, 1920–1926', *Acadiensis* 23, 2 (Spring 1994): 27.

61. Cited in Ian McKay, 'The Realm of Uncertainty: The Experience of Work in the Cumberland Coal Mines, 1873–1927', *Acadiensis* 16, 1 (Autumn 1986): 52.

62. PANS, RG 21, series A, vol. 38, no. 13, Richard Brown diary, entry for 24 Feb. 1894.

63. *TJ*, 29 May 1889.

64. Lawrence Chrismas, *Alberta Miners: A Tribute* (Calgary: Cambria, 1993), 29.

65. As one woman wrote to the PWA's official newspaper in 1882, 'I am precluded by sex from joining your society.' *TJ*, 11 Oct. 1882.

66. Labour Canada Library, Annual Meeting of the PWA Grand Council, *Minutes*, 1907, 611.

67. Quoted in Harold W. Aurand, *From the Molly Maguires to the United Mine Workers: The Ecology of an Industrial Union, 1869–1897* (Philadelphia: Temple University Press, 1971), 37.

68. Cited in McKay, 'Realm of Uncertainty', 52.

69. R.A.H. Morrow, *The Story of the Springhill Disaster* (Saint John: R.A.H. Morrow, 1891), 83–4.

70. Ibid., 84–6; Scott, *Springhill*, 72.

71. PANS, MG 2, box 675, folder 1, F1/15295, A.M. MacLeod to E.H. Armstrong, 26 Jan. 1924.

72. Penfold, '"Have You No Manhood"', 21.

73. Ibid., 27.

74. Sydney *Post*, 4 Apr. 1925, cited ibid., 29.

75. 'Minutes of Evidence, Royal Commission on Industrial Disputes in the Province of British Columbia', Canada, *Sessional Papers*, 1904, vol. 38, no. 13, 36A, 4.

76. Halifax *Herald*, 31 Mar. 1909.

77. See Penfold, '"Have You No Manhood"', 30–2; David Frank, 'The Miner's Financier: Women in the Cape Breton Coal Towns, 1917', *Atlantis* 8, 2 (Spring 1983): 137–43.

78. Wylie, *Coal Culture*, 133–4. Lynne Marks observed that church groups offered the only organized associational life in small towns for married women in contemporary Ontario. See Marks, *Revivals and Roller Rinks*, 137.

79. David Alan Corbin, *Life, Work, and Rebellion in the Coal Fields: The Southern West Virginia Miners, 1880–1922* (Urbana: University of Illinois Press, 1981), 92–3.

80. John R. Hinde, '"Stout Ladies and Amazons": Women in the British Columbia Coal Mining Community of Ladysmith, 1912–1914', *BC Studies* (Summer 1997): 44. A One Big Union women's auxiliary was formed in Minto in 1926. Allen Seager, 'Minto, New Brunswick: A Study in Class Relations between the Wars', *Labour/Le Travailleur* 5 (Spring 1980): 110–11.

81. Penfold, '"Have You No Manhood"', 38–42.

82. See *TJ*, 11 May 1883, 21 Nov. 1888, 2 Jan. 1889; *CMR*, Dec. 1894, 237, for references to intoxicated boys.

83. See also *TJ*, 5 Oct. 1887.

84. McKay, '"Wisdom, Wile or War"', 21.

85. Victoria *Daily British Colonist*, 17 Mar., 5 May 1877.

86. Nanaimo *Free Press*, 25 Nov. 1912.

87. Hinde, '"Stout Ladies and Amazons"', 33–4.

88. Penfold, '"Have You No Manhood"', 33–4.

89. See, for instance, LC, *Evidence*; 'Minutes of Evidence, Royal Commission on Industrial Disputes in the Province of British Columbia', Canada, *Sessional Papers*, 1904, vol. 38, no. 13, 36A; Provincial Archives of Alberta (PAA), Royal Commission on the Coal Industry,

Report and Evidence; Commission on Miners' Old Age Pensions, *Report*; National Archives of Canada (NAC), RG 33, series 95, Royal Commission on Industrial Relations, 1919, *Minutes of Evidence*; Labour Canada Library, Royal Commission Respecting the Coal Mines of the Province of Nova Scotia, *Minutes of Evidence*, 1925.

90. Penfold, "'Have You No Manhood'", 36; Hinde, "'Stout Ladies and Amazons'", 33–4.
91. Seager, 'Minto, New Brunswick', 119.
92. McKay, 'Realm of Uncertainty', 24.
93. C.W. Lunn, 'From Trapper Boy to General Manager: A Story of Brotherly Love and Perseverance', Ian McKay, ed., *Labour/Le Travailleur* 4 (1979): 226; Bowen, Boss Whistle, 17.
94. Bercuson, ed., *Alberta's Coal Industry*, 84.
95. See P.C. Bailey, *Leisure and Class in Victorian England: Rational Recreation and the Contest for Control, 1830–1885* (London: Routledge & Kegan Paul, 1978). . . .
96. *TJ*, 13 Apr. 1881. The view of the miner as a degraded brute was captured in popular novels such as *Germinal* by Emile Zola and Hugh MacLennan's *Each Man's Son*.
97. On the traditional weekly 'idle spell' of urban craftsmen, often called 'Blue' or 'Saint' Monday, see Gregory Kealey, *Toronto Workers Respond to Industrial Capitalism, 1867–1892* (Toronto: University of Toronto Press, 1980), 54, 68; Bryan Palmer, *A Culture in Conflict: Skilled Workers and Industrial Capitalism in Hamilton, Ontario, 1860–1914* (Montreal and Kingston: McGill-Queen's University Press, 1979), 21.
98. *TJ*, 18 July 1883. Drummond failed to acknowledge that companies operated nineteenth-century mines irregularly.
99. PANS, RG 21, series A, vol. 38, no. 10, Richard Brown diary, entries for 21 Mar., 6 Jan., 17 Mar., 3 Apr., 1 May 1874.
100. Robert Drummond, *Minerals and Mining, Nova Scotia* (Stellarton, NS: Mining Record Office, 1918), 276–7.
101. *TJ*, 1 Aug. 1888.
102. Cameron, *Pictonian Collier*, 215; McKay, 'Realm of Uncertainty', 47.
103. PANS, RG 21, series A, vol. 38, no. 10, Richard Brown diary, entry for 4 May 1874.
104. PANS, RG 21, series A, vol. 38, no. 12, Richard Brown diary, entry for 2 Apr. 1881.
105. *TJ*, 13 Apr. 1887.
106. Macdonald, *Coal and Iron Industries*, 73.
107. David Frank, 'The Cape Breton Coal Miners, 1917–1926', PhD dissertation (Dalhousie University, 1979), 232; McKay, 'Realm of Uncertainty', 55–6.
108. See CMR, Dec. 1894, 236; CMJ, 15 June 1913, 381.
109. CMR, Sept. 1903, 198.
110. *TJ*, 8 Nov. 1882.
111. A circus, which the boys apparently found disappointing, closed the mine at River Hebert for a day. See *TJ*,

13 Aug. 1884. A baseball game once shut the Joggins mine. See Halifax *Herald*, 7 June 1906.
112. *TJ*, 25 Apr. 1883.
113. *TJ*, 17 May 1882.
114. *TJ*, 14 Jan. 1885.
115. *TJ*, 14 Sept. 1887.
116. *TJ*, 11 Oct. 1882.
117. *CMJ*, 15 April 1914, 254.
118. See Labour Canada Library, [Duncan] Royal Commission Respecting the Coal Mines of the Province of Nova Scotia, *Minutes of Evidence*, 1925, 2648–9, 2953.
119. *TJ*, 23 Dec. 1885.
120. *TJ*, 5 Oct. 1887. The Canada Temperance [Scott] Act had been declared in force in Pictou County in 1882. See *TJ*, 27 Sept. 1882.
121. *TJ*, 7 Mar. 1883.
122. Quoted in Den Otter, *Civilizing the West*, 164.
123. Quoted in Allen Seager and Adele Perry, 'Mining the Connections: Class, Ethnicity, and Gender in Nanaimo, British Columbia, 1891', *Histoire Sociale/ Social History* 30, 59 (May 1997): 66.
124. *TJ*, 21 Jan. 1885.
125. See Katherine Harvey, 'To Love, Honour and Obey: Wife-Battering in Working-Class Montreal, 1869–79', *Urban History Review* 19, 2 (Oct. 1990): 128–40.
126. *TJ*, 25 Apr. 1883.
127. *TJ*, 24 Oct. 1883.
128. *TJ*, 12 Aug. 1885.
129. On prostitution in the Alberta mining camps, see Den Otter, *Civilizing the West*, 174, 242–8; and Bercuson, ed., *Alberta's Coal Industry*, 190–1.
130. See Daniel Samson, 'Dependency and Rural Industry: Inverness, Nova Scotia, 1899–1910', in Samson, ed., *Contested Countryside: Rural Workers and Modern Society in Atlantic Canada, 1800–1950* (Fredericton, NB: Acadiensis Press, 1994), 129.
131. See Angus L. Macdonald Library, St Francis Xavier University, *Minutebooks*, Pioneer Lodge, PWA, 14 Aug. 1884.
132. Belshaw, 'Standard of Living', 61–2.
133. *TJ*, 12 Aug. 1885. Other reports of dog-fighting are found in the issues of 30 Sept. 1885 and 11 Jan. 1888; and in the Sydney *Daily Post*, 31 July 1909.
134. See *TJ*, 9 Jan. 1889; Nanaimo *Free Press*, 6 Feb. 1901.
135. Katherine I. McLaren, "'The Proper Education for All Classes": Compulsory Schooling and Reform in Nova Scotia, 1890–1930', MEd thesis (Dalhousie University, 1984), 33, 44–6.
136. Ibid., 54–5.
137. Paul Axelrod, *The Promise of Schooling: Education in Canada, 1800–1914* (Toronto: University of Toronto Press, 1997), 57–9.
138. McLaren, "'The Proper Education for All Classes'", 19.
139. *TJ*, 9 May 1888. See LC, *Evidence*, 437, 447.
140. LC, *Evidence*, 454.

141. *TJ*, 1 Apr. 1885.
142. Jack Lawson, *A Man's Life* (London: Hodder and Stoughton, 1932), 74.
143. Halifax *Morning Chronicle*, 4 Dec. 1890.
144. On this point, see Marks, *Revivals and Roller Rinks*, 81–5.
145. *TJ*, 8 Nov. 1882 (bowling alley), 19 Dec. 1888 (on the shooting gallery as a 'drop-in' for boys).
146. See *TJ*, 3 June 1885. On nineteenth-century courting, see W. Peter Ward, *Courtship, Love, and Marriage in Nineteenth-Century English Canada* (Montreal and Kingston: McGill-Queen's University Press, 1990), esp. chs 4 and 5.
147. *TJ*, 18 July, 31 Oct. 1883, 2 Jan. 1889.
148. *TJ*, 11 May 1883.
149. *TJ*, 21 Nov. 1888.
150. *TJ*, 2 Jan. 1889.
151. *CMR*, Dec. 1894, 237.
152. LC, *Evidence*, 437.
153. *TJ*, 24 Aug. 1887.
154. See Bryan Palmer, 'Discordant Music: Charivaris and Whitecapping in Nineteenth-Century North America', *Labour/Le Travailleur* 3 (1978): 5–62; E.P. Thompson, '"Rough Music": Le charivari anglais', *Annales. Economies. Sociétés. Organisations* 27 (1972): 285–312. Philippe Ariès remarked on how activities at one time common to all age groups eventually came to be confined to the young. See Ariès, *Centuries of Childhood: A Social History of Family Life* (New York: Knopf, 1962), 62–99.
155. *TJ*, 10 Sept. 1884.
156. *TJ*, 15 May 1889.
157. *TJ*, 2 Nov. 1887.
158. New Glasgow *Eastern Chronicle*, 30 June 1870; *TJ*, 28 Oct. 1885.
159. *TJ*, 6 June 1888.
160. *TJ*, 22 May 1889.
161. Nanaimo *Free Press*, 24 Mar. 1900.
162. *TJ*, 24 Apr. 1889.
163. Marks, *Revivals and Roller Rinks*, 15, 230–2 (Tables 3–5).
164. *TJ*, 2 Nov. 1887, 7 Mar. 1888.
165. Scott, *Springhill*, 50.
166. Labour Canada Library, Annual Meeting of the PWA Grand Council, *Minutes*, 1894, 281.
167. Labour Canada Library, Robert Drummond, 'Recollections and Reflections of a Former Trades Union Leader', unpublished manuscript (*c.* 1926), 198.
168. He first made the suggestion in *TJ*, 21 July 1880, when he observed that payday at Stellarton had been switched to Thursdays with considerable success, 'there being much less dissipation than has followed Saturday pay-days'.
169. Marks, *Revivals and Roller Rinks*, 109.
170. Lynn Bowen, 'Friendly Societies in Nanaimo: The British Tradition of Self-Help in a Canadian Coal-Mining Community', *BC Studies* no. 118 (Summer 1998): 67–92.
171. *TJ*, 15 Nov. 1882.
172. *TJ*, 7 Jan. 1885.
173. Cameron, *Pictonian Collier*, 328.
174. Lunn, 'From Trapper Boy to General Manager', 233.
175. O.R. Lovejoy, 'Child Labor in the Coal Mines', *Annals of the American Academy of Political and Social Science* 27 (1906): 297.
176. *The Bulletin* (Dartmouth), 15 Dec. 1886, cited in McKay, 'Realm of Uncertainty', 27; Frederick H. Sexton, 'Industrial Education for Miners', *Transactions of the Canadian Mining Institute* (1912): 594.
177. A Nova Scotian 'new model boy' is presented in Lunn, 'From Trapper Boy to General Manager', 211–40.

'Miss Remington' Goes to Work: Gender, Space, and Technology at the Dawn of the Information Age[1]

———— **Kate Boyer** ————

Introduction

Beginning at the end of the nineteenth century, the financial services sector began to undergo a technological 'revolution' with the introduction of new information and communication technologies such as the telephone, typewriter, dictaphone, and mimeograph machine. These technologies changed social–spatial relations within the white-collar workplace, the scope and scale of the networks of branch banking, and even how people thought about city life. At the same time as this process was occurring, the gender of labour within the financial services sector was also changing, such that by the end of the first quarter of the twentieth century most of the work taking place within white-collar offices was performed by women.[2] This paper concerns how these two processes impacted one another and how together they reshaped the spaces and experiences of the early twentieth-century, white-collar workplace.

A growing body of scholarship within (and beyond) geography has begun to theorize information technology and the information economy as spatial phenomena that create and foreclose opportunities at different scales.[3] Meanwhile, feminist geographers have long been interested in the workplace as a site for the production of identity.[4] Sharing elements with both these literatures while infusing complementary theoretical concerns and disciplinary traditions, scholars in science and technology studies and the history of technology have examined gender and the construction of sociotechnical systems in the workplace.[5] In this paper, I draw on and hope to link these lines of inquiry in geography on the one hand and science and technology studies on the other through an analysis of the interplay between technology and gender within the early twentieth-century information economy in what was the centre of the Canadian financial services sector at the time: Montreal.

I argue that the early twentieth-century financial services sector created new geographies of mobility and fixity that differed by sex and by scale. Specifically, the branch-banking system created a network in which men flowed through and women functioned as fixed points. This pattern was echoed at different scales, from the level of the body and the workplace up through spatially dispersed national-level networks, and was supported through regimes of temporal and spatial surveillance as well as rhetorics about women's supposedly staid nature. After introducing the broader project from which this paper is drawn, I will provide some background on Montreal at the time period under review. I will then turn to a consideration of social relations in the early wired workplace, and conclude by examining how women and men fit into the broader networks of branch banking that new information and communications technologies helped create.

Kate Boyer, '"Miss Remington" Goes to Work: Gender, Space, and Technology at the Dawn of the Information Age', *The Professional Geographer* 56, 2 (2004): 201–12.

The Study

This paper draws on research conducted for my doctoral dissertation on the feminization of clerical work in Montreal between 1900 and 1930, the central aims of which were to consider processes of identity formation in the early information technology workplace and link the feminization of clerical work to changing representations of women in the city more generally.[6] . . .

At the corporate archives under review I was able to draw upon materials such as employee files, company journals, photographs, internal correspondence relating to company policy and personnel issues, and records documenting company-sponsored extracurricular programs. The three companies, for which I had preserved information on individual employees in the time period considered, were the Bank of Montreal, Sun Life, and the Bank of Nova Scotia. At the Bank of Montreal I examined records for the 593 women employed between 1902 and 1923, gathering information on age at hiring, place of birth, and years of service. At Sun Life, I was able to chart the number of women employees between 1900 and 1930, though this company did not preserve any other data on individual employees.

The most detailed records of women employed as clerical workers in the financial service sector during this time were preserved by the Bank of Nova Scotia in files that typically included information on home address, religion, educational background, letters of reference, yearly evaluations, and salary information. Some also contained letters from managers of branch offices, personnel in head office, and employees themselves relating to employee behaviour. However, because the head office of this bank was not located in Montreal, the number of women in my sample was smaller at this institution than at others under review. From my reading of 2,880 of the 6,216 total employee files housed at this archive, I found records for 27 women who had worked at the Montreal Branch of this bank in the first third of the century. Though smaller in number than records from other corporations,

these documents were valuable because they illuminated the limits of acceptable behaviour in this workplace.

I approached print media not as a transparent window to past times and places, but rather, after Hall et al. and Tuchman, Kaplan-Daniels, and Benét, as a mediated site for reinforcing dominant social values.[7] In addition to being a fundamental part of their working lives, reading and writing were an important component of working women's leisure time. Moreover, newspapers served an important role in shaping ideas about city life. As Domosh has noted, 'the metropolitan press pioneered journalistic practices that satisfied people's need for information about the bewildering place they found themselves in, the other inhabitants, and themselves.'[8] Though written in reference to the nineteenth-century city, this observation holds true for the time period under review here. Based on an analysis of these sources, I argued that the feminization of clerical work created important new spaces for identity formation and heterosociability in the white-collar workplace; that this process opened up the city to women in new ways; and finally, that the early twentieth-century clerical workspace, and women clerical workers themselves, provide a useful vantage point from which to think about modern urban subjectivity.

Setting the Scene: Gender, Work, and Ethnicity in Early Twentieth-century Montreal

As today, early twentieth-century Montreal was a rich mix of language, religion, and ethnicity, with English-Protestant, French-Catholic, and Irish-Catholic constituting the three major cultural groups. Montreal was also home to significant Jewish, Italian, and other smaller immigrant communities.[9] Most Montreallers spoke French as their first language and claimed Catholicism as their religion. Of those claiming British origins, about two-thirds were Protestant, and one-third Irish-Catholic. While the Catholic Church controlled an impressive array of social institutions, economic power was concentrated in a bourgeoisie comprised largely of Anglo-Scottish Protestants, with Irish- and French-Catholics composing the majority of the middle- and working-classes.[10] Montreal served as the centrepoint both for the national banking and financial services industry, as well as for the smaller French banking system. The financial services sector overall was disproportionately English-Protestant in composition, both in terms of language spoken and religious–linguistic background of the workforce, though among clerical employees Irish-Catholics were overrepresented relative to the city as a whole.

The technological revolution that began in the late nineteenth century created an explosion of paperwork that required keeping track of and a concomitant explosion of low-paid, routinized office jobs in the financial services sector.[11] For class-conscious companies attuned to their public image, it made sense for companies to hire educated, middle-class women to perform office work. In the early twentieth century middle-class femininity still evoked Victorian notions of the 'cult of ideal womanhood', understood through attributes of piety and moral purity, domesticity, and submissiveness,[12] traits that companies in the financial services sector were happy to attach to their employees. And although considered morally superior to men, educated middle-class women were cheaper to employ than their male counterparts and could be paid wages equivalent to a male bricklayer. At the same time, viewed from the perspective of female job seekers, clerical work paid more than nearly any other type of job open to women, and companies did not lack for applicants to fill out their employment rolls . . . . By 1911, clerical work had become the third most important source of employment for women in Quebec after manufacturing and domestic service.[13]

Not unlike the North American economy of the late 1990s, the 1910s saw the emergence of an employment market that sucked workers in. Labour-saving innovations in agricultural technologies meant that fewer people were needed on farms, and increasing numbers of rural inhabitants, especially women, began to look for work in cities. At the same time, Montreal served as the major Canadian destination point for overseas immigration throughout this period. As early as 1901, one-third of the women claiming employment as clerical workers, stenographers, or typists on the Montreal census were born outside the city itself. Of the 588 women employed at the head office of the Bank of Montreal between 1902 and 1923 for whom place of birth is known, more than half were born outside of Montreal, with one-quarter hailing from the United Kingdom and smaller portions from the United States and other countries.

As a group, clerical workers in the early twentieth-century city were overwhelmingly young and single. Reinforcing the findings of Dagenais and Rudin, my research found that the average age at hiring for all women employed at the Bank of Montreal between 1902 and 1923 was 20 years old.[14] . . . The average length of tenure was two years, and over 98 per cent of these young women were single. Though for a small number of women, clerical work served as a means to remain financially independent throughout adult life, for most it represented a time of independence and relative freedom between young womanhood and married life.

While Victorian-era notions of idealized middle-class femininity based in domesticity, purity, and piety continued to circulate, by the 1910s, they were joined in the popular press by depictions of the 'New Woman' and independent working girl.[15] Liberated from family (who sometimes remained behind in the country or even in another province), the so-called New Woman enjoyed the pleasures of the city and a greater degree of freedom than her rural (or more traditional) sisters. The New Woman was marked by her sophistication, explicit rejection of Victorian gender stereotypes, and urban milieu.[16] As Elizabeth Wilson argues, rejection of traditional gender ideology is key to understanding the modern woman as a distinctly urban type: 'Since nature was altogether overturned in the city,' she argues, 'a new form [of] beauty and new form of sexuality were appropriate for its iron landscape, a form that combined masculine grandeur and strength with feminine allure.'[17]

Employed in the heart of downtown, this workforce of young, mostly single, clerical workers and other working 'girls' came to be constituted as an urban 'type' associated with New Womanhood and the nocturnal urban landscapes of an entertainment industry that was expanding at this time through cinemas, dance halls, and cabarets. Consider the following excerpt from a 1926 article in the *Montreal Daily Herald*:

> Eight o'clock and the entrance to each of the many theatres that open their jaws along St. Catherine Street holds its group of waiting ones, a stenographer waiting for her girlfriend, a saleslady keeping a tryst with her fellow. . . . [A] young sheik waits for a dance-hungry jazz baby inside the portal of the hall of the theatre just down the street.[18]

Similarly, a series of articles appearing in the national [magazine] *Maclean's* in 1931 comparing office work to marriage for young women offers a vivid example of how the freedom enjoyed by clerical workers was contrasted in popular media to the constraints of life for the young mother at home. Entitled 'This Bondage' (referring to married life), the article is accompanied by an image of a young woman flanked by two young children and shackled to a ball and chain labelled 'home'. From her imprisonment on one side of the text, she looks wistfully toward a busy office on the other side of the page, as if recalling a memory from an earlier time. Through advice columns, pieces with such titles as 'Saturday Talks to Business Girls', and articles chronicling the need for more working women's clubs in the city, newspapers of the day cast clerical workers as a recognizable urban type, characterized by their youth, freedom, and (importantly) their unmarried status. This contrasted both the confined lives of

their 'married sisters', as well as notions of middle-class femininity that located women's worth in their identities as . . . mothers and wives.[19]

Space, Technology, and Gender in the Early White-collar Office

In contrast to the freedom by which clerical workers were portrayed in the popular press, women's widespread entrance to the financial services sector as employees was happening at the same time as the widespread adaptation of principles of scientific management, or Taylorism, to the white-collar workplace.[20] The goal of scientific management was to increase productivity, an activity that required devising and vigilantly employing systems for tracking progress, output, and employees themselves.[21] In the financial services industry this meant employing punch clocks and hall passes to track worker's movements in time and space and establishing standards such as words-per-minute to measure productivity.[22] At Sun Life, one of the largest employers in early twentieth-century Montreal, employees were not allowed to leave their departments unless on company business, and department heads were instructed to report offenders.[23] Loitering in locker rooms, washrooms, and corridors was specifically forbidden, and employees wishing to leave the building during business hours required a pass from the department head, to be presented to the hall porter in exchange for passage through the building. Though I did not find any specific evidence of this motivation on the part of management, forbidding workers to congregate away from their workstations during the business hours may have also served as a strategy to deter unionization. In addition to monitoring employees' movements within the building, workstations were arranged to be efficient and cost-effective. At most of the corporations under review by the 1920s, stenography and clerical work was centralized within company headquarters, and performed at desks in large, open-floored workspaces. The Bank of

Nova Scotia had a typing pool by 1911,[24] and in that same year the Sun Life employee journal (then *Sunshine*) described the 'army of typewriters', and typing pools filled with women.[25]

Though clerical work offered women better wages than other kinds of jobs open to them, within any individual company, women were concentrated at the bottom of the managerial hierarchy. Workers in these jobs were seen as needing more supervision and were subjected to more stringent regimes of spatial and temporal control relative to those higher up the management ladder. Workers in these jobs were also disproportionately women. In contrast to the small desks and open-floor plans in which women clerical workers laboured, management (at Sun Life and elsewhere) typically worked in large offices decorated so as to evoke middle-class domestic space.[26] Freed from the typewriter or dictaphone, these men worked at desks designed for conversing, reading, and thinking, in offices equipped with doors and secretaries to buffer and regulate contact with others. Meanwhile, at the bottom of the organizational hierarchy, clerical workers were 'tied' or tethered to spatially fixed pieces of equipment such as a typewriter or dictaphone, in workspaces that more easily lent themselves to visual and auditory surveillance.[27] For such employees, location and productivity were intimately linked: for those whose work was identified most closely with a certain piece of machinery, being anywhere but at one's workstation meant not 'doing one's job'. Thus, in contrast to the highly *mobile* nature of women's lives as suggested by 1901 census and birthplaces of Bank of Montreal employees noted earlier, within the space of the office, clerical workers were allowed relatively little spatial freedom. Through the close connection to the machines they worked with, clerical workers functioned as 'part of the machinery' in a way that recalls nineteenth-century textile mills.

As clerical work became increasingly feminized throughout the early twentieth century, women also came to be viewed as having a certain degree of expertise regarding the technologies they used. As an illustration of this point, consider the following two advertisements for Remington typewriters, the first from 1888 and the second from 1910. The first advertisement hails from a time not long after the typewriter had been invented and before its use was widespread in offices. This was at the beginning of women's entrance into the clerical sector. As Figure 1 illustrates, the advertisement depicts a woman in shadowtone seated at a typewriter inside a house. She is being observed through a window by a man who does not understand that she is typing, but mistakenly thinks she is playing the piano. This early ad constitutes a clear effort not only to inform consumers about a product, but also to link that product with middle-class femininity. By locating their product in the middle-class home (and thus, material comfort) and linking it to an activity already associated with respectable middle-class womanhood (and an appreciation of arts and culture), the ad sought to portray typewriting as an activity that would reinforce conceptions of middle-class femininity rather than challenge them (presumably even when the activity took place *outside* the home).

As typewriter use became more widespread and women's presence in offices became commonplace, advertisers no longer had to sell consumers on the appropriateness of women typists. In the second image (from 1910) the typist has become a respectable office worker (and product spokesperson), the idealized 'Miss Remington' (Figure 2). Because Miss Remington has been working in an office for some time (despite her young appearance), she has gained experience evaluating office machinery, and, as we are told, she is familiar not only with the new model but with its predecessors as well. From the side of the frame, Miss Remington advises us that the new model 10 is 'a brand new proposition', offering the buyers 'something new and better for his money than he has ever before obtained'.[28] We are invited to take Miss Remington's word for it, based on her status as an expert user.

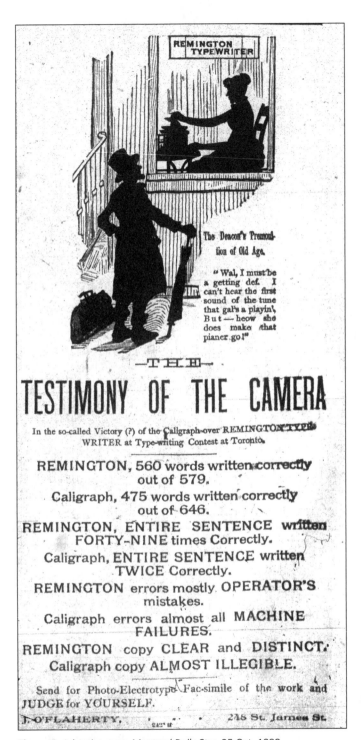

Figure 1. Advertisement, *Montreal Daily Star*, 25 Oct. 1888.

Figure 2. Advertisement, *Montreal Daily Herald*, 9 Jan. 1910.

Yet this technological expertise had its limits. Arguably, the intended goal of women becoming 'part of the system' was to disencumber men's minds from the prosaic end of office work, so that they could concentrate on the 'real' (read, masculine) work to be done. At the same time as quotidian technologies such as the typewriter were becoming ever more closely associated with women's work, projects of city and nation-building—and the technologies that enabled both—continued to be viewed as men's domain. Indeed, at least to some, scaled, gender differences in the ability to understand and use technology were not culturally determined, but inborn. This view can be seen in a 1931 article on why women could not become managers, in which an anonymous manager at the Canadian Imperial Bank of Commerce argued in the pages of his company journal that women were unfit to manage because they had not gained (nor were capable of acquiring) the 'right kind of knowledge'.[29] 'Boys and men,' the author claimed, acquired this knowledge 'by their very nature', because 'from earliest boyhood', males take an interest in animals, material things, and in the working of machinery. As an illustration, the author enclosed a test comprised of questions on industry, manufacturing, trade, and agriculture that prospective managers could take.

Explaining why men could be expected to answer these questions while women could not, he argued that the young boy, in contrast to the young girl, 'goes as a matter of boyish interest where these things are going on, asks questions and imitates such activities in his play'.[30] Applying this point to the work of bank managing, the author stressed the importance of knowledge about broader systems of manufacturing and production to the banking business and the work of investing. Surely, he argued, this knowledge was as foreign and unknowable to women as the remote lumber camps that managers were required to visit. In this way, the author located the experiences and knowledge required for managing a bank in spaces that were off limits to 'respectable' women.

Though 'Miss Remington' may have known her typewriters, as gender stereotypes of the day would have it, the workings of technology, city building, forestry, and trade, together with sites where this knowledge could be procured, were beyond her grasp as a respectable, homebound, middle-class female. To summarize: in contrast to both the highly mobile nature of so many clerical workers' lives—migrating from farms and even from overseas—and media representations highlighting this group's freedom, within the workplace itself, clerical workers were spatially fixed: 'tied-down' to their machines and workstations. In addition, women and men were posited as having quite different relationships to the different technologies that enabled networked branch banking. While women were free to claim authority over small, discrete pieces of office machinery, comprehending the broader sociotechnical systems of which those machines were a part was still considered men's work.

Gender and Networked Branch Banking

In addition to creating new geographies of opportunity and constraint at the level of the workplace, the feminization of clerical work created new geographies of mobility and fixity that differed by gender at the broader scale of networked branch banking. Enabled by new information and communications technologies, branch banking served to reconcentrate power, in terms of people, information, and capital, in 'command and control' centres in larger cities.[31] Making spectacular use of interior steel-frame construction developed in the late nineteenth century, head offices gave companies new symbolic significance on the urban landscape and introduced ideas about rationality, modernity, and in the Canadian case, empire, in physical form. Head offices represented the power of both the company itself (as a logo on stationery and company products), as well as the city in which that company was headquartered, thus contributing to a process of skyline-based urban branding.

Though situated in urban areas rich in services and amenities, the trend in the case of the companies under review was for head offices to function as much as possible as total worlds, in which employees could engage in both work and non-work activities. For example, according to E.F. Chackfield, an engineer reporting in 1931 on the structural marvels of the Sun Life Insurance Company head office in the *Municipal Review of Canada*, the 24-storey structure amounted to no less than 'a city within a city'.[32] Assuring readers that the 35 acres of interior space was every bit as impressive as its exterior, the author highlighted the 38 elevators, five miles of telephone cables, and three basements housing entertainments such as archery ranges, shooting galleries, and a bowling alley, all to amuse the 10,000 to 12,000 employees in off hours.[33]

By drawing on what was then technology's cutting edge, head offices could keep employees linked to each other and the outside world, while at the same time satisfying as many employee needs as possible (including dining, sports, and other leisure activities), in-house, under watchful eyes. Descriptions such as these highlight the fact that not only were twentieth-century head offices impressive, they were impressive in a way that older examples of corporate architecture were not. They suggest a system for measuring the value and importance of commercial space based on magnitude of scale and level of technological sophistication that would endure throughout the century and beyond.

While information had to be managed in centralized head offices, early twentieth-century banking was also marked by the expansion of networks to hinterlands and overseas in order to extract profit from an ever broader territory. For the larger companies, the goal was clearly to be global. For example, Sun Life had branches in Britain, the United States, Asia, and the Caribbean by the 1920s, and as early as 1912 the

Bank of Montreal had 167 branch offices nation-wide, as well as branches in Great Britain, the United States, and Mexico, and affiliate branches in major cities in Asia, Europe, Australia, New Zealand, Argentina, Bolivia, Brazil, Chile, Peru, and British Guiana.[34]

In the companies under review, transferring between different branches was how one advanced up the managerial hierarchy. Transferring provided a way to familiarize management trainees with different positions within the company, standardize practices across the corporate network, and strengthen corporate allegiance. As Benedict Anderson has observed, spatially mobile employees can be thought of as human 'nodes', which strengthen a sense of shared corporate identity.[35] As they moved from one place to another within the network, everywhere meeting people with whom they shared common cultural references, these mobile male employees (and their wives and children) built webs of community nationally and internationally.

Yet women were barred from transferring. Although this can be explained in part by the fact that women were not put on management tracks as a matter of policy in the time period under review, I also found evidence suggesting a reticence to transfer women on principle. For example, records from the Bank of Nova Scotia Archives suggest that requests from women seeking to transfer within the same job category during this period were routinely denied, even when applicants offered to cover their own travel and relocation expenses.[36] Although I was not able to find a corporate policy on this issue, we can gain some insight from a 1927 article in the Royal Bank employee magazine entitled 'The Duties of the Country Junior':

> As regards promotion, it should be remembered that in one respect the female employees are at a disadvantage. A young man entering banking with the intention of making it his life-work is prepared to undertake service at any branch, however remote,

whenever directed to do so by Head Office . . . the circumstances and inclinations of female employees, as a rule do not permit them to serve in any but the branch or branches located in their hometown or city.[37]

As this passage suggests, within the middle-class ideology that informed gender relations at this time, women were imagined to be 'naturally' more immobile and 'home-based' than men, even when they were at work. Thus, whereas men flowed through the networks created by early twentieth-century branched-banking systems, women were positioned as fixed points within them: echoing their spatial fixity at the level of individual offices discussed earlier.

Conclusions

Through an analysis of textual and visual print media, company journals, and employee records, I hope to have shown that the spaces and technologies that sustained the information economy in the early twentieth century were not politically neutral, but rather, that they actively helped produce asymmetries of power and opportunity. As I have argued, women in the early wired workplace were more likely to be 'tethered' to specific machines in the office, and, owing to rules barring their advancement, were subject to higher levels of surveillance and corporeal constraint than their male counterparts. This stood in sharp contrast to actual levels of mobility among this population as suggested by the census and employee records, as well as the freedom by which female clerical workers were characterized within the popular press of the day. I have also argued that the new technologies that enabled the expansion of branch banking came to have gendered associations, which also differed by scale. Whereas large-scale work of city building and infrastructural development were conceived of as . . . male activities, downstream office technologies were feminized.

Finally, I have argued that women and men were positioned differently within the broader networks that branch banking created. In addition to advancing goals of profit-making and augmenting imperial glory, networked branch banking constituted a system for career advancement that worked to constrain women at various scales, both physically and metaphorically. While men moved through the system, making human networks and moving up the career ladder, women were conceived of as fixed points, tethered to their branch and hometown as they were to their typewriter or dictaphone. In these ways, new technologies reinforced power relations of class, sex, and ethnicity, even as they opened new opportunities for both sexes. As the digital information economy continues to take shape, I hope this example from the past can serve as a reminder of the importance of interrogating the relations between space, gender, and technology in the workplace.

Notes

1. My thanks to two anonymous reviewers for their helpful commentary and suggestions on earlier drafts of this paper.

2. See L. Fine, *Souls of the Skyscraper: Female Clerical Workers in Chicago 1870–1930* (Philadelphia: Temple University Press, 1991); G. Lowe, *Women in the Administrative Revolution: The Feminization of Clerical Work* (Toronto and Buffalo, NY: University of Toronto Press, 1987); and A. Kwolek-Folland, *Engendering Business: Men and Women in the Corporate Office, 1870–1930* (Baltimore: Johns Hopkins University Press, 1994).

3. See S. Graham and S. Marvin, *Splintering Urbanism: Networked Infrastructures, Technological Mobilities and the Urban Condition* (London: Routledge, 2001); M.-P. Kwan, 'Time, Information Technologies and the Geographies of Everyday Life', *Urban Geography* 23, 5 (2002): 471–82; W. Mitchell, *City of Bits: Space, Place and the Infobahn* (Boston: MIT Press, 1996); and J. Wheeler, Y. Aoyama, and B. Warf, eds, *Cities in the Telecommunications Age: The Fracturing of Geographies* (New York: Routledge, 2000), to name just a few.

4. See K. England, 'Suburban Pink Collar Ghettos: The Spatial Entrapment of Women?' *Annals of the Association of American Geographers* 83, 2 (1993): 225–42; K. England, 'Girls in the Office: Recruiting and Job

Search in a Local Clerical Labor Market', *Environment and Planning A* 27 (1995): 1995–2018; S. Mackenzie, 'Building Women, Building Cities: Toward Gender Sensitive Theory in the Environmental Disciplines', in C. Andrew and B. Milroy, eds, *Life Spaces: Gender and Household Equipment* (Vancouver: University of British Columbia Press, 1998), 13–30; L. McDowell, 'Social Justice, Organizational Culture and Workplace Democracy: Cultural Imperialism in the City of London', *Urban Geography* 15, 7 (1994): 661–80; and L. McDowell, *Capital Culture: Gender at Work in the City* (Malden, MA: Blackwell, 1997).

5. See C. Cockburn, *Machinery of Dominance: Women, Men, and Technical Know-how* (London: Pluto Press, 1985); F. Kittler, *Gramophone, Film, Typewriter* (Stanford: Stanford University Press, 1999); and C. Marvin, *When Old Technologies Were New: Thinking about Electric Communication in the Late 19th Century* (New York: Oxford University Press, 1988).

6. K. Boyer, 'The Feminization of Clerical Work in Early 20th-century Montreal' (PhD dissertation, McGill University, 2001).

7. See S. Hall, C. Critcher, T. Jefferson, J. Clarke, and B. Roberts, *Policing the Crisis: Mugging, the State, and Law and Order* (London: Macmillan Press, 1978) and G. Tuchman, A. Kaplan-Daniels, and J Benét, eds, *Hearth and Home: Images of Women in the Mass Media* (New York: Oxford University Press, 1978).

8. M. Domosh, *Invented Cities: The Creation of Landscape in 19th-century New York and Boston* (New Haven and London: Yale University Press, 1996). See also G. Barth, *City People* (New York: Oxford University Press, 1980).

9. See P. Linteau, *Histoire de Montréal depuis la confederation* (Montreal: Boréal Press, 1992); C. McNicholl, *Montréal: Une société multiculturelle* (Paris: Editions Belin, 1993); and S. Olson, 'Ethnic Strategies in the Urban Economy', *Canadian Ethnic Studies* 33, 2 (1991): 39–64.

10. See J. Dickinson and B. Young, *A Short History of Quebec: A Socio-economic Perspective* (Toronto: Copp Clark Pitman, 1988), and A. Germain and D. Rose, *Montréal: The Quest for a Metropolis* (New York: Wiley, 2000).

11. G. Lowe, *Women in the Administrative Revolution*, and G. Lowe, 'Mechanization, Feminization, and Managerial Control in the Early 20th Century Canadian Office', in C. Heron and R. Storey, eds, *On the Job: The Labour Process in Canada* (Toronto: McGill-Queen's University Press, 1984).

12. See R.S. Cowan, *More Work for Mother: The Ironies of Household Technology from the Open Hearth to the Microwave* (New York: Basic Books, 1983); L.K. Kerber, 'Separate Spheres, Female Worlds, Woman's Place:

The Rhetoric of Women's History', *Journal of American History* 75 (1988): 11; M.L. Roberts, 'True Womanhood Revisited', *Journal of Women's History* 14 (2002): 150–7; B. Welter, 'The Cult of True Womanhood', in *Dimity Convictions: The American Woman in the 19th Century* (Athens: Ohio University Press, 1976).

13. Census of Canada. 1911. Vol. 4, Table 11.

14. M. Dagenais, *Division sexuelle du travail en milieu bancaire: Montréal, 1900–1930*, memoir présenté a l'Université du Quebec à Montréal comme exigence partielle de la matrise en histoire Université du Québec à Montréal, 1987; M. Dagenais, 'Itinéraires professionnels masculins et féminins en milieu bancaire: le cas de la Banque d'Hochelaga, 1900–1929', *Labour/Le Travail* 24 (1989): 45–68; and R. Rudin, 'Banker's Hours: Life behind the Wicket at the Banque d'Hochelaga, 1901–1921', *Labour/Le Travail* 18 (Fall 1986): 63–76.

15. See E. Freedman, 'The New Woman: Changing Views of Women in the 1920's', *Journal of American History* 61 (Sept. 1974): 372–93; C. Smith-Rosenberg, 'The New Woman as Androgyne: Social Disorder and Gender Crisis, 1870–1939', in C. Smith-Rosenberg, *Disorderly Conduct: Visions of Gender in Victorian America* (New York: Oxford University Press, 1985); and E.W. Todd, 'Art, the "New Woman," and Consumer Culture', in B. Melosh, ed., *Gender and American History since 1890* (New York: Routledge, 1993).

16. E. Wilson, 'The Invisible Flâneur', *New Left Review* 191 (Jan/Feb 1992).

17. Ibid., 128.

18. *Montreal Daily Herald*, 7 Jan. 1926, 3.

19. A. Douglas, *The Feminization of American Culture* (New York: Knopf, 1977).

20. G. Lowe, 'Mechanization, Feminization, and Managerial Control'.

21. A. Pred, *Lost Words and Lost Worlds: Modernity and the Language of Everyday Life in Late 19th-century Stockholm* (Cambridge: Cambridge University Press, 1990).

22. M. Banta, *Tailored Lives: Narrative Productions in the Age of Taylor, Veblen, and Ford* (Chicago: University of Chicago Press, 1993). See also Kwan, 'Time, Information Technologies and the Geographies of Everyday Life'.

23. *Company Rules and Regulations*, circa 1920, Box 406, Sun Life Archives.

24. G. Lowe, 'Class, Job and Gender in the Canadian Office', *Labour/Le Travail* 10 (Autumn 1982): 11–37.

25. *Sunshine*, Nov. 1911, 142. See also Florence M. Richards, 'Half A Century of Girls', *The Sun Life Review*, Jan. 1945, 23. Both: Sun Life Archives.

26. Kwolek-Folland, *Engendering Business*.

27. For more on gender, space, and power in the white-collar workplace, see R. Pringle, *Secretaries Talk: Sexuality, Power, and Work* (London: Verso, 1989); D. Spain,

Gendered Spaces (Chapel Hill and London: University of North Carolina Press, 1992); and A. Van Slyck, 'Gender and Space in American Public Libraries, 1880–1920', Working Paper No. 27 (Southwest Institute for Research on Women: University of Arizona, 1992).

28. Whether the juxtaposition of Miss Remington and the promise that the model 10 offers 'a brand new proposition to the buyer' is intended as sexual innuendo is not clear. For more on the interpretation of visual sources, see G. Rose, *Visual Methodologies: An Introduction to the Interpretation of Visual Materials* (London: Sage Publications, 2001).

29. Anonymous Canadian Bank of Commerce bank manager, 'Women Bank Managers', *The Caduceus* 12, 3 (Oct. 1931): 51–3, quoted passage, 51.

30. Ibid.

31. P. Knox, *Urbanization: An Introduction to Urban Geography* (Englewood Cliffs, NJ: Prentice Hall, 1994).

32. E.F. Chacksfield, 'A City Within A City', *The Municipal Review of Canada* 27, 3 (Mar. 1931): 12–13.

33. Ibid.

34. *Report of Annual General Meeting 1912*, Bank of Montreal Archives.

35. B. Anderson, *Imagined Communities: Reflections on the Origin and Spread of Nationalism* (London: Verso, 1983).

36. Cases 28, 31, and 50, All Bank of Nova Scotia Archives.

37. W.L.G. Cumming, 'The Duties of Country Junior', *The Royal Bank Magazine* (Aug. 1927): 8. Royal Bank Archives.

15

A Platform for Gender Tensions: Women Working and Riding on Canadian Urban Public Transit in the 1940s

——— Donald F. Davis and Barbara Lorenzkowski ———

Canadian use of urban public transit peaked during the 1940s. So too did Canadians' frustrations with it. With people fully employed and automobile use suppressed by tire, gasoline, and vehicle shortages, the overcrowding of buses and trams was so intense that even the 'language of the ladies' had become 'awful'. As the *Toronto Telegram* reported in 1946, one lady 'told another lady to shut her mouth', during an altercation begun by the one climbing up the other's back 'in striving to enter the street car'. The *Telegram* fretted that the 'gnawing neurosis' induced in the women passengers by excessive crowding would soon require streetcars to carry the notice: 'Ladies will kindly refrain from using abusive language.' Overcrowding was having dire implications for traditional gender roles.

As millions of riders competed for physical space, they were also redefining the meaning of public space and the appropriate behaviour within it for 'ladies and gentlemen'. Public transit in Canada had always been a socially contested terrain: in the past it had been a public forum for the debate over industrial discipline, as the burnt and overturned streetcars of 1880–1920, a totem for the 'labour question', attested. On the buses and streetcars of the 1940s, by contrast, Canadians fought over such issues as sexual harassment and the rights of smokers and shoppers, as well as the employment of women drivers and conductors. In short, public transit provided a platform for negotiating and modifying Canadian gender relations.[1]

. . .

The war . . . created opportunities for women in an industry in which they had before then (with some exceptions during the First World War) been employed strictly to type, take dictation, and roll coins.[2] Now they became transit guides and conductors, moving into jobs that admittedly did not require much of a shift in the gender stereotype of woman as man's helpmate. The women who worked in transit garages and repair shops more obviously challenged traditional gender roles. As for female bus drivers and streetcar 'motormen', they had one of the most public platforms in 1940s Canada on which to mount their challenge to the sexual division of labour.[3]

At war's end, women transit workers were let go. By 1949, women retained only one important public role in Canada's urban transit industry, that of passenger guides for the Toronto Transportation Commission (TTC), selling tickets and helping travellers to find their way into

Donald F. Davis and Barbara Lorenzkowski, 'A Platform for Gender Tensions: Women Working and Riding on Canadian Urban Public Transit in the 1940s', *Canadian Historical Review* 79, 3 (1998): 431–65. © 1998 University of Toronto Press. Reprinted by permission of University of Toronto Press (www.utpjournals.com).

the vehicles and around the system. This occupation was so stereotypically 'feminine' that one is tempted to concur with historian Ruth Roach Pierson that, while 'the war effort necessitated minor adjustments to sexual demarcations in the world of paid work, it did not offer a fundamental challenge to the male-dominated sex/gender system.' Yet the temptation to dismiss the survival of the TTC Guide Service into the post-war era as a non-event in the history of both public transit and Canadian women should be resisted, for as historian Jeff Keshen has argued, after the war it was impossible for 'things to return to square one'.[4] Nor was the partial 'feminization' of the transit system in English Canada's national metropolis all that minor a change. This article contends that the guides helped to assure the remarkable post-war success of the TTC. As long as their role lasted, the guides made public transit a more welcoming place for women—a more 'feminine' system in effect. Some readers may balk at the notion that 'mere' guides could have played an important role in the evolution of Canadian transit systems after the war. After all, these women were not system managers; they were hourly rated employees. Yet the work of sociologists Michel Crozier, Michel Callon, and Bruno Latour tells us that 'actors' at all levels of a bureaucracy or technological network have the capacity to shape it socially.[5]

In sum, this article discusses three main themes: first, a crisis in gender relations on public transit triggered by unprecedented wartime crowding; second, the employment of women as drivers and conductors (that is, as platform workers) as well as passenger guides; and third, the exceptional decision of the Toronto Transportation Commission to preserve those values, labelled 'feminine', that women workers *and* riders brought to its wartime system. The goal here is to shed light not only on Canadian gender relations and on a group of women workers hitherto in the historical shadows, but also on the evolution of urban mass transit during the 1940s and on the collective Canadian decision to forsake public transit after the Second World War.

. . .

Canadians described urban transit in the 1940s in dehumanizing terms. They called the streetcars 'cattle cars', and the passengers who perennially blocked the entrance, a 'herd of stupid oxen'. Commuters felt like sardines. 'In the street car there's standing room only,' Gwen Lambton, a Toronto war worker, recalled; 'we're packed like sardines. . . . The used smell of people who have been up all night, their sweat (and mine) is nauseating, but at least I can't fall.'[6] Canadians were urged to grin and bear this crush. Worse, they were told that, contrary to their actual experience, they were already grinning and bearing it. The *Vancouver Sun* on 9 October 1943 ran a large advertisement entitled 'The Greatest Democracy in the World', asserting that the Vancouver public had accepted the necessity of changes to their working hours; they had 'accommodated themselves to fewer stops; . . . speeded up their use of the street car; . . . filled both ends of the cars'. Yet those upbeat words were accompanied by a downbeat drawing that showed weary, miserable-looking people. The drawing, captioned 'OMNIBUS', came with a subtext that explained the stoic, long-suffering looks:

The word 'Omnibus' in Latin meant 'for all.' So the modern street car and bus are 'for all.' People of every class, worker and professional man, woman welder and club woman, automobile owner and pedestrian rub shoulders on their way downtown and home. There are no classes among street car riders and bus riders. Everyone is equal. Everyone is sharing his ride in their great common vehicle of the time.[7]

The *Sun* asked its readers to 'carry the spirit' of democratic equality into every other aspect of the war effort.

By acknowledging the extraordinary nature of the class mixing and egalitarianism of wartime public transit, the newspaper was actually pointing to the heaviest burden imposed by the crush: the psychological loss of 'cultural privacy'. Cultural privacy was defined in 1971 by transportation critic Tabor Stone as the 'need and desire of individuals to be among other persons who share their values, norms, beliefs, and standards of behaviour, and to exclude from their presence individuals with other norms and standards'. In the 1940s, Canadian women and men often resented intrusions into their physical and cultural space by people of different age, class, ethnicity, culture—and sex. With vehicles too crowded for men and women to stake out separate spheres by congregating in front or by pushing through to the rear—or even by travelling at different hours—a struggle for social space was inevitable.[8]

Two groups found the crush loading especially vexatious in the 1940s: the 'shoppers', gender-typed as female; and the 'smokers', gender-typed as male. Both became acceptable targets for abuse as each sex vented its resentments about crowding. Attitudes towards shoppers and smokers were complex. Let us start with the female 'shoppers' who used public transit to carry home their purchases. For many, shopping by public transit was a new and unwelcome necessity, the wartime rationing of gasoline and tires having eliminated both home delivery and the family automobile as options. As 'shoppers' did their unaccustomed errands along unfamiliar routes, they found that their cultural privacy was threatened.[9] The time and space that women could call their own were greatly reduced. By 1943, the evening rush 'hour'—traditionally between 5:00 and 6:00 p.m.—had lengthened to three hours or more, as the major employers in a dozen or more Canadian cities joined the dominion government's plan to 'stagger' the start and end of the workday of 424,000 workers.[10]

It became difficult for shoppers to find a time when they were not competing with commuters for space. In Windsor, by December 1942 there were standing passengers 'at almost any hour'. Windsor was, to be sure, especially crowded. Elsewhere, seats were still sometimes available

during the off-peak hours. Yet shoppers, especially those with jobs or children, were not always able to complete their journeys between 10:00 a.m. and 3:00 p.m., because they had responsibilities that might prevent an optimal travel schedule. Wartime shortages also made shopping more inefficient and time-consuming. Working women became used to buying their groceries after work and then taking the homeward tram after 5:30 p.m., by which time passenger volumes had fallen sufficiently for them to have a shot at a seat. Staggered hours made it extremely difficult for working women to find either the time or the private space for shopping. Stigmatized by their boxes and bags, they became 'shoppers', their right to ridership in clamorous dispute.[11]

. . .

Gendered notions of politeness generally took a beating in the 1940s. As Mrs D.B. White of Ottawa remarked in 1943, 'The cars and buses are so crowded these days, that even the men have to stand!' She added that although a few men would surrender their seats, those who did were 'looked upon by their fellows as particularly odd specimens of the prehistoric animal; and by the ladies with a surprise bordering upon insult'.[12] In 1943 Ottawans could still joke about this 'standing' issue between the sexes. However, by the sultry summer of 1944 tempers had reached the boiling point. A flurry of letters in the Ottawa press that August attested to the frustration and fury with which men and women observed changing gender relations on the very public, very crowded platforms of mass urban transit. Helen Scott set off Ottawa's debate over gender roles in public transit with a letter on 18 August describing boorish behaviour that included sexual harassment:

I can stand to have men sit right in front of me and not bother to offer a seat, but what I can't stand is when they eye every girl standing within the general vicinity, up and down and back again. Besides making me so angry that I would love to slap them, this is most embarrassing. But they don't even stop there. I've seen elderly women, laden down with parcels, get on the street-car and then have to stand and be jostled by the crowd . . . Numerous times I have been just going to get on the street-car when a man came rushing up, elbowed me aside, and rushed madly down the aisle to grab the first available seat.[13]

This letter hit a nerve, not least among those men who addressed the allegation of sexual harassment in their reply to the editor. None denied harassment. They either justified it or placed the onus on women to avoid it. Gerald Birch, though he endorsed equal rights, did so in order to argue that with rights came duties, one of which it seemed was to compete on equal terms for a streetcar seat. Birch countered: 'And so the girls are being stared at and it really peeves Miss Scott. Would she then kindly tell me why the girls spend hours beautifying their body beautiful for the apparent purpose of attraction and when they do get it, scorn it?' If they want to be ignored, let them 'wear something more concealing.'[14] W.L. Farmer claimed to sympathize with Miss Scott, 'one of the few refined ladies among our very young modern generation', yet described her letter as 'pathetic to say the least'. He further accused women, who had won many rights, of taking for themselves habits that belonged exclusively to men:

Smoking, drinking, wearing slacks and shorts (the latter so brief), a loose kind of conversation, yes and all this . . . on streetcars. And in all women have acquired more masculinity in the past twenty years than men were able to lose in a thousand years. Oh! for the days of feminine charm, when tobacco and beer dared never so much [as] to skim the sweet innocence of a maiden's lip; when conversation and dress were modest, when manners were the order of the day

. . . Aye! men had an eye for feminine charm. But the sparkle has been dulled by the sight of a lot of high-ball guzzling, cigar toting mamas parading everywhere in shorts with the utmost disregard for the next fellow's feelings. Women tried competing with the opposite sex and they've got the competition with all its consequences . . . Now, tell me *why* should a man give his seat to an equal?[15]

In effect, Farmer was asserting that women should count themselves fortunate to attract male attention, considering how unsexed they had become. Or was it oversexed? Those 'shorts' obviously bothered him in the hot summer of 1944. Of course, because of gender roles in the 1940s, women could not announce their sexual availability. If they did, or if they smoked, or if they insisted on sexual equality, they apparently should not expect respect.

. . .

Many male commuters were angry during the 1940s—definitely about transit crowding, and probably also about feminine intrusion into their cultural privacy and social space. The bitter, defensive tone of men's remarks about women's traditional priority in seating also revealed anxiety over their own failure to meet traditional gender expectations, an anxiety that inevitably surfaced in civilian male circles in wartime. (Interestingly, none of the males who complained to the press claimed to be a soldier.) They were undoubtedly also bothered, to varying degrees, by the platform that public transit provided for growing numbers of women workers to make known both their existence and their claims to equal treatment. Nevertheless, the wartime discourse about women transit riders did not focus on the workers among them. It targeted instead the hapless shoppers, women who were being condemned for remaining faithful to pre-war gender roles. For decades women had been prized for being domestic consumers. Now their consumer role interfered with the war effort. While historians have emphasized the positive reinforcement to homemakers from government propaganda extolling their role in the war effort, one must wonder whether insults hurled their way for doing their family's shopping did not outweigh any flattery from the elites.[16]

Shoppers were not the only riders to incur the wrath of fellow passengers, for smoking had also become a flashpoint for gender tensions. In the 1940s smoking was still considered a gendered habit, even as Canadians recognized that women increasingly indulged in it. Smoking areas on trams were a man's world. Calgary males, for example, later became nostalgic about their 'smokers', as these enclaves disappeared with the trams themselves after the war. A long retrospective in the *Calgary Herald* of 18 February 1956 acknowledged that the 'smoking compartment was filthy, most of the time', and that it 'smelled of stale smoke'. And yet, 'the ride in the smoking compartment was a social occasion, particularly in the morning.' As the men gossiped about the weather, politics, exotic travel experiences, and the transit service, 'time passed quickly as well as pleasantly.'[17]

The 'stern of an Ottawa street car' was also a 'sort of travelling club for smokers' for five months a year, concluded the *Ottawa Journal* in October 1945. It editorialized: 'Especially is the morning smoke appreciated by those who have a short interval between breakfast and the office, and the man who sets out at the same time each day finds acquaintances in the back of the car. As the smoke billows out the open windows there is talk of fishing, of gardening, of politics . . . and world affairs are given a going-over.'

The *Journal* thought that women could enter this space: 'Sometimes a woman sits there, but it is assumed that she likes smoke, or at least doesn't object to it.'[18] But, like most men's clubs in the 1940s, Calgary's smoking compartment was 'strictly a male preserve', according to the *Herald*:

Occasionally a woman tried to take a seat in the smoker, when the rest of the car was perhaps overloaded . . . Once in a while there would be some frustrated suffragette, who wanted to show that women were smoking too and entitled to the same rights as men, who would barge in and try to make as though she was really enjoying herself. But the atmosphere, both the smoke and the heavy chill that descended when she entered, discouraged the girls.[19]

Realistically, women must have felt unwelcome anywhere the air was 'blue' with smoke. Indeed, in Ottawa they clogged the front of streetcars, a newspaper editorialist remarked, rather than 'move farther down the aisle because, perhaps, by so doing they eventually land[ed] in the bay at the back which is usually occupied by men'— that is, by smokers.[20]

The male tobacco privilege, whether it existed by law or by neglect, came under attack as transit became more crowded during the Second World War. By May 1945, 21 of the 33 transit operators polled by a bus journal had banned smoking. They all reported cracking down on the practice, but men were resisting. Twenty-six of the systems reported difficulty in making their rules stick, especially in cities like Hamilton and Port Arthur (Thunder Bay) which had many manual workers and servicemen. The Sudbury-Copper Cliff Suburban Railway said that it had failed to suppress smoking because 'most of the passengers are miners who have not been able to smoke all day.' The Calgary Municipal Railway complained that it had difficulty restricting smoking to the rear vestibules of streetcars, despite periodic checks by police officers, because its 'own employees [were] offenders to some considerable degree.'[21]

The smoking debate in Edmonton had a distinctly gendered dimension: indeed, the increase in opportunity for female workers on its municipally owned tram system was explicitly linked to the decrease in opportunity for male smokers. Until the war, Edmontonians had agreed to restrict smoking to the rear compartment, but wartime crowding brought confrontation.

In September 1940 the Woman's Christian Temperance Union urged city council to ban smoking on trams 'during such time as the windows have to be closed'. Their letter asked for 'a just recognition that non-smoking patrons have some rights, and that young children who use the street railway service have a right to tobacco-free air'. In October the police, in confirmation that smokers were invading the main body of the cars, promised a crackdown. Yet a city commissioner reported in January 1942 that women were still 'especially annoyed' by the large number of men puffing away well forward of the smoking compartment.[22]

. . .

. . . An 8 October [1943] news report announcing majority support on city council for prohibition pointed out that it was not only the rear entrance that doomed smoking, but also the hiring of the 'conductorettes'. They could not be expected to do their work enveloped in smoke. On 25 October 1943 Edmonton council finally prohibited smoking on urban public transit. This particular gender struggle for space had a clear victor.[23]

It might be expected that Edmonton's men would vent their anger over lost privileges at the women conductors, who were literally supplanting the smokers. Yet women *shoppers* took the brunt of male frustrations in Edmonton, as elsewhere. Women *workers* apparently bothered men less in the 1940s than is often assumed, unless of course the women in question threatened a man's *own* job.

While male and female passengers frequently defamed each other, they almost always had a kind word for women streetcar staff. As a public platform for gender conflict, Canadian mass transit displayed more a battle over gendered space than over occupational roles. This pattern becomes clearer as the experience of other cities with women conductors and drivers is examined. In the next section the narrative shifts perspective, as the nature of the sources requires the story to be told from the companies' point of view

rather than, as would be ideal, from that of the women workers who 'invaded' (as the *Winnipeg Free Press* put it) 'one of the last jobs held exclusively by men in Canada'. These women workers, like the smokers and shoppers, reshaped public transit as a social space as they entered it, experienced it, and even as they left it. Glimpses into their lives appear in the next few pages, but much of their history is yet to be learned.[24]

Canadian transit operators were as slow as one of their vintage trams to move towards hiring women platform workers. In most cases, they hired their first female conductors in the summer of 1943, by which time the number of gainfully employed women in the nation had already neared the million mark (rising from 638,000 in August 1939).[25] In January 1943, when 94 per cent of American transit companies were already employing more than 11,000 women, of whom 718 were operating vehicles, Canada still had not a single woman platform worker. Canadian transit companies explained their lack of interest in female help by pointing to the age profile of their male employees; to the fact (as a Montreal Tramways executive put it in June 1941) that 'no new transportation employees [had] been engaged or trained, in many properties, for almost ten years.' Consequently, Canadian transit was, as the TTC's general superintendent remarked later that year, 'particularly fortunate in the respect that the average age of its employees [was] relatively high and not many [were] likely to be enlisted in the armed forces or be attracted to other employment by promise of temporary advantage'. Yet the manpower situation was similar in the United States: a substantial number of American transit employees were too old for the draft. Even so, it is possible that one major difference in the conscription policies of the two countries—the fact that the United States initiated its military draft in September 1940 while Canada waited until June 1942—explained the keener American interest in hiring female platform workers. An alternative explanation would point to the sheer conservatism of Canadian transit operators, a conservatism that had made them slower than Americans to embrace the trolley coach in the 1930s.[26]

. . .

. . . [T]ransit companies appeared to regard the decision to hire female operators and conductors as radically innovative and inherently risky. In August 1943 Winnipeg Electric told its passengers that the original reaction to the proposal to put women on the streetcar platform had ranged from 'mild scepticism to outright scorn'. To ease such qualms, transit journals ran a series of positive articles on the performance and reception of women transit employees in the United States and, later, in Canada.[27] Meanwhile, the dominion government's manpower policies were pressuring Canadian operators to hire womanpower. By mid-1943 the men being sent to transit companies were over 45 years old and, in the opinion of the transit association's Special Sub-Committee on Manpower, of 'very poor' calibre. It advised companies to hire women, paying them on an equal basis with the men. Union opposition had in the meantime collapsed, since the only realistic alternative to hiring women was a much longer working day for the remaining men. Consequently, systems in Victoria, Vancouver, Winnipeg, Windsor, Kitchener, Toronto, and Sydney had committed themselves by July 1943 to hiring women for platform or garage work. Before the end of the year, women were working as conductors, streetcar motormen, or bus drivers in Edmonton and St Catharines, Ontario, as well. As of March 1944, 12 Canadian transit companies were employing 263 women as streetcar operators and conductors, 70 women as bus drivers, and 154 women in maintenance work. As most of these women worked in just four cities, the numbers suggest that, in the 1940s, Canadians remained more hesitant than Americans to give women a public role in public transit.[28]

After some discussion, the principal transit operators in Montreal and Ottawa both decided against hiring women. Montreal Tramways announced that it was not considering the use of women even to sell tickets on street corners. Presumably, the company was still mindful of French-Catholic reservations about women working in as public a sphere as mass transit. It also dared not upset its unions, especially after a strike in March 1943 proved that it had backed the losing side in their jurisdictional disputes. In Ottawa the street railway, apparently fearful of being permanently saddled after the war with platforms requiring two operators, refused to hire women as conductors. As for Toronto-style passenger guides to ride the cars on an ad hoc basis and keep order as needed, the company may have shared the opinion of Ottawa's *Evening Citizen* that 'Lady Hostesses . . . would simply get in the way of squeezing one more passenger on board.' Ottawa and Montreal had plenty of company in spurning women transit workers: only a minority of Canadian transit systems hired female conductors and drivers. There must have been a generalized resistance to giving women such a public platform on which to demonstrate their ability to do 'man's work'.[29]

What resistance there was seems to have been restricted to the corporate boardroom and the union hall, for the public manifestly welcomed 'the feminine twist' in transit wherever women were employed. This positive response should have been expected, given the widespread recognition that women workers were performing an important wartime duty. Female conductors in Toronto interviewed in September 1943 said that there was 'hardly any trip' during which 'some one doesn't congratulate us.' For example, an elderly man told TTC conductor Elsie Waterford, 'I have been riding these street cars for twenty-five years and I think you girls are doing a wonderful job.' According to a Toronto transit executive, 'the people [were] taking . . . splendidly' to female bus drivers in that city. Vancouver's 'electric guides' quickly garnered 'several letters of commendation' from the public. Women conductors were praised in Edmonton for noticeably speeding up loading and unloading. There seems, then, to have been little public resentment of female platform staff.[30]

Transit companies generally gushed over the women's performance: in August 1943 the *Winnipeg Free Press* quoted the transit company's instructor, E.F. Hales, as stating that he had 'found no trainees quicker to learn than the women employees. He noted that they listened very attentively to what is said, and demonstrate themselves as very apt and quick to learn.' Hales further said that 'the advantage a man might have in his natural mechanical ability is more than made up for by the women in their quickness and ability to learn.' Women actually listened, Hales said, 'they don't just say "yes! yes!" all the time when they really don't know what I'm talking about,' as men apparently did. The female conductors were 'doing a splendid job', Winnipeg Electric affirmed the following October. In late September 1943 the Toronto Railway Club quizzed transit executives about the performance of the new female workers. H.W. Tate, assistant manager of the TTC, responded: 'There have been no problems as far as women are concerned . . . At the present time they are very satisfactory—in fact more so than we expected.' Transit companies consistently reported that women operators had at least as good an accident record as the men—a significant virtue, given the shortage of replacement vehicles and parts. In late 1944 the TTC revealed that its 'women operators [had] been found highly satisfactory, and their accident ratio [had been] even somewhat less than that of the men bus drivers with the same length of service.' Though Winnipeg Electric stated in December 1943 that female streetcar drivers had more accidents than men, it affirmed that the 'men [had] been involved in more serious accidents than the women.' In 1945 it praised women operators for being as 'good as, and in some respects better than, male employees'. In June 1944 the Niagara and St Catharines system reported that women bus drivers were 'more courteous' than its men, and as 'accident free'.[31]

These sorts of direct, favourable comparisons obviously threatened males, and they often came with a negative qualifier. Thus, Niagara and St Catharines added that women took longer to train. It was also reported in Windsor that the work of women bus cleaners had not been 'entirely satisfactory' until the company had hired 'two older women to act as matrons'. As for those Toronto women bus drivers with the exemplary accident record, it was pointed out that they were also said to be 'on the cautious side' (which did not sound entirely complimentary); and their male rivals were depicted by TTC's superintendent of traffic as being of low calibre, not the 'type of individual' who would have been hired 'before the war'. Assistant manager Tate elaborated: 'At the present time, the men we are getting into the organization are the last selection and the women are the best of the women; so if you make a sawoff of the two, I think you are on the good end.' In other words, the 'best' woman was as good as the 'last' man. And even then, Tate said, women performed well because 'their reputation [was] at stake'—that is, the reputation of their entire sex. No wonder they were overachievers.[32]

This perception—that they had the pick of Canadian womanhood—must have influenced the attitudes of transit managers towards their female staff. They could admire the performance of exceptional individuals without having to revise their opinions about women's overall suitability to work on the public platform. Ironically, women fostered this prejudice by the high numbers in which they sought—and were rejected for—transit work. For example, 'some 200 women' responded to Winnipeg Electric's first appeal in mid-July 1943 for women streetcar and bus drivers. Of these, the company 'selected ten as suitable applicants for traffic work' and another 10 as bus cleaners. Subsequent praise for the work of the first four women operators to emerge from this winnowing process did not, therefore, outweigh the company's public conclusion that 'there was a lack of first class [female] applicants for traffic work.' Similarly, the TTC, in reporting on the attrition rate among its female hirings, chose not to emphasize that 86 per cent of its streetcar staff were still working for it on 1 April 1944 (which meant that women had about the same persistence as wartime men in these jobs), but rather commented on the fact that only 70 per cent of its qualified women bus drivers had stuck with the job. They were quitting, the TTC figured, 'probably due [to] the more strenuous physical demands of that work, and partly due to the proportionately greater amount of rush hour work'.[33]

. . .

Managements clearly were displeased with the costs incurred in training platform workers during the war. The extra week or so must have been especially irksome, given the fact that they had not hitherto deigned to pay their trainees. Undoubtedly, the training experience reinforced the managers' prejudices against both middle-aged men and women. These two groups had, of course, the misfortune to serve their apprenticeships at a time when service conditions made it exceptionally difficult to impress their masters. While one could emphasize the positive—that women platform workers received superb training during the war, with even conductors being required in Toronto, Vancouver, and Winnipeg to qualify as drivers—realism demands recognition that transit managers probably looked forward to the day when they could trim their training budgets by hiring young, male workers once again. In the meantime, they hired women. Winnipeg appears to have had 53 platform workers at the peak, just under half of them operating streetcars, the rest conductors; as well, 29 women cleaned and tidied its vehicles. Although Victoria had three such cleaners (in January 1944), Vancouver had none; it did, however, have 40 'conductorettes', with 15 more in training. Edmonton, like Vancouver, used women primarily as conductors—there were 60 of these in April 1944—but an unknown number of women (and men) were also hired during the war to stand by the track switches, turning them

manually for approaching cars. Taken together, these cities probably had fewer than 200 women working for them at any one time. A scattered few worked on smaller systems such as those in Sydney, Kitchener, St Catharines, and Windsor.[34]

The numbers suggest that the majority of Canada's female transit workers had jobs in Toronto, inasmuch as its Transportation Commission hired 721 women during the war to do 'work usually done by men'. At the high point, the Toronto system had 340 female street railway and bus drivers, according to the press. Some sense of the overall distribution of its female workforce can be obtained from the TTC's own count in October 1945 . . . of the women it had employed to do 'men's work'. The count omitted female secretaries, stenographers, and receptionists at head office. The omission suggests that the TTC was not so much interested in determining how many women it was employing (a number it did not publish and perhaps did not compile) as in charting the female incursions into male space.[35]

Toronto's data indicate that transit women prized some jobs more than others, notably those which required technical skills and offered a diversity of challenges (repairwomen, handy-women, and the mechanics' helpers). They also had a preference for trams. On the other hand, women tended to leave jobs that reminded them of housework (the three sorts of 'cleaners') or involved especially heavy work, as did truck driving in the 1940s. Since many buses operated only during peak hours, driving them was exhausting work, the stop-and-go traffic requiring constant wheel and gear play; consequently, bus drivers had the second highest turnover of any of the female occupations reported by the TTC. If women themselves had arrived at a mutual conclusion with their employers that bus driving was not 'women's work', this finding would have eased the conscience of male managers as they pressured women at war's end to retire from male-gendered jobs or to transfer to 'positions more suitable for women'. Moreover, every transit company expected soon to scrap all or most of its streetcars.[36]

Transit men seem to have regarded bus driving by women as particularly invasive of their space; at least, it was the most threatening to their own masculinity. A bus driver commanded a free-wheel vehicle, alarmingly liberated from the steel and electric network that had hitherto guaranteed due subordination to the centralized, hierarchical, and male system; and unlike trams, buses could leapfrog each other. One male driver in 'a certain Canadian city' complained of a woman driver who had been running behind him: 'These dames aren't so dumb. She's been tagging behind me since 7:30 this morning so that I can pick up all her passengers and she doesn't have to risk getting tangled up. She's supposed to be 12 minutes ahead of me, but what can you expect?' A bus journal concluded that his complaints proved that 'man's feeling of security is a precious thing . . . not to be trifled with.' Like most urban bus drivers in the 1940s, this man had probably started out as a streetcar motorman, his security already 'trifled with' by orders to qualify on the new type of vehicle or retire. He may have had doubts about his suitability for his new occupation even before women entered it. In any case, the most hostile remarks towards transit women typically involved buses. For example, a representative of Toronto's electric railway and motor coach union told the National War Labour Board in November 1944: 'We hear lots of sarcastic remarks about women doing our jobs, but I can tell you that women operators are not satisfactory. They are wrecking equipment . . . They haven't the strength to shift gears and handle heavy buses.'[37]

It was rare for a transit man to broadcast such views, for it was unnecessary to denigrate women to ease them out of transit jobs at the end of the war. The women themselves were supposed to realize that they had been temporary replacements in, as the Toronto *Globe and Mail* described the TTC in October 1945, a 'strictly a "for-men-only" organization'. Winnipeg Electric, having told the Canadian Transportation Association in

November 1943 that it was 'not hiring women with any idea of employing them permanently', justified its 1945 decision to *stop* hiring them with the simple justification that men were now available. In Edmonton the street railway simply stopped hiring conductors in 1944, as it looked towards a return to one-man operation. Meanwhile, the TTC, having never disguised its belief that women's employment was 'of an emergency character', and that the jobs were 'for the duration' only, saw no contradiction in praising women for their 'emergency duty' and 'sacrifices', even as it claimed that women now 'were all eager and willing to step aside and let the boys have their jobs back again'.[38]

Were they indeed 'eager and willing'? Certainly, some female transit workers considered, as did Clara Clifford, their job to be 'a war measure'. Yet Clifford worked into 1946, deciding to leave (the TTC did not lay off its female employees) only after an inebriated passenger had accused her of 'taking a job now from a man'. 'This gave me food for thought,' she recalled. Yet she resented the drunk's double standard: 'He did not think . . . [of] the four years that I went through this cold to get him to where he wanted to go.' Some women also pressured female platform workers to leave; a 'middle-aged lady' in December 1945 expressed the widely held sentiment: 'It's time a lot of these girls were sent back to the farms. The war's over . . . Let the girls get themselves husbands, stay home and make room for men to get jobs.' The women workers who refused to heed this cultural message were transferred to more 'fitting' work at war's end on the TTC. Elsewhere, they were laid off.[39]

It is not known how many female platform workers actively resisted their gendered 'destiny'. There must have been some who fought to stay in 'male' jobs, inasmuch as few, if any, women entered the paid labour force primarily out of a sense of patriotic 'sacrifice'. When Canadian women were asked what motivated their entry into the transit industry, they stressed the personal satisfaction they derived from their work.

Streetcar operator Elsie Waterfield responded: 'They didn't want to depend on their children. They wanted to be independent.' The work also suited their interest in 'mechanical work'. Some women said that they had always wanted to drive a streetcar or that they enjoyed meeting the public. Others pointed out that work on the tram platform gave them an opportunity 'to show all the men who thought they couldn't do it that they could'; these women saw themselves as pathfinders for their sex through men's space. Personal improvement also showed up in the reminiscences: 'I was so withdrawn before I went to work,' recollected an erstwhile conductor. 'It gave me all the confidence in the world. I was able to cope with everything—including drunks.'[40]

Money also mattered, as companies advertising 'Good jobs at good wages' understood. Women platform workers emphasized the financial benefits of their jobs: 'I put in every hour I could work because I wanted to buy a home for a family,' recalled TTC conductor Clara Clifford. Urban transit was one of the few wartime occupations in which women got equal pay for equal work, thanks to the street railway unions having made their co-operation conditional on the sexes being treated equally, with respect not only to wages but also to seniority and shift work. The unions wanted to ensure that their employers had no economic reason to prefer female to male labour. Pay equity made transit work attractive to women, especially since the typical platform worker was married, and her husband in the military. These women looked to their job to supplement their dependant's allowance, and some of them undoubtedly had to be told at war's end to resign. Hints about their feminine 'duty' to cede their job to a returning veteran would not have sufficed.[41]

The Toronto Transportation Commission had been unusually open to women workers, and so its efforts at war's end to shut the door on them must have been especially unsettling to the organization. Or the TTC management may have had more opportunity than smaller systems to appreciate the contribution that female

employees could make as a *social class*—rather than as *exceptional individuals*—to the well-being of their system. Whatever the motive, it was apparently only on Toronto transit that women retained a role on the public platform in the two decades after 1946. The first TTC guides had started work in April 1942 at busy spots in the downtown area, standing on the sidewalks to sell tickets, make change, and give information on routes and destinations, in order to speed up the service by reducing the number of transactions and inquiries at the fare box. In November 1945 'a new group of girls was formed, to work at points radiating from the center of the city during the . . . rush hours.' The 23 new 'passenger guides' (thus named to distinguish them from the more stationary 'information and ticket guides' working downtown) were not tied to a specific location; they had 'considerable latitude', as *Canadian Transportation* reported the following February, to ride the cars and buses 'within their prescribed' areas, looking for congestion and opportunities to 'be of service' to the passengers. Once on board, they continued to sell tickets and give out information while simultaneously persuading women to move to the back and men to stub out their illicit cigarettes. The guides were praised in February 1946 for having helped lost children to find their school or mother, an army nurse to carry her 'heavy suitcases', and a soldier to retrieve a typewriter forgotten on a tram.[42]

The TTC prized its guides, considering them a prime asset to be featured on ceremonial occasions. For example, in June 1947 it was a guide who held the official ribbon that Toronto's mayor cut to inaugurate the city's first modern trolley coach service. And in March 1954 two files of guides and male inspectors lined the path leading 'dignitaries', including the provincial premier, to the ceremonies that marked the opening of Canada's first subway line. Two smiling guides were at the head of the file, visually in charge not only of the women but also of the male inspectors, who were the company's most senior and respected employees in traffic operations.[43]

. . .

Although the post-war viability of Canadian transit depended on retaining the loyalty of female riders in off-peak hours, only in Toronto did the system actively cater to their needs. The TTC guides made travel more pleasant for women—and for male non-smokers. They reduced shoving and enforced queues, to the obvious advantage of the very young, the elderly, and the small of frame. They persuaded women to move back in the cars, thereby reducing the buffeting they took from men pushing to the rear. They 'sweetly' told men to stop smoking. They patrolled the interior of vehicles, giving women a greater sense of security on the one-man trams and buses of the post-war era. They gave travel directions, to the advantage of women who, as shoppers or mothers, were more likely than their husbands to be venturing into unknown territory. Finally, it is crucial to note that most of the reported instances of special courtesy and generosity on the part of the guides involved other women. There must have been many women (as well as men) whose fidelity to the TTC was reaffirmed by experiencing or witnessing one of the passenger guides perform an act of basic human kindness such as this one, recorded by *Canadian Transportation* in February 1946:

A very poorly dressed woman got off a car with heavy bundles on a bitterly cold evening. She seemed ill and tired. The guide took off her own rubbers and gloves and put them on the woman, and ascertaining she lived only two blocks from the main thoroughfare, she carried the parcels and took the woman home. At the door, while the woman was returning the rubbers and gloves, she burst into tears and said, 'I never had anything as nice as this done to me before.'[44]

Only the TTC provided service of this quality to urban commuters in Canada. It had 'feminized' its system the most during the Second World War, and remained easily the most feminized

afterwards. The TTC's embrace of 'feminine' values, personified in the tact, cheerfulness, helpfulness, and kindness of its passenger guides, must have been an important asset in transit's post-war struggle to retain enough female patronage to remain economically viable. To be sure, the TTC was doing a lot of things right in the immediate post-war era (including its modernization program), and its regendering in the 1940s was not the sole explanation for its success. Still, the guides did constitute an outreach to women and an attempt to ease the gender tensions among its passengers that overcrowding had produced. On other Canadian systems, passengers were left to fend for themselves.[45]

It is surprising that the wartime crowding does not figure more strongly in accounts of the decline of public transit, and the explosive growth in auto sales in the late 1940s. After all, even a Winnipeg Electric engineer had advised the Canadian Transit Association in late 1944 that he had been 'on our cars when they were so crowded that I felt that a personal indignity had been visited upon me by our own company'. He then added: 'If I had any choice I would not have chosen our service.' Post-war prosperity actually gave Canadians that choice, and they opted for the motor car en masse.[46]

Public transit in the 1940s was indeed an 'indignity', and until historians fully assimilate this fact into their accounts, their explanations of transit's post-war decline will be incomplete and unpersuasive. It was not just the economics of transportation or the politics of subsidies that determined the decision to ride; it was also deep-felt, individual attitudes towards privacy and social space. To understand the widespread rejection of public transit, we must be able to imagine ourselves a reviled, wartime female 'shopper' laden with parcels, one of 65 standees in a 45-seat streetcar, with one man beside her blowing smoke in her face, another two men pressed against her nether regions, and a dozen people blocking her path to the exit. Our historical imagination must also encompass the beleaguered male smoker and the 'hapless male' described in a plaintive letter from an Ottawa man in 1947:

One has only to board a crowded car today to see how some women will out-do themselves to make some harried male feel small and cheap so that he is more or less obliged to give up his seat to the triumphant female . . . Some women—the obviously independent type—do not expect a man to give up his seat to them. When a tired young man stands up and graciously offers his seat to one of them, she turns him down and remarks with a superior smile, 'I'd rather stand, thank you.' Men, viewing a spectacle like this, have reason to think twice before standing up to be the target for amused glances and sly comments from sitting passengers.[47]

. . .

Not surprisingly, Canadians . . . had difficulty getting past the idea of transit work as strictly 'men's work'. The ideology of women's and men's 'proper' sphere resurfaced in 1944–5, as a powerful 'reconstruction' discourse demanded women's post-war return to the home. The story of the women platform workers who were forced out of the paid labour force or into lower-paid, less satisfying work told a familiar tale. The individuals involved clearly paid a high price for the nation's gender bias. So too did Canada, as transit's failure to listen to the women of Canada before 1941 or to give women a working role in the system after the war (outside of Toronto) contributed to public transit's post-war slide into subsidy and senescence.[48]

Notes

1. *Toronto Telegram* editorial reprinted in *Ottawa Morning Journal*, 12 Feb. 1946. All Ottawa press items come from the City of Ottawa Archives (COA), Ottawa Electric Railway Scrapbooks. . . .

2. An exception to the rule were female bus entrepreneurs in North America. See Margaret Walsh, 'Not Rosie the Riveter: Women's Diverse Roles in the Making of the American Long-Distance Bus Industry', *Journal of Transport History* 17 (1996): 43–56. . . .

3. There exists a well-developed body of studies on the gendered construction of skills. See, for example, Joy Parr, *The Gender of Breadwinners: Women, Men, and Change in Two Industrial Towns, 1880–1950* (Toronto: University of Toronto Press, 1990); Ava Baron, ed., *Work Engendered: Toward a New History of American Labor* (Ithaca, NY: Cornell University Press, 1991).

4. Ruth Roach Pierson, *'They're Still Women After All': The Second World War and Canadian Womanhood* (Toronto: McClelland & Stewart, 1986), 216; Jeffrey Keshen, 'Revisiting Canada's Civilian Women during World War II', *Histoire Sociale/Social History* (Nov. 1997). . . .

5. Michel Crozier, *The Bureaucratic Phenomenon* (Chicago: University of Chicago Press, 1964); John Law, ed., *Power, Action, and Belief: A New Sociology of Knowledge?* (London: Routledge & Kegan Paul, 1986); Wiebe Bijker et al., eds, *The Social Construction of Technological Systems: New Directions in the Sociology and History of Technology* (Cambridge, MA: MIT Press, 1987); Wiebe Bijker and John Law, eds, *Shaping Technology/Building Society: Studies in Sociotechnical Change* (Cambridge, MA: MIT Press, 1992).

6. Montreal *Gazette*, 24 Sept. 1948; Ottawa *Morning Citizen*, 7 Dec. 1948, 12 Nov. 1942; Gwen Lambton, 'War Work in Toronto', in Ruth Latta, ed., *The Memory of All That: Canadian Women Remember World War II* (Burnstown, ON: General Store Publishing House, 1992), 33.

7. *Vancouver Sun*, 9 Oct. 1943.

8. Tabor R. Stone, *Beyond the Automobile: Reshaping the Transportation Environment* (Englewood Cliffs, NJ: Prentice Hall, 1971), 100.

9. Modern prejudice envisages the 1940s shopper as someone with hatbox in hand, but she was more likely to have the evening's meal or a scarce commodity like sugar or coffee in her bag. . . .

10. *Chatelaine*, 22 Nov. 1942, 72, 75; City of Calgary Archives (CCA), City Clerk's Fonds, box 245, file 2245, City Clerk of Winnipeg to City Clerk of Calgary, 16 Aug. 1943; National Archives of Canada (NAC), RG 28, vol. 270, file 196–17–4, Department of Munitions and Supply, Press Release 593A, 19 Sept. 1945. . . .

11. *Bus and Truck Transportation in Canada* (BTT), Dec. 1942, 29, Feb. 1944, 40–1.

12. Ottawa *Morning Citizen*, 17 May 1943. . . .

13. Ibid., 18 Aug. 1944.

14. Ibid., 21 Aug. 1944. Birch was using the 'potent weapon of humiliation'. This weapon, as Karen Dubinsky has argued, 'touched all those who went public with their

stories of sexual conflict'. Karen Dubinsky, *Improper Advances: Rape and Heterosexual Conflict in Ontario, 1880–1929* (Chicago: University of Chicago Press, 1993), 164.

15. Ottawa *Morning Citizen*, 22 Aug. 1944.

16. The widespread negative attitudes towards female shoppers contrasted markedly with government propaganda efforts to recognize women's traditional domestic services (i.e., thrift and price monitoring) as socially necessary. See Pierson, 'They're Still Women', 41; *Chatelaine*, Nov. 1942, 72, 75, June 1944, 76. . . .

17. *Saturday Night*, 30 Nov. 1912, 29, 4 Nov. 1922, 23; *Edmonton Journal*, 31 Jan. 1942; Centre d'archives Hydro-Québec, file F6/16173, 'Rules and Regulations for the Government of Employees of the Hull Electric Company' (1913); *Calgary Herald*, 6 Dec. 1949, 18 Feb. 1956. . . .

18. Ottawa *Morning Journal*, 5 Oct. 1945.

19. *Calgary Herald*, 18 Feb. 1956. This article was prompted by the elimination of the last smoking vestibules. The 'clubhouse' theme also appeared in a *Herald* article of 6 Dec. 1949.

20. Ottawa *Morning Citizen*, 18 Nov. 1942.

21. *BTT*, May 1945, 72; City of Halifax Archives. City Council Minutes, 12 Nov. 1943, 338 (thanks to Kimberly Berry for this reference); CCA, City's Clerks Fonds, box 386, file 2532, 19 May 1947; CCA, Calgary Transit, Series III, box 82, file 859, Superintendent's Office Bulletin, 27 Oct. 1947. . . .

22. *Edmonton Journal*, 24 Sept., 10 Oct. 1940, 31 Jan., 30 Sept. 1942.

23. Ibid., 18 Aug., 4, 8 Oct. 1943; *Edmonton Bulletin*, 4, 8 Oct. 1943; City of Edmonton Archives (CEA), City Council Minutes, 25 Oct. 1943.

24. *Winnipeg Free Press*, 14 Aug. 1943.

25. C.P. Stacey, *Arms, Men and Governments: The War Policies of Canada, 1939–1945* (Ottawa: Queen's Printer, 1970), 416. This number did not include the 750,000 women working on family farms and the 43,000 women in the armed forces.

26. *Canadian Transportation* (CT), Feb. 1942, 90, May 1943, 245; *Proceedings of the 37th Annual Meeting of the Canadian Transit Association*, 1940–1, 110.

27. Canadian transit executives apparently had forgotten or chose not to recall that 12 women had served as streetcar conductors in Halifax for a year after the explosion of 6 December 1917. They were paid off 'when the men came home'. . . . See *Canadian Railway and Marine World*, Feb. 1933, 71; Provincial Archives of Nova Scotia, MG 9, vol. 229, Nova Scotia Tramways and Power Company Ltd, *Annual Report of the President and Directors for the Year Ended Dec. 31st, 1917*, 1–2; Halifax *Mail-Star*, 2 Dec. 1958; George Dillon and William Thomson, *Kingston Portsmouth and Cataraqui Electric Railway* (Kingston: Canadian Railroad History

Association, 1994); Vancouver *Province*, 17 July 1917 (Moose Jaw). (Thanks to Kimberly Berry and Steven High for the Great War references.)

28. *BTT*, July 1943, 37; Aug. 1943, 20; Vancouver Public Library, Harold Till, *Vancouver's Traffic History, 1889–1946* (n.d.), 60; Public Archives of Manitoba, P608 Amalgamated Transit Union, Minutes of 13 Apr. 1943; *CT*, July 1943, 378, Aug. 1944, 441; Toronto *Globe and Mail*, 12 July 1943; *Winnipeg Free Press*, 15 July 1943; Vancouver *Province*, 11 Aug. 1943; Kitchener *Daily Record*, 12 June, 7 July 1943. . . .

29. Montreal *Gazette*, 17 May, 19 June 1943; The Clio Collective, *Quebec Women: A History* (Toronto: Women's Press, 1987), 277–84; Alison Prentice et al., eds, *Canadian Women: A History* (Toronto: Harcourt Brace Jovanovich, 1988), 299; Ottawa *Evening Citizen*, 29 Nov. 1945; NAC, MG 28, I103, vol. 230, file 7, A.R. Mosher, 'A Public Statement on the Montreal Tramways Strike', 5 Apr. 1943.

30. Toronto *Daily Star*, 22 Oct. 1943; *CT*, July 1943, 378, Nov. 1943, 590, Jan. 1944, 30; Toronto *Globe and Mail*, 10 Sept. 1943; Ottawa *Morning Citizen*, 18 Oct. 1943; Ottawa *Evening Citizen*, 30 Nov. 1943 (latter two for Edmonton); Kitchener *Daily Record*, 7 July 1943; NAC, AV, tape R8547, Elsie Waterford reminiscences.

31. *CT*, Oct. 1943, 542, Nov. 1943, 590, Jan. 1944, 28–30, June 1944, 330, June 1946, 328; Winnipeg Free Press, 14 Aug. 1943; *BTT*, June 1944, 42.

32. *BTT*, June 1944, 42; *CT*, Nov. 1943, 590, Dec. 1943, 653.

33. *CT*, Dec. 1943, 653, Jan. 1944, 27, June 1944, 330; *Winnipeg Tribune*, 15 July, 5 Aug. 1943; *Winnipeg Free Press*, 14 Aug. 1943. The male turnover was 2.3–2.5 per cent per month in 1943.

34. *CT*, Jan. 1944, 30, Feb. 1944, 82, June 1946, 328; NAC, MG 30 B137, Norman D. Wilson Fonds, vol. 18, file 19, Thomas Ferrier to Edmonton City Commissioners, 19 Apr. 1944; Colin K. Hatcher and Tom Schwarzkopf, *Edmonton's Electric Transit* (Toronto: Railfare Enterprises, 1983), 116; *Edmonton Journal*, 10 Jan., 29 Mar. 1944.

35. *CT*, Nov. 1945, 637; Toronto *Globe and Mail*, 6 Oct. 1945. The TTC's reliance on women workers was not unusual for a Toronto company: in October 1943, more than 40 per cent of Toronto's manufacturing workers were female—the highest percentage for any Canadian city. NAC, MG 28 I103, vol. 362, General Part I, 1942–57, Department of Trade and Commerce, Dominion Bureau of Statistics, Employment Statistics Branch, 'Sex Distribution of the Persons in Recorded Employment at Oct. 1, 1943' (Ottawa: King's Printer, Dec. 1943).

36. *CT*, Nov. 1945, 637.

37. *BTT*, Sept. 1943, 25; Ottawa *Evening Citizen*, 1 Nov. 1944.

38. Toronto *Globe and Mail*, 6 Oct. 1945; *CT*, Oct. 1943, 542, Dec. 1943, 654, June 1946, 328, 334; *Edmonton Journal*, 10 Jan., 7 Dec. 1944, 21 Nov. 1945.

39. NAC, AV, tape R8546, reminiscences of Clara Clifford; Ottawa *Morning Citizen*, 1 Dec. 1945.

40. *Winnipeg Free Press*, 5 Aug. 1943; Toronto *Daily Star*, 22 Oct. 1943; *Winnipeg Tribune*, 5 Aug. 1943; NAC, AV, tapes R8546–7, reminiscences of Elsie Waterfield and Clara Clifford.

41. NAC, AV, tape R8546, reminiscences of Clara Clifford; *CT*, Jan. 1944, 27–9, Feb. 1944, 82, June 1946, 328; *Bus Transportation*, Dec. 1944, 35; *Edmonton Journal*, 10 Jan. 1944; Vancouver *Province*, 11 Aug. 1943; *BTT*, July 1943, 37. . . .

42. Only single women were employed as passenger guides, in keeping with the post-war trend against hiring married women. See NAC, AV, tape R8546, reminiscences of Clara Clifford; *CT*, Feb. 1946, 84, 86, Jan. 1949, 30; Toronto *Globe and Mail*, 19 Jan. 1943; Ottawa *Morning Journal*, 30 Nov. 1945; *BTT*, Aug. 1949, 42. . . .

43. Mike Filey, *The TTC Story: The First Seventy-five Years* (Toronto: Dundurn Press, 1996), 72, 89. The TTC guides lasted until March 1995, when the service ended for budgetary reasons. Information from Ted Wickson, the former TTC archivist.

44. *CT*, Feb. 1946, 86.

45. This conclusion raises the question of whether any American transit system had female guides immediately after the war and whether its ridership also held up unusually well. Unfortunately, the sources used here, including *Transit Journal* and *Bus Transportation*, allow us only to pose, not answer, this question. . . .

46. *CT*, Dec. 1944, 663. Motor vehicles in Canada rose in number from 1.5 million in 1945 to 2.6 million in 1950. F.H. Leacy, ed., *Historical Statistics of Canada*, 2nd edn (Ottawa: Statistics Canada, 1983), T147–78.

47. Ottawa *Evening Citizen*, 24 Nov. 1947.

48. Transit's story must have been repeated in countless other industrial sectors. Yet historians have tended to assume rather than prove that the post-war departure of women from entire occupations damaged society and the economy. In effect, there has been a liberal and individualistic focus, rather than a communitarian one, to the research. Among the few studies to examine the economic damage resulting from women's return to home and hearth in North America are Lewis Humphreys, 'Women and Government Intervention in the Canadian Labour Force, 1941–1947', MA thesis (Dalhousie University, 1986); Sherrie A. Kossoudji and Laura J. Dresser, 'Working Class Rosies: Women Industrial Workers during World War II', *Journal of Economic History* 52 (1992): 431–46.

16

Privilege and Oppression: The Configuration of Race, Gender, and Class in Southern Ontario Auto Plants, 1939 to 1949

——— **Pamela Sugiman** ———

Over the last few decades, attempts to theorize the relationship of race, gender, and class, and discussions of the centrality of these forces in shaping our lives have become increasingly sophisticated and passionately debated. . . .

There is a need then for social historians and social scientists to rethink some of the old conceptual categories, with an eye to understanding the ways in which race, gender, and class, as historically configured, have structured the economic institutions that govern our lives. How, for example, has this nexus organized wage-earning and shaped workers' experiences in this country? Moreover, what is the link between the gendering and racialization of capitalist workplaces and the politicization of the worker, the development of a worker consciousness, and the collective mobilization of the working class? Importantly, how can we theorize this link between structure and lived experience without reverting to old additive or multiplicative analyses based on the equation race + gender + class or race x gender x class?[1]

This paper offers an examination of the ways in which the matrix of race, gender, and class has structured the automobile manufacturing industry of southern Ontario, a work setting that has long been racialized and gendered.

Since the beginnings of the industry, white men have dominated the auto manufacturing workforce. Anyone who was not white and male was in the minority, different, an intruder, treated as unequal. In the auto plants of southern Ontario, two such 'minorities' existed. One, small groups of women, many of whom were born in Canada of Anglo-Celtic and Eastern European descent, worked in McKinnon Industries of St Catharines, Ontario, and the General Motors Company of Canada (GM)'s manufacturing facility in Oshawa, Ontario.[2] Two, even smaller pockets of black men, mostly Canadian-born, were concentrated in janitorial jobs and various types of foundry work in McKinnon Industries and the Ford Motor Company of Canada, as well as some smaller auto foundries in Windsor.[3]

In earlier research, I documented the experiences of white, women auto workers, tracing changes in both their position in the industry and their perceptions and politics over the course of several decades.[4] This study is an attempt to reconstruct a small part of the lives of black men, on the job and in their union, at a time when their numerical presence in the auto plants was at its peak, throughout World War II and into the post-war period.[5] It is based on a review of union

---

Pamela Sugiman, 'Privilege and Oppression: The Configuration of Race, Gender, and Class in Southern Ontario Auto Plants, 1939 to 1949', *Labour/Le Travail* 47 (Spring 2001): 83–113. © Canadian Committee on Labour History. Reprinted by permission of the publisher.

documents, as well as the oral testimonies of 12 black men who were employed in the industry during these years.[6] . . .

Oral testimony is a valuable methodological tool to unearth the histories of invisible groups who, by virtue of their small number, have escaped scholarly attention.[7] Due to the hegemony of whiteness in the auto plants, black auto workers have almost no place in Canadian labour history. Jobs in auto manufacturing have been viewed as 'naturally' white (and male); analyses of the racialization and gendering of workplaces have been confined to those settings in which women and people of colour are numerically dominant.[8] Yet in spite of the scant numbers of black men in the plants, auto manufacturers drew on widespread cultural beliefs about race and gender, and exploited and reinforced the structural inequalities that working-class blacks faced in wartime southern Ontario. Employers manipulated these beliefs in hiring workers, allocating them to jobs, and establishing the terms of their employment. In doing so, management was central to the construction of difference among workers—a notable achievement given the striking social homogeneity of the workforce as a whole.

Considering the industrial backdrop that employers had set in place prior to the emergence of the United Automobile Workers' Union (UAW), I also comment on the ways in which black men, as individual workers and subsequently as trade unionists furthering collective goals, coped with, and at times resisted their racial subordination. . . . Industrial unionism played a central role in shaping these strategies of coping and resistance. Yet the UAW posed contradictions. While the union served as an ally, offering both a philosophical commitment to social (racial) equality and justice, and the material resources and tools with which to seek it, the UAW also contained the struggle to racialize worker resistance.[9] Union leaders lacked an adequate understanding of racial and sexual discrimination, and they typically reduced both to class relations between workers (as a homogeneous entity) and their

employers. Furthermore, the union constructed a false dichotomized 'choice' between racial (and sexual) *difference* on the one hand and *equality* on the other. Believing in the importance of a unified 'workers' consciousness', UAW leaders, at times, posited difference or divisions within the working class as a threat to the labour movement.

An understanding of the social meaning of racial and sexual difference is central to an analysis of the workplace, working people, and their struggles. When we recognize these differences, we uncover many parallel, but separate working-class realities. The distinctive experiences of black men in the industry can be attributed to the particular ways in which race, gender, and class, both as subjectivities and social processes, have converged at different moments and touched the lives of workers, as well as shaped the larger historical scenario.

. . .

Constructing Difference among Auto Workers

Though data on the demographic composition of auto plants in Canada is based largely on anecdotal evidence, it is undeniable that employers used race and sex as criteria in filling jobs. Prior to World War II, in the pre-union period, sizable communities of black families lived in the auto towns of St Catharines and Windsor. St Catharines, a small city near Niagara Falls, was the home of McKinnon Industries. Windsor, a mid-sized city that is situated across the river from Detroit, was the location of the Ford Motor Company of Canada, Chrysler Canada, and a number of affiliated auto foundries such as Auto Specialties, Walker Metal Products, and Malleable Iron.

Despite the strong presence of the auto companies in their communities, however, most blacks understood that auto employment was unattainable to them. Before World War II, only a handful of blacks worked in auto [plants]. . . . In the 1920s, two black men, members of the

Nicholson family in St Catharines, poured iron in the McKinnon foundry. They may have been the only two 'coloured men' employed by the company at this time. In the 1930s, McKinnon Industries hired a large number of Armenians. These men, most of whom were recent immigrants to Canada, lived in company housing on Ontario Street, which was located opposite the plant. They occupied many of the jobs that increasing numbers of blacks would later fill. In the 1920s, some black men also found work in the Ford Motor Company, though their exact number is not known. Auto employees Lyle Talbot and Rod Davis, respectively, had a father and grandfather working in Ford.[10] Talbot's father was hired in 1919 and worked as a machine operator in the transmission department until 1947.

With the outbreak of World War II, employers were forced to alter their hiring policies in response to stepped-up production demands and the temporary departure of many prime-age, white, male employees. Thus, the doors to the auto plants opened a crack for some of those workers who had long been on the outside. For instance, during this time, Ford hired a number of Chinese men in its Windsor plant. Proud of this move, company publicists featured a photograph of each of their 56 Chinese workers in its monthly magazine, *Ford Times*. Ford described the employment of these men as a patriotic gesture in the context of war.[11]

During these years, the company also continued to hire black men in relatively small, but growing numbers. In the United States, the well-known industrialist Henry Ford had established a reputation for providing jobs to 'Negroes', a move indicative of his paternalistic relationship with the African-American community.[12] In 1941, blacks constituted roughly 10 per cent of the workforce (11,000 workers) in the Ford Motor Company in the United States.[13] While Henry Ford also upheld this reputation in Canada, the numbers of blacks in the Windsor plant seem almost insignificant in comparison to

those in the United States. For example, when Lyle Talbot began to work at Ford (Windsor) in 1940, he joined roughly 200 black men.[14]

McKinnon Industries was the other major employer of black men in the auto industry. In 1938, the company hired approximately 80 men, many of whom were black, in its foundry division.[15] Richard Nicholson, relative of the two Nicholsons who worked at McKinnon in the 1920s, was one of these recruits. Shortly after joining the company, he witnessed the entry of several more blacks. According to Nicholson, roughly 15 to 20 black men were hired in McKinnon Industries during World War II. By 1943, there were at least 40 to 50 black men out of a total workforce of 4,500.[16]

Of the 'Big Three', Chrysler Canada had the most overtly racist hiring practices.[17] In fact, the company did not hire a black worker until it was pressured to do so by law in the 1950s. In 1951, the Ontario Fair Employment Practices Act[18] was passed and in 1953, a federal Fair Employment Practices Act was set in place. According to the latter piece of legislation, any company that had a contract with the Canadian government was prohibited from engaging in racially discriminatory hiring practices. Thus, in October 1953, for the first time in its history, Chrysler Canada hired three black men to work on its assembly lines.[19]

None of the companies, however, offered employment to black women. According to a report by Lyle Talbot, former Ford employee and president of the anti-racist organization, the Windsor Council on Group Relations, at a time when many employers badly needed to replenish their diminishing supply of workers, 'the doors of virtually every factory in the Windsor area were closed tight against coloured girls and women.'[20] In fact, of the 50 shops in Windsor that were under UAW contract, not one employed a black woman in either office or factory. Talbot noted that, '[i]t was common knowledge of the coloured people of Windsor that their women-folk were hardly ever sent to factories, stores or offices' by the federal government wartime agency, the National Selective Service (NSS), because of a 'gentlemen's agreement'. In those few cases where the NSS did send black women for jobs, the employers had apparently reprimanded NSS officials. World War II 'broke the barrier' for 'coloured men' only.[21]

On the whole, personnel managers asked job applicants few questions about their employment experience or other personal qualifications. (In men of all races, employers overlooked the unique talents of the worker, i.e., skills for the job.) In working-class men, auto employers sought 'human machinery' to perform labour that had been organized for profit-making only.[22] Yet in specifically pursuing 'coloured men', on occasion, management was underlining the salience of race in this class context. Richard Nicholson worked in the foundry in St Catharines for 36 years. He remembers his entry into the company.

I heard the rumour . . . that McKinnon Industries was hiring blacks. . . . They were looking for *coloured people* to work in the foundry so I went down there to Ontario Street and 'bingo!' I got hired right away because I was a big lad and everything [emphasis mine].

During the war years, auto manufacturers recruited black men through various government and community networks. Many men found their jobs by way of either the NSS, district service clubs, or ministers of black Baptist churches. When neither the NSS nor the neighbourhood rumour system yielded sufficient numbers of black males, however, employers resorted to more active and direct means of recruiting, reaching out beyond local communities. Local folklore tells us that years ago, recruiters for McKinnon Industries went to Toronto to find black men. Then in 1940, under the exigencies of war, they travelled to Nova Scotia as part of a further recruitment drive.[23] The NSS paid the men's passage from Nova Scotia to St Catharines, a distance of close to 2,000 kilometres. At various points in time,

McKinnon managers also recruited black men from Fort Erie and Niagara Falls.[24]

'Foundries Is Made for Black Men'

Automakers took special measures to locate black male labourers largely because they wanted them to fill the most undesirable jobs in the plants—jobs that few white men wanted. In the auto plants of Ontario, racial segregation was never enforced as a matter of company policy nor was it written into collective agreements (as it had been in the United States). Yet management used informal, unspoken means of exclusion to place blacks in one of three areas: the heat treat, the powerhouse, or the foundry. Within various departments or divisions, some black men could also find work as janitors.[25] According to Lyle Talbot, who temporarily worked in each of these jobs, they were all bad places to be. The powerhouse was dirty.

[T]hey'd get all kinds of soot from the smoke. . . . In the powerhouse, there was a big pile of coal out in the yard, and big transformers that were run by coal, heat. Black men worked in a tunnel where the coal was brought in on a conveyor from the coal pile into the big furnaces that generated the heat for the power. The men had to make sure that the coal did not fall off the conveyor going through.

The 'heat treat's the same thing,' Talbot added. This is where they treated the metal with heat in long ovens. The worst of the three areas, however, was the foundry—'where all the heavy, slugging, dirty work' went on.[26] The vast majority of the black workforce was situated in the foundry.[27] And there, along with Armenians, they typically performed the least desirable job of iron pouring.

The men poured their own iron and you had to go out and shift the moulds—had a plate on top about that thick and go on top of the moulds for them to pour the iron. Sometimes they'd be pouring and the mould would be bad and as they poured in the iron would burst out the side and sometimes, as soon as that iron, just a drop, would hit . . . the concrete it would look like fireworks.[28]

GM worker Richard Nicholson commented on the relationship between race and job allocation:

In 1938 . . . when I went to General Motors, they hired us blacks for one reason. They didn't lie to you. When they hired me, they told me . . . 'We got a job for you in the foundry. It's a hot job. It's a hard job.' . . . [T]hey kept calling in blacks, more blacks. They would've hired more blacks if they could have got 'em because that was where you were supposed to be—right there in the foundry.

Black working-class men had little choice but to accept these hot, hard jobs. Typically, prior to finding employment in the auto industry, these men worked as bellhops or elevator operators in local hotels, and general labourers on railroads, in carnivals, and on farms. They also washed cars by hand, peddled wares on the streets, and collected metal in alleyways for resale.[29] Most of this work was seasonal. Auto employment not only offered higher wages, but more importantly, it was comparatively steady work. The black community faced intense racism in the labour market, a situation that resulted in extreme economic hardship.

Compounding the labour force requirements of auto manufacturers and the dire economic straits of most black workers, employers upheld a particular vision of black masculinity that rested in part on the belief that a 'coloured man' was most suited to hard, dirty, and physically demanding jobs.[30] Before foundries became highly automated, many of the operations required enormous physical strength (lifting castings and pouring iron, for example). And the dominant cultural image of a black

man was that of a strong, robust, and muscular worker. Moreover, foundry work was performed at extraordinarily high temperatures and thus demanded tremendous physical stamina. Some company officials claimed that coloured men, in particular, could endure these excesses because of a genetic predisposition to withstand heat.[31] According to auto worker Cassell Smith,

At that time the foundry there was smoky and dusty and the workers they'd get in there wouldn't stay long. . . . So they decided, we [black men] could stand it . . . that was the purpose of it because they figured, being black, you know, you could stand the heat . . . that they're all the same . . . people in Africa stand a lot of heat.

Exhibiting a racialized paternalism, some managers publicly showcased 'their' hard-working black employees. In doing so, they presented black masculinity in a hyperbolic form—using a racial stereotype to magnify the image of the unskilled working man.[32] In the eyes of some observers in the plants, these men were little more than powerful, labouring bodies. GM foundry employee Richard Nicholson recounted,

. . . quite a few white people come over and watch you work. Take pictures. They've got pictures of me down there now. Take pictures of us doing this heavy job. And they'd just sit back and say, 'Look at them guys work!' Visitors . . . the foremen or the general foreman [would] bring people in and say, 'Let's show you how we do it—how our boys do it.' They all look at one another and they used to be taking pictures of us guys all the time—the kind of work we was doin'.[33]

These men were highlighted for displaying manly brawn and to some extent they themselves expressed pride in their ability to perform work that involved remarkably high levels of physical exertion.[34] Yet at the same time, black men were objectified by employers. Managers who put the men on public display for performing hard, dirty, hazardous labour—work that they had little choice but to perform—paradoxically reinforced the notion that black males possessed a heightened masculinity while at the same time they emasculated these men in denying their 'humanness', in constructing them as 'beasts of burden'. Employers contributed to the construction of a racialized masculinity, a masculinity that embodied racial and class subordination.

The Privileges of Manhood

Being a man, however, did bring with it some privileges. It was because of their *sex* that these men were hired in the auto industry. As noted, even during World War II, black women faced formidable obstacles in finding any kind of factory employment in Windsor and elsewhere in Canada. Their sexual status furthermore ensured that black men would possess specific job rights, rights that were denied the small numbers of white women who had been allowed to work in some auto plants largely because of their privilege as a race.

Sexual inequalities were blatant in collective agreements between the UAW and auto manufacturers. Notably, contracts upheld sex-based job classifications and non-interchangeable, sex-based seniority. Moreover, it was not until 1954 that UAW leadership in Canada formally challenged company restrictions on the employment of married women.[35] Unlike their union sisters, men (of all races) were rewarded for being married. Assumed to be breadwinners, black men held departmental, and ultimately plant-wide seniority rights, received the same wages and piece rates, and in theory, could occupy the same job classifications as all other male auto workers. There is no evidence that during these years, any of the local collective agreements between the UAW and the Big Three automakers in Canada openly made distinctions among workers on the basis of *race*. GM worker Richard Nicholson explained that in

the past, differences in monetary rewards among the male workforce were based on an employee's family responsibilities only:

> The white boys I worked with and the black boys, we'd always see one another's cheque. . . . We all get the same [pay]. . . . The only difference would be in deductions. If you have more kids than the other guy, you have a dollar or two more because they didn't take as much money off ya.

Married or single, male auto workers received higher than average wages for working-class men because of the successful efforts of the UAW to secure a family wage. The family wage demand was premised on the assumption that workers (men only) must be paid a relatively high rate because of their responsibility, as head of a household, for the economic welfare of a wife and children.[36] It was this ideology of the male breadwinner that in turn provided the rationale for women's lower rates of pay. In the words of Windsor-based auto worker Howard Olbey, in the Ford Motor Company, 'it was all man to man.'

Manhood, of course, is historically contingent. In the United States, black men encountered brutal and overt forms of racism both in the plants as well as within their own union locals.[37] Between 1944 and 1946 alone, the UAW International Fair Practices Department (IFPD) reported 46 complaints at 41 different American UAW locals throughout its jurisdiction. Rank-and-file members lodged 27 of these complaints against management exclusively. These centred around the company's refusal to hire certain persons. In addition, workers filed 14 complaints directly against both management and the local union for failing to act on grievances. They directed five complaints concerning racially segregated meetings and the like against local unions exclusively. Most Fair Practices cases were racial, with a few based on religion and political affiliation and one made on the ground of nationality.[38]

In Canada, however, the racialization of the automotive workforce did not have the same implications as it did south of the border. Because black men in both the plants and in the wider communities of St Catharines and Windsor were so few in number, employers did not use them to undercut white men by paying them lower wages or hiring them as strikebreakers.[39] Thus, the political and economic positioning of Canadian black men was significantly different than those in the United States. In the Canadian plants, white working men consequently did not seem to perceive black workers as a serious threat. One could surmise that white unionists opposed racially discriminatory contracts in an effort to ensure that employers never would use black men as a cheaper, politically docile labour source. There is no evidence, though, to suggest that management in Canada either attempted to use black men as such, nor that UAW leaders weighed this possibility in any kind of public forum. In this particular historical context, and specifically in this sphere of social life—the paid work setting—the social meaning of gender (manhood) and race (blackness), and their configuration, permitted the elevation of black men to the *formal status* of white working-class men.

'We're All Brothers with the Union'

The vehicle by which all male auto workers secured various rights and entitlements in the workplace was the UAW, and there was a strong connection between belonging to the union and being a working-class man. Masculine bonds strengthened union ties and, in turn, union affiliation and masculinized class-based allegiances played an important part in reinforcing gender-based solidarities among these groups of men. Indeed, it is difficult to disentangle unionism from 'brotherhood' during these years. The industrial trade union was very much a masculine institution, not only because the vast majority of UAW members and leaders were men, but

also because these men built their unionism around a place in the sexual division of familial labour, recreational pursuits, cultural forms of expression, strategies of resistance, and a political agenda that spoke to many of the shared experiences of working-class men.[40]

. . .

Black men . . . had an ambivalent relationship to the UAW. After all, the upper echelons of the union bureaucracy were dominated by white men, few of whom challenged the informal discriminatory measures that kept black workers in perilous foundry jobs and out of the preferred skilled trades.[41] Yet black men's awareness of racist undercurrents within the labour movement did not diminish their strong commitment to industrial unionism and (unlike women members) they became actively involved in mainstream union politics at the local level. In fact, during World War II, their level of UAW office-holding was notably high in proportion to their numbers in the plants.

Of the 12 men interviewed for this study, nine had once held an official position in the local union structure. This finding is striking given that these men were not selected for study on the basis of union involvement.[42] . . .

To the UAW, racial discrimination was a serious matter with clear moral, political, and economic ramifications. The union's critique of racial segregation and inequality rested on several interrelated themes, each of which highlighted the deleterious consequences of racism. First, UAW discourse on race was highly moralistic, and was expressed in passionate, emotional language. Appealing to workers' basic sense of right and wrong, and underscoring the moral authority of industrial unionism, official UAW statements espoused an essential immorality of racism in industry. In policy statements and public addresses, UAW International leaders posited racial discrimination as 'cancerous', 'evil', 'infectious', a 'poison', and 'an act against humanity'.[43] They argued that any good trade unionist should take a stand against racism as a matter of good conscience and out of a commitment to one of the most fundamental philosophies of their union—that of 'brotherhood'.

Second, in statements about race, representatives of the UAW International often delivered an ideological message about the union's interests and responsibilities beyond the walls of industry. Reflecting the larger wartime political context, as well as their own factional interests, UAW President Walter Reuther and his caucus linked racism to Nazism and Communist influence on American society. They furthermore defined racial discrimination, especially segregation, as a threat to North American patriotism and standards of 'freedom and justice'. Proponents of racist attitudes and acts were often referred to as 'defilers of democracy' and thereby 'un-American'.[44]

At the same time, the union addressed race as an economistic/industrial relations issue, a view that had been promoted by Reuther since the late 1930s.[45] UAW records contain a series of diatribes by leaders asserting that it was 'illogical' and 'stupid' for trade unionists to foster or maintain racial divisions between workers because of the potential impact of such divisions on the economic security of white male workers, the future bargaining power of the union, and labour solidarity.[46] The doctrine of the UAW International was that racial discrimination and divisions were rooted in class-based economic inequalities and thus racial harmony necessitated a critical examination of the actions of employers. UAW statements on racial discrimination during the 1940s largely targeted the companies, if not in instilling racial hatred, then at least in exacerbating and profiting from it. Industrial strife and racial strife, according to UAW leaders, went hand in hand. One problem could not be solved apart from the other. Often, such arguments of economic and political expediency were used to reinforce appeals to workers' moral conscience. In a 1941 union publication, for instance, a black worker in the United States stressed the value of unity among workers, if not for decency, then at least for the paycheque.[47]

Admittedly, the UAW was not an oasis of racial harmony. The UAW Fair Employment Practices Department had only limited authority to intervene in regional affairs,[48] the myriad UAW policy statements and public addresses of the war and post-war years were largely rhetorical and were in fact dismissed by many local and regional union leaders,[49] and in any case, these messages most likely conveyed far greater meaning in American plants than in the Canadian Region. When regional directors or rank-and-file members proved uncooperative, however, the UAW International could take decisive action and they did promote the general view that the United Auto Workers union stood in strong support of social justice—especially racial justice—and unequivocally opposed racial discrimination.[50] Notably, official UAW discourse identified racial discrimination, unlike sexual discrimination, as a social/economic/political problem rather than an unfortunate, but largely taken for granted, feature of the times. The official UAW position was that all *male* union members must be treated the same.

Importantly, in Canada, this philosophical commitment to racial equality was reinforced by contract clauses that were premised on a commitment to impartiality and the broadly defined goal of equal opportunity among male members. Many black workers were aware that their UAW representatives were likely to play out their own racial prejudices on the shop floor and in the union. According to GM foundry worker Richard Nicholson, 'there's a lot of things goes on behind your back.' Nicholson believed that union reps would sometimes tell a worker that they had looked into a grievance when they clearly had not. In his view, such inaction made the grievant himself responsible for taking the initiative. Most interview informants, therefore, placed a strong emphasis on the theme of self-determination. At the same time, however, they highlighted the union's role in putting in place the machinery for equity. And this machinery, they believed, could be mobilized in attempts to secure either the hard-won rights of black workers or racial justice on a collective-scale.

Many black men were aware of the limits of such contract clauses and, as previously mentioned, they recognized the informal barriers to equal outcomes. This knowledge undoubtedly circumscribed their 'choices' as auto workers. Over the course of many decades in the auto plants, most black men remained where they had started—in the foundry. According to former Ford and Auto Specialties employee Elmer Carter, '[T]heir idea was, "well, the white man don't want you up there no how, so why . . . put yourself in a position where you know you're not wanted."'

A small number of men, however, protested vociferously about these hurdles and they turned to the *collective agreement* to support their claims. In particular, black auto workers in Canada attributed their ability to move out of a bad job and into a better one to the UAW's commitment to the seniority principle, as well as union-negotiated rules about job posting and transfer rights. Elmer Carter further commented,

> [W]hen I left Auto Specialties and I went to Ford's, there was a lot of different jobs that there was all white people on. . . . There was a lot of coloureds that worked at Ford's. . . . I had a couple of jobs at Ford's that a lot of coloured fellas didn't have and they'd say, 'How did you get that job?' I said, 'Well, I just put in for it' and I got it because by then see jobs would have to be posted in the shop . . . they went by seniority.

Lyle Talbot made similar observations about his 30 years at the Ford plant. He stated,

> The only changes I saw were the changes the union brought about, like equal pay, equal opportunity. For instance, if a job came open, that's in the bargaining unit. . . . If you had the qualifications, they had a phrase. The union had a phrase called 'willing and able'. If you were willing and able to do the job, the company had to give you a chance on it.

> I can think of . . . four jobs that I got that the company said I wasn't able to do . . . but the union insisted that they give me a chance.

Most black workers believed that the union contract could be used as a tool to protect their rights, in spite of the actions or inaction, prejudices or indifference, of individual men. The collective agreement was a tool for the achievement of a better life, a measure of dignity, and equal opportunity at work—an instrument that, when pressured, some (white) union leaders would put to use. Given that the formal equal status that black auto workers had in the workplace did not extend into the community, it seemed reasonable to believe that the trade union was an imperfect but important ally. According to John Milben, a foundry worker for 31 years, '[t]he union was a hundred per cent behind us. . . . Fairness. We're all brothers with the union.'

Race, Brotherhood, and Resistance

The UAW, however, played a contradictory role. While the union served as an ally, its philosophy of *brotherhood* was restrictive in its emphasis on *sameness* among workers. Likewise, the UAW definition of *equality* was narrow, not accounting for (racial or sexual) *difference*. Like women members, black men thus faced many dilemmas. They recognized the need for a separate forum for organizing yet they feared ghettoization and accusations of fostering divisions within the working class and threatening worker solidarity. While class-based and gender-based solidarities were openly celebrated, bonds based on race remained unspoken. This workplace/union scenario had significant implications for race consciousness and black workers' resistance.

Throughout the 1940s and 1950s, many black auto workers in Canada adamantly denied difference on the basis of race, and this clearly impeded efforts to mobilize in protest of racial discrimination. The denial of racial difference was most likely a means of coping with the hegemony of whiteness. Within a predominantly white setting, it represented an attempt to shield oneself from racist attacks, to avoid exacerbating racial tensions, and to assimilate (and thereby become invisible), or at least escape further marginalization in the plant and union. According to Richard Nicholson,

> The blacks never all gathered together 'cause we used to say to one another, 'We're not gonna all sit in a huddle—all of us together.' Like, it looks like you're discriminating yourself. Like you're all together. You know what I mean? I would talk to more white people than I did black people, really because I worked with white people and my boss was white.[51]

Living and working in communities in which racial difference and equality were dichotomized, and where 'Canadians' were perceived as 'white' and not foreign-born, many workers were caught in a dilemma between calling attention to their 'blackness' on the one hand—something that must have been at the core of subjectivity—and being a Canadian, a good trade unionist, and equal to their white brothers on the other. Auto foundry employee Howard Wallace rejected the designation 'black', equating it with American civil rights activists. Wallace preferred to be called 'coloured', something which he, in a seemingly contradictory way, associated with acceptance into mainstream respectable Canadian society. He remarked,

> I never heard tell of no 'black' man in the 1940s. Never heard tell of no black man. We always wanted the name of 'coloured' man. . . . The only time you hear of 'em say a black man, it started in the United States. They started it. There's a lot of fellas over there the colour of you but they call themselves black men. Why? I do not know. Well, educated and everything . . . I'm no black man. . . . [A] lot of people like to call themselves black 'cause they call themselves black over the River. . . . Either call me a coloured man or call me a Canadian. But I'm just what is anybody else in Canada.

Wallace's reflections make a potent statement about black identity in Canada.

It is impossible, however, for a 'visible minority' to achieve invisibility or complete assimilation. Very few black workers escaped *informal* displays of racism within the plant. Some men recollected that supervisors and co-workers alike participated in a variety of overt racist acts, largely in the form of derogatory jokes and name-calling. In retrospect, though, these men minimized the importance of such acts in shaping their workplace experiences. Some even bragged about their ability, as individuals, to counter and ultimately develop an immunity to such racist behaviour. According to Lyle Talbot,

> . . . you could handle those guys. You know. I've had guys call me 'black bastard' on the job. It didn't bother me at all because I knew that whatever my comeback was, it was just as good as theirs. . . . I had fellows that didn't like working with me, but there was nothing they could do about it. I knew it and they knew it.
>
> . . .

Individual resistance of this kind helped black workers to invalidate racial harassment and restore some dignity—dignity lost by a host of insults and injuries experienced both within the factory and in the wider community.

Racial prejudice was sometimes brutal and openly expressed, and racial boundaries were strongly upheld in the towns of Windsor and St Catharines. Blacks faced blatant discrimination in housing, schools, churches, recreational facilities, the job market, and in intimate relationships. They were, for example, barred from certain residential areas and ghettoized in others, turned away from restaurants, hotels, and bowling halls, and in some drinking establishments they were placed in a separate area called the 'jungle room'.[52]

Given the extent and impact of racism in their lives as a whole, it is striking that the men had so little to say about its effect on *workplace relations*. It is especially remarkable that most informants claimed that on the whole there were no racial tensions whatsoever among auto workers.[53] An Auto Specialties foundry worker for over 30 years, Howard Wallace stated, 'you'd see some white fellas or some foreign fellas. They all worked, you know. They all worked together. . . . They all got along. What gets me is they all got along good together.'

Many black men viewed the workplace as separate from the rest of the community, and claimed that the factory was one of the only arenas in which they could exercise their rights and even feel a camaraderie with white men. Auto Specialties worker John Milben related how he would 'feel bad' when he was forced to drink beer in a back room, sit apart from white soldiers in a restaurant, and live on a 'black street' in Windsor. Yet in contrast, 'it was nice in the foundry [he said]. Everybody was treated good. They had a cafeteria there. We sat and ate together. . . . And we'd drink beer together.'

Admittedly, direct racism on the shop floor did not reach the same level of intensity in Canada as it did in the American auto plants. And it is likely that to these men, racial tensions in southern Ontario plants seemed insignificant in comparison to the racial strife they heard about through the American popular media and UAW International press. The scale and intensity of racism in the United States most likely denied many black workers in Canada a sense of entitlement to public and collective outrage against the racism that touched their own lives. Given this, UAW leaders and local civil rights activists would occasionally remind Canadian Region members that while racial discrimination had taken a different form in Canada than south of the border, it nevertheless existed and should be challenged.

Moreover, the workers' descriptions of racial harmony within the plant underscore the fluidity of the concept of discrimination itself. Perceptions of discrimination are products of historical negotiation and as such are always changing. In the past, workers' conceptualization of racial discrimination did not encompass 'workplace harassment'. According to foundry employee Mahlon Dennis, during the war years and into the post-war period, racial harassment was simply 'not an issue'. Harassment is 'more of a recent thing,' explained Dennis. 'I can't recall during the period I was involved in human rights, whether there was anything mentioned about harassment . . . mostly . . . it dealt with the employment situation and housing accommodation.' Racial slurs, jokes, put-downs, even the occasional physical assault by another man, were not only part of the masculine culture of the auto plants, but they were also endured as part of the everyday experience of people of colour in Canada—one of the hardships of the times. As Lyle Talbot's . . . remarks suggest, it was up to individual men, manly men, to handle this.

Furthermore, the impact of the random racial attack by a co-worker or supervisor was softened somewhat by the men's formal equal rights and place in the industry. For the small group of black men who were 'privileged' to find work in the auto plants, the outcomes of racism were not directly economic. Formal contract rights (which secured economic equality) mediated the informal, day-to-day experience of racial prejudice.

Many black workers lamented the unrelenting power of racist oppression but reasoned that in light of the small but significant gains that they had made in the course of their own lives, it was best to 'turn the other cheek' to it. Getting a job in a car plant was among the most notable of these gains. Just as it mediated the impact of direct racial prejudice on the shop floor, the 'privilege' of auto employment and equal status as a UAW member, paradoxically, set limits on the racialization of black men's collective resistance. As Mahlon Dennis explained, coloured people couldn't complain about racial discrimination in employment during World War II because they were being hired. Former GM coremaker Cassell Smith stated, nothing's happening, so don't go throwing your strength. . . . You're going to aggravate something that way. . . . Be prepared for it but as long as things are quiet, let them stay. That's my opinion. I'm not saying I'm right. . . . A person can go and stir up a lot of trouble where there isn't any. . . . So as long as it's quiet and all, leave it. . . . This fighting. They talk about equal rights. This fighting for equal rights is going to be a lifetime thing.

. . .

The position of black men in auto plants was ambivalent. While they recognized that UAW leaders often failed to advocate their specific concerns as a race, most black auto workers exhibited a strong commitment to the ideological principles of industrial unionism. The UAW reinforced in them a sense of their own legitimacy in the union and industry, and this was something on which a handful of individual men would ultimately draw in their attempts to uphold their equal rights as *workers*. It was the UAW philosophy of social justice, class-based solidarity, and brotherhood, along with the privilege of holding a relatively well-paying automotive sector job, that furthermore bolstered unity among these male industrial workers. Most importantly, it was the union that provided black male workers the equity machinery (namely, the collective agreement) with which to challenge employers in their fight against multiple oppressions. The collective agreement, however, is an instrument that took white working men's experiences as the standard for the industry and it therefore left untouched and unremarked upon, the many elusive dimensions of racial oppression.

Conclusion

From the beginnings of the auto industry in Canada, employers have contributed to the *construction of difference* within the working class. These differences were based on race, gender, and family status, as well as skill. While auto manufacturers hired white male breadwinners to fill the vast majority of jobs in the industry, they also recruited extremely small numbers of black men (and white women) to perform work that many white men either rejected or were temporarily unavailable to perform. While these two groups of workers met a need on the part of capitalists, management clearly regarded each as marginal to the industry, different, and unequal to the core workforce. Both black men and white women were defined as the 'other', a socially created category that was itself broken down along lines of race and gender.

The history of black men in auto work is one of many contradictions. Such contradictions are the outcome of the changing configuration of race, gender, and social class. While black men were intruders in the homogeneous white world of the auto plants, their status as wage-earning men/union brothers accorded them various rights and entitlements that were denied (white) women workers. Given their positioning in the industry during the war and throughout the post-war years, black men did not constitute a political or economic threat to white workers in Canada. There is no evidence that management attempted to use blacks to lower wage rates, replace white employees, or to act as 'scab' labour during strikes. Moreover, racial segregation and exclusion were so pervasive and strictly upheld in the wider society—in intimate relationships, recreation, housing, education, and religious institutions—that the presence of scant numbers of black men in the foundries was not raised by white trade unionists as a matter of serious consequence. Race acquired a particular, distinctive meaning in man-to-man relations—in the masculine worlds of auto manufacturing and the UAW. The social and political implications of race in these settings permitted black men to be elevated to the formal status of white men, a status that was based on gender privilege, and class, and gender solidarities.

Formal equal rights in union contracts (equal wages and equal seniority rights), though, did not shield black men from face-to-face indignities on the plant floor, nor did they protect the men from the hazards of working in bad jobs, or the economic impact of stunted opportunities within the firm. Gender and class shaped the content of the racism that these men experienced; they did not protect them from it.

Moreover, racialized and gendered experiences have played an important part in configuring the resistance strategies adopted by this group of workers. Black auto employees faced an elusive form of discrimination. At work, they possessed formal 'equal rights', but found themselves confined to the worst jobs in the plants. As UAW members, they were committed to class-based struggles, relying heavily on equal opportunity and brotherhood as guiding principles, and the collective agreement as an instrument of justice. Yet at the same time, they participated in a union politics that at the local and regional levels was lacking in racial content. In both spheres, black men denied racial difference, though daily they were confronted with the hegemony of whiteness. A tiny group of black auto workers thus concentrated their efforts in challenging racial inequalities outside the workplace, particularly in housing and recreation. These activists emerged from a workplace politicized by industrial unionism, yet their struggles were not factory-based, and thereby left unchallenged an important element of their oppression as workers. In a sense, within the factory, equal opportunity served a defusing, perhaps depoliticizing function.

Race and gender shape working-class experience. Whiteness and masculinity were undeniably central features of auto work. The primacy of one of these constructs over the others has sometimes been debated, but this is not at issue here for there is no neat formula that can be consistently applied to understand their alliance. It is more useful to observe how the racialization of gender and the gendering of race have changed over time, and have taken on meaning in different spheres of social existence. When we examine the ever-changing nexus of race, gender, and

class, we understand the relationship not merely as one of multiple oppressions, but as something more complex—one in which people can be simultaneously victims and agents, privileged and oppressed.

. . .

Notes

This is a revised version of a paper presented at the annual meeting of the American Historical Association, 2–5 January 1997. For comments on earlier drafts of this paper, I would like to thank Robert Storey, Joan Sangster, and Alice Kessler-Harris, and four anonymous reviewers for *Labour/Le Travail*. Thanks also to Hassan Yussuff, students in the CAW Workers of Colour Leadership Training Programme, and the many workers who graciously agreed to share with me their stories. This research was funded by an Arts Research Board grant and a Labour Studies Programme research grant at McMaster University.

1. R.M. Brewer, 'Theorizing Race, Class and Gender', in R. Hennessy and C. Ingraham, eds, *Materialist Feminism* (New York, 1997), 238.
2. McKinnon Industries was originally a subsidiary of General Motors and later became a General Motors plant.
3. Small numbers of Armenian, Chinese, and Chinese-Canadian workers were also employed in the southern Ontario auto industry during World War II. However, I have chosen to focus here on black workers because they represented the largest minority, with the longest history in the plants.
4. P. Sugiman, *Labour's Dilemma: The Gender Politics of Workers in Canada, 1937–1979* (Toronto, 1994).
5. Unlike their American counterparts, these workers were so few in number, so seemingly marginal to either the company or the union, that their unique histories have never been traced. Paradoxically, they are workers whose difference made them highly visible in the workplace; yet this difference has rendered them largely invisible in Canadian labour history. Currently, there are no published scholarly accounts of the ways in which race has been used in structuring the auto industry in Canada. . . .
6. It was extremely difficult to locate black men who had worked in the auto industry during the period of study. Given the harsh conditions of their work, a sizable number of these workers left the auto industry after World War II. Also, many of the men who remained in the plants suffered from serious health

problems such as silicosis. Many of these men had died before this project was undertaken. By the time all of the interviews for this study were completed, several participants had died.

7. For an insightful discussion of the use of oral testimony, see C. Van Onselen, 'The Reconstruction of a Rural Life from Oral Testimony: Critical Notes on the Methodology Employed in the Study of a Black South African Sharecropper', *Journal of Peasant Studies* 20, 3 (1993): 494–514.

8. See D. Roediger, *The Wages of Whiteness: Race and the Making of the American Working Class* (London, 1991); D. Roediger, *Towards the Abolition of Whiteness* (London, 1994).

9. I wish to thank Joan Sangster for bringing this point to my attention.

10. Rod Davis was a participant in a session of the CAW Workers of Colour Leadership Training Programme.

11. 'Gung Ho', *Ford Times* 3, 5 (Oct. 1943): 12–14; 'Heart Strings Stretch from Windsor 'Round the World . . .', *Ford Times* 2, 2 (Nov. 1942): 3–4. . . .

12. For a discussion of the relationship between Henry Ford and the African-American community, see L. Bailer, 'Negro Labor in the American Automobile Industry', PhD dissertation (University of Michigan, 1943); K. Boyle, '"There Are No Union Sorrows That the Union Can't Heal": The Struggle for Racial Equality in the United Automobile Workers, 1940–1960', *Labor History* 36, 1 (Winter 1995): 5–23; A. Meier and E. Rudwick, *Black Detroit and the Rise of the UAW* (New York, 1979); B.J. Widick, 'Black Workers: Double Discontents', in Widick, ed., *Auto Work and Its Discontents* (Baltimore, 1976), 52–60.

13. Widick, 'Black Workers: Double Discontents', 53.

14. Interview #2, 30 May 1994.

15. Archives of Labor and Urban Affairs (ALUA), UAW Canadian Region Series III, box 70, Report of UAW Local 199, District Council Minutes (1939).

16. ALUA, UAW Research Department, acc. 350, box 11, 'Questionnaire on Employment in UAW-CIO Plants, Employment, Women and Negroes, UAW Regions 4–9A' (Apr. 1943).

17. In September 1949, Canadian Region Director George Burt reported to the Region 7 Staff that the Chrysler Corporation of Canada 'does not hire Negroes' and that 'in Windsor most of the Negroes are in foundries.' ALUA, UAW Canadian Region Collection, box 39, file 1, 'Minutes, Region 7 Staff Meeting' (1947–50). . . .

18. The Fair Employment Practices Act, 1951 was enacted to prohibit discrimination in employment on the grounds of a person's race, creed, colour, nationality, ancestry or place of origin. The Act covered application forms and advertisements. It did not include 'sex' as a prohibited ground of discrimination.

19. ALUA, UAW Region 7 Toronto Sub-Regional Office Collection, box 9, 'Minutes, Staff Meeting' (26–7 Oct. 1953), 6.

20. Lyle Talbot Private Collection, untitled document (Mar. 1950). . . .

21. Interview #12, 20 Feb. 1995.

22. I wish to thank *Labour/Le Travail* reviewer #2 for bringing this point to my attention.

23. This finding was generated through a series of informal classroom discussions that I held with participants in the current CAW Workers of Colour Leadership Training Programme. . . .

24. Interview #1, 18 Oct. 1990; Interview #12, 20 Feb. 1995; for example, as well as private conversations with various black CAW members who are currently living in St Catharines and Windsor.

25. *Ford Graphics* 6, 13 (15 July 1953): 6.

26. For a discussion of foundry work in early twentieth-century Canada, see C. Heron, 'The Craftsman: Hamilton's Metal Workers in the Early Twentieth Century', *Labour/Le Travailleur* 6 (Autumn 1980): 7–48. . . .

27. Black men in the United States were also concentrated in foundry work, as well as wet-sanding operations, material handling, and janitorial assignments. See Boyle, '"There Are No Union Sorrows"', 8; Widick, 'Black Workers: Double Discontents', 53.

28. Interview #12, 20 Feb. 1995.

29. Richard Nicholson, Mahlon Dennis, Howard Olbey, John Milben, Clayton Talbert, Elmer Carter, and Howard Wallace all reported to have performed at least a couple of these jobs before securing auto employment. Many men had worked four or five such jobs.

30. For a discussion of race and images of masculinity in the contemporary period, see among others, R. Staples, 'Masculinity and Race: The Dual Dilemma of Black Men', *Journal of Social Issues* 34, 1 (1978): 169–83.

31. Interview #1, 18 Oct. 1990; Interview #7, 3 Aug. 1994.

32. This idea was articulated by *Labour/Le Travail* reviewer #2.

33. Interview #1, 18 Oct. 1990.

34. In his account of metal workers in Hamilton, Ontario, during the early twentieth century, Heron argues that the pride of moulders in steel foundries 'fed on the physical demands of the work, which was notoriously heavy, dirty, and unhealthy'. See Heron, 'The Craftsman', 11.

35. In the GM Oshawa plant, before, during, and after the war, most women were confined to either the sewing department or the wire and harness department. For the duration of the war, some women also worked in GM's aircraft division, a makeshift facility that was designed exclusively for the production of war materials. In McKinnon Industries, women worked in a

wider range of departments. Nevertheless, they too were confined to far fewer jobs than men. . . .

36. For a more detailed discussion of the family wage, see B. Bradbury, *Working Families: Age, Gender, and Daily Survival in Industrializing Montreal* (Toronto, 1993), ch. 3; N. Gabin, *Feminism in the Labor Movement: Women and the United Automobile Workers, 1935–1975* (Ithaca, NY, 1990); M. May, 'Bread before Roses: American Workingmen, Labor Unions, and the Family Wage', in R. Milkman, ed., *Women, Work, and Protest: A Century of U.S. Women's Labor History* (Boston, 1985), 1–21; R. Milkman, *Gender at Work: The Dynamics of Job Segregation by Sex during World War II* (Urbana, IL, 1987); J. Parr, *The Gender of Breadwinners: Women, Men, and Change in Two Industrial Towns, 1880–1950* (Toronto, 1990); B. Palmer, *Working-Class Experience: Rethinking the History of Canadian Labour, 1800–1991* (Toronto, 1992).

37. . . . Boyle, '"There Are No Union Sorrows"'; K. Boyle, *The UAW and the Heyday of American Liberalism, 1945–1968* (Ithaca, NY, 1995); Meier and Rudick, *Black Detroit and the Rise of the UAW*; Widick, 'Black Workers: Double Discontents'.

38. ALUA, Emil Mazey Collection, box 11, file 11–6, FEPC 1946–47–2, 'First Annual Summary of Activities, International UAW-CIO Fair Practices Committee' (15 Oct. 1944 to 15 Feb. 1946). See also ALUA, UAW Research Department Collection, box 18, file: Minorities, 1942–47, 2 of 2, 'Fair Practices and Anti-Discrimination Department', UAW-CIO to UAW-CIO International Board Fair Practices Committee (10 Dec. 1946); ALUA, UAW Research Department Collection, box 18, file: Minorities, 1942-47, 1 of 2, 'UAW Fight Against Intolerance', Address by George W. Crockett (4 Nov. 1945); ALUA, Emil Mazey Collection, box 11, file: 11–6, FEPC, 2, 'Fair Practices Committee Decisions' (1946–47); ALUA, UAW Fair Practices Department—Women's Bureau, box 2, file: 2–17, Quarterly Reports (1946), 'Report of UAW-CIO Fair Practices and Anti-Discrimination Department to the International Executive Board', 10 Dec. 1946; AULA, UAW Research Department Collection, box 11, file: 11–20, UAW Fair Practices and Anti-Discrimination Department, 1947–58, 'Summer School Course in Workers Education'.

39. There is evidence that employers used black workers as 'scabs' in some UAW plants in Canada. For example, at the Walker Metal Foundry, black men were first hired as a result of a strike by a white male workforce. Interview #5, 29 June 1993. However, these cases were rare. There is no evidence that this was a serious consideration at General Motors, Ford, or Chrysler during the period of study.

40. See Sugiman, *Labour's Dilemma*, ch. 2.

41. See Boyle, '"There Are No Union Sorrows"', for a discussion of the opposition of skilled trades to African-Americans.

42. The level of participation of workers of colour, however, dropped in the following decades. To this day, workers of colour remain under-represented in the Canadian Auto Workers Union, especially in local office.

43. See, for example, ALUA, UAW Research Department Collection, box 9, file: 9–24, Discrimination Against Negroes in Employment, 1942–47, 'R.J. Thomas to All UAW-CIO Executive Board Members and Department Heads, 25 Nov. 1943'; ALUA, UAW Research Department Collection, box 18, file: Minorities, 1942–47, 1 of 2, 'UAW Fight Against Intolerance', Address by George W. Crockett, Director, UAW-CIO Fair Practices Committee, 4 Nov. 1945.

44. For example, ALUA, UAW Research Department Collection, box 18, file: Minorities, 1942–47, 1 of 2, 'UAW Fight Against Intolerance', Address by George W. Crockett, Director, UAW-CIO Fair Practices Committee, 4 Nov. 1945.

45. See Boyle, '"There Are No Union Sorrows"', 109.

46. For example, ALUA, UAW Research Department Collection, box 11, file: 11–20, Fair Practices and Anti-Discrimination Department, 1947–58, 'Summer School Course in Workers Education'; ALUA, Emil Mazey Collection, box 11, file: 11–6, FEPC, 1946–47–2, 'First Annual Summary of Activities of the International UAW-CIO Fair Practices Committee'; 'UAW Seeks to Prevent Hiring Discrimination', *Michigan Chronicle*, 8 Sept. 1945.

47. 'UAW Seeks to Prevent Hiring Discrimination', *Michigan Chronicle*, 9 Aug. 1945.

48. See Boyle, '"There Are No Union Sorrows"', 114.

49. Boyle, *The UAW and the Heyday of American Liberalism*.

50. Ibid., 118.

51. This position stands in contrast to black immigrants, largely from the Caribbean, who began to secure employment in the auto industry during the 1960s and 1970s.

52. For example, W.A. Head, *The Black Presence in the Canadian Mosaic: A Study of Perception and the Practice of Discrimination against Blacks in Metropolitan Toronto*. Ontario Human Rights Commission (Toronto, 1975); B.S. Singh and Peter S. Li, *Racial Oppression in Canada*, 2nd edn (Toronto, 1988), ch. 8; W.S. Tarnopolsky, *Discrimination and the Law in Canada* (Toronto, 1982); R. Winks, 'The Canadian Negro: A Historical Assessment', *Journal of Negro History* 53 (Oct. 1968): 283–300. Extensive accounts of racial discrimination in Ontario were also given in Interview #1, 18 Oct. 1990, Interview #2, 30 May 1994; Interview #8, 5 Aug. 1993.

53. Among others, Rick Halpern documents a history of interracial co-operation among some groups of industrial workers. . . . See R. Halpern, 'Interracial Unionism in the Southwest: Fort Worth's Packinghouse Workers, 1937–1954', *Organized Labor in the Twentieth Century South* (Knoxville, 1991), 158–82. . . .

17

Placing the Displaced Worker: Narrating Place in Deindustrializing Sturgeon Falls, Ontario

Steven High

To tell a story is to take arms against the threat of time, to resist time or to harness it. The telling of a story preserves the teller from oblivion; a story builds the identity of the teller and the legacy he will leave in time to come.

Alessandro Portelli[1]

The identity of places is very much bound up with the histories which are told of them; how these histories are told, and which history turns out to be dominant.

Doreen Massey[2]

. . .

The 'displaced worker' entered our everyday language in the 1940s with the economic upheaval that accompanied the war. One of the earliest published references that I have uncovered was a July 1942 article in *Barron's* that spoke of the US government's efforts to assist people displaced in the conversion to a war economy.[3] Displaced workers took on new prominence in the early 1960s with the upheaval that accompanied trade liberalization. Government programs in the United States and Canada were created to assist long-service workers who lost their jobs to imports. Since then, the 'displaced worker' label has come to apply to all those caught up in layoffs and in mill or factory closings.[4] The US Department of Labor, for example, has sponsored biannual 'Displaced Workers Surveys' since 1984.[5] These statistics and others

generated like it in Canada are sifted through by economists and social scientists for significant patterns. Displacement is almost always measured in narrowly economic terms. Who was displaced? How many? How long were they unemployed? What were their earnings once re-employed? The numbers are then broken down into the usual categories of sex, race, age, occupation, and region. In my view, the reliance on the aggregate and the abstract has contributed to an impoverished view of dis*place*ment that equates worker dis*location* with an event (a mill or factory closure) and the subsequent absence of paid employment rather than as a social and spatial process that is highly meaningful.[6]

Life history interviewing provides an opportunity to explore the cultural meaning of displacement from the vantage point of those most directly involved: workers themselves. Until recently, I have interviewed displaced workers decades after their mill or factory 'went down'. Some of these men and women found new jobs. Others never found steady work again. Despite the time that had passed, these interviews were highly emotional undertakings. Anger and loss punctuated many of the stories told. Yet nothing prepared me for the raw emotions encountered in the Sturgeon Falls project. Sturgeon Falls is a town of 6,000 located between Sudbury and North Bay, in northern Ontario. We began interviewing displaced workers within a year of Weyerhaeuser's closure of the corrugated paper mill in December 2002. Life history interviewing continued as efforts to reopen the century-old mill petered out and it was pulverized into dust and trucked away. By 2005, we had interviewed over 60 people. Several interviewees demanded to know if we had any connection to the company before agreeing to participate. A number of others declined to be interviewed out of fear that they would not be able to control their emotions. To deepen the conversation further, I conducted follow-up interviews with 15 of the mill workers in 2006. Most interviewees were still in mourning and their profound sense of loss permeated everything spoken. The resulting interviews record some of the thoughts, feelings, and attachments that workers had *at the time* of displacement or shortly thereafter.

It should come as no surprise that mills and factories are highly meaningful places for those who toiled there. This is particularly true of long-service workers who have spent 20, 25, or even 30 years in a given workplace. I cannot think of a single industrial worker with whom I have interviewed in the past decade who has not used home and family metaphors to describe their attachment to people, place, and product. Their intent is clear: the job meant more than a paycheque. Other historians have found much the same thing. In their now classic study of the Amoskeag textile mill published 30 years ago, Tamara Hareven and Randolph Langenback wrote that textile workers exhibited a 'highly developed sense of place' and formed tightly knit groups.[7] Place attachment is a complex phenomenon that involves affect, emotion, feeling, and memory. Places are thus seen, heard, smelled, felt, otherwise experienced and imagined.[8]

My own thinking on place identity and attachment has been profoundly influenced by British geographer Doreen Massey. In her brilliant essay 'Places and their Pasts', which appeared in *History Workshop Journal* in 1994, Massey argued that place identity is constructed out of a particular constellation of social relations, meeting and weaving together. Places don't just exist on a map but *in time* as well. . . . Larger social, economic,

and political forces are thus integral to the making of places. Yet the past of a place is 'as open to a multiplicity of readings as is the present. Moreover, the claims and counter-claims about the present character of a place depend in almost all cases on particular, rival interpretations of its past.'[9] Places are thus products of history and so exist in time and space.[10]

What is largely missing from the scholarly discussion of place-making, however, is its flip-side: the unmaking or demolition of place. What happens when places are lost to us and these ties are forcibly broken? If place attachment is a symbolic bond between people and place, this bond is often severed in times of sudden social or economic crisis such as a mill closing. People then attempt to re-create these attachments by remembering and talking about these places.[11] How was the mill spoken of during the interviews? Do former paper workers define themselves as displaced? Or, do they display a heightened attachment to mill and factory? Are these two reactions mutually exclusive?

In responding to these questions, I will listen to many voices but most deeply to those of Hubert Gervais and Bruce Colquhoun, the two worker-historians at the Sturgeon Falls' mill. They are the keepers of the 'mill history binder', a memory book in photographs and documents. The binder (one of the biggest that I have ever seen) was first put together by Hubert Gervais in 1995, updated in 1998 for the mill's centennial, and revised since then by Bruce Colquhoun. What is interesting here is how the two men and others treated the binder in the months and years that followed the closure: it was spoken of with great reverence, in a whisper. It was as if the mill history binder had become a surrogate for the mill itself.[12]

Mill/Town

The bonding of people with their workplaces insures that periods of major economic and social change are periods of major spatial change as well.[13] The power of place was everywhere apparent in our conversations with displaced workers and their families. It infused their language and structured their stories. Mine, mill, or factory closings challenge our sense of place at the deepest level: 'workers lose a social structure in which they have felt valued and validated by their fellows.'[14] The mill's closure therefore hit interviewees hard. Randy Restoule spoke for many when he said: 'I felt a deep loss. The fact that everyone else was leaving . . . All your friends are gone. And like I said before, the reason that you keep going in a job is because of friends.'[15] In the beginning, people spoke of the mill in the present tense as part of their 'today' but soon shifted to the past tense. As you can imagine, the mill's demolition unleashed strong emotions. Bruce Colquhoun related this story:

> When I stopped by on Ottawa Street on the far side of the mill and I take some pictures. I met with some of the older guys there who are retired. One guy looked up at me who was sitting in his car. I went over and talked to him and he says, 'You know Bruce. I never thought I'd live to see the day that they'd tear that mill down.' Then, tears are coming down. He says, 'I gotta go.' He took off. I never thought I'd see that place taken down either.[16]

Places exist at varying scales in the plant shutdown stories recorded. At times, displaced workers attached themselves to a particular department inside the mill (like the paintline) or to the mill as a whole. At other times they identify more strongly with the town, region, or nation. All of these local and trans-local identifications provide the men and women interviewed with a sense of belonging in a time of catastrophic change. In this section, we focus on people's strong attachment to the mill community and their sense of distance from the larger local community.[17]

Sturgeon Falls was a single-industry town like many others. The corrugated paper mill was the town's largest employer and offered the best wages. Most of the interviewees went to work in the mill straight out of high school. At its peak in the 1950s and 1960s, it employed 700 people and provided revenue to farmers in the surrounding rural areas who supplied the mill with much of its wood supply. Nearly every family in the town was once connected to the mill in some way. Over the years, however, employment levels dropped off until there were only 150 left. The mill's conversion to recycled paper from virgin wood in the early 1990s, and the closure of the hardboard mill, cut the plant's ties with farmers. As a result, the shrinking circle of 'mill families' became increasingly isolated from other residents.[18]

With the mill's social and economic dominance fading, it became possible for residents to imagine the town's future without the mill. Sturgeon Falls' identity as a mill town thus eroded over the years of decline. It remained the town's largest private sector employer, but not by much. The mill's closure in 2002 and its subsequent demolition, albeit unfortunate, only confirmed this new reality in the minds of many. There was no going back. For mill workers and their families, however, the town's indifferent response to the mill's closure came as a stunning blow.

One of the remarkable discoveries of our project is that the plant shutdown stories told by unionized production workers, salaried staff, and locally recruited managers follow the same narrative path. They all call the mill 'home' and co-workers 'family'. They are all rooted in place. There are differences of course, though these are never consistent. Several former mill managers, for example, seemed more forgiving of the company. The mill was old and it was small. The free market must be respected. Yet the 'we' in their narratives consistently referred to the mill workers and their families irregardless of workplace hierarchies. This cross-class attachment to place was also evident in the frequent use of 'our mill' in the interviews. 'All of those people that I worked with at that mill for 25 years,' recalled Mike Lacroix, 'are people that I went to school with, people that I knew . . . their families. I knew their fathers. I knew their kids. I knew them all. They were "born and raised". We worked together. I spent more time with the boys at the mill than I spent with my own family.'[19] He called it a 'little family'.

The reason for this submergence of difference within the mill is two-fold. In part, it was a product of the shared experience of displacement. Locally rooted managers were in much the same boat as unionized production workers. The old differences between unionized 'staff' (or 'company people') and the 'shop floor' ('workers') blurred once the mill closed. The closure appeared to pit residents against a non-resident company; Canadians against Americans (Weyerhaeuser was US owned). The second factor that needs to be considered relates to the web of kinship ties that connected many of the mill employees together. Almost all of the Sturgeon Falls mill workers that we interviewed listed other family members, past and present, who worked at the site. 'Some families had three or four brothers working in the plant at the same time,' recalled Percy Allary.[20] It was commonplace. Several interviewees could name three generations of mill workers in some local families. Bruce Colquhoun's father and grandfather, for example, worked in the mill before him. Family memories of the mill often went back generations. Just how tight-knit the workforce had become quickly became apparent to mill managers brought in from the outside. 'The first thing I learned,' said mill superintendent Gerry Stevens, was 'don't say anything about anybody because they are probably related.'[21]

Most interviewees were hired on at the mill with the help of their fathers or, in a few cases, their mothers. Mike Lacroix's father and two uncles worked at the mill but it was his father who got him in. But he did so on the condition that his son work hard and be on time: 'Back then, the old man, he said "You know, if you are getting in there, you better not screw up. If you screw up you will have to deal with me." . . . You didn't want to

make your dad look bad.'[22] This informal practice, common everywhere, was eventually formalized. It became plant policy to hire summer students on the basis of the seniority of their mill-working father or mother as well as their level of education. Otherwise the hiring issue risked causing bad blood. 'I always hated to play God,' recalled a relieved Ed Fortin—the mill's long-time personnel director.[23] No distinction was henceforth made in the hiring of the children of mill managers or production workers. 'It was easy after that,' he said. Other students in Sturgeon Falls, however, were out of luck. The mill's hiring policy made it a very closed shop indeed.

The mill therefore loomed large in the oral narratives of former employees, casting its shadow over the town. For more than a century, the rising smoke from the stack provided a reminder of the jobs that the mill provided. Smoke signalled prosperous times; and its absence has always been a danger signal in industrial towns and cities.[24] We were repeatedly told that the mill's smokestack and water tower could be seen from anywhere in Sturgeon Falls. In actuality, the mill was set apart from most of the town by the Sturgeon River and its high embankment. One could therefore only see these physical landmarks in certain areas and not at all from downtown streets. These remarks are therefore more an indication of the mill's local social and economic dominance, and its centrality in the lives of mill workers and their families, than a realistic assessment of its physical presence. It need not be taken literally.

Yet Sturgeon Falls was a colonized landscape. The mill had several distant owners over its 104 years of operation. The Spanish River Pulp and Paper Company (1920s), Abitibi (1929–79), MacMillan Bloedel (1979–99), and Weyerhaeuser (1999–2002) were all multi-site producers of newsprint and other paper products. Until the final years, the English-speaking mill managers were recruited from outside the locality. They once lived in 'the compound', a residential section of company-owned houses adjacent to the mill. Most are reputed to have promptly left

Sturgeon Falls upon retirement, if they had not already been transferred to another site.[25] Few Franco-Ontarians, who constituted the bulk of the locally recruited workforce, made it into management—though this began to change in the final decade. The social structure of the town therefore resembled that of other mill towns in northern Ontario and Quebec during the 1950s and 1960s. In fact, one of the superintendents interviewed had worked in Chicoutimi until Quebec's Quiet Revolution made life difficult for a unilingual Anglophone.[26] He initially found a familiar social landscape in Sturgeon Falls, but the language issue followed him across the Quebec–Ontario border when a fight erupted in the town in 1970 over French-language schooling. Until then, the town's only high school was English. In this regard, the mill changed much more slowly than the town itself.

The Making of the 'Mill History' Binder

At the time of the mill's closing, I was teaching history at Nipissing University located 25 minutes drive east in North Bay. I closely followed the efforts to reopen the mill in the local newspaper. Much of what I read was familiar to me. The workers and their union wrapped themselves in the Canadian flag in the hopes of forcing Weyerhaeuser to sell the plant as a going concern. The old opposition between 'American bosses' and 'Canadian workers', however, did not bring province-wide or national attention to this local struggle.[27] So the workers went to court. It was while these efforts to reopen the mill were continuing that we began to interview workers about the closure. It was our hope that the story would have a happy ending, as sometimes happens.[28]

I first met Bruce Colquhoun in late 2003 at the 'Action Centre', a job assistance centre operated by the paper workers union for the former mill workers. Dave Hunter, a local resident who assisted with this research project in its early days, first told me about the 'mill history

binder'—the largest binder he had ever seen. I really HAD to see it. He also told me that everyone he approached to be interviewed told him to first talk to Bruce, one of its compilers. I of course agreed. We met one wintry day in the Action Centre, a big room with tables arranged end-to-end in long rows. There were three or four other men in the room when I was introduced to Bruce and his huge black binder.

Bruce Colquhoun and the others treated the mill history binder as a sacred text or shrine to the mill: their voices lowered to a whisper and Bruce turned the pages with loving care. I instinctively did the same, as it was immediately apparent to me that this binder meant a great deal to these men.[29] It was like a giant memory book, with clippings of old news stories, photographs, and photocopied material on the mill found in the old *Abitibi Magazine*. Over the next two hours, Bruce told me stories as he slowly turned the pages. A soft-spoken man, Bruce noted that the mill history binder was treasured by the mill workers and their families. He related how he would sometimes get requests to borrow the binder to show a visiting family member or a grandchild. Sometimes former mill workers just wanted to re-visit their old lives inside the mill.

. . . The mill history binder can be read as a deep expression of place attachment. Historians sometimes look down on 'amateur' historians or 'collectors'. They are usually untrained—in the sense of not having graduate degrees in history—and are said to produce flawed research that is sentimental, celebratory, excessively detailed, or lacking in analysis. The mill history binder could be criticized on any one of these counts. Yet to do so would be to ignore what it is: a storehouse of memories from and for a workplace community that was shattered by a decision taken far-away. How displaced workers related to this memory book in the months and years following the closure tells us a great deal about the hold that the mill had on them.

The visual language of the mill history binder reminds me of a school yearbook, a family photograph album, or scrapbook—each image has a story attached to it. In her book *Suspended Conversations*, art historian Martha Langford asks what makes the photograph album so special: 'Well, memories of course.'[30] The album 'preserves the life story of the departed within a concrete and bounded report'.[31] The mill history binder serves much the same function: keeping its main protagonist, the mill itself, alive. In so doing, the binder came to symbolize their continuing connection with the past. People's attachments to specific places are not constant: we are most conscious of the sense of belonging that we derive from a place when this connection is most at risk. Place attachment is often 'activated retrospectively'.[32] Yet the mill history binder differs from a yearbook or photograph album insofar as its very openness, the refusal to 'close' the meanings or additions, suggests that the binder served a very different function than that of Langford's albums.

We know a great deal about the making of the mill history binder from a series of interviews that we conducted with the two worker-historians involved, Hubert Gervais and Bruce Colquhoun. Hubert grew up in the nearby village of Field, before starting to work at the mill on 29 April 1963 as an 'office boy'.[33] He worked in the mill's offices for the next 35 years. Bruce, by contrast, followed his father—who had been one of the first hired when the mill reopened in 1947 after being shut for 15 difficult years—onto the mill's shop floor. He worked in the maintenance department as an 'oiler', oiling and greasing machines all over the plant. The job took him everywhere. The two men—one Francophone and the other Anglophone; one an office worker and the other a production worker—thus neatly mirrored the social structure of the mill, albeit in reverse. They were interviewed on several occasions, alone and together, between 2003 and 2006. In all, there are probably 10 hours of recorded conversations. We also asked our other interviewees about the binder.

In an interview over lunch at a popular local restaurant, I asked Bruce and Hubert why they undertook the mill history project. Why was it important to them? To this, Bruce answered: 'I like history too, like Hubert. I wanted to know about the mill. I had always looked around and seen the old stuff in the mill. I don't know. I was doing my family history too. Hubert would help me out at the time and he showed me what he had done until 1976.'[34] Bruce asked if he could take the story up to the present. At this juncture in the interview, Hubert piped in to say Bruce was after him for a few years to do so. Hubert explained: 'I was retiring. I wanted to give it to somebody who was interested.'[35] Bruce therefore became the mill's historian upon Hubert's retirement in 1998.

The first history binder's existence was announced in the mill's newsletter, in a story entitled 'Our Mill—Way Back Then'. Employees were told that Hubert had 'compiled a book of old photos and articles from the old *Abitibi Magazine* dating from 1949 [to] 1969' and advised that 'anyone interested in looking at this book may do so in the main office lobby.'[36] There appears to have been only one or two copies made. That month, the town's weekly newspaper, *The Tribune*, published a piece by Hubert Gervais entitled '1898–1947: A Bit of the Sturgeon Fall Mill's History'.[37] It consisted of a chronology of the mill's development in the first half century.

. . .

If the first mill history binder failed to reach much beyond those who flipped through its pages in the mill's offices, it still resonated with Bruce Colquhoun. Upon his retirement in 1998, Hubert agreed to let Bruce bring the history of the mill up to date. In August, the two men were approached by the mill manager to finish the history in time for the mill's centenary later that year. For Bruce:

It was in August or September of that year, that mill management approached him [Hubert] and asked him if he would write a complete history of the mill, and if he could do it by October. It was on that date back in 1898, that our mill was born, and they wanted to put out a book [to] commemorate the first 100 years. It would be a monumental task to get the history written in time for the 100th anniversary, but, Hubert took up the challenge. The result of his hard work is one extremely well-written and documented history book, with lots of old photos included.[38]

Twenty copies of the second history binder were made, one for each department in the mill. 'Hubert kept one and since I am now the designated mill historian, I too, received a copy,' noted Bruce. 'Everyone here loved it. He had done a wonderful job.' Copies of the 1995 and 1998 binders were eventually donated to the local museum and to the public library by the mill manager, as a lasting contribution to the history of the town.[39]

After 1998, the mill history binder continued to evolve under the stewardship of Bruce Colquhoun. We will discuss its contents in the next section, but Bruce explains its production this way:

Later that year, Hubert called me to say that he had about 200 *Abitibi* magazines ranging in years from 1947 [to] 1969. Each of them had a page or two on our division in them. He gave them to me, and what I saw was 'FANTASTIC'. Here was a pictorial and written history of our mill, during some of the years that Abitibi owned it. I showed some of them to Marc Cote, Mechanical Superintendent. He was amazed with them. Marc and I photocopied each and every page that had something to do with Sturgeon Falls. Since there was 20 copies of Hubert's book, we decided to make 20 copies of each page. We put them in plastic sheet protectors, then in 3" binders, and distributed them the same way as was done with Hubert's book. Everyone loved them. They saw pictures of their fathers, mothers, grandparents, aunts, uncles, brothers, sisters, and even some of themselves. There is well over 200 pages of pictures and history. I combined Hubert's book and the Abitibi pages, and, together,

they filled a 5" binder. I am continuing on with the history, and Hubert is helping me with it. Every once in a while he calls me to say that he has found another picture or a historical fact. If it wasn't for Hubert, we wouldn't know what we now know about our mill. I would like to take this opportunity to say, on behalf of everyone at the mill, a heart-felt THANK YOU to Hubert.[40]

The Mill History binder's very existence is an act of defiance in the face of the erasure that accompanied the mill's closing. Hubert Gervais had begun to collect historical and pictorial materials in the 1970s and gathered them into an 'archive' kept in the old transformer building that once stood at the base of the mill's water tower. By the time that the mill closed, the space was filled with boxes dating back to Spanish River days. The mill's records were shredded or shipped off to destinations unknown after the closure. I managed to get into the mill on two occasions while the demolition company was 'preparing the site' by stripping the interior. I saw hundreds of blueprints piled high on the floor in the engineering offices, ready for destruction. Some of these plans dated back to the 1920s. I asked the Weyerhaeuser official on-site if it would be possible to save this heritage, offering to go through the materials myself. He refused, albeit politely.

The company did not succeed in destroying everything, however. Through Hubert's perseverance, and the clandestine help of another staff member, he spirited a box filled with the mill's newsletter—*The Insider*[41]—out of the closing plant. It had to be done quietly as the mill manager had earlier turned down their request for the materials in a fit of pique. One day when the mill manager was out of town, Hubert was told to drive his vehicle up to the door where the contraband was delivered.[42] In interviewing people, we discovered that many others had secreted away documents as well: a file here or a box there. Whenever possible, I copied the material—filling 28 large and small binders of my own—and urged the rescuers to donate the originals to the local museum. There should be a law against companies stripping industrial communities of their pasts. Weyerhaeuser owned the mill for only three years, yet it destroyed a century-long record of work and production without hesitation.

Narrating Place in the Mill History Binder

. . .

Hubert Gervais's original version of the binder was focused on corporate ownership, work process, natural disasters, and the mill's physical structures. There are therefore chapters dedicated to the mill managers, sawmill waste utilization, the primary treatment plant, renovations to the main office, as well as the floods of 1928, 1951, and 1979.[43] The focus is resolutely on the mill buildings and machines, not the mill workers themselves. It therefore resembles the kind of institutional history that one would expect to find from seeing the corporate logo of MacMillan Bloedel on the binder's front cover. This would be a mistake, however, as Hubert's narrative details the history of the mill itself and not those corporations that would claim it. It is the story of the making of the Sturgeon Falls paper mill— its industrial processes, production records, and other significant moments.

After 1998, the mill history became less a narrative history of 'the mill' and more of a yearbook that was peopled with mill workers and their families. With Hubert's help, Bruce Colquhoun inserted 200 pages from *Abitibi Magazine* that recorded the social world tied to the mill.[44] An open invitation to the mill workforce produced other photographs and documents. These new additions were organized year-by-year within the existing chapter structure but the years were marked. These pages revealed the social world that existed in and around the mill. Many of the photographs marked ritualized moments: production records, retirement parties, service

awards, scholarships to the children of employees, and the like. Anniversaries and other commemorative activity were now included. In 1968, for example, Abitibi Price commissioned a 10 x 14 foot mosaic of the mill in the high school, composed of 15,036 one-inch tiles, based on the sketch by the school's principal, Frank Casey. Other celebrations now appeared, including photographs of mill workers and their families. Bruce Colquhoun opened the binder to other workers, appealing for help in *The Insider* newsletter. The wording of the public call noted that Bruce was 'compiling a historical book of the mill' and that he was looking for 'pictures and or information about this division starting in 1976'. He specifically asked for 'old articles from newspapers or pictures about the people of the industry'.[45] Other mill workers appear to have responded to the call. People submitted a variety of things: 'I got guys with their moose in there. Little girls. New babies. One guy got mad at me. He says, "How come my picture is not in there?" I said, "Well you didn't give it to me."' Newly inserted documents included a photocopy of the 'First Board Made No. 2 Hardboard Machine, October 16, 1963'. The board had a number of signatures on it. Finally, Bruce included lists of local union executive members and shop stewards as well as other union milestones.

During one of our interviews, I asked Bruce Colquhoun and Hubert Gervais how they decided what to include in the binder. Both men insisted that everything went in: 'It's all history. It's the past.' For Bruce, 'The mill is not just the mill. It is all of Sturgeon and West Nipissing.' As a living memorial to the mill, the binder's evolving contents reflected the interests of the two co-authors. With the inclusion of visual and textual sources related to the mill workers and their families, the mill history binder changed substantially in the years that followed. This subtle shift occurred during a period of heightened conflict within the workplace and the uncertainty that accompanied Weyerhaeuser's 1999 purchase of MacMillan Bloedel and with it the Sturgeon Falls mill.

It took Bruce Colquhoun hours to prepare each of the 20 binders. A 3" binder was no longer sufficiently large, however, so he had to buy a 5" binder. He went and saw Marc Coté, his superintendent, for permission to purchase these binders, which cost $35 apiece. 'I was very shy about asking for stuff,' he said. Bruce got two. When the mill's communications officer later asked to see the binder, Bruce agreed to bring it in. The man then said that he wanted to take a look at it, but Bruce refused. The man insisted, saying that it was 'mill property'. Only then did Bruce relent and agree to show the binder to him.

Once recovered, these old stories were a hit on the shop floor. Several interviewees expressed fond memories of the binder:

> Everybody likes to read about the mill. We photocopied all the Sturgeon papers there and brought them into the mill and guys were freaking out. 'Oh my God there is my dad.' 'There's my grandfather.' 'My aunt and uncle.' And that's because of Hubert and [inaudible] that they have the *Abitibi Magazine*.[46]

While the mill still operated, Randy Restoule used to lug it into the operator's booth where he worked. He noted that the mill workers looked at it 'when they could'. The mill history resonated most with Ruth Thompson. One of the few women employed in the mill, she loved to look at the binder while on the job: 'Something like that I related to because I love to hear stories of just things that happened, people's lives . . . What it was like ages ago. It showed the pictures of the logging operations and the old trucks. The clothes the old guys wore. I loved that book.' Thompson particularly liked to see the photographs of her co-workers from 'ages ago when they were young' and liked to see the clothes that they wore in the 1950s and 1960s, especially during the 'hippy times'.

Those family stories that risked being lost, as few people had cameras in those days, were now being recovered. Bruce explained his family's deep connection to the mill: 'I worked [there] for 29 years. My dad worked there for 41 years. My grandfather worked there.' In these comments, we see that the mill history binder was very much a family album like any other. One photograph showed Bruce's own father in 1952. But Bruce was amazed to find his grandfather there as well: 'My dad's dad. He worked there as an electrician.' Joseph Colquhoun was congratulated on the birth of a baby boy. Later, he was honoured for saving the life of another worker. He received a gold watch and a commendation. A proud grandson, Bruce included a copy of the Spanish River Medal for merit with blue ribbon, a certificate of commendation, that was awarded to his grandfather, Joseph Colquhoun, for saving the life of a co-worker in July 1924.

What are the politics of the mill history binder? Is it another case of 'smokestack nostalgia'? The mill history binder was institutionally sanctioned, but it differs from the slick corporate image-making typically found in corporate publications of all kinds. First, the binder was never a public relations exercise. In fact, it was self-consciously produced by and for the mill workers themselves. Its loose format, a binder, and the nature of its distribution within the mill ensured that nobody could possibly confuse it with Weyerhaeuser's glossy commemorative book *Tradition Through the Trees*, published on its corporate centennial in 2000.[47] The mill history binder therefore acted as a rear-view mirror for mill workers and their families, relating the history of the place. These galleries of work and friendship provided a sense of pride in their work and in their shared history. The mill's production records were their collective achievements as were the photographs of smiling retirees and service award recipients. There is none of the anger or loss that was so apparent in the interviews. Yet it is not a joyful history— the mass layoffs and eventual closure of the mill ensured that the mill workers flipping through its pages had a nostalgic reaction to its contents. Without question the two worker-historians felt empowered by the existence of the binder. Their special status within the mill community was widely acknowledged. People constantly advised us to 'ask Hubert' or 'go see Bruce' when we asked questions about the history of the mill. . . .

During one of our meetings, I asked Bruce and Hubert if mill managers ever attempted to influence what went into the binder. It turns out they had. Both men, however, expressed some delight in recounting how they overcame these hurdles. For example, Bruce told us this story:

Scott Mosher [the mill manager at the time, said] 'I want to see everything before you put it in that book. I want to approve it.' And, I said, I work 8 hours a day and I don't have time to run in here 'is that okay.' And next day, 'is that okay.' 'We are not having classified secrets . . . I am not going to bad-mouth you . . . It is just the facts of the history of the mill.' He said, 'Don't go to extremes, we will pay for the ink and that for your cartridge but don't go to extreme. Don't go out and buy a $500 printer.' I said, 'I got a printer.'[48]

In the end, Mosher agreed to pay for the paper and cartridges. With this, Bruce shifts to a more conciliatory posture, adding: 'He was good. I didn't like the idea that he wanted to control everything there for awhile.' This story was followed by another confrontation—this one with the mill's final manager when Bruce was again told to hand over the binder:

He said, 'I've seen that binder.' He says, 'I want it.' ['No,' Hubert laughs] He says, 'Why not? It's the mill property. . . . That paper is my paper.' He says, 'Yes we'd pay for the paper.' 'You didn't pay for the paper,' I said. 'That paper is my paper.' He said, 'We'd paid for the binder.' 'Fine, I'll give you the binder back.' He'd say, 'We'd pay for the ink.' I said, 'I'll buy you a cartridge. You're not getting that binder.' He says, 'That's mill property, Bruce.' I said, 'No it isn't! It's at my place.

You are going to need a court order to get it out of my yard.' [laughs] I said, 'You're not touching that binder.'[49]

It was at this moment that the mill manager decided that Bruce and Hubert would not get their hands on the mill's newsletter. As already mentioned, the whole run of *The Insider*—which was produced throughout the 1990s—was rescued anyway. Both men took some joy out of their belief that an earlier plant manager now wants 'to see the binder bad'. But it was not '*for him*', it was theirs. The contents of the mill history binder are thus an expression of Bruce and Hubert's profound attachment to the mill and the people who worked there. In many ways, it has been their personal response to the mill's closing.

A Living Memorial

One question that I have had on my mind from my very first meeting with Bruce Colquhoun at the Action Centre, was 'Why hadn't they updated the binder to include the mill's closure and aftermath?' Every time I ask the question, I get the same answer: to do so would have been to admit that the mill was dead and their workplace community with it. Both men feared that this would signal the end of their efforts. It was still 'too soon'. They 'weren't ready'. Much the same thing happened when I asked if they intended to publish the binder in some way. Bruce told me that this would make it impossible for him to continue to add to its contents. It would freeze it forever. He did not want this—not now. It would stop being a living memorial to the mill and to the mill families. To my knowledge, Bruce Colquhoun still has not inserted the news stories, photographs, and other materials (such as a photocopy of the last roll of paper produced at the mill, signed by the workers) that he has collected. It remains a living memorial to what was, a book frozen in time.

'Voices must be heard for memories to be preserved,' notes art historian Martha Langford. For the family photograph album to fulfill its function, it must continue to live: 'Ironically, the very act of preservation—the entrusting of an album to a public museum—suspends its sustaining conversation, stripping the album of its social function and meaning.'[50] Martha Langford's words made sense to me the first time that I read them, largely because I had heard Bruce Colquhoun and Hubert Gervais make much the same point on several occasions. The mill history binder, like the photo albums Langford speaks of, has its roots in orality—workers remember by visual association. 'The showing and telling of an album is a performance,' writes Langford.[51] As long as the mill history binder continues to be interpreted for others, the conversation continues and the old connection to place remains. Yet in not taking the story up to the mill's closing and the painful aftermath, Colquhoun and Gervais have detached the mill history binder from its present context. The conversation contained in the binder may not be 'suspended' but it is certainly circumscribed. Everyday patterns of remembering, and place-making, are of course politically charged. . . .

We asked our interviewees about the memory book. Almost everyone knew what it was. It was a 'great big binder', recalled Raymond Marcoux. Ray Lortie likewise remembered the book well, covering as it did the mill's entire lifespan. Several interviewees had their own copies—whisked away, no doubt, from the closing mill. 'They showed them to me,' declared student interviewer Kristen O'Hare. Others had little to say about the memory book. A few never heard of it. For his part, Lawrence Pretty told us that one of his children recently used the binder for a school project on the history of the mill. He was not alone.

Once the mill closed, Hubert Gervais shifted his focus to documenting the demolition with his own camera. Over the six months that it took the company to completely demolish the mill, leaving the mill's hydroelectric plant and a big hole in the ground, Hubert took an astonishing 1,400 photographs of the mill.[52] He began taking pictures from outside the fence in July 2004, returning each day. One day he entered the mill property through the front gate. The security guard, who had been there while the mill was active, let him through after he explained that he was taking pictures for 'the book'. Yes, the mill history binder. 'Sure go ahead, take all the pictures,' she replied. As he walked onto the site, a contractor's truck came up to him and he was asked his business. Hubert was then invited to trade access to the site for the right to use these images in company promotion.[53] He accepted: 'I was there everyday. From the [time] they started to the time they quit [in November 2004].' Hubert observed that the demolition company seemed to work 'back in time'—dismantling the newest parts of the mill before tackling the oldest parts. He decided not to go the day that they demolished the main office, but had someone take pictures for him. On the day that the giant stack was toppled, Hubert took a piece of the rubble as a souvenir. There were always five or six cars parked outside the fence as others watched at a distance.

Conclusion

All blue-collar workers, to some degree, are attached to locality by ties of family and friendship, work ties, or by affect.[54] The act or process of displacement, or the putting out of place, is thus an integral part of 'industrial restructuring', 'globalization', or whatever other label that we want to apply to economic change. Capitalism destroys the old in order to make the new.[55] The urge to reaffirm and celebrate industrial history in the face of the crisis in North American manufacturing and the resource sector is not limited to Sturgeon Falls, Ontario. In Pittsburgh, for example, the impulse to commemorate steelworkers—'to fix their historical identity forever in a didactic monument'—arose from the demise of a living industrial culture that could nourish such memory from within.'[56] What is different about the mill history binder is the insistence on keeping it open to additional materials and available to other mill workers. It serves to keep the mill alive in their memories, even as the mill itself has been erased from the physical landscape.[57] A sense of place would be impossible without memory.[58]

Place is more than a static category, an empty container where things happen. It must be understood as a social and spatial process, undergoing constant change.[59] Place is therefore contingent, fluid, and multiple. Like the piece of rubble picked up by Hubert Gervais during the mill's demolition, the binder has become a last vestige, or remnant, of what was: a site of memory 'in which a residual sense of continuity remains'.[60] Yet the place being remembered is fixed to happier times before the mill's closing. Like the makers of other commemorative monuments, the co-creators of the mill history binder aim to 'create a stable and coherent past sealed off from the vicissitudes of change.'[61] The place that was the Sturgeon Falls mill, an active industrial site for more than a century until it closed in December 2002, is thus forever frozen in time. Doreen Massey's notion of place as existing in time and space is thus made manifest.

I would like to thank all of the men and women who agreed to be interviewed for this project. I would especially like to thank Hubert Gervais, Bruce Colquhoun, and Wayne LeBelle. Dave Hunter and Kristen O'Hare provided invaluable research assistance. . . .

Notes

1. Alessandro Portelli, '"The Time of My Life": Function of Time in Oral History', *International Journal of Oral History* 2, 3 (1981): 162.

2. Doreen Massey, 'Places and their Pasts', *History Workshop Journal* 39 (1995): 185.

3. Albert Fancher, 'Placing the Displaced Worker', *Barron's* (27 July 1942).

4. According to the US Bureau of Labor Statistics, 'displaced workers are defined as persons 20 years of age and older who lost or left jobs because their plant or company closed or moved, there was insufficient work for them to do, or their position or shift was abolished.' US Bureau of Labor Statistics, 'Displaced Worker Summary' *News* (15 Sept. 2006).

5. Steven Hipple, 'Worker displacement in the mid-1990s', *Monthly Labor Review* (July 1999): 15.

6. Charles Koeber makes this last point. See his 'Corporate Restructuring, Downsizing, and the Middle Classes: The Process and Meaning of Worker Displacement in the "New Economy"', *Qualitative Sociology* 25, 2 (Summer 2002). . . .

7. Tamara Hareven and Randolph Langenback, *Amoskeag: Life and Work in an American Factory City* (New York: Pantheon Books, 1978), 12. . . .

8. Historian Joy Parr is conducting some of the most interesting research into the senses, see her 'A Working Knowledge of the Insensible: Radiation Protection in Nuclear Generating Stations, 1962–1992', *Comparative Studies in Society and History* 48 (2006): 820–51.

9. Massey, 'Places and their Pasts', 183.

10. In her study of the working-class Hilesluis district of Rotterdam, sociologist Talja Blokland asks how place-making includes and excludes the process of shared remembering engaged in by long-time residents in the ice cream parlour and in other public spaces served to define these places as theirs. In so doing, the stories told by white 'regulars' powerfully excluded recent immigrants from the conversation and from the venues themselves. Talja Blokland, 'Bricks, Mortar, Memories: Neighbourhood and Networks in Collective Acts of Remembering', *International Journal of Urban and Regional Research* 25, 2 (June 2001): 279.

11. John Dixon and Kevin Durrheim, 'Displacing Place-Identity: A discursive approach to locating self and other', *British Journal of Social Psychology* 39 (2000): 27–44. Rituals and storytelling are important in establishing and maintaining the symbolic bond between individuals or groups and physical sites. 1. Setha M. Low and Irwin Altman, 'Place Attachment: A Conceptual Inquiry', in Altman and Low, eds, *Place Attachment* (New York: Plenum Press, 1992), 2. Yi-Fu Tuan, 'Place: An Experiential Perspective', *Geographical Review* 65, 2 (Apr. 1975): 151–65. . . .

12. Social psychologist Setha Low suggests that we treasure these memories all the more, 'recreating' it through memory, in her 'Symbolic Ties that Bind', in Altman and Low, eds, *Place Attachment*, 167.

13. Doreen Massey, *Spatial Divisions of Labour: Social Structures and the Geography of Production* (London: Macmillan, 1984), 11. . . .

14. Kathryn Marie Dudley, *The End of the Line: Lost Jobs, New Lives in Postindustrial America* (Chicago: University of Chicago Press, 1994), 47.

15. Randy Restoule interviewed by Kristen O'Hare, 5 Aug. 2004.

16. Bruce Colquhoun interviewed by Kristen O'Hare. For more on the phenomenon of former workers watching the demolition of their former mills or factories, see Steven High and David W. Lewis, *Corporate Wasteland: The Landscape and Memory of Deindustrialization* (Toronto: Between the Lines Press, 2007), ch. 1.

17. John C. Walsh and Steven High, 'Rethinking the Concept of Community', *Histoire sociale/Social History* 32, 64 (1999): 255–74.

18. For more on this divergence, see High, *Corporate Wasteland*, ch. 4.

19. Mike Lacroix interviewed by Kristen O'Hare, 4 Feb. 2004.

20. Percy Allary interviewed by Kristen O'Hare, 9 June 2004. See also the follow-up interview conducted by Steven High, June 2005.

21. Gerry Stevens interviewed by Kristen O'Hare, 2 June 2004.

22. Mike Lacroix interviewed by Kristen O'Hare, 4 Feb. 2004.

23. Ed Fortin interviewed by Kristen O'Hare, 5 Aug. 2004.

24. Having grown up in a forestry town (Thunder Bay) myself, I remember my economics teacher dramatically throwing open the windows of our school classroom to let the mill's sweet sulphur scent waft in. 'Smell that,' he said. 'That is the smell of money.' The point was not lost on us.

25. Local historian Wayne LeBelle had a great deal to say on this point in the various interview sessions.

26. Gerry Stevens interviewed by Kristen O'Hare, 2 June 2004.

27. For more on this see Steven High, *Industrial Sunset: The Making of North America's Rust Belt, 1969–1984* (Toronto: University of Toronto Press, 2003).

28. Two regional cases stand out in this regard, at least within the forestry sector: Kapuskasing, Ontario, and Temiscaming, Quebec. See Thomas M. Beckley and Naomi T. Krogman, 'Social Consequences of Employee/ Management Buyouts: Two Canadian Examples from the Forest Sector', *Rural Sociology* 67, 2 (2002): 183–207; and the documentary film *Temiscaming, Québec* (1975) directed by Martin Duckworth for the National Film Board.

29. It mattered to me too. I never came across anything quite like it in 15 years of research into mill and factory closings.

30. Martha Langford, *Suspended Conversations: The Afterlife of Memory in Photographic Albums* (Montreal: McGill-Queen's University Press, 2001), 3.

31. Ibid., 63.

32. Setha M. Low, 'Symbolic Ties that Bind', in Altman and Low, eds, *Place Attachment*, 167.

33. Hubert Gervais interviewed by Kristen O'Hare, 12 Mar. 2004.

34. Interview with Bruce Colquhoun and Hubert Gervais at Gervais Restaurant, Steven High, 18 Dec. 2004.

35. Ibid.

36. *The Insider*, May 1995. In the possession of the author. My copy of these documents will be donated to the Sturgeon Falls House Museum at the project's conclusion.

37. Hubert Gervais, '1898–1947: A Bit of the Sturgeon Fall Mill's History', *The Tribune*, 30 May 1995.

38. Bruce Colquhoun and Hubert Gervais. The 'Mill History' Binder (2005 version). In the possession of the author of this article as well as in that of its authors.

39. Interview with Bruce Colquhoun and Hubert Gervais at Gervais Restaurant, Steven High, 18 Dec. 2004.

40. Bruce Colquhoun and Hubert Gervais, The 'Mill History' Binder.

41. *The Insider* was published during the 1990s.

42. Interview with Bruce Colquhoun and Hubert Gervais at Gervais Restaurant, Steven High, 18 Dec. 2004.

43. For more on photographic image worlds see David E. Nye, *Image Worlds: Corporate Identities at General Electric, 1890–1930* (Cambridge: MIT Press, 1985).

44. The mother of one of the Sturgeon Falls workers had been the magazine's editor so he had the originals. It took Bruce three nights, staying late, to make all the photocopies. There were 20 binders. 'I put them all in binders and plastic sleeves. We made 20 copies of each page.' Interview with Bruce Colquhoun and Hubert Gervais, Steven High, 18 Dec. 2004.

45. *The Insider*, 18 Sept. 1998.

46. Interview with Bruce Colquhoun and Hubert Gervais, Steven High, 18 Dec. 2004.

47. Joni Sensel, *Tradition Through the Trees: Weyerhaeuser's First 100 Years* (USA: Documentary Book Publishers, 2000).

48. Interview with Bruce Colquhoun and Hubert Gervais, Steven High, 18 Dec. 2004.

49. Ibid.

50. Langford, *Suspended Conversations*, 5.

51. Ibid.

52. Hubert Gervais interviewed by Steven High, 22 June 2005.

53. The photographs can be found on the demolition company's website: http://www.environmentalhazards.com/demolition/ weyerhaeuser.htm.

54. Andrew Herod, 'Workers, Space and Labor Geography', *International Labor and Working Class History* 64 (Fall 2003): 112.

55. David Harvey notes that place attachment and displacement are an integral part of capitalism. See David Harvey, *Spaces of Global Capitalism: Towards a Theory of Uneven Geographical Development* (London

and New York: verso, 2006) 81. The term 'creative destruction' was coined by Joseph Schumpeter, *From Capitalism, Socialism and Democracy* (New York: Harper, 1975 [1942]).

56. Kirk Savage, 'Monuments to a Lost Cause: The Post-Industrial Campaign to Commemorate Steel', in Jefferson Cowie and Joseph Heathcott, *Beyond the Ruins: The Meanings of Deindustrialization* (Ithaca: Cornell University Press, 2003), 248.

57. Its closure and subsequent demolition destroyed this spatial fix, leaving people without a 'framework for memories'. The destruction of the steel mill had this effect in Homestead, Pennyslvania, say Judith Modell and John Hinshaw, 'Male Work and Mill Work: Memory and Gender in Homestead, Pennyslvania', in Selma Leydesdorff and Luisa Passerini and Paul Thompson, eds, *Gender and Memory* (New Brunswick: Transaction Publishers, 2005).

58. Joan M. Schwartz makes precisely this point in 'Constituting Place of Presence: Landscape, Identity and the Geographical Imagination', in Marlene Creates, *Places of Presence: Newfoundland Kin and Ancestral Land, Newfoundland 1989–1991* (St John's: Killick Press, 1997).

59. Walsh and High, 'Rethinking the Concept of Community'.

60. Pierre Nora, 'General Introduction: Between Memory and History', in Nora, ed., *Realms of Memory: The Construction of the French Past* Volume 1 (New York: Columbia University Press, 1996), xv.

61. Savage, 'Monuments to a Lost Cause', in Cowie and Heathcott, *Beyond the Ruins*, 238.

18

—— Visualizing Work ——

From the late nineteenth century to the present day, employers have used photographs and other visual materials for a wide variety of purposes. Public relations departments employed such images not only to sell products or services but also to project their own workers and work spaces as healthy, happy, and inviting. Since the vast majority of historical images of waged work are handed down to us from company archives or originated as commissioned material by employers, historians need to be aware that such representations of labour are inherently problematic. All of the images in this section are formal representations of waged work and, therefore,

share this concern. Although such illustrations can shed some light on the organization of work space, it is important to be aware that, whether these images are embodied in advertisements or photographs, it is the company's point of view that is being presented to the public.

In addition to the specific questions below, it is worthwhile considering some of the broader issues of absence in these images. What kinds of work were not typically photographed or advertised? How might workers themselves have represented their own work differently? Where does unwaged labour fit into our visual understanding of work?

Series 1: Rural Landscapes

The conditions of rural life underwent significant changes in the late 1800s and early 1900s. While there were variations across the country, especially as new areas were being colonized by agricultural settlement, farmers increasingly moved towards a global market economy, spurred by increased mechanization and what contemporaries called 'scientific agriculture'. The moral economy of rural labour discussed by Catharine Anne Wilson in Chapter 10 did not disappear, but it began to play a more limited role in everyday farm life. In this era of change, manufacturers needed to sell and advertise their goods in such a way as to balance the appeal of modern labour-saving machines with nostalgic understandings of the 'farm' as an anchor of stability even in times of economic upheaval. They had to promote the betterment of the rural ideal

while also celebrating the modern, industrial know-how which made their products possible to produce and, in turn, useful to the farmer.

Advertisements such as those in Figures 1, 2, and 3 were used in periodicals, distributed at fairs and exhibitions, appeared on broadsheets, and were featured in an ever-expanding range of ephemera given to farmers by salesmen such as postcards, greeting cards, and pocket calendars. Such a small selection of images does not teach us very much about how technology actually changed farm life, but it does provide insight into the ways in which workers and the sites of rural work were invested with deep socio-cultural meanings.

1. How are these technologies framed by gender, race, and class ideals? Why would advertisers do this?
2. How does each advertisement present the rural landscape as progressive and modern?

How are work and workers represented within this landscape?

3. What elements of rural work are missing or are deliberately marginalized by these advertisements?

Series 2: Industrial Spaces

The process of industrialization transformed the Canadian economy in the late nineteenth century, but industrial work spaces continued to evolve well into the twentieth century. The scale of industrial production expanded dramatically as industries consolidated, built increasingly larger factories, and turned to 'scientific' management techniques that 'rationalized' the workforce. Rather than being dispersed across many different sites, work was centralized by industrial architects who designed large-scale workplaces that brought together power plants, machine shops, manufacturing, and transportation facilities.

The following images were published in a glossy corporate brochure promoting Algoma Steel, based in Sault Ste Marie, Ontario. Very little text accompanied the images, which were intended to portray the company's extensive assets and demonstrate large-scale capacity for potential investors and customers. Since the company commissioned all of these photographs, it is important to consider how the camera directs our view and what principles are being embodied by the cultural aesthetics of the photographer.

1. In its 1938 promotional material, the majority of images published by Algoma Steel were external images of buildings, as shown in Figures 4 and 5. Carefully examine the perspective and camera angles of these two images. What message is being presented about the company?

2. Figures 6 and 7 offer different perspectives on the interior working spaces of Algoma Steel. What purpose do these images serve?

3. What role do the workers play in these photographs? Where do they appear and how is their relationship to the machinery of the industrial workplace portrayed?

Series 3: Selling Service

With the introduction of Pullman sleeping cars in the late nineteenth century, Canadian railway companies started to employ black porters to offer service to first-class passengers. While some were recruited from the United States and the Caribbean, many African-Canadians also found employment in this position. Porters were responsible for cleaning, stocking, and heating or cooling the cars, as well as taking care of passengers' needs. Their duties could range from polishing shoes to mixing drinks to caring for those suffering motion sickness. Although black railwaymen performed a wide variety of jobs for Canadian railway companies, their most public role was as porters, a position that was racially defined by the turn of the century.[1] Black porters remained a significant presence on railways even after World War II, as demonstrated by these four photographs taken in the late 1940s or 1950s as publicity material for Canadian National Railways (CN).

1. How can you tell that these photographs (Figures 8–11) are staged and not simply snapshots of everyday life?

2. Examine the sequence of the four photographs. What is the narrative or story that the company is trying to portray? Why would CN want to link the porter's home life with his work?

3. In these photographs, how are the spaces of home and work gendered? How do these representations of black porters compare with Pamela Sugiman's analysis of masculinity and black auto workers (Chapter 16)?
4. What was the audience for such images? How might people have read these photographs differently in the 1950s from how we might interpret them today?

Series 4: Business at Work

In the first decades of the twentieth century, a revolution in corporate management and administration led to a dramatic expansion of paperwork, from general records and bookkeeping to marketing and investment management. In this period, clerical workers as a profession grew by more than 80 per cent and numbered over 100,000. Such a rapid growth was only possible by allowing large numbers of women into what had formerly been a male work space. As the 'feminization' of clerical work proceeded, men found themselves struggling to define new codes of masculinity that stressed the 'rationality' of business.

Women did not, however, enter on equal terms. Employed for less pay and blocked from career advancement, women clerical workers were often viewed as transitory, entering the workforce as young adults but expected to withdraw once they were married. The public visibility of office workers also raised questions regarding sexuality, dress, and outward appearance.

Figures 12 and 13 offer contrasting images of two Montreal offices, one from 1924 and one from the late 1950s or early 1960s. The changing technologies of the workplace are evident in both photographs and are the subject of Figure 14, an advertisement for Gestetner.

1. Comparing Figures 12 and 13, what similarities and differences do you find in the physical layout of office space?
2. From Figures 12 and 13, how is the physical space within the office gendered? How does the spatial ordering of the office reflect the hierarchical relations between those who work within it?
3. In its advertisement (Figure 14), how does Gestetner use body language and positioning to sell copy machines? How are the roles of office workers and managers gendered, both in the image and in the text?

Note

1. Sarah-Jane (Saje) Mathieu, 'North of the Colour Line: Sleeping Car Porters and the Battle against Jim Crow on Canadian Rails, 1880–1920', *Labour/Le Travail* 47 (Spring 2001): 9–41.

Figure 1. 'National Cream Separator Manufactured by the Raymond Mfg. Co. of Guelph Limited', 1908. Baldwin Room Broadsides and Printed Ephemera Collection, Toronto Public Library.

Figure 2. 'The Aspinwall Potato Planter', 1885. Archival and Special Collections, University of Guelph Library. XA1 RHC A0389, MM 15 (Massey Manufacturing Co. 1891 catalogue).

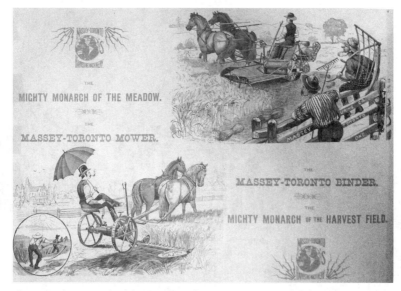

Figure 3. 'The Monarch of the Meadow: The Toronto Mower and The Massey-Toronto Binder: The Mighty Monarch of the Harvest Field', 1891. Massey-Harris-Ferguson, Archival & Special Collections, University of Guelph Library. XA1 RHC A0389, MM 13.

Figure 4. 'New Coke Oven Battery', *Algoma Steel Corporation Limited: Its Works and Properties, June, 1938* (Sault Ste Marie: Algoma Steel, 1938), 25.

Figure 5. 'Machine Shop and Tool Room', *Algoma Steel Corporation Limited: Its Works and Properties, June, 1938* (Sault Ste Marie: Algoma Steel, 1938), 49.

Figure 6. 'Teeming Heat of Steel into Ingot Moulds', *Algoma Steel Corporation Limited: Its Works and Properties, June, 1938* (Sault Ste Marie: Algoma Steel, 1938), 34.

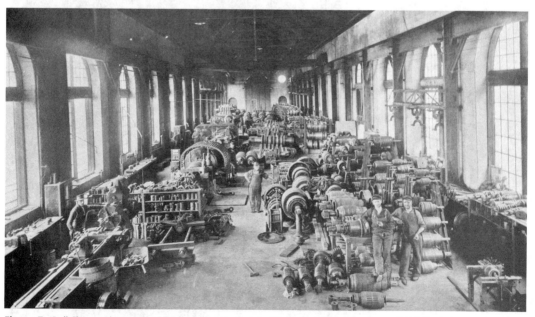

Figure 7. 'Roll Shop', *Algoma Steel Corporation Limited: Its Works and Properties, June, 1938* (Sault Ste Marie: Algoma Steel, 1938), 53.

Figure 8. CN porter and family at table. Canadian Science and Technology Museum, CSTM/CN collection/Musée des sciences et de la technologie du Canada, MSTC/CN collection, image 49315-2.

Figure 9. CN porter and family at doorstep. Canadian Science and Technology Museum, CSTM/CN collection/Musée des sciences et de la technologie du Canada, MSTC/CN collection, image 49315.

Figure 10. CN porter on train. Canadian Science and Technology Museum, CSTM/CN collection/Musée des sciences et de la technologie du Canada, MSTC/CN collection, image 49315-8.

Figure 11. CN porter at work. Canadian Science and Technology Museum, CSTM/CN collection/Musée des sciences et de la technologie du Canada, MSTC/CN collection, image 39403.

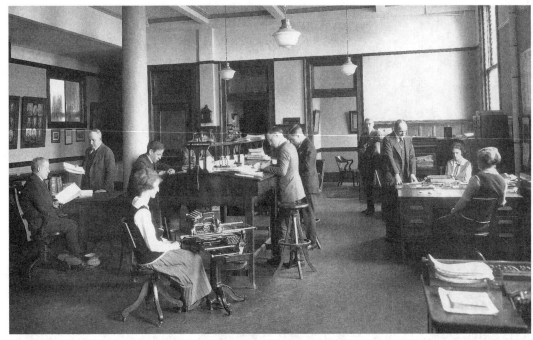

Figure 12. An office in Montreal, 1924, Wm. Notman & Son. McCord Museum, Montreal, view–21089.

Figure 13. Office, c. 1950s–1960s. Canadian Science and Technology Museum, CSTM/CN collection/Musée des sciences et de la technologie du Canada, MSTC/CN collection, image 55246.

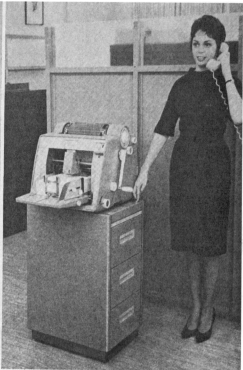
Figure 14. Gestetner, 'Clean, Clear Copies?', *Maclean's*, 8 Nov. 1964.

Part Three

—— **At Play** ——

While the social history of home and work emerged as serious fields of research in the 1970s, the social history of play did not move into the mainstream of scholarly study until the late 1980s and early 1990s. Historians of home and work had certainly mentioned leisure activities, such as sport and tavern life, but these were considered to be merely a part of some other history of family, class, gender, or ethnicity. Indeed, it is significant that the history of sport in Canada emerged from university kinesiology and physical education programs rather than history departments. Social historians began to take the history of play more seriously in the 1990s, a shift partly inspired by the work of cultural anthropologists which convinced historians that the ways in which a society plays and the rules that govern that play reveal much about the structures of social organization. By the end of this decade, our understanding of Canadian social history was enriched by the study of spaces such as roller rinks, exhibitions, tourist destinations, and sporting fields. The best of this literature focused on how power was exerted on and through these spaces, and here attention to government regulation and cultural hegemony was especially dominant. In the twenty-first century, this interpretive stance has been deepened and in some cases redirected by considering play as performance, a scholarly shift that is also identifiable in anthropology, cultural studies, and human geography. In these recent works, power flows not only from the state and cultural elites but is also experienced between and among individuals engaged in the same forms of play within the same social space.

This historiographical development makes it both possible and necessary to ask: What has it meant, historically, for Canadians to 'play'? In the articles that follow, the social history of play refers to the social history of leisure, of recreation, of having fun. This might include a wide range of activities, such as tobogganing or going out to the movies. But the meanings of play are far more complex and deep than the pure joy of fun. For example, dance halls, gaming houses, taverns, and even donut shops were all spaces subjected to the anxious watching of those who worried about what these spaces were doing to the moral, spiritual, and physical health of both individual bodies and the nation.

As a result, several of the readings in this section demonstrate how the social history of play was at the centre of the moral geography of the modern city. From the later decades of the nineteenth century, a wide range of voices insisted that the experiences and spaces of pleasure had to be balanced against and guarded from the experiences and spaces of danger. By the early 1900s, a whole series of reform movements and public health initiatives were devoted to producing more 'good' spaces and containing (if not eliminating) the 'bad'. For some the response to modern urban life was to forsake the city altogether and temporarily search out wilderness spaces to revitalize and reinvigorate mind, body, and spirit.

The concept of play as a social space is complicated by the fact that it overlaps many of the areas of study we have already examined. What functioned as leisure for some people served as work for others, while some forms of recreation were framed as proper pursuits within the home. These essays, therefore, offer an opportunity for readers to question the very division of these worlds and to examine how play was constituted by the shifting relations between home and work. They also afford the chance to think about how the imaginings of a moral geography sought to structure experiences and identities while also being contested and negotiated by a whole range of actors and organizations. This process takes on a unique form in Colin Howell's chapter, where travelling athletes and spectators combined to forge a regional identity around sport in the Maritimes and New England states that, in some ways, superseded the national boundary that differentiated Canadians from Americans on the map.

Many of the readings thus also call attention to how the performances of play produced contact zones of power and identification. Here we discover a variety of exchanges, such as those between exotic dancers, their bosses, and patrons in one of Vancouver's night-clubs and between campers, counsellors, and directors at Ontario summer camps. But how open were spaces like summer camps and nightclubs? How did leisure and recreational activities create boundaries of community that included but also excluded at the same time? What did contemporaries think about these communities of play, especially those that featured people of different ethnic or racial identities, from different classes, and from both sexes?

These questions help make clear that having fun in Canada has been fundamental to the experience of social history, but such encounters also offered platforms for performing identities—identities of gender, race, class, sexuality, and indeed the self—while also making visible the power relations that could affirm and/or challenge broader structures of social organization. Although the study of performance compels historians to look closely at specific sites of play, our readings also consider these sites within larger systems of governance and popular culture. Vancouver's nightclubs and Ontario's summer camps were not independent islands. Rather, we are encouraged to think of each as nodes in a network of spaces and places within the moral geography of Canada.

Further Readings

Bouchier, Nancy B. *For the Love of the Game: Amateur Sport in Small-town Ontario, 1838–1895*. Montreal and Kingston, 2003.

Dubinsky, Karen. *The Second Greatest Disappointment: Honeymooners, Heterosexuality, and the Tourist Industry at Niagara Falls*. Toronto, 1999.

Heron, Craig. *Booze: A Distilled History*. Toronto, 2003.

Howell, Colin. *Northern Sandlots: A Social History of Maritime Baseball*. Toronto, 1995.

McKay, Ian. *The Quest of the Folk: Antimodernism and Cultural Selection in Twentieth-Century Nova Scotia*. Montreal and Kingston, 1994.

Marks, Lynne. *Revivals and Roller Rinks: Religion, Leisure, and Identity in Late Nineteenth-Century Small-Town Ontario*. Toronto, 1996.

Moore, Paul S. *Now Playing: Early Moviegoing and the Regulation of Fun*. Albany, 2008.

Morton, Suzanne. *At Odds: Gambling and Canadians, 1919–1969*. Toronto, 2003.

Rudy, Jarrett. *The Freedom to Smoke: Tobacco Consumption and Identity*. Montreal and Kingston, 2005.

Strange, Carolyn. *Toronto's Girl Problem: The Perils and Pleasures of the City, 1890–1930*. Toronto, 1995.

Walden, Keith. *Becoming Modern in Toronto: The Industrial Exhibition and the Shaping of a Late Victorian Culture*. Toronto, 1997.

Wall, Sharon. *The Nurture of Nature: Childhood, Antimodernism, and Ontario Summer Camps, 1920–55*. Vancouver, 2009.

19

'Our Winter Sports': The Montreal Winter Carnivals

—— **Gillian Poulter** ——

For an ethnic group to become a group and not merely a collection of people it must identify itself, and be identified by others, as constituting a category different from other categories of the same type . . . In short, it must have a strongly developed consciousness of kind.

Chris Shore, 'Ethnicity as Revolutionary Strategy'

Young Downylip was a familiar caricature figure to readers of the *Canadian Illustrated News* in the early 1870s. On his 'first visit to Canada' in 1872, he enthusiastically accepted invitations to try out all the winter sports—skating, tobogganing, the Tandem Club Drive, and snowshoeing—as well as being a guest at an 'Evening Party'. Alas, Downylip was not Canadian and it showed. Every outing ended in embarrassment and disaster. None of the sports 'seem[ed] to agree with him'. And no wonder! These hearty Canadian sports were too physically challenging for a foreigner who lacked the Northern flare for the outdoors. So, with never-failing courtesy, his Canadian escorts picked him up and got him safely home (Figure 1).

Of all the indigenous sports, tobogganing was the most accessible. Although snowshoeing, hunting, and lacrosse were popular activities among men of the commercial and professional middle classes, active participation was restricted to those who were mature enough and physically able. In contrast, tobogganing could be enjoyed by women, children, and even the elderly, and it was not restricted to the middle classes because it required very little in the way of equipment; any steep slope offered hours of potential fun. These qualities made it an ideal activity to share with visitors like Downylip. At the Winter Carnivals held in Montreal in the 1880s, tobogganing was presented as a distinctively Canadian sport, and visitors of both sexes were encouraged to try it out to see for themselves what it felt like to be 'Canadian'. By this time, however, tobogganing had evolved from the classless, free-wheeling children's game of 'olden times'; now it had been given 'English character' and transformed into a highly organized club sport, with specialized equipment and codified behaviours.

It is impossible to explore the emergence of tobogganing as an organized sport without considering the Montreal Winter Carnivals and the role indigenous winter sports played in them generally. The carnivals were held when the moon was bright at the end of January or beginning of February in 1883, 1884, 1885, 1887, and 1889.[1] The 1884 carnival attracted the most visitors (approximately 60,000), but the 1885 carnival reached the most elaborate form. Most of my discussion and analysis will focus on the 1885 carnival since it is in the contrast between the East and West End Committee events of that year that internal tensions around differing concepts of national identity are revealed. Eva Mackey

Figure 1. Young Downylip was the invention of William Ogle Carlisle, who told of his young hero's excellent adventures in the snow in a series of cartoons published in 1872 and 1873. Carlisle makes a clear distinction between the clumsy performance of this young visitor and the confident proficiency of his Canadian hosts. Illustration: William Ogle Carlisle, *Young Downylip's First Visit to Canada—His Tobogganing Experience.* Source: LAC, *Canadian Illustrated News* 5, 8, (128), 24 Feb. 1872, No. 2495.

points out that in tracing the cultural politics of national identity, 'the central issue is to examine who decides when and how ["others"] are or aren't represented, or are or aren't managed, in the interests of the nation-building project.'[2] My contention is that the carnivals were a performance of Canadian identity given by middle-class British colonists for the benefit of an international audience. They were a self-conscious display of civic pride and national identity—an invitation to visitors from abroad to come and experience the thriving, modern, Canadian metropolis of Montreal. As historical antecedents, Native people had no part to play in such a scene. Despite the success of the carnivals, accounts of the events in the popular press show that the veneer of civic unity was very thin and that the Canadian identity constructed by the middle-class sports clubs was fragile and contested.

Tobogganing

The toboggan, or sled, was originally an Indigenous tool used to transport goods over the winter snows.[3] It was adopted first by French and then by British colonists and became a favourite winter amusement, especially for children. Although tobogganing was an ancient activity in Canada, it was claimed to be unknown to Americans before the 1883 carnival. According to the *Canadian Illustrated News*: 'To hosts of our American cousins the very name is unknown . . . This is a purely Canadian sport . . . These long Indian sleds, thin as wafers, strong as steel . . . afford an amount of exhilarating fun that is peculiar to themselves.'[4] Tobogganers initially used the *traine sauvages* of Native manufacture and took advantage of natural hills and slopes. In *Over the Snow*, a booklet written to promote the 1883 carnival, the ubiquitous George Beers explained for the benefit of American visitors that in his schooldays McTavish's Hill and the Côte-des-Neiges road were favourite Montreal tobogganing hills. Agnes Macdonald, second

wife of Prime Minister Sir John A. Macdonald, also reminisced about tobogganing, or 'coasting', on unprepared slopes 'in the more primitive days of Canada' for the readers of *Murray's Magazine* of London (1888). . . .

In the effort to bring a British sense of order and regulation to colonial society, tobogganing, like snowshoeing and lacrosse, was 'tamed' by being organized into a middle-class club sport that was carried out in a specific location and subject to particular behaviour and technological 'improvements'. In the process, its history was appropriated. Ed Ruthven, writing for the Toronto publication *The Week*, encapsulated the history of tobogganing for his readers but entirely left out its Native origins: 'It used to be necessary to have a hill and to slide down it until the snow was packed hard enough to make the exercise a pleasure. After a time rich men who did not happen to have hills at hand built slides for their children. The idea was taken up and big slides were built for the amusement of grown people. This was expensive, however, and gave the rich people a monopoly of the sport. Tobogganing clubs were then formed among the young men to put the fun on a more democratic basis.'[5]

. . .

Organized toboggan clubs emerged in the late 1870s, probably as a way for snowshoe club members to share respectable middle-class recreation with their families. The Montreal Toboggan Club was the first club formed, being inaugurated in 1879 with three slides on Mount Royal near Côte St Antoine. . . . Instead of allowing tobogganers free rein on the hills, the clubs built a series of ice chutes separated from each other by low ice walls. . . . The drop was steep and long; Ruthven found it 'more than merely exhilarating. A quarter of a mile in fourteen seconds, the first part of the journey down a hill the descent of which is like falling off a roof of a four-storey house, is calculated to quicken the pulse to a point which "exhilaration" is not sufficiently strong to do justice to. . . .'[6] Not much could be done to change the design of the old birchbark sleds. By 1888 toboggans were still being made to order by Native artisans,[7] but various manufacturers tried using different types of wood. . . . Even steel was used in what must have been a dangerous and ill-fated attempt to modernize toboggans and make them more scientific.[8] More successful was the effort to make toboggans more comfortable, feminine, and aesthetically pleasing with the addition of velvet cushions.

Carnival visitors could take a short bus or cab ride to any of the club slides, where, assisted by helpful club members, they could use the facilities at no cost during carnival week.[9] The woods and wide slopes of Mount Royal Park stood in for the Canadian wilderness, so visitors from abroad and other parts of the Dominion were able to both observe what Canadians did in their national landscape and try out how it felt to be one. . . . [F]orming clubs and building slides and clubhouses was a marker of class; it was a means by which club members differentiated and separated themselves from citizens of the other classes. By demarcating specific areas as club property and by adopting blanket suit costumes, the professional and commercial middle-class tobogganers were in no danger of having to share their slides with 'the great unwashed'.

Tobogganing extended to women the experience of being indigenized and performing identity. Organized sport was a means by which male gender roles had been defined, enacted, and displayed, and women's exclusion heightened masculinity. Moreover, the scientific discourse that constructed women as frail and physically incapacitated had kept them on the sidelines.[10] But as the Downylip cartoons show, in the last two decades of the century, attitudes toward women's participation in physical activities were changing, and respectable female behaviour in public included a measure of active participation. This was partly in response to fears that the Anglo-Saxon race was in decline in relation to others and that female health needed to be improved and invigorated in order to increase family size. . . .

By all accounts, tobogganing was 'a new sensation' for Americans, especially for young women, who were urged to sample the thrill of tobogganing described in surprisingly eroticized terms. The *Canadian Illustrated News* of 27 January 1883 promised: 'She will experience a sensation—short, sharp and singular—that she will not forget for many a day.' The Montreal *Gazette* of 5 February 1884 described it as 'a soft push, a gentle movement, which grew into a fearful rush then a bump, causing a tighter grip on the rungs, a whirl of fine snow in the face, lights passing in a more rapid succession than telegraph poles on a flying train, faster and faster they go and intenser grows the excitement, gradually the terrific speed slackens and with almost a regretful sigh that the slide was not prolonged, the end is reached.' . . . [T]obogganing presented unique opportunities for intimate chats and body contact that would have been considered scandalous in other circumstances. One commentator explained: 'Young ladies never look so piquant as they do in blanket suits—then hauling the toboggan uphill just gives the opportunity for a confidential chat denied in all formal meeting places. When Florence or Charlotte has to be tightly encircled by the grasp of an admiring pilot, down the glittering descent, the pair feel the mutual dependence and responsibility, which often leads them to courtship in earnest.'[11] . . .

The Roman Catholic bishop of Montreal, Mgr Edouard-Charles Fabre, however, saw this mixing of the sexes on the slopes as morally dangerous and feared women would adopt dissipated masculine habits and tastes. He issued a circular ordering his clergy to discourage tobogganing because it was too violent an exercise for their health and a risk to their virtue.[12] The New York *Sun* had no qualms about the effect of tobogganing on women's health. On the contrary, a writer commented on the natural beauty of Canadian girls, praising their bright red cheeks and flashing eyes as being the product of healthy outdoor exercise rather than a reliance on cosmetics, as seen among their American counterparts.[13] The souvenir booklet for the 1880s Winter Carnivals frequently referred to the healthy, rosy cheeks of young Canadian girls, whose 'faces are ruddy from exercise, and eyes are flashing with healthful excitement. A Canadian belle in white blanket suit, gaily trimmed, and with pale blue tuque jauntily set upon her head, stepping springingly along with mocassined feet is a sight worth going to Canada to see.' The pluck and courage of Canadian girls was also remarked upon: 'Nothing astonishes our winter visitors more than the indifference to danger, and the genuine delight in hard, rough pleasure shown by our Canadian girls.' Canadian ladies displayed much more confidence on the slopes than did American women: 'There is something of a national relish in their demeanour . . ., with the Americans, however, it is different. They peep down the shoot with tremulous emotion.'[14] The stereotype of Canadians as healthy, vigorous lovers of the outdoors could be extended to women at times. It was the female members of the party who got Downylip out of his scrapes, showing again that when an immature male displayed deficient manliness, nationality could overcome the disadvantages of gender. Nevertheless, the toboggans on which visiting women rode were usually commanded by men, who steered either by trailing one foot behind or by using short sticks to guide the sled down the run.[15]

Tobogganing . . . was an Indigenous activity that had been tamed, organized, and made more scientific. The organization of clubs was so central to this project of cultural colonization that tobogganing was hardly thought to have existed before they were formed, and the Native origins and French Canadian usage of toboggans was relegated to a dim and distant, primitive past. What made it especially potent as a cultural performance was that almost anyone (or, at least, anyone from the right social strata) could try tobogganing and find out what made Canadians distinctive.

The Winter Carnivals

The huge task of organizing and running the Winter Carnivals was a testament to the energetic voluntarism of the Montreal professional and commercial classes, even if some were motivated by a soupçon of self-interest. The connection between the sports clubs and local business is indicated by the fact that the first public dinner held at the Windsor Hotel when it was completed in 1876 was sponsored by the Montreal Amateur Athletic Association (MAAA).[16] Five times during the 1880s, a stalwart army of volunteers from a variety of Montreal sports organizations staged these six-day winter festivals, showcasing their city each time to an estimated 50,000 visitors from America, Europe, and elsewhere in Canada. According to Robert D. McGibbon, who was credited with initiating the Winter Carnivals in 1883, their objective was to overcome negative stereotypes of the Canadian climate and 'to make Montreal a winter resort' so that visitors might see for themselves how Canadians could enjoy the winter and appreciate its health-giving benefits.[17] To this end, the week was deliberately designed as a replica of the Montreal winter season. As a writer in the Montreal *Gazette* of 27 January 1883 explained, 'with the exception of the Ice Palace and some other features introduced to enhance the interest of the occasion, the Carnival is in reality only a panorama or general view of the recreations which, to our young and healthy especially, make our Canadian winter a season of delight.'

The five carnivals had very similar programs. With few variations, a typical week included the opportunity for visitors to try their hand at tobogganing on one of the toboggan club slides and to participate in an informal snowshoe tramp. They could watch snowshoe races, hockey matches, curling bonspiels, horse races on the river, and skating competitions. They were invited to attend fancy-dress skating carnivals, musical concerts performed by snowshoe club members, or if they were sufficiently wealthy, a society ball.

There were parades of all kinds of sleighs and horse-drawn vehicles in the streets, nightly fireworks displays, and, the highlight of the week, the attack and defence of the Ice Palace . . ., followed by a torchlight procession of snowshoers.

. . .

The Montreal Winter Carnivals were neither true carnivals nor traditional agrarian French-Canadian festivals, or fetes. Carnivals are popular festivities, occasions for overindulgence in all the fleshly sins. Carnival street parades and festivities are unruly, full of the bizarre and the grotesque, because carnival is a space and time of inversions, where the world is turned upside down and where status and rules are disrupted and undermined.[18] In keeping with British sensibilities, the Winter Carnivals showed little sign of the carnivalesque precisely because of the middle-class organizers' desire to avoid and eliminate disorder and spontaneity.[19] Guests for the fancy-dress ball in 1885 paid a hefty $6 for men and $4 for women to attend and they were *obliged* to wear fancy dress, whose design was 'subject to the approval of Costume Committee'. It was forbidden to wear masks; no 'negro characters' were allowed, except by special permission; there could be no religious orders, imps, or devils, no men dressed as women, and only two snowshoe costumes per club.[20] Thus, to avoid any chance of a breach of decorum, all the traditional elements of inversion and subversion were excluded, as were the popular classes themselves.

More accurately, then, the carnivals were civic festivals staged as tourist attractions to put Montreal on the North American tourist map and stimulate the local economy. Although the pecuniary incentive was downplayed by carnival organizers, who claimed to be inspired by the desire 'to prove that the people of Montreal can be hospitable, without the vulgar object of money-making', there is no doubt that the financial advantages of the carnivals were appreciated.[21] Local workers were employed cutting ice blocks, clearing snow, constructing the ice monuments, putting up flags and bunting, and

so on, but organizers and newspaper reporters commented mostly on the benefits of the carnivals to the railways, hoteliers, merchants, and businessmen.[22] Furriers were particularly busy selling coats, wraps, hats, and gloves to the inadequately clad American visitors. Photographers such as William Notman, a member of the Ice Palace Committee, sold photographs of the Ice Palace and other attractions, as well as souvenir portraits of visitors in 'Canadian' winter costume. Souvenir programs and special carnival numbers printed by local newspapers were another big seller. Souvenir sales generally were boosted by the carnivals, and the designs considered emblematic of Canada show how central indigenous winter sports were to Canadian identity. A jeweller, for example, made up silver brooches, earrings, and pins featuring toboggans, snowshoes, lacrosse sticks, moccasins, and ice palaces.[23] . . . Indian work and curiosities such as moccasins embroidered with colourful porcupine quills were also popular with visitors.[24] Bishop's *Winter Carnival Illustrated* (1884) noted the number of toboggans that had been taken home as mementos, along with the 'toy snowshoes made by the Indians', indicating that local Native groups were taking advantage of the opportunity, too.[25] Visitors generally shared the British tendency to conflate First Nations and French Canadians as primitive exotics. Ruth Phillips contends that British buyers were just as keen to purchase birchbark and moose-hair wares produced by French-Canadian nuns as they were to buy Native souvenirs. They commented 'with as much curiosity on the customs and exotic appearance of the *habitant* farmers as they did on the local Indians'.[26]

There was more to the carnivals, however, than commercialism and civic boosterism. . . . [A] desire to display and confirm identity, both national and class, was clearly evident. . . . Hence there are other questions that need to be asked. Why was it 'natural' that winter sports would be the central feature of the carnivals? How do the events and public spectacles chosen to make up the program fit within the context of the history of such 'invented traditions' in Montreal? The role of performance and the agency of the audience in the construction of meaning should be considered, for to perform is both to do and to show. Furthermore, 'the observation of the deed is an essential part of the doing,' and repetition of the performance is equally essential.[27] Judith Butler points out that 'performativity is . . . not a singular "act" for it is always a reiteration of a norm or set of norms . . . a performative is that discursive practice that enacts or produces that which it names.'[28] The carnivals were not just an expression or reflection of the financial and class interests of the professional and commercial middle classes; the performative nature of the events was itself an agent in the construction and dissemination of Canadian national identity.[29] Members of the audience identified the performers as people like themselves acting as Canadians, which signalled to them how to act Canadian. In emulating this performance of national identity, they became both pedagogical objects and performative subjects. The carnivals took place during a period of international nation-building, when Canada was pursuing a national policy designed to foster domestic manufacturing and markets, thus forging an independent course that would protect Canadian industry from American economic forces and signify independence from Great Britain. The Montreal middle classes that ran the sports clubs, along with the growing class of white-collar clerks, bookkeepers, and salaried employees who made up the bulk of their membership, wanted to establish their identity as members of a civilized, progressive, modern nation that cherished its connection with the British Empire yet had its own identity distinct from Britain and the United States.[30] They wanted to overturn the negative connotations attached to the image of Canada as a snowy northern waste. A writer in the *Canadian Illustrated News* of 27 January 1883 predicted the favourable impression American visitors would receive of Canadians: 'Visitors will learn that our cold climate does not interfere with the warmth of our feelings or the delicacy of our social intercourse. The evidence of wealth and prosperity which they behold on all sides will show our more southern neighbours that snow and ice are no bar in our commercial development or financial progress.'

. . .

The Carnival Program

. . . [The carnivals] were *winter* carnivals because winter and winter sports were the unique signifiers of Canada, employed even as the subject of sculptures modelled in sugar for banquet centrepieces. Snowshoeing and tobogganing were principal events in the carnivals because they were distinctive as national characteristics as well as being novelties that would attract American visitors. Lacrosse, the indigenous *summer* sport, was represented at the 1884 carnival by a match played on ice. It aroused much attention but was not repeated in subsequent years since it was felt the audience had not sufficiently understood the game. No doubt it was included due to its importance as a national signifier, and it should be remembered that many of the snowshoers also played lacrosse. But whereas curling, skating, and sleighing were activities available elsewhere in North America, snowshoeing and tobogganing were specifically Canadian winter sports that had to be experienced in situ.[31] Since the purpose of the carnivals was to overcome unfavourable stereotypes of the Canadian climate by showing visitors how Canadians survived and even enjoyed the winter season, winter sports were the ideal medium.

. . .

Since the Winter Carnivals were designed to represent the winter season in Montreal, and since the majority of the carnival organizers were themselves leading members of the snowshoe clubs, it is not surprising that snowshoe club concerts, tramps, and races, torchlight snowshoe processions, and the 'living arch' were all incorporated into the carnival program. Along with tobogganing, these represented the Indigenous pole of Canadian identity. The British pole was evidenced through the 'civilized' and orderly manner with which the carnivals were conducted and through the numerous references to royalty, which made it clear that Canadians were a special type of British subject. Royal emblems competed for precedence with snowshoes, toboggans, and tuques as ornaments on arches, parade floats, and street decorations as well as at the ice rinks. British flags were flown in the streets alongside the American and Dominion flags; at the Victoria Skating Rink . . . in 1885 a bust of Queen Victoria sculpted in ice took centre place, flanked by ice sculptures of male and female snowshoers. . . . The participation of the governor general and his party at the carnivals was always noted in the press accounts. Lord Lorne was unable to attend the first carnival, but Lord Lansdowne's participation in 1884 as Honorary Patron gained him great popularity. He agreed to accept membership in a new toboggan club named in his honour, and with his wife he officially opened the Lansdowne Toboggan Club slide . . . by taking the ceremonial first run down its slopes. Predictably, both were said to have been greatly amused by the experience. In participating in these Indigenous activities, the royal representatives conferred upon them the royal seal of approval, confirming their respectability and legitimacy.

The Carnival Visitors

. . .

The carnivals were oriented to attract 'others' more than 'us', for the local audience of Montreal citizens was small—one estimate is that only 7.6 per cent of the spectators lining the streets were Montreal citizens—although, of course, they were present in large numbers as participants in the events.[32] Those in the audience were thus a very select group made up only of people who

could afford the time and expense of attending carnival events. Nevertheless, contemporary commentators lavished praise on 'the heartiness of all classes in adopting and urging it [the carnival] to accomplishment and the pride manifested in the assumption of their respective parts'.[33] It is doubtful that members of the working classes felt this way. To be sure, the carnivals provided an opportunity for temporary work during the winter period when work was scarce. Workers certainly assumed 'their respective parts': male labourers were employed in preparing the streets and the ice monuments . . ., while women worked in the kitchens and sculleries of Montreal homes and hotels, cooking, sewing, and cleaning for thousands of visitors. However, the wealthy danced or skated in extravagant costumes worth more than an unskilled female worker could earn in a year, so the cost of participating in most of the carnival events was quite beyond the means of the popular classes.[34] . . . Only the fireworks displays and street parades were totally free and did not require special equipment or clothing; but even they took place during the working day or in the central areas of the city where few of the poorer classes lived.[35] In fact, workers were actively discouraged from attending events. Admission tickets to events such as the Native Concert in 1884 were deliberately kept high to ensure that 'the rowdy element known as "the gods"' would not disrupt the sensibilities of their social betters.[36] The toboggan club slides were free to visitors, but Montreal citizens had to be members, at a cost of $2–$4 for a man or $5 for a family.[37] Even the lower ranks of the professional and commercial middle classes had difficulty participating because they had to be at work during the day, except on the half-day public holiday declared by the mayor of Montreal each year. In 1884 a hockey match scheduled for four o'clock on Friday afternoon had to be called off because the bank clerks who made up one of the teams were not let off work on time.[38]

The local audience for the Winter Carnivals was therefore drawn largely from the same social strata as the participants and organizers, and this excluded the majority of Montreal's citizens. On the other end of the scale, it was only the upper echelon members of the sports clubs who could afford to attend the society events, and even so, very few of them appear in the guest lists for the Grand Ball of each carnival. . . . Thus the carnivals were not popular festivals but events where social classes were clearly differentiated. . . . In Montreal's case the local and visiting audiences were drawn from precisely the same sector of society that was on show. Their active participation in tobogganing, snowshoeing, and other carnival events authorized and legitimized the particular vision of Canadian national identity with which they were presented.

Responses to the Carnivals

. . .

. . . [A]lthough there was much enthusiasm for tobogganing as a thrilling and characteristically Canadian activity, it was *organized* tobogganing the promoters had in mind. Spontaneous tobogganing on city streets was frowned upon now that the clubs had built artificial slopes, and a commentator in the *Gazette* of 28 January 1885 complained about the lack of 'respect for the rights of pedestrians' by 'young men . . . pushing through the crowd dragging their toboggans behind them with such carelessness that other people were injured'. He continued: 'If they have not sense enough to take the roadway when the sidewalks are crowded the police ought to compel them to do so.' Here is illustrated the struggle for control of behaviour on the streets of industrial cities. The expectation was that the respectable tobogganer belonged to a toboggan club and stored his sled in the clubhouse rather than bringing it with him each time. Furthermore, the writer assumes a certain set of rules about proper behaviour in crowds, where communal order should prevail over aggressive individualism. A similar complaint about the 'breach of ordinary respect for the liberty of the pedestrian' was made

against the owner of the Snowshoe Cafe, who had hosed down his fabric awning to make an ice grotto. Although the restaurant was praised for its *interior* decorations, the owner was criticized for forcing pedestrians off the sidewalk.[39] Occasionally, members of the poorer classes attempted to resist middle-class control. In 1885 one of the snowshoe clubs held a Music Festival at the Drill Hall . . ., on the way to which 'a crowd of roughs amused themselves by tripping up the snowshoers as they marched past.' At the Drill Hall some 'thought to force an entrance without paying and policemen were obliged to use their batons to enforce good behaviour from the rowdies'. Middle-class sentiments were offended, not least because some ladies were 'badly bruised in the crush at the door'.[40] The lack of lenience given to these offenders illustrates the class hierarchy operating in Montreal.

It was not unusual for behaviour that was castigated and punishable in one class to be condoned in another. Six American visitors 'created a sensation' in St James Street by hiring a sleigh and a hurdy-gurdy grinder to supply music while they toured the streets, smoking cigars and stopping frequently for 'refreshments'. Although the court recorder had announced publicly that drunkenness and disorder would be dealt with very severely during the carnival to uphold the honour and reputation of the city, these men were indulged because of their class and nationality. Instead of being punished by the usual fine of $5 or 15 days imprisonment for drunkenness, or being the brunt of disapproving remarks in the newspaper, 'the steady going wayfarers [on St James Street] laughed heartily at their jovial eccentricities.'[41] Their deviant behaviour was not exactly condoned, but it was interpreted as harmless eccentricity rather than disorder. . . .

Ethnic Rifts

The predominantly middle-class, English-speaking, Protestant, Anglo-Saxon/Celtic organizers of the Winter Carnivals assumed that the version of Canadian identity they projected through the events was one that united both English- and French-speaking Canadians as members of Northern races. . . . However, analysis of some of the carnival events shows that significant social and ethnic divisions were discernible in 1885. Generally speaking, the area east of St Laurent Boulevard was predominantly francophone; and the area to the west was predominantly anglophone. However, this was not an absolute division. There were also mixed areas, and many French Canadians lived in the west of the city below Bonaventure Street. Moreover, within the anglophone group there were significant ethnic divisions between Anglo-Protestants and Irish Catholics.[42] But, although the social geography of the city was not in reality neatly divided along linguistic lines between francophone/east and anglophone/west, it was clearly perceived that way by carnival organizers. In 1885, the East End Committee was formed to organize a series of events in the area east of St Laurent since in previous years French-Canadian businessmen had complained that none of the carnival events had taken place in 'their' area.[43] These attractions were designed to mirror those planned for the West End. . . . Analysis and comparison of these events show that two opposing narratives of nation were being created; the French-Canadian concept of Canadian identity was quite different from that promulgated by the English-speaking inhabitants of Montreal and was rooted in a different version of Canadian history.

French Canadians were proud of their long history in Canada and their rural roots, but the romanticized version of Old Quebec being propagated by writers such as Philippe-Joseph Aubert de Gaspé and historian Francis Parkman did not accord with the modern, progressive image British colonists wanted to portray.[44] . . . The anglophone carnival organizers sought to show that French Canadians had been elevated by giving them 'our English character' and that now Montreal society was characterized by its modern

progress, civility, respectability, and social order. In the literary supplement to the *Montreal Daily Star*'s carnival number of 1885, S.E. Dawson reviewed the changes that had 'transformed into a commercial city of the most modern type the quaint medieval town which in 1760 surrendered to the arms of Great Britain'. This was not, he claimed, change caused by growth in size or wealth but more 'a transformation of character'. Practical common sense, commercial enterprise, improved urban planning, political awareness, and scientific know-how were all improvements that he believed had been brought to Montreal by the British.[45] . . . To propagate this modern image, anglophone organizers would sanction the inclusion of an activity like snowshoeing or tobogganing that was historically primitive but only if its present-day execution was civilized and orderly.

The desire to present an impressive and orderly spectacle is particularly evident in the organization of the Tandem Club sleigh parade. Saturday afternoon sleigh promenades were a feature of the Montreal season, an opportunity for the fashionable and wealthy members of the club to show off their magnificent 'winter equipages', 'good horses', 'rich robes and furs', and the 'incomparable designs' of their vehicles on Beaver Hall and St James Streets.[46] Some of the wealthiest families in the city were represented in the exclusive Tandem Club, and the ordering of the parade indicates the importance attached to social hierarchy and status.[47] In the 1883 and 1884 parades there had been some dissatisfaction because the elegant sleighs of the rich, drawn by four or more horses, had been mixed in with humble dog carts, and carters carrying paying customers had nudged their way into the procession. The 1884 parade had been very long, and the congested streets caused gaps to develop in the procession. Organizers in 1885 were anxious to prevent this from occurring again.

An elaborate plan was drawn up for the 1885 Grand Sleigh Parade in an attempt to overcome these faults. No cab sleighs or single-horse sleighs were to be allowed unless 'specifically designed as a characteristic feature of the Carnival'.[48] The parade was to be carefully sorted out in descending rank, from Mr Andrew Allan's 'dashing six-in-hand' complete with postillion riders, followed by the four-in-hands, several floats sponsored by snowshoe clubs . . . and so on down to the comical habitant sleigh of Mr Henry Judah, whose passenger was a man dressed as 'a good imitation of ancient rural femininity'.[49] . . . According to the *Montreal Daily Star* of 29 January 1885, 'the various arrangements were followed to the letter, a distance of over ten paces being maintained between each sleigh,' but perhaps the parade was a little less orderly than the organizers had planned because the next day a Montreal *Gazette* reporter praised the 'co-mingling of all manners and conditions' as being 'typical of everything in our flourishing Dominion'.

The Farmers' Drive, organized by the East End Committee in 1885, was planned with a different objective. The interpretation presented by the francophone press was that the display would give visitors 'an exact idea of our old customs and the lives of our fathers' and would mix the social orders rather than separating them out.[50] This was far more in keeping with French-Canadian traditions and was the first time that Montreal had had the appearance of carnaval, claimed a *La Presse* writer, who saw the Farmers' Drive as completely eclipsing the Tandem Club Drive. The random rather than ordered mixture of sleighs carrying entire farming families side by side with elegant tandems bearing passengers in rich fur coats, participants in bizarre costumes, and an antique covered wagon dating from 1824 driven by 'un vrai "habitant"' reportedly delighted the crowd. The presence of women in this parade was unique, being acceptable only because they were in the company of their husbands and children. Thus their presence was historical and allegorical.[51] The Quebec branch of Le Canadien Snow Shoe Club (one of the few specifically francophone clubs) also

drew attention to the history of French Canada by entering a float with an ancient canoe that had been used to carry mail from Quebec City to Point Levis for 40 years. French Canadians thereby sought to root their separate identity in remembering pre-Conquest New France as a golden age—a tactic also used at the time by the Roman Catholic Church, which sought to stem the exodus of its flock to industrial cities in the United States by advocating a return to the land and traditional rural way of life. The ultramontane clergy promoted colonization of the provincial hinterland through urging the Quebec government to provide land subsidies and to build roads and railways into the backwoods in order to guarantee the survival of French Canada and thereby strengthen church control.[52]

The English-speaking press had a different interpretation of the Farmers' Drive. British colonists wanted to take on the French-Canadian reputation for being a hospitable, fun-loving people but at the same time to emphasize the positive and transformative effects of the British Conquest.[53] Consequently, a Montreal *Gazette* report of 31 January disparaged the size of the Farmers' Drive parade as being 'not of the magnitude which the promoters might hope to see'. He added patronizingly that the 'luxury and variety portrayed in the grand [Tandem] drive of Thursday were absent of course'. A *Montreal Daily Star* report of the day before agreed that the turnout was much smaller than anticipated and noted that the drive got going only 'after numerous trifling delays'. Although the leading sleigh was drawn by 'six strong well-bred and well-fed farm horses', which were fine animals, they may not have 'matched exactly the graceful symmetry and slender outline which would have delighted the eye' of a British horse expert. Instead of interpreting the antique vehicles as reminders of the history of French Canada, the writer saw them as an indication of how improved farm transportation had become due to British influence. Similarly, ever mindful of the need to encourage immigration, he claimed that visitors must have been 'much impressed with the fine physique and fine turnout of the *habitants*', proof of the 'thriving condition' of agriculture under British rule.[54] Since habitants were said to be 'essentially an agricultural race, contented with things as they are', they had needed British know-how and initiative to bring them into the modern world.[55]

. . .

By visually contrasting themselves with the British . . ., the French-Canadian clubs contested the version of Canadian national identity the other clubs had proposed. Although visitors might have gained the impression that the races lived in harmony in Montreal, which was certainly the message carnival organizers sought to convey, this unity was an illusion. When carnival week was over, the organizers of the East and West End Committees held a dinner to celebrate the success of the carnival and toasted 'l'union la plus parfaite' that had never ceased to exist between them. Not everyone agreed. In reviewing the carnival, a writer in *La Presse* itemized numerous problems that had occurred in its organization and execution. He blamed these on the decision to organize events in the East and West Ends separately, which had led to a proliferation of attractions and competition for the audience. He recommended that there be a rest for a year or two so that Montreal could mend its rifts and do better next time.[56] For subsequent carnivals, the organization of events in the West and East Ends was combined under the control of the central Executive Committee—tacit recognition that the membership was in reality far from united, making separate activities too divisive an undertaking. Indeed, in 1887 a separate Board of Trade was formed by French-Canadian merchants to better promote their interests.[57] By 1889 the increasing cost of the carnival, the reluctance of the railways and hotels to provide financing, the difficulty of coming up with something new each year, and, most important, fatigue and infighting between the snowshoe clubs contributed to the demise of the carnivals.[58]

The End of an Era

For British colonists, the carnivals were the culmination of decades of inventing traditions built around interaction with the Canadian climate and landscape through participating in indigenous winter sports. Snowshoeing and tobogganing were opportunities to embody, perform, and display a 'native Canadian' identity that constructed Canadians as a special kind of British subject, different from both Britons and Americans. They were activities whose Aboriginal and French-Canadian associations had been overlaid with the British ideology of order and discipline. To a great extent, the carnival spectacles relied on an appropriated history of Canada that re-created both the stereotype of the jolly hospitality remarked upon by early British visitors to their new colony and the romanticized version of Old Quebec promoted in contemporary history, literature, and painting. But these historical and primitive associations had been 'improved' and made more modern and scientific by the application of rules and regulations and by the use of new materials and technologies. The Canadians referred to in the 1880s were generally English-speaking. They were also middle-class, Anglo-Saxon, Protestant, and predominantly male.

The carnivals were successful in disseminating to European and American visitors the 'native Canadian' identity constructed by the sports clubs. These visitors learned to recognize organized winter sports as distinctively Canadian. This identity gave the professional and commercial middle classes a consciousness of kind, but it ultimately failed to bring together diverse Canadians under one national rubric. Whereas the subversive and unruly aspects of carnivals and festivals are usually considered social safety valves that allow antagonisms to dissipate, the Montreal Winter Carnivals highlighted and entrenched social and ethnic divisions in the city. There was space for the wealthy elite to participate in the carnivals, but there was no place for the working poor, except as labourers. . . . The working classes were not invited to join in the enactment of national identity or even solicited as spectators who might approve of and emulate this dramatization of what it was to be 'native Canadian'. The increasing distance between the growing numbers of the 'middling sorts'—self-employed professionals or salaried and non-manual employees—and manual labourers who worked for daily wages was thereby evidenced on the streets of the city.[59] Women were no longer just spectators but could now participate in prescribed ways and were considered an asset to Canadian identity, but this was only true for women of the middle classes. Likewise, there was room for French-Canadian participation but not if it displayed a rival version of Canadian identity. In sum, the snowshoe clubs had invented traditions that spoke to their own class and to a similar class of foreign visitors, but these were used to exclude rather than include the lower classes and other ethnic and religious groups. The effect of this went both ways because, in excluding others, the middle classes felt a greater consciousness of kind. This was entirely consistent with the liberal model, which excluded these 'others' 'from the burdens and responsibility of full individuality', including enfranchisement.[60]

. . .

Notes

1. The 1886 carnival was cancelled due to the smallpox epidemic that raged in Montreal over the winter of 1885–6. The 1888 carnival was cancelled due to poor organization and lack of subscriptions.

2. Eva Mackey, *The House of Difference: Cultural Politics and National Identity in Canada* (Toronto: University of Toronto Press, 2002), 49.

3. The history of tobogganing in the French Regime and the derivation of toboggans, sleighs, and carioles is described by Jean-Paul Massicotte and Claude Lessard, 'La chasse en Nouvelle-France au XVIIe Siècle', *Canadian Journal of History of Sport and Physical Education* 5, 2 (1974): 18–30.

4. *Canadian Illustrated News*, carnival number and supplement, 27 Jan. 1883, 5, quoted by Peter L. Lindsay, 'A History of Sport in Canada, 1807–1867' (PhD diss., University of Alberta, Edmonton, 1969), 72–3.

5. Ed Ruthven, *The Week* (Toronto), 7 Feb. 1884, 158.

6. Ibid., 153–4.

7. Agnes Macdonald, 'On a Tobogan', *Murray's Magazine* (London) 3 (Jan.–June 1888): 78.

8. *Montreal Daily Star*, carnival number, 20 Jan. 1885, 2.

9. Samuel Edward Dawson, *Montreal Winter Carnival, February 4th to 9th, 1884*, supplement to Dawson's handbook for the City of Montreal ([Montreal]: Montreal Gazette Printing, [1884]), 15–18. Buses left the McGill Gates on Saturday afternoons and moonlight evenings during the winter months.

10. Patricia Vertinsky, *The Eternally Wounded Woman: Women, Doctors and Exercise in the Late Nineteenth Century* (Manchester, UK: Manchester University Press, 1990); Carroll Smith-Rosenberg and Charles Rosenberg, 'The Female Animal: Medical and Biological Views of Women and Their Role in Nineteenth-Century America', in J.A. Mangan and Roberta J. Park, eds, *From 'Fair Sex' to Feminism: Sport and the Socialization of Women in the Industrial and Post-Industrial Eras* (London: Frank Cass, 1987), 83.

11. *The Week* (Toronto), 15 Jan. 1885, 103. . . .

12. Sylvie Dufresne, 'Le Carnaval d'hiver de Montréal (1883–1889)' (MA thesis, Université du Québec à Montréal, 1980), 133.

13. Montreal *Gazette*, 27 Jan. 1883.

14. Dawson, *Montreal Winter Carnival*, 4; William G. Beers, *Over the Snow, or The Montreal Carnival* (Montreal: W. Drysdale and J. Tho. Robinson, 1883), 40; *Montreal Daily Star*, 6 Feb. 1884.

15. Macdonald, 'On a Tobogan', 84–5, explains the dangers and difficulties of steering.

16. Robert Rumilly, *Histoire de Montréal*, vol. 3 (Montreal: Fides, 1972), 91.

17. Montreal *Gazette*, 26 Jan. 1883, 8; 'The Origin of the Montreal Carnivals', *Montreal Daily Star*, 5 Feb. 1884.

18. Victor Turner, *Dramas, Fields, and Metaphors: Symbolic Action in Human Society* (Ithaca: Cornell University Press, 1974), describes carnaval as a liminal space where the normal rules of society no longer apply. The seminal description of the subversive power of carnival and the carnivalesque is Mikhail Bakhtin, *Rabelais and His World*, trans. Hélène Iswolsky (Bloomington: Indiana University Press, 1984). The American carnival tradition and its connection to French Canada are traced by Samuel Kinser, *Carnival, American Style: Mardi Gras at New Orleans and Mobile* (Chicago: University of Chicago Press, 1990), ch. 2. For a description of French-Canadian festivals, see Raymond Montpetit, *Le temps des fêtes au Québec* (Montreal: Éditions de l'homme, 1978), 169.

19. I cannot agree with Don Morrow's claim in 'Frozen Festivals: Ceremony and the *Carnaval* in the Montreal Winter Carnivals, 1883–1889' (*Sport History Review* 27,

2 [1996]: 188), that the 'carnivals were hollow dramas of Montreal sporting myths and activities that reflected, at various times, the essence of the spirit of carnival.' The Montreal sporting myths and activities were far from hollow dramas; they were cultural performances full of meanings for participants and spectators—meanings about identity and nation, not about 'carnival'.

20. Montreal *Gazette*, 24 Jan. 1885, 4.

21. Montreal *Gazette*, 7 Feb. 1884, 4.

22. This view was expressed in the Montreal *Gazette*, 26 Jan. 1883, 8; *La Presse*, 24 Jan. 1885 (*dernière*); and *La Minerve*, 28 Jan. 1885.

23. Montreal *Gazette*, 27 Jan. 1885, 5; 'Cochenthaler's Great Carnival Pin' and 'Snowshoe and Toboggan Jewellery', *Montreal Daily Star*, 31 Jan. 1884. . . .

24. Montreal *Gazette*, 24 Jan. 1883: 'The Indian curiosity store did a rising business yesterday.' Several advertisements for Indian work and curiosities appeared in *Souvenir of the Montreal Winter Carnival of 1884*. Macdonald, 'On a Tobogan', 84, remarks on the 'daintily embroidered' caribou- or moose-hide moccasins worn by the ladies.

25. *The Winter Carnival Illustrated, or Bishop's Carnival Illustrated* (Montreal: George Bishop, February 1884), 10.

26. Ruth B. Phillips, 'Nuns, Ladies, and the "Queen of the Huron": Appropriating the Savage in Nineteenth-Century Huron Tourist Art', in Ruth B. Phillips and Christopher B. Steiner, eds, *Unpacking Culture: Art and Commodity in Colonial and Postcolonial Worlds* (Berkeley: University of California Press, 1999), 37.

27. Tom F. Driver, *The Magic of Ritual: Our Need for Liberating Rites That Transform Our Lives and Our Communities* (San Francisco: Harper, 1991), 80–1.

28. Judith Butler, *Bodies That Matter: On the Discursive Limits of "Sex"* (New York: Routledge, 1993), 12–13.

29. The literature on the productive versus reflective work of fairs and exhibitions is reviewed by Keith Walden, *Becoming Modern in Toronto: The Industrial Exhibition and the Shaping of a Late Victorian Culture* (Toronto: University of Toronto Press, 1997), xiii–xiv.

30. Key organizers from the Montreal Snow Shoe Club included R.D. McGibbon, a lawyer; Hugh Graham, editor of the *Montreal Daily Star*; G.W. Beers, a dentist; and G.R. Starke, secretary of Dominion Transport. The St George's Snow Shoe Club was represented by S. Howard, an engineer; W.L. Mathews, manager of Dorion and Wright; and F.C. Henshaw, vice-consul for South America. The Argyle Snow Shoe Club was represented by C. Torrance, an entrepreneur. Other organizers included T. Brown, manager of Goodyear Rubber, who belonged to the Montreal Curling Club; C.P. Davidson, a lawyer, who was from the Victoria Skating Club; and A.W. Stevenson, an accountant, who came from the Montreal Amateur Athletic Association.

List compiled from Dufresne, 'Le Carnaval' (1980), 114 and Appendix 5.

31. The importance of curling as a carnival event declined rapidly each year. It was one of the major features of the first carnival but by 1885 was a minor event. . . .

32. Dufresne, 'Le Carnaval' (1980), 60–5. Figures for crowds were estimated by reporters and varied wildly; hence this is only an approximate figure. However, it does serve to highlight the very exclusive nature of the carnivals.

33. Montreal *Gazette*, 27 Jan. 1883, 4.

34. *Montreal Daily Star*, 24 Jan. 1885, reported that the cost of one fancy-dress costume for the ball was $250. . . .

35. Dufresne, 'Le Carnaval' (1980), 35–6.

36. Montreal *Gazette*, 6 Feb. 1884, 8.

37. *Montreal Daily Star*, 5 Feb. 1887, cited by Dufresne, 'Le Carnaval' (1980), 83.

38. Montreal *Gazette*, 9 Feb. 1884, 5. . . .

39. Montreal *Gazette*, 27 Jan. 1885, 5.

40. Montreal *Gazette*, 30 Jan. 1885, 5.

41. Montreal *Gazette*, 27 Jan. 1885, 5.

42. The ethnic makeup of the city can be shown by plotting the ethnicity of residents using Montréal l'avenir du passé (MAP), a digital database project compiled by Robert Sweeny, Sherry Olson, and Patricia Thornton. Database sources include: City of Montreal taxrolls, 1880; Lisa Dillon, the 1881 Canadian Census Project; the North Atlantic Population Project; and the Minnesota Population Center. Preliminary Version 13-MAY-2003 [computer file]. Montreal, QC: Département de Démographie, Université de Montréal [distributor].

43. *La Presse*, 28 Jan. 1885 (extra).

44. Francis Parkman's five-volume history, *France and England in North America*, was published between 1865 and 1892, and according to *The Week* (Toronto), 22 Jan. 1885, 136, he was becoming more popular each year as the historian of French Canada. Aubert de Gaspé's *Anciens Canadiens* was published in 1863 and quickly translated into English by Georgiana M. Penée and published in New York and Boston as *The Canadians of Old*. See Maurice Lemire and Denis Saint-Jacques, eds, *La Vie littéraire au Québec: "Un peuple sans histoire ni littérature"* vol. 3, *1840–1869* (Sainte-Foy, QC: Presses de l'Université Laval, 1990), 406–18.

45. Similar sentiments were expressed in a series of three articles published in the *Montreal Daily Star*, 5 Feb. 1884 . . .

46. *Canadian Illustrated News*, carnival number, 27 Jan. 1883, 50.

47. Susan Davis argues that parades are not just reflections of society but also public enactments patterned by and patterning social forces. Celebrations therefore shape the power relations in the city, although they are a selective version of local social relationships that

do not represent all communities; see her *Parades and Power: Street Theatre in Nineteenth Century Philadelphia* (Philadelphia: Temple University Press, 1986). . . .

48. Montreal *Gazette*, 24 Jan. 1885, 5.

49. Montreal *Gazette*, 30 Jan. 1885, 5. This was a rare example of the carnivalesque. . . .

50. *La Presse*, 24 Jan. 1885 (*dernière*).

51. *La Presse*, 31 Jan. 1885; Bonnie Huskins, 'The Ceremonial Space of Women: Public Processions in Victorian Saint John and Halifax', in Janet V. Guildford and Suzanne R. Morton, eds, *Separate Spheres: Women's World in the 19th-Century Maritimes* (Fredericton, NB: Acadiensis Press, 1994). . . .

52. French-Canadian attempts to promote nationalism emphasized rootedness in the land, shared language, faith, and laws. . . .

53. A similar argument is made by Daniel Francis, *National Dreams, Myth, Memory, and Canadian History* (Vancouver: Arsenal Pulp Press, 1997), 98. . . .

54. E.A. Heaman, 'Constructing Ignorance', working paper presented to the Canadian Historical Association, May 2003, argues that French Canadians, particularly habitant farmers, were increasingly construed as ignorant and backward by the British after 1760. . . .

55. A.M. Pope, 'French Canada and Its People', *Catholic World* 33, 197 (Aug. 1881): 702.

56. 'Le Carnaval', *La Presse*, 2 Feb. 1885. The English press had been particularly critical of delays; see, for example, 'Inauguration of the Condora', and 'The Tandem Drive', *Montreal Daily Star*, 30 Jan. 1885. Dufresne, 'Le Carnaval' (1980), 158–9, describes a number of conflicts between the two committees.

57. Paul-André Linteau, *Histoire de Montreal depuis la Confédération*, 2nd edn (Montreal: Boréal Express, 2000), 51.

58. Dufresne, 'Le Carnaval' (1980), 222–4.

59. Stuart M. Blumin makes this argument in *The Emergence of the Middle Class: Social Experience in the American City, 1760–1900* (Cambridge, UK: Cambridge University Press, 1989).

60. Ian McKay, 'The Liberal Order Framework: A Prospectus for a Reconnaissance of Canadian History', *Canadian Historical Review* 81, 4 (Dec. 2000): 626. McKay adds that although Catholics could not be excluded from the vote or political power, there was still 'a perceived tension between the demands of their faith and the claims of liberal individualism: they were, at least until the 1870s, in a sense probationary liberals' (625).

Borderlands, Baselines, and Big Game: Conceptualizing the Northeast as a Sporting Region

—— **Colin D. Howell** ——

Borderlands, baseball, and big game! Bluenose sailors, Boston Marathoners, Bobby Gimby, and the Bangor Mall! Other than alliteration, what unites these diffuse examples of northeastern popular culture, from sport to song to shopping expeditions? What might discussion of their interconnectedness offer us beyond a foray into postmodernist eccentricity or unfettered speculation? This study, part of an ongoing project on sporting culture along the Mexican- and Canadian-American borders over the past century, places borderland sporting life, in all its quirkiness, ambiguity, *and* significance, at the centre of historical inquiry rather than at the periphery.

Interest in borderlands studies as a way of inquiring into questions of power, conflict, identity, and cultural formation has grown significantly over the past decade. Along with the process of globalization the growth of ethnic nationalisms, the seeming fragility and impermanence of existing nation states, and the increasing mobility of peoples, ideas, and capital—the new interest in border relationships reveals a growing fascination with questions of cultural identity (or identities) and issues of national integrity.[1] Nations themselves, we are now told, are invented, imagined communities[2] that have the possibility of being reconceptualized quite differently from the way they are now perceived. The very meaning of borders in both the past and the present is now an issue of considerable controversy. According to W.H. New in

Borderlands: How We Talk About Canada, borders are metaphorical constructions, and borderlands are 'symptomatic of the contemporary condition, a condition of "interstititality", *in-betweenness*, an experiential territory of intervention and revision'.[3] But borders nonetheless distinguish one community from another. One need only think of the recent discourse over the treatment of suspected terrorists to know that borders carry powerful images of identity and differentiation. Borders, then, unite and divide—often at the very same moment.

In a recent article entitled 'How Canadian Historians Stopped Worrying and Learned to Love the Americans!', Phil Buckner has warned against accepting a notion that borders are 'artificial' impediments to closer and more 'natural' relations with friendly neighbours.[4] Buckner's argument is a useful counterweight to the attitude of those who would ignore differences in institutional arrangements, social and economic policies, and cultural values that derived from the experience of border making, but his blanket critique of borderlands historiography nonetheless obscures the complex and often ambiguous history of transnational interactions between America and her neighbours to both the north and south. This is especially the case with respect to social and cultural production. In fact, as becomes apparent with respect to sporting life, it is possible to write the history of borderlands interactions and yet maintain one's

Colin Howell, 'Borderlands, Baselines, and Big Game: Conceptualizing the Northeast as a Sporting Region', in Stephen J. Hornsby and John G. Reid, eds, *New England and the Maritime Provinces: Connections and Comparisons* (Montreal: McGill-Queen's University Press, 2005), pp. 264–79. Reprinted by permission of the publisher.

distance from the contemporary continentalist or global capitalist agenda.

A useful starting point for any discussion of sport in hinterland or borderland regions is the recent literature that has developed around the process of ludic diffusion, or the diffusion of sport. Several sport historians and sociologists have suggested that sporting culture radiates from the more developed nations outward to the rest of the world, and enters host cultures at the elite level, before descending through the social order and eventually reaching the working class and common people.[5] But a top-down approach to the development of popular culture often overlooks the complexity of the process of cultural formation and the lived social, cultural, and economic experience of local communities or hinterland regions, where history is made 'on the ground'. Of course, these contrasting orientations need not be mutually exclusive. The significance of the history of peoples on the margins and their cultural creativity—their agency, if you like—is that they can be seen as neither dependent upon nor independent of their relationship to the nation or the metropolis. This is particularly evident from a study of the barnstorming baseballists, big-game hunters, Bluenose sailors, and Boston Marathoners of the interwar years. Baseball, hunting, competitive international schooner races, and Maritime involvement with the Boston Marathon were essential components of the interwar conceptualization of the northeast as a transnational sporting region.

Of course, this imagined sporting community was not the only manifestation of the metropolitan influence over the Maritime provinces that Boston had exerted prior to this period—and would continue to exert more than 60 years after Confederation. Nor did it displace the presence and expression of other allegiances, particularly to Canada, in the sporting culture of the Maritimes. It does appear, however, that the assumption about a transnational northeastern sporting region was the *dominant* construction of the interwar years. The later emergence of nationalist

discourses in the 1960s, including Bobby Gimby's musical testimony to Canadian Confederation and the patterns of consumption that encouraged the development of the Bangor Mall, however, undermined such earlier configurations of sporting life in the northeastern borderlands and created new forms of cultural interaction between the Maritimes and New England.

Barnstormers

In 1936, just a year after his retirement from baseball, Babe Ruth climbed aboard the SS *Atlantic* in Portland, Maine, for a vacation trip to Nova Scotia. After arriving in Yarmouth, Ruth spent a few days in the southwestern part of the province in the company of friends and playing golf at the Digby Pines golf course. He then drove through the Annapolis Valley to Halifax before travelling to Westville in Pictou County to give a hitting exhibition. Although many Nova Scotians still recall this visit—and a second one in 1942 when Ruth helped open the new Navy recreation centre in Halifax—Ruth's connection to the Maritimes was more than simply incidental.

Born in Baltimore in 1895, Ruth had grown up along the city's rough-and-tumble waterfront where his parents ran a saloon catering to longshoremen, merchant sailors, roustabouts, and waterfront drifters. Considered an 'incorrigible youth', Ruth was consigned for most of his childhood after the age of seven to the Saint Mary's Industrial School for boys, a reform school run by the Xaverian Brothers religious order. The brothers had a lasting influence on Ruth. 'It was at St. Mary's,' Ruth wrote in his autobiography, 'that I met and learned to love the greatest man I've ever known . . . Brother Matthias of the Xaverian order.' Brother Matthias was born Martin Leo Boutilier in Lingan, Cape Breton, the son of a mining engineer with extensive family connections around the Bras D'Or Lakes. He and his older brother had both grown up playing pick-up baseball before entering the Xaverian brotherhood and following many of their Maritime compatriots before World War I down the road to the 'Boston States'. Indeed, a number of Ruth's major league colleagues had family in the Maritimes, among them two future Hall-of-Famers: Harry Hooper, whose father was a Prince Edward Island ship's captain, and Harold 'Pie' Traynor, whose father, Jimmy, had lived in Halifax before moving to Framingham, Massachusetts. Then, too, there was John Phalen 'Stuffy' MacInnes of Gloucester, a member of the Philadelphia Athletics' famed 'hundred-thousand-dollar infield', whose family had roots in Cape Breton, and who, after his playing days were over, returned briefly to coach semi-pro baseball in Nova Scotia. And finally, Ruth's first wife, Helen Woodford, whom he met in South Boston, had grown up in Nova Scotia and joined her family in the southward exodus from the Maritimes to Boston.[6]

Of course, given the demands of travel associated with a major league schedule, Ruth had little opportunity for summer visits to the province— in fact for summer vacations of any sort—during his 20-year career as a major league player. Had he not retired from baseball early in the 1935 season after a disappointing 28-game stint with the Boston Braves, however, he would no doubt have come to Nova Scotia with the Braves when they visited the province later that summer to play the Maritime champion, Yarmouth Gateways. A midseason junket to the Maritimes by a major league team would be incomprehensible today, but in the interwar years this was part of a broad tradition of itinerant baseball barnstorming that drew the northeast together as a sporting region, a tradition that endured until the 1950s. Both of Boston's major league clubs, the Braves and the Red Sox, regarded northern New England and the Maritimes as their hinterland and asserted that claim through numerous tours of the region and in their promotional materials. Most of these visits took place at season's end, but in 1935 the Braves came north to St Stephen, New Brunswick, in the middle of their summer schedule with the express purpose of challenging the

Maritime champion, and they followed up with a visit to Yarmouth to play the new champions the following summer.

Baseball connections between the Maritimes and New England were nothing new, however. As early as the 1870s, teams and players from the northeast were regular summer visitors to the Maritimes, and by the end of that decade imported professionals were beginning to show up in semi-pro lineups in Halifax, Moncton, Saint John, and Fredericton. Before 1900, travelling teams from Boston and nearby towns such as Haverford, Dorchester, and Lowell, as well as from Portland, Augusta, and Bangor in Maine, had helped create a shared baseball culture within which the border played a rather insignificant role. Various semi-professional leagues such as the Maine–New Brunswick League also spanned the border. In 1912, for example, the Saint John Marathons (winners of the Maine–New Brunswick league pennant) played a three-game series against the champion Lowell club of the New England League in what amounted to the minor league baseball championship of the Maritimes and New England.

After the war, New England teams flooded the region. In addition to the Braves and Red Sox, Eddie Carr's Auburn Club from Cambridge, Massachusetts, which the *Boston Post* dubbed the 'fastest amateur team around Boston', Bob Bigney's South Boston All-Stars, Dick Casey's Neponsett All-Stars, the James A. Roche team of Everett, Massachusetts, Frank Silva's Connecticut Yankees, and touring teams from Arlington, Dorchester, Quincy, Newburyport, Somerville, Malden, Salem, Taunton, and Attleboro would turn Maritime ball diamonds into 'burned over districts' of New England baseball barnstorming. They were joined, moreover, by various assemblages of African-American ballplayers from the so-called Negro leagues. As Chappie Johnson's Travelling All-Stars, the Philadelphia Colored Giants, the New York Black Yankees, the Ethiopian Clowns, and the Zulu Cannibal Giants barnstormed the province, they gave Maritime fans the opportunity to see leading stars of the Negro leagues, such as Bill Jackman and others, playing against their own clubs. Without question the most popular of these teams was Burlin White's Boston Royal Giants, who mixed straight baseball with clownish routines. These routines, or reams as they were called, demonstrated their baseball skills and dramatized their 'otherness' as a way of attracting fans to the park. The Giants returned to the Maritimes year after year during the thirties, playing over 300 games against predominantly white local teams. Despite the carnivalesque nature of these tours, which often involved the Giants mocking their white opponents, baseball fans in the Maritimes responded warmly to the Giants, and in the process contributed to an idealized image of the northeast as a region with a shared sporting identity that transcended both the border and the racial divide.[7]

This romanticized transnationalism, of course, stood in contrast to the discourses of betrayal and regional neglect that surrounded the place of the Maritimes within Confederation, and which had been given political expression in the Maritime Rights movement.[8] Indeed, the language of regionalism within Canada and linkages with New England resonated throughout the interwar years in the sporting pages of Maritime newspapers. In addition to the constant coverage of the baseball connection with New England, what is particularly striking is the absence of teams from the rest of Canada from Maritime baseball diamonds in these years. Indeed, the 1935 visit of the Montreal Dow team for two games marks the only instance of a team from elsewhere in Canada playing in the Maritimes and being reported in the region's newspapers during the entire period from the turn of the century to World War II.

Big-game Hunters

Another component of the interwar imagining of the northeastern borderlands as a sporting region is connected to baseball but not restricted to it.

To illustrate, let me return to Babe Ruth. Most Nova Scotians regarded Ruth's visits and those of the touring ball clubs from the United States as an indication of the region's modernity. To get to the Maritimes, these visitors took advantage of improved rail and highway systems. At the same time, the hotly contested matches seemed to demonstrate that Nova Scotians could play on a par with some of the best ballplayers in North America. The need to compete effectively with barnstorming clubs was thus something Nova Scotians took seriously. It is hardly surprising, therefore, that Claude 'Dingie' McLeod, the young pitcher who would serve up Ruth's plate offerings in Westville, would take the opportunity to show the crowd that he could strike out baseball's demigod. After a mixture of fastballs on the inside of the plate and curveballs away, Ruth had had enough. He walked out to the mound and told McLeod that he seemed to be missing the point. The crowd was there not to see him strike out, but to watch him hit home runs. 'So just give me some of those big drug store fastballs down the middle like you're supposed to do.'[9]

Of course one can find multiple meanings in incidents of this sort. For one thing, Maritimers' perceptions of the significance of these baseball interactions seem to have differed from those of the visitors. The fans in Westville may well have been delighted, even if a little embarrassed, to see one of their own reduce the Babe to the status of a mere mortal. Ruth, on the other hand, had come to the region not because of its modernity or the level of competition that ballplayers in the Maritimes could provide, but rather because it represented to him a natural sporting paradise where he could golf, fish, and hunt to his heart's content and at the same time bask in public adulation. Romantic images of northern New England and the Maritimes as a sportsman's paradise were commonplace in the interwar years, and local newspapers delighted in reporting on hunting trips involving American sporting celebrities. The *Sydney Record* of 13 November 1925, for example, reported on a moose-hunting expedition '40 miles into the wilds of Canada', more specifically into New Brunswick, involving Ruth and three of his baseball buddies. Apparently Ruth did not impress his guide, because he could only walk the first 15 miles into the bush and needed a horse to complete the other 25. He did, however, bag his moose, and later regaled the press with his triumph. 'As soon as I can get a freight train to carry the head back and get it stuffed, I'll show it to you,' Ruth gloated. 'The Yankee Stadium is the only place big enough to hold it.'[10]

Two years later the press reported on another post-season moosehunting trip by a group of players from the World Series champion Yankees and some of their former teammates. The players were accompanied by newspaperman William Slocum of the New York *Evening Telegram* and Dr J. Wolford, a big-game hunter and baseball devotee from Philadelphia. Wolford had led a group of baseball stars on a hunting trip to New Brunswick in 1924, an expedition that had brought down four bull moose and five deer. On this trip, Jack Doran, a catcher for the Fredericton Tartars, guided the hunters into the woods at Clarendon on the main line of the CPR. This was reported to be the same territory that heavyweight boxer Jack Dempsey had stalked a few years before and where 'the fistic star knocked out his first moose.'[11] There are a number of similar reports of baseball big-game hunters and other celebrities such as Zane Grey stalking the woods of Maine and the Maritimes.[12] Furthermore, the Boston Red Sox star Ted Williams purchased a summer camp on the Miramichi River in order to pursue his avocation as a fly fisherman after his retirement from baseball.

These stories of celebrity hunting trips reinforced musings about the region as a haven for American capitalists who, in seeking out the recuperative benefits of a natural paradise, might in turn come to recognize the potential for future resource development.[13] As Ian McKay has pointed out, the interwar period had witnessed a reconceptualization of the Maritimes as an idyllic paradise, a more authentic and simple place with a population living closer to nature than inhabitants of bustling North American cities. In the wake of deindustrialization and the consequent economic distress of the 1920s and 1930s, the language of industrial progress and modernity that had predominated before the war had given way to anti-modernist fantasies about the virtue and innocence of the Maritime folk.[14] Yet the romanticization of rural innocence often carried with it the thirst for commercial advantage. According to Beatrice Hay Shaw's *Nova Scotia: For Beauty and Business*, a 1923 publication promoting the province and its untapped resources, for example, the province offered American businessmen a respite from their hectic lives as well as a resource base ready to be exploited and developed. Shaw's imagery, in fact, bordered on the salacious. She depicted Nova Scotia as the innocent blue-nosed lady-in-waiting sitting patiently for 'the man of rod and gun. At this moment [she] holds her arms outspread, and bares her rich bosom to the world, calling to it to come and receive nourishment and life from her ripe breasts.'[15]

Indeed, in conceptualizing the northeast as a sporting region, Maritimers created a discourse that married anti-modernist assumptions about regional simplicity and a 'natural' lifestyle to a cautious hope of a future transformed by modern technology. Anti-modernism might have offered some consolation to a region that was already experiencing the destructive implications of industrial capitalist consolidation and the dismantling of its secondary manufacturing, but this nostalgia did not necessarily imply a rejection of all things modern.

Boston Marathoners

For most Maritimers, the city of Boston symbolized modernity and opportunity and acted as a safety valve for those unable to make a living in hardscrabble communities throughout the provinces. Centuries of economic interaction beginning in the seventeenth century and a history of widespread out-migration from the Maritimes to the northeastern United States in the decades following Confederation reinforced New England's metropolitan connection to its Maritime hinterland. Moreover, for many Maritimers in the interwar period, Boston seemed to exert a stronger and seemingly more benign influence than either Montreal or Toronto. While Toronto and Montreal were often criticized for their predatory behaviour in an age of deindustrialization, and while the rhetoric of Maritime Rights attributed the shortcomings of Confederation to Central Canada's broken promises, Boston was for many Maritimers literally their second home.

The seemingly benign nature of Boston's metropolitan authority explains in part both the fascination and the considerable involvement that Maritimers had with the Boston Marathon during the interwar years. Interest in marathon running at the turn of the century grew out of the sportive nationalism of the day and the inauguration of the modern Olympic Games in 1896. The brainchild of a French nobleman, Baron Pierre de Coubertin, the modern Olympics were associated with the classical symbols of Greek antiquity, not the least of which was the marathon run. At the 1896 games in Athens, the marathon distance was set at 24.8 miles, the distance a legendary Greek foot-soldier was supposed to have run across the plains of Marathon to carry to Athenians the news of the Greek army's victory over a mighty Persian invasion force. John Graham, manager of the American track and field team at the Athens Games and a member of the Boston Athletic Association (BAA) founded a decade earlier, was so impressed with the majestic spectacle that on his return he set about organizing the first Boston marathon, to be hosted by the BAA in 1897. It has been held annually without interruption ever since.

Boston's significant presence in the turn-of-the-century world of track and field was hardly surprising. The first US Olympic team had been an aggregation of students and 'gentlemanly amateurs' drawn largely from American northeastern

universities, including Princeton, Harvard, Yale, Boston College, and the Massachusetts Institute of Technology. Graham had taken with him a six-man delegation from the Boston Athletic Association, and they were accompanied by James Connolly of Boston's Suffolk Athletic Club. In the 12 track and field events at Athens in 1896, members of the BAA won seven gold medals, and Americans attending the games delivered the club cheer, 'B.A.A.-Rah-Rah-Rah', to an approving audience.[16]

Although the first Boston Marathon was won by New Yorker John J. McDermott, Canadians were prominent competitors in the years before World War I. Canadian Ronald MacDonald, a student at Boston College, won the 1898 race, and two years later a Canadian contingent led by John Caffery of Hamilton took first, second, and third places. Caffery won again in 1901. In 1907 Hamilton-based Onondaga runner Tom Longboat captured the crown. Three years later Fred Cameron of Amherst, Nova Scotia, became the first Boston Marathon champion to hail from the Maritime provinces, leading the race from beginning to end.[17]

Nova Scotia's interest in the Boston race intensified during the 1920s, spurred on by the remarkable success of home-bred marathoners Victor MacAulay of Windsor, Silas McLellan from nearby Noel in Hants County, and Billy Taylor and Johnny Miles from Sydney Mines. Of the four, Miles was the most accomplished, winning the event in 1926 and again in 1929 and becoming, in the words of local sportswriter Gee Ahearne, 'the long distance champion runner of the world'. Although the victories of Miles overshadowed the careers of MacAulay, McLellan, and Taylor, it is nonetheless worth remembering that Maritimers in the 1920s and 1930s applauded the accomplishments of all these fine runners. MacAulay's top five finish in the 1924 Boston Marathon catapulted him to a spot on the Canadian Olympic team that year. In 1925 he returned to Boston and finished a respectable seventh. Just two weeks after Miles's victory in the 1926 Boston Marathon, McLellan won the annual Italian Athletic Association 10-mile marathon in Lynn, Massachusetts, over Clarence DeMar, a multi-year champion of the Boston race. Billy Taylor finished second to Miles and ahead of DeMar in a race in Halifax in 1927 and joined the others on Nova Scotia's provincial team at Boston the following year. The province's 1928 team wore shirts emblazoned with a red maple leaf surrounded with 'Nova Scotia' in large black letters, dramatizing the tension that surrounded the relationship of the Maritimes to the nation itself.[18]

Maritime involvement in the Boston Marathon contributed to the imagining of the northeast as a coherent transnational sporting region. It also gave vent to the ambivalent allegiances and deep frustrations that accompanied post-war economic decline. Both the marathoners themselves and the newspapermen who reported upon them constructed stories that reinforced contemporary discourses about regional identity, national betrayal, and Maritime Rights. In many ways, Maritime sporting heroes and officials of the Maritime Provinces Amateur Athletic Association (MPAAA) became stalking horses of post-war Maritime regionalism. In the summer of 1924, for example, Victor MacAulay charged that Maritime athletes on the Canadian Olympic team had been discriminated against by head coach J.R. Cornelius. MacAulay complained that he had had to wear running shoes that were two sizes too large for him, and that Maritimers had received poor lodgings in comparison with athletes from central Canada and the west.[19] Charges of this sort led J.G. Quigley of the MPAAA to attend a meeting of the Canadian Amateur Athletic Union in 1925 where he called for 'Maritime Rights' for the region's athletes.[20] Silas McLellan lodged a similar complaint to that of Victor MacAulay during the 1928 Olympics. The third Canadian to finish in the Olympic marathon that year, McLellan complained that officials of the Canadian Olympic committee had woken him up at 11 o'clock at night to give him a rub-down, and made him

sleep in a room with five others. His complaint prompted A.C. Pettipas, Maritime representative on the Canadian Olympic Committee, to protest McLellan's shabby treatment.[21]

Issues of regional alienation and allegiance—not to mention the difficulties involved in making a living in a chronically depressed region where the British Empire Steel Corporation, the main employer in industrial Cape Breton, teetered on financial ruin—were equally evident in the career of Nova Scotia's premiere marathoner of the interwar period. When Johnny Miles, a 19-year-old delivery boy from Sydney Mines, won the Boston Marathon in 1926 in his first marathon competition, he became an immediate hero in his native province. For young working-class men such as Miles, running offered an inexpensive means of exercise since it required only a pair of shoes and the time and space to train, and victory in a big event could lead to a steady job. At the same time, the more accomplished a runner became, the heavier the financial costs associated with training. Unlike team sports such as hockey, football, baseball, and lacrosse, track and field offered few opportunities to make money from competition, and amateur athletes like Miles found themselves dependent on financial support from the community in order to defray travel and accommodation cost. In 1926, for example, Miles received financial assistance from his hometown and from the Cape Breton Club of Boston, before rewarding his supporters with a victory in the big race.[22]

When Miles and his parents returned from Boston, they were thrown into a dizzying whirl of local functions throughout Sydney Mines, North Sydney, Glace Bay, and Sydney. They also were inundated with invitations to compete in races across the Maritimes and New England. While he could not compete in them all, he did contest 19 major races in the northeast, until winter brought the 1926 racing season to a merciful close. The price of success was high. In return for financial support and media coverage, Miles and his family were expected to participate in the maintenance of their communities, local, provincial, or regional. The strain of this implied social contract, when combined with Johnny's hunger for success, took its inevitable toll. On 12 June, less than two months after his victory in Boston, Johnny collapsed just 220 yards from the finish line in a 10-mile race in Melrose, Massachusetts. According to the *Halifax Herald*, he suffered from heat exhaustion. Miles's biographer, Floyd Williston, suggested that Johnny had gorged himself on rich pastries at a reception earlier on the day of the race. Neither considered the likelihood that the public appearances associated with Johnny's 'social contract' were a factor contributing to his exhaustion.[23]

Just days after Miles's collapse in Melrose, press reports surfaced that he had received offers of financial support from track and field clubs in Boston and Hamilton, Ontario. Johnny's father expressed to the media his concern about the possibility of leaving Sydney Mines, but made it clear that the family would stay in Cape Breton only if he and his son were provided with steady jobs. 'There is absolutely no beating about the bush on this score,' he told the *Halifax Herald*. 'We either get jobs which will not have us tied down hard and fast in order to make a comfortable living or we change our place of residence. Hundreds who found themselves in exactly the same position as we are now have done just this, and why shouldn't we? I have received many promises in order that we might remain in Nova Scotia, but to date they have just been promises.'[24] Throughout the summer of 1926, negotiations continued between the Miles family and prospective clubs, and on 13 August the *Halifax Herald* reported that Miles had accepted an offer from the BAA. This report was premature, however. The family eventually declined that offer and returned to Cape Breton.[25]

Over the winter and into the spring of 1927, Johnny trained for the defence of his Boston Marathon title, supported by the Johnny Miles Training Fund set up by the *Halifax Herald*. The candid 'Gee' Ahem wrote that the family was in need of 'tangible' support and that all wellwishers should 'say it with cash'. Donations for the fund poured in from all over Nova Scotia and from Johnny's supporters in Boston. The publisher of the *Herald*, William Dennis, believed that support for Miles was warranted because he was both an 'asset and advertiser' to a province interested in attracting tourists.[26] An investment in Miles was thus an investment in one's self and one's country. The material circumstances that faced the Miles family were difficult to endure. Even when combined, Miles's father's mining pay and his pay as a clerk could not meet the costs of competing on a regular basis. Nor was it easy to raise money from Cape Breton miners, who faced wage cuts in their struggles with BESCO and themselves relied upon relief from across the country to battle chronic poverty. Still, over $1,500 was collected for the Miles family before their departure to Boston to train for the 1927 event.[27]

The 1927 marathon was run in what was unusually hot weather for Boston in April. Miles quickly succumbed, as steaming tar from the hot pavement seeped through the thin base of his shoes. Apparently his father had shaved the bottoms of his sneakers with a straight razor, hoping that thinner soles would translate into a faster time. Before he called it quits at the seventh mile Miles's feet were burned, blistered, and bloodied. He was not alone. More than a hundred runners dropped out because of the heat, including 35 before the second mile.[28] Nevertheless, his supporters were quick to criticize. Bill Cunningham, a *Boston Post* sportswriter and friend to Miles, suggested that 'Miles should have finished the race if he had to crawl across the line on his hands and knees after the hour of midnight with his bleeding feet wrapped in newspaper.'[29] There was initial underlying resentment in the Maritimes as well. It was as if Johnny had reneged on his obligation to those who supported him. Their disappointment quickly healed upon his return to Cape Breton, however. Ten thousand fans turned out to see him defeat Jimmy Henigan, United States 10-mile champion, and Clarence DeMar, eight-time winner of the Boston Marathon (including 1927), in a five-mile race at the Black Diamond track in Glace Bay. On Dominion Day another 10,000 people turned out in Sydney to witness his third-place finish behind Albert Michelson and Jimmy Henigan, and ahead of Clarence DeMar, who finished fourth.[30]

The race in Sydney was one of Miles's last in the Maritimes. In September he left for Hamilton to attend the Olympic trials. After a disappointing ninth-place finish in Hamilton, the Canadian Olympic committee suggested that he was in poor physical condition and requested that he remain there to train. His father also wanted him to stay in Hamilton, where he would work with top-notch trainers in first-class facilities and be given a job at International Harvester inspecting twine.[31] The Hamilton Olympic Club had been trying to recruit him for over a year. Although Miles did not make a formal public announcement that he would be leaving the Maritimes and taking up permanent residence, the invitation from Hamilton and the pressure applied by the Olympic committee made the decision to leave irresistible. His family soon followed him to Ontario, and they purchased a house adjacent to Hamilton Stadium where Miles frequently trained. He finished sixteenth at the Amsterdam Olympics in 1928.

Interestingly, after his departure, Nova Scotians began to cheer instead for runner Billy Taylor. Had Miles gone to Boston he would likely still have been regarded as a Maritimer in the Boston States; but for some, forsaking Nova Scotia for Ontario was tantamount to betrayal. Like Miles, Taylor was also a British immigrant, an ex-miner and ex-grocery clerk from Sydney Mines. After finishing second to Miles and ahead of DeMar in Halifax in 1927, it seemed that Taylor might well be the next Marathon Champion. In 1928 Taylor dominated Maritime races while Miles was winning his share in Central Canada. For Maritimers the 1929 Boston Marathon was Billy Taylor versus Johnny Miles. Miles won the race and set a course record, while Taylor finished

sixth.[32] In June the two appeared at the Black Diamond track in Glace Bay. Residents of the colliery districts cheered lustily as Taylor lapped Miles on the seventh mile of a 10-mile race that Taylor went on to win.[33]

While back in Cape Breton for the race Miles finally explained his decision: 'I never would have left the Maritime Provinces if there had been anything here for me or any prospects at all for my future . . . Every place I went to look for something in my line the answer was we have nothing for you just now.'[34] He raced for a few more years and finished fourteenth at the 1932 Olympics before retiring at 26. Miles went on to receive an MBA degree and was employed for 43 years with International Harvester.[35] Ironically, Taylor also left the region to further his career, moving to Montreal in 1930 to join the distinguished Campbell Park Athletic Club. After several victories, however, he died suddenly from complications after suffering sunstroke at a race in Montreal in June 1931.[36] That both Miles and Taylor finished out their athletic careers in other parts of Canada attests both to their national sensibilities and the limited employment opportunities available to them in Cape Breton. Nevertheless, for most of the interwar period, Maritime sporting connections with New England were more visible than those with the rest of the country.

Bluenose Sailors

In the post-Confederation years,[37] many Maritimers from ports such as Lunenburg, Yarmouth, and Gloucester, Massachusetts, who made their livelihood fishing or sailing the waters of Georges Bank and the Gulf of Maine, or carried on coastal commerce between Nova Scotia and New England, were also tempted down the road to the 'Boston States'. Not surprisingly, it was their pride in nautical skills or shipbuilding and the sense of competitiveness that accompanied the exploitation of marine resources, that provided the impetus for sporting competition across the international border. In 1905 a 360-nautical-mile sailboat race from Marblehead, Massachusetts, to Halifax was contested for the first time. The Marblehead race was held on a sporadic basis before and after World War I until the Boston Yacht Club and the Royal Nova Scotia Yacht Squadron agreed in 1939 to organize and sponsor the event. The race continues to be run even today on a biennial basis, and in recent years has featured over 100 boats in five divisions.

The connections between the Maritimes and New England were further consolidated after World War I when the schooner *Bluenose*, under the direction of Captain Angus Walters, made her reputation for speed on the open sea. Built in Lunenburg in 1921, the *Bluenose* won every racing competition she entered but one, and over the years established a secure place in regional folklore. The *Bluenose*'s reputation was founded largely upon her successes in the International Fisherman's Trophy Race, a contest first proposed by Colin McKay, one of the region's most influential socialist leaders, as a way of kick-starting the region's struggling post-war economy.[38] Dennis, publisher of the *Halifax Herald* and notable defender of regional causes, whether they involved Maritime Rights or the promotion of Johnny Miles, immediately saw the value of a series of races pitting Canadian fishing schooners against American vessels, in order to settle the claims of fishermen in Lunenburg and Gloucester as to who had the faster fleet. After the American vessel *Esperanto* won the first two races in the fall of 1920, work began on the construction of the *Bluenose* in Lunenburg's Smith and Rhuland shipbuilding yards, and she was launched in time for the 1921 fishing season. Once she met the requirement of a full season in the bank fishery, the *Bluenose* was ready to contest the International Fisherman's Trophy. She won the trophy for the first time in 1921, and never relinquished it until the series was brought to a close by the outbreak of war in 1939.

Dennis's promotion of a race involving fishing schooners at the very time that the fishery was being transformed by the introduction of the gas-powered fishing trawlers was just one manifestation of a broader construction of fishermen and life at sea as the embodiment of Maritime folk identity. According to Ian McKay, as Nova Scotia's post-war culture producers constructed anti-modernist images of a sturdy and virile folk, they offered a culture of consolation to a region suffering from deindustrialization and the failed promises of capitalist modernity.[39] It was not only Maritimers who found these romantic images appealing, however. Reporting on the 1922 series involving the *Bluenose* and the American vessel the *Henry Ford*, the Toronto *Globe* described rival captains Angus Walters and Clayton Morrissey as 'hard fisted, rollicking sailormen, whose vocation necessitates almost constant defiance of death, [and who] display a brand of sportsmanship that might well be emulated by certain others . . . in the sporting eye'.[40]

In the first few years of the competition, disputes arose concerning eligibility requirements for the race between those who celebrated the fishermen's skills at sea and members of the yachting fraternity who, in the tradition of the America's Cup competition, were more interested in improvements in racing technology. Dennis agreed that there had to be practical rules for the governing of competition, but insisted: 'They should be interpreted and carried out by men who know every phase of the fishing and shipping industry.' No yachtsmen, Dennis argued, should 'be connected with the competition in any capacity'.[41] Earlier, Halifax trustees of the international trophy had barred the Boston schooner *Mayflower* from the race because it had not abided by the rules requiring that vessels be working fishing schooners, and this decision was upheld by the United States Racing Committee, which barred the *Mayflower* from the American elimination finals.

Over the next 15 years, as the races continued without interruption and disputes over eligibility were held in check, the *Bluenose* came to symbolize the close association of Nova Scotia and

New England. Since 1937 the ship's image has been reproduced on the Canadian dime, and the *Bluenose II* was constructed in 1963 in the same shipyards as her predecessor. Although the replica never races, she continues to evoke romantic memories of an earlier age of sail and of past sporting glories.[42] As Cheryl Sullivan has written, 'People from all walks of life and from ports all over the world still respond to the romantic past which *Bluenose II* suggests. Millions of people have boarded her, sailed on her, or simply looked at her; and when the time comes for an extensive and expensive refit, it is to these people who feel an emotional connection to the *Bluenose* that the government turns.'[43]

Conclusion: Bobby Gimby and the Bangor Mall

In the interwar period Maritimers and New Englanders developed a sense of a shared sporting culture through connections on sporting diamonds, in hunting grounds, on the ocean, and along long-distance race courses. With the exception of ice hockey, which helped link Canada together through nationwide competition and weekly Hockey Night in Canada radio broadcasts beginning in the 1930s, the emerging national sport culture of the interwar period garnered little support in the Maritimes. Of course, sporting connections between the Maritimes and Canada can be found, especially in regard to Olympic competitions; yet interwar Maritime sporting allegiances were likely to be regional and transnational, rather than pan-Canadian. Only with World War II would the dominant assumption of the northeast as a coherent transnational sporting region begin to give way to alternative constructions. New patterns of consumption—and the growing influence of television—would lead to the perception that the Maritimes truly shared in a Canadian sporting culture. The post-war years also witnessed new patterns of migration that weakened transnational linkages.

Instead of making the traditional exodus to New England, Maritimers increasingly left the region in search of jobs in Toronto, and eventually in cities further west.[44] In the 1960s, moreover, amid the heightened nationalism of the day (evident in the flag debate, and the Expo 67 celebrations) the Canadian state took a more active role in the development of a national sporting culture. Canada Games competitions, the coming of two major league baseball franchises, coast-to-coast television diffusion of hockey and Canadian football, and the marginalization of hunting as a sporting pursuit prompted a re-imagining of the Maritime sporting universe. And so, as Maritimers followed Bobby Gimby in singing about their love of Canada at the 'hundredth anniversary of Confederation', or were 'goin' down the road' in new directions in search of work and well-being, their once intimate connections with northern New England were displaced by the occasional holiday shopping trip to the Bangor Mall.

Notes

1. See, for example, Jeremy Adelman and Stephen Aron, 'From Borderlands to Borders: Empires, Nation States, and Peoples in Between in North America', *American Historical Review* 104, 3 (June 1999): 814–41; and the articles by David Thelen, Bruno Ramirez, Ian Tyrrell, Robin Kelley, and Mauricio Tenorio Trillo in 'The Nation and Beyond. International Perspectives on United States History. A Special Issue', in *The Journal of American History* 86: 3 (Dec. 1999) 965–1187. . . .

2. Benedict Anderson, *Imagined Communities: Reflections on the Origin and Spread of Nationalism* (London: Verson, rev. ed. 1991: orig. pub. 1983). For a similar discussion in a Canadian context, see Daniel Francis, *National Dreams: Myth, Memory, and Canadian History* (Vancouver: Arsenal Pulp Press, 1997).

3. William New, *Borderlands: How We Talk About Canada* (Vancouver: UBC Press, 1998), 27.

4. Phillip Buckner, 'How Canadian Historians Stopped Worrying and Learned to Love the Americans', *Acadiensis* 25: 2 (Spring 1996): 117–40.

5. Allen Guttmann, *Games and Empires: Modern Sports and Cultural Imperialism* (New York: Columbia University Press, 1994).

6. Ruth's upbringing and his connection to the Maritimes are chronicled in Robert Creamer, *Babe: The Legend Comes to Life* (New York: Simon and Schuster, 1974); Robert Ashe, *Even the Babe Came to Play: Small-Town Baseball in the Dirty 30s* (Halifax: Nimbus, 1991; William Humber, 'Babe Ruth Comes to Canada in Search of ??', *Saskatchewan Historical Baseball Review* (1996): 24–35; and Colin Howell, 'The Man who Taught the Bambino: The Mystery of Brother Matthias', in William Humber and John St James, eds, *All I Thought About Was Baseball: Writings on a Canadian Pastime* (Toronto: University of Toronto Press, 1996), 149–52.

7. The baseball connection between New England and the Maritimes is addressed in fuller detail in Colin Howell, *Northern Sandlots: A Social History of Maritime Baseball* (Toronto: University of Toronto Press, 1995).

8. Ernest R. Forbes, *The Maritime Rights Movement, 1919–1927: A Study in Canadian Regionalism* (Montreal and Kingston: McGill-Queen's University Press, 1979).

9. Ashe, *Even the Babe Came to Play*, 102–3; Howell, *Northern Sandlots*.

10. *Sydney Record*, 13 Nov. 1925.

11. Ibid., 21 Oct. 1927; *Halifax Herald*, 1 Nov. 1924.

12. See, for example, the lengthy article entitled 'Where Gun, Canoe and Fishing Rod are the Tourist's Joy', in a special tourist edition of the *Halifax Herald*, 24 Mar. 1925.

13. James Morrison, 'American Tourism in Nova Scotia, 1871–1940', *Nova Scotia Historical Review* 2, 2 (Dec. 1982): 40–51.

14. Ian McKay, *The Quest of the Folk: Antimodernism and Cultural Selection in Twentieth-Century Nova Scotia* (Montreal and Kingston: McGill-Queen's University Press, 1994).

15. Beatrice M. Hay Shaw, *Nova Scotia: For Beauty and Business* (Halifax: Royal Print and Litho Ltd., 1923), vii.

16. Mark Dyreson, *Making the American Team: Sport Culture, and the Olympic Experience* (Urbana and Chicago: University of Illinois Press, 1998), 40–6.

17. A brief history of the Boston Marathon and the results of each race can be found at the official Boston Marathon website, www.bostonmarathon.org/history.htm. I am also indebted to my student research assistant Daniel Macdonald for collecting material relating to the career of Johnny Miles used in this essay.

18. *Halifax Herald*, 5 Apr. 1928.

19. Ibid., 29 July 1924.

20. Ibid., 19 Sept. 1925.

21. Ibid., 3 Sept. 1928.

22. Ibid., 13, 17 Apr. 1926; Williston, *Johnny Miles: Nova Scotia's Marathon King* (Halifax: Nimbus, 1990), 2.

23. *Halifax Herald*, 14 June 1926; Williston, *Johnny Miles*, 35.

24. *Halifax Herald*, 29 June 1926.

25. Ibid., 13 Aug. 1926.

26. Ibid., 7, 9, 19, 25 Mar. 1927.

27. Ibid, 7 Apr. 1927.

28. Williston, *Johnny Miles*, 44–5; Tom Derderian, *Boston Marathon: The History of the World's Premier Running Event* (Urbana, IL: Human Kinetics Publishers, 1990), 112–14; *Halifax Herald*, 20, 21 Apr. 1927.

29. Derderian, *Boston Marathon*, 114.

30. *Halifax Herald*, 2 July 1927.

31. Ibid., 10, 19, 24 Sept. 1927.

32. Ibid., 15, 18, 19, 20 Apr. 1929.

33. Ibid., 13 June 1929.

34. Ibid., 10 June 1929.

35. Derderian, *Boston Marathon*, 133.

36. Williston, *Johnny Miles*, 75–6.

37. Alan Alexander Brooks, 'The Exodus: Migration from the Maritimes to Boston During the Second Half of the Nineteenth Century', PhD diss., University of New Brunswick, 1977; Patricia Thornton, 'The Problem of Out-migration from Atlantic Canada, 1871–1921: A New Look', *Acadiensis* 15, 1 (Autumn 1985): 3–34; Betsy Beattie, '"Going up to Lynn": Single, Maritime-Born Women in Lynn, Massachusetts, 1879–1930', *Acadiensis* 22, 1 (Autumn 1992): 65–86.

38. Ian McKay, 'Of Karl Marx and the Bluenose: Colin Campbell McKay and the Legacy of Maritime Socialism', *Acadiensis* 27, 2 (Spring 1998): 3–25.

39. McKay, *Quest of the Folk*.

40. Toronto *Globe*, 24 Oct. 1922.

41. Ibid., 27 Oct. 1922.

42. James Marsh, 'The Bluenose'.

43. Cheryl Sullivan, 'The Paradox of *Bluenose II*: Antimodernism, Capitalism and the Legacy of the Schooner *Bluenose* in Nova Scotia', *Nova Scotia Historical Review* (1997): 2–22.

44. Gary Burrill, *Away: Maritimers in Massachusetts, Ontario and Alberta: An Oral History of Leaving Home* (Montreal and Kingston: McGill-Queen's University Press, 1992).

Totem Poles, Teepees, and Token Traditions: 'Playing Indian' at Ontario Summer Camps, 1920–55

——— Sharon Wall ———

In 1899 Pauline Johnson, famous 'Mohawk princess' and Aboriginal performer, paid a visit to the small northern Ontario town of Sundridge. As Johnson served up her fare of dramatic poems and recitations, one 10-year-old girl was particularly enthralled. Recounting the incident later in life, Mary S. Edgar, the young white girl in question, recalled, 'I was fascinated and wished I were related to her,' a longing only heightened by Johnson's later visit to the Edgar family home. Some 20 years later, little Mary's wish was, in one sense, granted. The summer of 1922 found the 33-year-old Edgar the director of a newly established summer camp for girls. There she presided over the camp's Indian council ring, crafted her own Indian legends, and entertained campers in her wigwam-style cabin. On a visit to the camp sometime in the interwar years, Chief Mudjeekwis of the Rice Lake Ojibway extended the hand of friendship and bestowed on Edgar the honour of an 'Indian' name. Over the years, in her role as 'Ogimaqua', Edgar, the white woman, would imaginatively weave herself and her campers into the family of 'Indians'.[1]

In her fascination with all things Indian, Edgar was not alone. At least as early as the 1890s white audiences throughout Canada, the United States, and Britain thronged local halls and auditoriums to see and hear celebrities like Johnson, whose appearances fanned the flames of interest in the performing Indian. In the same period, North Americans crowded into the rodeos and Buffalo

Bill shows that prominently featured Aboriginal performers. If, as with Edgar, this outsider fascination slipped into the desire for insider status, what most of these 'wannabee' Indians did with the impulse to 'go Native' is not well known. The story of Grey Owl's faux-Indian fame points in one direction, but it is unlikely that many took their enthusiasm to such extremes. For many who were not seeking wholesale changes of identity, playing Indian part-time would suffice.[2] Summer camp was one site in which this impulse could be readily indulged, a place where, it was understood, children learned to 'live like Indians during the camping season.'[3]

This article attempts to make sense of this curious cultural phenomenon, to place this cultural appropriation in a broad historical context. By exploring camps' Indian programming and representations of Native people in camp literature, it takes a critical look at the fascination with playing Indian. What becomes apparent is that the incorporation of so-called Indian traditions was part [of] a broader anti-modernist impulse in twentieth-century Ontario. Like the summer camp phenomenon as a whole, it reflected middle-class unease with the pace and direction of cultural change, with a world that appeared to be irrevocably industrial, decidedly urban, and increasingly secular. As historian Leslie Paris has concluded in the American context, racial play-acting at summer camp was not a matter of respecting the experiences of racial minorities.[4]

Sharon Wall, 'Totem Poles, Teepees, and Token Traditions: "Playing Indian" at Ontario Summer Camps, 1920–1955', *Canadian Historical Review* 86, 3 (2005): 513-44. © University of Toronto Press Incorporated. Reprinted by permission of University of Toronto Press Incorporated (www.utpjournals.com).

So also at Ontario camps, 'going Native' had little to do with honouring (or even accurately portraying) Aboriginal tradition, but much to do with seeking a balm for the non-Native experience of modernity. Above all, at summer camp playing Indian reflected modern desire to create a sense of belonging, community, and spiritual experience by modelling anti-modern images of Aboriginal life. These impulses point to a racialized expression of twentieth-century anti-modernism—one springing from adult experience, but articulating itself on the landscape of childhood. . . .

The first camps in Ontario, founded by charitable organizations, private individuals, and the YMCA, appeared at the turn of the century, but before the First World War they served a limited clientele composed mainly of older boys. In the 1920s there were significant developments, including the appearance of girls' camps, camps for a broader age range of children, and the establishment of several private camps whose directors would become important leaders in the field of camping. By the 1930s, the impulse to take children of all sorts 'back to nature' spawned something of a camping movement, with the newly established Ontario Camping Association playing a prominent role. Its efforts to educate the public about the benefits of camp and its attempts to raise standards of the camps themselves, seem to have paid off. In the early 1950s *Saturday Night* magazine claimed that 'between 5 and 7 per cent of all Canadian children attend a summer camp,' while a *Financial Post* article quantified this at 150,000 children. If one considers that a majority of Canadian camping took place in Ontario—one journalist estimating roughly 70 per cent by 1960—it would seem that the camp certainly had come of age by the end of this period.[5]

. . .

Playing Indian has most often been understood as a form of cultural appropriation, a practice that has been the source of intense debate among scholars, literary critics, journalists, and others. Hartmut Lutz, a German literary scholar,

provides a useful explanation of the concept: 'What is at issue . . . is the kind of appropriation which happens within a colonial structure, where one culture is dominant politically and economically over the other, and rules and exploits it. . . . It is a kind of appropriation that is selective . . . and that is ahistorical in that it excludes from its discourse the historical context, especially, here, the history of Native–non-Native relations.'[6] This is clear enough from other histories of 'playing Indian'—studies by Phillip Deloria and Shari Huhndorf among others—which show the phenomenon was clearly rooted in desires to fill the personal, social, and national aspirations of Whites. . . . Other scholars argue that the appeal of playing Indian was heightened as time went on by the marginalization, displacement, even death of real Aboriginal peoples. With the latter posing a decreasing threat to white society, negative images of Indians could now, more often, give way to positive ones.[7]

Though much useful analysis emerged from such studies, more explicit connection can yet be made between the phenomenon of 'playing Indian' and the broader context of twentieth-century modernity and anti-modernity. In the guiding work on the subject, Jackson Lears pinpointed anti-modernism's North American origins in the late nineteenth century. As a result of broad social changes wrought by industrialization, turn-of-the-century intellectuals, literati, and other members of the urban bourgeoisie suffered feelings of 'weightlessness' and 'overcivilization'. Their efforts to compensate, to replace 'weightlessness' with 'intense experience', took many forms, from renewed fascination with 'the simple life', to the arts and crafts movement, the revival of martial ideals, and explorations of medieval and Eastern mysticism. Scholars since Lears confirm that such responses were not a strictly American, nor Victorian, phenomenon. In early twentieth-century Nova Scotia similar quests for identity and meaning spawned what historian Ian McKay has termed a 'quest of The Folk'—a pre-modern incarnation of Nova Scotians, one that folklorists and cultural producers would claim as the region's true cultural core. Like the camp industry, this image had important economic implications, serving as the cultural myth that fuelled modern tourism in that province.[8]

. . .

The backdrop for the emergence of this strain of anti-modernist sentiment was a province that had seen rapid cultural change. Though the notion of 'modernity' is a notoriously slippery concept, suffice it to say that Ontario was very much a modern entity by the interwar years. To a greater degree than any other Canadian province, it was capitalist, industrial, and distinctly urban. In 1921, when 47 per cent of all Canadians were urban dwellers, the number in Ontario was at almost 60. By 1951, when the national average reached 62 per cent, in Ontario the figure was already 10 per cent higher.[9] Possibly more significant than the physical consequences of modernity was the shift in cultural consciousness that underlay them. At the broadest level, this entailed the unadulterated exaltation of reason and commitment to the rationalization of not only production, but ever-expanding realms of social life. In the realm of child psychology, professional experts preached the wonders of 'habit-training' by which children, no less than the tools of industry, could become efficient working machines. Interwar child-rearing experts agreed that what children needed was unbending and factory-like routine, not the emotional inconsistencies that marked traditional child-rearing. By rigid scheduling of the child's day, restrained shows of affection, and a reasoned rather than punitive approach, children would develop along healthy and predictable paths and grow into the reasonable, well-behaved citizens modern living demanded.[10]

. . . If modern expertise and professional advice promised to turn out well-adjusted children, other cultural developments seemed to threaten healthy child development. In camp literature, concern was expressed about the fact that, already in childhood, Canadians were becoming soft, habituated to technological comforts, and alienated from 'real' experience. 'Children today, especially in large cities, have little opportunity for really creative living,' one camp director lamented. 'Lights go on at a switch, heat comes when a knob is turned . . . [and] drama means sitting in the movies.'[11] Given twentieth-century understandings of child development—and of the lasting import of early experiences—the impact of these modern conditions was felt to be especially worrying. With few countervailing influences, many feared children would grow into adults incapable of enjoying life's simpler pleasures or of appreciating the importance of physical exertion and hard work. If the notion of childhood had always implied a degree of protection for the young, under conditions of twentieth-century modernity, the notion that children needed protecting from the very culture that surrounded them would deepen. To be a modern North American parent would be to contemplate no end of worries about the possible negative influences of modern culture.

Primary among these worries was children's presumed vulnerability to the lure of consumer culture. Paradoxically, having put an end to the most extreme forms of child labour, middle-class observers now worried about the uses to which children's expanding leisure time would be put. Crime comics and pulp novels, movie theatres and youth dance halls all worried bourgeois onlookers, some of whom worked to prohibit or restrict access to such attractions. On the other hand, proponents of 'rational recreation'—another modern innovation—took a positive approach, offering wholesome entertainment alternatives at local YMCAs, community centres, and post-war teen canteens.[12]

Founders of summer camps took this critique one step further, suggesting that what children needed was a complete break with city life and experience with more natural living. In this way of thinking, they were heavily influenced by Ernest Thompson Seton and, to a lesser extent, G. Stanley Hall. The widely sought-after Seton was popular as a naturalist, artist, master storyteller, and founder of the League of Woodcraft Indians. Seton's critique of modernity was inseparable from a marked romanticization of Aboriginal culture, one instrumental in fuelling youthful interest in 'going Native'. 'Our civilization is a failure,' he commented on one occasion, while his writings on Indian lore conversely idealized 'Indian life' and encouraged Euro-North Americans—especially children—in its emulation. His instructional manuals like *The Red Book: Or, How To Play Indian* were widely read at camp (and elsewhere), while in the case of at least one camp, he was brought on as temporary staff. Less directly, camps were likely also influenced by theories of 'race capitulation' popularized by Victorian psychologist G. Stanley Hall. In Hall's view, boys in particular needed to indulge their savage tendencies in childhood so that they might, as the human race itself had ostensibly done, progress beyond them to civilized adulthood.[13]

Emerging from a culture of increasingly secular proportions, with anti-modern concerns over childhood and a penchant for 'playing Indian', the camp offered itself as not only a physical escape from the city, but also—in its use of Indian programming—metaphoric release from the emotional confines of modern childhood. Here was a world, geographically removed from home and city, where the combination of newness and isolation offered the perfect backdrop for the construction of alternate identities. Indeed, as children first heard of these camps—Temagami, Keewaydin, Ahmek, and so on—the foreign nature of the experience was announced. Arrival at camp quickly confirmed that it was one designed to usher youth out of the modern world and into the realm of the Indian past. As they first passed though gates that demarcated the boundary between the two worlds, campers frequently encountered camp names constructed from purportedly 'Indian' languages. One camp director's son recalled, 'All the popular camps of the day had Indian names.'[14] Campers themselves were sometimes 'renamed', with Ojibwa, Algonquin, Cree, and Blackfoot commonly

marking their cabins or sections. Gazing about the grounds, children would quickly have noticed that not only names, but the material culture of camp—its teepees, totem poles, and sometimes whole 'Indian villages'—confirmed the Indian connection. At camps of all sorts, arts and crafts period saw children variously carving, painting, and constructing their own totem poles, teepees, and 'Indian heads'. As they went about their activities, children were reminded that the very earth on which they walked had once been 'Indian land'. This point was brought home in a special way to campers who thrilled at the chance to observe, listen, and learn from the Aboriginal staff employed at certain camps. Finally, campers would also have discovered the Indian council ring, set off geographically from the rest of camp. In this woodsy, chapel-like setting, 'young braves' would 'sit in solemn pageant' on their rough-hewn benches, awaiting the words of 'the chief' delivered from his sacred 'council rock'. Having been duly blanketed and face-painted, and sometimes in 'breech clouts', these make-believe Indians would make use of everything from tom-toms and rattles to shields and headdresses.[15]

While camps offered surprisingly similar renditions of Indian programming, boys and girls also encountered distinct aspects of 'Indianness' at their respective camps. At boys' camps the Indian was frequently represented as bearing a kind of violent hyper-masculinity, a model deemed particularly fitting for male campers. In keeping with theories of 'race capitulation', boys were encouraged to indulge their 'savage' impulses in games of 'scalping' and 'pioneers and Indians', which, in one case, was happily reported to include 'blood-curdling yells' from 'fierce-visaged boys of ten'.[16] Girl campers, on the other hand, were encouraged to emulate a very different sort of Indian. At their camps the emphasis on Native activities was on the development of artistic abilities, not on primitivist catharsis, with weaving and painting of 'Indian themes' being popular. Although sometimes providing campers with more independent models of girl-hood, the tone of other Indian programming was also more appropriately feminine. For instance, a description of 'Indian day' at Camp Tanamakoon had no savage or primitivist over-tones: '[The girls] had been in another world,' it was recounted, 'a world of quiet feet, gliding canoes and spirited dances.'[17]

Broadly speaking, and whatever its gendered components, the summer camp experience was understood as a recreation of the Indian way of life. 'The Native Canadians . . . were campers,' educator Mary Northway put it. 'In their small groups they lived a simple, outdoor life, striving against the elements and using natural resour-ces to furnish their existence.'[18] In this way of thinking, Indians were campers and campers were Indians. Nothing, it seemed, could be more 'Indian' than camping.

Meanings Behind the Masks

Indian programming was straightforwardly explained by administrators as having educa-tional value. . . .

. . . [S]trict attention to historical accuracy was, unfortunately, not the rule. Ironically, since praise of Indians had as its premise the presumably 'primitive', even ageless, nature of their practices, so-called Indian culture at camp was sometimes quite literally made up. Perhaps the most familiar example is the use of simu-lated Indian names. If certain camps were care-ful to choose names that had real meanings in indigenous languages, many others were happy enough if the overall effect was an Indian tone. Thus were born institutions like the New Frenda Youth camp and Camp Wanna-com-bak. . . .

Invention could also take more inadvertent forms, sometimes through careless blending of one Aboriginal tradition with another. All too often objects of Native material cultures were presented in utterly jumbled fashion. The desire to create an Indian atmosphere at Bolton, for instance, meant that the totem pole (a uniquely

West Coast tradition) and the teepee (used only by Plains groups) could be displayed unprob-lematically side by side, with an Omaha 'tribal prayer' thrown in for good measure. . . . In such cases, camps were not penetrating the intricacies of Native history or culture; rather, like those of a long line of explorers, settlers, and academics before them, their images of Native people were based on a fantastical amalgam of Aboriginal trad-itions projected onto one mythic Indian Other, another version of the white man's Indian.[19]

In all of these cases, the child's experience of this culture—and not its realistic depiction—was clearly the central concern, a point under-scored in the following advice:

If you have no serious objection to a little sub-terfuge, it is possible to enliven your Indian program . . . by 'discovering an Indian Burial Ground.' It can either just happen or you can make it known that this camp was once the home of such and such a tribe and that arrow heads, bits of pottery and other evidence has [sic] been found. . . . Please yourself how far you want to go with this kind of thing. Once started, the ball will continue to roll. Bones and all kinds of things will be brought to your attention for there's nothing excites a camper more than discovery.[20]

If discovery excited children, if Indian cere-monies awed them, and if games of scalping allowed them to let off steam, Indian program-ming was a success. In contrast to the regimen-tation recommended by child-rearing experts, campers were sometimes (though by no means always) encouraged to be excitable and to indulge in imaginative and often passionate play.

Clearly, Indian programming was not really about honouring Aboriginal traditions, but it was not without purpose or meaning in the life of the camp. Like anti-modernists of earlier periods, camp enthusiasts were on the trail of intense experience, which Indian programming offered in abundance. Council ring, for instance, could function not merely as Saturday night entertainment, but also as the symbolic centre of camp. It was here that important visitors were introduced, here that opening and closing ceremonies were held, here that directorships sometimes formally changed hands. In effect, council ring offered the ritual, solemnity, and spirit of communalism that such events demanded and seemed to be lacking in modern life.

. . . Indeed, part of the essential meaning of camp was that it was more than a collection of unconnected individuals; above all, it was a community. A common spiritual striving, broadly defined, was deemed invaluable in nurturing this sense of community, even at camps without a primarily religious focus. We see this at Ahmek where references to 'the value of persons', the search for 'higher values', and the indescribable 'camp spirit' suggested incorporation of a liberal, humanistic spirituality. Despite its distancing from institutional religion, this camp still ultimately claimed, 'To many counsellors and campers, Ahmek has been their one outstanding religious experience.' They were careful to add, however, that religion was a concept 'as flexible, changing and real as life itself'.[21]

. . .

At many summer camps the council ring ceremony was the central vehicle for channelling experience of this 'pure religion' to urban campers. Through it, campers could immerse themselves in ritual that contained no reference to Christian theology, but rather offered an air of novel freshness. The ceremony was often a weekly or bi-weekly event, held after dark, and involving the entire camp. 'It has been used as a vehicle through which much sound teaching can be given without effusive moralizing,' a short history of Bolton Camp explained.[22] At the Statten camps the ceremonies were treated with equal seriousness. Only those who had actively participated, it was claimed, could 'know the deep meaning of such an hour'.[23] Discussions of council ring's physical layout point out similar understandings of its import.

The area itself was treated as semi-sacred space, and the rituals it facilitated, as quasi-religious. 'The choice of a site for the Council Ring is important,' one handbook advised. 'Select an area reasonably remote from any buildings. . . . A flat space . . . surrounded by trees will lend enchantment. Atmosphere is very important. . . . Find another site for the ordinary camp fires and wiener roasts.'[24] Without question, the backdrop of nature was deemed essential in creating the desired atmosphere. At Bolton, this was achieved by situating the ceremonies 'in a most appropriate forest setting', while at Glen Bernard, Mary Edgar rejoiced in her discovery of 'the glen, a perfect amphitheatre for a Council Ring'.[25] According to this way of thinking, trees became markers of the borders of intimacy, rocks became symbolic altars to be used by presiding chiefs, and the wide open sky suggested the loftiness of the entire enterprise.

Organization of council ring proceedings points to further parallels with religious ritual, as well as that blend of catharsis and control, freedom and order that characterized the rest of the camp experience. The usual roster of activities included a dramatic fire-lighting ceremony followed by prayers to 'the gods', some form of camper recitations or reports (often of nature sightings), 'Indian challenges' or contests, and a sombre closing ceremony. All was to be guided by a strict 'order of procedure', in keeping with the belief that 'everything that is done at the council ring is deliberate,' or as it was put at Bark Lake Camp, 'everything on the programme is planned ahead.'[26] Creating the desired atmosphere also depended on knowing when to keep quiet and when to join in the noise-making. At certain points 'absolute silence' was considered something of an iron law, while at other times input from the 'braves' (like lay participation) was essential. As council ring's central organizing feature, the fire itself cannot be overlooked. Fire, which often holds a sacred place in religious ritual, here held pride of place, providing a circular and thus communal ordering to the ritual.

Before gaining entry to this sacred space, campers were expected to undergo transformation on several levels. If, broadly speaking, all of camp life reflected the desire to 'go Native', it was at council ring ceremonies that campers were, in essence, 'born again' as Indians. The first step in this process was external change. Here nature itself helped, eliciting positive reference to the Indian appearance of sun-browned campers. Suntans were assumed to be one of the healthy by-products of a summer at camp, providing not only physical benefits, but also the psychospiritual advantages of 'going Native', as both Deloria and Paris have shown. In the Ontario context, one mother and her children who returned from fresh-air camp were described as 'mortals from another world. The mother is browned by the kiss of summer winds. . . . And the children? They look like four little nut-brown papooses— as tough as nails—sparkling and effervescent.'[27] To compliment their Indian 'skins', campers anticipating council ring were expected to take on Indian dress. At Bark Lake Camp it was stated, 'Campers dress up in blankets, towels, feathers and war paint,' while photo evidence suggests that 'dressing up Indian' was also the routine at other private, fresh-air and agency camps.[28]

Other aspects of transformation were less visible, if no less real. Fundamentally, one was to be open to a new way of feeling and of experiencing the self. . . . More than anything, however, it required a willingness to be transported metaphorically to another time and place, to enter into a new state of mind, and to open oneself up to mystical experience. Directors . . . were also told that this required not only 'dress[ing] for the part', but also that the chief himself 'become enchanted' and open to 'the emotional appeal of the Red man'.[29] Judging from a description of council ring proceedings at Ahmek, director Taylor Statten apparently played his part well. 'Each week at camp seemed to await the Council Ring,' it was recalled.

One gathered a blanket and a flashlight and marched off to the Council Ring as an actor in a well-rehearsed play . . . somehow, the austere and [pervasive] presence of the Chief transformed the play into a realistic re-enactment of all Indian ceremonies of all time. The twentieth century slipped away in the darkness and all evidences of modern civilization were . . . somehow forgotten. . . . It was a shock returning from this other world in which we had all been participants . . . and the validity of the experience was owing to the magnificent skill of the Chief. He was really THE CHIEF.[30]

In this atmosphere, members of the camp community could find themselves emotionally stirred, personally connected, and perhaps even spiritually moved. . . . Here, without explicit reference to religion, one could taste the beauty of ritual, embrace feelings of awe, and experience the power of the communal event. In this context, Aboriginal people were far from mind and one's own experience, the focal centrepiece.

. . .

Playing Indian could engender experience; it could also inform identity at all manner of camps. As in the world of art, literature, and sport, proving one's connection to Indians was a surefire way to found a 'Canadian tradition' and to establish one's 'Canadian' roots.[31] To achieve this feat at camp, outdoor enthusiasts ignored their immigrant roots and constructed themselves— as those who chose to 'live like Indians'—as the figurative 'heirs' of Native tradition. . . . Director Mary Hamilton's account of Algonquin Park history is illustrative:

To the uninitiated the name of Algonquin spells Indian. One thinks of wise men of the forest who knew this country well and trapped and fished here in the days when all the wilderness of forest and stream belonged to them. These associations are true, but Algonquin Park is much more than an Indian hunting ground. It is an expanse of twenty-seven hundred square miles of forest. . . . It is a land that finds a place in history associated with the records of Champlain, it was the happy hunting ground of the Algonquin Indians. . . . In the days of Tom Thomson it became the gathering place for members of the Group of Seven.[32]

Clearly, there was tension here between giving the Aboriginal peoples their due and the construction of a narrative that assumed their eventual irrelevance. The same tone marked Mary Edgar's prompting to past campers: 'We need often to remind ourselves that this country which we proudly call "this land of ours" once belonged to the Indians,' that, 'it was the smoke from their camp-fires which first ascended to the sky.'[33] Clearly, camps had much in common with the salvage anthropologist who lamented, but also assumed the inevitability of, the Indian's cultural demise.[34] From this perspective, Indians were those of strictly pre-contact innocence. Any cultural change or adaptation on their part was read simply as decay. 'Real Indians', so it was understood, were no longer a people who 'lived among us' or who had a place in the modern world.

Having rendered contemporary Aboriginal peoples virtually invisible, white campers could now step in to fill the void as their remaining heirs. In doing so, they distinguished between themselves—true lovers of nature—from less-enlightened elements of their society. In a 1931 article, parallels were drawn between campers and early Aboriginal peoples. The author suggests that, like 'the redmen' of the past, it is now 'the new dwellers of the out-of-doors' who are being 'pushed further and further afield'. The enemies now are not from the east, but annoying cottagers from the south who 'bring with them their city habits and customs'. These philistines are described as 'inane bands of jazz-makers [who] violate the silence of the night', who bring 'hot dog stands and shabby food "joints"' to the wilderness, and ultimately, as 'idolaters in the temple of the Great Spirit'.[35] By contrast, camps painted themselves as respectful followers of Indian ways, inheritors of Native traditions and practices. In their use of the Aboriginal tumpline—a

heavy leather strap that was tied around goods, then around the forehead of the hiker—Camp Keewaydin considered itself to be 'the custodian of ancient practices and devices long since discarded elsewhere'.[36] At Bolton, campers who fished, tented, and chopped wood were depicted as receiving 'instruction in skills of the historic past', while CGIT [Canadian Girls in Training] campers were said to be learning to live 'as did their Indian brothers and sisters'.[37] Ultimately, if campers were the children of these earlier Aboriginal siblings, their role as inhabitants of Indian land—the entire country, of course—could be regarded as only natural. They were legitimate 'Canadians', and this was their home.

Such re-tellings, borrowings, and inventions were the base elements of camps' Indian programming. They suggest that the history of playing Indian is not only one of longing, but also of privilege. Clearly, dramatic re-inventions of campers as Indians merely emphasized the shared whiteness of the actors under the paint, to their freedom in taking 'Indianness' on and off at will. Indeed, it was precisely because they felt so deeply assured of their status as 'white' that they could play at being, and long to be, Indian. Camp enthusiasts were not seeking a true change of status, but a revised, more pleasing image of their own racial character. Through their role as summer campers, lovers of the outdoors claimed an identity that was vaguely countercultural but, at the same time, still clearly white. One would be hard pressed to argue, for instance, that playing Indian was a truly progressive form of 'transgression'—that it inverted and thus challenged the social status quo—even if it contained some carnivalesque features. As most scholars of American minstrel performances agree, when whites put on other racial faces, they were not making attempts at accurate representations of the Other or at honouring the experience of subaltern cultures. On the other hand, neither should their acts be read as simple denigration, since they also revealed a certain ambivalence towards racial Others. This included a privileged longing to experience racialized ways of being and acting normally deemed unacceptable within the dominant culture. . . .

Playing Indian at camp, like 'blacking up', represented a similar white, middle-class, and privileged longing to identify with the socially marginal, the 'low-Other' of Canadian society. Like the Setons and the Grey Owls they resembled, camp enthusiasts sought from Aboriginal peoples a connection to a time of pre-modern simplicity, a golden age of social harmony and calm. . . . In the context of the summer camp, Aboriginal peoples were seen as living the enviable simple life, and whites as those impoverished by modernity's flow. Indeed, at camp, anti-modernist tendencies were frequently expressed in racialized terms, with a simple, if unarticulated, equation undergirding common thinking on the question. Quite simply, white equalled 'modern', and 'Indian', 'premodern' or 'primitive'. Re-articulating much older primitivist tendencies in Western culture, twentieth-century camps in this way also fuelled their own unique version of primitivism.[38] From this perspective Indians were regarded as the quintessential primitives, identification with them as a way of distancing campers from distasteful elements of mainstream society. Note this description of the Aboriginal worker at Camp Keewaydin: 'The guide's values were different from those of a white middle- or upper-class young man,' it was explained. '[He] had no schooling but had been educated by Nature and life.'[39]

Admiration for this proximity to nature was coupled with romanticization of the Indian's presumed distance from modernity. The *Toronto Star*'s reading of the camp project at Bolton explained, 'City children . . . will learn there were no department stores, super-markets or Saturday matinees for the Indians.'[40] Where Aboriginal guides were employed, they were similarly praised for their total lack of implication in the culture of consumption. Keewaydin's camp historian claimed of their Native workers, 'The early guide never owned an automobile. He owned a canoe. With it, he earned his livelihood,

hunted . . . and engaged in any leisure activity.'[41] The Indian, then, was one who did not rely on the comforts of mass culture, but who instead accepted the challenge of real physical work. . . .

Paralleling camps' praise for the idealized Indian was a mock derision and scorn for 'the white Man'. In keeping with earlier primitivist tendencies, those who glorified the Indian also offered a social critique of their own society, however limited. In the case of playing Indian, this manifested as a semi-serious attack on 'whiteness', otherwise understood as symbol for implication in modernity. . . . At Bolton Camp, boys participated in dramatic re-enactments of historic Native–white conflicts, with one description noting 'the treachery of a band of marauding whites'.[42] Use of the derogatory *pale-face*—'pale-faced campers' or white visitors as 'chiefs in the pale-faced world'— also reveals attempts to look through Aboriginal eyes and to de-centre whiteness as the assumed vantage point.[43] Looking back on the dominant culture from this new perspective, campers could join in the performance of the fire-lighting ceremony, which bid them to declare, 'Light we now the council fire, built after the manner of the forest children. Not big like the whiteman's where you must stand off so front all roast and back all gooseflesh; but small like the Indian's, so we may sit close and feel the warmth of fire and friendship.'[44] Here, whiteness was represented as not only synonymous with ostentation, but also with a cold, impersonal culture, lacking in true intimacy. By superficially critiquing whiteness, members of the camping community could distance themselves from the hollowness of modern alienation and excess, essentially allowing them to re-conceptualize their relationship to modernity. Through the summer camp experience, white urban Ontarians could think of themselves as existing outside the limits of the dominant culture. Clearly, the critique was a shallow one that lasted only so long as one's stay in the woods. What made 'going Native' at camp such an act of privilege was that campers could comfortably go home to whiteness once returned to their urban environments, settings where the benefits or 'wages of whiteness' were generally irresistible. . . .

Assessing Impact

. . . [I]f Indian programming was of clearly adult origin, it also had its impact on children. That certain families patronized the same camps over several generations suggests that powerful loyalties engendered in childhood sometimes endured into adult years. Many children, it seems, were strongly affected by their stays at camp, and it is likely that lessons learned there— Indian programming included—followed campers into later life. Fitting as it did with the rough and tumble aspects of boy culture sanctioned in other social contexts, Indian programming was particularly popular with boys. At Bolton Camp, one observer remarked, 'The Indian Ceremonial has been of never-failing interest to the boys,' while participation in one 'Indian pageant' of 1938 was said to have given its male campers 'a thrilling experience, so thrilling indeed that many of them insisted on wearing paint, feathers and tomahawks for the rest of their stay at camp'.[45] Where Native guides were employed at more northerly, private camps, boys' fascination with the Indian could be intensified. In such cases, Aboriginal workers modelled an alluring masculinity based on their mastery of wilderness skills. At Camp Ahmek, Ojibwa canoeing instructor Bill Stoqua was described as 'a perfectionist'. Staff recalled, 'He had the style and the physique and the appearance. . . . [A]ll the campers thought if they could paddle like [him] they would have achieved something important.'[46]

When it came to council ring, boys and girls alike appear to have been moved by the ceremony, which some, looking back on it, place 'in the realm of the holy'.[47] Indeed, Taylor Statten claimed that 'no single activity contributes more to the camp sense of unity than the weekly Council Ring,' while YMCA Camp Pine Crest counted council ring 'among the most attractive all-camp activities'.[48] One Wapomeo camper, later director, recalls that this was no casual event. It was 'always done very precisely, very organised and well planned', she explained, 'Some of us were in fear and trembling that somebody would do the wrong thing and spoil the atmosphere.'[49] Other former campers agreed. According to one, 'We all behaved as if . . . in a church service,'[50] remaining quiet except when called on to sing or recite. Mary Northway recalls of council ring at Glen Bernard Camp, that it was 'awe-inspiring. At dusk in blankets the Big Chief (little Miss Edgar [the camp director]) turned us into Indians of a long ago time.'[51] In a lighter spirit, Jim Buchanan remembers council ring as 'a fun event and certainly . . . one of the highlights of camp'. He now admits he couldn't help indulging the idea of Taylor Statten as truly Aboriginal, even though he knew otherwise. 'In many respects he struck you as stoical [sic],' he now explains, '. . . that he actually had an Indian background . . . which he sure as hell didn't. But he seemed like he did.'[52]

Beyond the reaches of campers' childish psyches, playing Indian at camp had other repercussions. As we have seen, camp programming conveyed the same negative images and limiting stereotypes of Aboriginal peoples as those circulating in the wider society. In so doing, camps did more than shape attitudes of individual campers; at a broader level, they contributed to the ongoing rationalization of colonialism. Negative images of violence and savagery rationalized it from the humanitarian perspective, while positive stereotypes, by freezing Aboriginal peoples in time, suggested that such noble, pre-modern creatures couldn't hope to survive in a modern civilized society. Either way, the colonial project was naturalized; that is, it was simply the way things had to be. On the other hand, as with the colonial project in general, silences and omissions regarding the tragic history of Native–white relations did as much harm as these articulated messages. Indeed, perhaps more damaging than what camps had to say about the Indian was what they did not. Nothing, it seems, was ever said about the fact that, as white campers played at being Indian, contemporary Native children were the target of aggressive campaigns aimed to rid them of their 'Indian-ness'. Did campers have any idea, one wonders, that as directors donned Native headdresses, state laws attempted to bar Aboriginal peoples from appearing publicly in traditional dress? Were they ever aware that as they enthusiastically participated in Indian rituals, Native bands in western provinces were prohibited from holding their own sundance and potlatch ceremonies?[53]

Whether campers knew it or not, as they seasonally put on Indian skins, Aboriginals could not escape the taint of their Indian status. Even while scholars conclude that racial categories in general are 'shifting and unstable', and even 'appallingly empty',[54] for those racialized Others, the biological 'unreality' of race conflicted with its pressing social reality in their day-to-day lives. Take only the example of the Bear Island band of Temagami. By the time of this study, they faced an unenviable set of social and economic conditions. As the result of a long-outstanding land claim, the band had never been formally assigned reserve land. Despite this fact, they adapted gradually to the fact of white encroachment on their land, surviving on a combination of trapping and guiding, including even some employment at the area's summer camps. However, without clear hunting and fishing rights, the Temagami band faced continual harassment by local game wardens. Worse still, resource development in the area and the infiltration of white trappers in the 1930s put the supply of fur into serious decline, leaving many to survive increasingly on relief funds. Post-war years saw little improvement in these conditions. The province continued to equivocate on the issue of establishing a reserve, and problems of alcohol and family breakdown increased.[55]

During this time, the small but influential recreation-based community of Temagami did little to ameliorate and, in some ways, exacerbated the problems of the Bear Islanders. With their own eyes firmly on preserving the area as wilderness escape and/or tourist mecca, white cottagers and resort operators complained variously about Native health problems, their destruction of the visible shoreline, and abuses of alcohol in the Aboriginal community, calling for increased police and medical surveillance as solutions. Camp Keewaydin's employment of Bear Islanders gives some indication of how camp communities fit into this picture. At the camp's founding in the first years of the century, the administration considered Ojibwa men from Bear Island knowledgeable, experienced, and close at hand; in short, the ideal tripping guides. Primarily trappers, they spent the winter on their lines but were available and often looking for summer work. Over the years, however, Keewaydin's preference shifted away from the Bear Island band so that by the 1920s the camp no longer sought workers from within the local community. Although the camp historian is silent on the issue, it is quite possible that, given the situation already noted, the Bear Islanders were increasingly regarded as the undesirable sort of Indians, hardly the noble self-sustaining survivalists that camp life sought to glorify. As far as other questions are concerned—for instance, the Bear Islanders' outstanding land claim— there is no indication that the white community—camps included—had anything to say on the issue, much less that they played any role as advocates for Aboriginal rights. Reminding children that they walked on what had been 'Indian land' was portrayed not as a matter of controversy, as the basis for a critique of colonialism, or social redress, but rather as a mildly interesting (if unchangeable) anthropological fact. Were camp administrators aware of, or concerned about, the Bear Islanders' long outstanding land claim? Certainly, by the 1970s and 1980s some involved themselves in this struggle.[56] For this earlier period, however, decades still marked by a broad cultural confidence in the colonial project, nothing could be found to indicate camp concern about the social and economic predicament of their Aboriginal neighbours in Temagami.

In other contexts, the early post-war years saw the first indications that parts of the camping community were developing new sensibilities toward the design of their Indian programming. As early as 1946, educator Mary Northway attacked the 'distortion' of Native culture that she observed in camp programs. 'Isn't it too bad,' she observed, 'that the only conception some of our campers, living in haunts so recently inhabited by Indians, have is that Indians were a people who met on Saturday nights dressed in blankets from . . . the Hudson Bay store and engaged in marshmallow eating contests?'[57] Presumably in response to the shift in public consciousness, some camps moved to eliminate certain features of their Indian programming. In 1958 Mary Hamilton described the decision to do away with Indian council ring at Tanamakoon: 'The familiar "How! How!," the tribal set-up and the Indian names still exist,' she explained. 'As for the Indian council fire, it was shortlived. We decided not to be Indians any longer and proceeded to be our own natural selves.'[58] Other camps could be slower to initiate change. At the prestigious Taylor Statten camps, it was an Aboriginal youth who apparently articulated the first critique of council ring. In the early 1970s this counsellor-in-training, also daughter of the chief of the Ontarian Curve Lake band, complained to the camp administration: 'I was so shock [sic] to go to council ring last night . . . having to watch you people make fun of my people.'[59] Initially, the camp administration attempted to pacify the youth by removing the 'dress-up' element from the ceremony, but when this prompted others to complain that 'something was lost', the ritual was reinstated in its original form.[60] By the 1980s and 1990s, some camps—like Bolton—were more self-critical. There, council ring was not eliminated but modified; the use of broken English

was forbidden, and campfires were instituted, following non-Indian themes. . . . In the hot political context of late twentieth-century Native–white relations, clearly playing Indian was not always seen as harmless child's play. On the other hand, the issue is still contested, if silently; these traditions continue in many ways at different camps, with Aboriginal names and practices still in evidence. As late as 1994, Indian council ring was still going strong at Camp Ahmek, with staff carefully following Statten's original order of proceedings, and campers continuing to dress up in 'blankets, feathers, and paint'.[61]

Conclusion

The history of camps' Indian programming tells us something about the shifting nature of Native–white relations, but ultimately the history of 'playing Indian' is the history of whites and of white middle-class culture. One aspect was a recurring anti-modernist sentiment that presented itself as a strong, if sub-cultural, tendency throughout this period. The fact that camps did not disappear, but indeed proliferated in the 1950s and beyond, is just one indication that anti-modernism still figured in the post-war cultural landscape. Granted, infatuation with modernity in many forms was everywhere to be seen, but anti-modernism also percolated beneath the surface, raising questions and dampening the cultural optimism of the day.

In the interwar years this ambivalence revealed itself by the fact that while child care manuals counselled rigid and controlled approaches to rearing children, many also considered the temporary outlet of experiences like camp—its Indian programming included—as necessary antidotes. It is revealing to note that the diminishing importance of Indian programming coincided with not only a changing climate of racial politics, but also with the rise of more permissive, emotional approaches to child-rearing in the post-war period. Perhaps as children were treated less as machines and more regularly encouraged to be 'their own natural selves', the catharsis of playing Indian was deemed a more dispensable frill.

. . .

The common thread connecting this and other North American incarnations of anti-modernism was its ultimate social impact . . . Through the camp, modern ways of thinking, feeling, and imagining the self and racial Others were reinforced. Preoccupation with intense experience and with identity, and the belief that both were to be sought on the terrain of leisure, were all typical of the modern condition. That camp administrators were not above marketing this experience was also indicative of their times. Born of anti-modernism, the summer camp was a modern animal. Playing Indian in this setting was just one way it allowed for simultaneous expression of these competing cultural impulses.

Notes

My sincere thanks to the anonymous reviewers for their comments on an earlier version of this article. Thanks also to Cecilia Morgan and Gillian Poulter for their helpful comments and collegial support.

1. Mary S. Edgar, 'Our Indebtedness to Our Indian Friends', 72-007/5/16, Ontario Camping Association Papers (hereafter cited as OCA), Trent University Archives (hereafter cited as TUA). Hereafter, the quotation marks around the term 'Indian' will be implied.

2. Bobby Bridger, *Buffalo Bill and Sitting Bull: Inventing the Wild West* (Austin: University of Texas Press, 2002); Daniel Francis, *The Imaginary Indian: The Image of the Indian in Canadian Culture* (Vancouver: Arsenal Pulp, 1992), 115–23, 142–3 . . .

3. C.A.M. Edwards, *Taylor Statten* (Toronto: Ryerson, 1960), 88.

4. Independently, Paris and I have come to the similar conclusion that camps were shaped by simple life nostalgia, but also inextricably linked to the urban social worlds they claimed to be escaping. In addition to exploring racial play-acting in its Indian forms, Paris also traces the fascinating history of blackface minstrelsy at summer camp. Leslie Paris, 'Children's Nature: Summer Camps in New York State, 1919–1941' (PhD diss., University of Michigan, 2000). . . .

5. On camp statistics, see Nancy Cleaver, 'An Old Canadian Custom: Sending the Kids to Camp', *Saturday Night*, 19 Apr. 1952, 16; Peter Newman, 'Junior's $10 Million Adventure in the Pines', *Financial Post*, 5 June 1954, 5; 'Canada's Summer Indians Hit the Trail', *Star Weekly Magazine*, 11 June, 1960, 3. On the early camp movement, see essays in Bruce W. Hodgins and Bernadine Dodge, eds, *Using Wilderness: Essays on the Evolution of Youth Camping in Ontario* (Peterborough, ON: Frost Centre for Canadian Heritage and Development Studies, 1992), and Ontario Camping Association, *Blue Lake and Rocky Shore: A History of Children's Camping in Ontario* (Toronto: Natural Heritage/Natural History, 1984).

6. Hartmut Lutz, 'Cultural Appropriation as a Process of Displacing Peoples and History', *Canadian Journal of Native Studies* 10 (1990): 167–82. . . .

7. Philip Deloria, *Playing Indian* (New Haven, CT: Yale University Press, 1998); Shari Huhndorf, *Going Native: Indians in the American Cultural Imagination* (Ithaca, NY: Cornell University Press, 2001). . . .

8. T.J. Jackson Lears, *No Place of Grace: Antimodernism and the Transformation of American Culture, 1880–1920* (Chicago: University of Chicago Press, 1981); Ian McKay, *Quest of the Folk: Antimodernism and Cultural Selection in Twentieth-Century Nova Scotia* (Montreal and Kingston: McGill-Queen's University Press, 1994).

9. 'Urbanization', *Canadian Encyclopedia* (Edmonton: Hurtig Press, 1988), 2235.

10. Katherine Arnup, *Education for Motherhood: Advice for Mothers in Twentieth-Century Canada* (Toronto: University of Toronto Press, 1994), 84–116; Katherine Arnup, 'Raising the Dionne Quintuplets: Lessons for Modern Mothers', *Journal of Canadian Studies* 29 (Winter, 1994–95): 65–84; Cynthia Comacchio, *Nations Are Built of Babies: Saving Ontario's Mothers and Children* (Montreal and Kingston: McGill-Queen's University Press, 1993) . . .

11. Mary L. Northway, 'Tools for the Job', *Parent Education Bulletin* 13 (1941): 6.

12. Cynthia Comacchio, 'Dancing to Perdition: Adolescence and Leisure in Interwar English Canada', *Journal of Canadian Studies* 32 (1997): 5–35; David MacLeod, 'A Live Vaccine: The YMCA and Male Adolescence in the United States and Canada, 1870–1920', *Histoire Sociale/Social History* 11 (May 1978): 5–25; Margaret Prang, 'The Girl God Would Have Me Be: The Canadian Girls in Training, 1915–1939', *Canadian Historical Review* 66 (1985): 154–83 . . .

13. H. Allen Anderson, *The Chief: Ernest Thompson Seton and the Changing West* (College Station: Texas A&M University Press, 1986); Gail Bederman, '"Teaching Our Sons To Do What We Have Been Teaching the Savages To Avoid": G. Stanley Hall, Racial

Recapitulation, and the Neurasthenic Paradox', in *Manliness and Civilization: A Cultural History of Gender and Race in the United States, 1880–1917* (Chicago: University of Chicago Press, 1999); Deloria, *Playing Indian*, 95–110; Adele Ebbs, interview by Jack Pearse, 22 May 1986, 83-002/10/9, OCA Sound/Tape Collection, TUA; Edwards, *Taylor Statten*, 88 . . .

14. Bert Danson, 'The History of Camp Winnebagoe' (unpublished paper, 2000).

15. Neighbourhood Workers' Association (hereafter cited as NWA), 'The Story of Bolton Camp', in *After Twenty Years: A Short History of the Neighbourhood Workers Association* (Toronto: Family Services Association, 1938), 43, Family Services Association of Toronto Archival Collection (hereafter cited as FSATA); Hedley S. Dimock and Charles E. Hendry, *Camping and Character: A Camp Experiment in Character Education* (New York: Association, 1929), 74; W.J. Eastaugh, *Indian Council Ring* (Camp Ahmek: Taylor Statten Camps, 1938); Camp Pine Crest, 'Report of Craft Activities', 1951, 78-009/2/1, Camp Pine Crest Fonds, TUA.

16. NWA, *Annual Report: New Interests at Bolton Camp in 1935* (Toronto: NWA), 15, FSATA. On games of 'scalping', references to 'scalps' (made of hemp rope) on display in council ring, and to Native 'tribes' as 'mortal enemies', see Eastaugh, *Indian Council Ring*, 26, 31.

17. Mary G. Hamilton, *The Call of Algonquin: Biography of a Summer Camp* (Toronto: Ryerson, 1958), 149. . . .

18. Mary L. Northway, 'Canadian Camping: Its Foundation and Its Future' (paper presented to the Manitoba Camping Association Annual Meeting, May 1946), 1, 98-019/13/6, series E, Adele Ebbs Papers, TUA.

19. . . . On Bolton's Indian programming, see NWA, *Annual Report: Bolton Camp, Report of Operation, 1937* (Toronto: NWA), FSATA. On Ahmek, see Dimock and Hendry, *Camping and Character*, 73–5; 'The War Whoop', *Canoe Lake Camp Echoes* 4 (June 1931): 53, Ronald H. Perry Fonds, TUA.

20. Eastaugh, *Indian Council Ring*, 30.

21. Dimock and Hendry, *Camping and Character*, 141–2.

22. NWA, *After Twenty Years*, 43.

23. Dimock and Hendry, *Camping and Character*, 141.

24. Eastaugh, *Indian Council Ring*, 1.

25. NWA, *Annual Report: New Interests*, 8; Edgar, 'Our Indebtedness', 2.

26. Eastaugh, *Indian Council Ring*, 7; 'Notes on Programme: Bark Lake', 1948, 98-012/1/1, Ontario Camp Leadership Centre, Bark Lake Fonds, TUA.

27. 'Five Years of Drudgery Bring Proud, Brave Family to End of Their Resources', *Toronto Daily Star*, 30 Aug. 1927, 21. Deloria and Paris also note the symbolic importance of tans in connecting campers with a 'premodern time zone'. Deloria, *Playing Indian*, 106; Paris, 'Children's Nature', 243.

28. 'Notes on Programme: Bark Lake', 1948; Dimock and Hendry, *Camping and Character*, photo, 74; Bolton Camp photo albums, 1920s–1950s, FSATA. Camp Pine Crest, *Camp Pine Crest*, 1945, 78-009/2/4, Camp Pine Crest Fonds, TUA.

29. Eastaugh, *Indian Council Ring*, 1.

30. Eustace Haydon, 'Memorial Talk Delivered to Camp Ahmek: Founders' Day', 12 July 1959, in Donald Burry, 'A History of the Taylor Statten Camps' (master's thesis, University of Saskatchewan, 1985), 27. Emphasis in original.

31. Douglas Cole, 'The Invented Indian/The Imagined Emily', *BC Studies* 125/126 (Spring/Summer 2000): 147–62; Francis, *Imaginary Indian*, 190; Terry Goldie, *Fear and Temptation: The Image of the Indigene in Canadian, Australian, and New Zealand Literatures* (Montreal and Kingston: McGill-Queen's University Press, 1989) . . .

32. Hamilton, *Call of Algonquin*, 4.

33. Edgar, 'Our Indebtedness', 2.

34. For examples, see Peter Kulchyski, 'Anthropology in the Service of the State: Diamond Jenness and Canadian Indian Policy', *Journal of Canadian Studies* 28 (Summer 1993): 21–50; Andrew Nurse, '"But now things have changed": Marius Barbeau and the Politics of Amerindian Identity', *Ethnohistory* 48 (2001): 433–72.

35. 'Change', *Canoe Lake Camp Echoes* 4 (June 1931): 18, 82-016/2/8, Ronald H. Perry Fonds, TUA.

36. Brian Back, *The Keewaydin Way: A Portrait, 1893–1983* (Temagami: Keewaydin Camp, 1983), 37.

37. 'Pale-faced City Tikes Taught Indian Lore by Expert Woodsmen', *Toronto Daily Star*, 7 June 1950, 25; 'Calling All Campers', *Canadian Girls in Training Newsletter*, 1952, file 4, box 39, 85.095C, UCA/VUA.

38. On Western primitivism, see Bederman 'Teaching Our Sons', 112–17; Helen Carr, *Inventing the American Primitive: Politics, Gender and the Representation of Native American Literary Traditions, 1789–1936* (New York: New York University Press, 1996) . . .

39. Back, *Keewaydin Way*, 142.

40. 'Pale-faced City Tikes Taught Indian Lore', 25.

41. Back, *Keewaydin Way*, 141.

42. NWA, *Annual Report, 1937*, 8, FSATA.

43. 'Pale-faced City Tikes Taught Indian Lore', 25.

44. Eastaugh, *Indian Council Ring*, 7.

45. NWA, *After Twenty Years*, 43; NWA, *Annual Report, 1938*, 11, FSATA.

46. Ron Perry, interview by Bruce Harris, 2 Dec. 1981, 83-002/5/1, OCA Sound Tape Collection, TUA.

47. Shirley Ford, interview by author, 20 June 2000, Toronto.

48. Dimock and Hendry, *Camping and Character*, 321; Camp Pine Crest, 'Director's Report', 1950, 78-009/2/1, Camp Pine Crest Fonds, TUA.

49. Ebbs, interview by Pearse.

50. Jane Hughes, interview by author, 26 June 2000.

51. 'Northway Recollection of Glen Bernard Camp'.

52. James Buchanan, interview by author, 26 July 2000, Toronto.

53. Douglas Cole and Ira Chaikin, *An Iron Hand upon the People: The Law against the Potlatch on the Northwest Coast* (Vancouver: Douglas and McIntyre, 1990); Keith Regular, 'On Public Display', *Alberta History* 34, 1 (Winter 1986): 1–10; Glen Mikkelsen, 'Indians and Rodeo', *Alberta History* 34 (Winter 1986): 13–19.

54. Anne McClintock, *Imperial Leather: Race, Gender, and Sexuality in the Colonial Contest* (New York: Routledge, 1995), 52; Constance Backhouse, *Colour-Coded: A Legal History of Racism in Canada, 1900–1950* (Toronto: University of Toronto Press, 1999), 8.

55. Bruce W. Hodgins and Jamie Benidickson, *The Temagami Experience: Recreation, Resources, and Aboriginal Rights in the Northern Ontario Wilderness* (Toronto: University of Toronto Press, 1989), 210–28.

56. In the 1970s camp director and scholar Bruce Hodgins began researching his *Temagami Experience*, which took a sympathetic view of Aboriginal rights in Temagami. . . .

57. Northway, 'Canadian Camping'.

58. Hamilton, *Call of Algonquin*, 22.

59. 'Margo', quoted in Ebbs, interview by Pearse.

60. Ebbs, Interview, 20.

61. Liz Lundell, *Summer Camp: Great Camps of Algonquin Park* (Toronto: Stoddart Publishing, 1994), 104–6; Fred Okada, conversation with author, 15 Dec. 1998; Dale Callendar, *History of Bolton Camp* [1997], 11, FSATA.

22

At Play: Fads, Fashions, and Fun

———— Cynthia Comacchio ————

It is time that the civic conscience awakened to the debauchery and degrading circumstances of the dance halls . . . the reeking atmosphere . . . the absolutely inevitable stirring of sexual passion entailed in the so-called jitney and other similar dances.

Guelph Daily Mercury, 1921

In October 1921 a 'large gathering' reportedly collected in Guelph, Ontario, to hear a local preacher discuss the social and spiritual repercussions of the 'youth dance craze'. The speaker cited expert evidence, from 'authorities who had no interest in the religious aspects', who proclaimed young dance hall patrons to be 'failures in classroom and physical culture'. It was urgent that responsible citizens 'lend their influence in remedying these conditions'.[1] Such an impassioned outcry against dance halls cannot be dismissed as simply clerical duty in the salvation of young souls. The small-town preacher's dismay about the antics of modern youth was replicated across a multiplicity of discourses, religious and secular, 'expert' and non-expert. Its language of moral outrage and foreboding only thinly veiled the real issue: the youth autonomy symbolized by the 'palaces for pleasure' that were the burgeoning commercial amusement places of the time. Whatever these places sold as entertainment, they were important bases for a modern style of recreation that was very much geared to the young consumer, a vital emergent market for producers and sellers of goods as well as mass entertainment.

By the 1920s, Canadian adolescents were spending much of their leisure time, as well as greater amounts of money in the pursuit of leisure, apart from their families out of the home. With children at school and adults occupied by housekeeping and wage labour, truly free time was very much the dominion of the in-betweens. They were enjoying greater social freedom in the streets and public venues, and more selection in the widening array of modern amusements available as a result of technological advances and mass production. Along with their own enthusiastic participation, these factors were shaping a youth culture expressed through leisure activity, much of which involved cash transactions in commercial venues, a thoroughly modern and increasingly democratic endeavour.[2] This chapter considers how popular culture and modern adolescence became entwined in the public eye during these years, eventually coming to constitute the youth problem in essence. The matter of how the young had fun was grounded in larger issues of citizenship, national welfare, and the very nature of modernity, with its ethic of consumption and its 'new' and highly questionable morality.

. . .

By the 1920s, social scientists were presenting leisure as a positive social force that, by providing the necessary opportunities for human beings to recover and re-create their energies, could be martialled to reinforce the work ethic.[3] The challenge, yet again, was posed by modernizing forces. In conjunction with diminishing child labour and extended schooling, Canadian youth

Cynthia Comacchio, 'At Play: Fads, Fashion, and Fun', *The Dominion of Youth: Adolescence and the Making of a Modern Canada*, 1920–1950 (Waterloo, ON: Wilfrid Laurier University Press, 2006), pp. 161–88. Reprinted by permission of the publisher.

were confronted with unprecedented time on their hands to fill as they chose. Representing a realm of autonomy and choice, leisure held much potential for 'mismanagement' by people of all ages, but by none more than adolescents. Leisure had become a complicated matter, contributing, paradoxically, to the very confusion and disorder seen to characterize modernity: 'Our recreations include ten activities where [our] grandfathers knew one.' Because of their 'recreational illiteracy', Canadians appeared to be surrendering to 'all the mechanical gadgetry in which we seek stimulation for jaded play appetites'. Yet it was this very mechanized mode of living that made more important 'the need to develop vocational-creative abilities', to ensure 'a sort of safeguard for the soul, oppressed as it is by push buttons, levers and mass production'.[4]

. . . The greatest social danger of the day appeared to be the emergence of a 'multitude of people in all classes of society with no skill they can exercise, either for their own enjoyment or other people's benefit, but with plenty of money in their pockets for the purpose of readymade pleasures'. Work and play were ideally bound in a relationship geared toward the shaping of an efficient modern Canada, both productive and principled: 'Lack of all-round keenness in work and play is probably one of our greatest failings in the practice of citizenship.'[5] Canadians, and especially those in the critical adolescent stage, had to stop thinking about leisure 'merely in terms of play or pleasure', so that their pastimes would be at once restorative and productive. For the young, leisure would ideally constitute an enjoyable but otherwise stringent form of preparatory training for their all-important future roles, reinforcing ideals of bodily and mental fitness as well as citizenship goals. It was a tall order to place in the realm of fun.

. . .

Early twentieth-century changes in the organization of both work and leisure gave rise to a youth-oriented mixed-sex recreational arena, more removed than ever before from the watchful gaze of adults.[6] The abundant and varied diversions of the modern age—the dance halls, cinemas, spectator sports, automobile trips, and speakeasies—energized an emergent youth culture that would come to signify mass culture itself. By the early post-World War I years, mass culture was being identified as the modern demon animating the youth problem. Both popular culture and youth came to be demonized as a result. Increasingly, the law was applied to the problem. Seductive adolescent pastimes that took place in public spaces were legally proscribed in variations on Ontario's Minors' Protection Act of 1927: 'No child under the age of 18' was permitted entry into a billiard, pool, or bagatelle room 'for the purpose of loitering or to play billiards, pool or bagatelle therein'. The same Act outlawed tobacco sales to those under eighteen.[7] Discussions about modern youth made constant reference to the special attraction that mass culture, actuated by modern technology, held out to the young, who were more modern than their parents could ever hope to be. Critics worried that young Canadians were being sucked into the intensely materialistic, commercialized, immoral/amoral vortex of modernity. The youthful 'thirst for pleasure and luxury and money' was undermining 'the qualities of mind and character that must form the foundation for a race'.[8]

The movies stood unchallenged as the most potent of the new cultural forces affecting youth. Government reports, professional journals, popular magazines, the daily press, the nation's pulpits, and the House of Commons and provincial legislatures all resounded with moral indignation about the screen images that planted 'wrongful notions' in young minds, the new 'talkies' using dialogue to magnify the poisonous effects. The harvest sown by this filmic 'evil seed' was measured in the increase in theft and violent crime among boys and 'sexual immorality' among girls, upon whom Hollywood's effects were deemed 'constantly and seriously demoralizing'.[9] The tone and extent of the panic over movies also points to the great difficulty of dissuading Canadians, especially the young, from frequent cinema attendance. Marketing surveys of the time found that age was the single greatest factor in movie attendance.[10] A 1936 survey of 100 adolescents in Halifax found that 96 regularly attended the cinema, with 38 going at least once a week and roughly one-quarter at least once every two weeks; the remaining one-third attended twice a month 'or more often'. Murder, detective, and 'thrilling pictures' were favoured by both sexes. Among the girls, collecting photographs of film stars was also the most popular hobby declared.[11] From the perspective of those who would regulate all modern pastimes, the Canadian passion for cinema-going was sadly reflected in data revealing that, while regular church attendance drew 'scarcely half our people', over 90 per cent of Canadians were regular moviegoers, and fully 60 per cent of these were under the age of 18. Even during the Depression, most moviegoers attended once a month; in larger centres, the average attendance was 20 to 35 times per year.[12] Going to the movies had become an integral youth pastime. The cinema was affordable, accessible, and relatively tame as commercial amusements went. It permitted a public, safe (and dark) setting for the rituals of adolescent meeting and courtship.[13] Even the embarrassment of having to return soft drink and milk bottles, in great demand during the salvage campaigns of World War II, just to collect enough change to attend was considered worth doing for the pleasure of seeing the latest movie.[14]

. . . Calls for regulation rose to fever pitch in the aftermath of a fire at the Laurier Palace cinema in Montreal in January 1927, in which 78 children, one-third of them young teenagers between the ages of 13 and 16, perished at a Sunday matinee screening of the ominously titled comedy *Gets 'Em Young*. Despite the 1919 provincial legislation prohibiting those under 16 from attending films without adult accompaniment, and despite the owner's previous convictions under that law as well as for breaching fire regulations about crowding the aisles, the majority of the audience was both under 16 and unaccompanied.

According to the coroner's testimony at the inquiry, three-quarters were at the cinema without their parents' knowledge or permission. Most provinces subsequently tightened their regulations for licensing, inspection, and ages and hours of admission.[15] Ontario allowed no admission to any unaccompanied child under 15 except on Saturdays between the hours of nine in the morning and six in the evening, during which time a 'matron' was to be present in supervisory capacity. In addition to the usual difficulties of enforcement, even such legislation left considerable opportunity for movie attendance by children and youth. The law consequently did little to relieve adult anxieties about the dangers of overcrowding at theatres and even less in regard to the 'bad influence' of the movies on budding sexual and criminal proclivities.[16]

Since controlling the age of attendance was not particularly fruitful, the other favoured option was to control what was actually shown on the screen. There were censor boards in place in most provinces by 1914, but there was seemingly little faith in their efficacy, judging by the frequency of arguments for a single national board to ensure the uniformity and consistency believed to be needed.[17] Already by the war's end, public pressure had brought about amendments to censorship regulations, making them at once more precise and more encompassing. Most provinces imitated Manitoba's sweeping provisions of 1916: that province's censor board would not approve any film depicting scenes 'of an immoral or obscene nature,' or which indicate or suggest lewdness or indecency or marital infidelity or showing the details of murder, robbery, or criminal assault or depicting criminals as heroic characters', or, for that matter, 'any other picture' considered to be 'injurious to public morals, suggestive of evil to the minds of children and young people or against the public welfare'.[18] Ontario's board eliminated such scenes of depravity as that of a young woman picking up a man's watch from the floor beside her bed, and such subversive dialogue as a reference to 'old Comrade God Himself'.[19]

. . . Various rating schemes were initiated in the interests of educating a naive movie-going public, especially parents of children and adolescents. The nation's largest social service agency, the Canadian Council on Child and Family Welfare, began publishing a 'White List' of approved films for those under adult age in 1927. . . . In 1931, Charlotte Whitton, the council's executive director, complained that even the dissemination of this bimonthly select list of motion pictures saw 'little progress made . . . though existing in a field that cries out for service'.[20] Attempts to slay, or at least tame, the Hollywood dragon appeared futile. These were the films that people wanted to see; film producers and cinema managers were well aware of the importance of catering to their loyal young clientele.[21] . . .

. . .

Where 1920s films had glamourized youth, the most popular Hollywood movies of the Depression decade—the gangster films—idealized the modern urban outlaw, all too often cultivated from the ranks of male juvenile delinquents. During a time when some young people might well have wondered what could be achieved by hard work and law-abiding behaviour, the criminal gangs and activities depicted in these films might have appeared heroic. At bottom, they offered non-conformism as a means of escape from Depression dreariness. [Lewis] Jacobs believed that the 'indiscriminate rebellion against moral conventions' characterizing the jazz-age films was replaced in the 1930s by 'an earnest search for moral norms', resulting in both a new on-screen realism and also a 'powerful and unceasing censorship'. The new realism and the reinvigorated censorship crusade collided over the issue of gangster films.[22] To youth-watchers, the enthusiasm for these 'shoot 'em up' movies bespoke only young lives heading downward, the nation rapidly following suit. In the United States, with every step closely followed by Canadians, organized protest against gangster movies reached new volume over the release of the 1932 Howard Hawks film *Scarface*, starring Paul Muni as the Al Capone-like central figure.[23] The outcome was the Motion Picture Production Code, or Hays Code, endorsed by the industry's own Motion Picture Producers and Distributors of America and made mandatory in 1934, as well as the formation of the policing organization known as the League of Decency.

. . .

Movie-going topped the list both for young Canadians pursuing modern recreational opportunities and for the adults who strove to regulate that pursuit, but the so-called dance craze vied closely for that ranking. Dancing as a social activity was certainly nothing new. In the 1920s, however, it appeared to have 'a grip on our young people such as it never had before'.[24] The number of editorials, letters from irate readers, 'scientific' analyses, eyewitness accounts, and clerical admonitions reported in the popular press concerning the dance phenomenon of that decade is immeasurable. It was not only the seeming dance-obsession of the young that perturbed Canadians, but even more so the style of dancing, sometimes called 'whirling'. Modern dance appeared to be all about sex, a stylized public mating ritual that, bad enough in its lewd and suggestive bodily contact, was made all the worse because it was performed in darkened, often packed, too often unchaperoned commercial dance halls where cigarettes burned and illicit liquor flowed. Such 'fevered' dances as the foxtrot, the jitney, the Lindy hop, the bunny hug, the Charleston, and the truly heinous tango were linked with everything from juvenile delinquency through madness and 'race suicide', another obsession of the age and one closely linked to the young generation, future parents that they were.[25]

As was the case in regards to the movie-mania of the young, Canadian critics of popular culture were able to turn to American experts for the necessary 'science' to back their protests about the young generation's 'dance-o-mania'. Among the most fear-inspiring of these was a widely circulated tract by Dr R.A. Adams, self-proclaimed 'author, editor, lecturer on Higher Eugenics, Sex Hygiene Prophylactics and Social Economics'. Adams declared that 'the devil chose well' in making the dance 'one of his surest, truest and most potent instruments of destruction . . . of the bodies, minds, lives and souls, of men and women'. Here was an instrument that not only would ruin the present generation but, 'by means of Heredity, Pre-natal Influence and Defective Environment', would pass its degenerate effects to future generations. Devoting the better part of several hundred pages to the immorality of modern dance, vehemently sustained by racist condemnation of the 'Negro' origins of the 'habit', he continually conflated its health repercussions with its implications for the souls of white Christian youth.[26]

. . .

The fact that young dancers kept pace to the 'uncivilized' and 'primitive' strains and 'mad rhythms' of jazz and other 'Negro' music was equally objectionable to many observers. The earliest jazz musicians on the Canadian scene were American performers appearing on the vaudeville circuit in the mid- to late 1910s. Canadian musicians, as much as young music-lovers, quickly took up this cultural import. Jazz historians date the music's commercial beginnings in Canada to about 1917, at which point recordings of the music and the growth of commercial dance halls fuelled its popularity. The jazz phenomenon was further facilitated during the 1920s by radio broadcasting, the cheap cost of producing records, and rising radio and gramophone ownership.[27] Already in 1922, the American magazine *Photoplay* was reporting that the 18–30 age group accounted for 48 per cent of all phonograph and record purchases, although making up only 23 per cent of the US population.[28] In an evolutionary process hinging on youthful tastes and the youth market, the music industry increasingly responded to these with music and dance styles aimed directly at them and purposely distinguishing the new generational style from the old jazz, the 'crooners' of

the late 1930s, the big-band sound, swing jive, and ultimately the revolutionary 'youth sound' of the 1950s, rock 'n' roll.

The unrestrained, free-form, highly improvised syncopated rhythms of jazz signified the music of the modern age, and consequently of modern youth. Because the Great War drew away many of the nation's seasoned musicians, the development of jazz in Canadian cities, according to musicologist Mark Miller, was accelerated as they were replaced in the dance halls by 'younger men with the newer ideas of a generation maturing under the formative influence of jazz, a music that offered their youthful energies full release'. Among the best known of the early Canadian jazz bands was the Winnipeg Jazz Babies, who came together during that city's tumultuous spring of 1919, amidst the General Strike. The band was composed of seven teenage boys, the oldest only 18. They were regular performers at the city's Manitoba and Alhambra dance halls and earned wider renown through tours across the western provinces.[29] Montreal, with a growing community of single black men, many of them Americans imported to work for the railway, became the contemporary hotbed of Canadian jazz, although many of the 'white' clubs in the city, as across the continent, would not hire black or 'mixed' bands.[30] The Catholic Church in Quebec railed mightily against the wicked implications of jazz and dance for a devout, traditional, francophone society.[31] The *Vancouver Sun*'s music critic called jazz and the shimmy the 'twin sisters of corruption'. In an even more extreme—and racist—response, one letter writer to that newspaper pronounced it 'nigger trash', exposing his resentment that this 'vulgar music' was all that 'the average Vancouver dancing audience . . . care to hear.'[32]

While roused to panic over dancing, jazz, and the dance hall itself, the commentators were not, as was often the case, entirely misinterpreting the situation, even as they exaggerated the dangers to youth. During this period, the dance hall came to be a favoured stage for young people experimenting with a thrilling new generational style which served to define their own personal style—their personal 'aura', as the marketers of sex appeal called it—with due attention to appearance, technique, and attraction of the opposite sex. For contemporary youth-watchers, this very style became the visual symbol of troubling emergent attitudes toward leisure, sexuality, and personal fulfilment.[33] Modern 'dance hall girls' were surrendering to the odious flapper influence, and not only in their manner of dressing: more important, 'the very clothing worn is an indication of the character and the ideals which are actuating our growing girls.' The gauzy, strappy, short-skirted flapper costume bore witness to 'a degradation in the minds of young women suggestive of a return to animal instinct and opposed to the dictates of what we are pleased to call civilization'. The 'risks' taken by immodestly dressed girls were quite simply 'enough to make a mother's heart stop'.[34] But the boyish look of the day—deliberately downplaying traditional conventions of feminine beauty, freeing up both preparation time and physical movement—was a special generational marker for young women. For the first time in history, youth was setting the fashion pace. Age, class, gender, and race, however, weighted even the flimsiest of mass-produced items of fashion with different social meanings. Along with other elements of style such as smoking, drinking, and 'loose' attitudes toward fun and sex—if not necessarily loose behaviour—dress and coiffure signified the thoroughly modern girl.[35] Yet much of the flouting of gender-defined middle-class convention remained at this level of the symbolic. Very real restrictions on women's lives persisted, especially for girls still largely dependent on their families.

For the anti-dance set, the ideal was 'adequate philanthropic or civic provision for the normal demand for rhythm and music in recreation'. Until this noble objective was realized, public regulation of the commercial dance hall, by means of licensing to establish hours of operation and ages

of admittance, was critical. But 'the thing that would really alter' the situation was supervision by a chaperone who was 'doing it because of her motives and not for the money entailed'.[36] The chaperone would have 'control of the dances' and 'of correct methods of dancing', clearly intended in the moral and not the performative sense of correctness. But despite a great many determined resolutions by the Council on Child and Family Welfare and a variety of other interested groups, progress in regulating public dance halls as 'a menace to the physical and moral life of youth' was slow, piecemeal, and largely ineffectual. Requiring public halls to be registered, licensed, and inspected by provincial governments at least kept them under watch, a surveillance that could be extended through municipal bylaws, which were often more stringent in their requirements.[37] In Ottawa, the two dance halls that existed in 1929 were licensed by both city and province, with the municipality prohibiting the admittance of 'any unescorted woman'. They were also chaperoned and obliged to close at midnight.[38] Kitchener and Galt, Ontario, each hired a policewoman expressly to keep an eye on 'moral conditions' in and around the towns' dance halls. But Guelph residents lamented that no provision was made in its three dance halls 'to prevent, say, a drunken man from annoying girls. . . . There is no paid chaperone, there is not even a "chucker-out".'[39]

Dance fever continued to infect the young during the 'swing era' of the 1930s, notwithstanding Depression hardships and perhaps even because of them. Helped along by radio exposure and inexpensive recordings, popular music became increasingly accessible to young Canadians. In Regina, as a young teenager when the Depression began, one woman was more fortunate than most, in that her father kept his job, though at reduced wages: 'We didn't miss money that much,' she remembered, 'as long as we had money for the dance hall.'[40] . . . Young people could attend on their own, but most went with friends or as part of a couple: 'You could have a drink . . . Coke, 7 Up or Cream Soda . . . but no liquor. You could have chocolate bars and just dance and listen to the music really. . . . During my era it was only the boys that were drinking, maybe at sixteen or seventeen.'[41] . . .

The big-band sound, with its accompanying jitterbug dance style, continued into the war years, popularized in countless dance halls and high-school gyms by recordings of the American Glenn Miller band and tours by Guy Lombardo and His Royal Canadians. Writer Robert Collins looked back on his youth with a certain wistful nostalgia for the music of the war years, recalling the early 1940s as

a time of young men swirling young women through the intricate weaving patterns of the jitterbug, skirts planing out like saucers with a tantalizing flash of thigh. Of music forever linked to that war, wistful ballads of love and parting: 'I'll Be Seeing You' and 'White Cliffs of Dover' and 'When the Lights Go On Again'. A thousand pianists with a single accomplishment, a nimble left hand that could coax out the rippling, rumbling eight-to-the-bar of boogie-woogie. And the World War II anthem, Glenn Miller's 'In the Mood', soaring.[42] . . .

By the mid-1940s, the 'jazz babies' and swing enthusiasts were evolving into a generation of 'hepcats', a swelling new source of fandom for the crooners of the day. The biggest star among them was easily 'The Voice', as American singer Frank Sinatra was known by his adoring fans, the majority of whom were teenage girls. By this time, dancing and the dance hall seem to have lost some of their centrality in discussions of the youth problem. Jazz, swing, bebop, and their variations in modern popular music, as well as the related dance styles, were being appropriated into mainstream popular culture, which meant that adults were indulging in rather larger numbers. This co-option removed these music and dance styles from the domain of

adolescent transgression and generational style and rendered them reasonably 'safe' and more truly popular. . . . When Sinatra made his only 1944 Canadian appearance in Montreal, 'a wall of sound greeted him. . . . You couldn't hear a note for the shrieks and screams.' 'Frankie' was 'the male singer to whom we would compare all others and always find them wanting.'[43]

Though concerns emanated from press, pulpit, and psychologists about the effects of the Sinatra craze, with diagnoses of mass hypnotism, mass hysteria, 'mass frustrated love without direction', and even 'wartime degeneracy' regularly delivered, the hyperbole surrounding the moral, physical, 'mental hygiene', and 'race suicide' effects of popular music and its accompanying dance styles was actually quieting down by the war's end.[44] Like the high schools did, youth clubs and organizations incorporated dancing as a regular social activity, also mitigating its earlier 'immoral' representation. . . . The burgeoning 'teen club' or 'teen town' movement went the furthest—and was possibly the most successful of all the period's attempts at providing regulated and supervised youth havens for 'wholesome' dancing and other leisure activity. Although certainly not a long time in coming, it would take the next generation's rock 'n' roll fever to bring back the full force of adult apprehension about music and dance.[45]

. . .

The 1920s saw the beginnings of another new cultural trend: the equation of youth not only with the modern, but also with the aesthetic, particularly regarding fashion and standards of physical beauty. The young, fit, virile, and handsome male was idealized in the form of the 'matinee idol' and 'sex symbol' of the new age, notably the iconic Sheik, Rudolph Valentino, whose exotic and erotic qualities spoke to a forbidden racialized sexuality associated with a new breed of 'lounge lizards', 'cake-eaters', 'boy flappers', and 'tango pirates'. Young, lascivious, and mainly foreign-born or 'of foreign blood', these were dangerous men who waited to trap unsuspecting and naive white women. They were also men who danced 'divinely', transgressing traditional constructions of manliness. Yet the message was decidedly mixed: eugenicists obsessing about race suicide maintained that (white) male beauty should be interpreted as 'a sign of fitness for parenthood'.[46]

While the film idols, both male and female, were not themselves adolescents, their 'style' was sold as the style of young moderns and worthy of emulation as such. Hollywood became the new international fashion centre, a modern rival to Paris as style capital of the world, its films the ultimate means of popularizing new styles quickly and efficiently to all who could purchase a movie ticket. Especially keen to buy were the working girls whose precarious social status made shopping for up-to-date fashions a marker of identity as well as a pleasurable way to pass their time and dispense their earnings.[47] The descriptor 'young-looking', with its connotations of smooth skin, up-to-date hair and clothing, and a slender body, entailed new social pressures that would escalate over the course of the century. Youth itself became a modern consumer product to be purchased in everything from cosmetics, undergarments, and hair dye to fad diets, popular beverages, new exercise regimens, and even plastic surgery.

The American soft-drink manufacturer Coca-Cola was among the most effective of those companies that took up the modernity, youth, and beauty campaign. It employed young female models in calendars and advertising campaigns, commencing in earnest in the 1920s, when it also adopted youth slang in its target advertising. In turn, 'Coke' culture permeated youth culture with its own language and imagery. Hallmark Cards, for example, initiated a line of 'Betty Betz' greeting cards during the mid-1940s that were actively promoted as 'greeting cards that speak the Coke set lingo' and as 'groovy new greeting cards designed just for you [teenagers]'. The 'groovy' signifier was a cultural reference associated with late-1930s swing-jive musicians and their fans.

By making reference to 'the Coke set'—the Coca-Cola company's own invention—the Hallmark advertising campaign sold a 'groovy' youth subculture; the 'Coke date' came to mean a non-alcoholic but still 'cool' adolescent date.[48]

The movies were a prime engine of transmission for this modern association between age, personal beauty, and what came to be known as 'lifestyle', as well as a boon to entire industries devoted to the battle against aging and the ugliness and decrepitude that it was coming to stand for.[49] The film industry's establishment of youth as icon received a considerable boost from the concomitant growth in mass-circulation 'family' and 'ladies'' magazines, and of the advertising that they conveyed. As film stars became celebrities and idols rather than mere actors, they were increasingly seen off-screen endorsing products in the magazines. When readers were told that 'every woman and girl wants a Mary Pickford cap-craze of the age,' the message undoubtedly left its imprint. In the early twentieth century, Canadians were not only avid consumers of American film and magazines but could increasingly turn to made-in-Canada magazines. Magazines became market-directed, increasingly reliant on advertising revenue, and increasingly oriented to light reading as an important component of modern leisure.[50] Through mass media and advertising, myriad representations of 'youth as style' entered middle-class Canadian homes.[51] The new moving-picture medium, the newly popular magazine, and the burgeoning advertising industry reinforced circulating images of youth, thereby contributing to the intensity of public attention to the actual human subjects as well as to the commodification of youth as the latest product to enhance modern life or to make it truly modern.

If slowed somewhat by Depression spending restraints, the idea of 'youth fashion' (or, increasingly, 'teen-age fashion') was entrenched by World War II, as 1940s magazines and newspapers—advertisements and features alike—suggest. The bobby-soxers of the 1940s derived their name from the short rolled socks that many young women adopted in lieu of the silk or nylon stockings that wartime production regulations had more or less legislated out of being. Also popular, for casual wear at least, was clothing with writing on it, in particular the loose-fitting pullovers or 'sloppy joes' of the late war years. These became the uniform of teenage girls, along with 'a skirt, generally plaid, or matching the sweater, often pleated, coming to mid-knee or slightly above; pearls, or a detachable Peter Pan collar; white socks, and brown and white scuffed saddle shoes or polished loafers'.[52] The war and Hollywood were also normalizing the wearing of pants by women: in 1945, the 'must-have' item for adolescent girls was the plaid pedal-pusher, 'not a long short but more of a short slack'.[53]

Among young men, the generationally defined, countercultural, and oppositional posture adopted by the brotherhood of 'zoots' or 'zoot-suiters', while representing only a very small minority, caused all manner of disproportionate panic. Using fashion to distinguish themselves as young and non-conformist, even within their peer group, the zoot-suiters also flaunted a new variation on masculinity, and especially masculine sexuality, that was deeply troubling to many observers. The possibility that youthful sexuality might be a contributing cause of the zoot-suit troubles, which culminated in street violence in Toronto and especially in Montreal, is entirely plausible within the context of the wartime concerns—recirculated once again from the Great War—about a loosening of sexual morality. The zoot controversy was about the seeming desire of modern youth in general—though chiefly those who were male, urban, and often depicted as being (if not actually) of 'non-Canadian' or even 'non-anglophone' background—to set themselves apart in provocative subcultures.

Zoot suits made the news in the United States and Canada in the early summer of 1943. Put simply, this form of attire was adopted as a type of counter-uniform to the military apparel on display on the streets of wartime Canada by a 'jive-set' of young urban men also known as 'the boys with the reat pleats'.[54] Many of the anti-zoot contingent were irked by the defiantly unconventional outfit, fundamentally a caricature of respectable male business and 'Sunday best' attire—but also by their wearers' even more offensive stance in defiance of the Wartime Prices and Trade Board, which actually prohibited the manufacture of the suits. Zoot suits were not only immoral, they were illegal. Flustered board officials could uncover no evidence of their being manufactured on a large scale and surmised that 'the small tailor' might be hoarding fabric and making them for the black market, or even that 'many of them were evidently imported from the United States before our restrictions went into effect.'[55]

The zoot suit comprised pants 'with the ankles so tight they can hardly be pulled over the feet' and a long 'Prince Albert-type' jacket reaching to the knees and featuring exaggerated shoulder padding. Accessories included suede shoes, a wide-brimmed hat, usually of brown straw with a wide and 'noisy' hatband, and, 'zootiest of all', a watch chain descending to the shoes in a wide loop. This was the outfit of the urban dandy, unmanly in its various overstated details—a suit for lolling about street corners and smoky billiard halls, for drinking and 'cutting a rug' in dance halls, but not for working or fighting or carrying out the activities that proper adult males were supposed to carry out. Depending on the flourishes desired, it might cost anywhere from $45 to $80, easily a weekly pay packet, often two, for the young men who flaunted the ensemble. Some attributed its origins to Hollywood, and specifically to wartime star Clark Gable, who, it was announced, had 'exchanged his zoot suit for the uniform of the United States Army', thereby redeeming himself both as a man and as a patriotic citizen. Others theorized that the suits originated in Harlem, 'where the negroes congregate', immediately framing the outfit within popular understandings of racial inferiority. Thus, the zoot suit represented youthful wantonness, frivolity, and disrespect for authority as much as had the flapper outfit of the 1920s.[56] For their part, the younger generation saw the anti-zoot campaign, backed by government, police, and military force, as 'persecution of a minority', meaning 'teenagers in general'.[57] Wartime generational antagonism, already fuelled by public panic over juvenile delinquency, came to a head over the zoot.

. . .

During a time of national sacrifice, these young men in flamboyant clothing, many assumed to be 'of foreign birth' or otherwise not white (as well as being 'afficionados of jazz', which implied the same thing to many adults), greatly offended those whose own military uniform demonstrated maturity, patriotic duty, and a large measure of masculine heroism. In particular, the fight was on between servicemen of all ages and the 'slackers' in zoot suits, a significant proportion of whom were not even of military age.[58] If the question agitating 'Toronto's jive-set' was 'To zoot or not to zoot', the response on the part of city-based servicemen derived from 'strong feelings toward the rug-cutters'. Only because Toronto police 'stepped firmly on the boys with the reat pleats', according to the city's dance, pool hall and theatre managers, were the riots that plagued Los Angeles avoided.[59] Police had believed it necessary to remove jukeboxes from two popular recreational beaches, Sunnyside and Hanlan's Point, after sailors and other members of the armed forces had 'heaved zoot suiters into the lake or torn the clothing from them'.[60]

. . .

The real zoot-suit trouble seems to have centred in Montreal and environs. In late May 1943, an hour-long battle took place between 'boys' from the St Lambert suburb and other youths 'said to be zoot suiters from Montreal'. The street fight was claimed to have been the outcome of an effort by zoot-suiters to eject non-suit-wearing St Lambert youths from a restaurant, and involved an estimated 200 young rioters in total.[61] Further clashes, mostly between the standard enemy sides of zoot-suiters and servicemen, were

reported through the fall of 1943 and the winter of 1944. The apex was reached almost exactly a year after the St Lambert fracas, in late May and early June 1944, when the Montreal area was again the scene of street-fighting between zoot-suiters and servicemen, primarily sailors.[62] Initially, the city press identified the zoot-suiters as mainly of Italian background, with some francophones among them, while the soldiers and civilian non-zooters were declared to be mostly English-speaking 'Canadians'. In Verdun early in June, several hundred servicemen sought out zooters at nightclubs, poolrooms, and dance halls, beating them, stripping them, and shredding their despised suits. Dozens were injured, and more than 40—of whom 37 were sailors—were arrested.[63]

The subject was discussed at the highest military and political levels. An inquiry ordered by the Navy produced the predictable verdict that the zooters were a 'definite sect or clan of a subversive nature who aim at sabotaging the war effort by unwarranted attacks on service personnel.'[64] Their alleged 'Italian ancestry' was evidence of their ill will, disloyalty, and absence of patriotism; allegations that they were primarily francophone were cast in the same manner.[65] Justice Minister Louis St Laurent announced in the House of Commons that both the RCMP and Montreal police had dismissed 'racial' and political causes, and offered his own view that rivalry between servicemen and civilians over the city's young women was the true underlying cause, effectively construing the matter as one of youthful male sexuality. Whatever the ultimate explanation, what is important is that the zoot-suit riots stirred public anxiety—once again focused squarely on the youth problem—in an especially anxious time. Much as had happened in Los Angeles, the riots served, quite literally, to recapture public space for those who represented authority and the wartime necessity of civilian deference, while confirming for 'deviant' and often-times 'minority' youth that their own power to transgress would be carefully contained. The generational style adopted by this group of young men would not be countenanced by the generation in power at a time when national sacrifice and unity were the foremost priorities.

. . .

The reasons for such developments in the fashion retail industry had been uncovered by the marketing surveys of the 1920s: the growing purchasing power of youth, matched by the steadily growing demand on their part for selection, style, and quantity in their own wardrobes. The adolescent girl was found to have 'absolutely a minimum of six dresses', while her mother had only three; without the teenager, 'the industry would be practically on a housecoat basis.' Large department stores began to set up 'teenage councils'. . .; one of these closed its eighth annual meeting in 1946 with a council of 36 girls and 30 boys. Surveys were distributed, interviews were conducted, fashion shows and dances were staged, and the program kept two store employees fully employed for the entire year, because, put succinctly, 'the teenager is definitely a business entity.' Clearly this trend had gained a foothold in Canada some time before the supposed discovery of the teenager in the 1950s.

Targeted market research of this nature also persuaded Canadian clothing manufacturers and sellers that teenagers were not inclined to adopt American fashion trends outright, disliking, for example, the 'loud' colours that were popular among American youth.[66] Whatever the success of attempts to encourage an indigenous Canadian teenage style, the popular magazines aimed for a regional focus in their fashion features. *Chatelaine* printed a spread on youth fashion in western Canada, a region that was itself 'perpetually young in mood and action'. Readers were informed that western Canadian teens were 'knowledgeable about fashion'. The western girls unanimously reported that they desired 'all purpose' coats, 'something new in sweaters', and 'plaid skirts that won't make us look hippy'. While they preferred going bare-headed, they wanted 'a bit of veiling or a clutch of flowers on a half-hat' for date dresses and 'small felt rollers' for tailored suits. In fact, there was nothing particularly, recognizably 'western' in the clothes modelled by western teenagers in the photographs accompanying the article. As the writers themselves concluded, 'the clothes they like to wear, and the way they wear 'em, come together in that easy, feminine, yet purposeful young look which all *Chatelaine* teen-agers, cross country, have described as their target for fall '46.'[67] At the same time that the young were working on a distinctive generational style, they were also, on the whole, giving in to style conformity as promoted by the adults who made and sold 'teenage' products.

Because modern leisure was so intertwined with mass culture, it challenged the established relations of class, gender, race, and family, many of which were age-delimited, making it so fundamental and such an overwhelming part of the 'problem of modern youth' that the two became essentially the same problem. Whether consideration was given to movies, dance halls, music, or clothing styles, it was the moral implications of this emergent youth culture, with its sexual overtones and its association with working-class, uncultured, and possibly 'unrespectable' adolescents, that chiefly offended and challenged adult observers. The exact type of offence might change generationally, in keeping with the ephemeral nature of fads and fashions, but the tone of public discourses about them were echoed across succeeding generations.

However frivolous, morally suspect, and even 'dangerous' the cultural practices of the young across the decades studied here appeared, youth managed to play an important historical role as producers, consumers, and disseminators of new aesthetic forms, new products, new practices, and new values. The modern culture that they embraced and helped to shape was in many ways their own in the years since the Great War, the juvenilization of popular culture has been steady and unabated.[68] Yet however much, and however dangerously, adolescent independence appeared to be growing during these years, young Canadians remained largely under the governance of parents, teachers, employers, lawmakers, and other authoritative adults. Not having reached the age of majority, they had neither voice nor visibility in decision-making circles. By regulating commercial amusements through adult fiat—legislation, supervision, discipline and other forms of authority—and also by summoning up wholesome alternatives to these through school, church, and club, worried adults tried to limit the transgressive potential of youth leisure that so frightened them: an inappropriate crossing into the jealously guarded realm of adult privilege without the requisite, socially prescribed attainments that signified 'maturity' and citizen status, and equally without adult sanction. Legislative and voluntary attempts to regulate cinemas, dance halls, and other public places of amusement may have helped to keep these social spaces 'on the level', but they did not dissuade adolescents from frequenting them. Young people were formulating their own rites of passage into adulthood in newly important, if not altogether new, informal leisure institutions. While their critics feared the growing autonomy and market power of the young, it was, ironically, what the young lacked in power that made them focus their lives on consumption, fun, and the politics of play.[69]

Notes

1. 'Guelph Pastor Scores Dancing', *Guelph Daily Mercury*, 3 Oct. 1921, 3. . . .
2. W.S. Haine, 'The Development of Leisure and the Transformation of Working-Class Adolescence', *Journal of Family History* 17 (1992): 451; K. Peiss, *Cheap Amusements: Working Women and Leisure in Turn-of-the-Century New York* (Philadelphia, PA: Temple University Press, 1986); and for Canada, C. Strange, *Toronto's Girl Problem: The Perils and Pleasures of the City, 1880–1930* (Toronto: University of Toronto Press, 1995) . . .
3. D.G. Wetherell and I. Kmet, *Useful Pleasures: The Shaping of Leisure in Alberta, 1896–1945* (Regina, SK: Canadian Plains Research, 1990), 7–9.
4. B. Barnabas, 'Progress in Boy Guidance', *Social Welfare* (Nov. 1925): 37; 'Earning and Spending Health',

editorial, *Social Welfare* (Apr. 1931): 135; M.W. Beckelman, 'The Group Worker in the Modern Scene', *Canadian Welfare Summary* (July 1938): 61. . . .
5. H. Baker, 'Leisure', *Social Welfare* (June 1933): 211, 214; 'Caradog', 'The Citizen of Tomorrow', *Social Welfare* (Feb. 1931): 94.
6. D. Nasaw, *Going Out: The Rise and Fall of Public Amusements* (Cambridge, MA: Harvard University Press, 1993).
7. *Statutes of Ontario*, c. 71, 1927; also Manitoba, 14 Geo V, 1924 Regulation of Billiard and Pool Rooms; British Columbia, 2 Geo V, c. 28, 1912, Pool Rooms Act.
8. Hon. L.A. David, provincial secretary, Quebec, 'Opening Address', *Social Welfare* (Dec. 1921): 423.
9. G. Dickie, 'The Menace of Delinquency', *Social Welfare* (Apr. 1921): 185; 'Children at the Movies', *Child Welfare News* (Feb. 1930): 266. On film in Canada, see T. Magder, *Canada's Hollywood: The Canadian State and Feature Films* (Toronto: University of Toronto Press, 1993).
10. S.C. Hollander and R. Germain, *Was There a Pepsi Generation before Pepsi Discovered It? Youth-Based Segmentation in Marketing* (Lincolnwood, IL: NTC Business Books, 1992), 66.
11. Public Archives of Nova Scotia, Alexander Mowat papers, MG 2408, file 2, A. Mowat, handwritten survey notes, 'Outside School Hours', 3–4. . . .
12. W.M. Bellsmith, 'What of the Movie Censor', *Social Welfare* (Apr. 1931): 143. . . .
13. D. Fowler, *The First Teenagers: The Lifestyle of Young Wage-Earners in Interwar Britain* (London: Woburn Press, 1995), 105. . . .
14. M. Peate, *Girl in a Sloppy Joe Sweater: Life on the Canadian Home Front during World War II* (Montreal: Optimum, 1988), 71.
15. Library and Archives Canada, Canadian Welfare Council files, vol. 8, file 41, Montreal *Gazette* clipping, 'New Theatre Law Draft Commenced', (17 Mar. 1919), that indicated a $50 fine or one month's imprisonment to theatre owners for a first offence. See also '76 Perish in Montreal Motion Theatre Fire', *Globe*, 10 Jan. 1927, 1. . . .
16. The age was raised to 16 in 1930, and attendance was also permitted between 9:00 a.m. and 6:00 p.m. on legal and public holidays; 'Amendments to the Theatre and Cinematographs Act', *Child and Family Welfare* (Nov. 1930): 30.
17. *Statutes of Manitoba*, 6 Geo. V, c. 109, 1916, Public Amusements Act; *Statutes of British Columbia*, 4 Geo. V, c. 75, 1914, Moving Pictures Act; *Statutes of Nova Scotia*, 5 Geo. V, c. 44, Act Respecting Theatres and Cinematographs; Ontario, 1 Geo. V, 1911, Theatre and Cinematographs Act. . . .

18. *Statutes of Manitoba*, 11 Geo. V, c. 46, 1921, An Act to Amend the Public Amusements Act; for similar wording, see *Statutes of Saskatchewan*, 21 Geo. V, c. 70, 1931, Act Respecting Theatres and Cinematographs. . . .

19. Public Archives of Ontario, RG 56 B-5, 1932-3, Box 2, Ontario Board of Censors, Elimination Sheets, June 1932.

20. 'Experiment in Approved Motion Pictures', editorial, *Social Welfare* (Apr. 1927): 395; Library and Archives Canada, Canadian Welfare Council, Proceedings and Reports of Annual Meetings, Report of the Executive Director, 1 Nov.–31 Mar. 1931, 9.

21. R.L. Briscoe, 'What the Censor Saves Us From', *Maclean's* (Nov. 1929): 28; Magder, *Canada's Hollywood*, details the futile attempts made by Canadians to hold off American domination; see also D. Nasaw, 'Children and Commercial Culture', in P. Petrik and E. West, eds, *Small Worlds: Children and Adolescents in America, 1850–1950* (Kansas City: University Press of Kansas, 1993), 19–25.

22. L. Jacobs, *The Rise of the American Film: A Critical History, 1921–47* (New York: Teachers College Press of Columbia University, 1939, 1948, 1967), 506–07, 509.

23. J. Springhall, *Youth, Popular Culture and Moral Panics: Penny Gaffs to Gangsta-Rap, 1830–1996* (New York: St Martin's Press, 1998), 136–40. See also J. McCarty, *Hollywood Gangland: The Movies' Love Affair with the Mob* (New York: St Martin's Press, 1993).

24. J. Strothard, 'The Most Urgent Reform Needed', *Social Welfare* (May 1920): 283.

25. G. Studlar, *This Mad Masquerade: Stardom and Masculinity in the Jazz Age* (New York: Columbia University Press, 1996), 150–98, ably deconstructs the 1920s 'dance madness'. . . .

26. Dr R.A. Adams, *The Social Dance* (Kansas City, KS: R.A. Adams, 1921), 3. . . .

27. M. Miller, *Such Melodious Racket: The Lost History of Jazz in Canada, 1914 to 1949* (Toronto: Mercury Press, 1997), especially 44–65. . . .

28. Hollander and Germain, *Was There a Pepsi Generation before Pepsi Discovered It?* 70.

29. Miller, *Such Melodious Racket*, 58–9; see also 'Winnipeg Jazz Babies Concert for Soldiers', *Manitoba Free Press*, 13 June, 1919, 8.

30. M. Reynolds, 'Toot Sweet: When Jazz Ruled Montreal', *The Beaver* (June/July 2001): 26–32. . . .

31. See A. Levesque, *La Norme et les deviantes: Des femmes au Quebec pendant l'entre-deux-guerres* (1991), trans. Y. Klein as *Making and Breaking the Rules* (Toronto: McClelland & Stewart, 1994), for discussion of the Quebec scene during the interwar years, especially as regards young women.

32. Cited in Miller, *Melodious Racket*, 64; R. Jamieson, 'Music: In the House, the Studio and the Concert Hall', *Vancouver Sun*, 28 Sept. 1919, 38; 'Music', letter to the editor, 31.

33. Peiss, *Cheap Amusements*, 88–90.

34. Strothard, 'The Most Urgent Reform', 285; 'Home Authority Is Lax', editorial, *Guelph Daily Mercury*, 21 Mar. 1921, 6.

35. N. Enstad, *Ladies of Labor, Girls of Adventure: Working Women, Popular Culture and Labor Politics at the Turn of the Twentieth Century* (New York: Columbia University Press, 1999), 9–10.

36. Strothard, 'The Most Urgent Reform', 285.

37. 'National Conference on Child Welfare', *Social Welfare* (Nov. 1922): 31. . . .

38. Library and Archives Canada, CWC, vol. 28, file 143, City of Ottawa Survey: Recreation, Memorandum to Captain Bowie, Recreation Division Advisory Committee, 1929, 4.

39. 'Mary Marston's Own Column', *Guelph Daily Mercury*, 28 Jan. 1921, 8.

40. Reminiscences of Wilda S., Living History Project, Riverview Health Centre, Winnipeg, MB, http://www.riverviewhealthcentre.com/livinghistory/wilda.html.

41. Ibid.

42. R. Collins, *You Had to Be There: An Intimate Portrait of the Generation That Survived the Depression, Won the War, and Re-invented Canada* (Toronto: McClelland & Stewart, 1997), 61.

43. Peate, *Girl in a Sloppy Joe Sweater*, 69.

44. Ibid., 85.

45. The more assertive sound of bebop, developed in New York during the early 1940s, also found devotion among Canadian youth by the late 1940s, as represented in recordings by Moe Koffman and Oscar Peterson. See M. Miller, 'Jazz', *Canadian Encyclopedia of Music*, www.canadianencyclopedia.ca

46. See C. Studlar, *This Mad Masquerade: Stardom and Masculinity in the Jazz Age* (New York: Columbia University Press, 1996), especially ch. 3, 150–98. Studlar notes the 1920 publication by American eugenicist Knight Dunlap, *Personal Beauty and Racial Betterment* (St Louis, MI: C.V. Mosby, 1920), 87–9, urges women to judge beauty according to a standard of 'highest' value, which also meant of the 'white race' (163).

47. B.B. Hampton, *History of the American Film Industry from Its Beginnings to 1931* (New York: Dover, 1970 [1931]), 223, observes that 'Cecil B. DeMille made it possible for every girl with the price of a theatre ticket to feast her eyes on fashion shows.' . . .

48. Hollander and Germain, 38–9. The 'Betty Betz' ad ran in 96 American newspapers, with total newspaper circulation approaching 30 million.

49. B. Haiken, 'Plastic Surgery and American Beauty in 1921', *Bulletin of the History of Medicine* 68 (1994): 429–53.

50. The Pickford cap campaign is discussed in Jacobs, *The Rise of the American Film*, 282; R. Johnston, *Selling Themselves: The Emergence of Canadian Advertising* (Toronto: University of Toronto Press, 2001), 229. . . .

51. Johnston, *Selling Themselves*, 228–9. . . .

52. Peate, *Girl in a Sloppy Joe Sweater*, 67.

53. Editorial, *Toronto Star*, 15 June 1945, 6.

54. 'Zoot Suit's Day Wanes, in Opinion of Tailors', *Globe*, 12 June 1943, 5.

55. Ibid., 5.

56. Ibid.

57. Peate, *Girl in a Sloppy Joe Sweater*, 122.

58. M. Mazon, *The Zoot-Suit Riots: The Psychology of Symbolic Annihilation* (Austin: University of Texas Press, 1984), 6–8, contends that most zoot-suiters in the United States were more likely rejecting adult ways than government policy; they were more a social than a political grouping. R.D.G. Kelley, 'The Riddle of the Zoot: Malcolm Little and Black Cultural Politics during World War II', in J. Austin and M.N. Willard, eds, *Generations of Youth: Youth Culture and History in Twentieth Century America*, sees the zoot suit's adoption by young male African-Americans as a 'signifier of a culture of opposition' (137). For the Montreal situation, see S.M. Durflinger, 'The Montreal and Verdun Zoot-Suit Disturbances of June 1944: Language Conflict, a Problem of Civil-Military Relations or Youthful Over-Exuberance?' in S. Bernier, ed., *L'Impact de la deuxième guerre mondiale sur les sociétés canadienne et québécoise* (Montreal/Ottawa: Université du Québec à Montréal

et la Direction Histoire et Patrimoine de la Défense Nationale, 1998). . . .

59. Editorial, *Globe*, 19 June 1943, 5.

60. Ibid.

61. 'Zoot Suit Wearers of Montreal Start Riot in St Lambert Suburb', *Globe*, 30 May 1944, 3. The newspaper reported one arrested, five injured.

62. Durflinger, 'The Montreal and Verdun Zoot-Suit Disturbances', 224.

63. This was reported in the *Verdun Messenger*, cited in Durflinger, 'The Montreal and Verdun Zoot-Suit Disturbances', 225.

64. Ibid. . . .

65. Ibid. The board of inquiry found the zooters were from varied ethnic backgrounds while the sailors were mainly anglophone. Five out of eight witnesses described the zooters as being of Italian background, two believed they were francophone, several described some as 'Jewish' or 'Syrian', and most agreed that they were predominantly English-speaking.

66. 'Teen-agers "Big Business"', *Toronto Star*, 15 June 1946, 12. Teenagers evidently bought 60 per cent of dress goods.

67. E. Kelly, 'Teen-Age Special: The West, Young Country, Young Fashions', *Chatelaine* (Sept. 1946): 8–9. All clothes modelled in this spread were 'courtesy of the Hudson's Bay Company'.

68. Austin and Nevin Willard, 'Introduction: Angels of History, Demons of Culture', in *Generations of Youth: Youth Culture and History in Twentieth Century America*, 30–1.

69. M. Brake, *Comparative Youth Culture* (London: Routledge and Kegan Paul, 1976). . . .

23

A Man's City: Montreal, Gambling, and Male Space in the 1940s

Suzanne Morton

Montreal in the 1940s was a man's city.[1] Guides such as *Montreal Confidential* directed tourists and businessmen to the city's most exciting clubs and districts while the short-lived American tabloid *Pic: The Magazine Men Prefer* offered its readers a photo essay on 'Montreal: Booming Paris of the West' featuring the city's gambling clubs and its most famous burlesque performer, Lily St Cyr of the Gayety Theatre.[2] The North American press often drew attention to the exotic nature of Montreal: as a bit of Paris in North America it was touted as one of the most vital centres of male sporting culture to survive on the continent. Its unique position as the only major city in North America where liquor flowed legally and continuously throughout the 1920s and 1930s and its geographic proximity to dry northeast American cities made Montreal a popular destination for parched tourists during prohibition. Moreover, unlike other Canadian and eastern American cities, Montreal was not dominated by the culture of a Protestant elite who demanded the enforcement of legislated forms of morality. The glamour and excitement of Montreal as an island of European libertine freedom in a generally repressive Protestant continent were widely incorporated into North American popular culture in examples which ranged from early Harlequin romances to Damon Runyon's short stories.[3]

In our attempt to understand the relationship between urban space and gender, much recent work has concentrated on women's or gay men's space in the city. The work of scholars such as Mary Ryan, Christine Stansell, Judith Walkowitz, and George Chauncey have altered the way we see the city as they examine the way women and gay men used urban spaces to create and reinforce their own identities.[4] This paper hopes to borrow from these insights and apply them to a specific Canadian city, Montreal in the 1940s, in an examination of male spaces associated with gambling. I want to argue that although these spaces could be and were further segregated by class, race, language, and age, they provided important settings which preserved a male sporting culture in a period historians have usually associated with the development of heterosocial or mixed-sex commercialized leisure. At the same time urban space was used by marginal women and gay men as a strategy to forge identity and of survival, this examination of semi-public male spaces illustrates the use of space in the city to reinforce privilege and as a form of continuity with older homosocial leisure patterns.

Gambling—in its various forms of bookmaking, cards, and a popular Montreal dice game called barbotte—was almost completely associated with men. A female reporter who published a series of articles on Montreal gambling in 1946 stated that she had met with her informants over coffee rather than enter their locations of business since she did 'not think women were allowed'.[5] Similarly, a long-time employee of one of the downtown's busiest betting establishments

Suzanne Morton, 'A Man's City: Montreal, Gambling and Male Space in the 1940s', *Power, Place and Identity: Studies of Social and Legal Regulation in Quebec*, eds. Tamara Myers, Kate Boyer, Mary Anne Poutanen, and Steven Watt (Montreal, QC: Occasional Papers of the Montreal History Group, 1998). Reprinted by permission of the author.

claimed that he had never seen a woman in his place.[6] Of course there were some exceptions, usually in the most exclusive establishments where women could be found on the arms of men at the barbotte table or the roulette wheel. There were also other forms of gambling which appealed specifically to or incorporated women, namely bingo and sweepstakes, but by and large, placing bets, playing cards, and rolling dice were activities men engaged in with other men. These forms of competitive games capitalized on notions of 'macho risk taking', aggressive behaviour, and courage.[7] What is remarkable and most important about gambling as a male activity is that in the words of one Montreal observer it 'extended to all classes, colors, creeds and nationalities'.[8] Gambling linked a diverse group of men and although there might have been particular class, race, or linguistic variations, the common locations of gambling in the city served as male space.

Gambling was one of the activities most associated with what has been described as nineteenth-century male sporting culture. According to Timothy Gilfoyle, male sporting culture linked various forms of gaming with communal drinking, commercial sex, and the celebration of male autonomy through sexual aggressiveness, promiscuity, and a renunciation of men's connection with their families. It thus posed a direct challenge to respectable bourgeois Christian morality.[9] Both Gilfoyle in his study of nineteenth-century prostitution and Elliot J. Gorn in his investigation into boxing during the same period argue that the nature of male sporting culture and its emphasis on masculinity diminished divisions based on class, ethnicity, and religion.[10]

Male-sporting behaviour survived in the twentieth century in forms other than gambling. The use of taverns as male space, for example, was regulated by discriminatory provincial laws which permitted women entrance only under specific conditions. Indeed the tavern, along with other examples of exclusively male space such as the locations of professional and amateur sports, and the culture around brothels, frequently overlapped with gambling activity.[11] Moreover, it is also well worth making the obvious point that male segregation within the city was not restricted to leisure activities as most occupations and many industries were in themselves gender-specific.

Although male sporting culture survived in Montreal, by the early twentieth century it was overshadowed by heterosocial forms of leisure. The nineteenth-century celebration of domesticity transformed middle-class and later working-class patterns of leisure and the advent of commercialized mass entertainment such as amusement parks, nightclubs, roller rinks, dance halls, and movie theatres popularized this new ideal and expanded the group of men and women who were likely to socialize together. These new semi-public commercial spaces have been recognized by Roy Rosenzweig and Kathy Peiss to have undermined the working-class tradition of same-sex leisure.[12]

In the 1940s, Montreal was still Canada's largest city, with a population of approximately one million people. This population was divided by many factors, including language, with approximately 65 per cent of the population French-speaking. So, in addition to the North American pattern of urban division along class and racial lines evident in Montreal in the wealthy districts of Westmount and Outremont or the concentration of visible minorities in Chinatown and black districts, language also divided the city along an east–west axis.[13]

Montreal's distinctiveness also was evident in its experience of the Second World War. Although the Montreal economy was focused on war production, there was greater ambivalence towards and more public dissent directed at Canada's involvement in the war than in other Canadian cities. Local full employment, the influx of a transient male military population looking for pleasure, and a political climate which did not necessitate wartime austerity meant that the licit and illicit branches of the Montreal entertainment industry prospered. One historian of jazz wrote that 'the sheer frivolity and extravagance of Montreal nightlife mocked the extortions [sic: exhortations] of Canadian leaders to sacrifice and sobriety.'[14] Prostitution experienced a crackdown in 1944 after the Canadian Army threatened to make Montreal out of bounds for its personnel unless immediate action was taken to curb the threat of venereal disease.[15] Public pressure to stop gambling was slower to take root and did not occur until after the war, when Montreal gambling kingpin Harry Davis was murdered in broad daylight in August 1946. The temporary enthusiasm for the enforcement of laws against gambling which followed was accompanied by public petitions from various reform coalitions requesting an inquiry into the deficiency and corruption in policing of commercial gambling and prostitution.

Organizations such as le Comité de moralité publique were able to capitalize on similar political pressures and concerns in the United States expressed in the Kefauver Commission into organized crime and were finally granted their own Montreal inquiry in 1950.[16] The Caron Inquiry operated from September 1950 to October 1954 and its mandate covered all aspects of gambling activities in Montreal in the 1940s.[17]

Most illegal forms of gambling were covered under the federal government's Criminal Code.[18] While the law did not prevent any individual from making a bet with another individual, it could intervene into any situation where it might be possible for a third party to make a profit off the wager. Gambling in itself was not illegal but participating in or operating any form of commercialized gambling contravened federal law. The criminal law also contained an implicit class bias as there was a means to bet legally on horse races at the racetrack for those who were able to attend daytime races and use the government-approved parimutuel machines (where the federal and provincial governments took their share of revenue). Conversely, those who could not

leave their place of work were breaking the law when they placed bets with a local bookmaker. This exception which allowed commercialized gambling under specific and limited conditions excluded most working-class participants. Thus, it is not surprising that most gambling probably took the illegal route.

Illegal commercialized gambling was thus an important component of the Montreal economy. Some contemporary observers even considered it Montreal's most important industry as it was alleged to gross over $100 million per year in the mid-1940s.[19] It was also an activity that in some sense was understood to be spatially defined. The very word 'underworld' and the common description in reference to the city's loose policing creating a 'wide open city' or 'une ville ouverte' reinforced this geographic and topographical connection. Certainly there was a paradox acknowledged in the description of gambling as simultaneously hidden from view (or underground) and operating in an exposed manner with little fear of police intervention. The importance of space and the feeble attempts to regulate it were also evident in the only tactic police used to control gambling and brothels during the 1940s: the padlock.

While the padlock now has infamous connotations connecting Premier Maurice Duplessis and his attempts to quiet political dissent within the province, the most common use (and misuse) of the padlock law in Montreal was to regulate offenders of public morality. Under the power of a municipal bylaw, gaming and betting houses on their third charge were to be physically closed by padlock for a specified number of days.[20] In order to prevent this potential interference with business, operators responded to potential closures by providing police with fictional addresses or placing apartment numbers on fake doors, broom closets, and even toilets.[21] This unsuccessful strategy for regulating gaming through the control of space was not restricted to Montreal and was implemented with somewhat more success in Toronto and Vancouver.[22]

In 1945, before any serious attempt to crack down on gambling, Montreal reporter Ted McCormack wrote, 'the gaming houses are scattered like raisins through the loaf of the town.'[23] While this was an appealing image and suggestive of the abundant sites available for gaming, it was not quite true. The location of betting and gaming establishments was not random and although there was no single 'men's district' in the city,[24] gambling activities were associated with specific neighbourhoods or districts. During the Caron Inquiry, 248 addresses were provided as locations of repeated raids between 1942 and 1950. Among the addresses cited, not a single address connected gambling to the wealthiest districts of Westmount or Outremont. Instead, the locations were concentrated in the red-light district around the intersection of Ste Catherine and St Laurent, the neighbourhoods immediately adjacent to the main train stations, the downtown theatre and nightclub district, and the area centred around the working-class commercial streets of Mont Royal and St Laurent. In addition to these specific neighbourhoods, prominent bookies and gaming houses also operated close to places where large numbers of men were employed such as the Angus rail yards, munition factories, and the Tramway depot.[25]

The Montreal geographic pattern of gambling conforms with the organizational characteristics noted by David C. Johnson in his study of American cities, where Johnson observes that the 'bright light districts' were embraced by criminal entrepreneurs. Here illicit activities operated beside legitimate enterprises, lending the illegal neighbours a sense of legitimacy and respectability. Proximity to train stations and hotels along with theatres, restaurants, and nightclubs generated a steady flow of sidewalk traffic that might be greeted on the streets with employees trying to hustle men inside.[26]

Not only were there apparent spatial concentrations of gambling in the city but the addresses also shared common legal pretenses such as so-called 'bridge clubs', bowling alleys, barbershops,

tobacco stands, and billiards parlours or pool halls. Of the establishments which can be identified in the Montreal city directory as operating some legitimate business as a front for or in conjunction with gambling activities, 54 were listed as bridge clubs, 14 as billiard parlours or pool halls, 11 as barber shops, eight as bowling alleys, and five as tobacco stores. These businesses, where illegal gambling activity repeatedly transpired, were occasionally even combined so that cigar stands also had their own pool tables.

In a day and age when men had their hair cut more frequently and cigarettes were more acceptable yet not available in food stores, barber and tobacco shops appeared on almost every corner. Their high customer turnover and male clientele made them perfect foils for collecting bets on races. An address on Ste Catherine Street West, where a bookie operated for at least 15 years, was listed in the city directory as a barbershop. A witness testifying before the Caron Inquiry stated that clients entered through the front of a barbershop to a larger room upstairs. The shop itself was large enough for three or four chairs but held only one for show.[27]

The link between barbershops and a male gambling subculture had been long established in Montreal. In the report of the 1925 inquiry into municipal policing, Judge Louis Coderre cited the example of a gambling house at the corner of Ste Catherine and Peel Streets 'camouflaged, and very poorly, as a barber shop'.[28] Coderre continued to draw the connection between betting houses and barbershops and tobacco stores, noting, 'Their doors are open to all, which shows how safely they can be operated.'[29]

Even if barbershops themselves were not the site of illegal gambling, they could be a good source for men looking for information about where to find some 'action'. When reporters for *La Presse* were seeking a barbotte game, they successfully approached the barber across from the Mont Royal Hotel for more information.[30] These networks went beyond information and could become personal. Montreal gambler Harry Ship stated that he had first met some of his later gambling colleagues hanging about the same barbershop on St Laurent.[31]

The shortage of outdoor play space in the nineteenth-century city generated the need for new forms of participatory leisure activities for working-class men. Leisure historian Steven Riess has described the process by which working-class sporting men and boys were gradually deprived of traditional recreational activities such as playing ball in the street through municipal bylaws which regulated the use of public space with the goal of fostering order and efficient commerce.[32] One of the results was the increased importance of the saloon or 'workingmen's club' which offered various forms of entertainment outside the home. The most famous saloon in late nineteenth-century Montreal was Joe Beef's Canteen located by the waterfront.[33] Entertainment in Joe Beef's Canteen in its most extreme form included watching live bears but this type of excess was gradually replaced with more sedate pleasures such as playing pool. Steven Riess has argued that in the United States, billiard parlours were 'probably more widely distributed than any other commercialized entertainment except perhaps movies'.[34] The number of pool halls continued to grow in the twentieth century as listings in the Montreal city directory increased from 39 businesses in 1920 to 117 in 1940.

Halls and parlours with only a few tables could not succeed as prosperous ventures unless the owner ran the business in combination with another activity catering to male sporting culture such as shoe shines, cigar stands, and lunch counters or he supplemented his income with illicit revenue.[35] Establishments were not usually permanent and the listing of billiard parlours in the Montreal city directory suggests a frequent turnover. The location of billiard halls, even if they were not involved in illicit activities, tended to overlap with the same districts as other gambling activity. The halls and parlours needed male patronage but did not need a great deal of space or capital to operate. This was in contrast to the operation of other leisure activities such as bowling alleys, which required the construction of special facilities for the sport.

In the nineteenth century, billiards and pool were much more of a cross-class male activity than bowling, which attracted only working-class participants. Alan Metcalfe has noted that billiards was very popular in Montreal and received prominent coverage in both the French and English newspapers of the 1870s.[36] The game not only bridged linguistic groups but also class extremes as it was played in the city's 'best' homes and hotels as well as its most seedy districts. Although the game was the same, its respectable status disappeared in its encounter with working-class players whose enjoyment of pool, in the eyes of middle-class moral critics, was inescapably bound with gambling and alcohol.[37] Even when pool halls and billiard parlours became independent from alcohol consumption, they retained their notorious reputation, perhaps because of the way in which these activities brought together men from a broad range of class backgrounds. A Montreal reformer in 1919 described pool halls as 'veritable nurseries of hell where boys as well as younger men congregate and learn the devious ways of vice and crime'.[38]

While billiards and pool remained an exclusively male activity, at least one form of bowling was transformed into a heterosocial and ultimately more respectable pursuit. By the 1940s, not all bowling alleys could be considered male space. Nascent sportswriter Trent Frayne observed in 1943 that on a visit to a bowling alley 'there were so many women there that I thought for an embarrassing moment I was in the lingerie department.'[39] World War II promoted the popularity of bowling among women but the feminization of the activity had begun in November 1909 when a Toronto bowling entrepreneur invented the modern game of five-pin bowling using a three- to four-pound ball. This lighter ball replaced the 16-pound ball used in 10-pin bowling and was intended to attract a more respectable clientele than the 'husky' and 'hairy-chested' working-class men who traditionally played the game. Ten-pin bowling remained a male preserve but five-pin bowling took off in popularity in the 1920s as women were introduced into mixed leagues and companies found the limited physical demands of bowling ideal for bringing together employees of various ages in industrial and commercial leagues. Thus, the influx of women, the presence of non-perspiring men, and the support of corporations elevated the status of the sport.[40] The continued presence of bowling alleys in the Montreal police reports suggests, however, that not all alleys were re-created into respectable homosocial space and certain establishments, probably those continuing to play the 10-pin game, continued to be sites of male sporting culture.

Except for the richest and poorest games, gambling brought together men from across the class spectrum. Crowded around a barbotte table might be 'businessmen, servicemen, playboys with their girlfriends, clerks, theatre ushers, taxi drivers, workers and so on down the line to just plain rummies'.[41] While Montreal police dismissed accusations of the vast numbers of returned soldiers and working-class family men who lost their pay envelopes in the city's illegal clubs, this denial contradicted the more frequent descriptions of the range of men brought together over the tables.[42] An aspect of the variety of men that gambling united was extreme upward and downward mobility; Montreal gamblers often came from nothing and claimed they quickly lost everything. Reports after Harry Davis's murder dwelled extensively on his impoverished childhood.[43] This unstable world of quick wealth and sudden poverty contrasted with the more rigid conception of status in the respectable world and made cross-class mixing possible.

Gambling could also bring together men across other divisions such as ethnicity and language. Here again there were variations. Certain clubs catered to specific ethnic groups such as the Jewish clientele attracted to the Laurier Bridge Club's pinochle games or the almost exclusively Italian and Syrian clientele of the Montsabre Club on St Denis Street.[44] These ethnic male enclaves were at least a partial reflection of residency patterns, as particular clubs served the men who lived in their neighbourhood. In light of the multi-ethnic character of Montreal, it is remarkable to observe not the existence of clubs serving specific communities but rather, the degree to which gambling brought men together. Male sporting culture in Montreal brought together a mixture of French, English, Jewish, Italian, Greek, and occasionally black men. The group of male gamblers conspicuously absent from this syndicate was the Chinese.

The only segregated gambling clubs in Montreal were those which served Chinese men and it is significant to note that in the petitions to establish the Caron Inquiry, the French and English reformers were largely silent on this issue. Until the concern about commercialized gambling and the peril of organized crime emerged in the 1940s, the gambling problem in Montreal had at times been synonymous with the Chinese community. An extreme gender imbalance in nineteenth-century immigration patterns to Canada and twentieth-century laws which prohibited legal Chinese immigration meant that the Chinese population of Montreal, as in other Canadian cities, was predominantly male. Thus, the particular combination of race and gender created a special meaning associated with Chinese gambling which differentiated it from gaming in the rest of the city. The general discourse against gambling was not applicable in Chinatown as it did not fit into concerns around organized crime or moral apprehension around men squandering family income. Nevertheless, the clubs of Montreal's Chinatown were presented in a particularly negative light, the danger of their racial exclusivity only compounded when they opened their doors to white clientele.[45]

In the minds of some critics, Chinatown itself was nothing more than a front for illicit activities as it harboured restaurants where one could buy lottery tickets but not obtain a cup of coffee.[46]

Anti-Asian sentiments meant that the Chinese clubs were among the locations most carefully policed. In the first six months of 1945 before a serious police crackdown on Chinese gambling in the city, 71 per cent of all men charged with keeping a betting or gambling house and 43 per cent of all gambling found-ins were connected to the Chinese communities.[47] This was at a time when the total Chinese population of the Island of Montreal comprised far less than 2,000 men or about 0.1 per cent of the population.[48] Obviously, police statistics do not reflect the distribution of gambling in the city, but rather the policy of municipal officials at a time when non-Chinese gambling establishments were operating in the open. Moreover, gambling in Chinatown almost disappeared completely after city police instituted a policy in July 1945 whereby any men caught in raids of Chinese clubs were brought to police headquarters, where their identities were verified and they [were] held overnight before being released on bail. In all other cases, gambling 'found-ins', usually hired by operators to be caught in planned raids, were granted bail on the spot and after providing false names would forfeit the bail (the money provided by the club owner or bookmaker) and avoid conviction. The distinct rules for policing Chinese gambling and the racial segregation of their establishments made Chinese gambling culture very different from that of other forms of male sporting culture in the city. The experience of the Chinese of Montreal challenged the universality of male sporting culture and provided an important exception of its inclusiveness.

In addition to factors such as class and race, time intersected with location to create distinct male space. Locales with a more gender-neutral function such as small groceries, confectionery shops, and lunch counters could be transformed by the time of day, the day of the week, and the season of the year. Bookies and gambling clubs in the downtown area, which catered to both the nightclub clients and daytime employees in offices and small manufacturing, often shared facilities

in order to make the most efficient use of expensive rental space. Bookmakers and their agents would open at 10:00 in the morning and would be busiest between three and six in the afternoon. Bookmakers were busiest on Saturdays, which coincided with free time and a new paycheque. In the evenings, barbotte or the card games would begin after the last race had been run. These operations opened around 8:00 pm and would run until 4:00 or 5:00 in the morning.

The daytime operation of betting on horses complemented the hours of small businesses such as barbershops and taverns, which were supposed to close at 10:00 p.m. On the other hand, pool halls and bowling alleys, with their later closing times, and private clubs, with no time restrictions, were more suited to the nocturnal hours of cards and barbotte.[49] The around-the-clock facilities available to men highlight the fact that at least some men were free to move around the city day or night. This temporal freedom meant that specific places could adopt different functions at different times.

The concept of a changing use of place also applied to the transmutation of space in the suburbs. While the notion of male leisure space is bound in our conception of the downtown core, an investigation into gambling also challenges our understanding of suburbs as only domestic space.[50] Elite gambling clubs catering to a male clientele operated just outside municipal police jurisdictions, a strategy which dated from the late 1920s when 'The White House Inn' operated in Lachine and continued in the 1940s when the 'swankiest' gambling club in Montreal attracted patrons to 'The Mount Royal Bridge Club' in the upper-middle-class suburb of Côte St Luc. A crackdown in Montreal policing in the 1940s also drove the city's largest and most important dice games, the barbottes, to the fringe areas of Côte de Liesse and Côte St Michel. These clubs were connected to the downtown by specially commissioned taxis which linked all Montreal gambling districts together through the transportation of clientele.[51] The presence of gambling clubs in areas associated with family life and respectability challenged any rigid or strict denotation of Montreal's moral geography.

Another understanding of Montreal's moral geography was that in the general absence of women, male spaces were frequently identified as dirty. Downtown operations usually had lunch counters, licensed by municipal authorities, which sold sandwiches, soft drinks, coffee, and cigarettes to men while they waited for the results of their races to come in.[52] With no apparent irony intended, municipal sanitary inspectors would occasionally remove or threaten the removal of lunch-counter licences for breaking the municipal code of health. For example, while no concern appeared to be directed towards criminal activities taking place all around, in June 1942 the operators of a large and permanent bookmaking establishment on Ste Catherine Street West received a warning that unless the rat droppings were cleaned up, rat holes filled in, and a sink installed, the lunch counter would lose its municipal licence.[53] Problems with cleanliness of lunch counters reveal a common characteristic of male spaces, which were often identified as dark and dirty.[54] Patrons at 1455 Bleury had to be asked specifically 'not to spit on the floor'.[55] Concerns around cleanliness suggest a level of male sociability, particularly in bookmaking shops, which was distinct from the act of placing the bet itself. Customers clearly sat around at tables provided by owners, perhaps drinking a Coke and eating a sandwich, while they waited for results to come in. At the Sportsmen's Club on Bleury, there were often informal card games taking place for which owners did not receive any percentage of the money played. This form of comradeship overcame physical conditions and probably added to the pleasure of the gambling experience. Participants were involved in an urban subculture, not strictly a business transaction.

Although male sporting culture was still spatially defined in Montreal in the 1940s, it was evident that it was a world in decline. Riess attributes the demise of the male sporting culture

to the rise of suburbia, as the relocation of many families from the city core interfered with easy access to separate male spaces. In Montreal, the Caron Inquiry acted as a springboard for the political career of Jean Drapeau, and the publication of the final report in October 1954 coincided with his election as mayor on a reform platform. Mayor Drapeau instituted 'un grand nettoyage', which curbed the most obvious examples of unofficial tolerance around gambling and prostitution. The Montreal reform administration ran concurrent with organizational changes taking place in commercialized gambling everywhere. By the early 1960s, the provincial gambling squad in Ontario would observe that 'the cigar store and pool room is [sic] vanishing.' Illegal gambling continued to be an important male activity but its space-specific culture diminished as bets were relayed by anonymous telephone contacts to the suburbs where bookmaking enterprises operated out of ordinary-looking houses.[56] Certainly, elements of this Montreal male sporting world of the 1940s still survive today in the city's Italian, Portuguese, and Greek cafés with their male-only clients crowded around card and pool tables. Another version of this bygone male world also survives in the novels of Mordecai Richler and Ted Allan.[57]

What did it mean to create and maintain urban space that excluded women? The persistence of male sporting culture in the twentieth century permitted the survival, reproduction, and reinforcement of this particular version of masculinity. Men continued to own all of the city in a way that was not possible for women. Enclaves associated with male sporting culture appeared to be particularly important for young men who were learning about masculinity. Bookmakers' establishments, pool rooms, bowling alleys, cigar stands, and taverns offered an opportunity to socialize with other men in an environment removed from the domestic sphere and the pressures of heterosocial leisure activities. In doing so, it strengthened notions of participants' masculinity and their power as it recreated a network of privilege and power. Although space could play an important role for the marginalized and the oppressed such as the Canadian Chinese community, it was also important to remember that it was used effectively by those who had power to perpetuate their position and preserve a form of masculinity which existed outside the bourgeois ideal. This need not be romanticized, as the practice reinforced and celebrated male privilege, aggression, and competitiveness. Divisions found in class, ethnicity, or sexual orientation should not be minimized, but the examination of gambling spaces in Montreal in the 1940s in particular suggests that with at least one important exception, men with a variety of identities shared the same physical space and a similar male sporting culture. There were limits to this commonality, as the exclusion of Chinese men reminds us, but placing a bet, staking a hand, or rolling the dice attracted, in the words of a Montreal novelist, 'men of various sizes, shapes, odours and auras'.[58]

Notes

1. I would like to thank Programme nouveau chercheur, Fonds pour la formation de chercheurs et l'aide à la recherche for funding this project and Mary Matthews, Tanya Gogan, and Tamara Myers for their research on the Enquête Caron.

2. Archives de la Ville de Montréal (hereafter AVM), P43, Enquête Caron, box 054–06–03–02, E–791; *Pic* (Mar. 1950); Al Palmer, *Montreal Confidential* (Montreal, 1950).

3. Ronald J Cooke, *The Mayor of Cote St Paul: A Harlequin Book* (Toronto, 1950); Damon Runyon, *Guys and Dolls* (Harmondsworth, 1956 [1931]). This Montreal has also been captured in William Weintraub's *City Unique: Montreal Days and Nights in the 1940s and '50s* (Toronto, 1996).

4. Mary P. Ryan, *Women in Public: Between Banners and Ballots, 1825–1880* (Baltimore, 1990); Judith Walkowitz, *City of Dreadful Delight: Narratives of Sexual Danger in Late-Victorian London* (Chicago, 1992); Christine Stansell, *City of Women: Sex and Class in New York, 1789–1860* (Urbana, IL, 1987); George Chauncey, *Gay New York: Gender, Urban Culture, and the Making of the Gay Male World, 1890–1940* (New York, 1994).

5. AVM, P43, Enquête Caron, box 054–06–03–01, testimony of Jacqueline Sirois, 3 July 1952, 16.

6. AVM, P43, Enquête Caron, box 054–06–03–01, testimony of Izzie Litwack, 6 Oct. 1950, 696.

7. John C. Burnham, *Bad Habits: Drinking, Smoking, Taking Drugs, Gambling, Sexual Misbehavior and Swearing in American History* (New York, 1993); Kathy Peiss, *Cheap Amusements: Working Women and Leisure in Turn-of-the-Century New York* (Philadelphia, 1986), 21.

8. Wilfred Emmerson Israel, 'The Montreal Negro Community', MA thesis (McGill University, 1928), 195.

9. Timothy Gilfoyle, *City of Eros: New York City, Prostitution, and the Commercialization of Sex, 1790–1920* (New York, 1992), 81, 98–9. Male sporting culture is described by Timothy Gilfoyle as centred on a variety of gaming such as 'horse racing, gambling, cockfighting, pugilism and other "blood" sports'.

10. Gilfoyle, *City of Eros*, 102, 104; Elliot J. Gorn, *The Manly Art: Bare-Knuckle Prize Fighting in America* (Ithaca, NY, 1986).

11. Montreal gamblers in the 1940s had close connections to boxing and the operation of city nightclubs, restaurants, and cabarets. Although there were some links between the gambling fraternity and narcotics in the 1930s, with a few significant exceptions, most Montreal gamblers seemed to be distanced themselves from illegal narcotics and prostitution in the 1940s. In the testimony of alderman Frank Hanley, himself a former jockey, he acknowledged a connection with two of the city's most prominent gamblers through boxing connections. AVM, P43, Enquête Caron, box 054–06–02–01, 1952–2Z, testimony of Frank Hanley, 27 June 1952, 20, 56.

12. Peiss, *Cheap Amusements*; Roy Rosenzweig, *Eight Hours for What We Will: Workers and Leisure in an Industrial City, 1870–1920* (Cambridge, 1983).

13. Israel, 'Montreal Negro Community', 185; Paul-André Linteau, *L'histoire de Montréal depuis la Confédération* (Montreal, 1992).

14. John Gilmore, *Swinging in Paradise: The Story of Jazz in Montréal* (Montreal, 1988), 90.

15. Suzanne Commend, 'De la femme dechue à la femme infectieuse: perception sociale et repression de la prostitution montréalaise pendant la Seconde guerre', MA thesis, (Université de Montréal, 1996).

16. William Howard Moore, *The Kefauver Committee and the Politics of Crime, 1950–1952* (Columbia, MO, 1974).

17. Danielle Lacasse has written on aspects of this inquiry relating to prostitution in *La prostitution féminine à Montréal, 1945–1970* (Montreal, 1994). See also François David, 'Le Comité de Moralité Publique de Montréal', *Cultures du Canada Français* 8 (1991): 84–95.

18. *The Criminal Code and Other Selected Statutes of Canada* (Ottawa, 1951), ch. 36, ss. 225–36.

19. Ted McCormack, 'Gambling in Montreal', *Maclean's*, 15 Sept. 1945, 5.

20. No. 921: 'By-Law to authorize the Recorder's Court of the City of Montreal to order the temporary closing of certain immovables' (17/1/1927), *By-laws of the City of Montreal. Compilation of all By-laws to date* (Montreal, 1931).

21. AVM, P43, Enquête Caron, box 054–04–02–01, testimony Lionel Elie, 3 Oct. 1950, 305–14; box 054–03–03–02, E-19, E-20, E-21, E-22, Padlock Registers 1932–48.

22. *Vancouver Sun*, 18 July 1940, 5.

23. McCormack, 'Gambling in Montreal', 7.

24. Phillip Thomason, 'The Men's Quarter of Downtown Nashville', *Tennessee Historical Quarterly* 41, 1 (1982): 48–66. This district in nineteenth-century Nashville was marked by tailors, tobacco shops, saloons, and barbershops.

25. AVM, P43, box 054–05–02–01, testimony of Omer Dufresne, 2 Feb. 1951, 75; box 054–01–03–01, 1952–94, testimony of Albert Langlois, 15 Sept. 1952. This absence of gambling establishments in Westmount, Outremont, and Notre Dame de Grâce was reinforced by inquiry witnesses.

26. David R. Johnson, 'The Origins and Structure of Intercity Criminal Activity 1840–1920: An Interpretation', *Journal of Social History* 15, 4 (Summer 1982): 596.

27. AVM, P43, Enquête Caron, box 054–04–02–01, Barney Shulkin, 28 Sept. 1950, 363. A parallel example of a billiard parlour with only one pool table but many tables for card games was brought to the attention of the Coderre Inquiry in 1925. *Montreal Star*, 14 Mar. 1925, 55.

28. *Montreal Star*, 14 Mar. 1925, 54; translation of Coderre's judgment.

29. Ibid., 55.

30. AVM, P43, Enquête Caron, box 054–05–02–02, 1952–78, testimony of Raymond Taillefer, 10 Apr. 1951, 28.

31. AVM, P43, Enquête Caron, box 054–06–02–01, 1952–46, testimony of Harry Sharp, 22 July 1952, 357.

32. Steven A. Riess, *City Games: The Evolution of American Urban Society and the Rise of Sports* (Chicago, 1991), 72–3.

33. Peter Delottinville, 'Joe Beef of Montreal: Working Class Culture and the Tavern, 1869–1889', *Labour/Le Travailleur* 8, 9 (Autumn–Spring 1981–2): 9–40.

34. Riess, *City Games*, 75.

35. Ibid.

36. Alan Metcalfe, *Canada Learns To Play: The Emergence of Organized Sport, 1807–1914* (Toronto, 1987), 138.

37. Riess, *City Games*, 73–4; Delottinville, 'Joe Beef'.

38. E.I. Hart, *Wake Up Montreal!* (Montreal, 1919), 16.

39. B.T. Frayne, 'Set 'em Up', *Maclean's*, 1 Feb. 1943, 13.

40. Larry Gough, 'Sallys in our Alleys', *Maclean's*, 1 Jan. 1944, 15, 26; Lizebeth Cohen, *Making a New Deal: Industrial Workers in Chicago, 1919–1939* (Cambridge, 1990), 179.

41. McCormack, 'Gambling', 7.

42. AVM, P43, Enquête Caron, box 054–03–03–01, D–147. Handwritten note from Captain O'Neill.

43. For example, see *The Standard*, 27 July 1946.

44. AVM, P43, Enquête Caron, box 054–03–02–02. Complaints, 1947, re: 6968 St Denis.

45. Kwok B. Chan, *Smoke and Fire: The Chinese in Montreal* (Hong Kong, 1991); Denise Helly, *Les Chinois de Montréal, 1877–1951* (Quebec, 1987). See also Kay Anderson, *Vancouver's Chinatown: Racial Discourse in Canada, 1875–1980* (Montreal, 1991). Chinatown held its own particular dangers with concern around opium and mixed-race prostitution.

46. Robert A Percy, 'Dufferin District: An Area in Transition', MA thesis (McGill University, 1928), 106.

47. AVM, P43, Enquête Caron, box 054–03–02–01, Morality Squad Reports, 1945.

48. According to the 1941 census there were 1,844 Chinese living on the Island of Montreal out of a total population of 1,116,800. In 1951 this number had fallen to 1,142 men and 292 women out of a total population of 1,320,232. Canada, *Census*, 1941, vol. 1, Table 32, 'Population by principal origins for census sub-districts'; *Census*, 1951, vol. 1, Table 34, 'Population by origin and sex for counties and census divisions, 1951', 34.9–34.10.

49. Montreal Bylaw 1103 (12/1/1931).

50. Veronica Strong-Boag, 'Home Dreams: Women and the Suburban Experiment in Canada, 1945–60', *Canadian Historical Review* 72, 4 (Dec. 1991): 471–505.

51. AVM, P43, Enquête Caron, box 054–04–02–01, testimony of Lizzie Hitwack, 11 Oct. 1950, 874. Not only were the suburbs an important site of gambling, but testimony before the Caron commission also suggested that at least some gamblers were model family men who commuted into the city each day for work. One of the city councillors representing the predominantly English suburb of Notre Dame de Grâce, which itself had no reported gambling activity, claimed that 'most of the bookies' in Montreal lived in his district with their families. According to the councillor, 'They do business in town and they live in the suburbs.' AVM, P43, Enquête Caron, box 054–06–02–01, testimony of John Edward Lyall, 27 June 1952, 64.

52. AVM, P43, Enquête Caron, box 054–04–02–01, testimony of Edgar Bruce Murdoch, 29 Sept. 1950, 182; testimony of Samuel Hyams, 2 Oct. 1950, 232.

53. AVM, P43, Enquête Caron, box 054–05–03–01, E–420. Inspection reports for 286 Ste Catherine West. This book operated between 1932 and 1946.

54. AVM, P43, Enquête Caron, box 054–05–02–01, testimony of Albert Hotte, 6 Feb. 1951, 17. Sanitary inspector re 327 Ste Catherine East.

55. AVM, P43, Enquête Caron, box 054–03–03–02, E–95. Photos from 1455 Bleury, 5 Sept. 1946.

56. Alan Phillips, 'Gambling the greatest criminal conspiracy of them all', *Maclean's*, 7 Mar. 1964, 15.

57. Ted Allan, *Love is a Long Shot* (Toronto, 1984); Mordecai Richler, *Apprenticeship of Duddy Kravitz* (1959), *Son of a Smaller Hero* (1955), and *St Urbain's Horseman* (1971).

58. Allan, *Love is a Long Shot*, 29.

24

Drinking Together: The Role of Gender in Changing Manitoba's Liquor Laws in the 1950s

——Dale Barbour——

Home wrecker or harmless social lubricant? When Manitobans discussed revising their liquor laws in the 1950s their language was alive with gendered implications. Since the nineteenth century, liquor had been tied to masculine space—men joined together to drink, while female drinkers were eyed with suspicion and, in the view of the middle class, members of the working class, male and female, should never meet over alcohol.[1] It was a situation that was enshrined in law in Manitoba in 1928 when public drinking was confined to all-male beer parlours. But by the 1950s the gender line was wearing thin. Men and women were drinking together, pouring drinks under the table in supper clubs or sneaking drinks outside of dance halls, in defiance of both convention and the law. But even as Manitobans discussed where women should be able to drink, they also considered where they couldn't—the all-male beer parlour. Of course, gender does not operate in a vacuum—as much as the beer parlour was masculine, it was also working class. The downtown location of these beer parlours allowed speakers to avoid using the term class in their critiques, even though they meant it just the same.

I am primarily concerned with the city of Winnipeg in the 1950s. I have tapped the *Winnipeg Tribune* archives, specifically the liquor clipping files from 1943 to 1957, and the 1955 *Report of the Manitoba Liquor Enquiry Commission*, headed by former Manitoba premier John Bracken, as primary sources.[2] This study is centred on the commission, but I am less interested in the policy process than I am in the language used by people both for and against more liberal drinking laws, including the language of the report itself.

I will be using Kathy Peiss's concept of homosocial and heterosocial space, as outlined in *Cheap Amusements: Working Women and Leisure in Turn-of-the-Century New York* as a theoretical base for my discussion. Heterosocial refers to the mixing of both genders while homosocial refers to the social mixing of people of one gender and not, it should be noted, to sexual orientation.[3] In *Cheap Amusements*, Peiss traces the transition of leisure spaces in North American industrial cities from being focused on homosocial activities to those that were heterosocial.[4] She describes late nineteenth-century male public leisure as a homosocial affair—a saloon culture of camaraderie, frivolity, and the trading of rounds of drinks. It was not a place for women and those who did partake risked being labelled prostitutes.[5] Instead of the saloon, women frequented new, alcohol-free, commercial entertainments such as dance halls and movie theatres. Within these spaces, a dating culture emerged in which courting was removed from the scrutiny of parents and taken into the public sphere.[6] But as Carolyn Strange illustrates in *Toronto's Girl Problem: The Perils and Pleasures of the City, 1880–1930*, the rise of women as social actors and their movement

Dale Barbour, 'Drinking Together: The Role of Gender in Changing Manitoba's Liquor Laws in the 1950s'. Reprinted from *Prairie Metropolis: New Essays on Winnipeg's Social History*, eds Esyllt W. Jones and Gerald Friesen (University of Manitoba Press, 2009). Used with the permission of the publisher.

into this evolving heterosocial public space weakened patriarchal control over their leisure time and, it was feared, emphasized their sexuality.[7] In response, a discourse was constructed 'that linked women's pleasure to immorality and their independence to danger'.[8]

Prohibition marked a definitive encounter between the law and drinking culture. Prince Edward Island was the first to initiate it in 1901 and Quebec was the last in 1919.[9] Manitoba enacted prohibition in 1916, but the era was short-lived. Mirroring a trend that took place across the country, Manitoba ended prohibition in 1923 by allowing the sale of liquor in government-run stores and then, in 1928, went further to allow the sale of beer by the glass in the new beer parlours. The end of prohibition did not mean a return to the saloon. Instead, new laws were introduced in the hope that a new kind of drinking place would be established. While the rules varied across the country, there was one matter on which all provinces could agree: women would be permitted to enter beer parlours only in a highly regulated setting, if at all.[10] British Columbia and Ontario created all-male beer parlours that had a separate section for women and their escorts.[11] Men could not enter the women's side on their own and women were not to stray into the men's side. This division of space by gender had the side effect of opening space for gay, lesbian, and transgendered people to slip through regulation that was targeted primarily at preventing 'improper' heterosexual activity rather than homosexual contact.[12]

The Manitoba Liquor Act of 1928 did include provisions for similar gender segregation in Manitoba's beer parlours.[13] And in 1928 a Winnipeg Beach hotel briefly opened a women's beer parlour. But being unaware of the ins and outs of the new law, the female proprietor failed to obtain a proper licence and the women's beer parlour was promptly closed.[14] No other businesses followed up on the attempt, and Manitoba's beer parlours were constituted as all-male establishments.

By the end of the 1940s, boundaries were crumbling. Mariana Valverde describes the growth of an 'enlightened hedonism' after the Second World War and links the new cocktail lounges that emerged in 1947 in Ontario and after 1957 in Manitoba with consumer culture:[15] 'Class, sex, and gender had to be simultaneously reorganized in relation to spirits drinking in order to make the cocktail lounge possible. In respect to sex and gender, heterosexuality in the context of public drinking, which in the era of beer parlors had been associated with prostitution, was now revalorized and made central to the new legal category of the cocktail lounge. But this was a new, historically specific form of heterosexuality, namely the post-war heterosexuality associated with middle-class consumerism and early marriage.'[16] The bar had been forbidden in beer parlours but its return to the new cocktail lounges did not so much signal the return of the saloon but rather its final burial as a working-class masculine institution. As Valverde notes, 'the class and gender meanings of spirits drinking dramatically shifted in the post-World War II period.'[17] It was assumed that respectable customers—read middle-class customers—could discipline themselves to a greater extent than beer parlour patrons could.[18]

Mixed-gender drinking was not an issue for the *Winnipeg Tribune* in the 1940s. Articles fretted about the amount of revenue the province was bringing in from liquor sales and whether this was morally acceptable, but the question of whether men and women should drink together hardly entered the public discussion.[19] In some ways the concept slid into Manitoba by stealth when social and ethnic clubs were allowed to serve alcohol in 1928.[20] Winnipeg Centre MLA Stephen Juba noted that the social clubs catered to different classes in the community and created inequity because members could drink in mixed company while the general public lacked the same privilege.[21] Meanwhile, Winnipeg North Liberal MLA Frank Chester argued in 1950 that ethnic clubs in the north end of the city were not being granted the same liquor privileges as other clubs. The Liquor Commission said bluntly that it was because clubs in North Winnipeg were 'admitting practically anyone' and 'practically became mixed beer parlors'.[22] The position of the ethnic and social clubs at the regulatory and legal edge of society provided the early entry points where mixed drinking could emerge.[23] This space grew exponentially when veterans' clubs were allowed liquor licences and the possibility of mixed drinking in 1953.[24]

Whether ethnicity was an entry point for alcohol or simply a scapegoat is debatable. Canadian Temperance Federation general secretary Rev. John Linton linked ethnicity to changes in liquor culture in 1956 when he warned the province to tread carefully when it came to changing liquor laws. Linton argued that the increased number of drinkers could be blamed on the 'breakdown of taboos' in two world wars and the 'influx of settlers from European countries where patterns of drinking were different'.[25] Of course, linking ethnicity to alcohol was nothing new—it had been a focus in the arguments of groups such as the Dominion Alliance in arguing for prohibition at the turn of the century.[26]

Ethnic and social clubs were the legal places where people could drink in mixed company. However, people were ignoring the law and drinking together at dances, supper clubs, and socials. As one woman interviewed by the *Winnipeg Tribune* said: 'I'm a member of a club licensed to serve beer to men and women and it's worked out very well there. And I don't like going to supper dances and thinking we've got to finish that bottle that's under the table.'[27] Breaking the law by drinking under the table was a given. Even the Women's Christian Temperance Union acknowledged that people were ignoring the law: 'The management serves the mixer and the patrons bring their bottles. We are thus rearing a generation of law-breakers.'[28] Alcohol was part of heterosocial space by the early 1950s. The only question was whether society at large was prepared to acknowledge it.

The public acceptability of alcohol in heterosocial space would be the central question

when the Manitoba Liquor Enquiry Commission was convened in 1954, though gender was only referenced in one of the several questions placed before it. Retired politician John Bracken was picked to head the commission. Premier of Manitoba between 1922 and 1942, Bracken had been in power when the post-prohibition liquor law was drawn up in 1923 and when it was amended in 1928. He was renowned as a 'teetotaller' and acknowledged that his party had been in favour of prohibition but, through the laws passed in 1923 and 1928, had solidified the Manitoba government's role as the barkeeper of the province.[29]

The tenor of the Report of the Manitoba Liquor Enquiry Commission—or Bracken report—was set in part one, entitled, 'The Basis of the Liquor Problem and Traditional Ways of Dealing With It.'[30] Nearly 350 pages of the 751-page Bracken report outline the dangers of alcohol consumption, a situation not lost on reviewers such as Manitoba Co-operative Commonwealth Federation (CCF) leader Lloyd Stinson, who called it a 'textbook of temperance'.[31] Under the section 'The Problem as Interpreted', the report offers a glossary of technical terms. With respect to why there needed to be a 'control law' for liquor, the report states: 'Because the "liquor" here referred to means alcoholic beverages, the trade in which for several hundred years has been considered by all countries to require control because of its anti-social effects.'[32] The definition for 'tension': 'Nervous state arising from the inhibitions of modern society, complexities of modern life or the worries of business or other affairs. Said to be one of the chief causes of drinking; and the lessening of which considered to be the chief benefit, though a temporary one, from drinking.' The definition for 'skid row' is also included: 'The part of the population which has been completely demoralized by alcoholic consumption; the part of a town frequented by such persons.'[33]

These definitions can be read alongside the language of the rest of the report. Liquor consumption, the report notes, can reduce intelligence and in turn impair moral sense: 'The moral restraint which prevents anti-social action and even a depraved course of action is no longer active.' And what is the impact of this progressive deterioration of one's moral sense? 'Improper advances may be made to respectable women, or the drinker may seek questionable sexual outlets which his normal restraints would forbid.'[34] Tapping Freudian terms, the report suggests that when alcohol is 'sufficiently present in the nervous system, the "censor" [Freud's term], whose function it is to "restrain or divert inappropriate sexual impulses," is off guard'. And from there: 'The close association between the brothel and the bar has been widely observed.'[35] These comments are telling because they speak to why mixed drinking was considered a threat, particularly in beer parlours. The view was not only that every woman who entered alone was a potential prostitute, but that men might lose their moral sense due to alcohol and commit immoral sexual acts with women who were present. Women when mixed with alcohol were a moral threat to men, and men who were drinking could not be trusted in the presence of women.

The Bracken report put its own spin on what it saw happening in the world. It ticked off changes ranging from social dislocations following the Second World War to an increase in leisure time and social events, and to a trend towards the use of alcohol at social events, coupled again with the 'tensions of modern life'.[36] It noted: 'The effects of two world wars on two succeeding generations do not disappear over night: that such consequences have always shaken previous concepts of morality is a matter of history, and on top of this in our case has come a period of economic prosperity unprecedented in our time. The ethical standards of a previous era have thus suffered from the clash of many forces never before witnessed on such a scale in this part of the world.'[37] Later the report notes: 'society has made remarkable economic gains in recent years and will make more; but social gains have not kept pace with them.'[38] There is an ambivalence about modernity within the Bracken report, an ambivalence reflected in the definition of terms such as 'tension'.

Race enters this exchange primarily through the discussion around Aboriginal people.[39] While the federal government granted Aboriginal people access to alcohol in 1951, it fell to the provinces to make the changes in their own jurisdictions. For Manitoba, that meant the Aboriginal question was part of the Bracken report and the general liquor laws discussion. Within that discussion, Aboriginal people were defined, and 'othered', almost entirely by race. The notion that Aboriginal people did not have the 'moral capabilities' to handle alcohol was repeated in a number of *Tribune* articles.[40] In contrast, gender almost never entered the picture. If Aboriginal people had any gender it was inevitably male.[41] Secondly, while women are quoted in the discussion around mixed drinking parlours, Aboriginal people are never quoted directly about whether they feel they should have drinking rights.[42] The closest we come to a quote is second hand and offered by Anglican Rev. R.T. Milburn who quotes an Aboriginal person on The Pas Indian Reserve as having said: 'It's not very dignified for me, as a man, to pay $2 for an 80 cent bottle of wine, drink it in hiding in a hurry and then run back to the reservation.' Access to alcohol was portrayed as being critical for defining masculinity, which meant that denying Aboriginal people legal access to alcohol was an infringement on their masculinity.[43] The quote is found in an article headlined, 'Probe Chief Seeks Indian Pow-Wow on Fire Water'. The play on traditional stereotypes and othering through use of antiquated terms hardly needs pointing out.

The Bracken report outlined the distribution of beer parlours within Winnipeg. Due to licensing restrictions, the vast majority of beer parlours were exactly where they had been in 1928—huddled downtown in the area between the CN and CP railway stations. 'The neighborhood beer parlor with its healthy atmosphere of friendly neighborliness has, therefore, not developed,' the report noted. It went on to say, 'some of the licensed parlors are now in undesirable locations and are of an unpleasant and socially questionable type.'[44] The downtown beer parlours were thus cut off from the wealthy areas of the city, a case of spatial segregation by class. The Bracken report did not use the term 'skid row' in this instance, but that's probably what it had in mind.[45]

A 'committee of five men interested in social problems' visited Winnipeg's beer parlours in the winter of 1954–5 at the behest of the commission. The term 'social problems' suggests what the committee expected to find. Its report constructs a class-based masculine culture in which 'laboring class' patrons attended the parlours. The report describes with almost anthropological precision the behaviour of the patrons.[46] Social clubs and veterans clubs, while discussed in the report, did not warrant a visitation.

It was to the working-class beer parlour that the Bracken Commission turned when contemplating the flaws and possibilities of liquor laws. The regulation of alcohol has historically focused on controlling space—creating 'a kind of moral architecture to shape customers' (and owners') behaviour'.[47] This concept wasn't lost on the authors of the Bracken report. With respect to Manitoba's drinking establishments, they noted that beer parlour restrictions that forbid food, frivolity, music, entertainment, or games of any sort ensure that only one activity is possible: 'All in all it may be said that Manitoba beer parlors are places where men may drink and drink and may do nothing else.'[48]

Throughout the discussion in the 1950s, normalized heterosexuality was held up as the model of what mixed drinking could accomplish. When drinking was promoted, it was inevitably something that a husband and his wife did together. It was an argument that assigned women the role of moderating influence. The International Union of United Brewery, Flour, Cereal, Soft Drink and Distillery Workers argued in 1950 that '"Mixed" parlors and sale of beer with meals will do much to make drinking here "the civilized and pleasurable custom it should be."'[49] Meanwhile, United College professor R.N. Halstead suggested alcohol needs to be 'placed

before the public in places where a person can dine and drink in the presence of his wife and friends'.[50] Winnipeg alderman H.B. Scott also had lofty expectations of what the introduction of women would do for mixed drinking parlours and cocktail bars: 'profanity would disappear' and 'drunkenness would decrease'.[51] Women were part of the new moral architecture being considered for drinking establishments. In this discussion, we hear echoes of Adele Perry's *On the Edge of Empire: Gender, Race, and the Making of British Columbia, 1849–1871*: 'White women's importance lay not as autonomous political subjects but rather in their ability to shape and control white male behaviour, as *objects* that would shape the behaviours and identities of the true *subjects* of colonization, white men.'[52] Nearly 100 years later, the same discourse was alive and well, with women called upon to tame men. Of course, the possibility of women getting drunk was never part of the discussion.

Even when supporters of mixed drinking did argue from a pure 'equality' point of view, they centred the argument within the traditional heterosexual home. As an unnamed source quoted in the *Winnipeg Tribune* said in 1953: 'Women are now represented in every sphere of government, business and professions and, as homemakers, they are said to control the spending of 80 per cent of the family income. Surely, with that record, it is safe to assume they are mature enough to drink intelligently.'[53] The Manitoba Provincial Council of Women and the Manitoba Women's Institute surveyed 2,460 women and found that the majority in Winnipeg favoured some form of mixed drinking. The people in favour suggested that the 'wife should be able to go in, rather than to sit in the car waiting for her husband.' As with most arguments in favour of mixed drinking laws, the discussion was framed around a husband and wife. The notion of a single woman going in to meet a single man was not put forward.[54] Those speaking against mixed drinking used similar language to make their points: 'who would look after the children?' It 'would tend to break up the home'. Or, playing on the fears of dangerous heterosexuality, that it was simply 'demoralizing'.[55] Similarly, the United Church of Canada quoted the Bracken report in arguing that there is a 'close association between the brothel and the bar'.[56] The discourse linking prostitution to alcohol would be repeated often by critics of more liberal drinking laws, but with little uptake among the general public.

In the run-up to the release of the Bracken Commission, a survey of people reported that they expected little change. Implicit in their pessimism was the view that the existing laws were antiquated and that more liberal drinking laws represented modernity. The commission's ambivalence about modernity seemed apparent to all. As a 'businesswoman' stated: 'How can we expect a fair liquor law with a teetotaler like Bracken heading the commission? We'll be stuck with a horse and buggy law forever.' Similarly a 'housewife' said, 'I guess the recommendations will depend on what the temperance people think' and a 'salesclerk' added, 'No change. Manitoba leaders are too frightened of the old-fashioned thinking that's popular in this province.'[57] Even temperance supporters linked access to alcohol with modernity. In an appearance before the commission in 1954, Women's Christian Temperance Union executive member Mrs W.W. Thompson had to state repeatedly to the commission that the WCTU had only 200 members. They were incredulous, having expected it to represent a larger force. Thompson explained the dwindling numbers of the group: 'The old people are dying and the young people—I imagine a good many of them are drinking, so they won't join.'[58]

When Bill 14, outlining the new liquor laws, was brought forward in February 1956, the lead for the story was: 'A blueprint for future drinking customs in Manitoba—relegating the present drab all-male beer parlors to a minor role—was unveiled by the provincial government Thursday.'[59] Similarly, when the report was released in September 1955, the *Winnipeg Tribune* headed off its article by mentioning that 'it urged equality of drinking on a sweeping basis for every Manitoban including women and Indians over 21.'[60]

After all the discussion on beer parlours, they were the one establishment that was almost ignored by the changing laws. The report called for mixed drinking in restaurants and the new cocktail lounges, but beer parlours were denied that option. Some male citizens had warned the commission that 'to allow mixed drinking in parlors would destroy this last "stronghold for males only."'[61] In fact, the addition of a supper-hour closing and increased food and drink options were the only significant changes made to beer parlours. Linking of masculinity to space certainly seemed borne out in Winnipeg by men's comments on supper-hour closures at the beer parlour: 'It just isn't self respecting for a man to leave a parlor this early,' and 'my wife will figure something's wrong when she sees me coming home.'[62] But the rationale for keeping women out of beer parlours went beyond nostalgia for lost masculine space: 'The Commission, having surveyed the on-premise picture as a whole, felt that, while some of the present beer parlors were attractive, many were not acceptable for women. We decided, therefore, that though women must be recognized as citizens having equal rights with men, the privilege of public drinking should not be extended to them in beer parlors.'[63]

To put it more succinctly, women were equal but still in need of protection. We shouldn't be surprised. Women were considered vulnerable to men when alcohol was involved—a critical discourse when beer parlours were being labelled as strictly masculine space. Beer parlours in Winnipeg were marked by class. When the report stated that it did not want women going into beer parlours, what it was really stating was that it did not want women in working-class establishments. However, women would be allowed to drink in new establishments, with the hope that these new spaces would be better, due to the proximity of food and their sex's 'moderating influence'.[64] The province was still in the business of trying to control space, and this time women were being used as part of the control mechanism.

For its part, the Bracken report offered one other explanation for opening up the liquor privilege in Manitoba: people simply were not obeying the old laws. As Bracken noted: 'We cannot hope to hold people to a law they do not believe in. We hope, by producing facts and figures with our report, to make the people of Manitoba say, "this is a good law, we'll go along with it."'[65] Rather than legislated moderation, the Bracken report argued for self-control.[66] In practice the law still attempted to control space in all the new establishments and even outline exactly what new foods could be introduced to beer parlours.

On 1 March 1957, following local option votes across the province, new drinking establishments began opening their doors. In Winnipeg, the Royal Alexandra Hotel's dining room could now serve liquor. The *Winnipeg Tribune* focused its story on a couple, Mr and Mrs G.R. Saunders of Winnipeg, as they shared a bottle of wine in this 'new and exciting experience'. With 20 members of the staff watching, waiter Mauro Martinelli paused until the stroke of 12 and then 'tipped the first few drops into a glass, Mr Saunders tasted it, savored it, and nodded assent'.[67] The *Winnipeg Tribune* trumpeted it as a 'new era in the history of Manitoba' and a 'revolution'. It was both and neither. Heterosexuality was triumphant. Drinking spaces were redefined as heterosocial space, but it was the man who gave approval for the wine. For all the new heterosocial space that had been created, gender hierarchies were still in place.

The most interesting parts of the 1950s liquor discussion in Manitoba were happening under the table. Critics tried to restrain the debate with familiar suggestions that alcohol and women bred prostitution. Men, of course, could not be trusted around women because once they were into the sauce they would lose their moral judgment. Even the argument for equal access to alcohol was made in specific gendered terms: that women who could be trusted to raise children and run a household should be able to handle the responsibility of drinking alcohol, or that a man and wife ought to be able to have a drink together. Women in this discussion were always part of something more, whether it be family or marriage. And socialized drinking was always discussed in the context of a married couple sharing a drink. How those couples might have met was a question that was rarely put on the table. City police morality inspector Peter Cafferty offers a glimpse in a report to the Manitoba legislature in 1950 focused on the abuse of banquet permits: 'There are cases where 400 or 500 persons are assembled in a hall, 50 to 75 per cent women and girls, and it's an easy matter to make money on sale of liquor.'[68] Clearly, they were not all walking into these banquets as married couples, and not all the women—indeed few, if any—were prostitutes.

The reality was that men and women were meeting over drinks in the 1950s, whether through clubs, banquets, or the smuggled bottle of alcohol that was poured under the table in a supper club. The Bracken report acknowledged this reality when it said a law was only enforceable when it met with approval from the people. By the time the province of Manitoba was drafting its revised liquor laws, alcohol and heterosocial space were already united. But still, what of all the problems associated with alcohol that were spelled out at length in the first half of the Bracken report? Blame the beer parlours. The sins of alcohol were visited upon the working-class beer parlours, just as the saloon had born the brunt of prohibition anger. The beer parlours were irredeemable masculine space. And in the end, that homosocial nature was their undoing, for while clubs and dance halls could be sold as locations for proper heterosexuality, the beer parlour never could. So in the 1950s, as heterosocial space—space for marriage and space, though they were loath to admit it, for dating—grew, the homosocial space of the beer parlour was the odd 'man' out.

Notes

1. Joan W. Scott, 'Gender: A Useful Category of Historical Analysis', in Sue Morgan, ed., *The Feminist History Reader* (New York: Routledge, 2006), 133–48.

2. 'Bracken Heads Liquor Probe', *Winnipeg Tribune*, 13 Apr. 1954.

3. Kathy Peiss, *Cheap Amusements: Working Women and Leisure in Turn-of-the-Century New York* (Philadelphia: Temple University Press, 1986), 4–5.

4. Ibid., 40.

5. Ibid., 28.

6. Beth Bailey, *From Front Porch to Back Seat* (Baltimore: Johns Hopkins University Press, 1988), 13.

7. Carolyn Strange, *Toronto's Girl Problem: The Perils and Pleasures of the City, 1880–1930* (Toronto: University of Toronto Press, 1995), 3 and 5.

8. Ibid., 10.

9. Craig Heron, *Booze: A Distilled History* (Toronto: Between the Lines, 2003), 180.

10. Robert A. Campbell, *Sit Down and Drink Your Beer: Regulating Vancouver's Beer Parlours, 1925–1954* (Toronto: University of Toronto Press, 2001), 59, 63, and 75.

11. Heron, *Booze*, 290.

12. Campbell, *Sit Down and Drink Your Beer*, 75–6.

13. Geoffrey Bernard Toews, 'The Boons and Banes of Booze: The Liquor Trade in Rural Manitoba, 1929–1939', *Manitoba History* 50 (Oct. 2005): 20–1.

14. Val Werier, 'Behind the News: Law Allows Women Beer By the Glass', *Winnipeg Tribune*, 20 Sept. 1952.

15. Mariana Valverde, *Diseases of the Will: Alcohol and the Dilemmas of Freedom* (Cambridge: Cambridge University Press, 1998), 97.

16. Ibid., 158.

17. Ibid., 159.

18. Campbell, *Sit Down and Drink Your Beer*, 108.

19. "Liquor Nets $4 ½ Million In Province', *Winnipeg Tribune*, 28 Feb. 1946; 'Manitoba Spending on Liquor Attacked', *Winnipeg Tribune*, 14 Feb. 1949; 'Mixed Drinking Question not Topical', *Winnipeg Tribune*, 10 Mar. 1949; and 'Province Says No to Cocktail Bars', *Winnipeg Tribune*, 29 Mar. 1949. (Don't mistake the 'No' for a policy statement. The story was gleaned from an exchange between governing and opposition parties.)

20. Val Werier, 'Mixed Drinking? We've had it for Many Years', *Winnipeg Tribune*, 20 Aug. 1955.

21. *Report of the Manitoba Liquor Enquiry Commission*, 20.

22. 'Liquor Probe to Study Hotel Control', *Winnipeg Tribune*, 26 Oct. 1950.

23. Valverde, *Diseases of the Will*, 97.

24. Juba was elected as Winnipeg mayor in 1956, just as the local option votes were giving the thumbs up to mixed drinking in Winnipeg.

25. 'Temperance Leader Urges Hold-Off on New Outlets: "All Canada Eyes Liquor Session"', *Winnipeg Tribune*, 20 Feb. 1956.

26. Heron, *Booze*, 168.

27. 'The Women want Mixed Drinking', *Winnipeg Tribune*, 18 Nov. 1953.

28. 'WCTU Approves Selling Cocktails', *Winnipeg Tribune*, 21 Oct. 1954; 'Request Changes', *Winnipeg Tribune*, 22 July 1954.

29. 'Bracken Heads Liquor Probe', *Winnipeg Tribune*, 13 Apr. 1954.

30. *The Report of the Manitoba Liquor Enquiry Commission*, 5.

31. 'Stinson Attacks Liquor "Remedy"', *Winnipeg Tribune*, 29 Feb. 1956. Stinson was critical of its recommendations. He was pleased with the temperance elements.

32. *Report of the Manitoba Liquor Enquiry Commission*, 32.

33. Ibid., 36 and 39.

34. Ibid., 40, 45, 47, 48, and 106.

35. Ibid., 49, 55, 73, 216, and 226. 'On Guard Manitoba! It All Began in a Glass of Beer', *Winnipeg Tribune*, 19 Sept. 1956.

36. *Report of the Manitoba Liquor Enquiry Commission*, 256.

37. Ibid., 266.

38. Ibid., 349.

39. The report does comment on liquor habits across the world, and some of the comments, particularly around the Irish, play into ethnic stereotypes. See *Report of the Manitoba Liquor Enquiry Commission*, 171, 173, 175, and 178.

40. Gordon Sinclair, 'Selkirk Bootleg Outlets Scored', *Winnipeg Tribune*, 16 July 1954. 'Local Option Vote Set to Permit Treaty Indians to Drink Liquor', *Winnipeg Tribune*, 16 Apr. 1956.

41. 'Inquiry Favors Sale of Liquor to Indians', *Winnipeg Tribune*, 9 Nov. 1951.

42. I reviewed the *Winnipeg Tribune* clipping file 'Liquor category' between 1943 and 1957 and found no interviews with Aboriginal people.

43. Gordon Sinclair, 'Probe Chief Seeks Indian Pow-Wow on Fire Water', *Winnipeg Tribune*, 7 Aug. 1954.

44. *Report of the Manitoba Liquor Enquiry Commission*, 407–08.

45. Campbell, *Sit Down and Drink Your Beer*, 108–09.

46. *Report of the Manitoba Liquor Enquiry Commission*, 413–14.

47. Heron, *Booze*, 281.

48. *Report of the Manitoba Liquor Enquiry Commission*, 282 and 404.

49. Ben Lepkin, '"Mixed" Parlors Urged', *Winnipeg Tribune*, 12 Dec. 1950.

50. '"Saloon Era" Liquor Laws Under Attack', *Winnipeg Tribune*, 20 Nov. 1952.

51. 'Ald. Scott Wants Winnipeggers to Have Say on Bars: Let People Set Own Liquor Rules', *Winnipeg Tribune*, 15 July 1954.

52. Adele Perry, *On The Edge of Empire: Gender, Race, and the Making of British Columbia, 1849–1871* (Toronto: University of Toronto Press, 2006), 146. Emphasis in original.

53. 'The Women Want Mixed Drinking', *Winnipeg Tribune*, 18 Nov. 1953.

54. 'Liquor Outlet Hike Opposed by Women', *Winnipeg Tribune*, 27 Oct. 1954.

55. Ibid.

56. Peter Desbarats, 'Wets Start Gentle Drive In Favor of More Outlets', *Winnipeg Tribune*, 17 Oct. 1956. 'On Guard Manitoba! It All Began in a Glass of Beer', *Winnipeg Tribune*, 19 Sept. 1956.

57. 'Nobody Seems Very Hopeful', *Winnipeg Tribune*, 30 July 1955.

58. 'WCTU Approves Selling Cocktails', *Winnipeg Tribune*, 21 Oct. 1954.

59. '"Social Glass" Outlets Urged', *Winnipeg Tribune*, 24 Feb. 1956.

60. 'Self-Control Drinking Set for Manitobans', *Winnipeg Tribune*, 3 Sept. 1955.

61. 'New Pub Game: Beat the Clock', *Winnipeg Tribune*, 17 July 1956.

62. Ibid.

63. *Report of the Manitoba Liquor Enquiry Commission*, 434.

64. Ibid., 436.

65. George Brimmel, 'They Study Laws . . . But Drink Probers Won't Enter Pubs', *Winnipeg Tribune*, 24 Sept. 1954.

66. *Report of the Manitoba Liquor Enquiry Commission*, 100.

67. 'Glass of Wine Heralds Era', *Winnipeg Tribune*, 1 Mar. 1957.

68. 'Morality Chief Charges Banquet Permits Abused', *Winnipeg Tribune*, 25 Oct. 1950.

25

Manipulating Innocence: Corruptibility, Youth, and the Case against Obscenity

————— **Mary Louise Adams** —————

In 1949, a Toronto man wrote to the Ontario Government Censorship Bureau (a bureaucratic entity that, in fact, did not exist) to protest the availability of cheap pulp paperbacks. 'These books,' he wrote, 'many of them filthy in the extreme, have alluring colour covers, and any adolescent can buy publications for 25 [cents], that his parents would be shocked to read.'[1] His complaint was one of many received by the Ontario Attorney General's office in the post-Second World War period when, after years of paper shortages and restrictions on trade, Canadian newsstands were opened to a huge range of mass-market publications from the United States. Concerned citizens, as individuals and as members of a wide spectrum of organizations, condemned the 'licentiousness of magazines',[2] the 'flood of objectionable literature',[3] 'porno-graphy for profit',[4] and, among other things, the transformation of Canada into 'an open end[ed] sewer' for filth from the United States.[5] For the most part, these objections were articulated through a discourse of concern for youth who, it was assumed, had relatively unlimited access to inexpensive printed material over which their parents and teachers had little control.

In the 1930s and 1940s, mass-produced literature had flourished, especially in the United States. The creation of new genres and new approaches to marketing and distribution combined with improvements in printing techniques to make the publication of comics and paperbacks increasingly profitable.[6] After the war, Canadian newsstands felt the full impact of this growing sector of the US publishing industry. The market for so-called 'real literature' was swamped by 35-cent pulp novels, 15-cent magazines, and 10-cent comics that were readily available in drugstores and cigar stores. In Ottawa, for instance, a single news and magazine distributor received 3,800 copies of *Women's Barracks*, a 1952 pulp novel title.[7] In 1950, a researcher for the Toronto Board of Education counted 135 different comics for sale in that city, and he estimated their readership at more than 500,000 individuals each month.[8] To put these figures into perspective, the Canadian distribution of hardcover books was limited to 2,000 bookstores, while magazines and pulps could be bought at more than 9,000 outlets.[9]

Alongside this boom in pulp publishing, so-called sexy magazines were also becoming increasingly visible. As a 1952 *Reader's Digest* article said, such questionable material was nothing new; what had changed was its accessibility. In the years before the Second World War, 'girlie' magazines had been available only in (male) adult environments like 'barbershops, saloons and army posts'. By the 1950s, however, these magazines were being sold right at the corner drugstore, on the same shelves as family magazines and 'useful books'.[10] In 1953 the launch of the 'tasteful' and expensively produced *Playboy* solidified the trend.

Fears about the power of mass media to divide parents from children were not unique to post-war North America.[11] They had followed the emergence of novels in the nineteenth century, and of silent films in the 1910s and 1920s. They would re-emerge over television in the late 1950s and the 1960s. We see them today in discussions about rock videos, Nintendo games, and the Internet. Writing about the British campaign against horror comics of the mid-1950s, Martin Barker says that 'each rising mass medium in turn has been targeted in the name of revered values.'[12] But, he adds, parental and social concerns are less a factor of the medium that spawned them than they are of the values assumed to be threatened by it. Where turn-of-the-century working-class parents worried that commercial entertainments such as cheap movies undermined traditional gender roles and put their daughters in too close proximity with boys,[13] middle-class parents of the 1950s worried about standards of sexual behaviour and whether the pulps encouraged their children towards deviance. In both cases, the medium was an easier target of popular protest than the general social context which spawned it.

Post-war discourses about the 'corruptibility' of youth, and their need for protection from sex as it was portrayed in various forms of pulp literature, were able to provide the impetus for broad-ranging initiatives of moral and sexual regulation that targeted adults as much as they targeted young people themselves. Discursive constructions of youthful innocence helped to set the boundaries of normative sexuality, thus marginalizing non-normative forms of sexual expression by people of all ages. Without the concepts of youth they were able to mobilize, these regulatory discourses would never have been so widely circulated.

Post-war discussions about the effects of indecency and obscenity on young people occurred in a variety of contexts. Here I pay particular attention to three of these: efforts in the late 1940s to restrict the circulation of comic books, especially crime and horror comics; the proceedings of the 1952 Senate Special Committee on Salacious and Indecent Literature; and a 1952 trial over obscenity that took place in Ottawa. Each of these illustrates the way 'youth' was used as a rhetorical trope in attempts to maintain dominant sexual and moral standards.

. . .

The Threat of Indecency, or Why the Concern about Obscenity?

What counted as harmful literature in the late 1940s and the 1950s was a wide range of material, although the exact details of its content is not always easy to ascertain. As they do today, standards of decency and propriety varied widely—even within class and ethnic groupings. Certainly there did not exist agreed-upon definitions—even in law—of either indecency or obscenity. What I am concerned with here, however, is not so much the actual content of materials that were thought to be indecent or obscene, but the language and discursive strategies used to present them as such. How was it that social critics were able to generate concern about particular types of publications? My findings are similar to those of Martin Barker in his analysis of the British campaign against horror comics. Barker found that arguments against the comics were based more on popular ideas about the young people who were assumed to be reading the comics than about the content of the books themselves.[14] In Canada, post-war debates about the moral effects of mass-market publications crystallized concerns about the nature of youth, their relationship to sexuality, and the place and character of sexuality in Canadian society.

Two distinct, but related, efforts to clean up Canadian newsstands suggest that different media came under scrutiny at different times. In the late 1940s, crime comics were the major concern, until a 1949 amendment to the Canadian Criminal Code almost completely eliminated them from the newsstands. In the 1950s, cheap paperbacks and what were referred to as 'girlie magazines' took their turn as targets of public protest and condemnation. Disapproval of these publications was institutionalized in the 1952 Senate Special Committee. While these two episodes of moral concern exploited a variety of regulatory strategies—some shared, some not— the ideologies that helped to construct them were remarkably similar.

Anti-indecency campaigns (I use the word 'campaign' with hesitation—it suggests perhaps too organized a shape for what were often contradictory efforts) relied heavily on representations of young people as in need of both protection and control, particularly in the realm of sex and morality. Teens were assumed to be impressionable—'born imitators'—in ways that adults were not. Adolescence was seen as a time of both sexual and moral development,[15] the success of the former depending to a great extent on the success of the latter. With the proper guidance, teenagers could learn to control their unfolding sexuality. However, this belief that teenage morality was a blank slate meant that teens were open not only to 'proper' influences but to 'improper' ones as well. Their moral immaturity—or moral innocence, as it was more likely to be called—was said to leave them vulnerable to harmful sexual attitudes that might lead to degeneracy and delinquency. As one magazine journalist claimed, 'The love comics are to the girly magazines what elementary schools are to high schools. If a child's taste is formed by love and crime comics, he or she will continue to crave lurid, unreal, violent and sexy material in print.'[16] And such material, apparently, could skew an adolescent's understanding of her own social climate: 'The mass production and distribution of sensational novels depicting lewd, repulsive and perverted behaviour of the characters as a normal way of life has superseded all other worthwhile publications offered for sale in Canadian stores. Men and women are portrayed as monsters of perversion and the women pictured as Lesbians and modern Messalinas.

Added to this is the continuous suggestion that crime and perversion is [sic] normal. . . .'[17]

More than anything else, it was normality that was deemed to be under threat from the pulp publications. They were accused of making immorality seem normal, of shifting the boundaries of what was seen to be acceptable: perverts might cease to be perverse; abnormality might fail to operate as a negative marker of sexual and moral difference from the norm; monogamous heterosexual marriage might end up as just one of many forms of sexual expression. Arguments about the dangers of indecency suggested that a whole process of moral degeneration would be put into effect if 'immature' teenagers read pulps, absorbed their sordid values, and carried them into the 1960s.

Young people were widely regarded as products in which adults invested sums of time and money, along with material, emotional, intellectual, and spiritual resources. Parents considered it their right to make these investments exclusively or to have them made by other adults of their choosing. In this context, teenagers' reading of comics or dime-store novels turned the publishers of this literature into trespassers and usurpers of parental prerogative. The publishers were guilty of competing with and disrupting the influences of the home, the church, the school. A widely circulated 1952 resolution from the town council of Timmins, Ontario, included the following justification for regulatory measures against obscenity: 'And whereas, millions have been spent on excellent universities, high schools and public schools to educate our children to become law-abiding, productive and lovable citizens, who are our most sacred investment, and who should not be exposed to an education, through the reading of filthy literature, stories of compromising situations, and details of sex crimes, which tend to undermine our whole educational system. . . .'[18]

Some thought that bad literature was powerful enough not just to threaten but to cancel the efforts of church, school, and home to educate young people about proper forms of sex and family living. Members of the Canadian Committee for the International Conference in Defence of Children worried that indecent literature might turn young people from the goals adults had set for them: 'high ideals, noble emotions and constructive action directed to the general good'.[19] Pulp literature was seen as competition for approved forms of sex education (however limited these were) that promoted the normalization of sexual and moral standards. The outcome of this contest could affect 'the whole moral tone of the nation'.[20] 'Civilized life', 'democracy', and 'freedom' were all thought to be dependent upon a particular, dominant version of morality. As long as this was challenged by the salacious materials on the newsstands, the future itself seemed to be threatened.

During the early years of the Cold War, statements about 'threats' to the nation often concealed fears about Communism, and the discussion about printed indecency was no exception to this. A direct relationship was assumed between a particular version of moral health and Canada's strength as a nation. Demoralization, in both senses of the word, was assumed to be a prime strategy of infiltrating Communists. In their 1953 report, members of the Senate Special Committee on Salacious and Indecent Literature stated that 'in the world-wide struggle between the forces of darkness and evil and those of good, the freedom-loving, democratic countries have need of all the strength in their moral fibre to combat the evil threat, and anything that undermines the morals of our citizens and particularly of the young is a direct un-Canadian act.'[21]

During the proceedings of the committee, chair J.C. Davis (who took over after the death of J.J. Hayes Doone, the instigator of the project) expressed his own racist version of this position, without any opposition from his colleagues: 'This is a Christian country, and we have to fight the powers of darkness from non-Christian countries. The morals of this country have to be strengthened to keep us strong. We are being attacked at

the very roots by the influx of indecent literature and we have to stop it one way or another.'[22]

Notions of 'threat to the nation' operated discursively in much the same way as the more frequently cited 'threat to youth'—by stirring up moral indignation that might lead to calls for protective regulation. Moreover, each of these phrases could be used to underscore the gravity of the other: a threat to the nation was perceived to be a threat to teenagers and youth. Who could not be moved by the vulnerability of young people, struggling towards maturity? Who did not want them to develop to their full potential? Who could abandon the goals of those who had died so recently on European battlefields? Who could abandon their sons and daughters to an atmosphere of immorality and indecency that was assumed to be the antithesis of a democratic society? The crusade against obscenity and harmful literature was built on, and gained its momentum from, these kinds of discursive attachments. Notions of patriotism and 'Christian values' were called on to underscore arguments against the mass-market publications. They lent weight to an issue that might otherwise have appeared to be trivial.

The Canadian Fight against Crime Comics

In Canada, the fight to ban crime comics, although not entirely cohesive, was broadly based. As the product of well-organized efforts by individuals and groups it certainly had significant effects. The man most often identified with the crime comics campaign was E. Davie Fulton, Tory member of Parliament from Kamloops, British Columbia. Fulton claimed that national interest in the matter had been 'aroused' by the Federated Women's Institutes, the Federation of Home and School Associations, the Ontario Teachers' Federation, Parent-Teacher Federations, and the Imperial Order Daughters of the Empire (IODE)—all of them middle-class and predominantly female organizations.[23]

Comic books were by no means new in the late 1940s, but their content had undergone substantial change since they first appeared in the 1920s as bound collections of newspaper strips. In 1938 readers were introduced to Superman, the first superhero (created by Jerry Siegal and Toronto-born artist Joe Shuster). By 1941, American publishers were putting out 168 different titles, and by the middle of the war, National Periodical Publishers claimed sales of more than 12 million comics per month.[24] At its peak, in the post-war decade, it is estimated that the US comics industry was producing 60 million comics per month.[25]

. . .

After the Second World War, the patriotic superheroes took a back seat to new narrative genres. Crime, horror, and love comics became especially popular, launching a wave of public concern. New titles appeared regularly, and many readers increased their consumption by exchanging copies with friends. As Fulton said, the whole process of buying, reading, and trading could occur outside parents' control. Newspaper and magazine articles frequently played up the fact that comics were not a large part of adult culture. Parents and teachers were often described in the act of 'discovering' a 'hidden stash' in a child's room or school desk. Apparently many were 'shocked' by what they found: drawings of women that emphasized their breasts and buttocks; detailed stories about crime, including murder and rape; titles like *Tales from the Crypt*, *Haunt of Fears*, *Crimes by Women*, *Heart Throb*, and *Flaming Love*.

Toronto Board of Education trustee W.R. Cockburn was typical of those who spoke out against comics. In 1945 he raised concerns about them with the board's Management Committee, saying they were 'degrading and detrimental to the welfare of our youth'.[26] Complaining that Biblical comics were largely unavailable in Toronto, Cockburn showed his colleagues comic books he had been able to buy in the city—*Daring*, *Human Touch*, *Black Terror*, and *Boy*

Commandos—saying, 'They're nothing but a lot of rot about daggers and guns.' A similar argument was endorsed in 1947 by the members of the IODE's National Education Committee, who lamented the eclipsing of funny comics: 'Instead we have "Superman" and gangs of thieves, G-men and sadistic murderers who carve their way through the "funny pages" talking plain talk, and giving people "the works."'[27]

While views like those expressed by Cockburn and the members of the IODE were widely reported on, they were not shared by everyone. In 1949, *Chatelaine* ran a story by Mary Jukes called 'Are Comics Really a Menace?'[28] In an attempt to interrupt prevailing anti-comics discourse she claimed that psychologists, teachers, and parents 'do not look upon this form of entertainment as dangerous [despite] the daily papers continu[ing] to turn up stories tying juvenile delinquency to the reading of certain types of comics'. In a poll of 2,000 of its readers, *Chatelaine* found that 'they are wholeheartedly in favor of real comics; they don't feel that all comics should be scrapped because of the few horror numbers.' Of course, the acceptability of 'real' (funny?) comics was precisely the point the IODE had been trying to make. Fulton, Cockburn, and the others who raised their concerns publicly didn't think all comics should be scrapped; their goal was to influence policies that separated the 'good' (what they called 'real') comics from the 'bad.' . . .

Portrayals of crimes, overly graphic representations of women's bodies, and a rarely defined immorality were the main concerns of the anti-comics crusaders. Today, post-war comics seem an odd mix of provocativeness and predictability. In Canadian titles, at least, the good guys and gals always won—even if it wasn't until the last frame—and, generally, crime didn't pay. But such morally acceptable endings were invariably preceded by fights, killings, and other dirty deeds, depictions of scantily clad women, and graphic or textual sexual innuendo. 'Barry Kuda', a story in a 1946 issue of *Unusual Comics* (Bell Comics, Toronto), shows how these 'dangerous' elements were combined: 'What made the walls of Queen Merma's palace tremble as she held a farewell banquet for Barry Kuda and Algie? Barry was soon to learn, when the banquet hall became a scene of boiling terror and Sato's awful army, with their bodies glowing red hot, fought to brand the Queen's domain with THE SYMBOL OF SIN!'[29]

As Sato's volcanic eruption destroys Merma's palace, the blond and muscular Barry Kuda (wearing a wrestling-type singlet and shorts) carries the slim, white, long-haired Merma (wearing bikini shorts and conical breast-coverings) to safety. Barry returns to the palace to fight the devilish Sato, complete with horns, and to find his friend Algie. But Barry's plan is foiled when he is frozen stiff in his tracks by one of Sato's men.

In the meantime, Sato himself has gone in search of Merma.

> Merma: What do you want, Sato? Keep away! What can you gain by killing me?
> Sato: But—I'm not going to kill you, my dear. It's lonely in Volcania! I'd like a real queen for a wife!
> Merma: No! No! Not that! Barry—Bar—

Her cries are to no avail. Merma gets frozen too. In the next frame, she is lying helpless on a table, Sato's doctor hanging over her scantily clothed body. When her 'frozen flesh is thawed', he gets ready to inject her with the blood of one of Sato's guards so that she will be able to survive in their underworld. 'Oh. No! No! Barry! Algie! Help!'

The scene shifts to the outside of the palace where Barry has managed to thaw himself out, find his friend, and kill some of Sato's minions. Bodies are flying in all directions. And just in time, Barry and Algie run through the carnage to find Merma, who is about to receive the injection of devilish blood. 'Help No—Oh, Barry! Thank Heavens!' Sato is vanquished, Merma is saved, and Barry and Algie are feted as heroes.

. . .

Opponents said that the comics 'glamorize[d] crime, brutality and immorality'[30] and gave young people 'a wrong idea of the civilized way of life'.[31] Adult commentators tended to take the view that young readers (blank slates that they were assumed to be) passively absorbed whatever the comics put before them and that, once exposed to crime, sex, and violence on the page, children and teens would develop a taste for it and be moved to re-enact it in daily life.

In June 1948, Fulton first introduced the issue into the House of Commons, arguing that crime comics were leading Canadian young people into delinquency. While this flagging of possible moral degeneration got the issue on the government's agenda, it was not enough to convince the Minister of Justice, J.L. Ilsley, of the immediate need for suppression. The minister claimed that his own research, including queries to the provincial Attorneys General, had not uncovered any conclusive evidence of the link between reading crime comics and subsequent delinquent activity. Ilsley quoted Dr C.M. Hincks, general director of the National Committee for Mental Hygiene, who said: 'It has never been scientifically established that crime or thrill stories either in movies, radio or comics have contributed to delinquency. Prohibiting publication is an admission of failure on the part of the family and the educational system in encouraging the development of wholesome and healthy interests.'[32]

Ilsley's stance on comics was a 'scientific' one versus the decidedly moral approach adopted by Fulton. Originally, Fulton had attempted to take a more 'rational' approach. Before introducing his bill, he requested statistics on delinquency from the Minister of Justice. But the figures he received, for crimes committed by people under the age of 18, did little to help his case. In 1945 there had been 3,934 convictions; in 1946 there were 3,682; and in 1947 there were 3,350.[33] Despite Fulton's continued claims to the contrary, the actual incidence of delinquency was falling. According to sociologist Augustine Brannigan, this trend in delinquency rates was consistent for the years 1942 to 1949, and the figures remained 'relatively low' until the mid-1950s.[34] Still Fulton persisted, appealing to common-sense notions of what was good for young people, of how easily they might be corrupted, and of how dangerous the effects of comic books were:

I just want to give an example from the one [comic book] I have in my hand. It starts off on the inside cover with the picture of a man striking a match and staring at it. The caption over the next picture is, 'Tonight I dreamed of a blazing moon like a fiery wheel in the sky—burning trees were crashing about me,' and the caption is illustrated. The next picture portrays him walking to a slum tenement, and he says, 'I saw an old condemned building. Nobody would care if it burned down.' The next picture shows this man holding a burning match, and the caption says, 'Tonight I stole into the cellar of the condemned building and set my first fire.' That is a fine thing to put before a youngster of twelve or so, who perhaps has just struck his first match.[35]

Eventually, Ilsley conceded that legislation was necessary. Apparently, his change of position came after he received a selection of comics from Fulton—*Crime* and *Crime Does Not Pay*—comics which Ilsley characterized as a flagrant abuse of freedom of the press. But Ilsley wanted to take his time over the new law, and the conclusion of the comics debate was held off until the next parliamentary session. By the time that session was underway, Ilsley had retired from politics and been replaced as Justice Minister by Stuart Garson. Fulton introduced his private member's bill once again, and a full-scale debate of crime comics occupied the House for several days.

MPs rallied to the call to protect youth from 'the trash you get in these dime crime comic books'.[36] In a particularly evocative, though not entirely typical, contribution to the Commons debate, Daniel McIvor, MP for Fort William, described the crime comics as a tactic of 'the devil'. He said, 'You can almost hear him saying, "Get them young. That is the time to get them." Our Sunday school teachers can work their heads off and

still not succeed in combating an agency such as obscene literature. It is a curse.'[37]

Many of the MPs admitted to having made studies of crime comics at their local drugstore or in their home ridings. They argued their support for Fulton's bill on the basis of personal experience and gut reaction. They waved (unnamed) comics at their colleagues and read statements from concerned constituents. Howard C. Green (Vancouver-Quadra) read from a letter from 'a mother in Vancouver, who, by the way, is the daughter of a distinguished Canadian authoress': 'I know you are as anxious as any conscientious parent to see our Canadian children rescued from the evil effects of these criminal immoral magazines. I believe a big house-cleaning of our magazine and paper-back 25-cent books is overdue. We busy ourselves building youth centres, working in church to show our young people the guide posts to clean living, and all the time a stream of filthy books is allowed to come into our country.'[38] The MPs mobilized common-sense assumptions about shared moral principles: 'I know it would disgust everyone in the House and it would disgust the average man and woman right across Canada.'[39] There was much mutual congratulation on the 'high level' of the debate, and there were commendations for Fulton from the other MPs and for the Minister of Justice for bringing the bill to the House.

Bill 10 was passed in December 1949. It amended section 207 of the Criminal Code, which dealt with obscene literature: 'to cover the case of those magazines and periodicals commonly called "crime comics," the publication of which is presently legal, but which it is widely felt tend to the lowering of morals and to induce the commission of crimes by juveniles.'[40] While the actual wording of the amendment was broad and vague, its inclusion in the general section on 'obscene literature' is telling. Subsection one of section 207 would be contravened by anyone who 'prints, publishes, sells or distributes any magazine, periodical or book which exclusively or substantially comprises matter depicting pictorially the commission of crimes, real or fictitious, thereby tending or likely to induce or influence youthful persons to violate the law or to corrupt the morals of such persons'.[41] Even in law the moral capacities of young people were what set the bounds of decency. Under such a broad definition, fairy tales and news articles might have been subject to prosecution. Of course, they were not. Crime comics, on the other hand, rapidly disappeared from Canadian newsstands. At the end of 1950, a researcher for the Toronto Board of Education claimed to have found no crime comics for sale in the city.[42]

Fredric Wertham and *Seduction of the Innocent*

One of the main proponents of the theory that comics were dangerous literature—the reading of which could lead otherwise normal youngsters to perform criminal or sexually immoral activities—was Dr Fredric Wertham, senior psychiatrist for the New York City Department of Hospitals from 1932 to 1952. In 1948, the year E. Davie Fulton introduced his bill into the Canadian House of Commons, Wertham published five articles in popular American magazines denouncing comics in general and crime comics in particular.[43] In the House of Commons debates, Fulton referred to Wertham and cited his American 'evidence' as support for the proposed amendment to the Criminal Code.

Wertham outlined his position in detail in his 1954 book, *Seduction of the Innocent*, which was a featured selection for the Book-of-the-Month Club that year.[44] The book mentions E. Davie Fulton and the passage of Bill 10, quotes from *Hansard*, and speaks in glowing terms throughout most of a chapter about the work against comics that had been done in Canada, both in Parliament and among ordinary citizens:[45] 'No debate on such a high ethical plane, with proper regard for civil liberties but with equal regard for the rights and happiness of children, has ever taken place in the United States.'[46]

It is impossible, here, to do a full critique of Wertham. Nevertheless, it is important to

consider his work because it was so influential on Canadian activists. He was quoted in the House of Commons debates. He was referred to and cited by people writing to the Ontario Attorney General. He corresponded with members of the British Columbia Parent-Teacher Federation, including a Mrs Eleanor Gray, who was mentioned by name in *Seduction of the Innocent*. In a letter he wrote to thank Gray for a Christmas card, Wertham acknowledged his own importance in the international debate on comics when he wrote, 'P.S: If you wish to, you may quote any part of this letter in any way you wish.'[47]

According to Wertham, comic books affected reading skills, desensitized young people to violence, and led to delinquent behaviour, psychological difficulties, and problems in sexual development. While delinquency, illiteracy, and sex each get their own chapter in *Seduction of the Innocent*, concerns about sexuality appear throughout the book, as does the evocative sexual language that Wertham used to build his case. For instance: 'I have come to the conclusion that this *chronic stimulation, temptation and seduction* by comic books, both their content and their *alluring* advertisements of knives and guns are contributing factors to many children's maladjustment.'[48] At times he was even more blatant, writing, for instance, that children 'give up crime-comic reading like a bad sexual habit.'[49] But what operates as a literary device on one page becomes fact on another—for Wertham, reading comics *was* a bad sexual habit. In a chapter entitled, 'I want to be a sex maniac!' he says that 'an elementary fact of [his] research' is that 'comic books stimulate children sexually.'[50] Wertham took it as self-evidently bad that 'children' should be sexually 'turned on'. Reading comics, he said, impedes 'the free [sexual] development of children' and causes 'sexual arousal which amounts to seduction'.

Wertham's tendency to refer to children, while offering case studies of adolescents, was a rhetorical technique that helped to support his main argument that comics 'seduced' the 'innocent'. To have referred to adolescents would have been to refer to young people who were already in the process of becoming sexual, who were somewhat less than sexually innocent. In invoking 'children', as an imperilled group, Wertham heightened the sense of moral outrage implicit in his writing. The slipperiness between the terms 'child' and 'adolescent' that is evident in Wertham's text is not unique to him, though he manipulates it to his advantage in a remarkable fashion. That adolescence was considered by many to be a transitional 'stage' between childhood and adulthood contributed to the slippery usage. Definitions of adolescence as transitional meant that while adolescents were not children, they continued to be affected by notions about childhood—for instance, the ambiguous concept of childhood innocence.

. . .

Certainly, Wertham was not the only one to believe that comics had a negative effect on children's sexuality, but he was the only one to state his concerns so explicitly. While other commentators spoke demurely of the links between comics and perversion or comics and immorality, Wertham spoke explicitly about masturbation, sado-masochistic fantasies, homosexuality and homoeroticism, prostitution, and sex crime. Though his concerns were numerous, underlying them all was the risk that young people were being exposed to things of which they apparently had no prior knowledge, things that he felt were not suitable for children (however defined), including, and especially, their own sexual feelings. He cites numerous cases where boys and girls recounted to him masturbatory fantasies which were 'aggravated' by reading comics. Even in those cases where young adults seemed to have emerged from their comics-reading years unharmed, Wertham held steadfastly to his position that they might, nevertheless, end up with sexual troubles: 'But is it not one of the elementary facts of modern psychopathology that childhood experiences very often do not manifest themselves as recognizable symptoms or behavior patterns in childhood, but may crop up later in adult life as perverse and neurotic tendencies?'[51]

Wertham's analysis rested on a simple construction of monkey read, monkey do, based on his clinical observation of troubled youth. He was particularly concerned about what he saw as the tendencies of the various forms of comics to encourage homoerotic attitudes. Would the millions of comics circulating across North America lead to an increase in the number of sex deviates? Wertham claims that certain types of comics tended to fix boys in their pre-adolescent phase of disdain for girls—what other writers frequently called the 'normal' homosexual phase of heterosexual development.[52] It seems that homoerotic attitudes were caused, in part, by 'the presentation of masculine, bad, witchlike or violent women. In such comics women are depicted in a definitely anti-erotic light, while the young male heroes have pronounced erotic overtones.'[53]

Wertham lamented the fate of adolescent boys, who lived with their own fears of becoming homosexual. Apparently such boys were likely to become 'addicted' to the 'homoerotically tinged type of comic book', a habit which could only lead to homoerotic fantasies, followed inevitably by guilt and shame as they learned of social taboos against sexual deviation. Certainly, homosexually inclined boys had few other sources to turn to for acknowledgement of their desires, and, given the social climate, they may have felt shame about their reading habits. But, of course, Wertham was not concerned about the discriminatory social conditions and widespread intolerance that led to those feelings of oppression; he was concerned about the tenor of the comic books. Singled out as exemplary of those needing to be cleaned up were the 'dangerous' chronicles of the Caped Crusader and the Boy Wonder.

Wertham's discussion of Batman is a prime example of 1950s moral panic about sex perversion—four and a half pages of 'expert opinion' on the 'Ganymede-Zeus type of love-relationship'. His arguments about the dangers of Batman drew on the most stereotypical signifiers of homo-ness and on a macho individualist version of masculinity more suited to the receding frontier than to post-war domesticity and middle-class corporate life.

> At home they [Batman and Robin, aka Bruce and Dick] lead an idyllic life . . . They live in sumptuous quarters, with beautiful flowers in large vases, and have a butler, Alfred. Batman is sometimes shown in a dressing gown. As they sit by the fireplace the young boy sometimes worries about his partner: 'Something's wrong with Bruce. He hasn't been himself these past few days.' It's like a wish dream of two homosexuals living together. Sometimes they are shown on a couch, Bruce reclining and Dick sitting next to him, jacket off, collar open, and his hand on his friend's arm.[54]

Moreover, Robin was often shown standing with his legs apart, 'the genital region strictly evident', and Batman, in their crusading adventures, frequently came to Robin's rescue. By Wertham's definition, the stories contained no 'decent, attractive, successful women', evidence of an anti-woman attitude he equated with the homoerotic theme. Boys exposed to this pastiche of codes and signifiers would, no doubt, be incited to homoerotic fantasies. And, Wertham claimed, he had the case studies to prove it.

While girls are mentioned infrequently in *Seduction of the Innocent*, they too were at the mercy of the comic-book publishers, perhaps even more so than boys. Wertham contends that female character development was more severely affected by comics than was male character development, primarily because of the nature of female superheroes.[55] He considered characters like Wonder Woman so far outside normal constructions of femininity that girls would be thrown into a spin of mental torment if they should ever endeavour to identify with their heroines.

Resting on his claim to 'professional' knowledge, Wertham 'outs' Wonder Woman, asserting that her lesbianism is 'psychologically unmistakable'. Apparently, Wonder Woman 'is always a horror

type. She is physically very powerful, tortures men, has her own female following, is the cruel, "phallic" woman. While she is a frightening figure for boys, she is an undesirable ideal for girls, being the exact opposite of what girls are supposed to want to be.'[56] One could make much of the 'supposed to' in this sentence. Is Wertham responding to women's and girls' dissatisfaction with post-war discourses on femininity? Is the powerful Wonder Woman a symbolic foreshadowing of the eruption of 1960s feminism? Is this why Wertham is careful not to make any mention of Wonder Woman's sidekick, the pudgy, bon-bon eating Etta?

In the context of post-war psychological discourse, so-called normal sexuality, as we have seen, was not a given; it needed to be fought for and nurtured. 'Normal' sexuality was thought to be the culmination of a precarious developmental process that might easily be sent astray. Outside influences could stall or preclude the attainment by adolescents of sexual maturity. Comics, at least as Wertham and his followers understood them, were clearly in this category of outside threat. What was thought to make comics especially dangerous was the fact that they were deliberately aimed at a young readership. While their content was 'tame' when compared to, say, sex magazines, the moral imperative to clean comics up was considerable because of the long-term consequences they might have had on the 'immature' characters of their intended young audience. The perceived unambiguous relationship between comics and youth was critical to the success of the anti-comics activists. Certainly the passage of the Fulton bill was a major victory for them. More importantly, concerned citizens were also able to exert tremendous pressure directly on the publishers. In 1954, the publishers developed their own production code, similar to that used in the film industry. Overseen by the Comics Magazine Association of America, the code included guidelines such as the following:

- All characters shall be depicted in dress reasonably acceptable to society.

- Illicit sex relations are neither to be hinted at or portrayed. Violent love scenes as well as sexual abnormalities are unacceptable.
- Respect for parents, the moral code, and for honorable behavior shall be fostered. A sympathetic understanding of the problems of love is not a license for morbid distortion. [57]

While campaigns against the perceived immorality in other types of reading material also drew on discourses about young people's vulnerability to corruption, the frame of the discussion was not the same as it had been in the fight against comics. Unlike the market for comics, the market for sex magazines and pulp novels was not primarily made up of children and teenagers. To talk about protecting young people from the influence of these adult publications was to admit, on some level, a loss of control over young people by adults and a failure to maintain the innocence the campaigns claimed they were protecting. Would the truly innocent youth read such things? It was a contradiction the campaigners never addressed.

. . .

A central feature of the moral panic over indecency was that nowhere in these discussions were the definitions of immorality and indecency at issue, nor was the need of Canadians to be protected from them questioned. Immorality and indecency were assumed to be known and harmful categories; all that needed to be asked—by concerned senators, editorial writers, or parents—was how they could best be dealt with. This limited frame of reference is blatantly obvious in the evidence from an Ottawa obscenity case that ran concurrently with the first round of the Senate hearings. In the trial evidence, one sees how this truncated debate was made possible by ideas about the relationship between youth and sexuality. Indeed, one can also see that had it been possible to step outside prevailing discourses of childhood and adolescence, the trial might never have occurred.

Lesbianism as Obscenity or *Women's Barracks* as a Threat to Girls

In March 1952, National News Company, an Ottawa distributor, was charged under section 207 of the Criminal Code with 11 counts of having obscene matter in its possession, 'for the purpose of distributing'. Seven 'girlie' magazines and four pulp novels were named in the charges. All were eventually found to be obscene by Judge A.G. McDougall, and National News was fined a total of $1,100.[58]

Among the novels was *Women's Barracks*, written by an obscure French author named Tereska Torres.[59] Its story is similar to the one told in Torres's 1970 autobiography about her time in the women's section of the Free French Army during the Second World War.[60] The novel follows a group of women who spent several years together in a London barracks. We read of their work assignments and drills, of their hopes for France, and their social and sexual lives. The characters are a mixed lot, mostly young heterosexuals, though there are two lesbians and an 'older' (40-year-old), sexually experienced woman named Claude who has affairs with men and women. Several of the heterosexual women have affairs with married men, one of them gets pregnant out of wedlock, all of them drink. In the midst of this, the narrator operates as the moral centre of the book. She distances herself from the other women and their sexual and emotional experiments—engaging in none of her own—trying to maintain her ideals about love, fidelity, and marriage.

To the present-day reader, Torres's prose is far from lurid. Nevertheless, *Women's Barracks* was packaged in typical 1950s pulp style and marketed as 'THE FRANK AUTOBIOGRAPHY OF A FRENCH GIRL SOLDIER'. While the allusions to sex in the book are many, the details of it are few. In her foreword to the book, Torres links the sexual activity and its emotional fallout to the adversities of war; in 'normal' circumstances, she suggests, little of this activity would have taken place.[61]

When the book first came to trial, Crown Attorney Raoul Mercier's strategy was a simple one. He wanted to prove, simply, that the book had been for sale in a particular cigar store, that the store had been supplied by National News, and that copies of the book had been found on the premises of the distribution company. He was confident that the judge would find the text itself obscene when he came to read it.

. . .

Under the law, no one could be convicted on an obscenity charge if they could prove that the 'public good' had been served by the act in question. This was the grounds of the defence strategy pursued by National News's lawyers, G.W. Ford and J.M. McLean. As they put it, even if Torres's book was technically obscene, it still might have fulfilled a social purpose.[62] Expert witnesses were called to explain just what that purpose might have been. The Crown Attorney, wanting equal time, revised his original strategy and called his own experts to prove the first lot wrong. All told, the trial gave rise to a substantial, public, documented discussion of lesbianism.

While lesbianism is clearly not the focus of the novel, it was the focus of courtroom debate. A copy of the novel is filed with the court transcripts at the Archives of Ontario. Inside the front cover are the initials 'R.M.', presumably referring to Crown Attorney Raoul Mercier. Throughout the text are underlinings and annotations in both pencil and black pen. Fifteen pages are marked with tags made out of sticky tape, possibly pages from which Mercier might have wanted to read in the courtroom. On all but two of these pages, there is some reference to lesbianism.[63] In the margins Mercier has written: 'lesbianism' and 'sex act' (each of these is repeated several times); 'lesbian crave' (56); 'ménage à trois' (87); 'homosexual' (32); 'act of lesbianism' (125). The one scene of lesbian seduction is marked 'all previous chapters lead to but this one climax' (46); passages prior to this are marked 'preparation' (34) and 'build-up' (12 and 36), presumably referring to the scene of lesbian seduction. There are no tags on the parts where heterosexual women find themselves pregnant, or where they discuss their plans to sleep with married men, or where they attempt suicide. The definition of immorality at work here is too narrow to include them. For Mercier, what made this book obscene was its discussion of lesbianism.

Even one of the expert witnesses for the defence, Toronto *Globe and Mail* writer J.A. McAree, claimed that lesbianism was the 'theme' of the book.[64] Certainly, he and his colleagues did nothing to challenge the alignment of lesbianism with immorality. In fact, the basis of defence arguments was that Torres's novel served the public good by warning its readers, especially young women, about the dangers of lesbianism.

Allan Seiger, a professor at the University of Michigan, tried to underscore the relationship of the lesbian activity to the war: 'These women are to be regarded, I think, as much casualties of the war as other soldiers.'[65] John Bakless, a journalism professor at the University of New York, stated that the book presented the lesbian episodes as being 'positively repulsive to any normal male or female'.[66] He also said that in 'the context of the book as a whole they clearly point out that the wages of sin is death.'[67] But, asks Mercier, is it not likely that

> a little girl who is not maybe a French woman in the same barracks, but who is in [a] convent or in a boarding school reaching the puberty age, does not know anything about these things, reads this passage from this book, wouldn't you say they would be willing to indulge in this practice to see if it is as described?
>
> A: I have read that book through, and I wouldn't want to be near a lesbian. Don't forget what happens. . . .
>
> Q: And you do not think they would be tempted to try lesbianism?
>
> A: No, sir, there is disaster there too plainly, and it is only with sympathy and regret that you can read it. . . .[68]

What happens is that Ursula, the 16-year-old, sleeps with Claude, the older bisexual woman, and falls in love with her. Claude 'toys' with Ursula emotionally. In her tormented state, Ursula is unable to muster feelings for a male Polish soldier who is pursuing her. Later, she tries to have sex with a male French sailor. But she is not up to it, and he ends up treating her like a little sister during the several days and nights they spend together. After this, Ursula's affections for Claude diminish. She falls in love with the Polish soldier, they plan to marry, they have sex, she gets pregnant, and he goes off to the front and is killed. In despair, she kills herself. It is a disaster, certainly. But the sequence of events is hardly caused by her one night of lesbian sex.

However, it is not Mercier's reading of the plot that stands out here; rather it is his attempt, and that of his opponent, to present the text as having powerful social consequences. What might the book do to young women in particular? Oddly, it is Mercier and his collection of expert witnesses who argue that the picture of lesbianism painted by Torres is an inviting one. Indeed, its attractiveness is what makes it dangerous. They refer several times to the passage where Ursula finds herself in bed with Claude—the only explicitly 'lesbian sex' scene in the book. (Not surprisingly, the markings in the margins of Mercier's copy of the book become quite frenzied at this point):

Ursula felt herself very small, tiny against Claude, and at last she felt warm. She placed her cheek on Claude's breast. Her heart beat violently, but she didn't feel afraid. She didn't understand what was happening to her. Claude was not a man; then what was she doing to her? What strange movements! What could they mean? Claude unbuttoned the jacket of her pajamas, and enclosed one of Ursula's little breasts in her hand, and then gently, very gently, her hand began to caress all of Ursula's body, her throat, her shoulders, and her belly. Ursula remembered a novel that she had read that said of a woman

who was making love, 'Her body vibrated like a violin.' Ursula had been highly pleased by this phrase, and now her body recalled the expression and it too began to vibrate. She was stretched out with her eyes closed, motionless, not daring to make the slightest gesture, indeed not knowing what she should do. And Claude kissed her gently, and caressed her. . . . All at once, her insignificant and monotonous life had become full, rich and marvellous. . . . Ursula wanted only one thing, to keep this refuge forever, this warmth, this security. (45)

What would become of a normal teenage girl who read this passage? Adult women, surely, would have the moral strength to resist the temptation such a positive image might hold. But teenagers, their moral characters not yet fully developed, would be less able to distinguish right from wrong. According to Isabelle Finlayson—Crown witness, mother of two, and member of the Ottawa school board and numerous women's groups—teens had not had enough experience to 'be expected to form their [moral] standards, therefore, they would take it [the lesbian sexual activity] as a proper conduct, as conduct accepted generally'.[69] Finlayson seems to be saying that teens had not yet had time to bring their standards in line with socially approved ones. They were still, in a sense, moral works-in-progress who might choose pleasure over indignation and denial.

According to Rev. Terrence Findlay, another Crown witness, the danger of the seduction scene was that a young girl might read such a passage and be enticed to experiment. A young girl, he said, is only 'beginning to form within her' a knowledge and experience of sex and is, therefore, 'intensely curious'. Findlay suggested that if a girl had not already received training about the dangers of lesbianism, the book might 'have a tendency to suggest to that girl that here is a way of satisfying sexual desires without the danger of consorting with male companions'.[70]

This kind of literature, he said, tended to sway normal girls towards the abnormal, by making the latter seem both attractive and possible.

Ford tried to counter Findlay's position by emphasizing the 'normality' of most teenaged readers. Is it not likely that the pleasure of the seduction scene would be annulled by the scene where Ursula finds herself unable to have sexual relations with the French sailor? For Ford, these two scenes are intimately linked—lesbian sex leads to frigidity with men. Would not a 'normal teen-age girl' with 'normal sexual reactions' be 'nauseated' by Ursula's 'abnormal relations'—the latter phrase referring both to sex with a woman and an inability to have sex with a man?[71]

Ford wanted *Women's Barracks* to be taken up as a cautionary tale that might warn young women of the dangers of lesbianism, and in this way might serve the public good. No one disagreed with him over the need for this, although Crown witnesses rejected Torres's book as appropriate to the task. But, asked Ford, were they not all better informed on the subject after having read the novel? Isabelle Finlayson, in particular, claimed she had known nothing about lesbianism before she read the book. How then, asked Ford, could she possibly have warned her daughter of lesbian dangers? Ford's argument had nothing to do with the book's effects on Finlayson herself; as an adult she was assumed to be beyond its influence, capable of reaching her own conclusions on such a vexing moral issue. Someone like Finlayson, well schooled in popular discourses about sexual deviance and perversion, would have been able to see past the pleasure of the seduction scene to the downfall which would inevitably follow. A teenaged girl, on the other hand, needed to have that downfall made explicit. According to Ford, Torres's novel did just that. It provided the context that schoolgirl gossip and curbside chatter about lesbianism might not.

Judge McDougall did not accept Ford's case. In his judgment he wrote:

[The book] deals almost entirely with the question of sex relationships and also with the question of lesbianism. A great deal of the language, and particularly the description of two incidents of unnatural relationships between women, is exceedingly frank. The argument advanced before me was that publicity should be given to the question of lesbianism in order that it might act as a deterrent influence and in this respect would be a matter of public good. The dissemination of such information is no doubt a matter that should receive proper attention from a medical and psychological standpoint, but the manner in which the material is presented in this book does not comply with those standards in any manner.[72]

The underlying assumption, on both sides, indeed the basis of the obscenity charge, was that a pulp novel could have a harmful impact on young people who read it. The test of obscenity used by Canadian courts demanded that Davis and Ford take this as their starting point. In 1953, *Women's Barracks* was the focus of another trial in St Paul, Minnesota, where notions of the corruptibility of young people were not embedded in the definition of obscenity and therefore had no sway over the final judgment: 'In conclusion, therefore, it is the opinion of the Court that the book, *Women's Barracks*, does not have a substantive tendency to deprave or corrupt by inciting lascivious thoughts or arousing lustful desire in the ordinary reader in this community in these times. It is the finding of the Court that the likelihood of its having such a salacious effect does not outweigh the literary merit it may have in the hands of the average reader.'[73]

Notions of adolescence as a time of rapid and profound change echoed widespread fears about change in the society at large. As the progression of one's adolescence was seen to determine the shape of one's adulthood, so too the collective progress of living, breathing adolescents was thought to indicate the shape Canadian society would take in the future. In this sense, youth operated as a metaphor for the development of the society as a whole: if they turned out all right, it was assumed the nation would be fine, too. But, after two decades of turmoil, such an outcome was not guaranteed.

It is in this context that ideas about the moral and physical capacities of young people were able to help constitute the limits of sexual discourse. The desire to 'protect' youth and the future they were assumed to represent helped to motivate broad-ranging initiatives of moral and sexual regulation—such as the conviction of National News, the banning of crime comics, and the implementation of the Senate Special Committee—that took not only youth but adults as their objects. Common-sense ideas about the nature of adolescent moral and sexual development contributed to the setting of limits on how and where sexuality could be expressed or represented and by whom. Some adults saw teenagers as being under the control of their blossoming sex drives. These adults wanted to set limits on public discussions of sexuality because they feared it would set teens off on an orgy of experimentation. Other adults were less concerned about the impulses of puberty and the exigencies of hormones than they were about teenagers' moral immaturity. They worried that boys and girls faced with sexual information or images would be unable to distinguish right from wrong and thus might 'innocently' engage in questionable activities. In both perspectives notions of sexuality as potentially dangerous, as destabilizing and morally charged, combined with ideas about the nature of puberty and adolescent development to curtail public discussion of sex.

The relationship between discourses about sexuality and discourses about youth—especially the way these combined to conduct social anxieties around a broad range of issues—was central to the generation of the moral panic around obscenity. At stake in the furor over mass-market publications were accepted standards of sexual morality, standards that affected both young people and adults. Indecent material, in its various guises, offered competing ways of making sense of sex, morals, and relationships. Comics and trashy novels contradicted the many

efforts to transform teenagers into 'fine moral citizens' that were commonplace in English Canada during the late 1940s and 1950s. The discourses made available in the pulps threatened the complex of processes through which particular forms of heterosexual expression were normalized. Comics, girlie magazines, and trashy novels suggested alternative ways of organizing sexuality, ones that might upset the dominance of a family-centred, monogamous heterosexuality. At bottom, indecent literature challenged dominant sexual and moral standards and these, as much as individual young people, were assumed to need protecting.

Notes

1. Letter to 'Ontario Government Censorship Bureau' (a bureaucratic entity which did not exist—the letter was directed to the Attorney General), 20 June 1949, Archives of Ontario (AO), RG 4–32,1949, no. 270.

2. Paul Guay, President of Press and Cinema Services (Canada's equivalent to the League of Decency in the United States), Ottawa Archdiocese of the Catholic Church, Brief submitted to the Senate Special Committee on Salacious and Indecent Literature; see Canada, Senate, Special Committee on Salacious and Indecent Literature (hereafter Special Committee), *Proceedings*, 3 June 1952, 10.

3. Letter to Attorney General Dana Porter from a 'citizen' in Stoney Creek, 8 Nov. 1955, AO, RG 4–32, 1955, no. 25.

4. 'Notes taken at a meeting on 24 February 1956, during which a delegation representing a number of [Ontario] civic and religious groups presented a brief to the Attorney General re: salacious literature': AO, RG 4–02, file 91.7.

5. BC Provincial Congress of Canadian Women, Brief submitted to the Senate Special Committee on Salacious and Indecent Literature, Special Committee, *Proceedings*, 11 Feb. 1953, 41.

6. For a discussion of the evolution of mass-produced pocket books and the various technologies that have made it possible, see Janice A. Radway, *Reading the Romance* (London: Verso, 1984).

7. The book was *Women's Barracks* by Tereska Torres, and the distributor was National News Company. See *The Queen v. National News Company*, 514, AO, RG 4–32, 1953, no. 830. There are no records of how many copies were sold.

8. 'Comics as Yule Gift to Clergyman-Trustee, Tely's Palooka Fan', *Toronto Telegram*, 13 Dec. 1950.

9. Senate, Special Committee, *Report*, 29 Apr. 1953, 243.

10. Margaret Culkin Banning, 'Filth on the Newsstands', *Reader's Digest* (Oct. 1952): 150.

11. James Gilbert, *A Cycle of Outrage: America's Reaction to the Juvenile Delinquent in the 1950s* (New York: Oxford University Press, 1986), 3.

12. Martin Barker, *A Haunt of Fears: The Strange History of the British Horror Comics Campaign* (London: Pluto, 1984), 6.

13. Kathy Peiss, *Cheap Amusements: Working Women and Leisure in Turn-of-the-Century New York* (Philadelphia: Temple University Press, 1986).

14. Barker, *Haunt of Fears*, 87.

15. See Paul Landis, *Adolescence and Youth* (New York: McGraw-Hill, 1947), 47.

16. Banning, 'Filth on the Newsstands', 150.

17. Congress of Canadian Women, Submission to the Senate Special Committee on Salacious and Indecent Literature, Special Committee, *Proceedings*, 25 June 1952, 149.

18. Resolution from the Town of Timmins, Ontario, about indecent literature, AO, RG 4–32, 1952, no. 59. Endorsed by at least 32 other municipalities, it urged the government to survey and censor magazines in order to eliminate 'all that which is undesirable and unfit for consumption by the children of this Province'.

19. Canadian Preparatory Committee, International Conference in Defense of Children, Submission to Senate Special Committee on Salacious and Indecent Literature, Special Committee, *Proceedings*, 25 June 1952, 161.

20. Christian Social Council of Canada, Brief presented to the Senate Special Committee on Salacious and Indecent Literature, Special Committee, *Proceedings*, 17 June 1952, 77.

21. Special Committee, *Report*, 246.

22. Special Committee, *Proceedings*, 25 Apr. 1953, 221.

23. Canada, House of Commons, *Debates*, 21 Oct. 1949, 1043.

24. Patrick Parsons, 'Batman and His Audience: The Dialectic of Culture', in Roberta E. Pearson and William Uricchio, eds, *The Many Lives of Batman: Critical Approaches to a Superhero and His Media* (New York and London: Routledge and the British Film Institute, 1991), 68–9; Bill Boichel, 'Batman: Commodity as Myth', in Pearson and Uricchio, eds, *The Many Lives of Batman*, 6.

25. John Bell, *Guardians of the North: The National Superhero in Canadian Comic-book Art* (Ottawa: National Archives of Canada, 1992), 18. Bell's booklet is the catalogue from an exhibition of the same name at the Canadian Museum of Caricature during the summer of 1992.

26. 'Trustee Calls "Comic" Books "Degrading and Detrimental"', *Globe and Mail*, 26 Sept. 1945.

27. Cited in Brief presented to Special Committee of the Senate by the IODE, 1952, AO, RG 4–02, file 91.7.

28. Mary Jukes, 'Are Comics Really a Menace?', *Chatelaine* (May 1949): 6–7.

29. *Unusual Comics* (Sept.–Oct. 1946), Bell Publishing.

30. 'Comic Book Study Urged for Effect on Children', *Globe and Mail*, 11 Aug. 1950.

31. 'Board Debates Comic Books', *Globe and Mail*, 10 Jan. 1951.

32. Canada, House of Commons, *Debates*, 14 June 1948, 5201.

33. Ibid., 9 June 1948, 4935.

34. Augustine Brannigan, 'Mystification of the Innocents: Crime Comics and Delinquency in Canada, 1931–1949', *Canadian Justice History* 7 (1986): 118.

35. Canada, House of Commons, *Debates*, 8 June 1948, 4932.

36. Statement by G.K. Fraser, MP for Peterborough West, ibid., 6 Oct. 1949, 580.

37. Ibid., 4 Oct. 1949, 517.

38. Ibid., 7 Oct. 1949, 624.

39. Statement by G.K. Fraser, MP for Peterborough West, ibid., 6 Oct. 1949, 580.

40. Canada, House of Commons, Bill 10, 1949.

41. Ibid.

42. 'Comics as Yule Gift to Clergyman-Trustee'.

43. Parsons, 'Batman and His Audience', 71.

44. Fredric Wertham, *Seduction of the Innocent* (New York and Toronto: Rinehart, 1954).

45. Ibid., ch. 11: 'Murder in Dawson Creek—Comic Books Abroad'.

46. Ibid., 282.

47. Copy of letter from Fredric Wertham to Mrs T.W.A. [Eleanor] Gray, 14 Dec. 1953. The letter is appended to a letter from Mrs Gray, on behalf of the British Columbia Parent-Teacher Federation, to the Attorney General of Ontario, 4 Feb. 1954, AO, RG 4–32, 1954, no. 26, box 98.

48. Wertham, *Seduction of the Innocent*, 10; emphasis mine.

49. Ibid., 81.

50. Ibid., 175.

51. Ibid., 177.

52. For an example of this, see Maxine Davis, *Sex and the Adolescent* (New York: Permabooks, 1960), 62.

53. Wertham, *Seduction of the Innocent*, 188.

54. Ibid., 191.

55. Ibid., 99.

56. Ibid., 34.

57. 'Code of the Comics Magazine Association of America', 26 Oct. 1954, AO, RG 4–02, file 76.12.

58. *Regina v. National News Company Limited*, 8 Oct. 1952, AO, RG 4–32, 1953, no. 830.

59. Tereska Torres, *Women's Barracks* (New York: Fawcett, 1950). While published by a New York company, the book was printed in Canada. There is a copy of the

novel, with margin notes by the Crown attorney, on file with the court transcripts. AO, RG 4–32, 1953, no. 830.

60. Tereska Torres, *The Converts* (London: Rupert Hart-Davis, 1970). The text on the front cover of the book jacket reads, 'The autobiography of Tereska Torres, author of "Women's Barracks"'.

61. Torres, *Women's Barracks*, 5.

62. *R. v. National News*, 16.

63. The other two tags mark a slang reference to prostitution and a scene where a young woman loses her virginity with a man.

64. *R. v. National News*, 29.

65. Ibid., 44.

66. Ibid., 64.

67. Ibid., 54.

68. Ibid., 64.

69. Ibid., 380.

70. Ibid., 361.

71. Ibid., 365.

72. A.G. McDougall, 'Judgment re: Women's Barracks', 22 Nov. 1952, AO, RG 4–32, 1953, no. 830.

73. Judgment from a trial in St Paul, Minnesota, 16 June 1953, quoted in Torres, *Women's Barracks*, 11th printing, June 1958, inside front cover.

26

Spectacular Striptease: Performing the Sexual and Racial Other in Vancover, British Columbia, 1945–75

── Becki Ross and Kim Greenwell ──

In the late 1940s, in the words of *Vancouver Sun* night-beat reporter Jack Wasserman, 'Vancouver erupted as the vaudeville capital of Canada, rivaling and finally outstripping Montreal in the East and San Francisco in the south as one of the few places where the brightest stars of the nightclub era could be glimpsed from behind a post, through a smoke-filled room, over the heads of $20 tippers at ringside. Only in Las Vegas and Miami Beach, in season, were more superstars available in nightclubs.'[1] Fellow Vancouver journalist Patrick Nagle recalled a 'show business railway' that moved largely American performers, including showgirls and striptease headliners, up and down the Pacific coast from San Francisco to Las Vegas to Seattle and on to the lush, mountain-ringed port city of Vancouver, British Columbia.[2] The city's geographical proximity to the western United States meant that talent flowed steadily south-to-north across the US/Canada border much more than it flowed east-to-west beyond the physical and symbolic barrier of the perilous Rocky Mountains. American entertainers rehearsed new material in Vancouver, often at discounted rates for discerning fans; at the same time, the burgeoning nighttime entertainment scene supplied opportunities for aspiring local talent. Professionally staged female striptease began to prosper inside the maturing city's nightspots and it contributed greatly to Vancouver's growing reputation as 'home to the hottest nightclubs north of San Francisco'.[3]

Despite the city's history as a key node in entertainment circuits, commercial striptease remains an unexplored contribution to Vancouver's social and economic heritage. We explore one aspect of the staging and status of striptease in postwar Vancouver. From a rich store of archival documents and 40 interviews conducted from 1999 to 2003 with retired dancers, club owners, booking agents, and musicians, we unsettle the hegemonic notion of 'stripteaser' as a homogeneous category of identity and occupation. Specifically, we examine how processes of racialization shaped the production and perception of striptease in Vancouver, differentiating the ways in which white dancers and dancers of colour negotiated strategies of success and survival in this highly competitive industry. Our single city focus provides a window onto both transnational, circuit-wide trends and the specificities that made Vancouver stagings unique. We employ the racialized (and classed) geography of the city as an analytical frame, focusing on striptease in two spaces—the supper clubs of the predominantly white and affluent uptown West End and the 'ethnic' working class nightclubs within and around Vancouver's Chinatown in the downtown East End. . . .

We begin our inquiry after 1945, in the context of the demise of classic burlesque and the crystallization of professional female striptease as a financially rewarding, though risky, career choice. Nineteen seventy-five marks the endpoint

Becki Ross and Kim Greenwell. 'Spectacular Striptease: Performing the Sexual and Racial Other in Vancouver, B.C., 1945–1975', *Journal of Women's History* 17:1 (2005), 137–64. © 2005 Journal of Women's History. Reprinted with permission of The Johns Hopkins University Press.

of both an era and our study, with the mid-1970s heralding radical transitions: the shift in the stripping business to full nudity; the replacement of live musical accompaniment with tapes and disc jockeys; the relocation of the industry from independent, free-standing nightclubs to an ever-proliferating number of hotel 'peeler pubs'; the re-staging of performances to include pole, table, and lap dancing, spreading or 'split beavers', and showers on stage; and the cross-national movement of migrant dancers from Japan, Eastern Europe, the former Soviet Union, and Latin America in the 1980s and 1990s.[4] Revisiting the three-decade span from 1945 to 1975—a time of considerably more continuity than change in the business—we focus on what Canadian former dancer Lindalee Tracey has described as a golden era, 'before striptease fell from grace because the world stopped dreaming'.[5] Our findings suggest that the 'gold' of this golden era was unevenly distributed among dancers. White striptease dancers dominated the 'A-List' headliner category in ways that exposed the racial grammar of post-war 'glamour' and 'sexiness'—a grammar that simultaneously encoded dancers of colour as 'novelties' with limited marketability. Further, inequalities embedded in racialized discourses of desirability had material effects: dancers of colour earned less money, were relegated to 'B-List' East End and Chinatown clubs, and were unable to invest in the same fancy costumes and props or to enjoy the same lighting, stages, and dressing rooms associated with West End marquee status. We argue that stripteasers of colour negotiated different discursive fields— both literally and figuratively—experiencing and resisting the exhibition of their bodies differently than white dancers. At the same time, we examine how some white dancers performed 'exotic' racial Otherness in ways that avoided the indelible stigma of non-whiteness in a city dominated by Anglo-Canadians until the mid-1970s, at which point waves of Asian and other non-European immigration propelled significant demographic changes.[6]

Post-war Vancouver Heats Up

The post-war business of bump and grind in Vancouver stirred opposition as it had decades earlier before the rough-edged frontier town donned a mid-century patina of sophistication. Always teetering on the edge of legality and never granted the same respect afforded 'legitimate' small business operators, nightclub owners faced persistent pressure from anti-vice factions to clean up the acts. Police raids, arrests, and nightclub closures engineered to stamp out immorality and revitalize law and order discourse were commonplace in Vancouver and elsewhere throughout this period.[7] The State Burlesque Theatre was raided by the Vancouver Police Department's Morality Squad in 1946 and again in 1950, 1951, and 1952; each time its license was revoked due to an 'indecent strip act'.[8] Twenty years later, the Café Kobenhavn pushed the erotic envelope to include full nudity in 1971, and two dancers were charged with obscenity under the Canadian Criminal Code. Far from succumbing to the concerted proliferation of speech and acts intended to repress and prohibit it, striptease flourished in the city's entertainment venues. Vancouver's economy thrived upon the employment options that erotic spectacle guaranteed while moral reformers protested that the 'lewd and obscene' public performances destroyed communities, family values, and the nation. Undaunted by criticism and police incursions, nightclub owners began to bill female striptease as enticing adult entertainment for locals and tourists alike in the late 1940s and early 1950s. The profitability of the industry revealed the hypocrisy beneath the hysteria and helped cement the prevailing image of an increasingly cosmopolitan Vancouver at once culturally and sexually permissive. By the early 1950s, the fast growing city of 400,000 inhabitants not only had drive-in movie theatres, 19,000 neon signs, the refurbished Orpheum Theatre, and the newly built Empire Stadium (site of the 1954 British Empire and Commonwealth

Games), but also a range of nightclubs to choose from and a bevy of striptease artists to behold.

As a number of studies have shown, striptease dancers—members of the 'second-oldest profession'—were, and largely still are, perceived as sex deviants.[9] Striptease has long conjured negative stereotypes of female dancers as prostitutes; nymphomaniacs; survivors of broken homes and sexual abuse; degraded victims of men's immoral lust; home wreckers; drug users; and dangers to the social order, the family, and the nation. Notwithstanding the fame and fortune garnered by a handful of striptease queens—Americans Sally Rand, Ann Corio, Margie Hart, Georgia Southern, and Gypsy Rose Lee—in the 1930s, 1940s, and 1950s, erotic dancers across North America laboured under the shame attached to the stigma of being of a 'stripper'.[10] And yet stripteasers negotiated the male-dominated business with courage and savvy, balancing moral condemnation of their overtly sexual behaviour with their love of dance, music, applause, and (varying degrees of) notoriety. To Canadian ex-dancer Margaret Dragu, striptease performers played the role of conscientious objector by bravely testing and defying society's sexual limits, and they experienced outsider status as 'sexual offenders'.[11] In effect, the business of striptease, like the city of Vancouver itself, was a jumble of contradictions: it promised women more lucrative dividends than any other service work in the 'pink ghetto' at the same time that it produced them as sexual others whose acts triggered competing meanings of adulation and contempt. Attention to the social and geographical distribution of the 'heat' referenced in Vancouver's risqué reputation reveals an industry as structured by inequalities as it was solidified by stigma.

The Racialized Spaces of East v. West

After World War II, the production and consumption of female striptease in Vancouver was split along racialized lines of perceived prestige and class. All erotic dancers were measured against the idealized contours of slim, white, young, glamorous, and heterosexy femininity defined and upheld by men in the homosocial game of buying and selling erotic fantasy to other men. White 'features' or 'A-dancers' with their elaborate costumes, props, and sets were featured at high-end Vancouver nightclubs—the Cave Supper Club (1937–81), the Palomar Supper Club (1937–51), the Penthouse Cabaret (1947–present), and Isy's Supper Club (later Isy's Strip City) (1958–76) in Vancouver's affluent and predominantly white West End. Beginning in the late 1940s, the Italian- and Jewish-Canadian men who owned these clubs—Joe Philiponi, Isy Walters, and Sandy De Santis, among others—took their cue from the magnetic influence of Las Vegas and began to book big-name striptease dancers. Most sought after were 'classy' American headliners. . . . Until the mid-1970s, all of the most famous erotic dancers who performed in Vancouver were white, American-born women who milked Canadians' fascination with talent imported from south of the 49th parallel. Scantily clad, plumed, and spangled, they worked a circuit that moved south-to-north across the Canada/US border; a select few worked an international circuit that included bookings in Europe. These extraordinary headliners were professionally managed, commanded celebrity status, and invested a considerable percentage of their substantial earnings back into their careers, including expensive gowns, choreography, props, music, and makeup. Salaries were as high as $2,000 to $4,000 per week, and until the arrival of recorded music and disc jockeys in the mid-1970s, they were accompanied on stage by the top-ranked (male) jazz musicians in the city.[12]

As city residents demonstrated a hearty appetite for bump and grind, a localized industry of dancers, choreographers, makeup artists, and costume designers sprang up to supplement imported acts with regional talent. Vancouver choreographer Jack Card attained widespread renown for the elaborate Ziegfeld-inspired production numbers he staged at the Cave and Isy's (Figure 1). With striptease increasingly showcased on a nightly basis, white women from the city and surrounding area could secure regular gigs in the West End clubs. But the West End clubs were not the only places where striptease was staged. Card admitted that women of colour were overrepresented in the 'B-list' and 'novelty act' categories and routinely limited to employment in a tightly knit circuit of less 'respectable' East End clubs.[13] These nightclubs were owned by men of colour—Chinese, South Asian, and African-Canadian—marginalized in similar (but not identical) ways as the women of colour they employed.[14] Throughout the 1950s, 1960s, and 1970s, small nightclubs such as Lachman Das Jir's Smilin' Buddha (1953–89), Leo Bagry's New Delhi (1956–73), Ernie King's Harlem Nocturne (1957–66), and Jimmy Yuen's Kublai Khan (1960–80) in the East End's working-class Chinatown and Main Street neighbourhoods

played up the 'ethnic status' of their performers—not only stripteasers but also masters of ceremonies, singers, musicians, and comics— in a bid to net prospective patrons' entertainment dollars. Here, in the 1950s, striptease dancers earned an average of $50 to $100 for six nights a week which increased to $600 to $800 per week by the mid-1970s, although dancers of colour we interviewed noted that they were paid less than their white counterparts and the quality of their working conditions was poor compared to the white-owned West End clubs. Card explained that performers at the East End clubs simply had to make do without the elaborate stage lights, collapsible stairways, velvet curtains, big orchestras, professional choreography, and handsome paycheques that the almost exclusively white dancers at the Cave and Isy's enjoyed. Moreover, denied liquor licences until the late 1960s (more than a decade longer than their West End rivals), East End clubs were subjected to much more

Figure 1. The Jack Card Dancers, Isy's Supper Club, c. 1965. Photographer unknown.

intense police surveillance and raiding even as they were able to use the 'forbidden' aura of the unlicensed bottle club to promote themselves as an illicit alternative. African-Canadian club owner of the Harlem Nocturne, Ernie King, harbours bitter memories of this disproportionate attention: 'No one was harassed more than me. No one. It got to the point the cops would harass me two or three times a night. Because I was the only man that owned a black nightclub!'[15]

In 1967, an article in the Vancouver *Province* noted: 'As a tourist attraction, Chinatown probably ranks second only to Stanley Park, and so contributes greatly to Vancouver's fame abroad. With its restaurants, stores and nightclubs, it adds entertainment spice for resident and visitor alike. . . . Few Vancouverites are unfamiliar with the color and romance of Chinatown.'[16] . . . In competition with their more prestigious West End counterparts, East End clubs were both tainted and made titillating by their location in the Chinatown area. Their tendency to trade in the allure of sexual and racial Otherness indeed may have bolstered racial stereotypes, but likely served as a shrewd strategy in a city rife with (often enforced) 'ethnic enclaves'. For many people of colour in Vancouver, the cheaper, more accessible, and less formal East End nightclubs were considered 'the place to be'. Indeed, the very names of the clubs—Kublai Khan, New Delhi, Smilin' Buddha, and Harlem Nocturne—belie the myth of Chinatown's homogeneity and suggest that in the area's nightclub scene, a diverse group of communities of colour converged, carving for themselves a social and economic space that was unavailable in other parts of the city.

At the same time, these venues also marked a popular destination for middle-class white Vancouverites and tourists who crossed the city after seeing the 'big stars' at the Cave and Isy's, much as white New Yorkers travelled to such Harlem nightspots as the Hot Feet, the Clambake, and the Cotton Club, and white San Franciscans sought entertainment in the city's Chinatown clubs.[17] For some white residents, voyaging from

Vancouver's West End to East End nightclubs was entangled with racialized and classed notions of 'slumming it' because the East End clubs were located not only in Chinatown, but also adjacent to the area's historic skid road, Vancouver's first so-called slum district. Inhabited by waves of immigrants, unemployed poor, and mobile male labourers—loggers, sailors, fishers, mill workers, cannery workers, and miners—the East End's skid road was dotted with cheap, single-room occupancy hotels and lodging houses dating to the early twentieth century.[18] By the 1950s, the area was widely perceived as a dangerous and disorderly home to male addicts, criminals, alcoholics, and sex deviates who frequented nearby nightclubs and engaged in other morally suspect activities. The historic separation of Vancouver's East End from the West End along class lines was simultaneously rooted in racial segregation: small communities of Chinese- and African-Canadians had residential and commercial interests in the eastern working-class districts of Chinatown, Strathcona, and Hogan's Alley, and they both owned and supported nightclubs, restaurants, groceries, and laundries after World War II. Coincidentally, the city's police station was located on the edge of Chinatown, affording the overwhelmingly white police force easy access to what they deemed the 'trouble zone' of the East End.[19] Intersecting notions of gender, sexuality, race, and class thus fused the 'pathological masculinity' of skid road with the resilient imagery of Chinatown as a 'vice town', and ensured the quasi-illicit reputation of East End clubs, enhanced by nightclub owners' tendency to publicize promises of more skin and raunchier acts than could be found 'uptown'.[20] While dancers of colour had few options outside performance in these venues, white dancers regarded East End clubs as shady destinations that they generally sought to avoid. In the business from the early to mid-1970s, April Paris recalled that the East End clubs failed to eschew 'that opium-tinged' connotation and seemed like 'dark and strange places' to her and other white performers.[21]

'Racy' Acts: Black Stripteasers and the White Imagination

Although East End nightclubs may have seemed off-limits to such white dancers as April Paris, these were the venues where stripteasers of colour, particularly black women, were most likely to find employment. Jack Card stated that most of the city's black striptease performers danced at the Main Street and Chinatown clubs, sometimes finding extra work at the carnival 'girlie shows' of the Pacific National Exhibition.[22] . . . This is not to say that black women never appeared at Vancouver's West End clubs. Josephine Baker, famous burlesque dancer and American expatriate, performed at the Cave in 1955, more overdressed than underdressed. At 49, her status as an international vedette still assured her top billing in the nightclub's advertisement—a status earned through earlier acts in which she catered to the fantasy of the jungle animal, dancing in banana skirt and feathers to feed white audiences' appetite for the spectacle of 'savage' sexuality.[23] At the same time, however, it is likely that Baker's performance in Vancouver stirred antiblack sentiment, coming only a few years after singer Lena Horne was denied a room by racist proprietors at the Hotel Vancouver, the George Hotel, and the Devonshire Hotel. This and other anecdotes of racism in Vancouver's more affluent clubs suggest that the East End's ethnically diverse venues may have offered a safer, less hostile environment in which black performers could work. At the same time, club owners in this area readily exploited certain racialized stereotypes when it proved to be profitable. In contrast to the white-owned West End clubs, the East End clubs openly promoted dancers of colour, especially black women, as 'Harlem cuties', 'ebony sexologists', and 'Afro-Cuban specialists'.[24]

While not international stars, stripteasers such as Coffee, Zoulouse, Sugar, Coco Fontaine, Lottie the Body, Choo Choo Williams, Miss Wiggles, Lawanda the Bronze Goddess, Mitzi Duprée, and Miss Lovie were among the black women

(both American and Canadian) who danced in Vancouver. Born in 1929, Choo Choo Williams grew up in the black community of Amber Valley, Alberta. Her father was from Texas, her mother was from Oklahoma, and they were part of the migration of African-Americans who were promised free land for homesteading in Canada in the 1910s and 1920s.[25] After moving to Vancouver to marry band leader and trombonist Ernie King, Choo Choo began a 12-year dancing career (1954–66) as a professional showgirl, first at the New Delhi and the Smilin' Buddha nightclubs, and later, at the Harlem Nocturne, which she co-owned with King from 1957 to 1966. Williams was initially inspired to launch her striptease career after witnessing other black dancers 'shimmy and shake' at Vancouver's Pacific National Exhibition in the early 1950s: 'I went to the "Harlem and Havana" show at the PNE and I seen these girls up there wearing these costumes and dancing and shaking. I thought to myself, "Gee, do they make money doing that?" I thought, "Well, jeez, I can do that!" I seen this girl named August May Walker and she was cute. So I went and got myself some work.'[26]

With little money to spend on training or fancy costumes and accoutrements, Choo Choo Williams sewed her own lavish 'Carmen Miranda' outfit and did the limbo to a Latin beat: 'I had a sewing machine, so I made a turban, sewed a bunch of fruit on top. I had a chiffon skirt with hooks on the front, I'd take it off and dance. I had a leopard costume, I had bras and panties with sequins and fringes, fishnets. . . . I was pretty good for a country girl who had no training. As I got older, I got bolder (laughs).' . . . Not only was Choo Choo a contributing partner to the success of 'The Harlem' nightclub, but she also reaped other benefits from striptease dancing: 'I could be home with my kid in the daytime and then go out and dance at night. . . . I like music, I've always liked music, and I like dancing.'[27] Running the Harlem Nocturne, Vancouver's only black nightclub, was truly a family affair and Ernie King was Choo Choo's biggest fan: 'I used to like to watch the show. I got a kick out of looking at her. She could shake it up! She had some shake-up costumes! I wasn't jealous. She was being paid to dance, and I was being paid to play the trombone, and I'm playing the trombone on the stage above her and I'm keeping her in line!'[28] When she finished her floor show, Choo Choo changed her clothes and either worked as the cashier or waitressed at the club. Her religious parents in Edmonton, Alberta, disapproved of the Harlem Nocturne, and although they never said anything about their daughter's dancing 'with no clothes on', Choo Choo speculated that they viewed the entertainment business as Satan's work.

At the same time that King and Williams enjoyed a measure of fame in East End entertainment circles, each noted that the doors to the West End's Cave Supper Club and the Palomar Supper Club 'were pretty much closed to them'.[29] King had his own band, The Harlem Kings, and he recalled the barriers to better paying and more esteemed gigs in the West End supper clubs: 'I was qualified enough to play in the Cave, but they didn't want a guy like me. They knew our Black musicians had as much talent or more than anybody else. But the owners wanted an all-white band, not a colored band with me sitting in there. It was like two different worlds.'[30] Dancing at East End nightclubs, Choo Choo remembered that she was paid about $50 a week, sometimes $100 if it was a special gig. She stated that 'the white women probably made more money, but I didn't work with any. The only white women I worked with were singers, like Judy Hope and Eleanor Powell.'[31]

Miss Lovie was arguably Vancouver's most successful black dancer. She worked for 10 years (1965–75), first in the 'B-List' East End clubs and in the early 1970s in the West End's Penthouse Cabaret. She eventually shifted her career from stripteaser to master of ceremonies to singer, and, at one point in the early 1970s, to nightclub owner in Powell River on the province's Sunshine Coast. Born in Texas and raised in

Chicago by a working-class single mother, Miss Lovie was a pediatric nurse in Seattle when she discovered she could earn her weekly salary of $100 in three days as a striptease dancer. Miss Lovie recalled her start in the business: 'I met another dancer, Tequila. She was the one that told me, "Girl, you don't need to be at that. Get out of there, you dance too good!" So, I started dancing in a little club in Seattle, the Black and Tan with Big Mama Thornton on the bill.'[32] By the time Miss Lovie moved permanently to Vancouver in 1964, she had developed an act for the New Delhi Cabaret in which she sat on the floor, bikini-clad, facing away from her audience and rhythmically twitching the muscles in her legs and buttocks to the beat of numerous Conga drums. She explained her signature act: 'I made things happen with my body. I'd sit on the floor, I'd stick my legs up high, up above my head, and I'd make my butt pop. I made my buttocks work like drums through muscle control. I could move around the floor like a clock, in a circle. I did the splits. I used to do a lot of black light dancing, and I used to wear a lot of glitter all over my body. That use to be my thing: I glittered.'[33]

Miss Lovie quickly became a regular feature at East End nightclubs New Delhi, Kublai Khan, Harlem Nocturne, and the Smilin' Buddha, where she was advertised as 'the world's foremost exponent of Afro-Cuban dancing' and an 'Artist of Rhythm'. An advertisement for the New Delhi Cabaret appeared in the *Vancouver Sun* newspaper throughout the late 1960s (Figure 2).[34] Here, Miss Lovie poses on the ground, wearing a zebra-striped bikini top, fur anklets, bracelets, and ears. Another photograph of Miss Lovie in leopard-skin bikini remained on display in the window of the New Delhi long after she had retired from dancing. Like Choo Choo Williams, she was expected to embody an animal-like primitivism, and like other black dancers, she found steady work in the East End nightclubs.

Other black women were carefully contained and marginalized within the racialized category of 'novelty act'. Miss Wiggles stripped to pasties and g-string upside down with her head on a chair. Lottie the Body was an American dancer who, like Miss Lovie, invented a repertoire based in Afro-Cuban music and movement. She was also known to have balanced a chair in her teeth while nearly naked. A 'fierce performer' with a 'truck driver's mouth on her', Lottie danced at a range of East End nightclubs.[35] In the 2002 documentary film *Standing in the Shadows of Motown*, she described herself as 'one of the greatest exotic dancers in the world'. Uriel Jones, a Motown jazz musician and member of the legendary Funk Brothers, reminisced about Lottie: 'If she moved one cheek, there was a certain drum she wanted you to hit; if she moved her left foot you had to catch all of that stuff, plus keep in rhythm with the band.'[36]

Vancouver-based jazz drummer Dave Davies developed a special relationship with African-American dancer Lawanda Page in the 1960s: 'She was a big black woman. She and I were tight, tight friends for years. She used to be a stripper in the New Delhi Cabaret amongst other places. She had an incredible figure in those days and she called herself Lawanda the Bronze Goddess and she did a fire act. She'd light her finger and go around lighting guys' cigarettes in the club. Then the lights would go off and she'd light up the tassels on her pasties and spin them like propellers, in opposite directions. It was wonderful. After the gig, Lawanda and I would go back to the Regent Hotel, which was a sleazy place on Hastings Street. We'd sit up all night and talk while she sewed costumes. She was a real free spirit.'[37]

Perhaps most notoriously, African-American Mitzi Duprée, originally from Los Angeles, was a crowd favourite in Vancouver, across the province of British Columbia, and throughout Alberta. Beginning in the late 1970s, Mitzi dexterously sprayed ping pong balls and played 'Mary Had a Little Lamb' and 'Frère Jacques' on the flute with her vagina. Wildly popular, she was arrested for performing an 'indecent act' in Kamloops, British Columbia, in 1981, acquitted in 1982, and finally deported to the United States from Vancouver in 1984 after a conviction in Calgary, Alberta, for participating in an 'immoral, indecent or obscene theatrical performance'.[38] White women and women of colour alike recognized the wisdom of advice immortalized in song in the 1962 Hollywood film *Gypsy*:

Figure 2. Miss Lovie at the New Delhi nightclub, advertisement in the *Vancouver Sun* (14 Mar. 1969), 40.

'You've got to have a gimmick, if you want to get ahead.'[39] White female stripteasers borrowed from a rich reservoir of symbols of white glamour, pageantry, and feminine sophistication from performers at the Moulin Rouge, the Lido, the Folies Bergère, various nightclubs on the Las Vegas strip, and on Hollywood's silver screen. By contrast, dancers of colour did not and could not invent their gimmicks and stage personas from the same set of possibilities or expectations as did white dancers who exercised a near monopoly on glamour.[40] Sometimes subtly, sometimes blatantly, club owners, booking agents, promoters, and patrons pressured black dancers to incorporate props, costumes, music, and makeup that fit racialized and sexualized colonial tropes of African primitivism and hypersexuality.[41] Racist imagery and expectations routinely cast black women as tragic mulattas, comic maids or mammies, or oversexed jezebels. These narrowly defined roles constricted black women's power to perform unencumbered by white racist fantasies.[42]

Interviews with black dancers themselves, however, shatter any illusions of a uniform, shared black experience, and invite analysis attentive to contradictions. Miss Lovie argued that being an African-Canadian in Vancouver in the 1960s accorded her, and other black entertainers such as singer Ron Small and MC Teddy Felton, special status as a novelty. She reminisced: 'We were spoiled. Everybody wanted to be around you.' Far from making her feel tokenized, Miss Lovie said that the attention made her feel 'wonderful', and through her dancing, Miss Lovie may well have mined an otherwise rare opportunity to celebrate Afro-Cuban traditions of dance and music. At the same time, she shouldered a stigma that no striptease dancer completely eluded: 'I upset my family, that's why I did it in Canada. And my stepdad's a minister! Women were not supposed to go out and be assertive—you were a hussy! Strippers were the low side of the totem pole, though we didn't feel that way. We felt wonderful and we made good money.'[43]

Yet other black dancers have less rosy recollections about their experiences of a still predominantly white Vancouver. Coco Fontaine began dancing in Calgary, Alberta, in 1968, and she moved to work full-time in Vancouver in 1973. She described Miss Lovie as an important mentor who stood up for women of colour in the business. In the late 1970s, Miss Lovie helped Sugar, another black dancer from Montreal, lodge a human rights complaint against the discriminatory practices of a West End club, revealing that she was far from oblivious to issues of racism. Coco recalled feeling 'lots of really strong discrimination' and described Vancouver as 'quite racist'.[44] Painfully aware that 'there were only certain jobs Black women were allowed to get into,' she related a pivotal conversation with her mother, who had also worked as a burlesque dancer with the Royal American carnival shows: '"Mom, I can be a chambermaid all my life. Or I can dance." And my Mom just laughed and said, "Okay, if you're going to be one, be a damn good one!" And she gave me hints on how to dance.'[45] Club owner Isy Walters put Coco on the road for $350 a week 'to prove herself' in Kamloops, Fort St John, Prince Rupert, Nanaimo, and Granisle, British Columbia. 'In some places,' she remembered, 'we changed in the beer coolers.'[46] Walters invented her stage name, Coco Fontaine, and her birthplace, Chicago, in order to manufacture a more exotic mystique. For years, she performed four shows a night, six nights a week, largely on the road where she made a maximum of $800 per week before retiring from the industry in 1983. She noted that white feature dancers tended to work less—only three shows a night. At an average of $1,500 to $2,000 per week and up to $4,000 for Lili St Cyr, they were paid more and had first choice of music and colour of costumes in the mid-to-late 1970s.

Former booking agent Jeannie Runnells admitted that 'a lot of nightclubs didn't want Black girls, and it was harder for Black dancers to get booked in the "A"-rooms.'[47] White dancer Tarren Rae added that black dancers 'weren't as marketable'. She continued: 'Club owners were like, "drop one in there amongst the mix, but don't give me a whole line up. Don't give me two Black girls, or two Chinese girls."' Jazz pianist Gerry Palken added that 'Black dancers were expected to be more erotic, more loose, do more things that supposedly would turn men on.'[48] When asked whether she felt pressure to perform a primal, jungle bunny routine, Coco Fontaine laughed and said she did not need to be told. She 'danced primitive' on advice from her father to 'do what they expect you to do, but beat them at their own game'. As a born-in-Alberta girl dancing to the beat of the supposed jungle, she remembered laughing to herself and thinking, 'Oh god, you stupid fools.' With satirical parody disguised within their performances, black dancers resisted racialized, sexualized expectations internally at the same time that they staged them outwardly.[49] Still, none of the black striptease dancers who worked Vancouver venues achieved the stardom enjoyed by some of their white peers, although as Choo Choo Williams commented, light-skinned or 'high yellow' dancers were more likely to reach higher heights in the business than darker-skinned women. Working-class black dancers had more difficulty purchasing expensive costumes, dance lessons, props, and promotional photographs. Even if they possessed the material resources necessary to attain a career as a headliner, the colour line persisted, sutured into place by stubborn, racist beliefs about the 'nature' of black dancers and where they did and did not belong. Yet first-person accounts of Choo Choo, Miss Lovie, and Coco, among others, reveal resilient subjectivities that both accommodated and exceeded the terms of white voyeurism.

Beyond Black and White: Others Absent from the Spotlight

Despite the fact that so many nightclubs were located in and around Chinatown, none of our narrators have been able to recall more than a handful of Asian dancers. In fact, when Asian dancers were seen in Vancouver, it was most likely not in any of the Chinatown clubs, but rather as part of a 'song-and-dance' show playing at the Cave or Isy's such as the China Girls or the China Doll Revue, both of which advertised Asian women 'direct from New York'. In spite of Vancouver's growing Asian-Canadian population, few Asian women became professional strip-teasers. Like dancer Sen Lee Fu, memorialized as 'The Most Exotic Dancer of Them All' in burlesque memorabilia, and Tokyo and Japan who appeared in 1950s trade magazines, the handful of local Asian-Canadian women who found work in the business highlighted their exotic ethnicity in order to capitalize on their 'novel', albeit limited, marketability.[50] Interviewees tell of local Asian dancer Suzie Wong, who wore traditional Chinese dresses and used makeup to emphasize the shape of her eyes, and Damien, who incorporated fans and jade ornaments into her act.

Other women of colour were neither exoticized nor misrepresented on Vancouver's stages: they were simply absent, unrepresented as spectacles of even the most graphically racialized sexuality. Interviews suggest that only one or two First Nations women danced in Vancouver, and they were able to do so only because they were 'part-Native' and light-skinned enough to pass as white, or in the case of Tia Maria, to pass as Asian. The representation of Native women, or rather the lack thereof, in striptease performance suggests that while colonial discourse cast Native women as thoroughly sexualized, as historian Jean Barman has shown, it rarely cast them as 'sexy' in the idealized, ultra-feminine sense of the term.[51] The fact that a biracial First Nations dancer's best chance of success lay in passing herself off as anything other than Native reveals the uniquely denigrated status of Native women's sexuality in a province long steeped in anti-Indian discourse and practice.

Since we were able to interview only four women of colour about their experiences, we asked white participants in the business of striptease to speculate about the relatively small numbers of non-white dancers.[52] In the case of black women, for example, white narrators normalized the sparse representation by referring to the general absence of blacks in Vancouver. Yet this assumption that few black women were in the business because black people simply did not live in Vancouver is propped up by widespread ignorance of the history and existence of the black neighborhood, Hogan's Alley,[53] and the larger African-Canadian community in Vancouver. For white narrators, it was likely easier to reference a 'non-existent' black community in the 1950s, 1960s, and 1970s rather than to reflect critically on how the super-idealization of white, sexy female bodies (even those that staged 'exotic' Otherness only to discard it at night's end) operated both to shape the appetites and desires of Vancouver audiences, and to shrink opportunities for non-white dancers in the city.

In the case of South Asian and Asian women, white narrators cited the 'conservative' nature of 'those' cultures, and argued that these women's families would have objected to them working as erotic dancers. This argument fails to recognize that white Euro-Canadian women chose to dance for a living despite the fact that they too came from cultures that stigmatized their profession, and a hegemonic 'white Canadian' culture which still desires to exclude them from the 'national' historical memory. Indeed, whether or not Asian and South Asian women faced harsher prohibitions against careers in professional striptease than white women, the well-documented anti-Asian history of Vancouver suggests that the 'exoticized' ethnicity of all Asian dancers would have had limited purchase before an audience beset with warnings of immigrant, unassimilable 'hordes' from the East and the resilient imagery of 'yellow peril'.[54]

Impersonating the Exotic Other

Nightclub and carnival displays of Otherness also drew on the rich discursive tradition of

Orientalism. In his analysis of this discourse, Edward Said used a theatrical metaphor to describe understandings of the Orient in the European imagination. Representative figures or tropes such as the Sphinx, Cleopatra, Eden, Babylon, the harem, and others, he argued, are to the Orient 'as stylized costumes are to characters in a play'.[55] But throughout the history of carnivals, circuses, and sideshows in both Europe and North America, these stylized costumes were literally put on and the metaphor was performed before audiences hungry for the mysteries of the Orient. From the turn of the twentieth century onwards, dancing girls at Canadian and American carnivals were regularly described simply, but sufficiently, as 'Oriental dancers', and shows with such names as 'Persian Palace', 'Turkish Village', 'Little Egypt', 'A Trip to Babylon', 'Mecca', and 'A Street in Cairo' flourished. Here, the tourist discourse of escape used to lure white travellers to exotic destinations, especially robust after World War II, was materialized in Vancouver, where nightclub owners and Exhibition programmers marketed 'naked girls' from 'faraway villages' and 'palaces' as cheap alternatives to vacation sites and sights beyond provincial borders. In particular, the treatment of colonized India in shows worked implicitly to sanction British imperial rule and to promote the superiority of *British* Columbian spectators.[56] An intriguing facet of such shows is that Oriental dancers were often white women, participating in yet another long established carnival tradition—the impersonation of the Other by white performers. . . .

In 1945 Vancouver, white headliner Yvette Dare, whose trained parrot helped her to disrobe on stage, was billed as presenting a 'Balinese dance to the bird god'. In an interview in the *Vancouver Sun*, Dare admitted using brown makeup all over her body and revealed that Jeta, her parrot, was not actually from the 'exotic isle of Bali' as advertised, but rather was 'a New York department store bargain' who had 'never been nearer to Bali than Macy's basement'.[57] Such a confession reveals the complex character of white performances of racial Otherness. To deploy such 'exotic' trappings and then proceed to call your own bluff publicly suggests a uniquely situated form of 'passing' intended to deceive no one. Recalling her 'exotic' repertoire at the State burlesque theatre in 1951, chorus line dancer Nena Marlene noted the industry demands for Otherness, while she self-reflexively gestured to her own duplicity: 'Our line filled in between the comedians, the accordion player, and the magician, and before the headlining strippers.

We'd do Hawai'ian dances, and Indian tom-tom dances because we had to keep changing themes, but we weren't authentic one bit.'[58] (Figure 3) . . . Even in the mid-1970s, it was commonplace for dancers—including local, Vancouver-based women—to be billed as imports from the United States and abroad in order to ratchet up the 'exotica quotient' and re-stabilize the racialized norm that all-Canadian (white) girls were somehow innocent and immune from what was believed to be the sordid, commodified behaviour of (non-white) foreigners.

Figure 3. Nena Marlene strikes a 'Hawaiian' pose at the State Burlesque Theatre, Vancouver, British Columbia, c. 1951. Photographer: Jack Uter.

The Respectability Sweepstakes: Stubborn Legacies

As much as lines separating 'good girls' from 'bad girls' were drawn and re-drawn between 1945 and 1975, one taboo endured: the proper, self-respecting, morally upstanding, white Canadian woman did not undress in public with the explicit goal of sexually arousing men for a living. Ironically, after World War II, professional female figure skaters with the Ice Capades and Canadian Ice Fantasy,[59] fashion models, beauty pageant contestants, magicians' assistants, female trapeze artists, and baton-twirling majorettes also wore very skimpy costumes and traded on their (hetero)sexual allure.[60] According to jazz historian Sherrie Tucker, even female big-band jazz and swing instrumentalists in the 1940s and 1950s were promoted to 'look like strippers' with 'gowns revealing plenty of bosoms'.[61] However, the respectability of good girls (that is, non-strippers) who performed in beauty contests, parades, magic acts, fashion shows, musical combos, circuses, and figure skating spectacles was virtually guaranteed by the legitimizing stamp of their participation in 'family-oriented' entertainment in reputable venues. Of necessity, these mainstream female entertainers developed a keen sense of how to position themselves on the safe side of the (ever-shifting) class-specific, gendered, and racialized line dividing the tasteful from the vulgar.

From the late 1940s through the 1970s, television and Hollywood film popularized and glorified white female entertainers who knew all too well that their success hinged on adherence to strict norms of conventional (yet non-threatening) beauty and conservative gender roles.[62] Mass-market, post-war ideals of white, middle-class, full-time, suburbanized wifedom and motherhood were symbolized by Betty Crocker, June Cleaver, and Donna Reed, and propagandized in women's lifestyle magazines. In actuality, the domestic stereotype was displaced by female anti-war and union activists, *Playboy* models, munitions workers, and other non-conformists.[63]

Striptease dancers, both white and non-white in Vancouver, British Columbia, were denied association with bourgeois feminine respectability, especially after 'bottomless' performance was decriminalized in the early 1970s. Even in the context of women's liberation, the sexual revolution, and the relaxation of some gender and sexual mores, erotic dancers continued to provoke shock, anxiety, and moralizing judgment among feminists and non-feminists. No erotic dancer raising children, especially if she was non-white, was ever honoured for her role as mother and moral guardian of 'the race'. Perceived by many as no better than disgraced whores, dancers were positioned outside of discourses that elaborated what it meant to be a normal, moral, and patriotic Canadian citizen. At the same time, none of the 17 retired dancers we have interviewed ever considered herself a powerless dupe of patriarchal control, in spite of difficult, sometimes demoralizing working conditions, and a steady climate of moral opprobrium.[64] In the mid-1970s, a cross-racial union drive brought Coco Fontaine, Tia Maria, and Miss Lovie together with white dancers Lee, Tarren Rae, and Silver Fox. They fought for decent pay, decent dressing rooms with showers, and better treatment, recalled Coco Fontaine, 'because we were worth it'—although race-specific complaints were never publicly aired and a first contract was never secured.[65] Stymied by booking agents and club owners threatened by the labour unrest, the dancers nonetheless took pride in their rebellious campaign for justice.

In Vancouver, whether they drew audiences to posh, upscale, West End supper clubs or grittier, downscale, East End nightclubs, striptease dancers and their promoters capitalized on the cultural fascination with heterosexy female bodies. What made the 'naughty' art of striptease unique was the dancers' self-conscious, premeditated, and primary purpose to sell sexual thrills to voyeurs in the already excessively sex-saturated spaces of burlesque halls, stripclubs, and summer carnivals. White striptease dancers, including those who donned blackface or manipulated other non-white tropes, could take on the symbols and signifiers of the racial Other as erotic spectacle or play up the pageantry of white glamour. Indeed, they were not indelibly stigmatized by their skin colour as black dancers and Asian dancers were. However, even the most successful white dancers courted disapproval (and criminal sanctions) for disrupting definitions of white femininity and respectability. Yet, ironically, the stigmatization of stripteasers as deviant, abject subjects served to stabilize the colonial myth of white female sexual civility.[66] Those men (and women) who attended spectacular striptease at Vancouver nightclubs could rationalize their consumption of wayward sexuality by assuring themselves that good (that is, domesticized, genteel) white ladies would never perform commercial striptease unless coerced and/or drugged by pimps or mobsters, as popular lore would have it. And spectators could confirm racial and sexual stereotypes that 'coloured girls' on stage embodied a primordial foreignness appropriate to their licentious 'nature' in a city visibly governed by Anglo-Canadian elites. Patrons desired and disavowed stripteasers of colour whose bodies carried the weight of white cultural projections and preoccupations with difference and deviance. And yet African and Asian dancers in Vancouver from 1945 to 1975 negotiated racist and sexist expectations with humour, anger, courage, and irony; like other workers of colour in colonial contexts, they made difficult choices and concessions all along the way.

Inquiry into the post-war history of professional female striptease is enriched through attention to the complexity of memories narrated by retired dancers, club owners, choreographers, and booking agents. In Vancouver, British Columbia, all erotic dancers navigated the thorny business of male-controlled and racially segregated erotic entertainment. It was not until the mid-1970s that the racialized and class-specific stratification of commercial striptease was somewhat flattened out as hotel beer parlours proliferated across the lower mainland and independent nightclubs spiraled into oblivion. With more hotel stages than

dancers to fill them, white dancers and dancers of colour were booked into many of the same hotels, although white dancers were first offered the esteemed, local gig of 'house feature' and dancers of colour had to 'prove themselves' on the road. Before the explosion of hotel bars, dancers of colour were largely confined to the city's East End and Chinatown stages where prospects to attain marquee status, top salaries, and adequate working conditions were notably constrained. Our case study affords a window onto the post-war social organization of hierarchies of beauty, glamour, and sexiness: elite white club owners booked 'classy', Eurocentrically attractive and predominantly white striptease headliners for white, middle-class patrons. In so doing, they reproduced the classed and racialized divide that split the affluent West End from the impoverished East End. In a city scarred by more than a century of class and racial conflicts, some white Vancouverites were comforted by the association of working-class Chinatown with vice and immorality, and the physical and psychic distance of the East End from their tony neighbourhoods on the West side. Dancers of colour and white dancers were differently ensnared in these complex relations, and they resisted differently. The broad category of 'stripteaser' meant that all dancers shared many experiences, and our study invites us to reconsider received, racialized assumptions about the post-war 'golden era' of bump and grind.

Notes

We would like to thank the Social Sciences and Humanities Research Council of Canada (SSHRCC) for financial support, and Michelle Swann for research assistance. We would also like to acknowledge the trenchant, stimulating, and insightful feedback from anonymous reviewers, as well as the patient, talented editorial staff at the *Journal of Women's History*.

1. Jack Wasserman, 'Saloon Crawler's Notebook', *Vancouver Sun*, 19 Oct. 1971, A5.
2. Patrick Nagle, interview with Becki Ross, Victoria, British Columbia, 28 July 2000.
3. Wasserman, 'Saloon Crawler's Notebook', A5.

4. See Estanislao Oziewicz, 'Canada's Bare Essentials', *Globe and Mail*, 19 Feb. 2000, A15.

5. Lindalee Tracey, *Growing Up Naked: My Years in Bump and Grind* (Vancouver: Douglas & McIntyre, 1997), 210.

6. In 1951, the total population of British, French, and other Europeans in British Columbia was 93.2 per cent, the Asian population was 2.4 per cent, and the Aboriginal population was 2.2 per cent (other: 2.2 per cent); in 1961, British/French/other European was 93.4 per cent, Asian was 2.5 per cent, Aboriginal was 2.4 per cent (other: 1.7 per cent); in 1971, British/French/other European was 92.4 per cent, Asian was 3.5 per cent, Aboriginal was 2.4 per cent (other: 1.7 per cent). Cited in Veronica Strong-Boag, 'Society in the Twentieth Century', in Hugh Johnston, ed., *The Pacific Province: A History of British Columbia* (Vancouver: Douglas & McIntyre, 1996), 276.

7. Robert Campbell, *Sit Down and Drink Your Beer: Regulating Vancouver's Beer Parlours, 1925–1954* (Toronto: University of Toronto Press, 2001), 107–26. . . .

8. Arthur Moore to Chairman and Members of the Licenses and Claims Committee, City Hall, 5 Sept. 1946, 28–D, File 20, City Clerk fonds, Series 27, Vancouver City Archives; '5 Convicted of Indecent Stage Show', *Vancouver Sun*, 18 Jan. 1952, 25; and 'Burlesque Show Closed; Appeal Next', *Vancouver Sun*, 19 Jan. 1952, 6.

9. On striptease as the second-oldest profession, see Margaret Dragu and A.S.A. Harrison, *Revelations: Essays on Striptease and Sexuality* (London: Nightwood Editions, 1998), 23. On the construction of the stripper as sex deviant, see James Skipper and Charles McCaghy, 'Stripteasers: The Anatomy and Career Contingencies of a Deviant Occupation', *Social Problems* 17, 3 (1970): 391–405; and David Scott, *Behind the G-String* (Jefferson, MD: McFarland & Company Inc. Publishers, 1996), 37–8, 132–3.

10. On the pernicious imposition of shame, see Angela Latham, *Posing a Threat: Flappers, Chorus Girls, and Other Brazen Performers of the American 1920s* (Hanover, NH: University Press of New England, 2000), 113–18. . . .

11. Dragu and Harrison, *Revelations*, 53–7.

12. All examples of salaries are in Canadian dollars.

13. Jack Card, interview with Becki Ross, Kim Greenwell, and Michelle Swann, Vancouver, British Columbia, 28 Jan. 2000.

14. Jack Card, interview with Becki Ross, Kim Greenwell, and Michelle Swann, Vancouver, British Columbia, 14 Mar. 2000.

15. Ernie King, interview with Becki Ross, Vancouver, British Columbia, 4 Feb. 2002.

16. Cited in Kay Anderson, *Vancouver's Chinatown: Racial Discourse in Canada, 1875–1980* (Montreal: McGill-Queen's University Press, 1991), 206.

17. On racialized entertainment in post-war Montreal, Quebec, see Meilan Lam, *Show Girls: Celebrating Montréal's Legendary Black Jazz Scene* (National Film Board of Canada, 1998), filmstrip. On slumming, see George Chauncey, *Gay New York: Gender, Urban Culture and the Making of the Gay Male World, 1890–1940* (New York: Basic Books, 1994), esp. 246–7. . . .

18. See Jeff Sommers, 'Men at the Margin: Masculinity and Space in Downtown Vancouver, 1950–1986', *Urban Geography* 19, 4 (1998): 292.

19. See Greg Marquis, 'Vancouver Vice: The Police and the Negotiation of Morality, 1904–1935', in David Flaherty, ed., *Essays in the History of Canadian Law*, vol. 6 (Toronto: University of Toronto Press, 1995), 242–73.

20. On 'pathological masculinity', see Sommers, 'Men at the Margin', 292.

21. April Paris, interview with Becki Ross, Vancouver, British Columbia, 30 Aug. 2000.

22. Card, interview 28 Jan. 2000. On twentieth-century 'girl shows' at carnivals, circuses, and exhibitions, see A.W. Stencell, *Girl Show: Into the Canvas World of Bump and Grind* (Toronto: ECW Press, 1999).

23. See Phyllis Rose, *Jazz Cleopatra: Josephine Baker in Her Time* (New York: Doubleday, 1989), 12; and Andrea Stuart, 'Josephine Baker: Looking at Josephine', in *Showgirls* (London: Jonathan Cape, 1999), 75–110.

24. Advertisement, *Vancouver Sun*, 21 Feb. 1964.

25. See Bruce Shepard, *Deemed Unsuitable: Blacks from Oklahoma Move to the Canadian Prairies in Search of Equality Only to Find Racism in Their New Home* (Toronto: Umbrella Press, 1997).

26. Choo Choo Williams, interview with Becki Ross, Vancouver, British Columbia, 4 Feb. 2002.

27. Ibid.

28. Ernie King, interview with Becki Ross, Vancouver, British Columbia, 4 Feb. 2002.

29. Ernie King and Choo Choo Williams, interview with Becki Ross, Vancouver, British Columbia, 4 Feb. 2002. On black histories in Vancouver, see Wayde Compton, ed., *Blueprint: Black British Columbian Literature and Orature* (Vancouver: Arsenal Pulp Press, 2001), 95–120.

30. King, interview, 4 Feb. 2002.

31. Williams, interview, 4 Feb. 2002.

32. Miss Lovie, interview with Becki Ross and Kim Greenwell, Vancouver, British Columbia, 22 Sept. 2000.

33. Miss Lovie, interview, 22 Sept. 2000.

34. Advertisement in *Vancouver Sun*, 14 Mar. 1969, 40.

35. King, interview, 4 Feb. 2002.

36. See Paul Justman, *Standing in the Shadows of Motown* (Vancouver, British Columbia: Lions Gate Films, 2002), documentary film.

37. Dave Davies, interview with Kim Greenwell and Michelle Swann, Vancouver, British Columbia, 27 June 2000.

38. For press coverage, see 'Ingenious Mitzi Stirs Up Strippers', Vancouver *Province*, 4 Oct. 1981, and 'Stripper Bounced to the U.S.', *Vancouver Sun*, 28 July 1984.

39. Jules Styne and Stephen Sondheim, 'You Gotta Have a Gimmick', in *Gypsy*, DVD, directed by Arthur Laurents (1962; Burbank, CA: Warner Home Video, 2000).

40. See Peter Bailey, 'Para-Sexuality and Glamour', *Gender and History* 2, 2 (1990): 148–72.

41. On the imperialist exhibition of Sara Bartmann, an African woman captured by Dutch colonizers in the early nineteenth century, see Yvette Abrahams, 'Images of Sara Bartman: Sexuality, Race, and Gender in Early Nineteenth Century Britain', in Ruth Roach Pierson and Naupur Chaudhuri, eds, with assistance from Beth McCauley, *Nation, Empire, Colony: Historicizing Gender and Race* (Bloomington: Indiana University Press, 1998), 227. . . .

42. Patricia Hill Collins, *Black Feminist Thought: Knowledge, Consciousness and the Politics of Empowerment* (New York: Routledge, 1990), 67.

43. Miss Lovie, interview, 22 Sept. 2000.

44. Coco Fontaine, interview with Becki Ross, Vancouver, British Columbia, 20 Sept. 2000.

45. Ibid.

46. Ibid.

47. Jeannie Runnalls, interview with Becki Ross and Michelle Swann, Coquitlam, British Columbia, 21 June 2000.

48. Gerry Palken, interview with Becki Ross, Delta, British Columbia, 18 Feb. 2002.

49. Paige Raibmon makes a similar point in 'Theatres of Contact: The Kwakwa̱ka'wakw Meet Colonialism in British Columbia and at the Chicago World's Fair', *Canadian Historical Review* 81, 2 (2000): 186–90.

50. See Len Rothe, *The Queens of Burlesque: Vintage Photographs from the 1940s and 1950s* (Atglen, PA: Schiffer Publishing Ltd., 1997), 35.

51. See Jean Barman, 'Taming Aboriginal Sexuality: Gender, Power, and Race in British Columbia, 1850–1900', *BC Studies* 115/116 (Autumn–Winter 1997/98): 237–66. . . .

52. Richie Walters, interview with Becki Ross and Kim Greenwell, Vancouver, British Columbia, 8 July 2000; Ross Filippone, interview with Becki Ross, Kim Greenwell, and Michelle Swann, Vancouver, British Columbia, 15 June 2000; Runnalls, interview, 21 June 2000; and Card, interview, 14 June 2000.

53. See Cornelia Wyngarden and Andrea Fatona, *Hogan's Alley*, 1994, documentary film, available from Video-In, 1965 Main St, Vancouver, British Columbia, Canada.

54. On the racist, anti-Asian discourse of 'yellow peril', see Patricia Roy, 'The "Oriental Menace" in British Columbia', in John Friesen and Harry K. Ralston, eds,

Historical Essays on British Columbia (Toronto: Gage, 1980), 243–55. . . .

55. Edward Said, *Orientalism* (New York: Vintage Books, 1979), 71.

56. On how circus spectacles featuring 'Indian subjects' glorified British imperialism, see Janet Davis, 'Spectacles of South Asia at the American Circus, 1890–1940', *Visual Anthropology* 6 (Sept. 1993): 125.

57. Advertisement in *Vancouver Sun*, 12 May 1945, 6; Ray Gardner, 'After Dark', *Vancouver Sun*, 12 May 1945, 6.

58. Nena Marlene, interview with Becki Ross, Vancouver, British Columbia, 27 Feb. 2002.

59. On the careers of the Canadian Ice Fantasy skaters from 1952 to 1954, see Michael Scott, 'The Original Blade Runners', *Vancouver Sun*, 2 Feb. 2002, I8.

60. On the image of glamour constructed by and for white elite figure skaters Sonja Henie, Barbara Ann Scott, and Janet Lynn, see Michelle Kaufman, 'Gaining an Edge', in Lissa Smith, ed., *Nike is a Goddess: The History of Women in Sport* (New York: Atlantic Monthly Press, 1998), 159–68.

61. See comments made in the late 1940s by trumpeter and bandleader Joy Cayler about how she was promoted in the 'glossies', cited in Sherry Tucker, *Swing Shift: "All Girl" Bands of the 1940s* (Durham, NC: Duke University Press, 2000), 58–9.

62. See Susan J. Douglas, *Where the Girls Are: Growing Up Female with the Mass Media* (New York: Random House, 1994), 17–20.

63. Contributors to Joanne Meyerowitz's excellent collection, *Not June Cleaver: Women and Gender in Postwar America, 1945–1960* (Philadelphia: Temple University Press, 1994) acknowledge the conservatism of the post–World War II years, but argue persuasively for new, otherwise excluded histories of women in a complicated era. . . .

64. For stories of former dancers before 1980, see Ann Corio with Joseph DiMona, *This Was Burlesque* (New York: Madison Square Press, 1968); Misty, *Strip!* (Toronto: New Press, 1973); Annie Ample, *Bare Facts: My Life as a Stripper* (Toronto: Key Porter Books, 1988); Tracey, *Growing Up Naked*; Lucinda Jarrett, *Stripping in Time: A History of Erotic Dancing* (London: HarperCollins, 1997); and Dragu and Harrison, *Revelations*.

65. Coco Fontaine, interview, 20 Sept. 2000.

66. Anne McClintock, borrowing from Julia Kristeva, wisely theorizes the paradox of abjection: 'Abject peoples are those whom industrial imperialism rejects but cannot do without: slaves, prostitutes, the colonized, domestic workers, the insane, the unemployed, and so on.' *Imperial Leather: Race, Gender and Sexuality in the Colonial Context* (New York: Routledge, 1995), 72.

27

'Our New Palace of Donut Pleasure': The Donut Shop and Consumer Culture, 1961–76

Steve Penfold

In January 1966, Country Style Donuts invited consumers to its 'new palace of donut pleasure' in Oakville, Ontario, an affluent suburb 30 miles west of Toronto, by placing a half-page advertisement in the local newspaper. At this time, Country Style was an upstart chain with a handful of outlets in Ontario, and the company was no advertising innovator. In both idea and image, the ad was busy, addressing an astonishingly wide variety of potential donut eaters by delivering a 200-word pastiche of messages both practical and spectacular. At base, the ad simply announced the core features of a 1960s donut shop. It celebrated, for example, the tremendous variety and outstanding quality of the outlet's offerings, bragging loudly of 'over 56 varieties' (plus fancies) and repeatedly marshalling adjectives like 'mouthwatering' (twice) and 'fresh' (eight times). It suggested buying donuts for special occasions (like church socials) and for everyday routines (inviting regular customers to join the 'Coffee and Counter Club'). Short customer testimonials (presumably apocryphal) highlighted the many virtues of a Country Style shop declaring 'everything is so fresh and clean,' 'there's lots of parking space,' 'the best coffee I've ever tasted,' and 'so many varieties to choose from.' The last one summed the message up: 'Oakville needs something like this.'[1]

. . .

This chapter examines the early years of the donut shop in Canada, focusing on how it structured the consumer experience by offering a combination of convenience, pleasure, and sociability and tried to ameliorate—only half consciously—many of the cleavages and tensions of post-war consumer culture. . . . Throughout, I argue that the donut shop offered a consumer experience that, while in part new, was at the same time built on continuities with earlier forms of popular culture. As such, it exposed some of the tensions inherent in consumer culture; it also expressed the complex social dynamics that arose as various groups—businesses, but also families, youth, police, and government officials—struggled to make (and make sense of) the post-war geography of consumption.

'Markets Today Have a New Dimension'

When Country Style arrived in Oakville, the donut shop idea was not common in Canada, though neither was it entirely new. Before the 1960s, donut retailing had many levels: small bakers, variety stores, street vendors, grocery stores, and others. But except for donut outlets like Downyflake Donuts and Faymakers in Toronto and a few others scattered across big-city Canada, few entrepreneurs were drawn to the idea or the name 'donut shop'. With the advent of shopping malls in the 1950s, a few donut specialty shops began to appear in growing suburban areas. Charles Downyflake Donuts,

Steve Penfold, '"Our New Palace of Donut Pleasure": The Donut Shop and Consumer Culture, 1961–1976', *The Donut: A Canadian History* (Toronto: University of Toronto Press, 2008), pp. 51–97. © University of Toronto Press Incorporated 2008. Reprinted with permission of the publisher.

for example, opened in the Hamilton Shopping Centre in 1956 as an extension of a local coffee-shop business, using a DCA machine to grab the attention of mall patrons. The name was eventually changed to Sally's Donuts, and the outlet passed through several owners.[2]

. . .

Tim Hortons and Country Style, Canada's 'indigenous' companies, began in 1962 and 1963, and initially borrowed heavily from existing American chains. Jim Charade came to the donut business as salesman and donut plant manager for Vachon, the iconic Quebec snack food company. . . . After meeting hockey star Tim Horton . . ., Charade began to think that celebrity might be an effective marketing tool. The two men formed a partnership, renamed the donut shop Tim Horton Donuts and opened a handful of Tim Horton hamburger restaurants around greater Toronto. The hamburger outlets soon failed, and the donut business expanded slowly, finally opening its first franchise on Ottawa Street in Hamilton in 1964. Tim Hortons' main Canadian competitor, Country Style Donuts, began when its Canadian founder, Alan Lowe, spotted a small American chain that he figured he could franchise for the Canadian market. Over the next decade, a few independent shops joined these early franchisors, although independents seem to have been comparatively rare until the 1970s.[3]

Donut chains aimed to feed (and to feed off) Canada's burgeoning automobile culture. Motor vehicle registrations in Canada more than doubled between 1945 and 1952, and had doubled again by 1964, far outpacing population growth.[4] Car ownership continued to vary widely by region, type of municipality (urban, surburban, or rural), and income, but the automobile's triumph in everyday life was undeniable. What was particularly notable about car ownership after the war was how deeply it penetrated the populace. Rates of ownership relative to population recorded rapid and steady increases: in 1953, no province averaged one car

per household; by 1966, only Newfoundland and Quebec did not. Car ownership was especially common in metropolitan southern Ontario, where donut chains initially thrived.[5]

. . .

The car was much more than a convenient way to get to work. In Hamilton, Ontario, for example, traffic planners discovered in 1961 that the 'typical' family averaged more than six car trips a day, hinting at a transformation of social patterns that went beyond the daily commute.[6] Most exciting to retailers, of course, was the stretching out of shopping patterns. 'Since before the last World War, our market potentials are no longer . . . confined within city and town limits,' L.R. Atwater told the Toronto chapter of the American Marketing Association. 'Markets today have a new dimension. . . . The new dimension is travel time by automobile.' For Atwater, speaking in 1955, the main feature of this new style of commerce was the ability of traditional downtowns to reach out to their fringes, drawing in retail dollars from suburban and exurban areas still underserviced by commercial institutions.[7] But as the 1960s approached, the new dynamics of automobile commerce changed: consumers continued to stretch out their shopping, but increasingly bypassed traditional commercial areas for newer institutions. The shopping mall grew to rival the downtown retail district, keeping more dollars and more consumers in fringe areas, and haphazard auto-oriented commercial strips mushroomed on the outskirts of existing communities as retailers targeted booming residential populations.[8]

Donut chains positioned themselves at the heart of this burgeoning automobile culture. Dunkin' Donuts chose sites on streets where at least 15,000 cars passed by each day at no more than 40 miles per hour, figuring that anyone going faster would be unlikely to stop.[9] On its arrival in Canada from the United States in 1961, Mister Donut built free-standing outlets along busy suburban arterials or, less often, at the ends of strip malls on high-traffic roads. Aiming for such locations meant sharing space with other types of drive-in commerce. An A&W hamburger stand, a Midas Muffler outlet, two gas stations and a strip mall flanked the Mister Donut on Eglinton Avenue East in Scarborough.[10] . . . In Scarborough, the outlet at Kennedy Road and Progress (opened 1967) had all the features of a successful donut shop: on a high-traffic strip, just off Highway 401, and at an access point to a large industrial park.[11] . . . Many independent operators chose locations based on their own knowledge of the local community and their intuitive sense of changing geography, or by informally inspecting traffic flows near a potential location. Even into the mid-1970s, Tim Hortons found many of its locations by flying over a community for a bird's-eye view of busy streets.[12]

Besides establishing free-standing outlets on suburban strips, some donut companies opened outlets in new, enclosed shopping malls. Mister Donut's outlet in St Catharines—the first chain donut shop in the city—found a welcome home in the Pen Centre, a regional mall built on the site of an old peach orchard. In 1971, Tim Hortons located its twenty-fourth outlet in Sherway Gardens, a mammoth regional shopping mall 10 kilometres west of downtown Toronto. These indoor outlets were comparatively rare in Ontario; for the most part the chains targeted commercial strips and small plazas, where they opened free-standing outlets or storefront shops.[13]

. . .

The Geography of Convenience

Car culture, then, had many expressions. Whether a donut shop appeared on a suburban strip in a burgeoning metropolis or on the fringes of a smaller city, automobile convenience remained the key criterion for success. These donut outlets were small, typically between 1,200 and 1,400 square feet, including the production area. Their interior seating was relatively limited—often only 12 stools at the counter and a few tables. Building designs facilitated fast-in,

fast-out traffic rather than comfortable surroundings: the take-out area and display cases were directly in front of the door, while the tables and eat-in counter were placed off to the side. But if buildings were small, the parking lots were not, since even a good location was useless without adequate parking. Parking could be a particular problem on traditional strips, no matter how much they had adapted to serve the automobile. John Fitzsimmons, a regular at the first Tim Hortons franchise on Hamilton's Ottawa Street in the 1960s, remembered that the parking lot at the outlet was so small that cars often lined up into the street, especially during shift change at the Dofasco plant.[14]

Losing cars to line-ups in the street signalled a broader problem. Donuts were an impulse purchase—marketing studies backed up the common-sense view that most customers were attracted by the location rather than advertising or brand name[15]—so visibility and access from the street were crucial ingredients for a successful outlet. Donut shop design was a classic example of what Chester Liebs called 'architecture for speed reading'.[16] Pylon signs were designed for maximum efficiency in attracting motoring customers. They were tall and brightly lit and displayed a minimum number of words. Many of them spun, or were surrounded by flashing lights. Finally, the signs were placed out at the roadway rather than close to the shop.[17] Big, bright signs were useless, however, if the outlet itself was obscured. Alongside raw data from traffic counts, then, the Dunkin' Donuts real estate team considered the visibility of the outlet from either direction at a good distance down the road, since customers needed time to see the shop and slow down. In strip plazas, a location near the entrance was an absolute necessity. The Mister Donut at Kipling Plaza in suburban Toronto was sited right next to the parking lot entrance. At nearby Jane and Wilson, the same chain built a free-standing outlet at the edge of a strip plaza parking lot, positioned to capture drivers off Jane Street as well as shoppers as they came and went.[18]

Donut chains were merely one part of a new trend in the geography of convenience. Between the 1920s and the mid-1950s, roadside food service emerged haphazardly in Canada. Individual entrepreneurs dominated the trade, joined after the Second World War by a few small chains that spanned local markets.[19] Beginning around the mid- to late 1950s, however, existing American chains and new Canadian equivalents began to establish a real presence in Canada, altering the geographic dynamics of roadside commerce. . . . Companies like Red Barn Hamburgers, A&W Root Beer, Country Style Donuts, and Mister Donut reached out beyond a single city almost as soon as they began Canadian operations. American donut chains already had impressive reach in the United States, comprising dozens of outlets by the time they expanded into Canada in 1961, and they quickly formed nationwide aspirations north of the border. 'We aim to make Mister Donut a coast to coast franchise chain with units reaching from the Maritimes through Vancouver,' Canadian supervisor Joe Lugossy commented in 1965.[20] Smaller Canadian chains quickly reached out across space as well. In 1966, Country Style was only three years old, but it already had outlets in Toronto, London, and Sudbury.[21]

. . .

The Political Economy of Convenience

The geography of convenience . . . did not evolve through some inevitable process—it was *made* through conscious acts and choices. Entrepreneurial and business strategies relating to location, signage, access, and parking helped construct the geography of convenience, and the donut shop's place in it. These decisions, though, were reinforced by the actions and inactions of other groups and institutions.

In their practical daily decisions, for example, consumers helped reinforce the strategies of entrepreneurs. Albert DeBaeremaker was a construction worker in the 1960s, working many sites around Scarborough, Ontario. He remembered the way the Country Style at Progress and Kennedy—just south of Highway 401, right beside a large industrial park—served the car better than existing restaurants. 'In Scarborough, where you had a small restaurant, there was generally no parking,' he recalled. '[There was] maybe parking for one or two cars, [but at] a donut shop you could generally park 10 or 20 cars no problem. . . . The ones I went to generally had sufficient parking, because they were mainly built as a donut shop. . . . They were the only one in the area there where anyone could go close by and get a coffee.'[22] . . .

Choosing convenience reflected a kind of consumer agency, although not the form we have been trained to expect. When cultural studies scholars began to emphasize 'agency' as a theme in the 1980s, they argued that speaking to, for, and about consumers would reveal more interesting mass culture scripts, showing the reappropriation of commodities and the ironic play and transgression that shaped meaning in consumer societies. Their agenda was partly successful. While some academics now hope to swing the pendulum back towards the power of cultural producers, even scholars who are critical of cultural studies take pains to avoid dismissing consumer intelligence.[23] An additional problem was that cultural studies scholars tended to find agency in the behaviours they found most interesting, reporting the more transgressive and romantic examples and largely ignoring the mundane and routine ones.

But quite often, taking consumers seriously reveals much more pedestrian concerns: consumers might remember their first visit to a donut shop as dramatic, but their ongoing pattern was tied to convenience and routine. In 1969, Al Stortz of Welland, Ontario, owned an auto body shop on Niagara Street with his brothers. When Tim Horton himself came to Welland for the grand opening of outlet number 12 just up the street, Stortz went over, excited more by the great defenceman than by his donuts. 'I got his autograph, which I still have to this day,' Stortz told me, brandishing a letter from the Tim Hortons corporate headquarters to prove the point. He eventually became a regular—an ongoing pattern of consumption tied less to celebrity than to convenience and familiarity. He built few enduring friendships inside the shop but took salesmen there to talk business and became a familiar figure to the workers there. 'I was a regular at that shop back then,' Stortz remembered. 'I never knew the names of the girls, but they got to the point where they'd say "Hi Al" and have my coffee waiting when I came in.' A surprising number of early customers I spoke to remembered precise details about locations and parking lots but couldn't offer even the first name of another customer or staff member. . . .[24]

But to recognize that consumer choices helped shape the geography of convenience is not the same as saying that consumers produced it. Consumer choices were structured by other forces and institutions. A native of east Toronto, DeBaeremaker moved to Scarborough for cheap housing: as a construction worker, buying a house was a challenge, and he felt he could get the best deal by heading to the fringes. Once there, his consumer preferences became structured by a landscape that he did not make nor entirely choose, and his daily decisions about travelling and stopping were reinforced by public policies that opened roads to drivers and that allowed and even encouraged drive-in commercial development. . . .[25]

. . . Across Canada, provinces and municipalities were spending millions of dollars on both new roads and highways and on widening existing ones, often based on newly minted 'traffic plans' that assumed the automobile was the norm. The consulting firm Damas and Smith alone reshaped the geography of several cities and towns in southern Ontario, using the ostensibly objective tools of traffic counts and destination surveys to set the agenda for change. Based on this approach, consultants normally produced impressively detailed maps of drivers'

desires, with arrows and travel lines projected over the existing road grid (symbolically relegated to the background), less often asking questions about how to build communities to make other transportation options viable or to privilege, say, aesthetic considerations over the movement of automobiles.[26]

Commercial zoning policies reinforced these trends. . . . Scarborough placed few controls on commercial growth until well after the war; then, when borough zoning regulations became more systematic, they set minimum parking standards, defined rules for proper access, and downplayed calls by some residents for controls on signage and roadside advertising. By the 1970s, many municipal officials and some residents agreed that the borough's commercial policies had helped produce a landscape dominated by fast food, car dealerships, and parking lots. Yet there had been nothing conspiratorial about these decisions. Borough officials had often merely heeded what they believed was a widespread public consensus about the benefits of convenience in car culture. Indeed, when officials began to question this form of development, they discovered that public apathy was often the biggest barrier to change.[27] 'The commercial structure of Scarboro is one of the most visually assertive aspects of the Borough,' noted one planning study in 1976. '[T]he commercial fabric . . . appears as a sprawling mass of car lots, fast-food eateries, grocery facilities, and department stores. . . . Parking lots, garish colours, plastic facades, shout and cajole at the passers by. It is only within the inner confines of a few residential neighborhoods that one can seemingly escape the tentacles of this "commercial carnival."' Planners recognized that their evocative language was not likely to produce dramatic results: 'The majority of residents appear to be fairly neutral regarding the appearance of facilities such as . . . car lots, take-outs, and service stations.'[28] The tentacles weren't just reaching out. For many of the people in the 'inner confines' of those residential neighbourhoods, the 'commercial carnival' had its attractions.

'Give Ma a Treat!'

Donut shops arrived along auto-oriented commercial strips at a time of change in the consumption of their two core products, coffee and donuts. Traditionally, Canadians had been a nation of tea drinkers, perhaps because of British cultural influence. Even so, coffee's popularity increased steadily over the first half of the twentieth century . . ., finally surpassing that of tea after the war. Per capita consumption of coffee increased by over 40 per cent between 1953 and 1962, while tea drinking actually declined by 25 per cent.[29] By the end of that period, coffee had matched tea as a popular beverage, both in raw numbers and as cultural metaphor. The widespread standardization of between-meal breaks in workplaces, designated by the distinctly American term 'coffee break' rather than the more British 'tea time', perfectly captured the spirit of this new consumer preference. The distinction was more than semantic. By 1956, three-quarters of Canadian workers enjoyed coffee-break privileges and coffee made up half the beverages they consumed, five times as much as tea.[30] 'The coffee break is the greatest single cause for both the relative swing away from coffee in the home and for the increased consumption across the country,' one trade magazine reported of this development. 'More and more employers, realizing the value of the break period, have included them in the working schedule.'[31] . . .

Donut shops appeared, therefore, just as coffee was overtaking tea as the standard hot beverage for many Canadians. Tim Hortons' donut boxes urged customers to 'take your next coffee break at Tim Hortons,' and even if the Ottawa Street outlet in Hamilton was too far from large factories like Dofasco to attract workers during the day, it became a regular haunt for the merchants and retail workers along the commercial strip. No matter how busy the store got, someone from Canadian Tire managed to make a trip across the street to pick up drinks and donuts for all the workers. . . .

Today, it is only a slight exaggeration to say that donut shops are, in essence, efficient caffeine-delivery systems: donuts, bagels, muffins, and other offerings largely serve as marketing tools to sell coffee. But in the early days, although coffee was the most profitable item, selling donuts was still a core part of the business. Chains like Tim Hortons and Country Style came into a thriving donut market, riding the post-war crest of increasing sales first cultivated by industrial producers like Margaret's.[32] In addition to mere volume, donut shops had the advantages of freshness and variety. Indeed, if coffee signals the localization of vast networks of distribution, the donut . . . shows another powerful tendency in twentieth-century consumption: the multiplication of superficial choice. For the most part, donut wholesalers specialized in large volumes of limited lines—Val's in Edmonton, for example, sold only glazed cake donuts, while Margaret's produced just four varieties. Donut drive-ins, however, offered what seemed to consumers an astonishing array of choice, with toppings, dips, nuts, fillings, jams, powders, and sprinkles added and combined to transform a few basic shells into dozens of varieties.

Indeed, donut drive-ins seemed a perfect metaphor for the two contradictory impulses of consumer culture: they multiplied the variety and choice of goods even while homogenizing taste and fashion. From houses to cars to toasters, post-war mass producers offered a basic commodity with an increasing number of options and colours to give the appearance of maximum choice and varied design.[33] However mundane the particular example, the Country Style sign in front of each store—'Country Style Donuts, 56 Varieties, Superb Coffee'—announced three key pillars of mass consumption: brand name, near limitless variety, and the promise of consistent quality. That underneath 56 icings and glazes lay the same DCA or Jo-Lo mix used at Val's or Margaret's seemed less important to consumers than the almost revolutionary choice of flavours. For Tim Lambert of St Catharines, who grew up on Homestead Bakery's honey-dipped donuts, the spinning donut case at the Mister Donut at the Pen Centre was a minor consumer spectacle, highlighting the tremendous variety and choice available.[34]

. . .

Many promotional activities aimed to create a carnival atmosphere in the shops. Mister Donut advised its franchisees to mount such public relations stunts as 'Donut a Go Go' (complete with an 'attractive teenager' to impress the crowds), donut-eating contests to draw children and reward maximum consumption, and tie-ins with holidays, movies, and television shows. To spruce up its core product, the chain developed a heart-shaped donut. None of these suggested much utility in buying donuts.[35] Indeed, eating a donut was a classic consumerist activity, since it involved spending on a product with little intrinsic value.

But the question of consumer behaviour was never so simple. It may have been that desire had triumphed over need, and spending over thrift, but many donut eaters were in no position to throw their money around. For many families, eating out at a restaurant continued to be a special occasion, but since the donut was cheap (at about 10 or 15 cents in the mid-1960s, compared to 40 or more cents for a fast-food meal), a trip to the donut shop could be routine. The daughter of a truck driver and veterinarian's assistant, Jenny Bryce remembered eating out being an extremely rare and formal occasion—at the nice restaurants 'up along Parkdale Avenue' in Hamilton—but donut shops were not so out of reach.[36] In this sense, the petty consumption of the donut shop reflected the practical balancing of income and pleasure within working-class family economies in a consumer age.

Moreover, even treats had a certain utility, allowing customers to exchange small purchases for time. Surviving on volume, donut shops needed to discourage excessive lingering. Counters and stools and hardback chairs subtly encouraged turnover, and by 1970, 'No Loitering' signs had formalized the encouragement to eat and go, but the question of time

remained complex. In Don Mills, youth worker Jesse Dean discovered servers and customers at the Donut Hole practising a kind of moral economy of lingering: 'The regulars had a system worked out,' he reported. 'One cold drink was good for an hour of seating privilege. Then, the waitress would ask them to leave. Five minutes later, the youths returned and there was a repetition of the game one hour later. One of the most interesting things was the way the waitresses and youths managed to get along, always on a friendly basis, even when the youths had been expelled a number of times the same day.'[37] Of course, the power of consumer culture was that it offered both pleasure and utility in spending and buying. Going to a donut shop offered more than products to buy—it offered a social space to experience, one that drew together several broad social developments in post-war North America.

'Neither Very Rich Nor Poor'

. . .

Then as now, consumer culture was a fascinating riddle. Anyone driving past the plazas, supermarkets, and restaurants that lined commercial streets like Scarborough's Eglinton Avenue, Oakville's Lakeshore Road, or Welland's Niagara Boulevard could see that the mass market was a real thing, an economic formation that had been carved into the landscape by countless public and private decisions. Yet at the same time, words like 'mass' and 'consumer' were little more than rhetorical inventions, part of a convenient shorthand to draw together people with different incomes, tastes, and backgrounds, and thus constantly dissolved into more specific identities like gender, class, age, and ethnicity. . . . Donut shops were not a single social space and never served one homogenous taste.

. . . Despite the middle-market aspirations, the owners, servers, and customers I interviewed often portrayed the donut shop as a working-class institution. 'I just thought that we had to open one in Hamilton,' recalled Jim Charade of his decision to open the Ottawa Street Tim Hortons. 'It's a worker, blue collar kind of worker, and they come out of there at two-three o'clock in the morning and they have no place to go for a cup of coffee.' Such descriptions spoke of practical and unspectacular connections based on mundane daily rituals and conveniences rather than social status, cultural image, or grand claims about working-class families joining the post-war middle market. Workers also appreciated the informality of the shops, which, unlike restaurants popping up in plazas, had no pretensions about offering full meals. The first Ideal Donut in Winnipeg drew in a lot of workers from the nearby sugar plant: 'They would come in with boots and overalls and the place would clean up easily. . . . They felt comfortable, almost like a small town diner atmosphere . . . they wanted to know all the girls' names and they would joke around with each other.' Workers on the road congregated at donut shops: salesmen, hydro workers, cabbies, and truck drivers came up as the core business quite often in interviews and newspaper stories. 'The bulk of the business in the early days were truck drivers,' recalled Linda Lalonde of her Cornwall Tim Hortons outlet. 'I can remember taking calls for them in the early days. I felt like a dispatcher for Williams Transport, because all those guys came in and I'd say, "Call the shop, somebody's looking for you."'[38]

In interviews, almost everyone used the term 'working class' to mean 'working men'.[39] 'There were a lot of men in there,' remembered Sandy Willard of a Tim Hortons outlet in east Hamilton. 'When I went in, I was usually with my father or brother.' Smoking reinforced the male character of the shops—a characteristic not necessarily appreciated by people who had to spend long hours in the shops. 'Ninety-nine percent of the people who came in smoked, no question about it,' recalled one Tim Hortons owner. 'In the store, the donuts were tasting like smoke . . . it was just awful.' Smoking had two effects. First, it made the place dingy and dark, no matter how much daily cleaning was performed. Costas Kiriakopoulos

remembered 'ashtrays all over the counter' of his family's Country Style outlet at Lawrence and Weston in Toronto. The smoke got so thick that they had to periodically wash down the walls, which had become brown with nicotine. Second, smoking also reinforced the general maleness of the place, at least for some customers. 'Men smoked. It was the manly thing to do,' Ed Mahaj recalled of the Ottawa Street Tim Hortons in the early 1970s. 'You'd go in there if you had some time to kill. You'd order a coffee and light up a cigarette. . . . Everyone would be smoking . . . The one on Ottawa Street was always men.'[40]

The sit-down counter was the hub of male culture in the outlets, carrying considerable symbolic weight in memories of donut shop socializing. More than any other feature, the counter made the shop a social space, linking the donut shop with lunch counters and coffee shops even while distinguishing it from other drive-in restaurants. At Red Barn and McDonalds, customers were handed their food by an efficient male worker behind a cash register; at the donut shop, you could get service at the counter. 'It was a coffee shop, not a restaurant', remembered Lori Broadfoot, a server at Winnipeg's Ideal Donut in the early 1970s. 'You would serve a person and then you could stand and talk to them.' Even the shortest conversations across the counter, or seemingly trivial events like a server remembering a daily order, enhanced the donut shop's role as a social space. When repeated as part of a daily routine of working, commuting, or travelling, such cross-counter rituals allowed consumers to graduate from the status of customer to that of regular. . . .

The employment policies of donut shops cemented the male character of the sit-down counter. Fast-food companies like Red Barn and McDonald's deliberately avoided hiring female cashiers, fearing they would attract unruly teenage boys. Servers at donut shops, on the other hand, were exclusively female in the early days. Brief, informal conversations across the counter occasionally passed into longer flirtations. Jenny

Figure 1. Interior of Tim Horton Donuts, Kitchener, February 1969. With counters, stools, and simple menu boards, early donut shops borrowed designs from lunch counters and coffee shops. *Kitchener-Waterloo Record* Photographic Negative Collection, University of Waterloo Library.

Bryce made it clear that there were many attractions to being a high-school student working the counter at Tim Hortons #7 on Queenston Road in Hamilton. She remembered young men 'who came crawling out of those holes after Friday night's adventures. Actually, I went out with a couple of them that I'd met there—a couple of them at the same time . . . I didn't know they knew each other.' One day, she needed a ride home from work, so she asked 'one of those guys in the leather jackets. He used to just ride for pleasure and drink Coca-Cola and eat ice cream cones—he wasn't your real hood . . . I guess I vaguely knew who he was, but I knew [my friend] didn't think much of him. So I got a ride home from him one afternoon and the next thing you know, four months later [we got] engaged and a year later married. That was twenty-six years ago.'[41] No doubt for many servers, flirting

across the counter was an annoying (and perhaps, at times, disturbing) part of the job, but Bryce obviously thrived on it.[42]

Flirting between servers and customers was a stereotype of the earlier lunch counters. Though donut shops were a novelty in the 1960s, many of their key features were familiar to customers. Continuities between lunch counters, diners, and donut shops were mentioned in interviews almost as often as references to novelty. Sometimes, the connection was direct. Tom Busnarda, who grew up on Ottawa Street in Hamilton, described the way the first Tim Hortons picked up on but also reformulated the social function of existing neighbourhood restaurants:

Around the corner and up a couple of blocks was a restaurant called the Bright Spot. The Bright Spot was a twenty-four-hour restaurant that predates Tim Hortons. It was a hangout for all this element . . . that was . . . associated with the east end . . . of Hamilton, which of course is working-class poor. And slowly, Tim Hortons started to take that element from the Bright Spot and you could see a movement to Tim Hortons . . . The Bright Spot was probably a better place to be, because there was a full menu, but Tim Hortons was more accommodating in some ways of having people sit and not do much of a purchase, and having some place to go. [43]

. . .

A sense of place reinforced these associations. The staples of early donut shop design—small, utilitarian interiors with stainless steel and arborite fixtures, menu boards over the cash register, a straight or U-shaped counter with stools, and a few small tables in the corner—were also the mainstays of the coffee shops and lunch counters that had been common in urban neighbourhoods and fringe areas since before the war. There were quite practical reasons for adopting these layouts. Restaurateurs had known for years that stools encouraged a quick turnover of customers—as much as four times the rate of tables.[44] Moreover, it was economical for equipment companies to build to standard designs, and their prices and advice structured the decision-making of both chain and independent restaurant owners. Indeed, designing a low-priced, fast-service restaurant in this period was as much a mass phenomenon as making donuts: companies like Ontario Store Fixtures manufactured the same basic stools, counters, and fittings in varied colours, types, and sizes.[45] Most lunch counters, diners, and donut shops, then, developed a distinctive look not through dramatic innovations in layout or design, but by choosing blue instead of green, vinyl instead of plastic, straight instead of rounded counters, or booths instead of tables and chairs. But from these practical and economic decisions grew a sense of cultural familiarity and social similarity, one that connected donut shops with lunch

counters and diners in a seamless architecture of informal eating out.

Yet from a consumer's perspective, features like menu boards and sit-down counters were more than simple design decisions; they were also cultural cues, as much a part of the donut shop's commercial speech as advertisements and promotions. Indeed, in many ways the appearance of an outlet was *the* key element of its commercial speech, since few donut chains advertised heavily in the early days. Ron Joyce, for example, was quite explicit about viewing the outlet itself as the primary promotional vehicle for Tim Hortons.[46] From this perspective, the design and atmosphere of donut shops expressed the complex cultural dynamics of the post-war mass market. . . .

By the 1960s, . . . two trajectories of mass marketing made for a confusing and complex mix of donut shop patrons. On the one hand, the shops often acquired a reputation as male, working-class institutions; on the other, by adding tables to the lunch counter design, enforcing standards of cleanliness, serving the roadside market, pitching their advertising at baby-boom families, and seeking out locations in shopping plazas and middle-income neighbourhoods, they aimed for a broader clientele. The surviving evidence suggests that overall, the early market was only slightly tilted towards men and that the social use of the shop could depend on time and location.[47] Donut shop owners and workers often spoke of a basic rhythm to the day: truck drivers in early morning, salesmen later, housewives doing shopping in the afternoon, youth in the evening, bar patrons after midnight, cabbies after that. These memories may be too neat, but they do speak to the way that time could alter the basic character of the shop. Space mattered as well: despite being organized on a chain basis, one donut shop was not necessarily like another. One Mister Donut marketing study found that men comprised almost 70 per cent of customers at a typical free-standing outlet on a busy commercial strip, while a shopping centre location had the highest proportion of female customers.

Location also affected the class character of the shops. Chris Pappas owned a number of Country Style Donut shops around Toronto in the 1960s and 1970s, and found that no matter how much they targeted the transient, car-driving market with big parking lots and easy access, the social composition of the neighbourhood affected the customer base. 'It depended on the area where you were, of course,' he explained. 'If you are in a blue-collar area, then you get that type of people. . . . But over here at Dundas and Islington, we had a better clientele. . . . So it depends where you were.' This point reinforces the importance of local residents to the shop's profitability.[48]

What Pappas described was less a grand blending of different social groups into a broad middle class than the strategy of selling to what might be called a 'middle market in aggregate': different locations might attract different sorts of customers; cabbies and truckers might sit at the counter while families stuck to the tables; the morning might be given over to salesmen and the afternoon to female shoppers. Across the chain and through the day, customers spanned the middle market. How else to make sense of Country Style locations beside an industrial park in Scarborough and in the heart of Canada's most affluent community in Oakville? Two different places, same commercial institution. . . . For donut entrepreneurs, however, changing residential dynamics were less important than convincing everyone in the area to drive in and buy donuts. . . . But in the 1960s, class rarely arose as the key marketing problem. Their biggest challenges lay elsewhere.

'They Were Selling Drugs out of the Washrooms'

In early July 1970, during a confrontation in front of the Country Style on Lakeshore Road in Oakville, 19-year-old Peter Simpson was arrested by Constable Roy Bonham and charged with obstructing a police officer. The next day, no doubt to his horror, Simpson found his late-night confrontation on page one of both local newspapers, on the Metro page of the *Toronto Star*, and even on the TV news. All the commotion wasn't really about Simpson, however. It was the place, not the person, that attracted the attention. Judging by media reports around the time of Simpson's arrest, the Country Style at Brock Street and Lakeshore Road was a veritable snack food Sodom and Gomorrah. 'Violence, Sex on Oakville Street', screamed an *Oakville Beaver* headline on 2 July. 'A "circus" that includes amusements like stomping heads until bloody, sexual intercourse on lawns, and urinating on sidewalks came up before council last night,' the *Daily Journal Record* reported of the goings on around the Country Style outlet.[49] Clearly, the shop had become the site of one slice of night-time youth culture, but there was more going on than bad behaviour. As the events around the outlet took on the trappings of a moral panic and spun into a broader discussion about civility and rights, matters soon became explicitly political. At their root, however, the problems were commercial, growing from the inherent tensions of the early donut shop form.

Donut shops attracted young people like magnets. 'The Donut Hole . . . has become an informal drop-in for a cross-section of youths between the ages of 15 and 21,' reported Don Mills youth worker Jesse Dean in 1971, noting that the shops filled a gap in local recreational space. Oakville youth largely agreed, complaining of restricted movies, conservative parents, and few other leisure options than donut shops and fast-food outlets. If the typical outlet became a sort of commercialized drop-in centre, the parking lot became a kind of park. The horseplay at the Lakeshore Road Country Style was matched at the Tim Hortons across town. 'A group of eight boys were tossing a Frisbee around the parking lot of Tim Horton's donut shop until the cops came to break it up,' the *Journal Record* commented. 'What Oakville needs is some kids' space. . . . Just unstructured, open space to gather.'[50] Informal styles of leisure and complaints about alternative options had been staples of youth culture for much of the post-war period.[51] As they proliferated through the late 1960s, donut shops also served as sites of the emerging underground economy. 'We did have a problem with teenagers,' Anita Halaiko, who owned a Mister Donut with her husband in St Catharines, recalled. 'There was a drug problem there. They were selling drugs out of the washrooms, and they were very disruptive.' Drug culture in donut shops seemed to vary: during his summer in Don Mills in 1970, Jesse Dean found many stoned teenagers—'speeders' especially—in the Donut Hole, but relatively little actual drug selling (in contrast, 'deals were made openly' at Edward Gardens park up the street).[52]

Youthful behaviours like horseplay, rowdiness, and drug selling were products of the age, but they were triply encouraged by the donut shop form. As informal institutions of petty consumption entailing all-night hours, small purchases, a minimum of supervision, and an informal setting, donut shops naturally attracted young people looking to socialize. In building outlets that emphasized automobile convenience, moreover, donut chains built large parking lots that became spaces in their own right, facilitating all kinds of alternative activities. Finally, because of their locational strategies, donut shop neighbourhoods were teeming with teens. By 1970 the baby boom had subsided, but the peak of its demographic bulge was aging into and out of their teenage spending years. Young people were a lucrative market of their own, with abundant leisure time and—at least in the minds of marketers—considerable amounts of discretionary income, which they were more than willing to spend on fast food, especially if it bought them a period of socializing with friends. At the chain level, Mister Donut recognized the value of pitching advertising to the 'youth component' because donut eating was inversely related to age. At the outlet level, owners knew they needed youth spending. Chris Pappas, who took over the Oakville outlet amid the troubles, knew

that most local youth had cash in their pockets and were heavy spenders at the outlet.[53]

In a broad sense, these demographic, social, and economic forces brought Simpson to the front of the Country Style that evening in early July, but his confrontation with Constable Bonham flowed from the difficulties of regulating the geography of youth culture, a complex tangle of public and private jurisdictions. A donut shop parking lot was an open and accessible public space in appearance, but in law it was private property with a fairly simple regulatory regime: misbehaving youth could simply be banned from the lot by the owner. . . .

. . . Back in Oakville, Tim Horton dealt with news of the goings on around the Country Style by making a special trip to his nearby outlet to set a firm rule: 'no hippies'. . . . On 7 July 1970 . . . the Oakville council passed the only bylaw in history known to be aimed specifically at a donut shop, although naturally the language was much broader. 'No person,' the bylaw declared, 'shall by himself or with another or others, loiter on any sidewalk . . . so as to occupy more than one-half of the width thereof . . . [or] so as to interfere with any person's access to or from any private premises.' The bylaw further empowered the police, after delivering suitable warnings, to arrest 'any person apparently loitering' in contravention of the regulation, making that person liable for a fine of up to $300.[54] That evening, Simpson was arrested when he joined 35 youths hanging out on the sidewalk in front of the shop.[55]

Though not so surprising in a town that one academic called the 'last outpost of WASP society' and a 'place where observable reactions are almost sure to be at the maximum possible', the bylaw could easily be read as an extension of broader adult attacks on youth leisure, running from legal regulation through 'no hippie' policies to informal harassment by police. As such, it expressed the links between generational discord, consumer culture, and the most powerful political discourses of the day. Indeed, once Brock Street residents arrived at council, the debate quickly moved to first principles, playing on notions of freedom, rights, and order. Specific complaints from small to large—from squealing tires, horn honking, and shouting to swearing, sex, violence, and 'immodesty'—ran together. . . . Angry adults lamented the breakdown of authority and decorum. Councillor Michael Boyle blamed 'permissiveness' for Country Style's problems. . . . Youth responded to such attacks on their leisure habits with their own dramatic rhetoric. One youth reporter condemned Tim Horton's 'no hippies' policy by appropriating the language of civil rights: 'In the early 60's,' he reminded the great defenceman, 'many restaurants in the southern states had similar policies dealing with black people.'[56]

. . .

Two weeks into the troubles at the Oakville Country Style, Pappas took over the outlet at the behest of the chain's head office and proceeded to assure local residents that he would not tolerate rowdy behaviour. . . . For donut shop owners, questions of civility were refracted through their own economic interests. Everyone wanted youth to behave, since rowdiness caused trouble for neighbours and drove good customers away, but notwithstanding the occasional 'no hippie' policy, few owners were willing to ban them outright. Young people had money, and donut shops were almost perfectly suited to the patterns of youthful pleasure. In this sense, Peter Simpson stood at the margin between attempts to exploit the consumer power of youth and efforts to control and reform their behaviour. . . . In the end, these tensions were almost inevitable, built into the donut shop form, its market, its atmosphere, and its parking lots.

'Oakville Needs Something Like This'

Four years before Oakville's infamous bylaw, Country Style Donuts built its new 'palace of donut pleasure' at Brock Street and Lakeshore Road with asphalt, mortar, bricks, and arborite, but the *place* it assembled was constructed from the building blocks of post-war consumer culture. Donut shops were one attempt to capitalize on the growing middle market of consumers. This market was not just the dream of the sophisticated retail expert: less erudite entrepreneurs understood that tapping car culture meant reaching consumers with money to spend, and their decisions about locations carved the dream of reaching the middle-market consumer into Canada's commercial landscape. Yet in offering customers a counter, some tables, and large parking lots, donut shops became social spaces, assembled out of broad changes in space and time, architectural informality, cheap products, and the cultural categories of customers, who fit these new places into their daily routines and into their mental maps of informal eating out. In doing so, entrepreneurs and consumers created places that attracted many working men, but that also served a broader market of families— women, children, and teens, who found their own uses for these mass commercial institutions.

. . .

Notes

1. *Oakville Daily Journal Record (ODJR)*, 15 Jan. 1966, 5.
2. Mike Filey, *I Remember Sunnyside: The Rise and Fall of a Magical Era* (Toronto: Dundurn Press, 1996); Lynn Korbyn, co-owner, Sally's Donuts, early 1960s, interviewed by author, Hamilton, Ontario, 21 Feb. 2002.
3. On Charade and Horton, see Douglas Hunter, *Open Ice: The Tim Horton Story* (Toronto: Viking Press, 1994), 306–48. Information on Country Style's origins is from Kevin Watson, interviewed by author, 22 Oct. 1999. (Watson is the son of one of the early directors of the company, and worked in various positions in the Country Style headquarters until the late 1990s.)
4. F.H. Leacy, *Historical Statistics of Canada*, 2nd edn (Ottawa: Statistics Canada, 1983), series T147-194.
5. In 1953, Ontario had the highest penetration of automobiles, averaging 0.9 cars per family. In 1971, British Columbia led the provinces with 1.6 cars per family (at the time, the Ontario figure was 1.44). . . .

6. *Hamilton Spectator* (*HS*), 19 Aug. 1961, in 'Streets in Hamilton' Scrapbook, vol. 4, 1960–9, 69, Special Collections, Hamilton Public Library.

7. Atwater quotation from *Financial Post* (*FP*), 5 Nov. 1955, 30. Despite their status as emblematic of postwar commercial development, shopping malls were still few in number into the mid- to late 1950s. . . .

8. For an example of the evolution of auto-oriented strips, which often grew haphazardly to serve growing local populations that lacked sufficient commercial choices, see Adams Farrow Associates, *Yonge Street, Town of Richmond Hill, a Report* (Richmond Hill Planning Board, 1959), available in the Urban Affairs Branch, Toronto Public Library. . . .

9. Robert Rosenberg with Madelon Bedell, *Profits from Franchising* (New York: McGraw Hill, 1969), 149.

10. *Might's Toronto Directory* (Toronto: Might's Directories Limited), 1963.

11. *Vernon's London City Directory* (Hamilton: Vernon Directories), 1965. Gerald Bloomfield, 'Lodging at the Interchange in London, Ontario', *Canadian Geographer* 40, 2 (1996): 173–80 discusses the development of Wellington Street.

12. Allan Asmussen, co-founder of Donut Queen (Kitchener-Waterloo), 1968, interviewed by author, Waterloo, 10 Sept. 2001; Calvin LeDrew, owner, Donut Queen, Sydney, Nova Scotia, 1964–70, telephone interview by author, 8 Aug. 2001; *HS*, 17 Apr. 1977; Ron Joyce with Robert Thompson, *Always Fresh: The Untold Story of Tim Hortons by the Man Who Created a Canadian Empire* (Toronto: HarperCollins, 2006), 149.

13. On the Pen Centre, see John Jackson, *St Catharines: Canada's Canal City* (St Catharines: St Catharines Standard Ltd., 1992), 54.

14. John Fitzsimmons, interviewed by author, Hamilton, 25 Jan. 1998.

15. Mister Donut, *Highlights from a Market Analysis of Mister Donut Stores* (Fall 1966), 2, from private collection.

16. Chester Liebs, *Main Street to Miracle Mile: American Roadside Architecture* (Boston: Little Brown, 1985), 39.

17. In the early days, Tim Hortons signs spun around.

18. No specific measurements were provided for Dunkin' Donuts' visibility. Rosenberg, *Profits from Franchising*, 137. . . . The Kipling Plaza outlet and the Jane and Wilson outlet both still exist, as do the plazas, although the former is now a Dunkin' Donuts and the latter is a Vietnamese restaurant. That an old Mister Donut would be transformed into an ethnic restaurant is symbolic of the social changes in Toronto's suburbs.

19. Hi-Ho Drive-Ins around Windsor and White Spot Restaurants in Vancouver would be two examples of these local chains. For a discussion of roadside commerce in Canada, see Steve Penfold, 'Selling by the Carload: The Early Years of Fast Food in Canada', in Madga Fahrni and Robert Rutherdale, eds, *Creating Postwar Canada: Community, Diversity and Dissent* (Vancouver: UBC Press, forthcoming).

20. *TS*, 30 Apr. 1965, 10.

21. *Canadian Hotel Review and Restaurant* (*CHRR*), 15 Aug. 1961, 36–40; 15 May 1964, 42–7; 15 May 1966, 38–44; *CHRR*, 15 May 1968, 44–51; 15 Mar. 1970, 43–9; 15 Mar. 1971, 20–3. . . .

22. Albert DeBaeremaker, telephone interview by author, 18 Mar. 2000.

23. Mike Dawson's excellent study of tourism in British Columbia, which emphasizes the power of cultural producers, is one recent example. Michael Dawson, *Selling British Columbia: Tourism and Consumer Culture* (Vancouver: University of British Columbia Press, 2004), especially 13.

24. Al Stortz, interviewed by author, Welland, Ontario, 17 April 1998; DeBaeremaker interview.

25. On general issues of road planning in Metropolitan Toronto, see Timothy Colton, *Big Daddy: Frederick G. Gardiner and the Building of Metropolitan Toronto* (Toronto: University of Toronto Press, 1980); Christopher Leo, *The Politics of Urban Development: Canadian Expressway Disputes* (Toronto: Institute of Public Administration of Canada, 1977).

26. In the mid-1960s, Damas and Smith undertook traffic surveys and planning studies for several Ontario municipalities, including Sarnia, Cornwall, Oakville, Burlington, Brantford, Pembroke, Timmins, Georgetown, Renfrew, Port Colborne, Galt, Preston, and Smiths Falls. . . .

27. I discuss some issues of anti-drive-in sentiments in Steve Penfold, 'Are We to Go Literally to the Hot Dogs? Drive-ins, Parking Lots, and the Critique of Progress in Toronto's Suburbs, 1965–1975', *Urban History Review* 33, 1 (2004): 8–23.

28. Scarboro Official Plan Review, *Commercial Policy Study*, October 1976, prepared by James F. MacLaren Ltd. for the Scarboro Planning Board), 2–9, 4–17.

29. *CHRR*, 15 Dec. 1964, 8, citing a Bank of Montreal survey. . . .

30. *CHRR*, 15 Nov. 1965, 68; *Restaurants and Institutions* (*RI*), Feb. 1959, 11. . . .

31. *CHRR*, 15 Nov. 1956, 68. The Pan American Coffee Bureau, an organization of major coffee producers, apparently coined the term 'coffee break' in the early 1950s as a marketing effort. . . .

32. See Steve Penfold, *The Donut: A Canadian History* (Toronto: University of Toronto Press, 2008), ch. 1.

33. On the increasing use of options within a standard format, see Joy Parr, *Domestic Goods* (Toronto:

University of Toronto Press, 1999); James Flink, *The Automobile Age* (Cambridge, MA: MIT Press, 1998), ch. 12; and Gary Cross, *An All-Consuming Century: Why Commercialism Won in Modern America* (New York: Columbia University Press, 2000), 88–103.

34. Tim Lambert, interviewed by author, St Catharines, 19 May 1998.

35. Mister Donut, *Advertising and Promotions Manual*, 1967, from private collection.

36. Jenny Bryce, Tim Hortons server, early 1970s, interviewed by author, Selkirk, Ontario, 9 Jan. 1998.

37. North York Public Library, North York History Collection, Jesse Dean, 'Streetwork Report: Don Mills Youth Scene' (1971), 18.

38. Charade interview; Lori Broadfoot, server, Ideal Donuts, early 1970s, interviewed by author, Winnipeg, 19 Oct. 2001; Lalonde interview.

39. Diners had typically been male spaces. See Andrew Hurley, 'The Transformation of the American Diner', 1,286–8.

40. Sandy Willard, interviewed by author, Binbrook, Ontario, 21 Feb. 2002; anonymous former Tim Hortons franchisee, interviewed by author, 11 Aug. 2001; Kiriakopoulos interview; Ed Mahaj, interviewed by author, Oakville, Ontario, 6 Jan. 1998. In fact, women's smoking had achieved a certain respectability by this time, although it was not without ambiguities. See Jarrett Rudy, *The Freedom to Smoke: Tobacco Consumption and Identity* (Montreal and Kingston: McGill-Queen's University Press, 2005), 148–70.

41. Jenny Bryce interview. Note: For a short time in the early 1970s, Tim Hortons outlets served ice cream cones. . . .

42. Certainly the work was dangerous, especially travelling to and from late-night shifts. In 1965, one Mister Donut server was murdered on her way to a night shift in suburban Toronto. Her husband lamented that he normally drove her right to the outlet, but that he had to work a night shift that day.

43. Tom Busnarda, interviewed by author, Welland, 15 January 1998 . . .

44. *CHRR*, 15 Nov. 1945, 30.

45. Ontario Store Fixtures had a 'package plan', which it installed in restaurants across the country. *CHRR*, 15 June 1962, 44. See *CHRR*, 15 Jan. 1965, 2–23, for discussion of the various types of counters and stools.

46. Joyce, *Always Fresh*, 49–50, 107–08.

47. Ron Buist reports that the early customer base of Tim Hortons was 55 per cent men and 45 per cent women. Buist, *Tales from under the Rim* (Fredericton: Goose Lane, 2003), 203.

48. Mister Donut, *Highlights from a Market Analysis*, 4; Chris Pappas, interviewed by author, Etobicoke, Ontario, 7 Dec. 2000.

49. *Oakville Beaver* (*OB*), 2 July 1970; *ODJR*, 30 June 1970. Peter Simpson is a pseudonym. . . . [S]ince there is no analytic value in using his real name, I have changed it to avoid dredging up old embarrassments.

50. Dean, 'Don Mills Youth Scene', 10; *ODJR*, 29 Dec. 1970, 4; 7 Jan. 1971, 4; 15 May 1971, 4.

51. On the history of youth and leisure, see Tamara Myers, *Caught: Montreal's Modern Girls and the Law* (Toronto: University of Toronto Press, 2006); Michael Gauvreau, 'The Protracted Birth of the Canadian Teenager: Work, Citizenship, and the Canadian Youth Commission, 1943–1955', in Gauvreau and Christie, eds, *Cultures of Citizenship in Postwar Canada* (Montreal and Kingston: McGill-Queen's University Press, 2003), 201–38; Shirley Tillotson, *The Public at Play: Gender and the Politics of Recreation in Post-War Ontario* (Toronto: University of Toronto Press, 2000) . . .

52. Jesse Dean, 'Don Mills Youth Scene' (North York, 1970), 11. On St Catharines, see Halaiko interview.

53. *Mister Donut Market Analysis*; Pappas interview. On the timing of the baby boom, see Owram, *Born at the Right Time*, 4–5. . . .

54. Town of Oakville, Bylaw 1970-98, 'A Bylaw to Prohibit Loitering and Nuisances on Public Highways', passed 7 July 1970.

55. *TS*, 8 July 1970, 13. . . .

56. *OB*, 29 Oct. 1970, A28. On the power of civil rights language in Canada, see Owram, *Born at the Right Time*, 166–7.

28

—— Visualizing Play ——

Since the late nineteenth century, images of play have made their way into a variety of media. Among these are print advertisements, sports and soft news photography for print media, and, of course, television, where entire networks are devoted to the broadcasting of play. Some photographs of play and recreation are taken for family reasons, to memorialize vacations or particular events. Much imagery of play, however, has been produced by industries with an interest either in promoting leisure or using the idea of leisure time to sell consumer products and services. Despite this commodification of play (or perhaps because of it), Canadians experienced an expansion of leisure as a component of everyday life, especially among the working and middle classes. As the selections in this section make clear, however, play has historically been an ambiguous site, where power was exercised and social meanings were deeply contested.

The images presented here come from a wide variety of sources. It is worthwhile asking how newspapers, advertisements, public photographs, and private snapshots all constituted different perspectives on the many sites of play that emerged in the twentieth century.

Series 1: Bodies in Motion

The development of the bicycle in the late-nineteenth century was seen as a technological triumph of Victorian progress. Although largely regarded as a masculine activity in its early form, the introduction of the 'safety bicycle' in the late 1880s led manufacturers to focus on the 'lady cyclist' as an expanding market. Such technology was deeply gendered; unlike the preceding, difficult-to-master 'high wheeler' and 'boneshaker' models that had appealed to men, these new bicycles were easier to ride and their frame was dropped to allow women to wear skirts without breeching propriety. Despite facing criticism that women's presence on bicycles was unseemly, unhealthy, and immoral, manufacturers were eager to marry the modernity of bicycling with the image of respectable femininity.

Critics, and some proponents, saw women bicyclists as the public embodiment of an emerging 'New Woman' ideal, which challenged Victorian notions of female dependency by embracing women's suffrage, education, and dress reform. Whether women themselves found bicycling and the increased mobility it offered to be liberating or a form of regulation remains the subject of scholarly debate.

1. Examine the wide range of riders depicted in the Massey-Harris advertisement (Figure 1). How is the act of riding linked to the individual identities and vocations of those depicted? How are these relationships gendered?

2. How does the Dunlop tire advertisement (Figure 2) reflect the tensions between the emerging 'New Woman' and a reinforcement of Victorian codes of femininity?

Series 2: At the Cinema

Since the rise of the Nickleodeon theatres in the late 1800s, both urban and rural Canadians of all ages have gone to the movies. Providing inexpensive entertainment, these early theatres were often ramshackle affairs, perceived with disdain by reform-minded Canadians who associated these spaces with rather crude forms of popular culture and illicit behaviours. With the encouragement of Hollywood and in the context of a new age of mass consumerism, the 1920s and 1930s saw some remarkable innovation in the design and construction of cinemas. Just as was the case in new construction of department stores and multi-purpose arenas, new cinemas in larger Canadian cities were intended to cultivate a new consumer experience and to attract an expanded audience of moviegoers, especially from the middle and elite social classes.

The two images here date from the early 1930s and reflect how cinemas were designed and marketed. The first is an architectural rendering of Toronto's Circle Theatre, which opened in 1932. The second is an advertisement celebrating the renovation of Ottawa's Capitol Theatre in 1931. As you consider these images and their accompanying text, keep in mind that Canada was at the beginning of what became the Great Depression. Both images thus embody the spectacular and monumental elements of the new 'cathedrals of consumption' that assumed prominent places within Canadian cities in the interwar years.

1. What audience(s) are these images appealing to? What kinds of experiences are they presenting to the public?
2. How is the social space of the cinema ordered? How does this spatial ordering speak to the questions of identity and experience at the cinema discussed above? Be sure to consider the facade shown in the advertisement, the detailed interior that appears in the architectural drawing, and the text that speaks about these spaces.

3. In considering the advertisements in Series 1 and 2, what do you think are the strengths and limitations of advertisements as evidence for social historical research? What other kinds of historical information would you want to know about these advertisements in order to use them in writing a social history of play?

Series 3: Consuming Sports

Today, the celebrity status of sports stars is taken for granted. However, the commodification of professional sports evolved in uneven stages throughout the twentieth century, fuelled by shifts in consumerism, leisure, and especially the rise of mass media, including radio and television. The five photographs in this series reflect the public presentation of professional athletes to a wide audience in the 1950s, but they also tell us a great deal about the contested spaces of bodies and athletics in the post-war period.

Figures 5 and 6 are professional public relations photographs of two famous athletes. Barbara Ann Scott, an Ottawa-born figure skater, attracted worldwide attention when she became the first North American to win the European and World Championships and followed that feat with a gold medal at the 1948 Olympics. With her face on the cover of *Life* and *Time* magazines, Scott became known as 'Canada's Sweetheart' and turned professional in 1949, travelling in a number of ice revue shows in the 1950s. Maurice 'The Rocket' Richard led the Montreal Canadiens to eight Stanley Cups and was venerated by French-speaking Canadians, who rioted in Montreal when Richard was suspended for hitting an official in 1955.

The last three photographs offer a different visual perspective on the relationship between media and athletes. All three were taken by newspaper photographer Jack De Lorme for the Calgary *Albertan*. None of the athletes were famous, but all of them were professional: Barbara Baker was an American wrestler travelling through Calgary on tour; Gerry Musetti and

Don Bailey, also American imports, played for the Calgary Stampeders football club; and Hiromi Uyeyama was a touring jockey described as a member of the 'only Japanese trainer-jockey combination on the continent' and went by the nickname of 'Spud'. All three of these photographs were cropped and published in the *Albertan* in 1956 and offer a snapshot on how newspapers presented professional sports to their audience. These images, while made to appear spontaneous in nature, were just as carefully posed as the public relations shots of Scott and Richard.

1. Consider the various sports presented in these five images. Which are considered 'rough' and which are considered 'respectable'? How are athletes' bodies posed to reflect these differences?

2. In the article that accompanied Figure 7, Barbara Baker is described as an athlete who 'packs her 130 pounds into her 5'2" frame with nary a muscle visible anywhere'. Comparing Baker's portrayal with that of Scott (Figure 5), how and why are the two athletes presented differently?

3. How are masculinity and femininity constructed in these photographs? Where do these gendered constructions become ambiguous in the relationship between poses, bodies, and the sports involved?

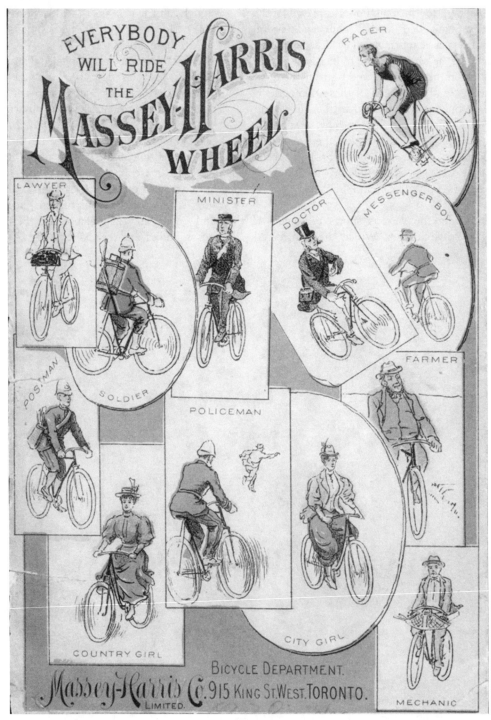

Figure 1. Massey-Harris Company, 'Everybody will Ride the Massey-Harris Wheel' Toronto Public Library, Baldwin Room Broadsides and Printed Ephemera Collection.

Figure 2. Dunlop Tires, 'You are Sure of . . .' *Massey Illustrated*, Mar. 1897.

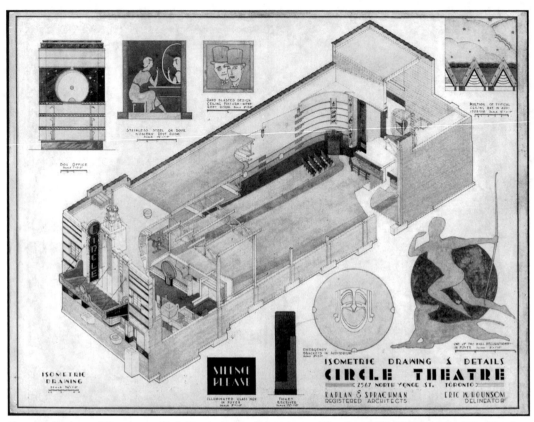

Figure 3. Kaplan and Sprachman, Circle Theatre Isometric Drawing and Details, s0881, fl0413, it0001 002, City of Toronto Archives. Massey-Harris-Ferguson Collection, Archival & Special Collections, University of Guelph Library.

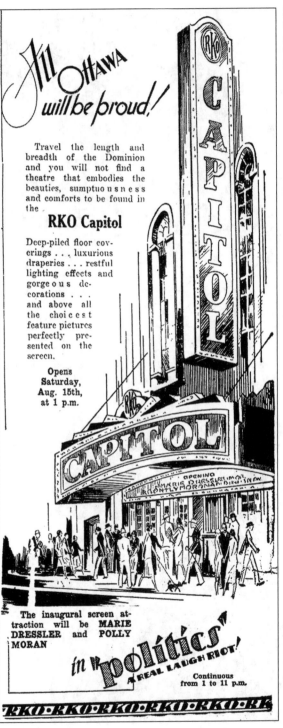

Figure 4. Advertisement for Capitol Theatre, *Ottawa Citizen*, 13 Aug. 1931. Also reprinted in Doug Fischer and Ralph Willsey, eds, *Each Morning Bright: 160 Years of Selected Readings* (Ottawa Citizen Group Inc., 2005), 262.

Figure 5. Barbara Ann Scott, Olympic and world champion figure skater, 1948.

Figure 6. Maurice 'The Rocket' Richard. Courtesy of the Hockey Hall of Fame, Toronto, 000038–0094.

Figure 7. Barbara Baker, wrestler, 1956, by Jack De Lorme. Courtesy of Glenbow Archives, Calgary, NA–5600–8349a.

Figure 8. Gerry Musetti and Don Bailey, Calgary Stampeders football, 1956, by Jack De Lorme. Courtesy of Glenbow Archives, Calgary, NA–5600–8062a.

Figure 9. Hiromi 'Spud' Uyeyama, jockey, 1956, by Jack De Lorme. Courtesy of Glenbow Archives, Calgary, NA–5600–8039d.